AVOIDING THE MIDDLE-INCOME TRAP IN ASIA

The Role of Trade, Manufacturing, and Finance

Edited by Bihong Huang, Peter J. Morgan, and Naoyuki Yoshino

ASIAN DEVELOPMENT BANK INSTITUTE

Asian Development Bank Institute
Kasumigaseki Building 8F
3-2-5, Kasumigaseki, Chiyoda-ku
Tokyo 100-6008, Japan
www.adbi.org

Contents

Tables and Figures

TABLES

FIGURES

Preface

The forces of economic convergence are powerful, but not all powerful. Most emerging economies in Asia have successfully moved from a low-income, high-growth state to a middle-income, middle-growth state through industrialization and globalization in the last few decades. Now, how to sustain sufficient economic growth to become a high-income country has become a key concern in the region. In fact, a lot of countries that were middle income in 1960 remained so in 2008. This refers to a phenomenon that has become known as the "middle-income trap" in which a country's growth slows down after its gross domestic product per capita reaches middle-income levels, making the transition to high-income levels difficult or unattainable. The middle-income trap can be defined in terms of both absolute- and relative-income levels.

The notion of a middle-income trap resonated widely with policy makers, especially in countries where growth had lost its luster. When former Prime Minister Najib Razak of Malaysia came to office in 2009, breaking from the "middle-income trap" and moving up toward high-income-nation status topped his reform agenda. Concerns about the middle-income trap also spread to Viet Nam's leaders in 2009 and appeared in South Africa's National Development Plan. In 2015, Lou Jiwei, then the People's Republic of China's finance minister, worried that his country had a 50% chance of falling into the trap in the next 5 to 10 years.

The Asian Development Bank Institute organized three conferences jointly with the National Natural Science Foundation of China and the *China & World Economy* journal: one in November 2015, one in April 2016, and one in December 2016 for academic researchers and policy makers to share their in-depth research and insights on the nature of the middle-income trap and ways to avoid it. Some of the most insightful papers from these three conferences were selected for inclusion in this book.

This book addresses a number of key issues relevant to understanding the middle-income trap and adopting policies to avoid it. What is the nature of the middle-income trap? What are the growth experiences of various middle-income countries? Which countries have been stuck in the middle-income trap? How can one distinguish between growth traps and the natural slowdown that any country can expect as it converges with leading economies? How does economic growth differ qualitatively between high-income and middle-income countries? What is the role of structural change and sectoral shifts in shaping a middle-income country's growth potential? Do demographics, migration, urbanization, and the labor market matter importantly for escaping the middle-income trap? How is the efficiency of the financial system related to the economic growth rate? What are the roles of manufacturing and openness in determining the innovation capacity of a country?

We thank Feng Xiaoming Feng and Zhinan Zhang of *China & World Economy* for their substantial support of this project. Yasuyo Sugihara, Ayako Kudo, and Yukiko Ichikawa provided able logistic support. Ainslie Smith was in charge of coordinating the editing, and Muriel Ordoñez and Jera Beah H. Lego were in charge of production.

We hope that this volume will contribute to the ongoing dialogue about how middle-income countries can graduate to high-income levels.

Bihong Huang
Asian Development Bank Institute

Peter J. Morgan
Asian Development Bank Institute

Naoyuki Yoshino
Asian Development Bank Institute

Abbreviations

2SLS	two-stage least squares regression
ASIF	Annual Survey of Industrial Firms
BE	between effect
CAFTA–DR	Dominican Republic–Central America Free Trade Agreement
CAGR	compound annual growth rate
CDM	Crepon, Duguet, and Mairesse
CE	competitive effect
CMD	credit market development
CPP	Chinese Pharmaceutical Patent
CRS	constant returns to scale
CSO	Central Statistical Organization
CUI	catch-up index
DEA	data envelopment analysis
DMU	decision-making unit
DSE	dynamic sectoral effect
ECI	economic complexity index
EME	emerging market economy
EU	European Union
FDI	foreign direct investment
FEM	fixed effects model
FIE	foreign invested enterprise
GDP	gross domestic product
GFDD	Global Financial Development Database
GMM	generalized method of moments
GNI	gross national income

GRDP	gross regional domestic product
GRP	gross regional product
GSDP	gross state domestic product
GVC	global value chain
HHI	Herfindahl–Hirschman Index
HP	Hodrick–Prescott
ICT	information and communication technology
IEF	Index of Economic Freedom
IFS	International Financial Statistics
IME	industry mix effect
IPC	International Patent Classification
IPR	intellectual property right
KI	Krugman Index
LAC	Latin America and the Caribbean
LBD	learning by doing
LBE	learning by exporting
LMIR	lower-middle-income range
LPG	labor productivity growth
MI	marketization index
MIC	middle-income country
MIT	middle-income trap
MLE	maximum likelihood estimation
NAFTA	North American Free Trade Agreement
NBSC	National Bureau of Statistics of China
NCE	new chemical entities
NDRC	National Development and Reform Commission
NERI	National Economic Research Institute
NGE	national growth effect
NIE	newly industrializing economy

NSS	National Sample Survey
ODI	outward direct investment
OECD	Organisation for Economic Co-operation and Development
OLS	ordinary least squares
PPP	purchasing power parity
PRC	People's Republic of China
PWT	Penn World Tables
QOG	Indicator of Quality of Government
R&D	research and development
ROA	return on assets
SAR	spatial autoregressive
SCM	subsidies and countervailing measures
SF	stochastic frontier
SIA	Secretariat of Industrial Assistance
SIPO	State Intellectual Property Office
SOE	state-owned enterprise
STAN	OECD's Structural Analysis Database
TFP	total factor productivity
TRIM	trade-related investment measure
TRIPS	trade-related aspects of intellectual property rights
UMIR	upper middle-income range
US	United States
VRS	variable returns to scale
WDI	World Development Indicators
WE	within effect
WIOD	World Input–Output Database
WTO	World Trade Organization

Contributors

David Bulman is an assistant professor of international affairs and China studies, and director at the Pacific Community Initiative at the School of Advanced International Studies at Johns Hopkins University, Washington, DC, United States (US).

Maya Eden is an assistant professor of economics at Brandeis University, Waltham, Massachusetts, US.

Libin Han is a post-doctoral fellow at the Antai College of Economics and Management of Shanghai Jiao Tong University, Shanghai, People's Republic of China (PRC).

Chun-Yu Ho is an assistant professor of economics, at the University at Albany, State University of New York, New York, US.

Anthony Howell is an assistant professor at the School of Economics of Peking University, Beijing, PRC.

Bihong Huang is a research fellow at the Asian Development Bank Institute, Tokyo, Japan.

Jiajun Lan is a PhD candidate at the Wang Yanan Institute for Studies in Economics of Xiamen University, Xiamen, Fujian, PRC.

Cheng Li is an associate professor at the Institute of Economics of the Chinese Academy of Social Sciences, Beijing, PRC.

Xin Li is an assistant professor at Antai College of Economics and Management of Shanghai Jiao Tong University, Shanghai, PRC.

Yu Li is an assistant research fellow at the Chinese Academy of International Trade and Economic Cooperation of MOFCOM, and a nonresident research fellow at the National Institution for Finance and Development, Beijing, PRC.

Ming Lu is a distinguished professor of economics, director of the China Centre for Development Studies at Shanghai Jiao Tong University. He is also an adjunct professor at Fudan University, Singapore Management University, and Dongbei University of Finance and Economics.

Jagannath Mallick is a consultant with the Department of Economics, Indira Gandhi National Open University, New Delhi, India. At the time of writing, he was an international fellow of the Japan Society for the Promotion of Science.

Peter J. Morgan is a senior consulting economist and co-chair for research at the Asian Development Bank Institute, Tokyo, Japan.

Ha Nguyen is an economist in the macroeconomics and growth team of the Development Research Group at the World Bank, Washington, DC, US.

Eva Paus is a professor of economics and Carol Hoffmann Collins director of McCulloch Center for Global Initiatives at Mount Holyoke College, South Hadley, Massachusetts, US.

Hua Shang is an associate professor at the Research Institute of Economics and Management of Southwestern University of Finance and Economics, Chengdu, Sichuan, PRC.

Quanyun Song is an assistant professor at the School of Finance of Southwestern University of Finance and Economics, Chengdu, Sichuan, PRC.

Dan Su is a PhD candidate at the Carlson School of Management of the University of Minnesota, Minneapolis, Minnesota, US.

Darius Tirtosuharto is an economist at the Economic Assessment Group, Department of Economic and Monetary Policy of Bank Indonesia, Jakarta, Indonesia.

Chen Wang is an associate professor at the School of Urban and Regional Science of Shanghai University of Finance and Economics, Shanghai, PRC. She also serves as a research fellow at the Department of Economics of Leiden University.

Xiaolu Wang is deputy director and senior fellow of the National Economic Research Institute of the China Reform Foundation, Beijing, PRC.

Yanrui Wu is a professor and head of the Department of Economics, Business School of the University of Western Australia, Crawley, Western Australia, Australia.

Yiyun Wu is an associate professor at the Policy Simulation Laboratory of the Social Sciences Academy, Zhejiang University, Hangzhou, Zhejiang, PRC.

Yu Wu is an associate professor at the Survey and Research Center for China Household Finance of Southwestern University of Finance and Economics, Chengdu, Sichuan, PRC.

Yang Yao is a professor at the National School of Development of Peking University, Beijing, PRC.

Naoyuki Yoshino is dean of the Asian Development Bank Institute, chief advisor of the Japan Financial Services Agency's Financial Research Center, chairperson of the Meeting of Japanese Government Bond Investors, and professor emeritus at Keio University, Tokyo, Japan.

Xiaojing Zhang is a professor and deputy director at the National Institution for Finance & Development of the Chinese Academy of Social Sciences, Beijing, PRC.

Weimin Zhou is an assistant professor at Antai College of Economics and Management of Shanghai Jiao Tong University, Shanghai, PRC.

Xiwei Zhu is a professor at the School of Economics of Zhejiang University, Hangzhou, Zhejiang, PRC.

CHAPTER 1

Introduction

Naoyuki Yoshino, Peter J. Morgan, and Bihong Huang

1.1 | Introduction

The "middle-income trap" (MIT) has become a popular theme in the literature and among policy makers, even though a precise definition of it and empirical evidence for it are hard to pin down.[1] The argument boils down to the view that high-income growth differs qualitatively from middle-income growth, and hence requires different factor endowments, industrial structures and policies, and that the transition cannot be taken for granted. Increased capacity to innovate is widely seen as vital to support higher value-added production. Since many policy makers aspire for their countries to achieve high-income status, understanding the factors that hinder or support this transition becomes crucially important. This volume presents recent research related to the MIT, with a focus on the experience of the People's Republic of China (PRC), whose policy makers certainly show great interest in the question. Some of the chapters were taken from three conferences sponsored by the Asian Development Bank Institute, the National Natural Science Foundation of China (Project 71133004), and *China & World Economy* journal, one in November 2015, one in April 2016, and one in December 2016.

---

[1]   The concept of the "middle-income trap" was introduced in Gill and Kharas (2007).

1.2 | Literature Review

Definitions

The term "middle-income trap" (MIT), first defined in Gill and Kharas (2007), usually refers to the phenomenon where some countries that have experienced rapid growth and reached the status of a middle-income country, but have not been able to move up to become high-income economies. In other words, these countries are caught in the MIT. The concept was elaborated on by Kharas and Kohli (2011) by raising the questions of "What Is the Middle Income Trap, Why do Countries Fall into It, and How Can It Be Avoided?" Since then, the concept of MIT has attracted more and more attention in academic research and political discussions, in particular, with respect to the growth performance of emerging market economies in Latin America and East Asia. Moreover, since the slowdown of the PRC economy after 2010, special attention has been paid to the question of whether the PRC is also an MIT candidate (see e.g., Wagner 2013, 2015).

Definitions of the middle-income range (MIR) and MIT are made either in absolute or relative terms (Im and Rosenblatt 2015; Glawe and Wagner 2016). The former is based on absolute thresholds of middle income whereas the latter refers to a country's per capita income relative to a reference developed country's (usually the United States [US]) per capita income. However, no consensus has been reached. The definitions of the absolute thresholds of the middle-income range vary substantially across studies. Many researchers (e.g., Felipe, Abdon, and Kumar 2012; Aiyar et al. 2013) adopt the yearly updated country income-class classifications published by the World Bank to define the thresholds. Table 1.1 lists the latest income threshold by the World Bank in 2016, which distinguishes four income categories based on real per capita gross national income. Eichengreen, Park, and Shin (2012, 2014) considered countries with a gross domestic product (GDP) per capita higher than $10,000 (GDP per capita in constant 2005 international prices) as having graduated from the middle-income group, while Aiyar et al. (2013) defined the MIR as being between $2,000 and $15,000 (also in 2005 constant international prices). Spence (2011) although not explicitly mentioning the MIT, referred to the MIR as $5,000 to $10,000.

Table 1.1: World Bank per Capita GNI Thresholds (2015 data)

Classification	Income Range
Low-income economies	< $1,025
Lower-middle-income economies	$1,026–$4,035
Upper-middle-income economies	$4,036–$12,475
High-income economies	≥ $12,476

GNI = gross national income.

Note: GNI calculated according to World Bank "Atlas method" to smoothen the effect of exchange rate fluctuations.

Source: World Bank. http://data.worldbank.org/about/country-and-lending-groups.

The absolute approach is widely employed to address the question of why some countries enter a long period of stagnation (Im and Rosenblatt 2015). Considering that the main development objective of less-developed countries is to achieve the living standards comparable to developed economies, some researchers use the relative approach to gauge how far an economy is away from reaching this goal (Cherif and Hasanov 2015; Cai 2012) or the income distribution across countries. World Bank (2013) took the US as the reference country and the range of middle-income as being roughly 5% to 45% of the US per capita income. It argued that the fact that very few countries that were in the MIR in 1960 had escaped to high-income status by 2009 was evidence of the MIT. Constructing a Catch-Up Index in which values are expressed as a percentage of US per capita income by using population and GDP data from the Maddison 2010 database,[2] Woo et al. (2012) classified economies having a Catch-Up Index between 20% and 55% as middle-income

---

[2]   https://www.rug.nl/ggdc/historicaldevelopment/maddison/releases/maddison-database-2010?lang=en.

countries. Employing data from the Penn World Tables 7.0, Bulman, Eden, and Nguyen (2014) set thresholds of 10% and 50% of US per capita GDP as the lower- and upper-middle-income range, respectively. Robertson and Ye (2015) argued that a country with a GDP per capita of 8%–36% of the US lies within the middle-income range.

The trap is characterized by its persisting character and difficulty of breaking out of it (Matsuyama 2008; Azariadiz and Stachurski 2005). According to Woo et al.'s (2012) definition in relative terms, an MIT period is longer than 50 years. Felipe, Abdon, and Kumar (2012) argued that the MIT period is longer than 42 years, strictly speaking, 14 years in the lower-middle-income range and 28 years in the upper-middle-income range. Chile and Mexico have stayed within the middle-income range for more than 60 years while Brazil's per capita income, after previously strong growth for about 3 decades, has remained nearly unchanged since it experienced the debt crisis in 1980 and remained at only 21.8% of the level of US per capita income in 2011 (Glawe and Wagner 2016).

Clearly, it is much easier to escape the MIT defined in absolute terms than in relative terms. The World Bank database lists fully 79 high-income countries as of 2015.[3] Moreover, the group continued to expand, as the British Virgin Islands, Nauru, and Gibraltar joined this club in 2015. As long as a country maintains some moderate growth of real per capita GDP it will eventually reach the high-income group; the only question is what time period is regarded as "too long," and this is subjective.

Converging to the income levels of the advanced economies such as the US is much more difficult, and it is well known that only a few non-Organisation for Economic Co-operation and Development economies have achieved this, mainly the Asian Tigers—Hong Kong, China; the Republic of Korea;

---

[3] World Bank. World Bank Country and Lending Groups. https://datahelpdesk.worldbank.org/knowledgebase/articles/906519.

Singapore; and Taipei,China. This is made more difficult by the well-known phenomenon of convergence theory, i.e., growth of per capita GDP tends to slow as income levels rise, reflecting diminishing returns from the potential for "catch-up" to the advanced economies. Nonetheless, some researchers find grounds to be skeptical about the existence of a trap between middle-income and high-income levels even in relative terms. Bulman, Eden, and Nguyen (2014) examined the growth performance of countries classified by the ratio of their per capita GDP to that of the US, but found that countries that grow fast continue to grow fast, and do not get "stuck" at any particular middle-income level. They concluded that becoming "trapped" at some middle-income level is not inevitable. However, they did find evidence that growth of high-income countries is qualitatively different from that of middle-income countries, so that appropriate policies probably are needed to ensure a smooth transition. Im and Rosenblatt (2015) explored both the absolute and relative thresholds of the "traps." Using transitional matrix analysis, they also found little support for the idea of MITs. They argued that focusing on the experience of a small number of fast "escapees" may be unhelpful, and that policies promoting gradual improvement may be more sustainable.

Which is more important—absolute or relative achievement? We would argue that, from the standpoint of welfare, achieving high-income status in absolute terms is probably the first and most important target. Once that has been achieved, countries have the luxury of worrying about how rapidly they are converging to the level of the most advanced economies. One might speak of a "lower-high-income trap." But this does not seem very meaningful or worrisome, and it is probably more important to focus on policies that maintain sustainable growth and improvement in incomes.

How to escape the middle-income trap

The notion of the MIT has also spawned a considerable literature about the reasons for it and the kinds of development and policies needed to escape it. The theories focus on the necessary political and institutional adjustments needed for a country to move from middle-income range to high-income range. Gill and Kharas (2007: 5) described MIT countries as being "…squeezed between the low-wage poor country competitors that dominate in mature industries and the rich-country innovators that dominate in industries undergoing rapid technological change." According to Kharas and Kohli (2011), countries fall into the MIT if they "cannot make a timely transition from resource-driven growth, with low-cost labor and capital, to productivity-driven growth." Similarly, Garrett (2004) argued that middle-income countries have to "find ways to 'tech up' and enter the global knowledge economy, so as to escape the trap of having to dumb down to compete in standardized manufacturing." Lin (2016) argued that the PRC needs to promote industrial upgrading to promote steady increases in total factor productivity. However, he is less convinced about the need to promote domestic innovation, suggesting that in many cases it may still be cheaper to import high-level technology.

1.3 | Chapter Summaries

The first two chapters examine the questions of the nature of the MIT and the fundamental factors that support or hinder sustainable growth, most notably the roles of the manufacturing and financial sectors and trade openness. The next two chapters analyze the effects of structural factors on growth, including the role of the manufacturing sector, the services sector, and globalization. The next five chapters consider the effects of government policy in fostering growth in the PRC. A common theme is that such policies may have unforeseen side effects which gradually undermine the effectiveness of such policies. This includes the effects of the *hukou* system and land-use policy in controlling the pace and distribution of urbanization as a part of overall development planning, and competition among provinces to imitate growth policies set by the central government regardless of local comparative advantage. The last two chapters focus on the role of finance in supporting innovation and growth.

The middle-income trap and factors affecting growth

Bulman, Eden, and Nguyen address the basic question of whether or not there is a "middle-income trap." The theory of the MIT suggests that the determinants of growth at low- and high-income levels may be different, and countries may struggle in the transition from growth strategies that are effective at low-income levels to strategies that are effective at high-income levels, and as a result may stagnate at some middle-income level. However, defining income levels based on per capita GDP relative to the US, they do not find evidence for unusual stagnation at any particular middle-income level. They do find evidence that the determinants of growth at low- and high-income levels differ. These findings suggest a mixed conclusion: middle-income countries may need to change growth strategies to transition smoothly to high-income growth strategies, but this can be done smoothly and does not necessarily imply the existence of an MIT.

Paus' chapter analyzes the reasons for the MIT in Latin America, where countries have been at the middle-income level for decades, and draws out lessons for Asia. She characterizes the MIT as a situation where a middle-income country can no longer compete internationally in standardized, labor-intensive goods because wages are relatively too high, but also cannot compete in higher value-added activities on a broad enough scale because productivity is relatively too low. The result is slow growth, stagnant or falling wages, and a growing informal economy. She argues that insufficient development of domestic innovation capabilities is at the heart of the MIT. In Latin America, it is the result of a market-led strategy that generated dismal productivity growth, rapid deindustrialization, a decline in export sophistication in many countries, poor innovation performance, and underinvestment in the requisite social capabilities. The current globalization context provides a challenging context for middle-income countries to narrow the capabilities gap, because they have less time to do so, with more players competing in the innovation space and technological innovation changing faster. She suggests that a comprehensive innovation-focused strategy with strategic active policies is the only way to escape the MIT. The nature of the production structure, already existing elements of an innovation ecosystem, and the possibilities for creating political coalitions in support of a systemic advancement of innovation capabilities are critical factors conditioning the escape from the MIT.

Structural factors affecting growth

Su and Yao revisit the role of the manufacturing sector during the middle-income stage of development. By exploiting a large macroeconomic and input/output data set with sectoral information, they find that, in the middle-income stage, the manufacturing sector tends to pull along all other sectors, including the services sector. Therefore a decline in the growth rate of the manufacturing sector will negatively affect the growth of all other sectors, in both the short run and the long run. They also investigate the possible mechanisms behind why manufacturing is central to development in a middle-income economy. They find that a larger share of manufacturing not only promotes the gross private-saving ratio, but also accelerates the pace of technological accumulation. This suggests that the manufacturing sector is still the key engine of economic growth for middle-income economies.

Mallick contributes to the debate on structural change effects versus labor reallocation effects on the regional disparity in productivity growth in India and the PRC. He uses secondary data at the state level in India and provinces in the PRC between 1993 and 2010. This chapter uses the general method of moment system estimator in a dynamic spatial panel data framework for the empirical analysis. The empirical investigations draw the four results. First, the shift–share analysis suggests that the low-income regions have higher structural change effects on labor productivity growth (LPG) than in the high-income and middle-income regions. Second, structural change has played an important role in boosting LPG. Third, the neighborhood effects also contribute positively to LPG. Fourth, human capital, investment in fixed asset, and foreign direct investment (FDI) have boosted LPG. Finally, he suggests that policy makers should consider the role of structural change effects along with the neighborhood relationship, human capital, physical investment, and

FDI for designing policies to reduce disparities in productivity growth, and hence economic growth; in turn, this will help to avoid the MIT.

Policy and the middle-income trap

Han and Lu observe that, since 2003, the PRC's central government has allocated more construction and-use quotas to inland provinces than elsewhere in an attempt to balance the growth gap between its coastal and inland regions. They use firm-level data from 2001 to 2007 to examine how this change in land policy has affected firms' investments and housing prices. They find that cities in which land-use quotas decreased experienced faster housing price growth than the cities in which land-use quotas increased after 2003. This sharp change in policy also highlighted two major channels of the effects of housing prices on capital investment by firms. In particular, higher housing prices increased firms' investment by providing a source of more valuable collateral, while crowding out other fixed capital investment. However, they find that the net effect of housing prices on investment is negative for economic growth.

Wu and Zhu investigate the trends and determinants of geographic concentration and industrial specialization in the PRC, using interprovincial panel data for the period 1999–2010. They find that after 2005 both geographic concentration and industrial specialization began to decline, resulting in an increased similarity of industrial structure among provinces. They hypothesize that the industrial policies of provincial governments are the cause of this phenomenon. The data are found to support this view, and the results are robust when using instrumental variables to deal with possible reverse causality and omitted variable problems. The underlying mechanism is that the policy of the central government, which is set to steer the direction of industrial development for several years to come, is an important reference document for all provincial planners. This policy therefore causes the less-developed regions to deviate from their comparative advantages and results in a combination of insufficient geographic concentration and inverse specialization in the PRC.

Chan and Wan argue that the PRC's urbanization in the early 21st century is not only a historic event of global significance, but, more importantly, it is also crucial to alleviating poverty and promoting domestic consumption and social stability in the country in the coming 2–3 decades. In the PRC, rural–urban segmentation has been a fundamental part of the PRC's state development strategy, but it has many uncommon features that are specific to the PRC and frequently misunderstood. The authors take advantage of the recent release of the 2010 census data at the county/subdistrict level to construct relatively consistent city population statistics that are close to those generally used for cities internationally. The new data enable the authors to sketch the broad contours of the PRC's urban system and to begin to explore a number of important issues relevant to current urbanization and *hukou* reform policies, such as "is the PRC successful in controlling the growth of large cities?" The authors argue that this policy was effective earlier, but continuing the across-the-board policy to limit the growth of large cities is likely to be ineffective and counterproductive. They argue that growth can be sustained only through easing of the *hukou* policy and gradual opening of the large cities, including the first-tier ones.

Tirtusuharto focuses on the impact of fiscal decentralization on the efficiency of fiscal resources at the regional level that will improve the probability of Indonesia avoiding the MIT. From a development standpoint, the implementation of decentralization was not only aimed to increase fiscal capacity and efficiency, but also to enhance institutional quality at the local level to support economic growth. A non-parametric method of data envelopment analysis is utilized to measure fiscal efficiency scores of state governments. In the second stage of empirical analysis, a Tobit panel model is constructed to find key factors that affect state fiscal efficiency in Indonesia. He finds that the degree of fiscal decentralization is the key determinant of state fiscal efficiency. Hence, despite the positive impact from fiscal decentralization in Indonesia, the expansion of the state's fiscal spending has caused some degree of inefficiency due to growing corruption and rent seeking. This could jeopardize the speed and extent of development in the Indonesian regions and also the transition into high-income levels.

Li, Wang, and Zhang analyze the economic effects of national city clusters
in the PRC, of which there were 20 in 2015. Based on panel data from 283
cities in the PRC over the period of 2003–2013, they examine whether
cities within those national city clusters have higher productivity than those
outside the clusters. They find that the national city cluster strategy initiated
in the PRC's 11th Five-Year Plan has not produced any significant impact
on labor productivity, possibly due to market segmentation, as well as the
relatively short track record of these clusters. However, one exception is the
Yangtze River Delta Urban Economic Coordination Committee—the most
developed national city cluster in the PRC, which has experienced steady
productivity improvement. However, this may reflect the longer time span of
this cluster compared with the others.

Roles of finance and innovation

Shang, Song, and Wu analyze the effects of credit market development
on PRC firms' innovative capacities. They argue that, in a more developed
financial market, investors will tend to allocate more credit to innovative
firms, i.e., those that are riskier but more productive. Using a large data set
of industrial firms in the PRC's 31 provinces, they find that credit market
development enhances the probability of firms' product innovation and
innovation outcomes. They further show that firms' credit constraints
and firms' performances are two channels through which credit market
development affects firms' innovative capacities. Their results are driven
neither by the increase in the quantity of credit, nor by the increase in the
number of firms in a province.

Ho, Li, and Zhou examine the effect of FDI on domestic innovation using a
data set covering pharmaceutical industries across 29 provinces in the PRC
over the period 1998–2007. They find that there is a negative horizontal
spillover effect of FDI on domestic innovation when the intellectual property
rights regime is weak. However, the spillover effect became positive when
the intellectual property rights regime was strengthened after the PRC's
accession to the World Trade Organization in 2001. They also find that

there is a positive upstream spillover effect of FDI on domestic suppliers of pharmaceutical intermediates. Taken together, their findings provide important policy implications on why the developing countries should encourage FDI and strengthen their intellectual property rights regimes in a coordinated way to enhance domestic innovation for promoting productivity and economic growth.

References

Aiyar, S., R. Duval, D. Puy, Y. Wu, and L. Zhang. 2013. Growth Slowdowns and the Middle-Income Trap. IMF Working Paper 13/71. Washington, DC: International Monetary Fund.

Azariadis, C., and J. Stachurski. 2005. Poverty Traps. In *Handbook of Economic Growth*, edited by S. N. Durlauf and P. Aghion. Amsterdam: Elsevier.

Bulman, D., M. Eden, and H. Nguyen. 2014. Transitioning from Low-Income Growth to High-Income Growth—Is There a Middle Income Trap. Policy Research Working Paper 7104. Washington, DC: The World Bank.

Cai, F. 2012. Is There a "Middle-income Trap"? Theories, Experiences and Relevance to China. *China & World Economy* 20(1): 49–61.

Cherif, R., and F. Hasanov. 2015. The Leap of the Tiger: How Malaysia Can Escape the Middle-Income Trap, IMF Working Paper WP/15/131.

Eichengreen, B., D. Park, and K. Shin. 2012. When Fast-Growing Economies Slow Down: International Evidence and Implications for China. *Asian Economic Papers* 11(1): 42–87.

———. 2014. Growth Slowdowns Redux. *Japan and the World Economy* 32: 65–84.

Felipe, J., A. Abdon, and U. Kumar. 2012. Tracking the Middle-income Trap: What Is It, Who Is in It, and Why? Working Paper 715. Levy Economics Institute of Bard College.

Garrett, G. 2004. Globalization's Missing Middle. *Foreign Affairs* 83(6): 84–96.

Gill, I., and H. Kharas. 2007. *An East Asian Renaissance—Ideas for Economic Growth*. Washington, DC: The World Bank.

Glawe, L., and H. Wagner. 2016. The Middle-Income Trap: Definitions, Theories and Countries Concerned—A Literature Survey. *Comparative Economic Studies* 58(4): 507–538.

Im, F. G., and D. Rosenblatt. 2015. Middle-Income Traps: A Conceptual and Empirical Survey. *Journal of International Commerce, Economies and Policy* 6(3): 1–39.

Kharas, H., and H. Kohli. 2011. What is the Middle Income Trap, Why do Countries Fall into It, and How Can It be Avoided? *Global Journal of Emerging Market Economies* 3(3): 281–289.

Lin, J. Y. 2016. Will China Continue to be the Engine of Growth in the World. *Journal of Policy Modeling* 38(4): 683–692.

Matsuyama, K. 2008. Poverty Traps. In *The New Palgrave Dictionary of Economics*, 2nd Edition, edited by S. N. Durlauf and L. Blume. Basingstoke, United Kingdom: Palgrave Macmillan.

Robertson, P. E., and L. Ye. 2015. On the Existence of a Middle-Income Trap. University of Western Australia Working Paper 13/12. Perth, Australia: University of Western Australia. (An earlier version of this article appeared in 2013 under the same title.)

Spence, M. 2011. *The Next Convergence. The Future of Economic Growth in a Multispeed World.* New York: Farrar, Straus, and Giroux.

Wagner, H. 2013. Challenges to China's Policy: Structural Change. *Comparative Economic Studies* 55: 721–736.

———. 2015. Structural Change and Mid-Income Trap—Under Which Conditions can China Succeed in Moving towards Higher Income Status. *European Journal of Comparative Economics* 12(2): 165–188.

Woo, W. T., M. Lu, J. D. Sachs, and Z. Chen. 2012. *A New Economic Growth Engine for China: Escaping the Middle-income Trap by Not Doing More of the Same.* Singapore and London: World Scientific Publishing Company and Imperia College Press.

World Bank. 2013. *China 2030: Building a Modern, Harmonious, and Creative High-Income Society.* Washington, DC: The World Bank.

CHAPTER 2

Transitioning from Low-Income Growth to High-Income Growth: Is there a Middle-Income Trap?

David Bulman, Maya Eden, and Ha Nguyen

2.1 | Introduction

Policy and academic communities in recent years have expressed growing concern that countries at middle-income levels may fail to generate enough growth to become high-income countries. In these countries, the policies that facilitated growth from low income to middle income might not facilitate a transition from middle income to high income, resulting in a "middle-income trap." But while theory suggests that growth determinants may differ by income level, empirical evidence for middle-income traps has not been conclusive.

Middle-income countries seek policies that can help them achieve strong and sustained growth and eventually help them join the league of high-income countries. Yet finding a set of appropriate pro-growth policies is a complicated task, particularly given the uniqueness of every country's institutional constraints. This chapter does not lay out specific policy recommendations; rather, it provides a set of stylized facts about middle-income countries and about fundamentals that might facilitate the transition from middle to high income. We focus on changes in relative income (i.e., how countries catch up to other high-income countries), rather than absolute income.

TRANSITIONING FROM LOW-INCOME GROWTH TO
HIGH-INCOME GROWTH: IS THERE A MIDDLE-INCOME TRAP?

15

We find mixed evidence regarding the existence of a middle-income trap—i.e.,
slowing growth that might cause middle-income countries to stagnate prior to
joining the high-income group. The predominant evidence against the existence
of such a middle-income trap comes from an examination of the growth paths
of successful transitions. We find that "escapees"—countries that "escaped"
the middle-income trap and became rich—tend to grow fast and consistently to
high income, and do not stagnate at any point as a middle-income trap theory
would suggest. In contrast, "non-escapees" tend to have low growth at all levels
of income. In other words, while the existence of a middle-income trap implies
that growth rates systematically slow down as countries reach middle-income
status, no such systematic slowdown is apparent in the data.

However, our analysis does show that successful middle-income countries
(i.e., those that "escape" and become high income) have different growth
fundamentals and different policy choices from unsuccessful middle-income
countries (i.e., those that are still middle income or that have become low
income). Among middle-income countries, descriptive analyses suggest
the following factors associated with higher growth: (i) economic structure,
and in particular a faster transformation from agriculture to industry;
(ii) higher export shares; (iii) lower inflation; and (iv) decreases in inequality
and dependency ratios.

We also find evidence that the effectiveness of different growth strategies may
vary across income levels. This is consistent with middle-income trap theories
suggesting that middle-income countries get stuck in the transition from growth
strategies that are effective at low-income levels to growth strategies that are
effective at high-income levels. While we do not find evidence of being "stuck,"
we do find evidence that such a transition may be needed.

We find that total factor productivity (TFP) growth is a much larger source of
economic growth, both in absolute and relative terms, in middle- and high-
income countries than in low-income countries.[1] This highlights the limits of

---

[1] This is true regardless if human capital is included or excluded from the production function
(see Data Appendix for more details).

capital accumulation (after all, investment has a decreasing marginal return) and suggests the important roles of education, research and innovation, and structural reforms. Figure 2.1 presents average contributions to annual growth in output per worker, by income level.[2] The light gray part represents average annual TFP growth and the dark gray part represents average annual growth of the capital–labor ratio (multiplied by the capital share). For low-income countries, the overwhelming majority of growth comes from capital accumulation. For middle- and high-income countries, however, the share of TFP growth is much larger.

Figure 2.1: Average Contributions to Growth, by Income Level

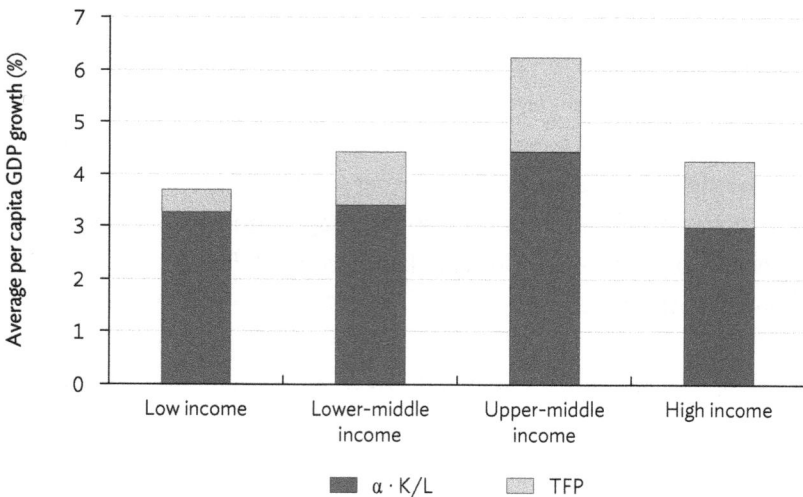

α = capital share, GDP = gross domestic product, K/L = capital per worker, TFP = total factor productivity. Source: Authors' calculations based on Penn World Table Version 7.0 (see Data Appendix).

---

[2]   Here, as in the rest of the chapter, we define low-income countries as those with per capita incomes less than 10% of the United States (US), middle-income countries as those with per capita incomes between 10% and 50% of the US, and high-income countries as those with per capita incomes over 50% of the US. Here, we further divide middle-income countries into lower- and upper-middle-income countries using a threshold of 30% of the US. Table A2.1 in the Appendix lists economies by income group at 2009. The categorization looks reasonable.

TRANSITIONING FROM LOW-INCOME GROWTH TO
HIGH-INCOME GROWTH: IS THERE A MIDDLE-INCOME TRAP?

17

The observation makes sense. For low-income countries, since the level of capital is still low, it is relatively easier to attract and accumulate more capital (think of giving farmers tractors). When the level of capital accumulation is higher, it is harder to attract investment because the return to capital now becomes lower (i.e., it doesn't help to give one farmer two tractors). To maintain growth, countries have to turn to other sources: better technologies, better management practices, and research and innovation. Our conjecture is that countries with better strategies to access or, even better, generate state-of-the-art technologies and management practices will be able to catch up to high-income countries.

While this aggregate finding is consistent with the above economic intuition, we fail to find strong support for it on a more disaggregated level. We conduct a regression analysis of growth determinants in low- and middle-income levels. Our findings do not support the hypothesis that innovation and human capital accumulation are more important determinants of growth for middle-income countries compared with low-income countries. Rather, the regressions suggest that growth of low- and middle-income countries may have to do more with the transformation of the economy: the growth effect of moving from agriculture to industry is stronger for middle-income countries than for low-income countries, while the growth effect of moving to services is weaker for middle-income countries.

The empirical analysis is not only of academic interest; a middle-income "trap" implies income stagnation for much of the 70% of the world's population currently living in middle-income countries. Such growth stagnation would have major human and global consequences. Understanding the correlates of successful middle-income growth helps points to directions for future work that develops policy frameworks. For example, the concept of middle-income traps is used to formulate policy recommendations for continued economic growth in the People's Republic of China (PRC) (World Bank 2013) and in Malaysia (Flaaen, Ghani, and Mishra 2013).

The chapter is organized as follows: Section 2.2 reviews related literature on the middle-income trap. Section 2.3 presents basic descriptions of income dynamics for a large set of countries, with a particular focus on the middle-income group. Section 2.4 contrasts middle-income "escapees" and "non-escapees" along several dimensions and compares middle-income country growth based on fundamentals. Section 2.5 presents regression results comparing growth determinants at middle-income and low-income levels. Section 2.6 concludes.

2.2 | Debating the Middle-Income Trap: Theory and Empirics

The term "middle-income trap" first appeared in the World Bank's *An East Asian Renaissance: Ideas for Economic Growth*, which stated that "middle income countries ... have grown less rapidly than either rich or poor countries" (Gill and Kharas 2007: 5). Since then, the concept of a middle-income trap has become increasingly popularized and discussed in both popular media[3] and academic literature, although a consensus on the validity of the concept has yet to emerge.

The middle-income trap concept has been debated from both theoretical and empirical angles. Theoretically, middle-income countries may face particular challenges in transitioning their economic growth models from strategies that were successful while they were poor to strategies that enable them to directly compete with high-income countries. In this sense, middle-income traps reflect the difficulty middle-income countries have competing with either low-wage economies or highly skilled advanced economies. These countries need different growth strategies, and these strategies are not readily available. At low-income levels, countries require structural transformation,

---

[3]   See, for example, *The Economist* (23 June 2011) for the People's Republic of China's "Middle Income Trap," and other media coverage for other countries (the Russian Federation, Malaysia, and Latin America).

TRANSITIONING FROM LOW-INCOME GROWTH TO
HIGH-INCOME GROWTH: IS THERE A MIDDLE-INCOME TRAP?

19

reallocation, and the availability of jobs. At middle-income levels, the gains from reallocating surplus labor begin to evaporate, in the vein of a Lewis–Kuznets framework—without surplus labor, wages begin to rise, making low-cost exports less competitive. Additionally, returns to capital begin to fall as the gains from technological imitation and importing foreign technology decline (Agénor and Canuto 2012; Kharas and Kohli 2011).

New sources of productivity, and particularly local innovation, are required to maintain growth and diversity exports. The previous section highlighted the greater contribution of TFP growth to overall growth for middle- and high-income countries. TFP growth slowdowns in middle-income countries are identified as a key cause for overall growth slowdown: Eichengreen, Park, and Shin (2012) found that, on average, 85% of a fast-growing economy's slowdown is attributable to TFP, and only 15% to capital accumulation. Daude and Fernandez–Arias (2010) showed that slow productivity growth, rather than factor accumulation, explains the inability of middle-income countries in Latin America to close the income gap with advanced economies. Felipe, Abdon, and Kumar (2012) found that countries that make it to the upper-middle-income group tend to have a more "diversified, sophisticated, and non-standard export basket" than those that remain stuck at lower-middle income levels.[4]

Combining the innovation and export approaches into a framework for middle-income growth, Kharas and Kohli (2011) argued in terms of the supply and demand needs of an economy, with low-income countries focused more on supply and high-income countries focused on demand. Low-income economies seek to maximize factor inputs through extensive growth while also focusing on the supply of an enabling institutional environment. Middle-income countries instead focus on demand: domestic demand through growth of the middle class, and new export demand focused on innovation and product differentiation. Creation of these new sources of demand requires

---

[4] Vivarelli (2014) provides a comprehensive discussion on the challenges faced by middle-income countries, with particular attention paid to the role of developing innovation capacity.

"modern and more agile institutions for property rights, capital markets, successful venture capital, competition, and a critical mass of highly skilled people to grow through innovations."

Although there is considerable theoretical evidence that middle-income countries need to transition growth strategies to maintain growth and become high income, empirical evidence that middle-income countries are more likely to stagnate than countries at other income levels has been less conclusive. There have been two general empirical approaches to identifying the existence of middle-income traps. The first strand does not explicitly refer to "traps," but rather analyzes cross-country growth dynamics across income levels, attempting to identify criteria for growth slowdowns and accelerations. The second strand directly confronts the definitional question implied by the middle-income trap hypothesis: are middle-income countries particularly cursed in failing to grow to high income? The first approach focuses predominantly on absolute incomes, comparing growth trajectories within a country. The second approach focuses predominantly on relative incomes, comparing growth to a high-income benchmark.

Considerable research has tried to document growth patterns for low- and middle-income countries. Pritchett (2000) showed that the patterns for developing countries are best characterized as volatile. While some countries have steady growth (hills and steep hills), others have rapid growth followed by stagnation (plateaus), rapid growth followed by decline (mountains) or even catastrophic falls (cliffs), continuous stagnation (plains), or steady decline (valleys). This suggests that econometric growth literature that makes use of the panel nature of data is unlikely to be informative—a point previously made by Easterly et al. (1993). In that paper, it is shown that growth is volatile across decades while country characteristics are much more stable, and growth is largely driven by external shocks. Pritchett and Summers (2014) followed and corroborated Easterly et al. (1993), finding a tendency for regression to the mean for fast-growing countries. The paper also found that income levels are poor predictors of growth slowdowns; the key is the fundamental difficulty of progress at all stages.

TRANSITIONING FROM LOW-INCOME GROWTH TO
HIGH-INCOME GROWTH: IS THERE A MIDDLE-INCOME TRAP?

21

Following Pritchett's (2000) suggestions, Hausmann, Pritchett, and Rodrik (2005) looked for instances of rapid, but sustained, acceleration in economic growth They found that growth accelerations tend to be correlated with increases in investment and trade, and with real exchange rate depreciations. Growth accelerations are also correlated with political regime changes and economic reforms. At the same time, growth accelerations are highly unpredictable; a majority of reforms do not lead to growth acceleration.

Related to growth accelerations, recent literature focused largely on middle-income countries specifically analyzing growth slowdowns. Eichengreen, Park, and Shin (2012) constructed a sample of cases where fast-growing economies slow down. They show that rapidly growing economies slow down significantly when their per capita incomes reach around $16,000 in year-2005 constant international prices. Since the PRC will soon reach this level of income, the paper implies that the PRC will likely witness a slowdown. In a recent paper, Cai (2012), through a discussion of many of the PRC's current problems, shared this concern. And in a more recent paper, Eichengreen, Park, and Shin (2013) instead identified two nodes for growth slowdowns, one at $10,000–$11,000 and one at $15,000–$16,000, concluding that middle-income countries experience slowdowns in stages rather than at a single point in time. Aiyar et al. (2013) looked explicitly at different growth patterns in middle-income countries, finding that growth slowdowns are more likely for middle-income countries than for low- or high-income countries. Using 42 explanatory variables to explain slowdowns, they found that small government size, deregulation, and infrastructure development are particularly important for middle-income slowdowns as opposed to low- and high-income slowdowns.

This literature on growth accelerations and slowdowns uses panel data to focus on growth patterns within individual countries; however, identifying an income-level "trap" instead requires comparing growth against a high-income benchmark, as income-level thresholds are frequently redefined. For instance, Eichengreen, Park, and Shin (2012, 2013) and Aiyar et al. (2013) focused on growth relative to previous growth; however, the authors did not control for levels of past period growth, so in their specification, slowdowns do not necessarily imply income-level traps, especially considering that middle-income countries in their data have higher first-period growth. For instance, a country that slows from 10% annual growth to 5% annual growth will still develop rapidly enough to catch up to high-income economies. Indeed, several countries forming the basis for the analysis of Eichengreen, Park, and Shin (2012, 2013) are now high-income economies, including the Republic of Korea and Taipei,China. The PRC, often the implicit (or explicit) focus of growth slowdown papers, has already slowed to a "new normal" growth path that is more than 3 percentage points slower than growth over the last decade, but this new "slow" growth of 7% would allow the PRC to reach high-income status in 8 years (absolute) or 16 years (relative to United States [US] income).[5]

Other literature on middle-income traps focuses specifically on the movement of countries to high-income status, defined by either absolute or relative income levels, i.e., thresholds based on constant dollar values and thresholds based on income relative to high-income countries. Felipe, Abdon, and Kumar (2012) grouped countries into four income categories—low, lower-middle, upper-middle, and high—and then defined lower- and upper-middle-income traps by the amount of time it takes a country to reach the next income levels: lower-middle-income countries that remain lower-middle income for 28 years are "trapped," as are upper-middle-income countries that have not become high income in 14 years. However, these thresholds are based on the median number of years that all countries spent at particular income levels—similar thresholds can be constructed at any income level, so it is not clear that there is any particular growth dynamic characterizing countries and middle-income levels. Note that in looking at absolute income, every country with even slightly positive growth will eventually become high income—so the criteria for a "trap" has to be the speed of this transition.

---

[5]   Here, the threshold for high income is based on the 2014 World Bank value of $12,746 gross national income (GNI) per capita using the Atlas method. The relative income threshold is based on 50% of US GNI per capita (at purchasing power parity), and assumes 2% annual US growth.

TRANSITIONING FROM LOW-INCOME GROWTH TO
HIGH-INCOME GROWTH: IS THERE A MIDDLE-INCOME TRAP?

23

More recently, Im and Rosenblatt (2013) discussed the definition of middle-income traps and explore both the absolute and relative thresholds of the "traps." Using a transitional matrix analysis, they also found little support for the idea of middle-income traps, and they demonstrated that transitions from lower-middle income to upper-middle income are as likely as transitions from upper-middle income to high income.

In sum, the existing literature identifies several theoretical reasons why middle-income countries may face particular challenges in maintaining high growth rates and transitioning to high income, but empirical evidence on a "trap" is mixed. We do not believe the theoretical and empirical findings are at odds. In the following sections, we demonstrate that, although empirically there is no evidence that middle-income countries are more likely to stagnate than countries at other income levels, nevertheless middle-income countries that grow fast and achieve high income have different growth fundamentals than low-income countries or than countries that stagnate at middle income: in other words, the theoretical concerns are valid, but countries can and have responded and avoid stagnation.

2.3 | Identifying a Middle-Income Trap: Basic Facts on Income Dynamics

In this section, we present some stylized facts on countries' income dynamics to identify whether such income dynamics correspond to an identifiable growth slowdown, or trap, at middle-income levels. The literature above highlights three potential approaches to identify an income trap: (i) slowdown relative to past growth, (ii) the persistence of an absolute income level, and (iii) the persistence of a relative income level. All three approaches have advantages, though they analyze different questions. For both theoretical and practical reasons, we believe that the use of relative income makes the most sense for determining whether a middle-income trap exists. Theoretically, as highlighted above, the key reason for a middle-income trap is failure to transition from low-wage growth strategies to high-wage growth strategies;

these wages are determined internationally on a relative scale. Practically, the use of an absolute threshold implies that any positive growth will eventually yield a transition to high income, even if such growth is well below the global and high-income average. For these reasons, we focus on relative incomes.

To identify income dynamics, we first divide countries into three relative income groups: low, middle, and high. Using a relative scale, low-, middle-, and high-income countries are those that have purchasing power parity (PPP) gross domestic product (GDP) per capita less than or equal to 10%, between 10% and 50%, and above 50% of US PPP GDP per capita, respectively. Table A2.1 in the Appendix lists all economies in these three categories in 2009 (including narrow relative income bins as well).

We remove oil exporters from our analysis for two reasons. First and most important, growth of these countries is driven largely by oil exports and not so much by fundamentals. Second, proceeds from oil exports can be very volatile, which would distort the persistence of countries' relative income. The Data Appendix provides a list of oil exporters removed from the sample.

Figure 2.2 shows economies' long-run changes of their income relative to the US. The log of per capita income relative to the US in 1960 is on the x-axis, with the 2009 value on the y-axis. Each axis is divided into three areas, representing the three income groups. Economies in the top-middle quadrant (in black) are those that "escaped" from middle income to high income over this period. The list of escapees includes Greece; Hong Kong, China; Ireland; Japan; the Republic of Korea; Puerto Rico; Seychelles; Singapore; Spain; and Taipei,China. Two countries that nearly make the list (the top of the middle quadrant) are Portugal and Cyprus, which are still classified as middle income in 2009. Table 2.1 summarizes the number of countries by income level and subsequent income transition in 1960 (and alternatively, in 1970, where we have more data).

TRANSITIONING FROM LOW-INCOME GROWTH TO
HIGH-INCOME GROWTH: IS THERE A MIDDLE-INCOME TRAP?

25

Figure 2.2: Relative Income Dynamics, 1960–2009

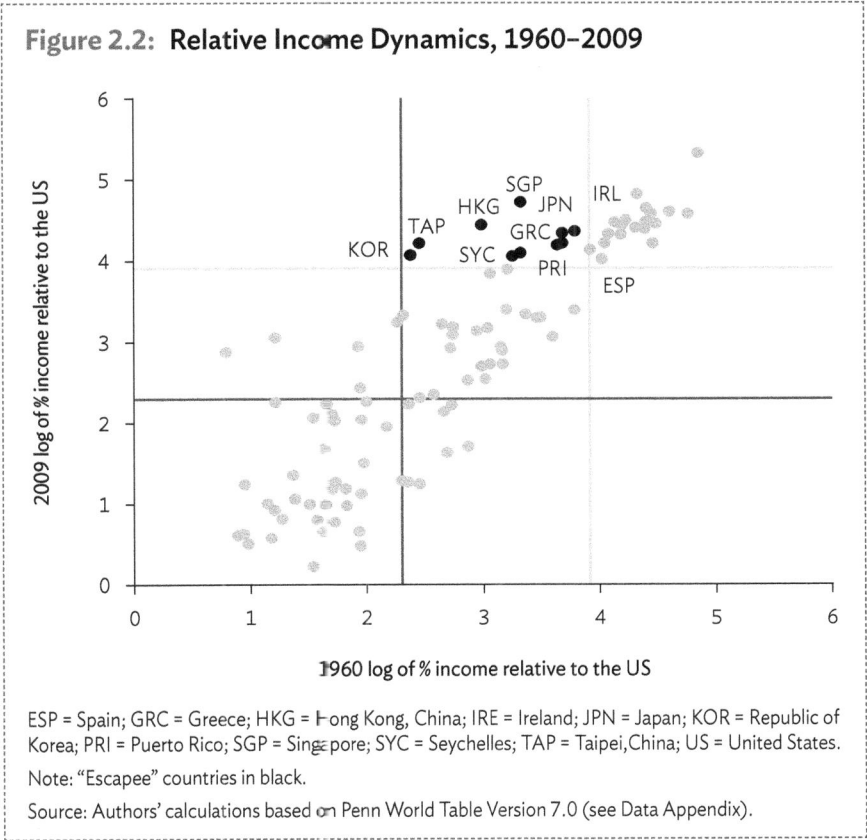

ESP = Spain; GRC = Greece; HKG = Hong Kong, China; IRE = Ireland; JPN = Japan; KOR = Republic of Korea; PRI = Puerto Rico; SGP = Singapore; SYC = Seychelles; TAP = Taipei,China; US = United States.

Note: "Escapee" countries in black.

Source: Authors' calculations based on Penn World Table Version 7.0 (see Data Appendix).

The predominant fact that emerges from Figure 2.2 and Table 2.1 is that relative income levels are highly persistent. All high-income countries in 1960 remained high income in 2009; a majority of middle-income countries remained middle income;[6] and only a handful of low-income countries joined the middle-income group. A concern is that there might have been more fluid movements of countries between 1960 and 2009—for example, some countries might have moved to high income and moved back, which Figure 2.1 would fail to capture. Figure A2.1 in the Appendix shows that there are few such movements. Almost all of the countries that have ever moved

---

[6]   A few middle-income countries declined to poor income groups (Bolivia, Ghana, Haiti, Honduras, Nicaragua, Paraguay, and Zambia).

into high income have stayed there. Two exceptions are the Czech Republic and Lebanon.[7] Another potential concern is that this persistence is an artifact of our selected middle-income threshold (i.e., 10%–50% of US per capita GDP). Figure A2.2 in the Appendix shows that this is not the case: relative income mobility is no more persistent for middle-income countries than other countries regardless of the threshold selected. In fact, through low and middle income, income levels become decreasingly persistent as countries get wealthier (i.e., low-income levels are the most persistent, lower-middle income levels are slightly less persistent, and upper-middle income levels are even less persistent).

Table 2.1: Countries' Income Distribution, 1960 and 1970

	Base Year	
	1960	1970
# of countries in sample		
Low income	42	59
Middle income	41	58
High income	19	26
Total	102	143
# (%) of income group transitions, base year to 2009		
Low → Low	37 (88.1%)	50 (84.7%)
Low → Middle	5 (11.9%)	9 (15.3%)
Low → High	0 (0.0%)	0 (0.0%)
Middle → Low	7 (17.1%)	8 (13.8%)
Middle → Middle	24 (58.5%)	41 (70.7%)
Middle → High	10 (24.4%)	9 (15.5%)
High → Low	0 (0.0%)	0 (0.0%)
High → Middle	0 (0.0%)	1 (3.8%)
High → High	19 (100.0%)	25 (96.2%)

Source: Authors' calculations based on Penn World Table Version 7.0 (see Data Appendix).

---

[7]   The Czech Republic was a high-income country (52% of the US) in 1990, but then it dropped to middle income throughout the 1990s and early 2000s, and, since 2005, it has again been high income. Lebanon became rich in the mid-1970s but went to middle income in the early 1980s as it had a long civil war in the 1980s.

TRANSITIONING FROM LOW-INCOME GROWTH TO
HIGH-INCOME GROWTH: IS THERE A MIDDLE-INCOME TRAP?

27

We also observe that escapees grow faster than non-escapees at all levels of income. Figure 2.3 shows the average annual growth rates at different per capita income levels relative to the US (shown in the x-axis). The dark gray columns are the average growth rates for countries that ever escape from middle to rich, and the light gray columns represent growth rates for those countries that never escape. The escapees do consistently much better than their non-escapee counterparts, and they do not exhibit significant signs of slowing down. In contrast, non-escapees have low and stable growth over all levels of income: they too do not show signs of slowing down at middle income.

Figure 2.3: Average Annual Change of Purchasing Power Parity GDP per Capita

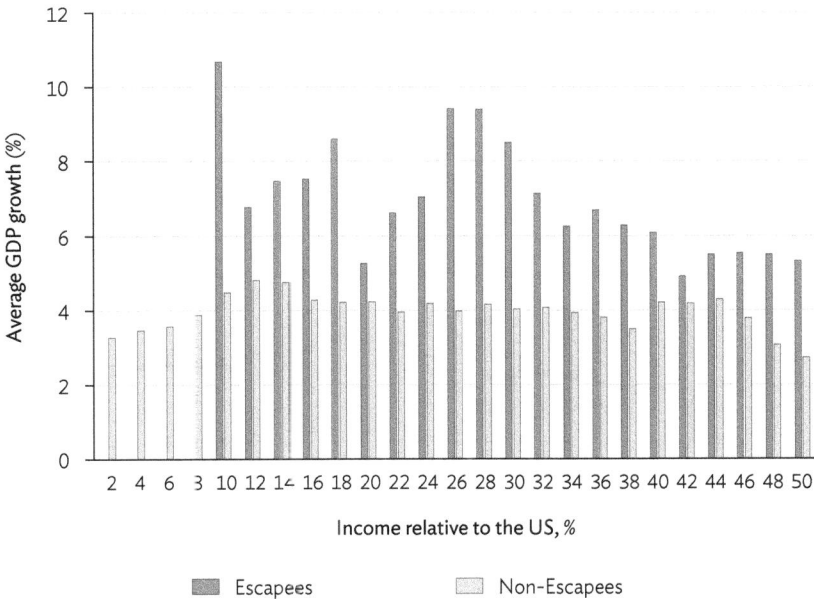

GDP = gross domestic product, US = United States.
Sources: Penn World Table Version 7.0; Authors' calculations (see Data Appendix).

Figure 2.3 presents evidence against the existence of a middle-income trap that causes growth to stagnate at a particular income level. Rather, non-escapees on average have slower growth at all levels of income, suggesting a persistent role of country-specific constraints and policy problems. A very familiar graph reinforces the point. Figure 2.4 shows the levels of PPP GDP per capita for escapees and some notable non-escapees over time. One can see that escapees, as a whole, grow strongly toward high income and do not see a "middle-income trap," while selected key non-escapees (Mexico, Malaysia, Brazil, and Turkey) experience relative stagnation for the entire period.

Figure 2.4: Income Dynamics of Escapees versus Non-Escapees

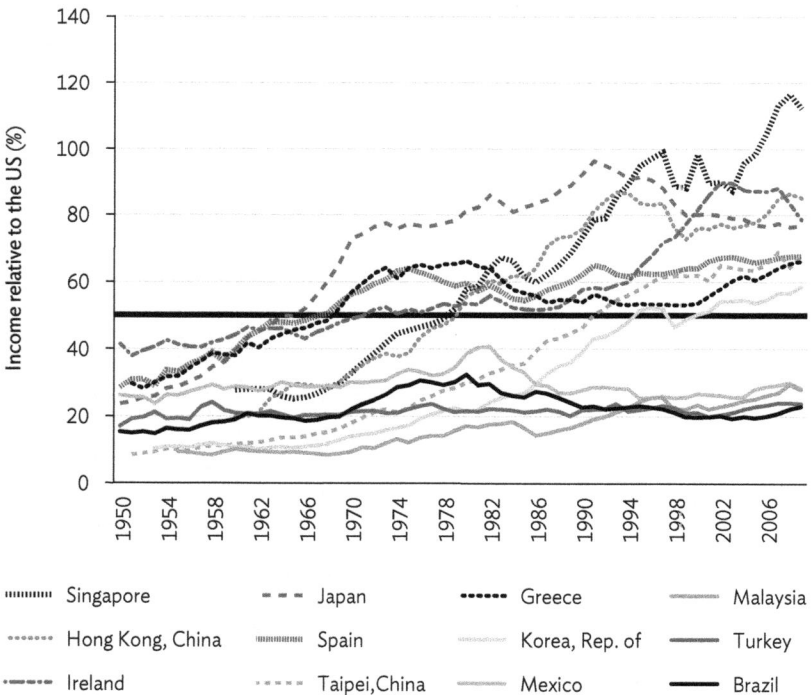

⁝⁝⁝⁝⁝⁝ Singapore	– – Japan	•••••• Greece	Malaysia
•••••• Hong Kong, China	⁝⁝⁝⁝⁝⁝ Spain	Korea, Rep. of	Turkey
•——•• Ireland	••••• Taipei,China	Mexico	Brazil

US = United States.

Note: The list of economies on the right-hand side is sorted by 2009 income level.

Source: Authors' calculations based on Penn World Table Version 7.0 (see Data Appendix).

TRANSITIONING FROM LOW-INCOME GROWTH TO
HIGH-INCOME GROWTH: IS THERE A MIDDLE-INCOME TRAP?

29

Another graph reinforces the notion that economies do not slow down at middle-income levels (relative to the US). Figure 2.5 shows a scatter plot of countries' subsequent 10-year average growth against (log of) countries' initial income relative to the US in 1960, 1970, 1980, 1990, and 2000. Evidence for a middle-income trap would imply a U-shaped curve, with countries systematically slowing down at middle-income levels. We do not see such evidence.

Figure 2.5: Initial Relative Income and Growth

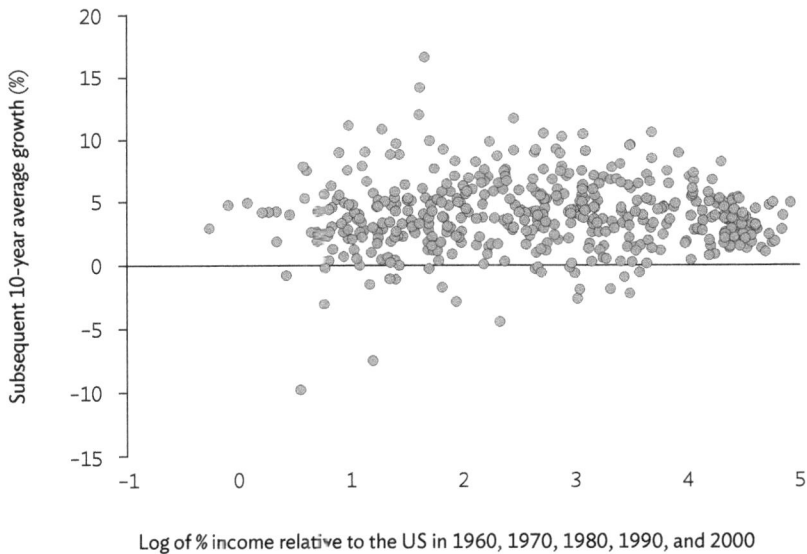

Log of % income relative to the US in 1960, 1970, 1980, 1990, and 2000

US = United States.

Source: Authors' calculations based on Penn World Table Version 7.0 (see Data Appendix).

For escapees, GDP growth was high and sustainable—strong growth in one period was followed by strong growth in the subsequent period—as if previous high growth paves the way for subsequent growth. This "momentum" hypothesis stands in contrast to the "regression to the mean" finding of Pritchett and Summers (2014). A look at all countries confirms empirically the momentum hypothesis: there is a correlation between previous growth and current growth. Figure 2.6 shows the scatter plot of a middle-income country's average decadal growth rates in two consecutive decades. The x-axis presents average growth over $t-10$ through $t-1$, while the y-axis presents average growth from $t+1$ through $t+10$, for all available years. The black dots correspond to those countries that escaped from the middle-income to the high-income group. For all middle-income countries, there is a significant, positive correlation between lagged and current decadal growth rates. The correlation coefficient for middle-income escapees is 0.47, while the correlation coefficient for middle-income non-escapees is 0.25.[8]

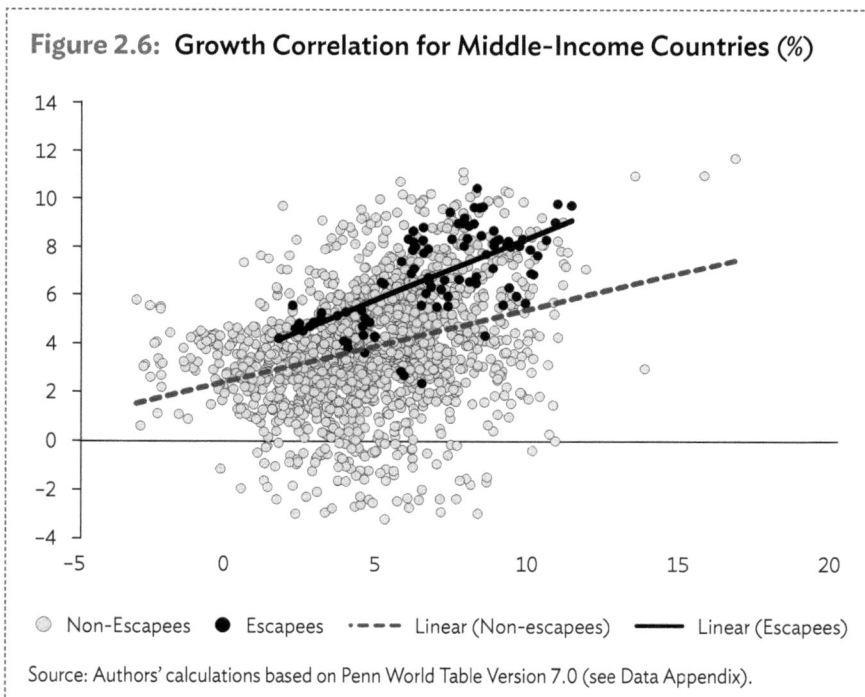

Figure 2.6: **Growth Correlation for Middle-Income Countries (%)**

Source: Authors' calculations based on Penn World Table Version 7.0 (see Data Appendix).

---

[8]   For all low- and middle-income countries, using non-overlapping decadal growth, the correlation coefficient between lagged and future growth is 0.19. Easterly et al. (1993) calculated the correlation coefficient between 1960s–1970s for developing countries as 0.1 and 1970s–1980s as 0.33.

TRANSITIONING FROM LOW-INCOME GROWTH TO
HIGH-INCOME GROWTH: IS THERE A MIDDLE-INCOME TRAP?

31

The positive correlation we find is particularly strong for escapees. Also for escapees, the dots are much more concentrated at the upper right end of the scatter plot, implying that the escapees' GDP growth is not only higher, but also more stable than that of other countries.

There are several possible economic interpretations for the persistence in growth. For example, it is possible that high growth provides more resources for investment (in infrastructure and education), paving the way for high growth in the next period. Political economy may also play a role: it may be politically easier for reforms to continue and deepen if they yielded economic success and high growth in the previous period.

2.4 | Comparing Middle-Income Average Growth Based on Fundamentals

What determines the ability of certain middle-income countries to persist in high growth? The previous section demonstrated that using a relative income standard, there is not an easily identifiable middle-income trap; instead, there are successful and unsuccessful countries at all levels of income.

Here, we first document several differences in fundamentals of escapees (middle-income countries that successfully transitioned to high-income countries) and non-escapees (middle-income countries that have yet to transition).[9] Such an exercise enables an identification of the underlying characteristics and sources of growth associated with movements from middle income to high income. Results from this analysis are shown in the Appendix, Table A2.2. In the table, significant differences (at 95%) between escapees and non-escapees are represented in bold text. In addition to the results for all middle-income countries, Table A2.2 also presents disaggregates

[9]   Unlike the previous list of escapees, which only included economies that "escaped" between 1960 and 2009, this list includes economies that escaped earlier as well as economies for which we do not have 1960 data. These include Austria; Bahamas; Spain; Finland; Greece; Hong Kong, China; Ireland; Iceland; Israel; Italy; Japan; the Republic of Korea; Macau, China; Malta; Puerto Rico; Singapore; Slovenia; Seychelles; and Taipei,China.

escapee and non-escapee fundamentals across four middle-income categories (10%–20%, 20%–30%, 30%–40%, and 40%–50% of US income).

This descriptive analysis reveals that escapees have higher GDP and TFP growth at all relative income levels. They have greater levels of human capital, experience a faster transformation to industry, are consistently export-oriented, have better macroeconomic management, and have more income equality and more growth-conducive demographic conditions. Additional details are discussed in the following subsections.

However, the approach represented in Table A2.2 suffers from a potential methodological shortcoming. If we think of escapees as rapidly growing countries, then the table basically shows that fast-growing countries have better fundamentals than slow-growing countries. These associations could be very misleading about the causal impact of the fundamentals. For instance, advocates like to point out that fast-growing countries like the Republic of Korea engaged in industrial policy, but this ignores the fact that many countries have experimented with industrial policy without growing rapidly.

The remainder of this section therefore looks at growth performance based on fundamentals, rather than the reverse. In the following discussion, each chart represents one potential determinant of future growth. Here, the dark gray bars represent average growth trajectories (future 10-year average growth rates) for countries with values below the median for that particular characteristic, and the light gray bars represent average growth trajectories for countries with values above the median. The error bars represent 95% confidence intervals. We separate results for lower-middle-income countries (10%–30% of US income) and upper-middle-income countries (30%–50% of US income) to see how growth determinants differ across the middle-income spectrum. Medians are calculated on an annual basis for lower- and upper-middle-income countries separately. So, for instance, in Figure 2.7A, the dark gray bars represent the average future 10-year average growth rates for all country/year observations in which the level of tertiary education is lower than the median value for all lower- and upper-middle-income countries in that particular year.

TRANSITIONING FROM LOW-INCOME GROWTH TO
HIGH-INCOME GROWTH: IS THERE A MIDDLE-INCOME TRAP?

33

Figure 2.7A:

Average Years of Tertiary Schooling Relative to the United States
(beginning of period)

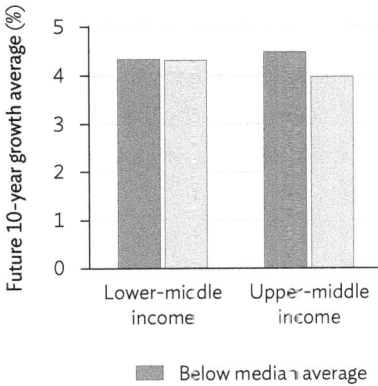

Figure 2.7B:

Number of Patents
(beginning of period)

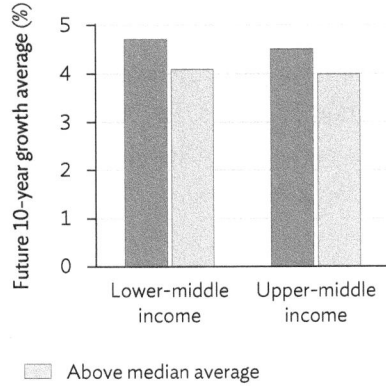

Below median average   Above median average

Notes: Error bars represent 95% confidence intervals. "Below" ("above") refers to observations below (above) the median in a given year for the given income group. "Beginning of period" indicates observations at the start of a given 10-year growth period.

Source: Authors' calculations (see Data Appendix).

2.4.1 Human Capital

The results in Table A2.2 indicate that escapees exhibit higher levels of primary, secondary, and tertiary education, and are also clearly differentiated from non-escapees by the number of patents they generate. Disaggregated results suggest that tertiary education is more important for escapees at lower-middle income levels, while patents are more prevalent for escapees at upper-middle income levels. This finding suggests that the quality of education is more important at middle-high income levels, consistent with the view that transition from middle to high income must be fueled by innovation-led growth.

Looking instead at growth performance based on fundamentals shown in Figures 2.7A and 2.7B, average years of tertiary education has little predictive power with regard to future growth; in the slight (not statistically significant) differences, upper-middle-income countries seem to suffer slightly from more tertiary education. With regard to patents, both lower-middle-income countries and upper-middle-income countries with above-median patents grow slower. This contrasts with the escapee vs. non-escapee results, which showed that upper-middle-income-level escapees have many more patents than non-escapees. The results in Table A2.2 were driven by the patent performance of the Republic of Korea and Japan, which is why this current exercise adds value.

2.4.2 Economic Structure

Countries that escape seem to show a clear and rapid transition from agriculture to industry, and this transition is particularly prevalent at lower-middle income levels (Table A2.2). Escapees tend to have larger industry sectors and smaller agriculture and service sectors, and they also have higher growth in industry and lower growth in agriculture and services. Buttressing these findings, Figures 2.8A and 2.8B show that lower-middle-income countries that see larger declines in the agriculture share and increases in the industry share grow much faster on average, while an increase in the share of the service sector translates into slower growth; these trends hold for the upper-middle income level, but are reduced in magnitude.

2.4.3 Openness

Escapees are significantly more export-oriented and have more undervalued currencies (defined as in Rodrik 2008). This undervaluation is particularly prevalent at lower-middle income (Table A2.2). For both lower- and upper-middle-income countries, export orientation is associated with higher growth and undervaluation is associated with lower growth (Figures 2.9A and 2.9B). These trends are particularly strong for upper-middle-income countries.

TRANSITIONING FROM LOW-INCOME GROWTH TO
HIGH-INCOME GROWTH: IS THERE A MIDDLE-INCOME TRAP?

35

Figure 2.8A:
Growth in Agriculture Share of GDP (concurrent 10-year annual average)

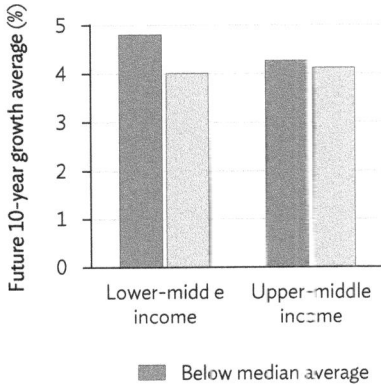

Figure 2.8B:
Growth in Industry Share of GDP (concurrent 10-year annual average)

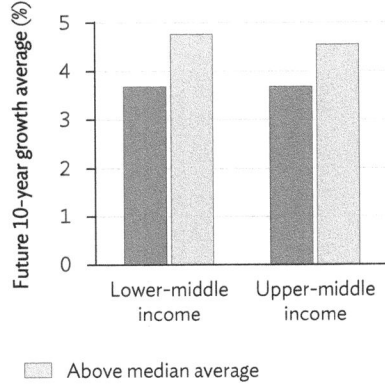

GDP = gross domestic product.

Notes: Error bars represent 95% confidence intervals. "Below" ("above") refers to observations below (above) the median in a given year for the given income group.

Source: Authors' calculations (see Data Appendix).

2.4.4 Macroeconomic Conditions

Escapees, and particularly upper-middle-income escapees, do not experience high inflation (Table A2.2). No middle-income "eventual escapee" ever experiences inflation over 20%, and by the time they reach upper-middle-income levels, they very rarely experience inflation over 10%. Even excluding the outliers (defined as the top 5% of observations), middle-income escapees experience lower inflation than non-escapees.[10]

---

[10] The top 5% of inflation observations for non-escapee middle-income countries (of nearly 2,000 observations) includes all countries with inflation over 85.7%. The top 5% outliers are not driven simply by a few countries with persistently high inflation (although many countries are indeed frequently delinquent); rather, 20 countries join the list at some point (Argentina, Belarus, Brazil, Bulgaria, Costa Rica, Croatia, Ecuador, Estonia, Latvia, Lithuania, Macedonia, Mexico, Peru, Poland, Romania, the Russian Federation, Suriname, Turkey, Ukraine, and Uruguay).

Figure 2.9A:
Exports as a Share of GDP
(concurrent 10-year
annual average)

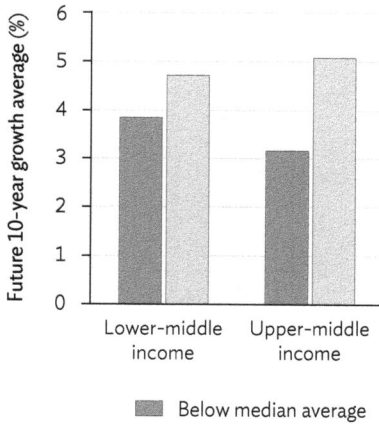

Figure 2.9B:
Log Undervaluation
(concurrent 10-year
annual average)

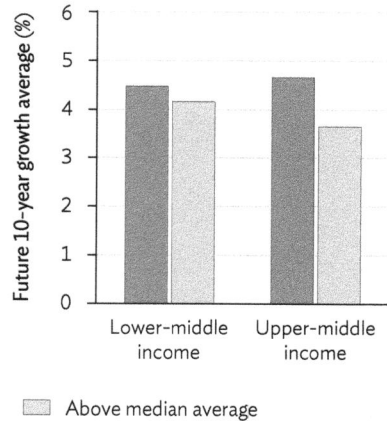

GDP = gross domestic product.

Notes: Error bars represent 95% confidence intervals. "Below" ("above") refers to observations below (above) the median in a given year for the given income group.

Source: Authors' calculations (see Data Appendix).

However, escapees have higher levels of external debt, which might be a result of greater access to outside markets or more financial development. Due to a lack of data, we cannot include other financial development indexes.

Looking instead at growth based on fundamentals, countries with lower levels of inflation grow significantly faster (Figure 2.10A). Inflation itself is fairly persistent, so it is not surprising that both lagged and concurrent inflation have negative predicted effects on growth. In contrast with the results for escapees in Table A2.2, Figure 2.10B shows, more in line with expectations, that middle-income countries with lower external debt grow significantly faster on average.

TRANSITIONING FROM LOW-INCOME GROWTH TO
HIGH-INCOME GROWTH: IS THERE A MIDDLE-INCOME TRAP?

37

Figure 2.10A:
Consumer Price Index
Inflation (concurrent 10-year
annual average)

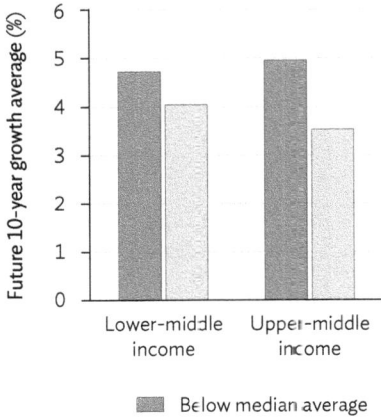

Figure 2.10B:
External Debt as a Share
of GNI (concurrent 10-year
annual average)

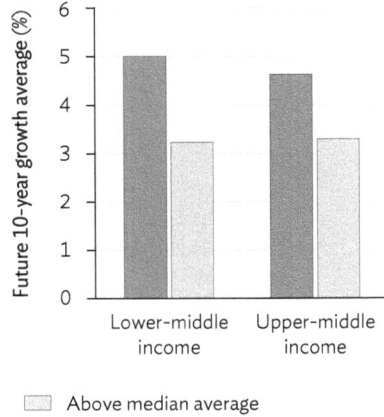

GNI = gross national income.

Notes: Error bars represent 95% confidence intervals. "Below" ("above") refers to observations below (above) the median in a given year for the given income group.

Source: Authors' calculations (see Data Appendix).

2.4.5 Governance and Politics

Levels of democracy and autocracy have little, if any, predicted effect on growth for either lower- or upper-middle-income countries (Figures 2.11A and 2.11B). There is some evidence that autocracy helps growth at lower-middle-income leve s but harms growth at upper-middle- income levels, but these differences are not significant.

2.4.6 Inequality and Demographics

Escapees have greater equality and lower age dependency ratios, and escapees at all middle-income levels are also less likely to see increases in inequality as well as decreases in the age dependency ratio (i.e., the so-called "demographic dividend") (Table A2.2).

Figure 2.11A:
Democracy Indicator
(beginning of period)

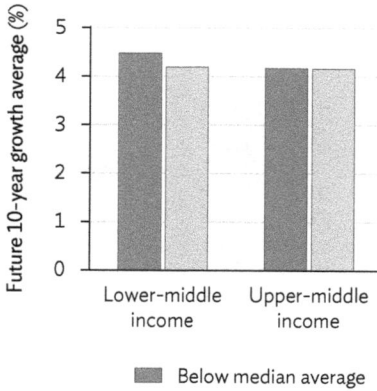

Figure 2.11B:
Autocracy Indicator
(beginning of period)

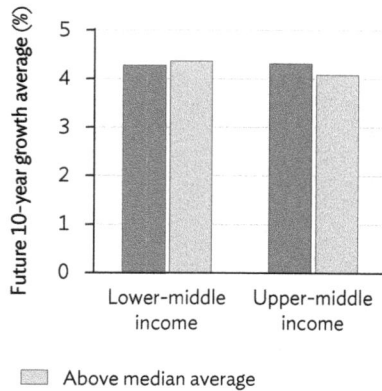

■ Below median average   □ Above median average

Notes: Error bars represent 95% confidence intervals. "Below" ("above") refers to observations below (above) the median in a given year for the given income group. "Beginning of period" indicates observations at the start of a given 10-year growth period.

Source: Authors' calculations (see Data Appendix).

Both the level of demographic characteristics at the beginning of the period and changes in demographic characteristics over the period affect growth (Figures 2.12A and 2.12B). Lower dependency ratios result in faster growth, and declining dependency ratios (the "demographic dividend") also translate into faster growth.

In terms of inequality, higher beginning-of-period levels are associated with slower growth, as are larger increases in the Gini coefficient (Figures 2.13A and 2.13B). The effect is particularly pronounced for Gini coefficient increases in upper-middle-income countries.

To sum up, the factors that stand out from the descriptive analysis in this section, as associated with growth for middle-income countries, are (i) economic structure, namely a faster transformation from agriculture to industry; (ii) export orientation; (iii) lower inflation and external debt; and (iv) decreases in inequality and the age dependency ratio.

TRANSITIONING FROM LOW-INCOME GROWTH TO
HIGH-INCOME GROWTH: IS THERE A MIDDLE-INCOME TRAP?

39

Figure 2.12A:
Age Dependency Ratio
(beginning of period)

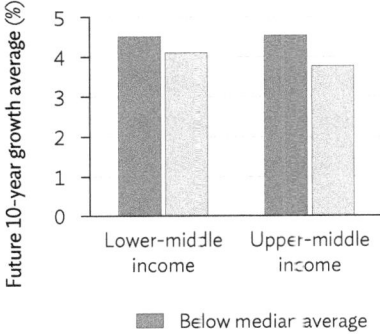

Figure 2.12B:
Change in Age Dependency
Ratio (concurrent 10-year
annual average)

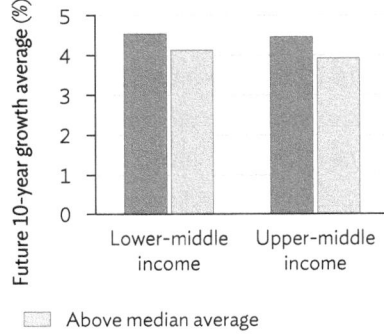

Below median average   Above median average

Notes: Error bars represent 95% confidence intervals. "Below" ("above") refers to observations below (above) the median in a given year for the given income group. "Beginning of period" indicates observations at the start of a given 10-year growth period.

Source: Authors' calculations (see Data Appendix).

Figure 2.13A:
Gini Coefficient
(beginning of period)

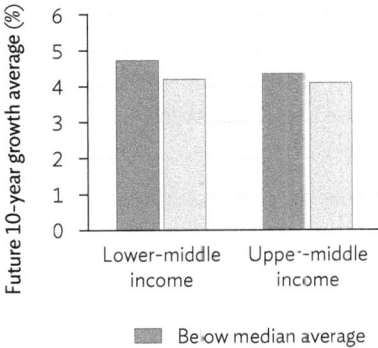

Figure 2.13B:
Change in Gini Coefficient
(concurrent 10-year
annual average)

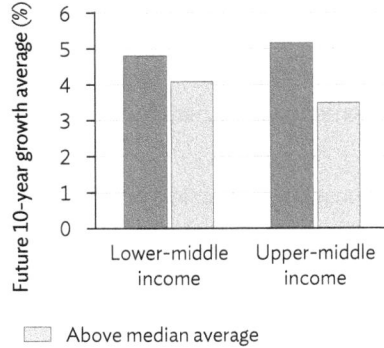

Below median average   Above median average

Notes: Error bars represent 95% confidence intervals. "Below" ("above") refers to observations below (above) the median in a given year for the given income group. "Beginning of period" indicates observations at the start of a given 10-year growth period.

Source: Authors' calculations (see Data Appendix).

2.5 | Regression Analysis

The differential growth performance suggests that there is room for a more systematic investigation. In this section, we run a pooled OLS regression on middle- and low-income countries, and interact the factors with a middle-income dummy to identify which factors matter for poor countries but not for middle-income countries and vice versa.[11] While we are aware that several issues exist with cross-country growth regressions (see Easterly et al. 1993), they nevertheless help to provide additional suggestive evidence for our exercises in the previous section. The regressions take the form:

$$Y_t = \alpha + \sum_i \beta_i X_{it} * MI_t + \sum_j \gamma_j C_{jt} + \varepsilon_t$$

The dependent variable (Y_t) is the overlapping decade average growth of annual PPP GDP per capita. To control for heteroscedasticity and within-country serial correlations in the error terms, we report robust Newey–West type t-statistics. The nine right-hand-side variables of interest (X_i), included together in each regression, are *Gini coefficient* (concurrent average level), *Fertility Rate* (5-year lag average level), *Age Dependency* (concurrent average change), *Agriculture share of GDP* (concurrent average change), *Tertiary education level relative to the US* (at the beginning of the 10-year period), Inflation (5-year lag average), *Polity score* (5-year lag average), *Trade share of GDP* (concurrent average level), and *Log of undervaluation* (concurrent average level). Since many of these variables can be endogenously determined with growth, the results reported here are best treated as associations. Please see the definition, the construction, and detailed data sources in the Data Appendix.

The baseline regression pools low- and middle-income countries and looks at these nine variables and their *interaction terms* with the middle-income dummy (M_{It}), along with controls (C_j) for lagged income growth and income relative

---

[11]   Our approach is related to Barreto and Hughes (2004) who showed differential growth determinants for underachievers (i.e., countries that grow more slowly than traditional characteristics predict that it should) and overachievers.

TRANSITIONING FROM LOW-INCOME GROWTH TO
HIGH-INCOME GROWTH: IS THERE A MIDDLE-INCOME TRAP?

41

to the US. The results are shown in Appendix Table A2.3. Along with the baseline regression results (column 1), Table A2.3 also presents results using absolute income as a control (column 2); not including the control for lagged growth (column 3); and regression results for both the low- and middle-income subsamples, excluding the interaction terms (columns 4 and 5, respectively).

As suggested by the "momentum" argument, *lagged 5-year growth* is significant in all specifications. This is consistent with the standard conditional convergence story, which suggests that growth rates of developing countries should decline over time (thus implying a serial correlation in growth levels). But the coefficient is nearly twice as large and is much more significant for the middle-income subsample than for the low-income subsample, implying that momentum may be more important for middle-income countries.

Generally, the following factors are significant for growth of middle-income countries: Gini coefficient (at the 10% level), fertility rate (at the 10% level), decline in the agriculture share of GDP (at the 5% level), and the trade share of GDP (at the 10% level). We discuss the important indicators in more detail below.

2.5.1 Structural Variables

In the baseline regressions, regardless of the controls or sample (low, middle, or both), the coefficient on the change in the agriculture share of GDP is significantly negative, suggesting that declining agriculture shares of GDP are important for growth (Appendix, Tables A2.3 and A2.4). The absolute coefficient for the low income-subsample is larger than that for the middle-income subsample. However, the interaction term (the middle-income dummy) is not robustly significant.

The industry share of GDP has a significant positive effect on growth for middle-income countries but has insignificant differential impacts on low- and middle-income countries (Appendix, Table A2.4). Interestingly, growth in the services share of GDP leads to a negative and significant coefficient on growth in middle-income countries. The interaction term is also significant and negative.

The regression results can be interpreted as follows: a decline in the share of agriculture or an increase in industry share is positively associated with growth both in low- and middle-income countries. However, growth in services actually harms growth in middle-income countries. This is probably because services in middle-income countries are still of lower productivity than industry; an expansion of services at the cost of manufacturing can actually hurt growth.

2.5.2 Human Capital and Inequality

The lagged level of years of tertiary education is insignificant in the pooled sample, as is the interaction term. This is consistent with existing literature: current measures of human capital have little effect on growth. Similarly, higher inequality does not seem to have an impact on most of the sample, except for middle-income countries. It has a negative coefficient but is only significant at the 10% level.

2.5.3 Openness

In the full regressions, trade has a negative but insignificant coefficient. In the middle-income subsample, however, trade has a slightly significant and positive association with growth. Similarly, we find the interaction term is positive, implying that trade has a stronger effect for middle-income countries than low-income countries. Undervaluation, on the other hand, has little impact on growth. However, the interaction term (the middle-income dummy) is negative and significant, implying that the benefit of undervaluation on growth (if any) is much smaller when a country is already a middle-income country.

TRANSITIONING FROM LOW-INCOME GROWTH TO
HIGH-INCOME GROWTH: IS THERE A MIDDLE-INCOME TRAP?

43

2.6 | Conclusion

In this chapter, we have attempted to answer two questions: Is there a middle-income trap? If there is a middle-income trap, what causes it? We answer the first question in the negative: countries that grow fast continue to grow fast, and they do not get "stuck" at any particular middle-income level. This suggests that becoming "trapped" in some middle-income level is not inevitable. However, this finding does not mean that no countries become *trapped* at a middle-income level. Indeed, middle-income countries that did not "escape" remain stagnant with low growth at all levels of relative income. Relative income levels are highly persistent, and transitioning from middle income to high income is hard.

Even in the absence of any evidence for a middle-income trap, it is worth exploring the different fundamentals of escapees and non-escapees, as well as the effects of different growth strategies at middle-income and low-income levels. We find that common wisdom largely applies: escapees have higher growth at all relative income levels, higher TFP growth, and experience a faster transformation toward industry. They have better macroeconomic management and greater income equality, and they are consistently more export-oriented. An alternative analysis focused on fundamentals also reveals that faster transformation to industry, low inflation, stronger exports, and reduced inequality are associated with stronger growth.

Cross-country growth regressions confirm that growth in middle-income countries is positively associated with industrialization, openness, and equality. However, we do not see clear associations between education and innovation to growth in middle- and low-income countries. We also find that transition toward service sector development can harm middle-income country growth prospects.

Most of the results in cross-country growth regressions are fragile (Levine and Renelt 1992; Sala-i-Martin 1997). However, both of these meta-studies find that country openness is robustly correlated with output growth, which is consistent with our results. The literature is silent on the robustness of agriculture share and growth.

One of the original theorists behind the middle-income trap describes it using an analogy from golf: "Not everyone falls into a 'trap,' but everyone's play is influenced by the presence of traps. Successful economies avoid falling into traps or escape rapidly, while unsuccessful (or unlucky) economies can get stuck for many years" (Kharas and Kohli 2011: 281). We agree, but we emphasize that traps at middle-income levels are no more likely than traps at other income levels; to continue the golf analogy, traps are scattered throughout the golf course, not only midway down the fairway. Avoiding these traps takes skill no matter where they are located, although approaches and club choice (i.e., economic strategies and policies) will differ as the green (high income) gets closer.

References

Agénor, P.-R., and O. Canuto. 2012. Middle-Income Growth Traps. World Bank Policy Research Working Paper 6210. Washington, DC: The World Bank.

Aiyar, S., R. Duval, D. Puy, Y. Wu, and L. Zhang. 2013. Growth Slowdowns and the Middle-Income Trap. IMF Working Paper WP/13/71. Washington, DC: International Monetary Fund.

Barreto, R., and T. Hughes. 2004. Under Performers and Over Achievers: A Quantile Regression Analysis of Growth. *The Economic Record* 80: 17–35.

Barro, R., and J.-W. Lee. 2011. A New Data Set of Educational Attainment in the World, 1950–2010. NBER Working Paper 15902. Cambridge, MA: National Bureau of Economic Research.

Cai, F. 2012. Is There a 'Middle-income Trap'? Theories, Experiences and Relevance to China. *China & World Economy* 20(1): 49–61.

TRANSITIONING FROM LOW-INCOME GROWTH TO
HIGH-INCOME GROWTH: IS THERE A MIDDLE-INCOME TRAP?

45

Caselli, F. 2005. Accounting for Cross-Country Income Differences.
    In *Handbook of Economic Growth*, edited by P. Aghion and S. Durlauf.
    Edition 1, Volume 1. Amsterdam: Elsevier.
Daude, C., and E. Fernández–Arias. 2010. On the Role of Productivity and
    Factor Accumulation in Economic Development in Latin America and
    the Caribbean. IDB Working Paper Series IDB-WP-155.
Easterly, W., M. Kremer, L. Pritchett, and L. Summers. 1993. Good Policy
    or Good Luck?: Country Growth Performance and Temporary Shocks.
    Journal of Monetary Economics 32(3): 459–483.
Eichengreen, B., D. Park, and K. Shin. 2012. When Fast Growing Economies
    Slow Down: International Evidence and Implications for China.
    Asian Economic Papers 11: 42–87.
———. 2013. Growth Slowdowns Redux: New Evidence on the Middle-
    Income Trap. NBER Working Paper 18673. Cambridge, MA:
    National Bureau of Economic Research.
Felipe, J., A. Abdon, and U. Kumar. 2012. Tracking the Middle-income
    Trap: What Is It, Who Is in It, and Why? Levy Economics Institute
    of Bard College Working Paper 715. Annandale-on-Hudson, NY:
    Levy Economics Institute.
Flaaen, A., E. Ghani, and S. Mishra. 2013. How to Avoid Middle Income
    Traps. Evidence from Malaysia. Policy Research Working Paper 6427.
    Washington, DC: The World Bank.
Gill, I., and H. Kharas. 2007. *An East Asian Renaissance: Ideas for Economic
    Growth*. Washington, DC: The World Bank.
Hall, R., and C. Jones. 1999. Why Do Some Countries Produce So Much
    More Output per Worker Than Others? *The Quarterly Journal of
    Economics* 114(1): 83–116.
Hausmann, R., L. Pritchett, and D. Rodrik. 2005. Growth Accelerations.
    Journal of Economic Growth 10(4): 303–329.
Heston, A., R. Summers, and B. Aten. 2011. *Penn World Table Version 7.0*.
    Center for International Comparisons of Production, Income and Prices
    at the University of Pennsylvania.

Im, F. G., and D. Rosenblatt. 2013. Middle-income Traps: A Conceptual and Empirical Survey. Policy Research Working Paper 6594. Washington, DC: The World Bank.

Kharas, H., and H. Kohli. 2011. What Is the Middle Income Trap, Why Do Countries Fall into It, and How Can It Be Avoided? *Global Journal of Emerging Market Economies.* September 3(3): 281–289.

Levine, R., and D. Renelt. 1992. A Sensitivity Analysis of Cross-Country Growth Regressions, *American Economic Review* 82(4): 942–963.

Marshall, M. G. 2011. Polity IV Project: Political Regime Characteristics and Transitions, 1800–2010. http://www.systemicpeace.org/polity/polity4.htm (accessed December 2016).

Milanovic, B. 2005. *Worlds Apart: Measuring International and Global Inequality.* Princeton, NJ: Princeton University Press. http://econ.worldbank.org/projects/inequality (accessed December 2016).

Pritchett, L. 2000. Understanding Patterns of Economic Growth: Searching for Hills among Plateaus, Mountains, and Plains. The World Bank Economic Review 14(2): 221–250.

Pritchett, L., and L. H. Summers. 2014. Asiaphoria Meets Regression to the Mean. NBER Working Paper 20573. Cambridge, MA: National Bureau of Economic Research.

Psacharopulos, G. 1994. Returns to Investment in Education: A Global Update. *World Development* 22(9): 1325–1343.

Rodrik, D. 2008. The Real Exchange Rate and Economic Growth. *Brookings Papers on Economic Activity.*

Sala-i-Martin, X. 1997. I Just Ran Two Million Regressions. *American Economic Review* 87(2): 178–183.

Vivarelli, M. 2014. Structural Change and Innovation as Exit Strategies from the Middle Income Trap. IZA Discussion Paper 8148. Bonn, Germany: Institute of Labor Economics.

World Bank. 2013. *China 2030: Building a Modern, Harmonious, and Creative Society.* Washington, DC: The Word Bank.

——. 2014. *World Development Indicators.*

Table A2.1: Income Categories, 2009

Low Income (38.6%)		
0%–2.5%	**2.5%–5%**	**5%–10%**
Zimbabwe	Mali	Zambia
Dem. Rep. of Congo	Rwanda	Sudan
Burundi	Benin	Pakistan
Liberia	Uganda	Nicaragua
Somalia	Tanzania	Kyrgyz Republic
Niger	Timor-Leste	Uzbekistan
Eritrea	Nepal	Moldova
Central African Republic	Afghanistan	Djibouti
Malawi	Kenya	Lao People's Democratic Rep.
Guinea–Bissau	Bangladesh	Philippines
Mozambique	Cote d'Ivoire	Viet Nam
Ethiopia	Lesotho	Papua New Guinea
Togo	Haiti	Syria
Madagascar	Gambia, The	India
Sierra Leone	Ghana	Morocco
Guinea	Senegal	Micronesia, Federal States of
Comoros	Mauritania	Mongolia
Burkina Faso	Cambodia	Swaziland
	Sao Tome and Principe	Honduras
	Cameroon	Bolivia
	Tajikistan	Paraguay
	Solomon Islands	Cape Verde
		Indonesia
		Sri Lanka

continued next page

Table A2.1: *Continued*

Middle Income (39.8%)			
10%–20%	20%–30%	30%–40%	40%–50%
Bhutan	Serbia	Chile	Poland
Kiribati	Belize	Belarus	Estonia
Fiji	Botswana	St. Lucia	Cyprus
Guyana	Jamaica	Latvia	Slovak Republic
Maldives	Mauritius	St. Kitts and Nevis	Portugal
Egypt	Brazil	Grenada	
Georgia	Turkey	Lebanon	
Armenia	Dominican Rep.	Lithuania	
Jordan	Panama	Russian Federation	
Namibia	Romania	Palau	
Dominica	Suriname	Croatia	
Ecuador	Costa Rica	Antigua and Barbuda	
Tunisia	Uruguay	Hungary	
Guatemala	Bulgaria		
El Salvador	Cuba		
Albania	Malaysia		
Samoa	Mexico		
Vanuatu	Argentina		
Ukraine			
Bosnia and Herzegovina			
Marshall Islands			
Montenegro			
People's Republic of China			
St. Vincent and the Grenadines			
Peru			
Colombia			
South Africa			
Macedonia			
Thailand			
Tonga			

continued next page

TRANSITIONING FROM LOW-INCOME GROWTH TO
HIGH-INCOME GROWTH: IS THERE A MIDDLE-INCOME TRAP?

49

Table A2.1: *Continued*

High Income (21.7%)				
50%–60%	60%–70%	70%–80%	80%–90%	90+%
Malta	Puerto Rico	France	United Kingdom	Austria
Barbados	Slovenia	Finland	Denmark	Switzerland
Czech Republic	Israel	Japan	Belgium	The Netherlands
Seychelles	Greece	Ireland	Hong Kong, China	United States
Korea, Rep. of	New Zealand	Germany	Sweden	Australia
Bahamas	Taipei,China		Canada	Macau, China
	Italy		Iceland	Singapore
	Spain			Norway
				Bermuda
				Luxembourg

Source: Penn World Table Version 7.0.

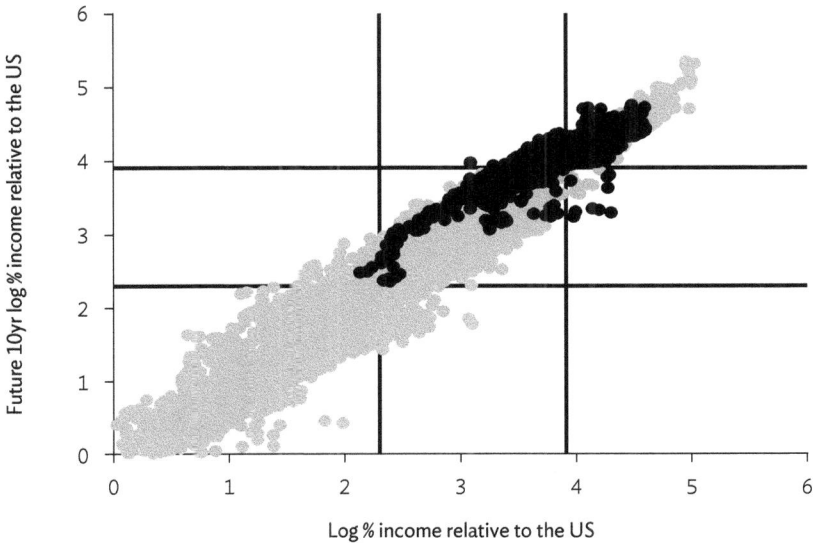

Figure A2.1: Relative Income in 10-Year Increments, 1950–2009

US = United States.
Sources: Penn World Table Version 7.0; authors' calculations.

Figure A2.1: The log of per capita income relative to the US in time t is on the x-axis, with the time t+10 value on the y-axis. The dots correspond to every possible 10-year period between 1950 and 2009. The countries in black are those that escape from middle to high income at any point. The black countries in the middle-right quadrant (i.e., those that went from rich to middle and at some point also went from middle to rich) are the Czech Republic (which got rich in the mid-1990s after dropping to middle in 1990) and Lebanon (which got rich in the mid-1970s and then went to middle income in the early 1980s).

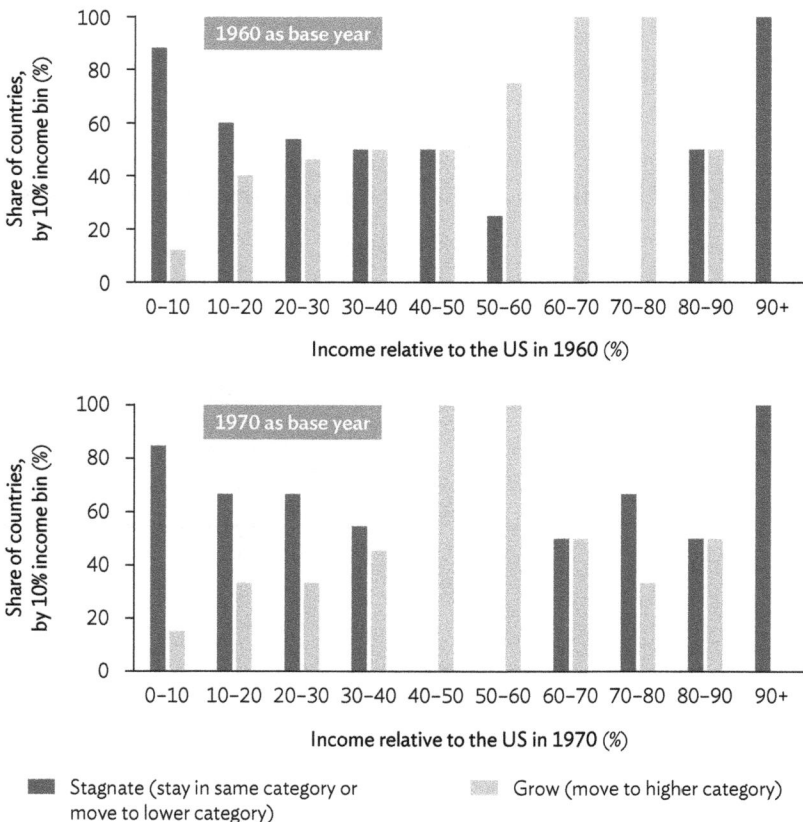

Figure A2.2: Income Mobility at Different Income Categories

US = United States.

Sources: Penn World Table Version 7.0; Authors' calculations.

TRANSITIONING FROM LOW-INCOME GROWTH TO
HIGH-INCOME GROWTH: IS THERE A MIDDLE-INCOME TRAP?

51

Table A2.2: Mean Value of Fundamentals for Middle-Income Escapees and Non-Escapees

	All Middle Income		10%–20% of US		20%–30% of US	
	Non-escapees	Escapees	Non-escapees	Escapees	Non-escapees	Escapees
Per capita GDP growth (%)	4.11	6.86	4.25	6.46	4.04	8.55
Total factor productivity (TFP) growth (%)	1.07	2.18	0.93	0.26	1.08	2.77
Average years of primary schooling relative to the US (%)	73.10	80.43	65.65	73.41	74.39	74.29
Average years of secondary schooling relative to the US (%)	31.00	43.10	28.46	33.72	32.01	45.94
Average years of tertiary schooling relative to the US (%)	17.20	22.46	14.71	21.99	18.04	23.11
Number of patents (1000)	1.79	6.97	2.26	1.33	1.53	1.44
Growth in agricultural share of GDP (%)	−2.68	−4.38	−2.20	−3.71	−3.00	−7.11
Growth in industry share of GDP (%)	−0.04	1.79	0.21	3.56	−0.07	1.53
Growth in services share of GDP (%)	1.19	0.19	1.18	0.90	1.11	1.05
Exports as a share of GDP (%)	36.78	57.83	36.05	20.69	33.28	67.80
Log undervaluation	0.17	0.24	0.11	0.28	0.25	0.32
CPI inflation (%)	18.67	6.75	14.55	14.33	27.31	9.15
External debt as a share of GNI (%)	46.72	9.74	44.34	NA	41.11	NA
Democracy indicator	5.02	3.81	4.16	1.21	5.27	2.51
Autocracy indicator	2.59	4.02	2.97	5.79	2.39	4.89
Gini coefficient	43.45	37.91	45.45	33.71	45.85	34.54
Age dependency ratio (%)	71.17	66.39	76.22	80.89	68.91	72.67
Change in Gini coefficient (%)	0.68	−0.32	0.76	0.47	0.58	−0.95
Change in age dependency ratio (%)	−0.96	−1.62	−0.98	−0.84	−0.87	−1.80

continued next page

Table A2.2: *Continued*

	30%–40% of US		40%–50% of US	
	Non-escapees	Escapees	Non-escapees	Escapees
Per capita GDP growth (%)	3.97	6.70	3.63	5.97
Total factor productivity (TFP) growth (%)	1.58	2.49	1.37	2.54
Average years of primary schooling relative to the US (%)	87.07	76.84	96.84	92.91
Average years of secondary schooling relative to the US (%)	30.99	46.89	43.11	44.78
Average years of tertiary schooling relative to the US (%)	19.61	20.33	26.62	23.84
Number of patents (1000)	1.77	3.42	0.50	12.21
Growth in agricultural share of GDP (%)	−2.90	−1.75	−4.30	−5.07
Growth in industry share of GDP (%)	−0.49	1.46	−0.75	1.56
Growth in services share of GDP (%)	1.41	0.05	1.21	−0.20
Exports as a share of GDP (%)	41.46	63.92	49.33	61.34
Log undervaluation	0.22	0.24	0.13	0.17
CPI inflation (%)	18.96	4.69	6.91	4.89
External debt as a share of GNI (%)	41.92	8.00	62.98	10.17
Democracy indicator	6.27	4.19	8.17	6.32
Autocracy indicator	2.32	4.00	1.21	2.16
Gini coefficient	37.62	39.44	29.08	40.38
Age dependency ratio (%)	66.20	66.86	51.04	59.55
Change in Gini coefficient (%)	0.47	−0.13	0.99	−0.54
Change in age dependency ratio (%)	−1.16	−2.81	−0.80	−1.31

CPI = consumer price index, GDP = gross domestic product, GNI = gross national income, NA = not available, US = United States.

Note: Numbers in bold indicate significant difference at 95% confidence.

Source: Authors' calculations (see Data Appendix).

TRANSITIONING FROM LOW-INCOME GROWTH TO
HIGH-INCOME GROWTH: IS THERE A MIDDLE-INCOME TRAP?

53

Table A2.3: Main Regression Results

	(1) Baseline	(2) Absolute GDP	(3) No Lagged Growth	(4) Low Income	(5) Middle Income
Gini – concurrent average level	-0.000 (1.03)	-0.000 (1.29)	-0.000 (0.58)	-0.000 (1.25)	-0.000 (2.40)*
Fertility – 5-yr lag average	0.001 (0.54)	-0.000 (0.13)	0.001 (0.64)	0.000 (0.16)	0.003 (2.16)*
Dependency – concurrent avg change	-0.179 (0.98)	-0.124 (0.67)	-0.245 (1.22)	-0.121 (0.56)	-0.144 (0.83)
Agr/GDP – concurrent avg change	-0.321 (5.12)**	-0.312 (5.03)**	-0.378 (5.44)**	-0.329 (5.19)**	-0.181 (3.90)**
Tertiary – lag 1-yr relative to US	0.001 (0.07)	0.001 (0.10)	-0.006 (0.51)	-0.005 (0.37)	0.005 (0.34)
CPI – 5-yr lag average	0.000 (1.44)	0.000 (1.45)	0.000 (0.01)	0.000 (1.08)	0.000 (0.67)
Polity score – 5-yr lag average	0.000 (1.45)	0.000 (1.36)	0.000 (1.12)	0.000 (1.36)	0.000 (1.76)
Trade/GDP – concurrent average level	-0.000 (0.86)	-0.000 (0.89)	-0.000 (1.10)	-0.000 (1.02)	0.000 (2.45)*
Log underval. – concurrent average level	0.004 (0.73)	0.004 (0.71)	0.004 (0.77)	0.003 (0.50)	-0.008 (1.41)
Variables Interacted with Middle-Income Dummy					
Gini – concurrent avg level	-0.000 (1.24)	-0.000 (1.07)	-0.000 (1.56)		
Fertility – 5-yr lag avg	0.003 (1.37)	0.002 (1.25)	0.004 (1.80)		
Dependency – concurrent avg change	0.009 (0.04)	0.019 (0.08)	-0.137 (0.49)		
Agr/GDP – concurrent avg change	0.147 (1.94)	0.125 (1.66)	0.235 (2.89)**		
Tertiary – lag 1-yr relative to US	0.000 (0.02)	0.010 (0.56)	-0.003 (0.18)		
CPI – 5-yr lag avg	-0.000 (0.88)	-0.000 (1.38)	-0.000 (2.07)*		
Polity score – 5-yr lag avg	0.000 (0.14)	0.000 (0.51)	0.000 (0.23)		
Trade/GDP – concurrent avg level	0.000 (1.85)	0.000 (2.04)*	0.000 (2.04)*		
Log underval. – concurrent avg level	-0.014 (1.78)	-0.016 (2.04)*	-0.022 (2.71)**		

continued next page

Table A2.3: *Continued*

	(1) Baseline	(2) Absolute GDP	(3) No Lagged Growth	(4) Low Income	(5) Middle Income
Controls					
Per capita GDP growth – 5-yr lag avg	0.191 (6.06)**	0.190 (6.09)**		0.145 (3.03)**	0.220 (5.46)**
Per cap. GDP (rel. US unless specified)	−0.000 (2.19)*	−0.000 (4.70)**	−0.000 (0.74)	0.000 (0.17)	−0.000 (2.20)*
Constant	0.040 (4.77)**	0.049 (5.73)**	0.042 (4.63)**	0.045 (3.07)**	0.035 (3.55)**
Observations	1682	1682	1686	823	859
Sample	L&M	L&M	L&M	L	M

agr = agricultural, avg = average, CPI = consumer price index, GDP = gross domestic product,
L = low-income countries, M = middle-income countries, US = United States, yr = year.

Notes: Robust z statistics in parentheses; * significant at the 5% level; ** significant at the 1% level.

Source: Authors' calculations (see Data Appendix for variable sources and definitions).

Table A2.4: **Growth with Different Structural Variables**

	Concurrent 10-Year Growth of Agriculture Share of GDP		
Variable	Full Sample	Low Income	Middle Income
Variable	−0.312 (4.25)**	−0.320 (4.18)**	−0.174 (4.97)**
MI*Variable	0.127 (1.60)		
Lag 5-yr avg growth	0.143 (4.25)**	0.103 (2.08)*	0.194 (7.61)**
Income relative to US	−0.000 (3.49)**		
Constant	0.037 (16.10)**	0.036 (13.88)**	0.028 (15.65)**
Observations	3,898	2,116	1,782

continued next page

TRANSITIONING FROM LOW-INCOME GROWTH TO
HIGH-INCOME GROWTH: IS THERE A MIDDLE-INCOME TRAP?

55

Table A2.4: *Continued*

Concurrent 10-Year Growth of Industry Share of GDP			
	Full Sample	Low Income	Middle Income
Variable	0.072	0.073	0.197
	(1.48)	(1.48)	(4.53)**
MI*Variable	0.124		
	(1.96)*		
Lag 5-yr avg growth	0.154	0.144	0.165
	(5.04)**	(3.10)**	(6.48)**
Income relative to US	−0.000		
	(1.21)		
Constant	0.036	0.036	0.033
	(16.53)**	(14.34)**	(21.48)**
Observations	3,893	2,111	1,782
Concurrent 10-Year Growth of Services Share of GDP			
	Full Sample	Low Income	Middle Income
Variable	0.093	0.098	−0.156
	(1.68)	(1.78)	(3.79)**
MI*Variable	−0.242		
	(3.57)**		
Lag 5-yr avg growth	0.159	0.151	0.166
	(5.07)**	(3.13)**	(6.53)**
Income relative to US	−0.000		
	(0.90)		
Constant	0.037	0.036	0.035
	(16.65)**	(14.07)**	(21.85)**
Observations	3,893	2,111	1,782

avg = average, GDP = gross domestic product, MI = middle income, US = United States, yr = year.

Notes: Robust z statistics in parentheses; * significant at the 5% level; ** significant at the 1% level.

Source: Authors' calculations (see Data Appendix for variable sources and definitions).

Data Appendix

Exclusion of Oil-Rich Countries

We identify oil-rich countries as those whose average oil exports, as a share of gross domestic product (GDP), exceed 30% or whose oil rents, as a share of GDP, exceed 29%, using the World Bank World Development Indicators data. With these criteria, the oil exporters are Algeria, Angola, Azerbaijan, Bahrain, Brunei Darussalam, Chad, Congo, Equatorial Guinea, Gabon, Iran, Iraq, Kazakhstan, Kuwait, Libya, Nigeria, Oman, Qatar, Saudi Arabia, Trinidad and Tobago, Turkmenistan, the United Arab Emirates, Venezuela, and Yemen.

International Growth Accounting Exercise

Baseline data used for growth accounting exercise, including per capita GDP, employment, and investment, come from the Penn World Table Version 7.0 (Heston, Summers, and Aten 2011).

Following Caselli (2005), capital stocks are generated using a perpetual inventory method:

$$K_t = I_t + (1 - \delta)K_{t-1},$$

where I_t is investment and δ is the depreciation rate. We assume 6% depreciation across countries. For countries with available investment data pre-1970, we calculate the initial capital stock as

$$K_0 = I_0/(g + \delta),$$

where I_0 is investment in its first available year and g is the average geometric growth rate of investment between I_0 and 1970. For those countries with investment data available starting only in the 1970s, we calculate K_t and K_0 with the same equations, but substitute g as the average geometric growth rate of investment between I_0 and 1980.

TRANSITIONING FROM LOW-INCOME GROWTH TO
HIGH-INCOME GROWTH: IS THERE A MIDDLE-INCOME TRAP?

57

Human capital data at the primary, secondary, and tertiary levels come
from Barro and Lee (2011). The data cover average years of schooling in
the population over 15 years old from 1950 to 2010, in 5-year intervals.[1]
Given the persistence of years of schooling data, we extrapolate data for
intervening years by assuming constant growth over each 5-year period. To
generate a human capital index, we follow Hall and Jones (1999) and generate
a human capital index as

$$h = e^{\varphi(s)},$$

where s is average years of schooling and $\varphi(s)$ is a piecewise linear function
with slope contingent on estimates for returns to different levels of schooling:
0.13 for $s \leq 4$, 0.10 for $4 < s \leq 8$, and 0.07 for $8 < s$.[2]

In the baseline growth accounting exercise, we exclude human capital
(its inclusion makes little difference, as shown below) and adopt a simple
Cobb–Douglas production function:

$$Y = AK^{\alpha}L^{1-\alpha},$$

Where Y is GDP, K is the aggregate capital stock, L is the number of workers,
and α is a constant representing factor shares. We then divide through by the
number of workers:

$$y = Ak^{\alpha},$$

where $y = Y/L$ and $k = K/L$. A represents the efficiency with which capital and
labor are used, and thus corresponds to total factor productivity (TFP).

---

[1] With our focus on middle-income and lower-income countries, and given lower tertiary
attendance rates in these countries, we focus on years of schooling in the 15+ population rather
than the 25+ population, as did Caselli (2005) and Hall and Jones (1999).

[2] From Caselli (2005): "International data on education-wage profiles (Psacharopulos 1994)
suggests that in Sub-Saharan Africa (which has the lowest levels of education) the return to
one extra year of education is about 13.4%, the World average is 10.1%, and the Organisation
for Economic Co-operation and Development average is 6.8%. Hall and Jones's measure tries to
reconcile the log-linearity at the country level with the convexity across countries."

We take growth rates of y and k and then estimate TFP as

$$TFP = gy - \alpha^{*}gk,$$

where the prefix g denotes annual growth rates. In this equation, following general practice, we set $\alpha = 0.33$. As a robustness check, we also calculate TFP including the human capital measure in the growth accounting exercise:[3]

$$y = Ak^{\alpha}h^{1-\alpha}$$

The TFP results across income levels are not greatly affected by such a change.

Inequality

Inequality data on Gini coefficients comes from Milanovic (2005). Milanovic calculates a variable "Giniall" that reports Gini coefficients from a wide range of nationally representative household surveys, covering 1,541 country/years. Given many missing observations and the relative annual persistence of Gini coefficients, we replace this "Giniall" variable by its running 5-year average.

Governance

Governance indicators come from the Polity IV database (Marshall 2011). The democracy and autocracy indicators are composite variables ("DEMOC" and "AUTOC" in the original data set) based on an additive 11-point scale (0–10). The included indicators for both composite variables can be found online (http://www.systemicpeace.org/inscr/anualv2010.pdf). The full "polity" score is calculated by subtracting a country's autocracy value from its democracy value.

---

[3] Here, h is the human capital measure described earlier, and can be seen as the human capital per worker; in other words, it is the "quality adjusted" workforce, Lh, divided by the number of workers.

TRANSITIONING FROM LOW-INCOME GROWTH TO
HIGH-INCOME GROWTH: IS THERE A MIDDLE-INCOME TRAP?

59

Undervaluation

Undervaluation is calculated following Rodrik (2008), where a "real" exchange rate is calculated as the actual exchange rate divided by the purchasing power parity conversion factor, using the Penn World Table Version 7.0 data. Unlike Rodrik, this index is calculated on an annual, as opposed to 5-year, basis. Given the Balussa–Samuelson effect, whereby non-traded goods are cheaper in poorer countries, Rodrik generates estimated real exchange rates by regressing the log of the real exchange rate on log per capita GDP, including fixed effects for the time period. The undervaluation index is calculated as the difference between the log real exchange rate and the fitted values from this regression (which correspond to the Balussa–Samuelson estimated real exchange rates). The undervaluation index is in log form, and positive values indicate higher levels of undervaluation.

Other Data

Additional data come from the World Bank World Development Indicators data set, and generally require no explanation. A full list of variables and data sources is presented in Table A2.5 for all variables whose calculation is not described.

Table A2.5: Variables and Sources

Variable	Source	Variable	Source
GDP and GDP growth	PWT Version 7.0	Patents	World Bank
Employment	PWT Version 7.0	Fertility	World Bank
Investment	PWT Version 7.0	Age dependency ratio	World Bank
Years of schooling	Barro and Lee (2011)	Exports/GDP	World Bank
Gini coefficient	Milanovic (2005)	Trade/GDP	PWT Version 7.0
Agriculture share of GDP	World Bank	Democracy indicator	Polity IV
Industry share of GDP	World Bank	Autocracy indicator	Polity IV
Services share of GDP	World Bank	Polity score	Polity IV
CPI inflation	World Bank		

CPI = consumer price index, GDP = gross domestic product, PWT = Penn World Table.

Source: Authors.

CHAPTER 3

The Middle-Income Trap: Lessons from Latin America

Eva Paus

3.1 | Introduction

This chapter analyzes the reasons behind the middle-income trap in Latin America and draws out lessons for Asian countries. An analysis of Latin America's experience is particularly instructive since countries in the region have, on average, been at the middle-income level much longer than Asian countries. And over the past 30 years, they have generally pursued a market-led model the results of which have been premature deindustrialization, a large informal sector, and a poorly developed national innovation system.

Since Gill and Kharas (2007) first introduced the notion of the middle-income trap, researchers, policy makers, and journalists alike have embraced the concept to capture the fact that—over the past half century—very few middle-income countries have become high-income, industrialized countries. The World Bank's *China 2030* report (2013) highlighted that of the 101 economies classified as "middle-income" in 1960 only 13 had become "high-income" by 2008. Other authors offer similar evidence (Felipe 2012; Im and Rosenblatt 2013).

The term "middle-income trap" captures a situation where a middle-income country can no longer compete internationally in standardized, labor-intensive commodities because wages are relatively too high, but it can also not compete in higher value-added activities on a broad enough scale because productivity is relatively too low. The result is slow growth and less potential for rising living standards for more people.

Why are middle-income countries in this predicament and how can they get out of it? The state of domestic productive capabilities is the key in answering both questions. Insufficient development of domestic productive capabilities for upgrading to higher value-added activities within and across sectors is at the heart of the predicament of middle-income countries. And comprehensive advancement of domestic innovation capabilities is the basis for moving forward.

The current globalization has made it more challenging for middle-income countries to narrow the capabilities gap. Engendering innovation on a broad scale is a complex process and requires time for learning, in the production process (Amsden 2001; Cimoli, Dosi, and Stiglitz 2009) and in building the necessary institutional structures that enable and support innovation (Doner and Schneider 2016). But the time available for achieving competitiveness in higher value-added activities has become shorter, with more players competing in international markets and technology changing faster. In addition, the rise of the People's Republic of China (PRC) has further increased the pressure on other middle-income countries, as this middle-income country is punching way above its weight in innovation. With more intense competition and rapidly changing goal posts, the escape from the trap is both more difficult and more urgent at this point in time.

All middle-income countries are facing this global reality. Yet, their ability to address it and avoid the middle-income trap differs. This ability is conditioned by the nature of a country's integration into the global economy and varies with path dependent economic structures, already existing elements of an innovation system and political constellations. In this chapter, I investigate the nature and interrelations of these factors in middle-income countries in Latin America and draw lessons for middle-income countries in Asia and elsewhere.

Most countries in Latin America and the Caribbean (LAC) are middle-income countries. Haiti is the only low-income country in the Western Hemisphere.

And even though Chile and Uruguay are classified as high-income countries, based on their income level, the development challenges they face are similar to the Latin American countries at the middle-income level.[1]

An analysis of the middle-income trap in Latin America is of particular interest since countries in the region have been at the middle-income level for a long time. In 2010, Paraguay and the Dominican Republic had been at the lower-middle-income level for 38 years, while Colombia and Peru had been middle-income countries for 61 years (based on the classification by Felipe 2012). In Asia, by contrast, the time span ranged from 6 years in Cambodia and Pakistan to 34 years in the Philippines. Nonetheless, shared middle-income status masks considerable differences among Latin American countries, in terms of income level and size (Table 3.1) as well as capabilities for moving forward. In this chapter, I generally focus on broad shared trends across countries rather than on country-specific conditions.

The chapter is structured as follows. In the next section, I briefly discuss the two different conceptualizations of the middle-income trap, one based primarily on neoclassical economics and the other on structural and evolutionary economics. I adopt the latter analytical framework with particular emphasis on the implications of the current globalization process for middle-income countries. In Section 3.3, I examine the manifestation and reasons of the middle-income trap in Latin America. In the last section I draw lessons for Asian countries.

3.2 | The Middle-Income Trap and Globalization

Moving from factor-driven to innovation-driven growth has always been the key challenge for middle-income countries. Yet it is only in the last few years that analysts have raised the specter of middle-income countries actually becoming trapped. Analysts agree, irrespective of their theoretical framework, that moving from a middle-income to a high-income economy involves the

---

[1]   Some of the small Caribbean islands are high-income countries as well.

Table 3.1: Income and Population in Major Latin American Countries, 2015

	GNI p.c.	GNI	Population
South America	(Atlas method)	(Atlas method)	
Argentina (UMIC)	12,460	541,107,693,169	43,416,755
Bolivia (LMIC)	3,080	33,036,925,034	10,724,705
Brazil (UMIC)	9,850	2,047,109,614,135	207,847,528
Chile (HIC)	14,060	252,439,621,752	17,948,141
Colombia (UMIC)	7,130	344,093,169,614	48,228,704
Ecuador (UMIC)	6,010	97,059,209,212	16,144,363
Paraguay (UMIC)	4,220	28,043,962,571	6,639,123
Peru (UMIC)	6,200	194,629,668,918	31,376,670
Uruguay (HIC)	15,720	53,928,953,514	3,431,555
Venezuela (UMIC)	NA	NA	31,108,083
Central America, DR			
Costa Rica (UMIC)	10,210	49,078,288,318	4,807,850
Dominican Republic (UMIC)	6,130	64,538,605,642	10,528,391
El Salvador (LMIC)	3,940	24,130,424,978	6,126,583
Guatemala (LMIC)	3,590	58,636,219,449	16,342,897
Honduras (LMIC)	2,270	18,361,664,576	8,075,060
Nicaragua (LMC)	1,870	11,244,356,510	6,013,913
Panama (UMIC)	12,050	47,341,547,302	3,929,141
Mexico (UMIC)	9,710	1,233,657,846,512	127,017,224
Latin America	8,939	5,657,765,221,594	632,959,079
Lower-Middle-Income Countries	2,035	5,955,948,420,932	2,927,414,098
Upper-Middle-Income Countries	8,429	21,693,419,635,830	2,573,612,474
Middle-Income Countries	4,925	27,193,921,095,750	5,521,156,908

GNI = gross national income, HIC = high-income country (GNI p.c. in 2015 above $12,475), LMIC = lower-middle-income country (GNI p.c. in 2015 between $1,026 and $4,035), NA = not available, UMIC = upper middle-income country (GNI p.c. in 2015 between $4,036 and $12,475).

Source: World Bank. World Development Indicators.

internalization of innovation-based activities on a broad scale. But they differ in their definition of the middle-income trap, the reasons behind it, and the policy recommendations for escaping it.

3.2.1 Different Conceptualizations of the Middle-Income Trap

Based on Paus (2014), I distinguish two different approaches to the trap. One approach is based mainly on neoclassical economics where the composition of production and export does not matter, and the context for learning and the specificities of the international situation are not relevant (e.g., Aiyar et al. 2013 Eichengreen, Park, and Shin 2013, 2011; Robertson and Ye 2013). The other approach rests on structural and evolutionary economics, where the nature of the production structure and the context for learning and international competitiveness matter (Paus 2014; Felipe, Abdon, and Kumar 2012; Foxley 2012; Gill and Kharas 2007; Ohno 2009; Yusuf and Nabeshima 2009). In both approaches, middle-income countries are facing slow growth, but the analytical framework for understanding the growth slowdown is different and so are the policy prescriptions.

In the neoclassical framework, the search for universal determinants of economic growth slowdowns across time and income levels assumes that period and region-specific factors as well as different policy strategies do not matter in explanations of different episodes of declines in growth. That is a questionable supposition. It is hardly coincidental that two-thirds of the growth slowdowns in middle-income countries identified by Aiyar et al. (2013) occurred after 1980, when many developing countries had to deal with the foreign debt crisis and followed market-led policies (the so-called Washington Consensus). More important, it is not clear what is added to our understanding when all countries that experienced a growth slowdown are characterized as having been in a middle-income trap; e.g., Australia, Austria, Belgium, Denmark, Finland, France, Israel, Ireland, Japan, the Republic of Korea, the Netherlands, New Zealand, Norway, Singapore, Sweden, the United Kingdom, and the United States (US) (Eichengreen, Park, and Shin 2013).

In the structural change approach I adopt in this chapter, analysts focus on the nature of the productive structure of the economy in the context of international competitiveness as the proximate cause for the middle-income trap. Economic activities differ with respect to returns, demand, and spillover potential. Thus, economic development is seen as a process where production is shifted increasingly toward activities with greater technological spillovers, increasing returns, and higher demand elasticities; in other words, toward higher productivity activities. Structural change is a driver of development, not just a byproduct (Ocampo, Rada, and Taylor 2009; Hausmann, Hwang, and Rodrik 2007; Shapiro and Taylor 1990).

Evolutionary economics emphasizes the process of technological learning, path dependency, and the cumulative interaction among the factors that shape the path of productive transformation (Nelson and Winter 1982; Dosi 1984). The advancement of productive capabilities takes time.

With an explicit focus on structural transformation and the needed accumulation of capabilities to achieve and sustain it, the middle-income trap is understood as a situation where a middle-income country can no longer compete internationally in standardized, labor-intensive commodities because wages are relatively too high, but it can also not compete in higher value-added activities on a broad enough scale because productivity is relatively too low. The "structural change cum learning" approach highlights that income convergence will be temporary unless it is based on capabilities convergence. The commodity price super cycle of the 2000s and its impact on growth in Latin America is a case in point. Between 2003 and 2007, Latin American economies experienced strong income convergence, but not capability convergence. When the commodity boom came to an end in the early 2010s, the capability deficiencies in Latin American countries came to the forefront in full force.

By its very nature a middle-income country has limited innovation capabilities. But these limited capabilities make it more challenging for a country to catch up in the current global context because competitive pressures and the speed of technological change have been increasing and the rise of the PRC has changed the global architecture of production (Paus 2014, 2012).

3.2.2 The Global Innovation Field: Many Players and Shifting Goals Posts

Over the last 30 years, widespread trade liberalization, the reduction in maritime transportation costs, and the rise in digital connectivity have increased the globalization of production and the number of producers competing in domestic and international markets. The transition in Central and Eastern European countries in the 1990s and the PRC's increased opening with its accession to the World Trade Organization in 2001 has led to the "Great Doubling," in the words of Richard Freeman (2007). The doubling of the global labor force intensified competitive pressures, especially in the production of labor-intensive products. As a result, prices of these goods have declined, in relative terms and sometimes also in absolute terms. For developing country exporters of manufactured goods, the terms of trade declined at an annual rate of 1.1% between 1980 and 2014 (UNCTAD 2016: x).

Since the PRC is the most populous country in the world, its opening to international trade has offered tremendous new export opportunities for the rest of the world. Yet, at the same time, the PRC's own export growth has intensified the competitive pressures on other middle-income countries, in their home markets and in third markets. The impact has been particularly consequential, as the PRC has been competing not only in standardized, low-tech products like non-design clothing, but also in high-tech products, particularly electronics and computer products. Between 2000 and 2014, the PRC's share in world imports of low-tech goods rose from 19.6% to 29.3%, while its share in high-tech imports increased from 6.7% to 27% (Figure 3.1).[2]

---

[2]   It is immaterial for the argument here that foreign transnational corporations are responsible for a significant share of exports from the PRC.

Figure 3.1: World Imports from the PRC as a Share of Total World Imports by Technology-Intensity of Products

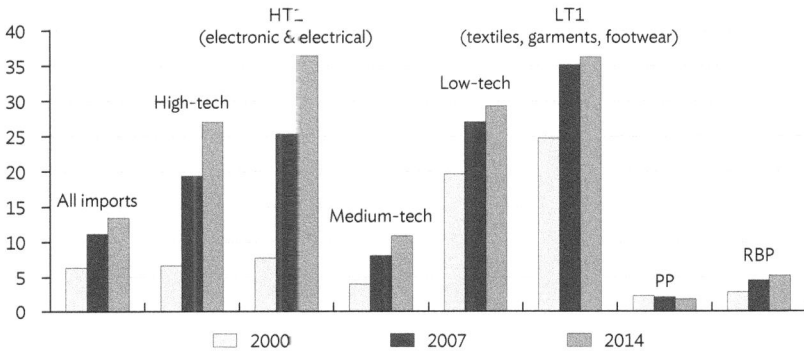

HT = high-tech, LT = low-tech, PP = primary product, RBP = resource-based product.

Source: Author's calculations based on UN Comtrade data. The technology classification is based on Lall (2000) who distinguishes between low-tech products, medium-tech products, high-tech products, resource-based products, and primary products.

In other words, the largest middle-income country looks in many ways like a high-income country, thus raising the innovation bar for the other middle-income countries.

In response to growing competitive pressures in international markets, more countries have emphasized competitiveness based on new ideas, new products, and new markets. Expenditures on research and development (R&D) are one indicator of such efforts. Historically, R&D expenditures as a share of gross domestic product (GDP) (R&D intensity) have risen with per capita income. The positive link is not surprising, since industrialized countries reached their high-income status and have remained competitive in high value-added goods and services based on a broad expansion of innovative activities. Yet, in the 2000s, the connection between R&D spending and income has become less tight, indicating greater engagement in R&D at all levels of income (Figure 3.2).[3]

---

[3]   Figure 3.2 includes data for all countries for which the World Development Indicators had data on R&D intensity for both 2000 and 2011.

Figure 3.2a: Research Intensity and GNI per Capita, 2000

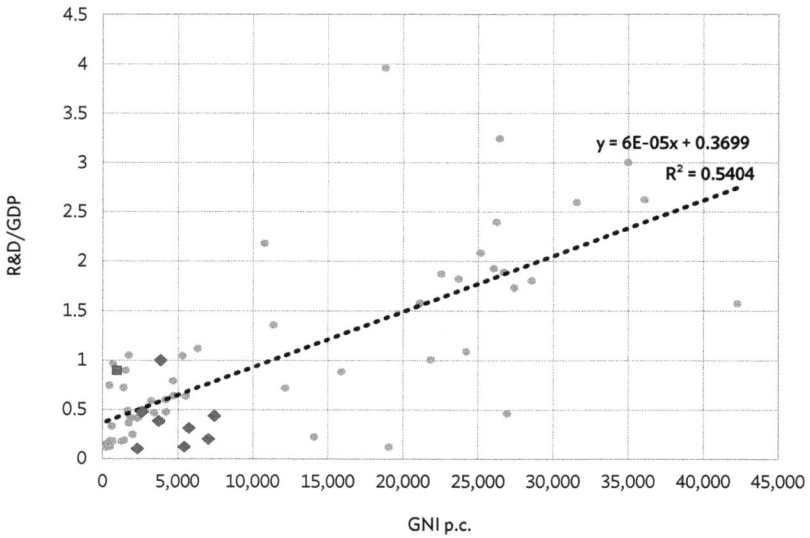

$$y = 6E\text{-}05x + 0.3699$$
$$R^2 = 0.5404$$

R&D/GDP

GNI p.c.

Figure 3.2b: Research Intensity and GNI per Capita, 2011

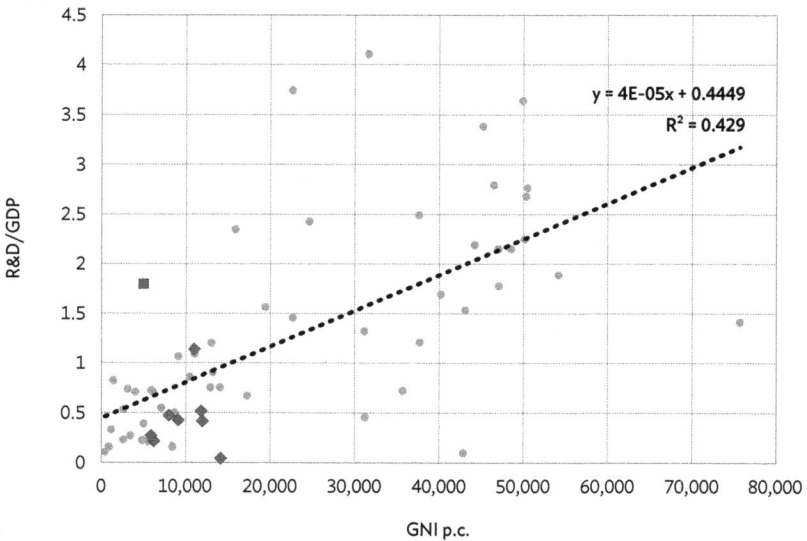

$$y = 4E\text{-}05x + 0.4449$$
$$R^2 = 0.429$$

R&D/GDP

GNI p.c.

GDP = gross domestic product, GNI p.c. = gross national income per capita, R&D = research and development.

Source: World Bank. World Development Indicators.

After the financial crisis of 2008, worldwide R&D expenditures expanded considerably. Between 2010 and 2014, gross expenditure on R&D increased by nearly 50%, from $1,216 billion to $1,803 billion. The PRC accounted for a third of this increase, making the country the second largest spender on R&D in the world, with $344 billion in 2014. The US is still the largest spender, with $485 billion.[4]

The more rapid technological change of the last 2 decades coupled with the "Rise of China" has engendered a "Red Queen Effect," where middle-income countries have to accumulate innovation capabilities faster just to stay in the same place. The predictions about the new technological revolution (Brynjolfsson and McAfee 2014; Ford 2015)—with the rise of robotics, digitization, artificial intelligence, and the Internet of Things—will further up the ante for capability catch-up. Countries that are at the forefront of widespread adoption of these technologies are expected to see considerable increases in productivity, which—in turn—will intensify the competitive pressures on middle-income countries. The PRC aims to become one of the frontrunners in the new technological revolution, again punching considerably above its weight (as measured by its GDP per capita).[5]

The upshot is that in the current globalization context there is less time for acquiring the innovation capabilities needed for catching up with high-income countries. That makes escaping from the middle-income trap both more challenging and more urgent (Whittaker et al. 2010; Paus 2014).

3.2.3 Policy Implications

The two approaches to the middle-income trap differ in the role they attribute to the state in a move to greater innovation-based growth. Scholars in the neoclassical tradition stress the importance of a good business climate and

---

4   R&D expenditures are measured in purchasing power parity (PPP) and from the Industrial Research Institute's *R&D Global Funding Forecast*, various years.
5   In June 2015, the PRC announced "Manufacturing China 2025," a sweeping strategy aimed to make the PRC the leading industrial power by mid-century, by combining smart manufacturing and "Industry 4.0."

investment in education and infrastructure. In the analytical frameworks based on structural and evolutionary economics, scholars also emphasize the importance of education and infrastructure. But they underscore the need for active government policies to lead and support firm learning and the advancement of the requisite social capabilities as well as institution building and coordination (Abramovitz 1986; Cimoli, Dosi, and Stiglitz 2009). Government policies are needed to provide assistance to firms through financial and other support when there are capability failures. And government institutions may need to take the lead in prioritized innovation areas because private producers deem the initial risk too high. Governments need to leverage macro policies, tax incentives, and protection of intellectual property, as well as selective targeted support to shape an incentive structure that is conducive to firm-level innovation (Stiglitz and Lin 2013).

3.3 | From State-Led Industrialization to Market-Led Industrialization: Latin America's Middle-Income Trap

The framework of structuralism and evolutionary economics summarized above informs the analysis in this section. I discuss the middle-income trap dilemma of Latin America with a focus on the history and nature of structural transformation in the region and the role of government policies in shaping the accumulation of productive capabilities and innovation.

Over the past 55 years, GDP per capita in Latin America has increased nearly threefold (measured in constant 2010 US dollars), from $3,621 in 1960 to $9,304 in 2015. But the growth performance differed considerably under the two different development strategies in the region: a state-led strategy from the end of World War II until the early 1980s and a market-led strategy thereafter (Figure 3.3).[6] Under the state-led strategy, governments adopted

---

[6]   I follow Bértola and Ocampo (2012) in using the term "state-led development" rather than "import-substituting industrialization." It focuses on the key role of government policies in support of industrialization and provides an apt juxtaposition to the market-led strategy that followed.

policies to promote industrialization and a more diversified economy to reduce the economies' dependence on primary products (agriculture, mining, and oil). They supported firm learning for structural change with import tariffs and quotas, subsidized credits and investments in education, infrastructure, and elements of an incipient innovation system. But with the external debt crisis of the early 1980s, governments changed to a market-led model. In the context of debt renegotiations, the World Bank, the International Monetary Fund, and the US Treasury demanded widespread liberalization of markets, in line with the rise of the neoliberal paradigm in the West, especially in the US and the United Kingdom.

Figure 3.3: **GDP per Capita in Developing Country Regions, 1960–2015 (in constant 2010 US dollars)**

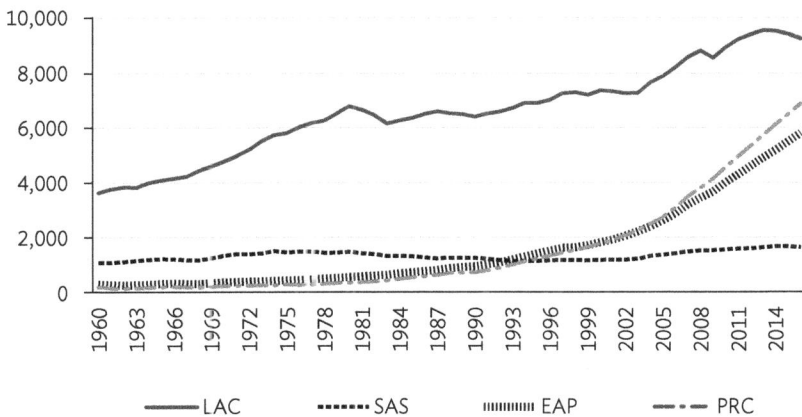

EAP = East Asia and the Pacific, GDP = gross domestic product, LAC = Latin America and the Caribbean, PRC = People's Republic of China, SAS = Sub-Saharan Africa.

Source: World Bank. World Development Indicators online (accessed 4 December 2016).

The adoption of a market-led model (the so-called Washington Consensus) included the lowering of tariff barriers, the reduction or elimination of public subsidies, the privatization of public enterprises, reduced public investment, and an open arms approach to foreign direct investment (FDI).

Though Latin American countries differed in the degree and speed with which they adopted the Washington Consensus, the development model generally shifted to a reliance on unrestricted markets. Trade and foreign capital were to become the drivers of growth and development, and the government's role in the economy declined drastically: as regulator, producer, and promoter of growth-enhancing structural change. Where the goal of the state-led model had been productive transformation over the medium to long run, the goal of the market-led model was the creation of comparative advantages based on international market prices.

Governments pursued trade and investment agreements, especially with the US, to gain market access. And though support for the development of dynamic comparative advantages was basically off the table for domestic producers, many governments offered special incentives to foreign investors, in the hope that they would bring new technology, fresh capital, and more employment. As a result, the playing field for domestic and foreign producers was often not even, but tilted toward foreign producers.

Brazil, the largest economy in Latin America, has been the most reticent in adopting the Washington Consensus. Successive administrations maintained a strategic role for the government in advancing structural transformation. Development plans prioritized specific sectors, and the national development bank BNDES continued to play a large role in funding the development of new comparative advantages. Other exceptions to the broad market liberalization and hands-off-government approach are sector-specific; e.g., the automobile sector under Mercosur (the Common Market between Argentina, Brazil, Paraguay, Uruguay, and Venezuela), the wine and salmon industries in Chile which was promoted by the country's development organization CORFO, and the wine industry in Argentina whose development was supported by the state of Mendoza.

The market-led model generated macroeconomic stability and an increase in static efficiency. But these achievements came at a steep cost, as the potential for advancing dynamic efficiency declined dramatically.

Washington Consersus policies engendered dismal productivity growth, rapid deindustrialization with a concomitant rise of the informal sector, a decline in export sophistication in nearly all countries, poor innovation performance, and underinvestment in the social capabilities needed for broad-based upgrading within and across sectors.

3.3.1 Labor Productivity Growth and Structural Change

Poor labor productivity growth over the last 20–30 years is the key indicator that Latin American countries are facing a middle-income trap. Between 1992 and 2015, labor productivity grew, on average, at a mere 0.74% per year. That places the region's performance only slightly above the poorest regional performers, the Middle East and North Africa (Figure 3.4). Labor productivity growth was considerably higher in South Asia, East Asia, and the average for middle-income countries. The PRC was the star performer, with an annual productivity growth rate of 8.2% over this period.[7]

Since different economic sectors have different productivity levels, we can look at aggregate labor productivity growth as the outcome of productivity growth within sectors and productivity growth, which results from the reallocation of labor across sectors. Between 1990 and 2005, the inter-sectoral component of productivity growth was positive in developing Asia, but negative in Latin America and Africa (McMillan and Rodrik 2011). In other words, in Asia, production and employment shifted from lower- to higher-productivity sectors. But in Latin America, labor shifted to lower productivity activities (Table 3.2). When we look at the 1990s and 2000s separately, a more complex picture emerges. While the inter-sectoral component was negative in the 1990s, it became positive in the 2000s in most Latin American countries. The employment-expanding sectors with above average productivity were public utilities, finance, insurance and real estate, and construction, but not manufacturing (Paus 2014).

---

[7] The data for total factor productivity (TFP) are equally disheartening. TFP increased from 1960 to the mid-1970s, after which it declined. In 2005, the level of TFP was lower than it had been in 1960 (Daude 2010).

Figure 3.4: GDP per Worker Employed in Developing Country Areas (average annual growth rate based on constant 2011 PPP)

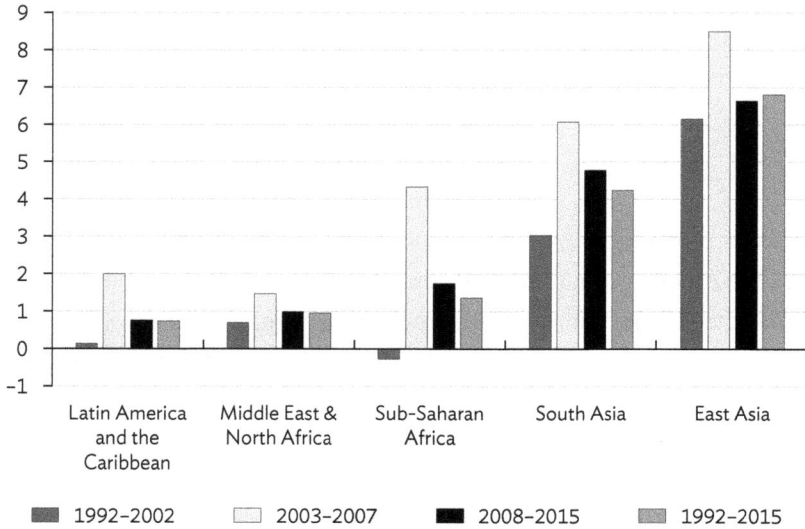

GDP = gross domestic product, PPP = purchasing power parity.
Source: Author's calculations based on World Development Indicators (accessed 5 April 2015).

Table 3.2: Decomposition of Labor Productivity Growth, 1990–2005 (%)

	Labor Productivity Growth (LPG)	Decomposition of LPG	
		Due to within Sector LPG	Due to across Sector Reallocation (Structural Change)
Latin America and the Caribbean	1.35	2.24	−0.88
Africa	0.86	2.13	−1.27
Asia	3.87	3.31	0.57
High-income countries	1.46	1.54	−0.09

Source: McMillan and Rodrik (2011).

To be sure, trade liberalization made the manufacturing sector in Latin America more productive. But the weight of manufacturing in the economy declined (Paus, Reinhardt, and Robinson 2003), and Latin America became the most extreme example of the widely commented phenomenon of premature deindust-ialization (Rodrik 2015). In contrast to countries in Asia, the share of manufacturing value added in GDP declined precipitously in Latin America during the 1990s (Figure 3.5). In 2015, the manufacturing share accounted for just 14.7 % of GDP in Latin America, even below the 14.9% for Organisat on for Economic Co-operation and Development (OECD) countries. An important question is whether other sectors (e.g., mining and high-tech services) can generate the same dynamic in the future that a dynamic man ifacturir g sector generated for today's industrialized countries and successful development latecomers in the past.

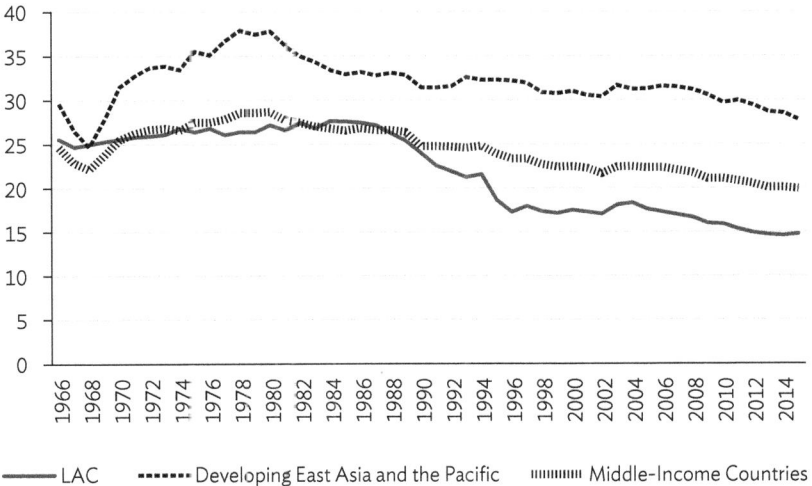

Figure 3.5: Manufacturing Value Added as a Share of GDP, Select Developing Country Areas, 1965–2015

——— LAC   ▪▪▪▪▪▪ Developing East Asia and the Pacific   ⅢⅢⅢⅢ Middle-Income Countries

GDP = gross domestic product, LAC = Latin America and the Caribbean.

Source: World Bank. World Development Indicators.

Under the state-led model government, policies were based on three central premises: (1) what a country produces matters for productivity and economic growth; (2) technological learning takes time and is cumulative; and (3) the accumulation of broad-based technological capabilities requires proactive government policies and the development of human resources, particularly through education and requisite infrastructure. The outcomes were growth-enhancing structural transformation and productivity growth.

Nonetheless, one of the biggest flaws in the implementation of the state-led model in Latin America was the absence of performance requirements or sunset clauses in exchange for tariff protection and other support measures.[8] In the Asian Tigers, in contrast, government support for the achievement of firm competitiveness in new activities was contingent on export performance and phased out over time. But in Latin America the absence of such requirements generated persistent and widespread inefficiencies and led to widely divergent productivity levels within and across sectors. Thus when governments liberalized imports and moved to a market-led model, many domestic producers found themselves unable to compete. And many producers—domestic and foreign—switched their sources from domestic to international suppliers, thus destroying national value chains and ushering in deindustrialization and growing informalization.

The differences in productivity levels among domestic companies have been persistently large. Micro and small enterprises constitute the majority of enterprises in Latin America. The gap between their productivity level and that of large companies is significantly larger than in developed countries (see Table 3.3). The deindustrialization process and reduction of government support for innovation also implied a loss of the technological productive knowledge that had been accumulated as well as a shrinking of the national innovation system that had started to develop incipiently under the state-lead model (Katz 2001).

---

[8]   The average unweighted nominal rate of protection in manufacturing in the 1960s was 264% in Uruguay (1968), 141% in Argentina (1958), 99% in Brazil (1966), and 83% in Chile (1961). The effective rates of protection were 384%, 162%, 118%, and 254%, respectively (Agosín 2013).

Table 3.3: Relative Productivity of Enterprise Groups Compared with Large Companies

	Microenterprises	Small Companies	Medium-Sized Companies	Large Companies
Argentina	24	36	47	100
Brazil	10	27	40	100
Chile	3	26	46	100
Mexico	16	35	60	100
Peru	6	16	60	100
Germany	67	70	83	100
Spain	46	63	77	100
France	71	75	80	100
Italy	42	64	82	100

Source: ECLAC (2010), Table II.7, p. 96

3.3.2 Changes in the Structure and Complexity of Exports

The poor productivity performance and premature deindustrialization in Latin America are also reflected in the structure of the regions' exports and their declining economic complexity relative to other countries. Under the market-led model, South American countries experienced a "re-primarization" of their exports, while Central American countries and Mexico became more integrated into global value chains, which are mostly dominated by US companies.

Most countries in South America reverted to comparative advantages in natural resources, with new ones like natural gas and soybeans added to the old ones like copper and iron ore. The PRC's high growth with its rising demand for natural resources was a key factor behind the commodity price boom of the 2000s. South American exporters of primary products benefited greatly from the increased export prices. But all Latin American countries saw a steep rise in imports from the PRC as well, which resulted in growing trade deficits for Latin America, with the exception of the top commodity exporters.

On the other hand, Central American countries, and to some extent Mexico, developed specializations in low-skilled, labor-intensive, assembly-based production as producers became integrated into global value chains (GVCs). The process was driven by privileged access to the US market through special provisions of the US tariff schedule and broad tariff-free access through the Caribbean Basin Initiative in 1984, and, in the case of Mexico, the North American Free Trade Agreement (NAFTA) with the US and Canada in 1994. During the 2000s, the free trade agreement between the US and Central America and the Dominican Republic (CAFTA–DR, passed in 2004) further cemented the region's integration into GVCs. Investors from Asia, including the PRC, increased productive investment in Central America— and Mexico—to take advantage of the tariff-free access to the US market. But these investments generally created few linkages with producers in the host countries.

The global value chain participation index of the World Trade Organization (WTO) shows the differences in the degree and nature of GVC participation in Latin American and Asian middle-income countries. The index is the sum of the two sub-indexes: the "backward participation index," which measures the share of foreign value added in exports, and the "forward participation index," which captures the domestic value added share in exports sent to third countries. Between 1995 and 2011, backward and forward participation indexes increased in both regions (Table 3.4).[9] Not surprisingly, the backward participation index is much higher for countries that process and reexport manufactured goods; these include Costa Rica and many countries in Asia. The forward participation index, on the other hand, is much higher in countries where exports are dominated by primary products: Chile and Colombia in Latin America, and Indonesia and the Philippines in Asia.

---

[9]   Table 3.4 includes all middle-income countries in Latin America and Asia for which the WTO has data on global value chain participation.

Table 3.4: Participation in Global Value Chains, Selected Countries in Latin America and Asia, 1995 and 2011

	Backward Participation		Forward Participation		Global Value Chain Participation Index	
	1995	2011	1995	2011	1995	2011
Argentina	5.7	14.1	12.2	16.4	17.9	30.5
Brazil	7.8	10.7	15.1	24.5	22.9	35.2
Chile	14.1	20.2	19.9	31.7	34.0	51.9
Colombia	8.5	7.6	15.4	30.2	23.9	37.8
Costa Rica	22.1	27.8	11.1	16.8	33.2	44.6
Mexico	27.3	31.7	11.1	15.1	38.4	46.8
Unweighted average	**14.1**	**18.7**	**14.1**	**22.5**	**28.2**	**41.1**
Cambodia	12.7	36.8	18.0	11.9	30.7	48.7
PRC	33.3	32.1	9.5	15.6	42.8	47.7
India	9.3	24.0	13.6	19.1	22.9	43.1
Indonesia	12.5	12.0	16.3	31.5	28.8	43.5
Malaysia	30.4	40.6	15.6	19.8	46.0	60.4
Philippines	29.8	23.5	12.8	27.4	42.6	50.9
Thailand	24.2	39.0	12.1	15.4	36.3	54.4
Viet Nam	21.1	36.3	13.1	16.0	34.2	52.3
Unweighted average	**21.7**	**30.5**	**13.9**	**19.6**	**35.6**	**50.1**

PRC = People's Republic cf China.

Source: WTO. Global Value Chain Statistics.

Differences in the economic complexity of countries' exports mirror differences in GVC participation. The Economic Complexity Index (ECI), developed by Hausmann and Klinger (2007) and available at the Atlas of Economic Complexity, captures both the ubiquity and the diversification of a country's exports. The authors suggest that the ECI reflects the complexity of the capabilities of the exporting country and its ability to produce more sophisticated goods in the product space. Research has shown that the ECI is strongly related with per capita income and a good predictor of future growth.

The graphs in the Appendix show the development of ECI rankings in Latin American and Asian countries over the past 50 years, i.e., the evolution of their export complexity relative to other countries. Under the state-led model the rankings had stayed more or less the same, and in the cases of Peru and especially Brazil, they had actually improved. But under the market-led model, the ECI ranking deteriorated for all South American countries. In Central America, in contrast, the ECI ranking improved for most countries around the turn of the century; and in Mexico, we see a high ECI ranking throughout the 1990s and 2000s. Yet, this improvement is not necessarily an indication of greater complexity of a country's collective capabilities. In a number of countries, it reflects increased production of manufactured goods in export-processing zones that have few linkages to the domestic economy.

In Costa Rica, the improved ranking is likely due to the growth of exports of medical devices and microchips, after Intel established its first test and assembly facility in Latin America in San Jose in 1997 which then triggered increased FDI in the assembly of medium and high-tech components. In Guatemala and Honduras, the sudden improvement reflects a change in how the countries reported their export data.[10] The case of Mexico demonstrates that a high ECI ranking need not go hand in hand with high economic growth. Between 1990 and 2015, Mexico's GDP grew at an average annual rate of only 2.75%. The disjuncture between ECI ranking and growth is due to the drastic increase in the import elasticity of demand for imports under the market-led model and the limited linkages between maquila production and the domestic economy (Paus and Gallagher 2008; Moreno–Brid and Ros 2009).

---

[10] Guatemala and Honduras started to include the exports from export-processing zones into the aggregate export statistics in the early 2000s. The magnitude of these exports, which consist primarily of clothing (produced with imported cloth and destined for the US market), likely explains the drastic improvement in rankings. In Guatemala, for example, clothing exports from export-processing zones were not included in the official data prior to 2002. The data show an increase in clothing exports from $42,403,436 in 2001 to $1,261,052,000 in 2002 (WTO, International Trade Data).

Under the market-led model, governments in Latin America (and elsewhere) welcomed FDI with open arms, expecting that technology transfer, capital infusions, and employment growth would generate stronger economic growth. But the experience of the last 3 decades has demonstrated that technology spillovers will only occur if domestic absorptive capacity exists; linkages will only develop if domestic producers are already competitive; and foreign companies will only invest in R&D in the host country if the country already has enough of an ecosystem conducive to innovation. In many Latin American countries, the technology benefits of FDI were limited or did not materialize.

In Asia, only three countries have experienced a fairly persistent improvement in the ECI rankings over the past 2–3 decades: the PRC, Malaysia, and Thailand. What this improvement tells us about the set of domestic productive capabilities depends here, too, on the extent to which export production is linked to the rest of the economy and dominated by domestic or foreign producers. In contrast to Malaysia and Thailand, the PRC has complemented a strategy of controlled opening to trade and FDI with an aggressive promotion of domestic innovation capabilities.

3.3.3 Domestic Innovation Capabilities

The discussion above highlights that the composition and sophistication of exports do not necessarily reflect the state of domestic productive capabilities. That disjuncture is underscored by the state of social capabilities that need to complement the advancement of productive transformation to higher value-added activities. I focus here on four indicators: R&D spending, patent applications, educational outcomes, and the state of infrastructure.

The R&D intensity in Latin American countries is lower than expected given their income level. All Latin American countries have an R&D intensity below 1% and lie below the trend line (the diamond symbols in Figure 3.2). The only exception is Brazil, where the R&D intensity is above 1%. But while the R&D intensity in Brazil increased from 0.99% in 2000 to 1.14% in 2011, it doubled in the PRC (the square symbol in Figure 3.2) from 0.9% to 1.79%.

Patent applications by residents in Latin America grew considerably between 1990 and 2014. But their share in total patent applications declined. The patent application picture for developing countries in East Asia and the Pacific seems to look better. However, once we exclude the PRC's patent applications, developing Asia looks even worse than Latin America (Table 3.5).

Table 3.5: Patent Applications by Residents and Nonresidents in Latin America and Asia, 1990 and 2014

	1990	2014
Latin America		
patent applications, residents (PAR)	4,588	7,345
patent applications, nonresident (PANR)	13,827	53,545
PAR/(PAR +PANR) (%)	24.9	12.1
PRA/world PAR	0.8	0.4
Developing East Asia and the Pacific		
patent applications, residents (PAR)	6,702	805,159
patent applications, nonresident (PANR)	10,262	155,059
PAR/(PAR +PANR) (%)	37.7	83.9
PRA/world PAR	1.1	47.0
Developing East Asia and the Pacific without the PRC		
patent applications, residents (PAR)	370	4,024
patent applications, nonresident (PANR)	5,957	28,017
PAR/(PAR +PANR) (%)	6.2	14.4
PRA/world PAR	0.1	0.2
PRC		
patent applications, residents (PAR)	5,632	801,135
patent applications, nonresident (PANR)	4,305	127,042
PAR/(PAR +PANR) (%)	57.5	86.3
PRA/world PAR	1.1	46.8

PRC = People's Republic of China.
Source: World Bank. World Development Indicators.

Table 3.6: PISA Results, 2015

	Math			Reading			Science		
	Average Score	Share of Low Performers (Below Level 2)	Share of High Performers (Level 5 or 6)	Average Score	Share of Low Performers (Below Level 2)	Share of High Performers (Level 5 or 6)	Average Score	Share of Low Performers (Below Level 2)	Share of High Performers (Level 5 or 6)
OECD average	490	23.3	10.7	493	6.3	8.3	493	5.5	7.8
B-S-J-G*	531	15.8	25.6	494	8.3	10.9	518	4.4	1.0
Singapore	564	7.5	34.8	535	2.8	18.3	556	2.0	24.2
Hong Kong, China	548	8.9	26.5	527	2.3	11.5	523	1.6	6.9
Taipei,China	542	12.7	28.1	497	5.4	6.9	532	2.7	15.4
Republic of Korea	524	15.4	20.9	517	4.1	12.7	516	2.9	10.6
Viet Nam	495	19.1	9.3	487	1.7		525		8.3
Thailand	415	53.8	1.2	409	17.9	0.3	421	13.0	
Indonesia	386	68.6	0.6	397	20.6		403	15.6	
Chile	423	49.3	1.3	459	8.7	2.3	447	9.9	1.2
Mexico	408	56.6		423	13.4	0.3	416	12.8	
Uruguay	418	52.4	1.7	437	15.5	2.5	435	12.3	1.2
Costa Rica	400	62.5		427	12.0	0.6	420	10.8	
Brazil	377	70.2	0.8	407	24.5	1.3	401	24.3	1.0
Argentina (Buenos Aires)	456	34.0	3.5	475	7.3	3.5	475	4.8	2.6
Colombia	390	66.3		425	16.8	0.9	416	16.2	
Peru	387	66.1		398	25.6	0.3	397	21.8	
Dominican Republic	328	92.5		358	41.3		332	55.4	

OECD = Organisation for Economic Co-operation and Development, PISA = Programme for International Student Assessment.

* Beijing, Shanghai, Jiangsu, Guangdong.

Note: Empty cells: data not reported because coefficient of variation was high.

Source: OECD (2016).

Secondary school enrollment rates have increased in Latin America, as has the average number of years of schooling. But the quality of outcomes is still fairly low. Compared with Asia, the OECD Programme for International Student Assessment (PISA) results for Latin American countries are generally lower in math and science, though not in reading. In math, the scores in Latin America range from a low of 328 in the Dominican Republic to a high of 456 in Buenos Aires. Among middle-income economies in Asia, the scores range from 386 in Indonesia to 531 in Beijing, Shanghai, Jiangsu, and Guangdong. Furthermore, in most Latin American countries, the majority of test takers performed poorly and only a very small percentage achieved at the high end (Table 3.6).

In the area of infrastructure, Latin America lags significantly behind middle-income countries in East Asia and elsewhere, in terms of quantity as well as quality. One of the main reasons is the decline in public investment. As governments sought to curtail fiscal deficits in the 1980s, a lot of the adjustment burden fell on capital spending. The weighted average of public investment in infrastructure for six major Latin American countries declined from 3% of GDP in the first half of the 1980s to less than 1% in the first half of the 2000s (Calderón and Servén 2012). Private investment made up for some of the decline in public investment, but it fell considerably short of compensating for it, with the exception of Chile. As a result, total investment in infrastructure fell from 3.6% to 1.9% of GDP between the early 1980s and the 2000s. The infrastructure deficits are most pervasive in roads and ports; in broadband coverage, countries in the regions are generally doing well.

3.3.4 Disillusion with the Market-Led Model

Over the course of the last decade, growing disillusion with the results of the market-led model has led to a resurgence of more activist policies for upgrading and structural transformation. But efforts in most countries are still limited, often piecemeal and disjointed, and not part of a more comprehensive long-term strategy (Peres 2011; Devlin and Moguillansky 2012). With the rise of left-leaning governments in several

Latin American countries during the 2000s, we saw an interesting dichotomy in development policies. There was an increased spending on social programs, with conditional cash transfer programs and greater emphasis on education. But the same governments generally did not promote comprehensive productive transformation sc as to generate more jobs at decent pay so that the children who receive more education on the basis of cash transfers will also have jobs in the future.

3.3.5 Inequality and the Middle-Income Trap

Since Latin American countr es have long been among the most unequal in the world, and since income inequality has risen in some Asian countries, most notably the PRC, the question arises whether there is a connection between inequality and the middle-income trap. The answer is complex, judging by the region's experience of the last decade and the arguments in the broader literature.

During the commodity boom of the 2000s, inequality declined in nearly all Latin American countries.[11] Lustig (2016) showed that inequality declined in countries with high growth ard in those with slow growth; in countries with left governments and in those with non-left governments; in commodity exporters and commodity importers; and in countries with stagnant minimum wages and in those with rising minimum wages. She argues that the decrease in inequality was mostly due to a decrease in inequality of labor income, which, in turn, was primarily the result of increased access to education. Other factors contributing to the decline were more progressive and larger government transfers and an increase in remittances.

In the extensive literature on the relationship between inequality and growth, we find theoretical arguments and empirical evidence in support of both a negative link and a positive link.[12] In the context of the analytical framework

---

[11] Between 2000 and 2014, Bolivia registered the largest decline with 0.85 percentage points and Costa Rica the smallest with 0.26 percentage points (Lustig 2016).

[12] For an overview see, for example, World Bank (2016, ch. 4).

for this chapter, however, the issue is not primarily about the link between inequality and growth. Rather the question is whether and how inequality affects the ecosystem for innovation.

Theoretically, there are four main channels through which inequality may impact innovation. First, high inequality may mean highly unequal access to education which, in turn, limits the accumulation of the human capital needed for innovation. Second, inequality may prevent the adoption of policies to advance innovation, if these policies threaten the power of the elite with de facto decision-making power (Flechtner and Panther 2015). Third, high inequality may make it difficult to raise the tax revenue needed for government investment in the advancement of needed social capabilities in education and infrastructure, if it requires higher taxes on the elite. And finally, high inequality may lead to political instability, which in turn makes it difficult to implement any long-term development strategy. Foxley (2012) argued that a reduction in the highly unequal distribution of income and opportunities in many Latin American countries is critical for maintaining/achieving social and political peace. That, in turn, provides the needed foundation for a development strategy aimed at increasing productivity and diversifying exports.

More detailed empirical research is needed, both in Latin America and in Asia, to determine the extent to which any of the factors discussed above constitute an important impediment for a specific middle-income country for escaping the middle-income trap.

3.4 | Lessons from the Latin American Experience

At the heart of the middle-income trap is the insufficient development of domestic innovation capabilities, which translates into low productivity growth. The outcomes of the development models that Latin American countries pursued over the past 60 years offer important lessons for escaping from the middle-income trap, in Latin America as well as in middle-income countries in Asia and elsewhere. Under the state-led model, governments recognized that the advancement of domestic productive capabilities in hitherto new areas requires incentives and space for firm learning (through protection, access to finance, and investment in requisite education and infrastructure). But, in contrast to the first generation of Asian Tigers, Latin American governments did not couple the incentives for learning with the imposition of discipline through sunset clauses and performance requirements to manage rents and simulate market pressures.

Rather than rectifying this critical flaw, most Latin American governments in the 1980s abandoned the model and opted to throw the baby out with the bathwater. Where the state-led model had offered "carrots" for learning, but no "sticks," the market-led model now offered "sticks," but no "carrots" for domestic producers to upgrade and learn and achieve competitiveness within and across sectors.

The Latin American experience demonstrates clearly that government leadership without mechanisms that simulate competition in protected domestic markets does not generate sustained productive transformation. But primary reliance on market forces without strategic government support for growth-enhancing structural change does not generate dynamic comparative advantages. The last 30 years in Latin America have shown that

(a) relying primarily on market forces cements static comparative advantages, but does not lead to broad development of higher value-added activities;

(b) securing access to developed country markets through trade agreements may lead to greater integration into GVCs, but—by itself—does not call forth upgrading in production;

(c) encouraging FDI with special incentives and bilateral investment treaties may indeed attract more FDI, but FDI per se does not generate significant linkages with the rest of the economy or engender technology transfer; and

(d) domestic innovation capabilities do not develop without proactive government policies at the meso, micro, and macro levels.

To avoid being trapped at the middle-income level, the development strategy for middle-income countries has to focus squarely on the promotion of domestic innovation capabilities in a systemic way. The implementation of such a strategy requires a renewed focus on active policies for productive transformation, for greater innovation in existing sectors and in support of a reallocation toward higher productivity sectors (Figure 3.6).

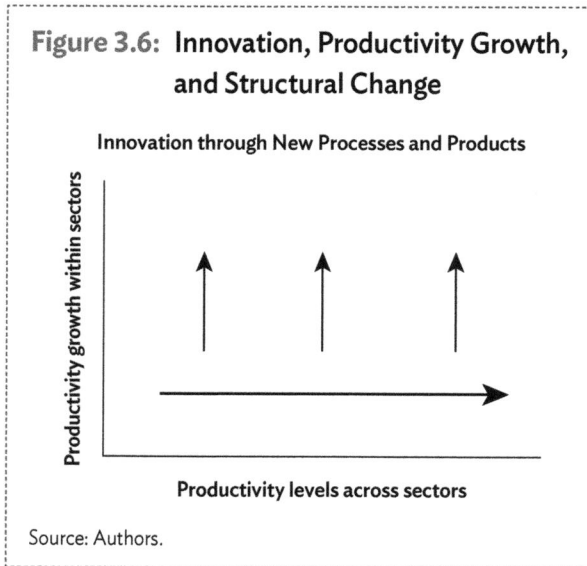

Figure 3.6: Innovation, Productivity Growth, and Structural Change

Source: Authors.

The large heterogeneity in capabilities and productivity among domestic firms means that the incorporation of knowledge developed elsewhere will continue to be important to increase productivity for many firms and to reduce the large productivity gaps among firms. Yet, it is more domestic creation of innovation that will be particularly important for moving forward. Innovation has to be a collective process where public and private actors interact and collaborate, initiatives have to complement each other, and the macro and micro incentives have to support innovation rather than discourage it. Local firms develop capabilities by learning in the production process and through internal R&D efforts as well as through interactions with other key actors in the economy: other domestic firms, foreign firms, research institutions, and universities. The meso and macro contexts have to make learning-by-doing at the micro level possible. That means that social capabilities have to evolve so that firms have the requisite information about technology and markets, have access to funding and the needed qualified personnel, and possibilities to collaborate with other firms or research entities in the innovation process. And the relative price and support structure has to be such that it makes the risk-taking of innovation not only possible, but also necessary.

The pervasiveness of coordination failures, capability failures, and market inadequacies as well as the need for non-marginal changes demand a proactive state for the achievement of broad-based upgrading. Horizontal and vertical policies are needed to advance social capabilities, support the development of local firm capabilities and establish a critical level of absorptive capacity, enable the affiliates of transnational corporations to upgrade production in the host country toward more sophisticated activities, and provide a set of economic incentives conducive to broad-based capability accumulation.

3.4.1 Horizontal Policies

There is widespread agreement on the value of horizontal government policies generally and horizontal policies for middle-income countries in particular: advancements in education, especially secondary and technical education, as well as infrastructure, particularly in information and communication technology; support for collaborations between and among private firms and research institutions, and support for engaging in R&D.

One horizontal policy of critical importance is the exchange rate policy. The exchange rate is the key relative price that determines the incentives and possibilities for producing tradable or non-tradable goods and services. McMillan and Rodrik (2011) pointed out that countries where labor moved from lower to higher productivity sectors (i.e., growth-enhancing structural change) tended to have undervalued exchange rates. By definition, not every country can have an undervalued exchange rate. However, it is clear that an overvalued exchange rate provides a major disincentive to upgrading and innovation in tradable sectors.

In countries where primary products make up a significant part of exports, the exchange rate is more volatile and prone to Dutch Disease impacts. Similarly, under open capital accounts and flexible exchange rates, large capital inflows can lead to overvalued exchange rates as well. Extended periods of overvalued exchange rates accelerated the deindustrialization process in a number of Latin American countries in the past.

The need for other horizontal policies will depend on country-specific conditions and constraints. Sometimes they extend to a whole region. For example, access to funding is a major problem for producers in Latin American countries. In the World Bank's Enterprise Surveys, a much larger percentage of firms reported access to finance as a major constraint in Latin America than in Asia (Table 3.7).

Table 3.7: Proportion of Firms Identifying Access to Finance as a Major Constraint, 2008–2015

Developed Countries (13)		East Asia (3)		South Asia (6)	
All firms	11.6	All firms	15.4	All firms	23.0
Large firms	9.1	Large firms	4.6	Large firms	20.8
Medium-sized firms	12.3	Medium-sized firms	18.6	Medium-sized firms	18.1
Small firms	12.1	Small firms	14.0	Small firms	26.0
Latin America and the Caribbean (31)		**Southeast Asia (9)**			
All firms	30.4	All firms	16.1		
Large firms	20.6	Large firms	12.1		
Medium-sized firms	29.0	Medium-sized firms	20.1		
Small firms	31.7	Small firms	16.2		

Notes: Number of countries in brackets.

Size categories: small: <20 employees; medium: 20–99 employees; large: >99 employees.

Source: UNCTAD (2016: 145) based on Enterprise Surveys of the World Bank.

3.4.2 Vertical Policies

Vertical policies, also often called active policies, target specific activities. The Latin American experience, especially in comparison with the first-generation Asian Tigers, demonstrates that targeted policies (as well as general protection policies) have to include performance requirements. Governments need to articulate and enforce what Amsden (2001) called "reciprocal control mechanisms."

In the current context, governments' financial constraints together with increased global pressures to increase innovation are making active policies particularly important. The key question, of course, is how to identify the activities where the pay-offs in terms of greater value-added production are largest and most likely to occur. The sectors in which to develop new indigenous production capabilities will depend on path dependency in country-specific contexts. There is no "one size fits all." Nonetheless, a reality and opportunity for all middle-income countries is the rapid growth of knowledge-intensive services and the blurring boundaries between such services and manufacturing (and agriculture). Lee (2013) argued that middle-income countries should leapfrog and focus on short-cycle technologies. Detailed studies are needed at the country and sector level to assess the potential for leveraging computerization, automation, and biotechnology for productivity increases. In the case of Argentina, for example, Anlló, Bisang, and Katz (2015) suggested interesting possibilities for significant productivity growth through precision agriculture.

The government needs to play a catalytic function where private sector risk is high and coordination of networked agencies and activities important. Indeed, Block (2011) and Mazzucato (2013) demonstrated the catalytic role that the US government has played in advancing innovation in new critical areas, by investing in the early-stage development in many industries.

Contrary to the perception of the US as a particularly liberal market economy, Block (2011: 6) argued that government business partnerships have been a constant in US history, but the "intensity and importance of the government role in driving innovation has intensified dramatically over the past seven decades."

Nonetheless, private–public partnerships may often help identify which activities should be targeted and with what measures. Private–public partnerships allow for real information exchange between business and government, can spell out allocative authority, and reduce barriers to rent-seeking (Schneider 2016).

Where a substantial part of production occurs in global value chains (e.g., in Central American and Asian middle-income countries), the key question is how to increase the share of domestic value added. Milberg, Jiang, and Gereffi (2014) argued that the failure of middle-income countries to move into more sophisticated parts of the value chain and establish brand recognition (in existing or new products) is one of the reasons of the middle-income trap in such countries. Yusuf and Nabeshima (2009) linked this failure explicitly to the failure to have built indigenous capabilities in design and innovation. But UNCTAD (2016) warned that intensified global competition and the reliance of transnational corporations on large first-tier global producers has increased the challenges for domestic firms in developing countries to capture more value added in the GVC.

With respect to FDI, governments need to pursue a strategic approach. That may mean targeting FDI in areas with the greatest potential for technological spillovers given the country's location-specific assets. It also means working with the affiliates of transnational corporations that produce in the country to support upgrading with complementary advances in social capabilities. In the context of GVC participation, Milberg, Jiang, and Gereffi (2014: 173) advocated managing the relationships between "foreign lead firms and domestic low value adding firms for the purpose of capturing more value added in the value chain."

3.4.3 South–South Connections

Regional integration can be a powerful tool for advancing the production of higher value-added activities. For example, in South America, where primary products dominate most countries' exports to the North, manufactured exports dominate the goods trade within the region.

Regional collaboration in research and development may be an area of real potential in the future, especially for smaller countries. The European Union has numerous programs to support joint cross-country research and innovation: the Research Framework Program, the Competitiveness and Innovation Framework Program, the Structural Funds, the Cohesion Fund, the European Agricultural Fund for Rural Development and the European Fisheries Fund (European Union 2011). It would be worthwhile to analyze these programs in greater detail to see what might be copied or adapted by middle-income countries that are members of regional agreements.

3.4.4 Policy Space for Active Government Policies

To implement active government policies for productive transformation toward a more knowledge-intensive economy, governments have to use all the policy space available to them and be creative in using it. The rules of the WTO—which came into effect in 1995—have restricted the policy space of governments for targeted policy support considerably. They disallow many key policies that development latecomers in the past have used to become high-income economies (Abugattas and Paus 2008). For example, trade-related investment measures (TRIMs) disallow preferential national treatment, performance requirements, and quantitative restrictions. That includes domestic content requirements and trade balance requirements. And the Agreement on Subsidies and Countervailing Measures (SCMs) prohibits the use of export subsidies.

Nonetheless, even though the policy space is reduced (and often narrowed further through bilateral trade and investment agreements), governments have not taken advantage of the policy space that still exists. Agosín (2013: 16), for example, argued that "most LAC countries have bound their tariff levels in the WTO at levels higher than those they use in practice, giving them some policy space to increase effective tariffs, if they chose to do so."

Furthermore, governments can provide subsidies for training and regional development. They cannot give preferential treatment to domestic producers, but they can treat domestic and foreign producers equally. They can support human capital formation, research and development, and capacity building. And they may demand that a foreign firm transfer technology, conduct a certain amount of R&D locally, or employ domestic workers to enhance their skills (Shadlen 2005).

Some countries have been creative in devising new rules or circumventing existing rules. Brazil, for example, had "voluntary" reciprocal agreements with transnational corporations, where the latter got access to the domestic market and, in return, had to meet requirements for local content and R&D (Schneider 2016). And the PRC has repeatedly used non-WTO conforming policies to advance domestic production capabilities in strategic industries. Oh (2015), for example, offered a detailed case study of the creation of the domestic wind turbine manufacturing industry in the PRC through the use of industrial policies that strategically disregarded WTO rules. When the US brought a complaint to the WTO and the dispute settlement body ruled against the PRC, the country complied. But by then domestic capability development had passed the critical initial learning stage.

3.4.5 Political Coalitions for an Innovation-Based Strategy

In the end, a necessary condition for escaping from the middle-income trap is the existence of a coalition of stakeholders that push for an innovation-focused strategy. There has to be a critical mass of national producers that have an interest in upgrading and innovation and would demand or support such a strategy, or at least parts of it.

In the case of Latin America, under the market-led strategy, many producers in the formal manufacturing sector were forced out of business or sold their businesses, often to foreign companies, to dedicate themselves to importing. The process of deindustrialization and informalization was often accompanied by denationalization, and foreign producers do not have the same interest in moving up the value chain in the host country. Increases in wages can serve as an incentive for upgrading. In Singapore, in the early 1970s, national wages were increased for exactly that purpose (Prime 2012). Theoretically, demands from labor unions for higher wages and better working conditions could provide incentives for producers to upgrade and increase productivity. But that has not happened in reality, as the deindustrialization process has gone hand in hand with a weakening of labor unions in most Latin American countries.

In some countries, it may be possible to identify common interests around a subset of issues, e.g., availability of financing, the formation of new clusters in areas of potential competitive advantage, or producers that are participating in GVCs. It may also be possible to expand from existing "pockets of excellence" by expanding linkages with the rest of the economy (see Sánchez–Ancochea 2012, on the Dominican Republic; Perez–Caldentey 2012, on Chile; and Abugattas 2012, on Jordan). Also if primary resources are owned by national producers, there will be a greater chance that they will be interested in developing new comparative advantages by incorporating information technology-based services or bio-technology.

Forging coalitions and building the institutional architecture in support of innovation is a challenging process. But no action or insufficient action on a broad innovation agenda will have undesirable consequences for all interest groups, as it will mean ongoing slow growth and stagnant or declining wages.

3.5 | Conclusions

In this chapter, I analyzed the reasons behind the middle-income trap in Latin America to extract lessons for escaping from the trap. The Merriam–Webster dictionary defines a "trap" as "something by which one is caught or stopped unawares; *also*: a position or situation from which it is difficult or impossible to escape."[13] Intense global competitive pressures and the rise of the PRC make it more challenging to escape, as they reduce the time for endogenizing and expanding innovation capabilities. But while it may be more difficult to escape, it is not impossible. The middle-income trap is not inevitable. Just as policy choice was an important factor behind economies facing the trap, a change in policies is the way to escape from the trap.

Middle-income countries need to embrace a capability-focused strategy to advance innovation, move up the value chain, and create decent jobs. The nature of the current production structure and location-specific assets that may be developed will shape the possible path of productive transformation; these are country-specific. Nonetheless, the compression of time for learning affects all countries. Countries where more elements of the requisite innovation ecosystem are developing already will have a better chance of escaping from the trap. The starting point, however, has to be the existence of political will to embark on an innovation-focused strategy with the requisite active policies to implement it.

References

Abramovitz, M. 1986. Catching up, Forging Ahead, and Falling Behind. *The Journal of Economic History* 46(2): 385–406.

Abugattas, L. 2012. Jordan: Model Reformer Without Upgrading? *Studies in Comparative International Development* 47: 231–253.

---

[13] http://www.merriam-webster.com/dictionary/trap?show=0&t=1383226418 (accessed 24 February 2017).

Abugattas, L., and E. Paus. 2008. Policy Space for a Capability-Centered Development Strategy for Latin America. In *The Political Economy of Hemispheric Integration. Responding to Globalization in the Americas,* edited by D. Sanchez–Ancochea and K. C. Shadlen. New York, NY and London: Palgrave Macmillan.

Agosin, M. 2013. Productive Development Policies in Latin America: Past and Present. Working Paper 382. Santiago: Facultad Eonomía y Negocios, University of Chile.

Aiyar, S., R. Duval, D. Puy, Y. Wu, and L. Zhang. 2013. Growth Slowdowns and the Middle-income Trap. IMF Working Paper WP/13/71. Washington, DC: International Monetary Fund.

Amsden, A. 2001. *The Rise of "The Rest": Challenges to the West from Late-Industrializing Economies.* Oxford, United Kingdom and New York, NY: Oxford University Press.

Anlló, G., R. Bisang, and J. Katz. 2015. Aprendiendo con el agro argentine. De la ventaja competitive a la ventaja competitive. BID. Documento para Discusión. (In Spanish).

Bértola, L., and J. A. Ocampo. 2012. *The Economic Development of Latin America since Independence.* Oxford, United Kingdom: Oxford University Press.

Block, F. 2011. Innovation and the Invisible Hand of Government. In *State of Innovation: The US Government's Role in Technology Development,* edited by F. Block and M. Keller. Boulder, CO and London: Paradgm Publishers.

Brynjolfsson, E., and A. McAfee. 2014. *The Second Machine Age. Work, Progress, and Prosperity in a Time of Brilliant Technologies.* New York, NY and London: Norton & Company.

Calderón, C., and L. Servén. 2012. Infrastructure in Latin America. World Bank Policy Research Paper 5317. Washington, DC: The World Bank.

Cimoli, M., G. Dosi, and J. E. Stiglitz. 2009. The Political Economy of Capabilities Accumulation: The Past and Future of Policies of Industrial Development In *Industrial Policy and Development,* edited by M. Cimoli, G. Dosi, and J. E. Stiglitz. *The Political Economy of Capabilities Accumulation.* Oxford, United Kingdom: Oxford University Press.

Daude, C. 2010. Innovation, Productivity and Economic Development in Latin America and the Caribbean. OECD Development Centre Working Paper 288. Paris: Organisation for Economic Co-operation and Development.

Devlin, R., and G. Moguillansky. 2012. What's New in the New Industrial Policy in Latin America? World Bank Policy Research Paper 6191. Washington, DC: World Bank.

Doner, R., and B. R. Schneider. 2016. The Middle-income Trap: More Politics than Economics. *World Politics* 68(4): 608–644.

Dosi, G. 1984. *Technological Change and Industrial Transformation.* New York, NY: St. Martin's Press.

ECLAC. 2010. *Time for Equality. Closing Gaps, Opening Trails.* Santiago, Chile: ECLAC.

Eichengreen, B., D. Park, and K. Shin. 2011. When Fast-Growing Economies Slow Down: International Evidence and Implications for China. NBER Working Paper 16919. Cambridge, MA: National Bureau of Economic Research.

———. 2013. Growth Slowdowns Redux: New Evidence on the Middle-Income Trap. NBER Working Paper 18673. Cambridge, MA: National Bureau of Economic Research.

European Union. 2011. *New Practical Guide to EU Funding Opportunities for Research and Development.* http://ec.europa.eu/research/participants/data/ref/fp7/204008/practical-guide-rev3_en.pdf (accessed 24 February 2017).

Felipe, J., A. Abdon, and U. Kumar. 2012. Tracking the Middle-Income Trap: What is it, Who is in it, and Why? Levy Economics Institute at Bard College, Working Paper No. 715.

Flechtner, S., and S. Panther. 2015. Global and Domestic Inequalities and the Political Economy of the Middle-Income Trap. Paper prepared for the World Congress of Comparative Economics, Rome, 25–27 June.

Ford, M. 2015. *Rise of the Robots. Technology and the Threat of a Jobless Future.* New York, NY: Basic Books.

Foxley, A. 2012. La Trampa del Ingreso Medio. El desafío de esta década para América Latina. Santiago, Chile: CIEPLAN.

Freeman, R. 2007. The Challenge of the Growing Globalization of Labor Markets to Economic and Social Policy. In *Global Capitalism Unbound. Winners and Losers from Offshore Outsourcing*, edited by E. Paus. New York, NY and London: Palgrave Macmillan.

Gill, I., and H. Kharas. 2007. *An East Asia Renaissance: Ideas for Economic Growth*. Washington, DC: The World Bank.

Hausmann, R., and B. Klinger. 2007. The Structure of the Product Space and the Evolution of Comparative Advantage. Center for International Development, Harvard University, Working Paper 128. Cambridge, MA: Harvard University.

Hausmann, R., J. Hwang, and D. Rodrik. 2007. What You Export Matters. *Journal of Economic Growth* 12: 1–25.

Im, F. G., and D. Rosenblatt. 2013. Middle-Income Trap: A Conceptual and Empirical Survey. World Bank Policy Research Working Paper 6594. Washington, DC: The World Bank.

Industrial Research Institute. R&D Global Funding Forecast, various years.

Katz, J. 2001. Structural Reforms and Technological Behaviour: The Sources and Nature of Technological Change in Latin America in the 1990s. *Research Policy* 30: 1–19.

Lall, S. 2000. The Technological Structure and Performance of Developing Country Manufactured Exports 1985-1998. *Oxford Development Studies* 28(3): 337–369.

Lee, K. 2013. *Schumpeterian Analysis of Economic Catch-up: Knowledge, Path Creation and the Middle-income Trap*. Cambridge, United Kingdom and New York, NY: Cambridge University Press.

Lustig, N. 2016. Poverty and Inequality after the Commodities Boom. Presentation at the Annual Conference of the Latin American Studies Association. New York, NY, May.

Mazzucato, M. 2013. *The Entrepreneurial State. Debunking Public vs. Private Sector Myths*. London, New York, NY, and Delhi: Anthem Press.

McMillan M., and D. Rodrik. 2011. Globalization, Structural Change and Productivity Growth. NBER Working Paper 17143. Cambridge, MA: National Bureau of Economic Research.

Milberg, W., X. Jiang, and G. Gereffi. 2014. Industrial Policy in the Era of Vertically Specialized Industrialization. In *Transforming Economies. Making Industrial Policy Work for Growth, Jobs, and Development*, edited by J. Salazar–Xirinachs, I. Nübler, and R. Kozul–Wright. Geneva, Switzerland: International Labour Office.

Moreno–Brid, C., and J. Ros. 2009. *Development and Growth of the Mexican Economy: A Historical Perspective*. New York, NY: Oxford University Press.

Nelson, R., and S. Winter. 1982. *An Evolutionary Theory of Economic Change*. Cambridge, MA: Harvard University Press.

Ocampo, J. A., C. Rada, and L. Taylor. 2009. *Growth and Policy in Developing Countries. A Structuralist Approach*. New York, NY: Columbia University Press.

Oh, S. 2015. How China Outsmarts WTO Ruling in the Wind Industry. *Asian Survey*. 55(6): 1116–1145.

Ohno, K. 2009. *The Middle-income Trap. Implications for Industrialization Strategies in East Asia and Africa*. GRIPS Development Forum, National Graduate Institute for Policy Studies, Japan.

Organisation for Economic Co-operation and Development (OECD). 2016. *PISA2015. Results in Focus*. https://www.oecd.org/pisa/pisa-2015-results-in-focus.pdf (accessed 24 February 2017).

Paus, E. 2012. Confronting the Middle-income Trap. Insights from Small Latecomers. *Studies in Comparative International Development* 47(2): 115–138.

——. 2014. Latin America and the Middle-Income Trap. Financing for Development Series. New York, NY: ECLAC, United Nations.

Paus, E., and K. Gallagher. 2008. Missing Links: Foreign Investment and Industrial Development in Costa Rica and Mexico. *Studies in Comparative International Development* 43(1): 53–80.

Paus, E., N. Reinhardt, and M. Robinson. 2003. Trade Liberalization and Productivity Growth in Latin American Manufacturing. *Journal of Policy Reform* 6(1): 1–15.

Peres, W. 2011. Industrial Policies in Latin America. World Institute
for Development Economics Research. Working Paper 2011/48.
New York, NY: United Nations University.

Perez Caldentey, E. 2012. Income Convergence, Capability Convergence,
and the Middle-income trap: An Analysis of the Case of Chile.
Studies in Comparative International Development 47(2): 185–207.

Prime, P. 2012. Utilizng FDI to Stay Ahead: The Case of Singapore.
Studies in Comparative International Development 47(2): 139–160.

Robertson, P. and L. Ye. 2013. On the Existence of the Middle-income trap.
Discussion Paper 13.12. Perth: Business School, University of
Western Australia.

Rodrik, D. 2015. Premature De-industrialization. NBER Working Paper 20935.
Cambridge, MA: National Bureau of Economic Research.

Sánchez-Ancochea, D. 2012. A Fast Herd and a Slow Tortoise?
The Challenge of Upgrading in the Dominican Republic. *Studies in
Comparative International Development* 47(2): 208–230.

Schneider, B. R. 2016. Upgrading in the 21st Century: New Challenges
for Industrial Policy and Institution Building. Background paper for
UNCTAD. *Trade and Development Report 2016*. Unpublished.

Shadlen, K. 2005. Exchanging Development for Market Access? Deep
Integration and Industrial Policy under Multilateral and Regional-
Bilateral Trade Agreements. *Review of International Political Economy* 12:
750–775.

Shapiro, H., and L. Taylor. 1990. The State and Industrial Policy.
World Development 18(6): 861–878.

Stiglitz, J., and J. Lin (eds.) 2013. *The Industrial Policy Revolution.
The Role of Government beyond Ideology.* New York, NY and London:
Palgrave Macmillan.

United Nations Conference on Trade and Development (UNCTAD).
2016. *Trade and Development Report 2016.* Geneva, Switzerland:
United Nations Conference on Trade and Development.

Whittaker, H., T. Zhu, T. Sturgeon, M. H. Tsai, and T. Okita. 2010.
Compressed Development. *Studies in Comparative International
Development* 45(4): 439–467.

World Bank. 2013. *China 2030. Building a Modern, Harmonious, and Creative Society.* Washington, DC: The World Bank.

———. 2016. *Poverty and Shared Prosperity 2016. Taking on Inequality.* Washington, DC: The World Bank.

World Trade Organization (WTO). Trade in Value Added and Global Value-Chains: Statistical Profiles. https://www.wto.org/english/res_e/statis_e/miwi_e/countryprofiles_e.htm.

———. Statistics on Merchandise Trade. https://www.wto.org/english/res_e/statis_e/merch_trade_stat_e.htm.

Yusuf, S., and K. Nabeshima. 2009. *Tiger Economies under Threat. A Comparative Analysis of Malaysia's Industrial Prospects and Policy Options.* Washington, DC: The World Bank.

Figure A3.1: Ranking in the Economic Complexity Index in South America, 1964–2014

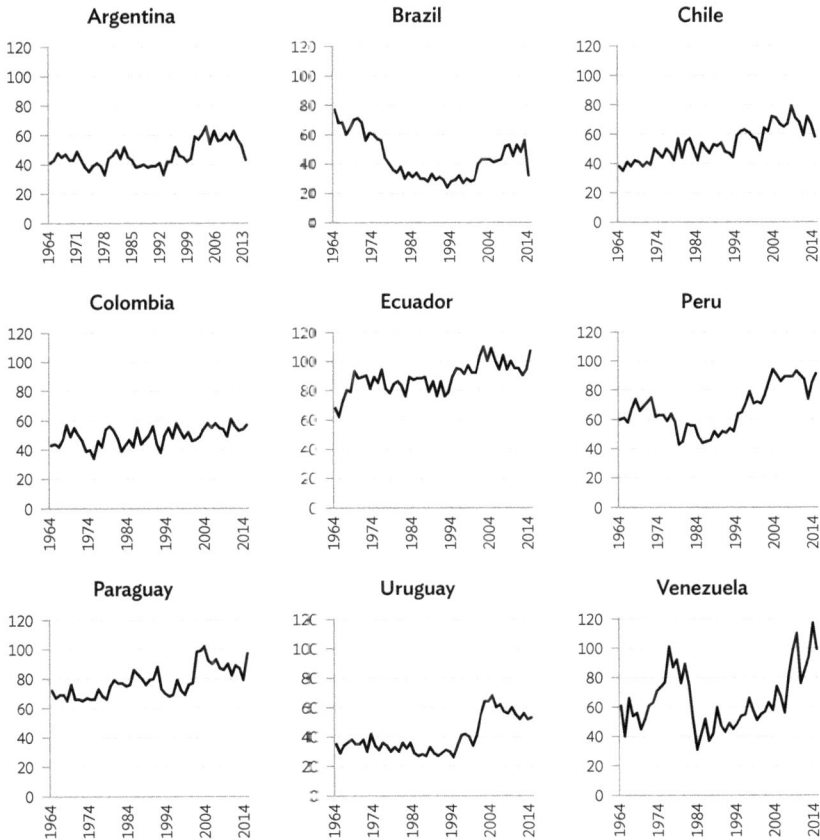

Argentina

Brazil

Chile

Colombia

Ecuador

Peru

Paraguay

Uruguay

Venezuela

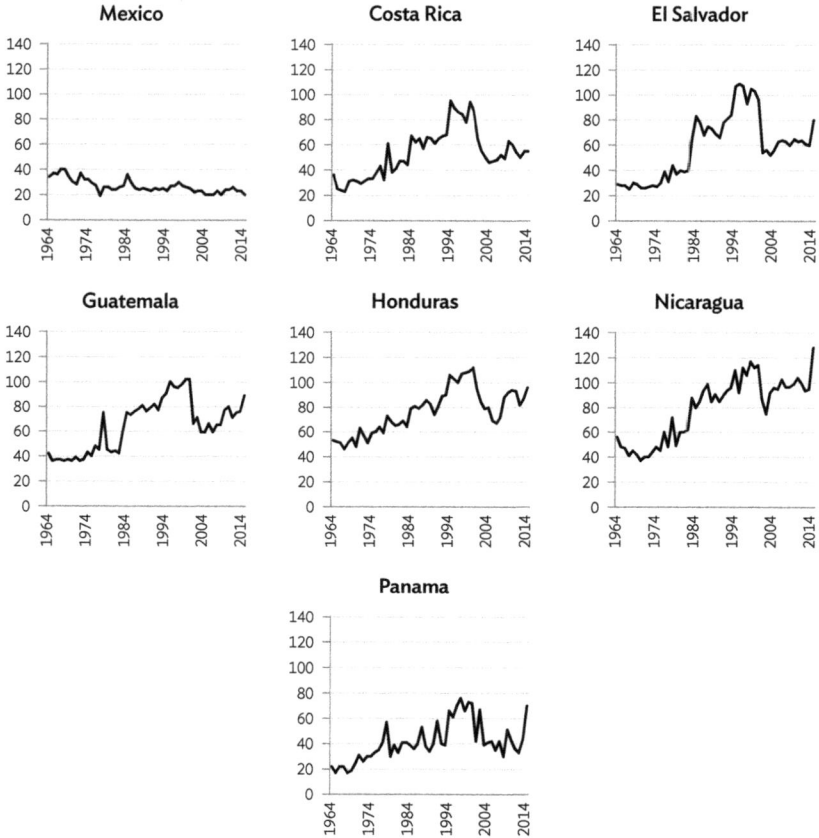

Figure A3.2: Ranking in the Economic Complexity Index in Central America and Mexico, 1964–2014

Figure A3.3: Ranking in the Economic Complexity Index in Asia, 1964–2014

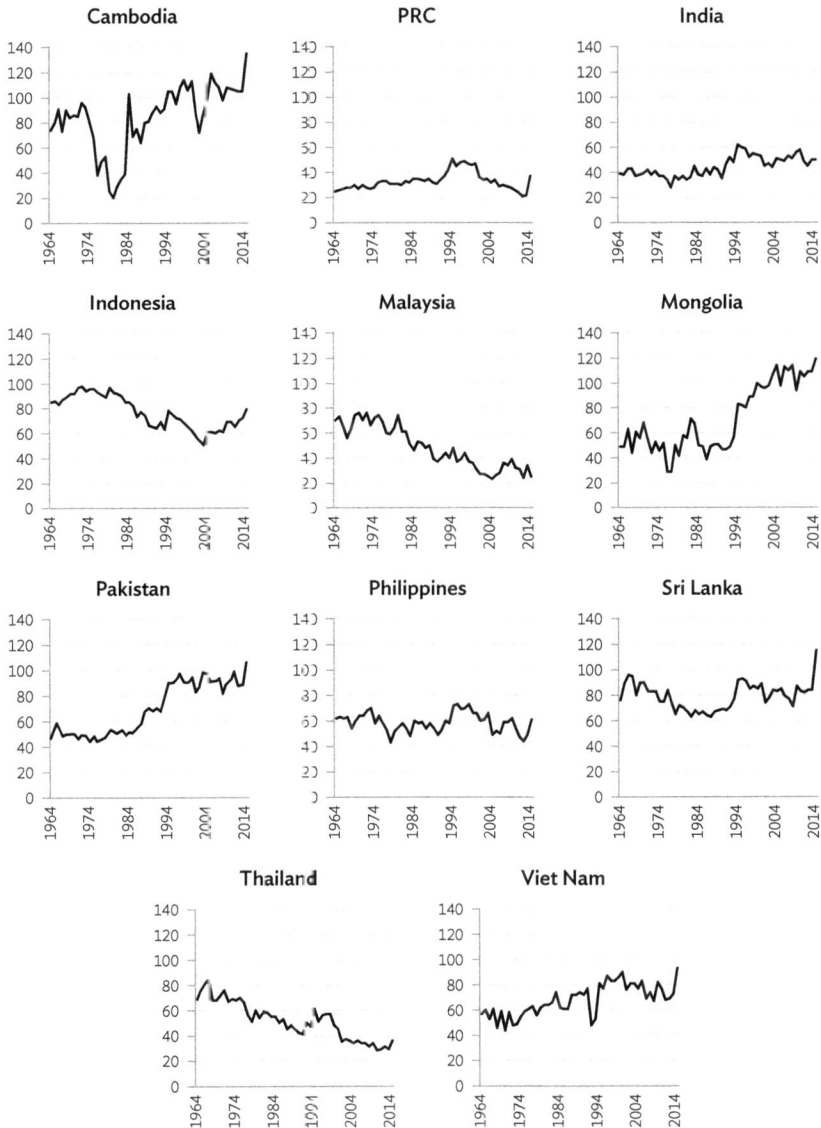

PRC = People's Republic of China.

Source: The Atlas of Economic Complexity, Center for International Development at Harvard University, http://www.atlas.cid.harvard.edu (accessed 24 February 2017).

CHAPTER 4

Economic Growth and the Middle-Income Trap: The People's Republic of China's Challenges*

Xiaolu Wang

4.1 | What Is the Middle-Income Trap and Why Do Countries Fall into It?

The so-called middle-income trap (MIT) is a common phenomenon but not a rule of economics. It describes a situation in which a country has developed into the middle-income stage, but its economic growth has significantly slowed or stagnated, and it has been unable to transform itself into a high-income country for a considerably long period. Typical examples are some of the Latin American countries in the second half of the 20th century, particularly from the 1970s until the 1990s, during which period they experienced very low, or negative, economic growth. Although their economic growth reaccelerated to some extent in the 21st century, none of those countries have so far been able to convert themselves into high-income countries.

Long-term stagnation occurs not only at the middle-income stage of development, but also at the high- or low-income stages, for different reasons and with different results. However, the phenomenon of MIT has a special meaning as it pertains to a country that is already on the track of economic

---

* An earlier version of this chapter was a paper written for the Asian Development Bank Institute (ADBI) research project: Middle Income Trap in Asia. The author is grateful for ADBI's support.

growth but stops halfway. Why is this the case? How can countries avoid this situation? There have been many different, even conflicting explanations and suggestions in economic studies. Further studies on this issue are needed, especially for a country like the People's Republic of China (PRC), which transformed itself into an upper-middle-income country over 3 decades of fast economic growth, and which aims to catch up with high-income countries.

Drawing the lessons from the Latin American countries that fell into MIT, a number of possible reasons for the MIT are as follows:

(1)   Extremely high-income inequality, severe social conflict, and labor disputes;
(2)   Government failure, collaborations between political power and large consortiums, leading to market monopoly, greater income inequality, and more social conflicts;
(3)   Populist governments with anti-market policies and excessive social welfare provisions that place a burden on economic growth;
(4)   Inappropriate macroeconomic policies, mainly excess money supply leading to hyperinflation or a debt crisis;
(5)   Unsmooth industrial transformation, when a country that moves up to the middle-income stage loses its original comparative advantage in cheap labor cost and is unable to establish a new comparative advantage;
(6)   An aging population causes a shortage in the supply of labor and human resources, which limits economic growth.

The above are some possible reasons for the MIT, although not necessarily all apply to each country falling into the MIT. Most of these facts relate to government policy and have an impact on income distribution. In those Latin American countries, great income inequality is likely to be a very important reason.

Table 4.1 lists eight Latin American countries' per capita gross domestic product (GDP) data from 1950 to 2008. They are Argentina, Bolivia, Brazil, Chile, Colombia, Mexico, Peru, and Venezuela—all with populations of over 10 million people. Per capita GDP data are mainly from Angus Maddison's calculation of international dollars in 1990 prices, at purchasing power parity (2001). These countries had been middle-income countries in the 1950s, with an average of GDP per capita of $3,330, and have remained middle-income countries until today. In particular, most of them experienced very low, or negative, economic growth from 1973 to 1998; on average their GDP per capita increased only by 1,000 international dollars during these 25 years. In 2008, their average GDP per capita in current prices was only $6,659.

Table 4.1: GDP per Capita of Latin American Countries
(International dollars in 1990 prices)

Year	1950	1973	1998	2008a	2008b
Argentina	4,987	7,973	9,219	13,991	7,200
Bolivia	1,919	2,357	2,459	3,057	1,460
Brazil	1,672	3,882	5,459	6,920	7,350
Chile	3,821	5,093	9,753	13,625	9,400
Colombia	2,153	3,499	5,317	7,500	4,660
Mexico	2,365	6,097	6,655	7,877	9,980
Peru	2,263	3,952	3,666	5,748	3,990
Venezuela	7,462	10,625	8,965	12,524	9,230
Average	**3,330**	**5,435**	**6,437**	**8,905**	**6,659**

GDP = gross domestic product.

Note: The year 2008 data (2008a) are calculated by the author using country growth rates of GDP per capita in 1998–2008 from the World Bank, and based on Maddison's calculation of 1998 data. These are not accurate calculations but close approximations as methods of calculation by Maddison and the World Bank are different. 2008b data are GDP per capita in current prices by the World Bank.

Sources: Maddison (2003); World Bank (various years), World Development Indicators.

All these Latin American countries have a common feature of great income inequality for a long period. Table 4.2 listed their Gini coefficients for the years corresponding (or close) to those in Table 4.1. It shows that the four countries with available data had an average Gini coefficient of 0.46 in 1950, 0.47 in 1973, and it increased to 0.55 in 1998. This indicates that the period of their economic stagnation was also the period they experienced increasing, and severe, income inequality. From 1998 to 2008, their average GDP per capita growth rate increased from 0.7% to 3.3%, while their income gap decreased from 0.55 to 0.52 on average. In fact, their average Gini coefficient of 0.52 was still significantly higher than the world average. In 2008, of the 145 countries for which data are available, only 25 have a Gini coefficient above 0.5, and most of the 145 countries' Gini coefficients are below 0.4 (World Bank 2011).

Table 4.2: Income Inequality in Latin American Countries: Gini Coefficient

Year	1950	1973	1998	2008
Argentina	0.412	0.353	0.522	0.458
Bolivia		0.420	0.585	0.573
Brazil	0.540	0.352	0.591	0.539
Chile	0.456	0.532	0.571	0.523
Colombia		0.591	0.575	0.585
Mexico		0.463	0.531	0.517
Peru		0.457	0.530	0.480
Venezuela	0.420	0.556	0.495	0.435
Average	**0.457**	**0.466**	**0.550**	**0.518**

Note: For countries where data were unavailable for the corresponding years, the closest year's data are used. Data sources: WIDER database; and World Bank, various years.

To compare with these Latin American countries, five East Asian economies and regions, i.e., Japan; the Republic of Korea; Singapore; Taipei,China; and Hong Kong, China had an average GDP per capita of only 1,614 international dollars (1990 prices) in 1950, only half that of the Latin American countries. Their Gini coefficient on average was 0.44, similar to the Latin American countries. But unlike the Latin American countries, their income gap continued to narrow afterward, dropping to an average of 0.36 in 1998. During the same period, their GDP per capita grew rapidly and achieved an average of above $18,000 in 1998, which means they had entered the high-income economies group. In 2008, their average GDP per capita exceeded $26,000, three times that of the eight Latin American countries. Both the economic performance and income inequality in the two groups of economies form a sharp contrast (Table 4.3).

Table 4.3: **Average Gini and Economic Growth Rate in Two Groups of Economies and Regions**

Average Gini	1950	1973	1998	2008
LA8	0.457	0.466	0.550	0.518
EA5	0.436	0.380	0.359	–
GDP per capita	1950	1973	1998	2008
LA8	3,330	5,435	6,437	8,905
EA5	1,614	7,766	18,082	26,286
Growth of GDP per capita		1950–1973	1973–1998	1998–2008
LA8		2.2%	0.7%	3.3%
EA5		7.1%	3.4%	3.8%

– = data unavailable, EA = East Asia, GDP = gross domestic product, LA = Latin America.
Note: GDP per capita is international dollars in 1990 prices, as in Table 4.1.
Data source: As in Table 4.1 and Table 4.2.

The above data do not mean that the large income inequality is the only reason why Latin American countries fall into the MIT. As pointed out above, there are other reasons, such as policies influenced by crony capitalism or extreme populism. Inappropriate macroeconomic policies leading to hyperinflation could be another factor. To assess to what extent such factors have contributed to economic stagnation, further research is needed.

4.2 | Structure Imbalance and Growth Slowdown in the PRC

The PRC experienced rapid economic growth at close to 10% annually for more than 3 decades, from 1978 to 2010, and successfully transformed from a low-income country to an upper-middle-income country. However, in recent years the impetus of economic growth has gradually weakened. From 2010 to 2016, the PRC's growth rates were 10.6%, 9.5%, 7.9%, 7.8%, 7.3%, 6.9%, and 6.7%. A continuous growth slowdown like this never happened in the preceding 3 decades. The effects of the PRC's expansionary fiscal and monetary policies have diminished. If this trend continues, the PRC may face economic stagnation and could even fall into the MIT.

The direct causes of the slowdown in economic growth are structural imbalance, as indicated by overinvestment and overcapacity in industry; a large housing stock in the real estate sector, which increased the leverage ratio; and substantial declines in productivity.

In terms of overcapacity, sectors suffering the most are iron and steel, cement, coal, nonferrous metals, flat glass, and other major raw materials industries, which experienced dramatic capacity expansion in past years. Taking crude steel as an example, in 2000 the nationwide total output was 131 million tons (MT), and in 2013 it had reached 813 MT, a more than fivefold increase. Over the same period, output of cement increased from 597 MT to 2,419 MT and coal from 1,384 MT to 3,974 MT. In 2015, output of crude steel, cement, and coal accounted for 50%, 58%, and 48%, respectively, of total world output.

Due to continued and massive investment, the rapid expansion of production capacity much exceeded demand growth, leading to large overcapacity in these industries. For example, it is estimated that production capacity of the steel industry in 2015 was 1,200 MT; about one-third of the capacity was unused. Coal, cement, plate glass, nonferrous metals, and other raw material industries are generally in the same situation. In fact, overcapacity exists in most industrial sectors, which leads to continuous price decreases of most industrial products.

Profits are falling, more and more firms make losses, and the solvency of firms is weakening.

In terms of the leverage ratio, calculated using the Central Bank's Social Finance data, indirect finance as a percentage of GDP increased from 110% to 208% during the period of 2000–2015. In fact, this is not a full calculation for the leverage ratio due to the data being incomplete. According to some calculations, the leverage ratio reached 260% in 2015. The rapid increase in the leverage ratio was mainly a result of continued loose monetary policy. With large overcapacity and decreasing returns to capital, firms' loan solvency is worsening and total debt is building up.

In terms of productivity, both the total capital–output ratio (capital stock/GDP) and incremental capital–output ratio (capital increment/GDP increment) increased sharply over the past 15 years. The incremental capital–output ratio was 2.7 in 2000 and increased to 7.1 in 2015, indicating sharply deteriorated input and output relations (Table 4.4).

Table 4.4: GDP and Capital Stock Growth, and Capital–Output Ratio in the PRC

	GDP growth (%)	Capital stock growth (%)	Capital–output ratio	Incremental capital–output ratio
2000	8.4	9.9	2.35	2.72
2005	11.4	13.7	2.60	3.07
2010	10.6	16.6	3.11	4.62
2015	6.9	12.5	4.12	7.09

GDP = gross domestic product, PRC = People's Republic of China.
Data source: the author's calculation based on data of the National Bureau of Statistics of China. http://www.stats.gov.cn/tjsj/.

The above data represent a situation of structural imbalance, largely due to excessive savings and overinvestment, and with large income inequality as the underlying reason. Continued loose monetary policy also played an important role in leading to the structural mbalance. In addition, excessive government intervention in business activities and in resource allocation pushed up the rates of savings and investment on one hand, and led to losses of allocative efficiency of resources on the other.

From 2000 to 2010, both the national savings rate and investment rate (as shares of GDP) increased from around 35% to around 50%, while the consumption rate dropped from 63% to 48%. The share of household consumption in GDP dropped from 47% to 36% during the same period (Table 4.5). The excessive increase of the investment rate and an excessively low consumption rate are the main causes of large overcapacity and economic weakness.

Table 4.5: Long-Run Changes of the Savings, Investment, and Consumption Structure in the PRC (%)

	1980	1990	2000	2010	2015
Savings rate	35.2	37.1	36.7	51.5	48.4
Investment rate	35.5	34.4	34.3	47.9	44.9
Consumption rate	64.8	62.9	63.3	48.5	51.6
Share of household consumption	51.1	49.4	46.7	35.6	38.0

Data source: NBSC (2016).

The rapid increases in the rates of savings and investment, and rapid decreases in the rate of consumption are related mainly to three facts:

First, the income gap continued to widen. During the 2000–2010 period, the Gini coefficient rose from 0.41 to 0.48 (National Bureau of Statistics of China [NBSC] data), and the income gaps both between urban and rural residents and between high- and low-income groups expanded significantly, meaning a change in the pattern of income distribution in favor of high-income residents. These weakened the relative consumption capability of middle- and low-income residents. Meanwhile, with effect of the law of diminishing marginal propensity to consume, high-income residents intend to use more of their increasing income for savings and investment, naturally leading to a lower average rate of consumption and higher rates of savings and investment.

Second, the incompleteness of social security networks in terms of coverage, dissatisfaction with public services, and fast increases in the prices of housing, medical services, and education, all added pressure on low- and middle-income residents. In response to these risks and unfavorable changes, they have to save more and consume less.

Third, during the same period, the disposable income of the government and the financial sector as a proportion of GDP rose from 15% to 21%, while the proportion of residents' income decreased from 67% to 60%; changes in the pattern of national income distribution have also weakened household purchasing power.

Increasing household savings are not the only reason for increases in total savings and investment. From 2000 to 2010, the household savings rate (household savings/household disposable income) increased from 31% to 42%, while the government savings rate (government savings/government disposable income) increased from –9% to 28%. The increase in government savings clearly exceeds that of household savings. Changes in the components of total savings show the same trend. The shares of the household sector and nonfinancial enterprise sector in total savings fell by 7 and 12 percentage points, respectively, whereas the shares of the financial sector and the government sector increased by 5 and 14 percentage points, respectively. The contribution of the government and state-owned enterprises in total capital formation also increased significantly. Clearly, the increases in the investment rate are more related to increases in government savings and government investment than they are to household savings.[1]

---

[1]   The rates of savings and investment data are from expenditure-approach GDP accounting and flow of funds statistics by the National Bureau of Statistics of China, see China Statistical Yearbook, various years, and the NBSC website. Data in the following are from, or calculated based on, the same sources unless specified otherwise.

Another way the government influences changes of the rate of investment, besides the direct increases in government savings and investment, is continued monetary stimulus. This had the effect of increasing nongovernment investment as well as increasing the debt ratio. In addition, the monetary stimulus resulted in bubbles, especially in that it caused dramatic increases in housing prices in large cities, brought high returns to investors in the short term, thus inducing people to invest in the real estate sector or stock market and push up their savings.

The government's industrial policy, its research and development (R&D) policy, and the regional development policies of local governments are all aimed at encouraging investment in certain industries, by certain enterprises, or in certain regions. These policies include preferential treatment to encourage investment in sectors selected by the government, special treatment for high-tech enterprises identified by the government, and local government subsidies or low land prices, etc. to attract investment.

That governments at various administrative levels are keen to expand investment is related to the performance evaluation systems of the government. Governments at higher levels in their evaluation of the performance of lower levels of government focus mainly on economic growth and investment outcomes. Although there have been changes in recent years, such as incorporating some other indicators into the evaluation systems, the overall situation remains the same. This also encouraged the different levels of governments to increase their intervention in resource allocation.

Particularly worrisome is that the PRC's loose monetary policy continues to result in a rising leverage ratio and increasing financial risks. This could lead to a major financial crisis or a bursting of the asset bubble, taking the economy into long-term depression, as happened in Japan in the 1990s, where it resulted in a 25-year period of very slow growth of below 1% on average. The key difference is that Japan was already a high-income country at that time, whereas in the case of the PRC the economy may fall into the MIT.

The slowdown in the PRC's economic growth in recent years cannot be explained by the normal business cycle; rather, it is the result of a structural imbalance caused by institutional and policy problems. Without further institutional reform and policy adjustments to rebalance the structure, it will be difficult to revitalize economic growth.

4.3 | Empirical Study: Key Factors Affecting the PRC's Total Factor Productivity and Economic Growth

In this study, we build a growth model and use the PRC's long-term time-series data to decompose total factor productivity (TFP) and to identify the factors influencing it, including institutional, policy, and structural variables, to examine the possibility of the PRC falling into the MIT. The model is constructed based on the human capital growth model by Lucas (1988). One important feature of the Lucas model, which distinguishes it from the well-known neoclassical growth model (see Solow 1956), is that it employs a human capital variable to replace the labor variable used in the neoclassical growth model. In addition to this, and considering the PRC's particular circumstances, a number of institutional and structural variables are included in the current model to test their possible effects on TFP changes. These variables represent the PRC's R&D investment, market-oriented reform, economic openness, urbanization, changes of government administrative cost, final consumption rate, and the leverage ratio, all considered, either theoretically or empirically, to have some possible effects on TFP changes in the PRC's circumstances.

The model is defined as follows:

$$Y = AK^{a_1} H^{a_2} H_a^{a_3} R^{a_4} e^{f(x)} \tag{1}$$

where Y is GDP at constant prices; A is a constant representing the level of productivity; K is fixed capital stock, calculated from data of both investment in fixed assets and fixed capital formation using the perpetual inventory method; H is human capital, defined as effective labor weighted by years of education; H_a is the average level of workers' education years, to test the possible spillover effect of human capital; R is the stock of technology capital, which is an accumulation of R&D investment over the years using the perpetual inventory method; and $f(x)$ is a subfunction composed of a number of institutional and structural variables, so that their possible effect on growth and TFP can be decomposed. The subfunction $f(x)$ is defined as follows:

$$f(x) = \alpha_5 m + \alpha_6 u + \alpha_7 f + \alpha_8 d + \alpha_9 g + \alpha_{10} l + \alpha_{11} c + \alpha_{12} c^2 + \alpha_{13} T \tag{2}$$

where m is the output share of the private sector in the industrial sector, to present the achievement of market-oriented reforms;[2] u is the rate of urbanization, as the proportion of urban population in total; f is the share of foreign capital in the total capital stock, calculated from FDI data; d is the trade dependency ratio, defined as a ratio of total value of imports and exports to GDP; g is the relative cost of government administration, as a ratio of government administrative expenses to GDP; l is the leverage rate, defined as total debt to GDP, calculated from the Central Bank Aggregate Financing to the Real Economy data; and c is the final consumption rate. The quadratic term of c is also included in the function to capture the possible nonlinear effect of the final consumption rate on TFP. Finally, T is a time series variable to capture the possible remaining part of TFP.

Bringing function (2) into function (1) and using the logarithmic form, we obtain function (3):

$$\ln Y = C + \alpha_1 \ln K + \alpha_2 \ln H + \alpha_3 \ln H_a + \alpha_4 \ln R + \alpha_5 m + \alpha_6 u \tag{3}$$
$$+ \alpha_7 f + \alpha_8 d + \alpha_9 g + \alpha_{10} l + \alpha_{11} c + \alpha_{12} c^2 + \alpha_{13} T$$

---

[2] As data for share of the private sector in the whole economy is unavailable, the private share in the industrial sector is used as a close proxy.

By taking the first order difference of equation (3) we can get an equation in the form of its rate of changes, theoretically without varying the values of the coefficients; then the second part of the right-hand-side equation, after capital and human capital variables, is an expression of TFP growth rate (denoted as *tfp*). Or in other words, it is the contribution of TFP to economic growth decomposed into influential factors:

$$tfp = \alpha_3 \Delta \ln H_a + \alpha_4 \Delta \ln R + \alpha_5 \Delta m + \alpha_6 \Delta u + \alpha_7 \Delta f + \alpha_8 \Delta d$$
$$+ \alpha_9 \Delta g + \alpha_{10} \Delta l + \alpha_{11} \Delta c + \alpha_{12} \Delta(c^2) + \alpha_{13} a \qquad (4)$$

After taking the first order difference, the original constant term becomes zero, whereas the first order difference of the original time trend becomes a new constant a. Equation (4) means that the TFP growth rate is a function consisting of possible spillover effects of human capital, technological progress led by R&D, and positive/negative effects of several structural variables on TFP. These variables are considered to be important in TFP changes and economic growth. In addition, the constant term a represent a possibly unexplained remaining part of TFP growth.

To empirically test the hypotheses of factors contributing to TFP growth, we have alternative ways, basically, either to empirically estimate Equation (3) and then calculate the sum of different effects on TFP growth, or estimate Equation (4) directly, based on proper assumptions. For a less complicated empirical equation and to avoid possible spurious regression in time series analysis, the second way is preferred.

To do this estimation, we first need to calculate the dependent variable *tfp*, i.e., the residual of GDP growth rate after deducting the contribution of capital and human capital to growth. On the basis of lots of growth analyses for the PRC in the literature, including the author's earlier estimations (see Wang 2000), three optional calculations for elasticity of capital and human capital, under the constant return to scale assumption, are used to test the stability of each influential factor's contribution to *tfp*. The elasticities used are 0.6: 0.4, 0.5: 0.5, and 0.4: 0.6, for capital and human capital, respectively.

$\Delta \ln H_a$ is dropped after the preliminary test as it lacks statistical significance. $\Delta \ln R$ is insignificant and replaced by its second-order differential, to test whether accelerated growth of technology capital stock has any effect on TFP changes. Both Δc and $\Delta(c^2)$ were 1-year lagged, to avoid a possible bi-causality effect on the dependent variable tfp (as it is a part of the GDP growth rate).

Historical time series data from 1950 to 2015 are used. All the raw data come from the NBSC (various years). GDP data for 1950 and 1951 are approximately estimated based on statistics of gross industrial output values, gross agricultural output value, and state investment in fixed assets in corresponding years, and GDP statistics in later years. The initial capital stock data are reestimated by the author with references to Chow (1993) and Wang (2000). The outcomes of the estimation are shown in Table 4.6.

Table 4.6 shows similar outcomes of the three estimations. Most estimates are significant and basically stable, only variations of Δu are larger. Of the estimates, $\Delta^2 r_{(t)}$, $\Delta u_{(t)}$, $\Delta g_{(t)}$, and $\Delta l_{(t)}$ are significant at the 1% or higher levels; Δm, Δc, and $\Delta(c^2)$ at the 10% level. $\Delta f_{(t)}$ and Δd are insignificant, although they are frequently found to have positive contributions in the growth literature on the PRC; hence, they are retained in the equation. The constant a is also insignificant and small in value. This suggests that TFP growth in the PRC has been well explained by the model, and there is little chance that there are important missing explanatory variables. However, a is retained in the equation as it may help to reduce errors in growth accounting and forecasts in the remainder of the chapter. The three estimations' adjusted R^2 are all above 0.6, indicating that the equation's explanatory power is satisfactory.

In the following, estimates of $tfp2$ from Table 4.6 are chosen to carry out growth accounting in different periods in the past. The PRC's TFP and economic growth rates are decomposed into various contributing factors (the outcome is shown in Table 4.7). The sum of factor contribution in the table is the sum of fixed capital and human capital contributions.

Table 4.6: Regression Results

Variable	Definition	tfp1 (K0.6, H0.4)	tfp2 (K0.5, H0.5)	tfp3 (K0.4, H0.6)
$\Delta^2 r_{(t)}$	See note 2	0.675 (8.26*)	0.685 (8.32*)	0.696 (8.34*)
$\Delta u_{(t)}$	Change urbanization rate	3.221 (3.26*)	3.740 (3.76*)	4.258 (4.22*)
$\Delta m_{(t)}$	Marketization (change private share in industry)	0.222 (1.67***)	0.230 (1.72***)	0.237 (1.75***)
$\Delta f_{(t)}$	Change foreign capital share	1.533 (0.84)	1.454 (0.79)	1.375 (0.74)
$\Delta d_{(t)}$	Change trade dep. ratio	0.083 (0.52)	0.081 (0.53)	0.085 (0.53)
$\Delta g_{(t)}$	Change gov. adm. cost	−12.24 (−4.48*)	−12.59 (−4.57*)	−12.94 (−4.64*)
$\Delta l_{(t)}$	Change leverage ratio	−0.336 (−3.61*)	−0.354 (−3.46*)	−0.341 (−3.29*)
$\Delta c_{(t-1)}$	Change consum. Ratio	3.431 (1.86***)	3.171 (1.70***)	2.911 (1.54)
$\Delta(c^2)_{(t-1)}$	Change quadra. $c_{(t-1)}$	−2.600 (−1.95***)	−2.410 (−1.79***)	−2.221 (−1.63)
a	Constant	−0.0066 (−0.81)	−0.0062 (−0.75)	−0.0057 (−0.69)
Obs.		65	65	65
Adj. R²		0.632	0.641	0.650

Notes: Data in parentheses are t statistics, * indicates a significance level of 1% or higher, ** a significance level of 5%, and *** a significance level of 10%; $\Delta^2 r_{(t)}$ = acceleration of technology capital growth.

Source: Author.

Fitted TFP is the sum of simulated positive and negative contributions of all variables that influence TFP. Calculated TFP is the explanatory variable *tfp2*, derived under the assumption of capital and human capital elasticities both being 0.5. The error term is the difference between fitted and calculated TFPs. Simulations using *tfp1* and *tfp3* are also carried out and had similar results to that using *tfp2*; for simplicity, these results are not listed in the table.

Table 4.7: Growth Accounting and Total Factor Productivity Decomposition by Periods (growth rate, %)

	1951–1978	1979–1990	1991–2000	2001–2010	2011–2015
GDP growth rate	6.65	9.05	10.44	10.51	7.83
Capital	3.50	4.33	5.21	6.62	6.79
Human capital	3.13	2.62	1.62	1.06	1.19
Sum of factor contribution	6.63	6.95	6.83	7.68	7.98
Technological progress	0.19	−0.43	0.91	0.16	−0.62
Urbanization	0.90	2.68	3.74	5.27	4.71
Marketization	−0.37	0.40	0.25	0.47	0.25
Foreign investment effect	0.00	0.45	0.52	−0.48	−0.57
Trade effect	0.00	0.13	0.08	0.08	−0.21
Government admin. cost	0.55	−0.79	−0.71	−0.28	0.41
Final consumption effect	0.23	−0.01	−0.02	−0.62	0.21
Leverage ratio	−0.49	−1.29	−0.47	−1.85	−3.19
Constant term	−0.52	−0.62	−0.62	−0.62	−0.62
TFP (fitted)	0.50	0.53	3.69	2.12	0.37
TFP (calculated)	0.02	2.10	3.61	2.83	−0.15
Error	0.48	−1.57	0.08	−0.71	0.52

GDP = gross domestic product, TFP = total factor productivity.

Notes:

1. The negative foreign investment and trade effects in recent years are due to declines in the foreign capital share and the foreign trade dependency ratio. The positive contribution of government administration costs is due to a decline in the relative government administrative cost as a share of GDP, and the same applies to others.

2. For some periods the sum of each item is slightly different from the total, due to rounding.

Data sources: Calculated from Table 4.5 and statistical data from NBSC.

One may find from the error terms in the last row of the table that there are larger errors between fitted and calculated TFPs in earlier periods before 1990, and the errors become smaller in later periods. This is possibly due to some unidentified effect of structural changes, but this also suggests that the model is generally suitable for forecasting TFP changes and economic growth in the future.

The main findings from the growth accounting and TFP decomposition are as follows:

(1)   Capital inputs still play the most important role in economic growth, having contributed more than 6 percentage points to the growth rate in recent years.

(2)   The contribution of human capital to growth has tended to decrease, due to a slowdown in growth of the labor force (human capital in this study is defined as the effective labor weighted by year of schooling), while improvement in human capital quality (education level) cannot fully compensate for the slowdown in labor force growth.

(3)   The regression results indicate that technology capital only makes a contribution to growth when it grows at an accelerating rate, which indicates that technological progress has not become an important driving force for TFP and economic growth. During the reform period, TFP increased significantly, mainly due to improvements in resource allocation brought about by institutional reform and structural change.

(4)   Urbanization has played the most important role in improving TFP, having contributed more than 4 percentage points in recent years. This is due to a reallocation of factors (mainly labor and land) from low-productivity agricultural sectors to higher-productivity urban nonagricultural sectors in the process of urbanization, which improves the overall resource allocation efficiency (see e.g., Lewis 1954). The urbanization process overall also benefited from market-oriented reform, which promotes the flow of factors between urban and rural areas.

(5)   Expansion of the market-oriented private sector of the economy made a significant contribution to TFP and economic growth, confirming that the efficiency of the private sector continues to be higher than that of the state-owned sector. An increase in the proportion of the private sector in total output of 1 percentage point increases TFP and the economic growth rate by 0.23 percentage points. This is mainly due to market allocation of resources and incentives to improve efficiency brought about by competition.

(6)   Economic openness (expansion of foreign investment and foreign
        trade) is likely to make some contributions to TFP, although this is
        not confirmed in the current study. The likely contribution has turned
        negative in recent years, because the foreign capital share and foreign
        trade dependency ratio decreased. In addition, due to the process of
        productivity convergence between domestic and foreign enterprises,
        the foreign investment and trade effects can be expected to gradually
        disappear.

(7)   Government administration costs (represented by government
        administrative expenses as a share of GDP) rose from the 1980s to
        the late 2000s, leading to an annual loss of TFP and economic growth
        of 0.3–0.8 percentage points. This proves that rising government
        costs (and greater government intervention in the market) reduce the
        efficiency of resource allocation. The powerful anticorruption campaign
        since 2012 has played a role in reducing the relative government costs
        in recent years, making a positive contribution of 0.4 percentage points
        to TFP. Whether this trend will continue depends critically on future
        government sector reform.

(8)   A simulation based on the regression result shows that the consumption
        rate (final consumption as a share of GDP) does have a significant
        nonlinear effect on TFP and growth, showing an inverse U-shaped
        curve, with the optimum point at 66% (corresponding to a savings
        rate of 34%). A consumption rate significantly higher or lower than
        the optimum value will reduce TFP, lowering long-run growth. In fact,
        this phenomenon had already been proven by the theory of economic
        growth; see Barro and Sala-i-Martin (1995) for the "golden role saving
        rate." In this study, we empirically tested and verified this theory using
        PRC statistical data.

        In the period of 2001–2010, the consumption rate in the
        PRC dropped by 15 percentage points, from 63% to 48%, and the
        corresponding savings and investment rates increased respectively by
        15 and 14 percentage points, drastically deviating from the critical value
        found above, thus leading to a serious structural imbalance, and TFP
        losing 0.6 percentage points per year in this period. After 2011, the

consumption rate rose slightly, and this made a positive contribution of 0.2 percentage points per year to TFP. However, the consumption rate in 2015 was only 52%, still well below the optimum rate of 66%. This indicates a large potential for a further recovery in the consumption rate, and a further decrease in the investment rate, through reform and structural adjustment. These will be conducive to future TFP and economic growth.

(9)   The rise in the leverage ratio in the PRC had a negative impact on productivity and growth in all periods. The sharp increase in the leverage ratio in the 2001–2010 period had a large negative impact on TFP, reducing its growth by 1.9 percentage points. The negative effect further increased to 3.2 percentage points in the 2011–2015 period. The high leverage ratio has become the main threat to growth and TFP. Excessive liquidity led to overinvestment, pushed up nonperforming loans, and expanded asset bubbles. Whether in terms of improving efficiency and maintaining healthy economic growth, or in terms of preventing financial crisis, it is necessary to maintain a neutral and stable monetary and credit policy.

(10)   To sum up the above findings, TFP was significantly higher during most of the economic reform periods than the pre-reform period, and this raised the economic growth rate by 2.1–3.6 percentage points per year until the late 2010s. However, TFP growth declined after 2000 and was around zero from 2011 to 2015.

As suggested by the outcomes of growth accounting, the decline in TFP growth and the slowing of economic growth had three major reasons, besides the possible effect of a fall in foreign investment and the foreign trade dependency ratio: (i) excessively high savings and investment rates and an excessively low consumption rate leading to overcapacity in industry and productivity losses; (ii) rising administrative costs and government intervention resulting in lower efficiency; and (iii) substantial increases in the leverage ratio that had a very negative impact on economic efficiency. These have resulted in a significant reduction in productivity growth, largely offsetting the positive contribution of other factors to TFP. In recent years, although the consumption rate has rebounded slightly and administrative costs fell, making some positive contribution to growth and TFP, this has been totally offset by the negative impact of a fast increase in the leverage ratio. It is clear that, without resolving these problems, the trend of declining TFP and economic growth rate will continue. Resolving these problems will be key to the PRC avoiding falling into the MIT.

4.4 | Forecasting the PRC's Future Economic Growth

The modeling analysis and growth accounting described above allow us to make a forecast for future economic growth up until 2020 and 2030, with a comprehensive consideration of important factors that affect TFP. The focus here is on the impact of the three major factors, i.e., the effects of a changing consumption rate, government administrative cost, and the leverage ratio, on future economic growth. Consider three scenarios in simulating future growth:

(1) **Regular scenario ("business as usual")**
     In this scenario, it is assumed that variables affecting economic growth (including production factors, institutional, policy, and structure variables) in the future will on the whole continue their trends seen in recent years. It is also assumed that, to reduce financial risk, there will be a minor adjustment to monetary policy to slow down the speed of increases in the leverage ratio. We cannot not totally rule out the future risk of financial crisis, but assume that within the period under consideration a financial crisis will not occur. Trends in other variables are expected to be as follows:

     (a) The savings and investment rates will continue to decrease. The annual growth rate of capital stock from 2011 to 2015 was 14.0% on average; it is expected to be 10.0% from 2016 to 2020, and 7.3% from 2021 to 2030.
     (b) Assuming that the rate of increase in the education level of workers remains unchanged, but the growth rate of the

working-age population will turn negative in the next 5 years, the annual growth rate of the human capital stock of 2.4% in the past 5 years will fall to an average 2.0% from 2016 to 2020, and 1.4% from 2021 to 2030.

(c)   With the economic slowdown, the urbanization process has been slower in recent years and is likely to slow further. It is assumed that the urbanization rate will increase by 0.9 percentage points annually from 2016 to 2020, and by 0.6 percentage points per year from 2021 to 2030.

(d)   As indicated by the increasing private share in the industrial sector, there has been continued progress with marketization, but this is likely to be slower in the future. It is assumed that the private share in industry will increase by 4 percentage points from 2016 to 2020 to reach 84%,[3] and increase further to 88% in 2030. The share of private enterprises in the overall economy is lower than that in industry, but the trend is expected to be basically the same.

(e)   Data show that growth of technology capital slowed in recent years, which had a negative effect on growth. This seems to be a short-run effect. It is assumed that in the next few years this negative impact will be offset by R&D acceleration and the effect will be neutral, and after 2020 it will accelerate to lift TFP growth by 0.5 percentage points per year.

(f)   The foreign trade dependency ratio is expected to continue to decline as it has done in the past few years, down 5 percentage points from 2015 to 2020, and further down 5 percentage points to reach 25% in 2030. The share of foreign capital in total capital stock will drop by 0.4 percentage points per year from 2016 to 2020, and by 0.1 percentage points per year from 2021 to 2030.

(g)   The ratio of government administrative costs to GDP decreased in the last few years due to the government's anticorruption campaign, and this is found to have a positive impact on TFP.

---

[3]   This share in the previous period was adjusted by the author to correct the inconsistency caused by changing statistical definition. The adjusted share in 2015 is 80%.

The same impact is assumed to be maintained in the coming few years, and it will gradually disappear after 2020.

(h)   The final consumption rate (1 year lagged) recovered slightly in recent years, making a contribution to productivity growth. However, due to an expected economic slowdown, the trend of consumption recovery is assumed to be slower in the future—an increase of 3 percentage points over the next 5 years is assumed; and another 3 percentage points increase from 2021 to 2030.

(i)   Over the past 5 years, the leverage ratio rose by more than 9 percentage points per year. Assuming the expected minor adjustment in monetary policy will slightly moderate its increase to 8 percentage points per year, it is forecast to reach 250% in 2020. After that, the trend of increase will slow further to 4 percentage points per year, reaching 290% in 2030.

(j)   The author assumes that structural adjustment in the coming few years will have a short-term negative impact on TFP and economic growth, which is expected to reduce the annual growth rate by 0.3 percentage points in the 2016–2020 period. This assumption also applies to other scenarios.

(k)   Simulation shows that in this scenario, economic growth will be weaker. The growth rate from 2016 to 2020 will be 5.5% on average (meaning the annual growth rate after 2018 will be below 5%), which will not achieve the government target of doubling GDP in 2020 compared with 2010. From 2021 to 2030, further structural adjustments and R&D progress will maintain the annual growth rate at 5.1% on average (see Table 4.8 for the growth forecast).

(2)   **Crisis scenario**

In this scenario, it is assumed that the trends of most factors influencing TFP after 2015 will be the same as in scenario 1, except that the leverage ratio will continue to rise by 10 percentage points per year to reach 260% by 2020 (a full calculation of the ratio should exceed 300% by 2018 or 2019) due to continued loose monetary policy targeted to maintain a certain level of short-run economic growth. A preliminary simulation shows that the rapid increase in the leverage ratio will have a strongly negative impact on economic growth from 2016 to 2020, leading to net TFP losses of more than 3 percentage points. International experience suggests that a continuously rising leverage ratio within an interval of 270% to 300% is very likely to lead to a financial crisis. This suggests that the next few years will be a high-risk period.

Although the predicted high TFP losses imply a financial crisis, our simulation cannot accurately predict the specific path of the financial crisis. But there is no doubt that in this situation factor inputs and some other structural variables will be affected and thus further affect economic growth. We therefore need to make some revisions to our previous assumptions on the basis of the most likely situation, as follows:

(a) The financial crisis will hit investment of enterprises, leading to a drop in the capital stock growth rate from 2016 to 2020 from 10% in the regular case to 8.3%, and further from 7.3% to 6.2% in the 2021–2030 period due to the lagged effect of the slowdown in investment.

(b) Due to a higher unemployment rate and slower growth of education inputs, the growth rate of human capital will be lower than that in scenario 1, dropping from 2% to 1.8% in the 2016–2020 period, and from 1.4% to 1.2% in the 2021–2030 period.

(c) The annual increase in the urbanization ratio will be down from 0.9% to 0.7% in the period of 2016–2020, and from 0.6% to 0.5% in the period from 2021–2030, as a result of slower employment creation in the urban economy.

(d) The withdrawal of foreign capital may affect economic growth by 0.1–0.2 percentage points annually.

(e) The financial crisis may break the rapidly rising trend of the leverage ratio; however, the monetary authority may tend to maintain a relatively loose monetary policy in the postcrisis period to help an economic recovery, leading to increases in the leverage ratio by 5 percentage points per year between 2021 and 2030.

(f) R&D expenditure of enterprises will be affected to a certain extent during the crisis and postcrisis periods.

(g) In a crisis, government reforms may be paused, slowing the reduction of government administration costs.

(h) Slower economic growth will have a direct impact on household consumption, assuming the trend of consumption recovery will continue but will be slower during and after the crisis.

Bringing these assumption revisions into the simulation, the results show that the economic growth rate will drop to 2.7% in the 2016–2020 period, and will be 3.0% in the 2021–2030 period. This means that the crisis will have a profoundly negative impact on long-run economic growth and change the growth trajectory. In other words, in this scenario, the PRC will fall into the MIT and stay there during the coming 15 years or longer period.

(3) **Reform and rebalancing scenario**

In this scenario, it is assumed that there will be major reforms and policy adjustments for structural rebalancing in the coming years, in three key areas described below. All other conditions are the same as in scenario 1.

(a) *Deleveraging*

Deleveraging is a difficult task that requires continued effort, including effective adjustment to make monetary policy neutral, cleaning up nonperforming loans, stopping support of inefficient enterprises, and improving external finance for small and medium-sized enterprises. Assuming that it will take a few years to stop the increases in the leverage ratio, by 2020 it will be no higher than 230% (based on a calculation of 208% at the end of 2015, from Social Financing statistics); and then fall to 200% or lower by 2030.

(b) *To promote consumption–savings structure adjustment via reforms*
     To improve the pattern of income distribution by pushing forward
     fiscal and tax reforms and public policy adjustment, to reduce
     government investment and increase social security and public
     service expenses, and to strengthen income redistribution, so as to
     promote the final consumption rate rising by at least 9 percentage
     points to reach 61% or higher by 2030, and savings and investment
     rates decreasing respectively to 39% and 36% or below.

(c) *To reduce administrative costs via government reforms*
     In recent years, great efforts to fight corruption have had the
     effect of reducing administrative costs and have positively
     contributed to TFP. To maintain this effect, further government
     reform is needed to improve government transparency,
     streamline government institutions, improve the budgetary
     system, and reduce government intervention in markets.

          If we assume that the government administrative cost
     (as a ratio of GDP) will continue to fall until 2020 at a slightly
     higher rate than in scenario 1, this effect will be only half in the
     2021–2030 period.

Simulations show that policy adjustment and reforms in these three areas
will have a very positive impact on economic growth in the medium and
long terms. Economic growth in the 2016–2020 period will be revitalized
to achieve 6.9%, and further accelerate to 7.8% in the 2021–2030 period.
This is a higher rate than commonly expected and can only be achieved
through great effort in terms of a series of policy adjustments and
institutional reforms.

Growth forecasts in three scenarios are shown in Table 4.8, and the three
different growth paths are illustrated in Figure 4.1.

There are large differences in the results of the three scenarios. In the reform
and rebalancing scenario, GDP in 2030 is 37% higher than in the regular
scenario and 92% higher than in the crisis scenario.

In the reform and rebalancing scenario, the PRC's GDP in 2030 is expected
to reach CNY203 trill on (in 2015 constant prices), which is 2.97 times that
in 2015. Using an exchange rate of 6.85:1 to convert it to United States (US)
dollars, it is equivalent to a per capita GDP of $20,500. Considering the
possible appreciation of the PRC's yuan in the long run, it is likely to be higher.
By that time the PRC will have joined the high-income country group.

Table 4.8: PRC Growth Forecast: Three Scenarios
(annual growth rate decomposition, %)

	Regular Scenario		Crisis Scenario		Reform and Rebalancing Scenario	
	2016–2020	2021–2030	2016–2020	2021–2030	2016–2020	2021–2030
Capital	4.9	3.6	4.1	3.1	4.9	3.6
Human capital	0.9	0.7	0.8	0.6	0.9	0.7
Sum factor contr.	5.8	4.3	4.9	3.7	5.8	4.3
Tech. capital	0.0	0.5	0.0	0.2	0.0	0.5
Urbanization	3.4	2.2	2.6	1.9	3.4	2.2
Marketization	0.2	0.1	0.1	0.1	0.2	0.1
FDI effect	−0.6	−0.2	−0.7	−0.2	−0.6	−0.2
Trade effect	−0.1	–	−0.1	−0.1	−0.1	–
Consum. rate	0.2	0.3	0.1	0.2	0.5	0.4
Gov. cost	0.4	0.0	0.3	0.0	0.5	0.2
Leverage ratio	−2.8	−1.4	−3.5	−1.8	−1.4	1.0
Time trend	−0.6	−0.6	−0.6	−0.6	−0.6	−0.6
Adjust. factor	−0.3	0.0	−0.3	−0.3	−0.6	0.0
Sum TFP	−0.2	0.9	−2.2	−0.6	1.3	3.6
GDP growth	5.5	5.2	2.7	3.0	6.9	7.8

FDI = foreign direct investment, GDP = gross domestic product, TFP = total factor productivity.
Note: For some periods the sum of each item is slightly different from the total, due to rounding.
Source: Author.

Figure 4.1: **Forecasted Future Growth in Three Scenarios (CNY trillion, 2015 prices)**

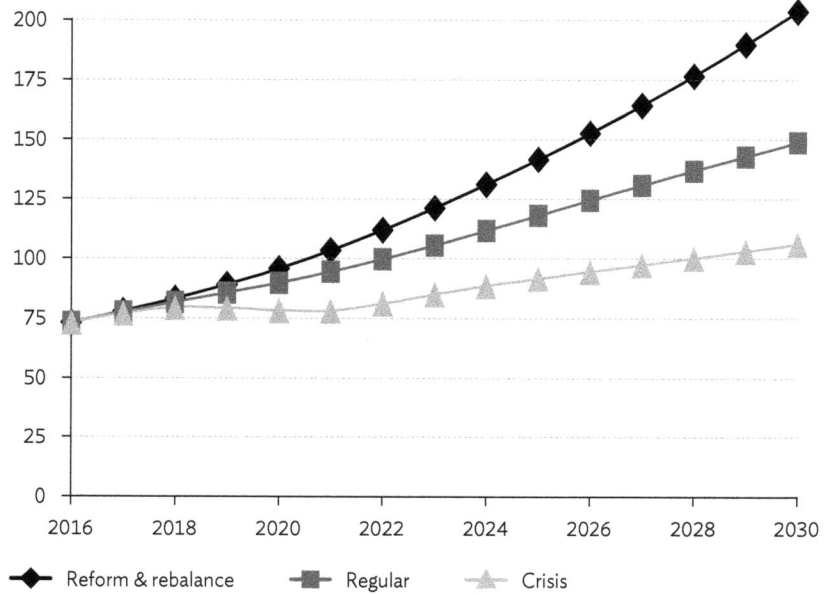

Data sources: Simulation result based on Table 4.8 and NBSC data.

In the crisis scenario, the PRC will soon enter a low-growth path, with GDP expected to reach only CNY106 trillion in 2030, or a GDP per capita of $10,700. This is clearly below the upper limit of the middle-income country standard, meaning that the PRC will be caught in the MIT for the next 15 years at least.

The result of the regular scenario lies between the two outlined above—GDP in 2030 is expected to reach CNY149 trillion, or a GDP per capita of $15,000. However, this is likely to be below the upper limit of middle-income countries by then.

4.5 | Summary

The first part of this chapter discusses the concept of the MIT and why countries get caught in it by taking into consideration international experiences. The evidence suggests that income inequality is a particularly important cause of falling into the MIT.

The second part describes the structural imbalances in the PRC that have led to a sustained slowdown of the PRC's economic growth and TFP losses in recent years. Data indicate that the fundamental reasons are overinvestment, underconsumption, and an undesirable income distribution. Governments at various administrative levels invest too much and stimulate economic growth too much, which is why there is excessive investment and overcapacity. This has weakened the market function of optimizing resource allocation, causing productivity losses. In particular, overinvestment and a loose money supply together have led to an increasingly high leverage ratio, resulting in high financial risks and a threat to the PRC's long-run growth path.

In recent years, structural rebalancing has made some progress, but further reform and policy adjustment is urgently needed. The loose money supply is still fueling increases in the leverage ratio, leading to higher financial risks.

In the third part, a growth model is estimated. Our empirical TFP analysis and growth accounting based on the PRC's long-term data over the past 65 years identify that excessively high rates of savings and investment and a very low consumption rate, rising government administration cost, and the continuously increasing leverage ratio, are the three major problems resulting in TFP losses and a slowdown of economic growth in the past.

Based on the modeling results, the fourth part provides results of the growth forecast under three scenarios. The outcome shows that, if current trends of factors influencing TFP continue, and there is only a moderate adjustment of monetary policy, the economic growth rate may drop below 5% by 2020 and the government target of doubling GDP in 2020 compared with 2010 will not be achieved. By 2030, the PRC may not have been able to join the high-income countries club.

If the rapid increases in the leverage ratio are not controlled, inefficient allocation of financial resources will further slow down economic growth and will likely lead to a financial crisis. The economy will likely get stuck on a low-growth track, meaning it will get caught in the MIT.

As another possibility, if reforms and policy adjustment for structural rebalancing can be effectively brought forward, to lower the very high rates of savings and investment and raise the consumption rate, to reduce the government cost and promote the role of the market in resource allocation, and to effectively adjust the monetary policy to deleverage, economic growth can be back above 7% after a few years of adjustment. Then by 2030, per capita GDP will reach $20,000 (in 2015 prices), and the PRC will join the high-income country club. This is certainly a more sustainable development path.

To avoid falling into the MIT and achieve the third scenario of economic growth, the necessary key reforms and policy adjustments can be briefly summarized as follows: (i) readopt a neutral and cautious monetary policy to deleverage and reduce financial risk; (ii) redirect government emphasis and resources from investment to public services, social security, and income redistribution to raise household consumption and reduce the rates of investment; and (iii) bring forward government reforms to reduce government administrative costs and allow the market to play a decisive role in resource allocation.

References

Barro, R., and X. Sala-i-Martin. 1995. *Economic Growth.* New York, NY: McGraw–Hill.

Chow, G. C. 1993. Capital Formation and Economic Growth in China. *Quarterly Journal of Economics* 108(3) (August): 809–842.

Lewis, W. A. 1954. Economic Development with Unlimited Supplies of Labour. *Manchester School of Economics and Social Studies* 22(May): 139–192.

Lucas, R. E. 1988. On the Mechanics of Economic Development. *Journal of Monetary Economics* 22: 3–42.

Maddison, A. 2001. *The World Economy: A Millennial Perspective.* Paris: Organisation for Economic Co-operation and Development.

National Bureau of Statistics of China (NBSC). various years. *China Statistical Yearbook.* Beijing: China Statistics Press.

———. http://www.stats.gov.cn/tjsj/.

Solow, R. M. 1956. A Contribution to the Theory of Economic Growth. *Quarterly Journal of Economics* 70(February): 65–94.

Wang, X. 2000. Sustainability of Economic Growth and Institutional Reform in China (in Chinese). *Economic Research* 7.

World Bank. various years. *World Development Indicators.* Washington, DC: The World Bank.

World Institute of Development Economics Research (WIDER), United Nations University. World Income Inequality Database. WIDER website.

CHAPTER 5

Manufacturing as the Key Engine of Economic Growth for Middle-Income Economies[1]

Dan Su and Yang Yao

5.1 | Introduction

Industrialization is viewed as the most important engine of economic growth. The unique characteristics of the manufacturing sector can be interpreted in many ways: rapid technological changes, economies of scale, and easy integration into global production networks (Lavopa and Szirmai 2014; Szirmai 2012). Additionally, some studies have empirically confirmed that transformation from agriculture to manufacturing, and further from manufacturing to services are the process of economic development (Chenery and Elkington 1980; Clark 1940; Fuchs 1981; Kuznets 1957). Therefore, it was recognized that "since the industrial revolution, no country has become a major economy without becoming an industrial power" (Lee 2005).

However, this rationale has been challenged. First, the importance of the services sector has been increasing since World War II. As shown in Figures 5.1 and 5.2, the world has seen a steady growth in services and a long-run decrease in manufacturing, regarding all three different indicators that measure economic composition. The literature has also confirmed this trend.

[1] We are grateful to Xiang Li, Wenquan Liang, Peter Morgan, and Ha Nguyen, as well as conference and seminar participants at the Conference on Escaping the Middle-Income Trap: Urbanization, Structural Change, and Sustainable Development in Asia, and Peking University for helpful comments.

Figure 5.1: The Share of Manufacturing in the World Economy

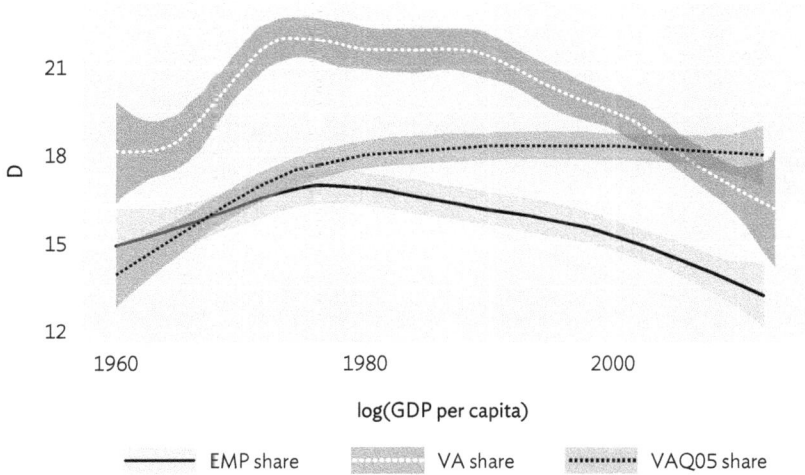

D = manufacturing, EMP = employment, GDP = gross domestic product, log = logarithm,
VA = value added, VAQ = value added in constant prices.

Note: This figure plots the world's fitted manufacturing share from 1960 to 2013. We use employment
percentage, nominal value-added percentage, and real value-added percentage as measures of
manufacturing share in the whole economy. We fit each series by using unweighted average and also
calculate the corresponding 95% confidence interval.

Source: Authors. See section 5.2.1.

For example, Dasgupta and Singh (2005) used the developing economies'
data to show that, contrary to the general conjecture, the growth rate of
the services sector in many developing economies is much faster than
that of manufacturing. Also, by investigating the historical data of the
United States (US), Buera and Kaboski (2012) found that growth in the
services sector share accelerates at a high-income level.

Second, the development of the information and communication technology
(ICT) sector demonstrates that the services industry could become the
new engine of economic growth in developing economies (Dasgupta and
Singh 2005; Fagerberg and Verspagen 1999; Lee and McKibbin 2014;
Maroto-Sánchez and Cuadrado-Roura 2009). One possible reason is that

Figure 5.2: The Share of the Services Sector in the World Economy

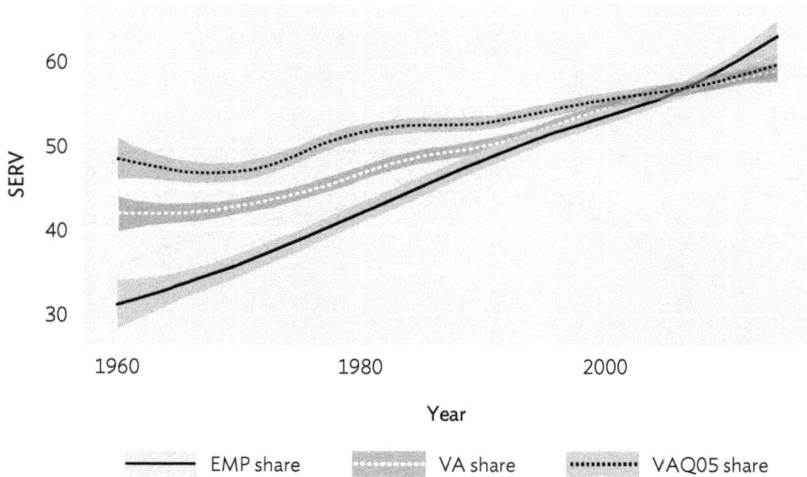

EMP = employment, SERV = services, VA = value added, VAQ = value added in constant prices.

Note: This figure plots the world's fitted services share from 1960 to 2013. We use employment percentage, nominal value-added percentage, and real value-added percentage as measures of manufacturing share in the whole economy. We fit each series by using unweighted average and also calculate the corresponding 95% confidence interval.

Source: Authors. See section 5.2.1.

manufacturing benefits the whole economy mainly through its role in trade and balance of payments, as business mostly takes place in manufacturing first (Dasgupta and Singh 2005). Therefore, as the ICT goods prove to be as tradable as manufacturing products, Dasgupta and Singh argued that the newly developed ICT sector could replace the critical role of manufacturing during economic development.[2]

---

[2]　Additionally, in a recent paper, Amirapu and Subramanian (2015) proposed that five essential characteristics allow a sector to serve as an engine of structural transformation and produce sustainable economic growth: high levels of productivity, dynamic productivity growth, expansion of the sector in terms of its use of inputs, comparative advantage for the host country, and exportability. Based on the case of India, they suggested that some services branches including finance, insurance, and real estate, could replace the role of the manufacturing sector.

Third, the economists' view of the services industry has changed. In the 1960s, many scholars regarded services as a stagnant industry. This argument, formally known as Baumol's disease in the literature, is mainly based on the fact that several branches of services, including education, health care, cultural services, and personal services, have relatively lower growth rates of productivity (Baumol 1967, 2001; Baumol and Bowen 1965; Pellegrini 2007). Therefore, they are particularly worried that deindustrialization will reduce the growth rate of the whole economy (Bluestone and Harrison 1982; Mishel 1989; Pugno 2006; Rowthorn 1987). However, few economists nowadays treat all services sectors as stagnant. On the one hand, services goods are increasingly viewed as intermediate inputs, which will result in significant benefits in terms of productivity and quality improvement throughout the economy (Chakravarty and Mitra 2009; Fixler and Siegel 1999). On the other hand, in many developing economies the services industries have seen sharp increases in productivity in the last few decades and have become increasingly important for their development.

Against this background, it is now a highly controversial question whether manufacturing should still be the focus of industrial policy in developing economies. In this chapter, we investigate the particular role of the industrial sector during the middle-income stage, and we attempt to contribute to the ongoing debate on the relative importance of manufacturing versus services. Our general conclusion is that manufacturing is the key engine of economic growth for middle-income economies. By exploiting a large cross-country data set at the sector level, we prove that for middle-income economies, manufacturing pulls along all other sectors. A(n) decline/increase in the manufacturing sector growth rate will negatively/positively affect the growth rate of the other sectors, in both the short run and the long run. This conclusion remains unchanged when we adopt different estimation techniques and model specifications. We also discuss the precise economic mechanisms through which the manufacturing sector works. We identify two possible ways and find that a larger share of manufacturing in employment can increase the gross private savings ratio, as well as accelerate technological accumulation. Compared with other sectors, the manufacturing industry has a higher demand for capital and investment, thus providing exceptional opportunities for capital accumulation. Also, the unconditional convergence characteristic of the manufacturing sector (Rodrik 2013) shows that this tradable sector has easier access to the world technology frontier. Thus a larger share of the manufacturing sector in the whole economy can speed up technological accumulation. Based on these findings, we conclude that the manufacturing sector remains central to middle-income economies' long-term development.

There are two reasons why we choose middle-income economies as the object of our study. First, the primary sources of economic growth of middle-income economies are completely different from those of developed economies, where knowledge-based innovation mainly drives growth. In contrast, increases in labor productivity in emerging economies mostly come from structural change or technology imported from developed economies. During this stage of rapid economic growth, easy adoption of world frontier technology is essential for middle-income economies. Admittedly, several factors, including the human capital level, the domestic political system, and the economic openness, may influence the transmission of foreign technology. However, industries also differ in terms of their ability to exploit world frontier technology. This makes certain sectors particularly relevant for middle-income economies in terms of achieving long-term economic growth. Second, sectoral heterogeneities and balanced growth are particularly important for the long-run performance of developing economies. Imbs and Wacziarg (2003) found that the evolution of sectoral concentration in terms of the level of per capita gross domestic product (GDP) follows a U-shaped pattern, which means that during the middle-income stage, economic activity is more equally spread across sectors. In this chapter, we investigate whether and how the development of the manufacturing sector is central during the middle-income stage.

Our findings have important policy implications. Whether manufacturing should continue to be the key engine of growth is now a critical question faced by many developing economies, including the People's Republic of China (PRC). Apart from the earlier literature that deals with this concept of *premature deindustrialization*[3] (Dasgupta and Singh 2006; Palma 2005; Rowthorn and Ramaswamy 1999), Rodrik (2016) documented a robust pattern of developing countries running out of industrialization opportunities sooner and being at much lower levels of income compared with those observed historically in developed economies. However, he stays on the fence regarding the economic consequences of premature deindustrialization. Based on current findings, he thinks that we should not be too worried about it, as improving domestic human capital and institutional quality can also induce moderate growth in the long run. But other scholars have shown great concern about this process in developing countries. For example, Cruz (2015) found that premature deindustrialization has been a major contributor to Mexico's economic stagnation. He concluded that the premature deindustrialization process has led to moderate economic growth and increased unemployment in Mexico. In the PRC, there is also a huge debate on where the PRC's industrial policies should be focused to promote growth in the new normal. As shown in Figure 5.3, the PRC has begun to deindustrialize at a much earlier stage than other East Asian economies. To assess whether this is a good sign requires further research.

This chapter also contributes to the recent discussion on the roles of manufacturing and services. In fact, the lack of consensus on the relative importance of these two modern sectors during a country's development reflects our limited understanding of how and why the manufacturing sector matters, especially for middle-income economies. Those well-documented patterns of structural transformation across industries are usually treated as empirical facts, rather than predictions derived from any particular theory.[4] Therefore, it remains questionable whether nowadays a developing country still needs to go through full industrialization before it gets rich.

---

[3] Deindustrialization is defined as the steady decline of both manufacturing output as a percentage of GDP (Tregenna 2009) and of manufacturing employment share (Cruz 2015; Palma 2005; Rowthorn and Ramaswamy 1999).

[4] There are many theoretical explanations for these structural change patterns, including differences in growth rates across sectors, changes in household preference, and globalization. Although these works provide convincing explanations for this primary–secondary–tertiary transition, there is no theory that shows us this transition process is closely related to the long-run growth rate of any developing economy.

Figure 5.3: The Pattern of Manufacturing Development in the PRC

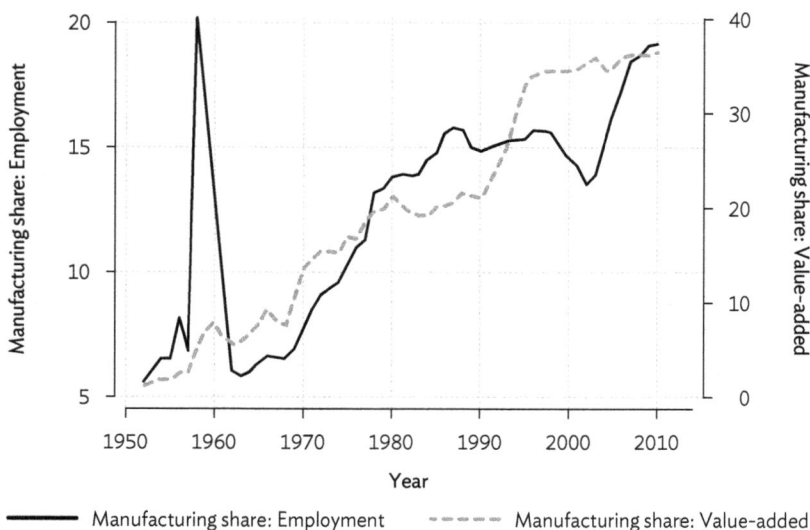

Manufacturing share: Employment ———   Manufacturing share: Value-added ----

PRC = People's Republic of China.
Note: This figure plots the manufacturing employment and real value-added share in the PRC since 1950.
Source: Authors. See section 5.2.1.

The rest of this chapter is organized as follows. Section 5.2 briefly describes the data we used, introduces the empirical methodology, and explains our major findings. Section 5.3 presents some evidence on the possible underlying mechanisms, and section 5.4 concludes.

5.2 | Empirics

5.2.1 Data

Following the work of Lavopa (2015) and many others, we construct a large data set with internationally comparable information on employment and value added at the industry level. The construction procedure is briefly explained as follows. First, we gather the value-added data of manufacturing

and service industries and transform them into constant terms based on
a variety of sources.[5] Then we use the World Bank's World Development
Indicators (WDI) data as the primary source, and extrapolate these series
by using the corresponding growth rate calculated from other databases.
Our final data set covers 158 economies from 1950 to 2013.[6] We use real
value-added growth rate and labor productivity growth rate of each sector
as two proxies for its economic performance. Throughout this chapter,
labor productivity is defined as real value added per person employed.

For detailed descriptions about data sources, as well the country classification
method used in this chapter, please refer to the Internet Appendix.[7]
Descriptive statistics for all variables used in our main regression are
reported in Table 5.1. In panels A and B, we present the statistics of two
country classification results according to the relative and absolute criterion,
respectively. Although there are modest discrepancies in the observations
and economies included, statistical characteristics do not change much
when we adopt different classification methods. For example, in the
relative criterion sample, the means of the manufacturing and services
sector value-added growth rate are 3.98% and 4.29%, respectively, and we
observe sizable standard deviations on these two variables. When we use
the absolute criterion, the means of manufacturing and services sector
value-added growth rate are 3.90% and 4.20%, respectively, with only slight
differences from those in the relative criterion sample. Similar conclusions
hold for other variables used in this chapter.

---

[5]   It includes the World Bank's WDI database, the World Input–Output Database, the World KLEMS
      Database, the European Union KLEMS Database, the Asian KLEMS Database, the Organisation for
      Economic Co-operation and Development's Structural Analysis Database (STAN), the Groningen
      Growth and Development Center 10-sector Database, and the UNIDO INDSTAT2 Database.
[6]   For most economies, the value-added data of the manufacturing and services sectors start in
      the 1970s.
[7]   https://www.tandfonline.com/doi/suppl/10.1080/13547860.2016.1261481/suppl_file/
      rjap_a_1261481_sm2703.pdf.

Table 5.1: Statistical Description

Panel A: Relative Criterion					
Variable	Obs	Mean	St. Dev.	Min	Max
Agriculture value-added growth (%)	2,068	1.911	7.613	−22.56	28.22
Manufacturing value-added growth (%)	2,271	3.975	8.134	−23.00	33.44
Non-manufacturing industry value-added growth (%)	2,052	3.882	9.411	−27.41	39.33
Services value-added growth (%)	2,007	4.289	4.336	−10.30	19.65
Agriculture labor productivity growth (%)	1,002	−3.576	15.18	−15.43	10.31
Manufacturing labor productivity growth (%)	1,002	−1.069	14.49	−8.287	9.050
Non-manufacturing industry labor productivity growth (%)	1,002	−2.136	14.45	−11.32	9.033
Services labor productivity growth (%)	1,002	−1.355	13.65	−3.211	4.322
Gross private savings ratio (%)	677	29.71	11.06	−40.08	99.94
TFP growth (%)	1,076	0.729	0.206	0.261	1.359
GDP per capita	1,095	12,804	6,772	1,624	35,828
Population	1,094	2.930e+07	5.440e+07	370,433	1.340e+09
Inflation (%)	699	28.75	170.1	−1.380	2948
Chinn–Ito Index	839	0.474	0.360	0	1
Deposit money banks' assets of GDP (%)	857	49.72	37.08	5.102	297.7
Domestic Credit to private sector of GDP (%)	909	76.90	640.2	1.126	13957
Real interest rate (%)	637	26.56	338.4	−98.93	6447
Dependency ratio (%)	961	61.02	16.23	34.49	102.2
Urban population of total (%)	961	65.67	15.81	16.48	100
Public expenditures on education and health of GDP (%)	345	8.896	2.797	2.585	24.74
Total investment share (%)	677	29.71	11.06	−40.08	99.94
Rule of law	1,582	4.248	6.650	−10	10
Human capital index	1,496	2.377	0.505	1.222	3.536

continued next page

Table 5.1: *Continued*

Panel B: Absolute Criterion					
Variable	Obs	Mean	St. Dev.	Min	Max
Agriculture value-added growth (%)	2,243	2.046	7.573	−22.56	29.82
Manufacturing value-added growth (%)	2,401	3.900	8.007	−24.05	31.53
Non-manufacturing industry value-added growth (%)	2,198	3.957	9.047	−27.44	38.95
Services value-added growth (%)	2,172	4.196	4.405	−11.68	21.38
Agriculture labor productivity growth (%)	975	−3.131	14.27	−14.61	10.24
Manufacturing labor productivity growth (%)	975	−0.740	13.15	−7.637	8.567
Non-manufacturing industry labor productivity growth (%)	965	−1.657	13.10	−9.252	8.828
Services labor productivity growth (%)	975	−0.859	13.52	−2.894	3.997
Gross private savings ratio (%)	659	29.24	12.47	−40.08	99.94
TFP growth (%)	1,052	0.736	0.212	0.261	1.359
GDP per capita	1,059	12,505	5031	2,207	30,691
Population	1,059	3.850e+07	9.730e+07	370,433	1.340e+09
Inflation (%)	648	32.28	181.2	−1.380	2,948
Chinn–Ito Index	782	0.464	0.354	0	1
Deposit money banks' assets of GDP (%)	801	46.03	29.48	5.102	164.2
Domestic Credit to private sector of GDP (%)	858	76.08	658.6	1.126	13,957
Real interest rate (%)	608	25.98	348.9	−1014	6,447
Dependency ratio (%)	915	59.99	14.70	34.49	102.2
Urban population of total (%)	915	66.95	15.09	24.14	100
Public expenditures on education and health of GDP (%)	313	8.549	2.823	2.585	24.74
Total investment share (%)	659	29.24	12.47	−40.08	99.94
Rule of law	1,657	4.027	6.672	−10	10
Human capital index	1,542	2.375	0.456	1.338	3.536

GDP = gross domestic product, TFP = total factor productivity.

Source: Authors. See section 5.2.1.

We also compute the correlation coefficients between each pair of our main variables of interest. Table 5.2 shows the correlation coefficients between manufacturing development and the development of other sectors as well as several growth determinants. The "annual" term here means we implement our computation by using all the available country–year observations.

Table 5.2: Correlations of Growth Determinants and Sectoral Development

Manufacturing	Agriculture		Other Industries		Services	
	Corr. Coeff	Rank Corr. Coeff	Corr. Coeff	Rank Corr. Coeff	Corr. Coeff	Rank Corr. Coeff
Panel A: Relative criterion						
Annual	0.0916*** (0.000)	0.1296*** (0.000)	0.0623*** (0.003)	0.3246*** (0.000)	0.3391*** (0.000)	0.4287*** (0.000)
Country averages	0.2714*** (0.000)	0.3625*** (0.000)	0.1313 (0.170)	0.2395** (0.011)	0.4731*** (0.000)	0.5353*** (0.000)
Panel B: Absolute criterion						
Annual	0.0903*** (0.000)	0.1517*** (0.000)	0.0567*** (0.001)	0.3281*** (0.000)	0.2396*** (0.000)	0.4296*** (0.000)
Country averages	0.2613** (0.011)	0.3544 (0.001)	0.1001 (0.342)	0.3069*** (0.003)	0.4918*** (0.000)	0.6310*** (0.000)

Manufacturing	Savings		TFP	
	Corr. Coeff	Rank Corr. Coeff	Corr. Coeff	Rank Corr. Coeff
Panel A: Relative criterion				
Annual	0.4140*** (0.000)	0.2171*** (0.000)	0.0864*** (0.000)	0.0953*** (0.000)
Country averages	0.1641*** (0.000)	0.2683** (0.026)	0.0817*** (0.000)	0.1396*** (0.009)
Panel B: Absolute criterion				
Annual	0.4073*** (0.000)	0.1933*** (0.000)	0.1218*** (0.000)	0.1451*** (0.000)
Country averages	0.1481*** (0.000)	0.2373** (0.032)	0.0814*** (0.000)	0.0813*** (0.001)

Note: ***, **, * denote statistical significance at 1%, 5%, and 10%, respectively. Calculated p-values are shown in parentheses.

Source: Authors. See section 5.2.1.

As for "country average" correlations, we first average the available information for each country, and then compute the cross-sectional correlation coefficients. We provide estimated coefficients of both Pearson correlation and Spearman Rank correlation. Again, panels A and B present the results of using relative criterion and absolute criterion, respectively. Based on Table 5.2, three general conclusions stand out.

First, manufacturing sector development is significantly related to each of the selected variables. Moreover, the correlation coefficients are always positive, no matter which calculation method we adopt. It indicates that a higher growth rate of the manufacturing sector is positively correlated with a larger private savings ratio, technological accumulation speed, and more rapid growth of all the other sectors. Second, we find that saving–manufacturing growth correlations are higher than total factor productivity (TFP)–manufacturing growth correlations, although they are all statistically significant. Also, services–manufacturing growth relationships are somewhat greater than agriculture–manufacturing and other industry–manufacturing correlations. This indicates that manufacturing is more closely related to the services sector. Third, when we investigate the sample of year-averaged observations, correlation coefficients slightly decrease for manufacturing–saving and manufacturing–TFP correlations. In contrast, sectoral relationships are much stronger when we use cross-sectional data.

5.2.2 Empirical Methodology

We are aware of the potential drawbacks of regression analyses in the existing literature that empirically study economic growth: highly correlated explanatory variables, country heterogeneity, reverse causality, and so on. In fact, many scholars have proven that the conventional ordinary least squares (OLS) estimation is only consistent under strict and unrealistic assumptions (Caselli, Esquivel, and Lefort 1996). To alleviate such concerns, we analyze each relationship by adopting a long-run Granger causality test and its different modifications. Granger causality tests allow for various dynamic specifications, which can be utilized to investigate the effects of the manufacturing sector in individual economies in a more appropriate way. Additionally, testing the existence of Granger causality can help to characterize the directional relationship between the variables we are interested in. A general representation of a dynamic time-series model linking two variables x and y is as shown as follows:

$$y_{i,t} = \alpha_{0,i} + \sum_{j=1}^{q} \alpha_{i,t,j}^{y} y_{i,t-j} + \sum_{k=1}^{p} \beta_{i,t,k}^{y} x_{i,t-k} + \varepsilon_{i,t}^{y} \tag{1}$$

$$x_{i,t} = \alpha_{0,i} + \sum_{j=1}^{m} \alpha_{i,t,j}^{x} y_{i,t-j} + \sum_{k=1}^{n} b_{i,t,k}^{x} x_{i,t-k} + v_{i,t}^{x} \tag{2}$$

However, such a system cannot be directly estimated without additional assumptions or restrictions on its parameters. Generally speaking, the assumption is relevant to the sample data and can be divided into two categories. If the sample covers a relatively long time horizon, one could impose the assumption of constancy in parameters over time but allow them to be variable across economies. And if the data set includes a rather large number of cross-sectional economies, one could allow the parameters to be constant across economies but differ over time. For the model used in the baseline regression, we introduce the additional assumptions of both no country and no time heterogeneity,[8] as our data set covers a large number of economies for a relatively long time. Therefore, the basic equation estimated for each pair of variables is shown as the following specification:

$$y_{i,t} = \alpha_{0,i} + \sum_{j=1}^{6} \alpha_{j} y_{i,t-j} + \sum_{k=1}^{6} \beta_{k} x_{i,t-k} + \varepsilon_{i,t} \tag{3}$$

In equation (3), $(y_{i,t}, x_{i,t})$ represents the growth rate of value added or labor productivity for each pair of sectors. As we noted before, the total economy is divided into four broad sectors—agriculture, non-manufacturing industry, manufacturing, and services. β_k here is also called the standard within-estimator in the literature. We choose the lag of six in our basic setup to balance the dynamic effects of dependent variable and the data availability.

---

[8]   In the robustness check, we implement the Granger causality test here under the assumption of constancy over time.

Following the literature (Attanasio, Picci, and Scorcu 2000), we also incorporate country fixed-effects in our regression model.

We construct two statistics here to make inferences. One is the sum of all β coefficients, which represents the short-run effects of variable x on y, and the other is calculated as $\sum_{k=1}^{6} \beta_k / (1 - \sum_{j=1}^{6} \alpha_j)$, which represents the long-run effects of changes in x on y after considering the persistence of the dependent variable. Null hypothesis for the former statistic is that the sum of all β coefficients are equal to zero, which is asymptotically consistent to a chi-square distribution. Null hypothesis for the latter statistic is that all β coefficients are jointly zero. We calculate the corresponding p-values for each statistic.

5.2.3 Empirical Findings

In this section, we discuss our main results of inter-sectoral linkages. The primary empirical results of long-run Granger causality by using value-added growth and labor productivity growth are presented in Tables 5.3 and 5.4, respectively. As we noted before, we estimate the dynamic model of equation (3) by using OLS with annual data. We include the lags of each variable up to the sixth order into the OLS regression, as well as the country-specific intercepts. Empirical results of other model specifications and estimation techniques are discussed in the robustness check section.

Conclusions based on panel Granger causality analysis are threefold. First, asymmetric Granger-causality relations among different sectors in the middle-income stage do exist. In Table 5.3, where we investigate the inter-sectoral linkages by using value-added growth data, the significantly positive signs of manufacturing industries in relation to other sectors indicate that there are substantial effects running from manufacturing growth to all other three sectors' development: if a country's manufacturing sector continues to grow fast, its services sector growth rate, as well as the agriculture and non-manufacturing sector growth rate, will be higher. This finding shows that the manufacturing sector is of great importance to a country's development.

Table 5.3: Long-Run Granger Causality Test: Value-Added Growth with Relative Criterion

	Agriculture	Non-manufacturing Industry	Manufacturing	Services
Short-run effect				
Agriculture	/	0.071	0.149**	0.178**
Non-manufacturing industry	0.007*	/	0.551***	0.616***
Manufacturing	0.006	0.040	/	−0.036
Services	0.069	0.064**	0.188***	/
Long-run effect				
Agriculture	/	0.043	0.090**	0.109*
Non-manufacturing industry	0.148	/	0.413***	0.457***
Manufacturing	0.007	0.045	/	−0.041**
Services	0.089	0.079***	0.218***	/

Note: ***, **, * denote statistical significance at 1%, 5%, and 10%, respectively.
Source: Authors. See section 5.2.1.

Table 5.4: Long-Run Granger Causality Test: Labor Productivity Growth with Relative Criterion

	Agriculture	Non-manufacturing Industry	Manufacturing	Services
Short-run effect				
Agriculture	/	−0.290	0.127	0.017
Non-manufacturing industry	−0.211	/	0.658**	−0.657
Manufacturing	0.137	−0.095	/	0.174
Services	−0.00004	−0.250	0.670***	/
Long-run effect				
Agriculture	/	0.043	0.090**	0.011***
Non-manufacturing industry	0.148	/	0.413***	−0.419
Manufacturing	0.007	0.045	/	0.677
Services	0.089	0.079***	0.218***	/

Note: ***, **, * denote statistical significance at 1%, 5%, and 10%, respectively.
Source: Authors. See section 5.2.1.

Moreover, due to small persistence in industry value-added growth rate, the long-term effect is slightly larger than the short-run effect. Also, when we switch to labor productivity data, we reach similar conclusions except that in the short run, we cannot observe significant effects of manufacturing growth in the agriculture sector. However, there exist major and positive effects after considering the persistence of agricultural labor productivity growth, which means that the development of manufacturing industry labor productivity is likely to benefit the agriculture sector in the long run. All these findings indicate that manufacturing sector development is central to the whole economy during the middle-income stage.

Second, such pulling effects are not only statistically significant but also economically significant. In the short run, a 1% level increase in the value-added growth rate of the manufacturing sector is likely to lead to a 0.149% increase in the growth rate of the agriculture sector, a 0.551% increase in the non-manufacturing industry, and a 0.188% increase in the services sector. Also, in the long run, a 1% difference in value-added growth rate in the manufacturing sector will generate a gap of 0.090% in the agriculture sector, a 0.413% gap in non-manufacturing industry, and a 0.188% gap in services. Such magnitudes are quite substantial. When we use labor productivity growth data, the empirical results in Table 5.4 also prove that the manufacturing sector has strong spillovers to and externalities for other sectors during the middle-income stage.

Third, the characteristics of all the other industries, including services, are different from those of manufacturing. Agriculture and non-manufacturing industry fail to contribute to the development of other sectors, which is in fact not a very surprising outcome. As for services, although it is likely to Granger cause the development of agriculture and non-manufacturing industry, it cannot provide significantly positive contributions to the development of the manufacturing sector. In the short run, there is no significant effect from services to manufacturing. However, in the long run, a 1% increase in the value-added growth rate of the services sector is likely to Granger cause a 0.041% *decrease* in the manufacturing growth rate. We obtain a similar conclusion when using the labor productivity growth rate as the dependent variable, but we are on the fence about the generality of this finding because we find that when we change our model specifications, the result changes. It turns out that the services sector can make a significantly positive, a significantly negative, or an insignificant contribution to the growth of the manufacturing sector. Therefore, we cannot draw any general conclusion from this baseline regression. However, the positive externalities of manufacturing to all other sectors are quite robust across different modifications in econometric methods.

All these findings indicate that the links between sectors may depend on the development stage. For developed economies, the services sector may contribute a substantial proportion to the growth of the total economy. But for middle-income economies manufacturing remains the key engine of growth. On the one hand, for middle-income economies, the tradable manufacturing sector is viewed as the primary channel through which a developing economy absorbs the best practices from advanced economies (Hausmann, Hwang, and Rodrik 2007; Jones and Olken 2005). Thus, it plays a significant role in adopting state-of-the-art technology from developed economies and diffusing the technology and knowledge across sectors. On the other hand, as industrialization progresses, the manufacturing sector increasingly stimulates demand for service inputs (Park and Chan 1989), thus further promoting the development of the services industry.

Our results are also consistent with many other papers that focus on the inter-sectoral linkages between the manufacturing sector and the service sector. According to Kaldor (1957) and many references therein (Naudé and Szirmai 2012; Szirmai 2012), manufacturing picks up services because the manufacturing sector has several important qualities that are not shared by other sectors. Therefore, they conclude that spillover effects are stronger in the manufacturing sector than in any other sectors. Guerrieri and Meliciani (2005) argued that the emergence of modern service activities depends on the improvement in the manufacturing structure. Park and Chan (1989) found that manufacturing development is important to both nonmarket services and market services because it provides an increased demand for those intermediate inputs. Based on this, they conclude that the development of the services sector depends more on that of manufacturing than vice versa. Szirmai and Verspagen (2015) proposed the same idea regarding the relation between these two important modern sectors.

5.2.4 Robustness Check

To test the robustness of our empirical findings, we conduct a range of tests. Generally speaking, those adjustments or modifications do not alter our essential conclusion that manufacturing is the key engine of growth in the middle-income stage. These tests are explained in detail below, and detailed results are presented in the Internet Appendix.[9]

First, we redo the Granger causality tests by using the sample of middle-income economies defined by the absolute criterion, and the results are summarized in Tables IA1 and IA2 (Internet Appendix). Certainly, there are notable differences between economies and their sample period when we adopt the alternative classification method, but it shows that our most important findings discussed in the last section do not depend on the choice of the classification method. Our results are quite robust, qualitatively and quantitatively.

Second, we use different numbers of lags in the regressions. In the baseline model, we use six lags. Here, we introduce four or eight lags in the regression to see whether different choices of lags will significantly change our results. The corresponding results are shown in Tables IA3–IA6, and we find that our basic conclusions are robust to alternatives of lag orders.

Third, in our basic model specification, the underlying assumption is that the size of the time span, as well as the number of economies in the cross section,

---

9   Tables IA1 to IA19 are available online. https://www.tandfonline.com/doi/suppl/10.1080/
     13547860.2016.1261481/suppl_file/rjap_a_1261481_sm2703.pdf.

is large enough. The minimum span of each economy included in our sample is 15 years. Although it seems relatively long, it is highly possible that our proposed within-estimator does not approximate well if the time span is in fact not long enough. A small T could lead to an asymptotic bias, which is the well-known Nickell bias documented in the literature (Nickell 1981). Therefore, we use the generalized method of moments (GMM) estimator developed by Arellano and Bond (1991) to deal with the potential effects of this Nickell bias. Based on the empirical results in Tables IA7 and IA8, we find that our conclusion still holds even after we control for this potential Nickell bias. Compared with the empirical results in the basic regression, there is only a marginal difference in the magnitudes of the estimated coefficients. It shows that the within-estimator used in this chapter has a small bias at most, if not none, which means that the size of the time span in our data is already long enough, and our basic model specification has controlled for the dynamics of dependent variables appropriately.

Fourth, we deal with the assumption of no country heterogeneity by allowing the coefficients of the dynamic model to differ in the cross-country dimension. We construct the mean-group estimators proposed by Pesaran and Smith (1995) and follow the corresponding statistical inferences to test whether this approach will alter the previous results. According to Attanasio, Picci, and Scorcu (2000), this framework is suitable for the analysis of heterogeneity among economies. A detailed discussion of the nature of cross-sectional heterogeneity would be particularly relevant if relaxing the homogeneity assumption leads to qualitatively different results. We present all the results in details in Tables IA9–IA16. In addition to the mean-group estimator and its statistical significance, we provide the quantiles' information on the estimated coefficients in the individual economy. According to Tables IA11 and IA15, which list the results of Granger causality tests on the effects from manufacturing to other sectors, the results on manufacturing's roles do not differ significantly from what was found by imposing the homogeneity assumption. The estimated coefficients are much larger than the baseline results, though. This is because the spillover effects of manufacturing are considerably significant in some economies. As for the services sector,

it shows negative impacts on manufacturing after we take the country
heterogeneity into account. According to the quantiles' information on
the estimated coefficients, there is indeed significant heterogeneity across
countries. Although the existence of country heterogeneity does not change
our most important conclusion, it alerts us to the fact that the precise
industrialization process in different economies may differ significantly.
We provide detailed discussion on this point in the Internet Appendix.

Fifth, we add some control variables in the regression. In addition to the
country fixed effect, we also include the year fixed effect to control for the
unobserved time trend. Moreover, we control for the consequences of
human capital and institutions by introducing them into the control variables.
The estimation results are shown in Tables IA17 and IA18. We find that
the empirical results do not change after we add these variables into the
regression, which supports our hypothesis that manufacturing sector has
substantial positive spillovers and externalities for all other sectors during the
middle-income stage.

Sixth, the services sector is highly diversified. Therefore, although we find
that the services sector as a whole cannot pull along the manufacturing sector
during the middle-income stage or other development stages, individual
branches of the services sector may have such ability. We use the cross-
country 10-sector database to implement our empirical analysis. We adopt
the same empirical methodology used in the baseline regression and
summarize the results in Table IA19. Generally, the basic conclusion remains
unchanged. For detailed discussion, please refer to the Internet Appendix.

5.3 | Underlying Mechanism

In this section, we attempt to identify several possible mechanisms through
which manufacturing development pulls along all other sectors during the
middle-income stage. Our discussion focuses on the relations between
manufacturing and domestic savings as well as TFP growth. We first provide a

conceptual framework in section 5.3.1 to explain why we think manufacturing development can increase the gross private savings ratio and TFP growth. Then, we briefly introduce the econometric methodology in the next subsection. Empirical results are shown in section 5.3.3.

5.3.1 Conceptual Framework

Manufacturing and Savings. Our first hypothesis is that manufacturing development can promote the incentives of gross private savings. Savings and economic growth are closely related. Capital accumulation has been proved an important determinant of economic growth, both theoretically and empirically. But this is true only if the economy is closed. Why is high domestic private saving valuable for developing economies, even if there is no restriction on international capital flow? We think there are mainly three reasons. First, it is related to the well-known Feldstein–Horioka Puzzle (Feldstein and Horioka 1980), which provides robust evidence that domestic saving and domestic investment are highly correlated. Although there is still no widely accepted explanation for this empirical finding, this documented relationship indicates that a higher local saving rate does matter for the long-term economic growth rate.[10] The second reason is raised in the debate on the benefits of capital account liberalization. In many papers the view is expressed that for developing countries, cheap international capital cannot help with the economic growth directly (Kose et al. 2009; Prasad, Rajan, and Subramanian 2007). Whether a country can make use of foreign capital depends on its financial system. Therefore, increasing domestic saving and improving the financial system are key to raising private domestic investment.

---

[10]   One possible explanation is *cofinance* proposed by Aghion et al. (2016). They think that in developing countries, foreign investment in fact requires the involvement of both a foreign investor and a local bank, because the former is familiar with the frontier technology, and the latter can directly monitor local projects. Therefore, in developing countries, local saving matters for innovation, and therefore growth, because it allows the domestic bank to cofinance projects and thus to attract foreign investment.

The third reason is that the capital to labor ratio or a country's endowment structure is essential to its industrial upgrading process (Acemoglu and Guerrieri 2008; Ju, Lin, and Wang 2015). According to Ju, Lin, and Wang (2015), this idea goes back to as early as the Rybczynski Theorem, which states that the capital-intensive sector would expand when the economy becomes more capital abundant. Therefore, as the domestic capital endowment increases, output will increase in every industry that is more capital intensive. All these arguments support the critical role of domestic saving in the development of a developing country.

But why is the manufacturing sector critical for raising gross private savings? The Permanent Income Hypothesis (Friedman 1957) and the Life-Cycle Hypothesis (Modigliani 1966) emphasize the important role of income growth for private savings and abundant empirical research have widely tested these two views.[11] However, we hold the view that those studies fail to account for the effects of the economic composition. We hypothesize that a larger share of manufacturing can promote gross private savings ratio. Our reasons are explained as follows.

First, in the manufacturing sector, there is a relatively high demand for capital since it requires high investment in machinery, equipment, and building materials (Rowthorn and Coutts 2004). Therefore, it provides great opportunities for capital accumulation. Second, the manufacturing industry has a more rapid technological growth rate due to its large economies of scale, which tends to increase the return on capital. Third, the manufacturing sector has a relatively low labor share, which leads to a low consumption rate and a high saving rate. A recent study by Gollin, Jedwab, and Vollrath (2016) showed that for countries that are highly dependent on resource exports, urbanization will be concentrated in those cities dominated by non-tradable

---

[11]   For example, Hall (1978), Bernanke (1984), Hall and Mishkin (1982), and many others have found that shocks to economic growth lead to changes in savings. Moreover, a large number of works, including Barro (1991), Gregorio (1992), and Barro and Sala-i-Martin (2004), prove that savings contribute a lot to higher economic growth rate in the short run.

services. Compared with cities that are more dependent on manufacturing, the saving rate is relatively lower in these "consumption cities" (i.e., cities with high consumption-to-income ratios). Last, compared with the agriculture sector, the manufacturing sector is much more spatially concentrated, which induces more rapid capital accumulation (Szirmai and Verspagen 2015). As a consequence, we think that the emergence of the manufacturing sector tends to lead to an increase in the private savings ratio.

Manufacturing and Total Factor Productivity Growth. Our second hypothesis is that manufacturing development can accelerate the pace of technological accumulation. Technological advancement, represented as TFP growth in the academic literature, is recognized as perhaps the most important factor for long-term economic growth. Considering its importance, many efforts are devoted to studying its determinants. Studies highlight the role of several important factors that promote productivity growth for developing economies, including trade openness, education, institutions, and so on (Acemoglu, Johnson, and Robinson 2005; Helpman and Grossman 1991; Loko and Diouf 2009). For developed economies, these findings are consistent with what endogenous growth theory predicts. However, those studies again fail to account for the effects of economic structure in the developing economies. We argue that the manufacturing sector can accelerate the pace of technological accumulation during the middle-income stage for the following reasons.

First, for middle-income economies catching up with high-income economies is a process of eliminating the productivity gap. However, different industries play distinct roles in this process. Many studies (e.g., Jones and Olken 2005; Rodrik 2013) have argued that the tradable manufacturing sector is the primary channel through which a developing economy absorbs knowledge and modern science from abroad. Additionally, unconditional convergence happens in the manufacturing industry (Rodrik 2013). It means that the manufacturing sector can obtain easier access to frontier technologies, which is essential for middle-income economies to catch up rapidly with the advanced economies.

Second, economies of scale, as well as its embodied and disembodied technological progress, can contribute to TFP growth in developing economies. Many papers stress the importance of embodied technological progress (Boucekkine, de Río, and Licandro 2003; Greenwood, Hercowitz, and Krusell 1997; Greenwood and Seshadri 2005), which means new machines that incorporate the latest technological advances are more crucial to the development of developing economies. For example, Phelps (1962) proved that the composition of technical progress matters a lot for developing economies and that a larger share of embodied technological progress will help the developing economies move more quickly to the high-income group. Another significant study consistent with our view is Greenwood, Hercowitz, and Krusell (1997), who conclude that embodied technical progress explains about 60% of the growth in labor productivity. Although several branches of services also offer except onal opportunities for disembodied technological advances, such as learning-by-doing, the manufacturing sector allows for a faster growth rate in both embodied and disembodied technological progress (Cornwall 1976).

Third, various works have shown that the vehicle of learning and adopting technology is an investment, rather than consumption (Arrow 1962; Boucekkine, de Río, and O. L candro 2003; Jovanovic and Rousseau 2002; Romer 1986). Therefore, the manufacturing sector, which calls for a higher level of capital and investment, takes on the central role of absorbing technology, as well as creating substantial externalities of knowledge flows to other sectors. These essential characteristics make the manufacturing sector crucial for TFP growth in all middle-income economies.

5.3.2 Econometric Methodology

In this part, we try to prove our hypothesis by investigating the relationship between a country's manufacturing share and its gross private savings ratio or TFP growth rate. In the earlier draft, we focus on the association between manufacturing growth rate and these two growth determinants (Su and Yao 2016). Although we find a significantly positive relationship using a variety of econometric methods, there is one major drawback to this approach—the manufacturing sector growth rate is highly correlated with the total growth rate of the overall economy, as well as that of all other sectors. Therefore, it is difficult for us to prove the increases in savings or TFP growth are a result of manufacturing development. Therefore, here we investigate the relation between economic structure and some growth determinants such as its gross saving rate and the TFP growth rate. We adopt the panel regression method to prove our hypothesis. Following the recent work of Acemoglu et al. (2015) who studied the effects of democratization on economic growth, our regression model for analyzing the panel data is as follows:

$$m_{i,t} = c + \sum_{j=0}^{p} \alpha_j m_{i,t-j} + \sum_{k=0}^{p} \beta_k y_{i,t-k} + \gamma MANFSHARE_{i,t} + \delta_i + \eta_t + e_{i,t} \qquad (4)$$

where $m_{i,t}$ is one of our variables of interest in country i in year t, i.e., gross private savings ratio or TFP growth rate. $MANFSHARE_{i,t}$ is our main variable of interest for manufacturing sector employment share in country i at time t. Besides, $y_{i,t}$ is the log of GDP per capita at year t for country i. Here we also include different lags of GDP per capita and dependent variable on the right side, to control potential residual serial correlation in the error term $e_{i,t}$. Country fixed effects δ_i and year effects η_t are incorporated into the regression to absorb the impacts of any time-invariant country characteristics and country-invariant time trends. $X_{i,t}$ are a bunch of control variables, which prove to be the key determinants of saving ratio and TFP growth in the literature. In this chapter, we use the following control variables: total population, capital account openness, the percentage of domestic banks' assets in nominal GDP, the share of private sector credit in GDP, real interest rate, dependency ratio, urbanization, total investment share, rule of law, and human capital.

5.3.3 Empirical Results

Tables 5.5 and 5.6 present the empirical results of using gross private savings ratio and TFP growth as the dependent variable, respectively. Here, the economies are classified by the relative criterion. In these two tables, columns (1) to (5) present the empirical results of different model

Table 5.5: Manufacturing Employment Share and Gross Private Savings Ratio: Relative Criterion

Dep: Gross private savings ratio (GPSR)	(1)	(2)	(3)	(4)	(5)
Manufacturing employment share	0.37***	0.36***	0.40***	0.47**	0.37*
	(0.001)	(0.002)	(0.002)	(0.017)	(0.080)
GPSR, 1st lag	0.54***	0.51***	0.50***	0.46***	0.38***
	(0.000)	(0.000)	(0.000)	(0.000)	(0.000)
GPSR, 2nd lag	0.02	0.02	0.02	-0.11	-0.17**
	(0.684)	(0.631)	(0.614)	(0.129)	(0.027)
GPSR, 3rd lag					0.07*
					(0.058)
log GDP per capita, 1st lag	-4.70	-4.44	-6.38	-0.59	-3.08
	(0.443)	(0.488)	(0.333)	(0.939)	(0.705)
log GDP per capita, 2nd lag	7.04	6.15	7.48	-1.52	7.86
	(0.249)	(0.344)	(0.261)	(0.858)	(0.505)
log GDP per capita, 3rd lag					-9.63
					(0.225)
Inflation rate (%)	-0.04**	-0.06**	-0.08**	0.07	0.08
	(0.028)	(0.032)	(0.018)	(0.267)	(0.199)
Chinn–Ito index	-0.63	-0.96	-1.30	-1.14	-1.04
	(0.494)	(0.340)	(0.225)	(0.345)	(0.388)
Deposit money banks' assets to GDP (%)	0.00	0.02	0.01	0.05*	0.07**
	(0.804)	(0.441)	(0.749)	(0.058)	(0.015)
Domestic credit to private sector (% of GDP)	-0.03***	-0.03***	-0.03**	-0.02	-0.02*
	(0.003)	(0.009)	(0.010)	(0.128)	(0.068)
Real interest rate (%)		-0.03	-0.04	0.10	0.13
		(0.409)	(0.349)	(0.228)	(0.126)
Dependency ratio (%)			0.14	0.18	0.13
			(0.234)	(0.347)	(0.505)
Urban population (% of total)			0.02	0.50**	0.46**
			(0.888)	(0.011)	(0.029)
Public health and education expenditure to GDP (%)				-0.11	-0.05
				(0.675)	(0.861)
Constant	-14.93	-10.61	-18.28	-28.26	4.73
	(0.245)	(0.487)	(0.290)	(0.495)	(0.916)
Country fixed-effect	YES	YES	YES	YES	YES
Year fixed-effect	YES	YES	YES	YES	YES
Observations	497	453	453	262	251
R-squared	0.87	0.87	0.87	0.94	0.94
Adj. R-squared	0.84	0.85	0.85	0.92	0.92

Dep = dependent variable, GDP = gross domestic product, log = logarithm.

Note: ***, **, * denote statistical significance at 1%, 5%, and 10%, respectively. Calculated p-values are shown in parentheses.

Source: Authors. See section 5.2.1.

Table 5.6: Manufacturing Employment Share and Total Factor Productivity Growth: Relative Criterion

Dep: TFP growth rate	(1)	(2)	(3)	(4)	(5)
Manufacturing employment share	0.24** (0.046)	0.22* (0.087)	0.25* (0.059)	0.26* (0.053)	0.27** (0.046)
TFP growth rate, 1st lag	0.18*** (0.000)	0.18*** (0.000)	0.17*** (0.001)	0.17*** (0.000)	0.16*** (0.002)
TFP growth rate, 2nd lag					0.01 (0.918)
log GDP per capita, 1st lag	−21.09*** (0.004)	−21.38*** (0.007)	−22.99*** (0.006)	−24.08*** (0.004)	−21.91** (0.011)
log GDP per capita, 2nd lag	12.01* (0.093)	11.25 (0.145)	13.60* (0.094)	15.02* (0.068)	0.65 (0.958)
log GDP per capita, 3rd lag					12.65 (0.110)
log population	−2.80 (0.506)	−4.70 (0.332)	−8.00 (0.130)	−5.54 (0.425)	−5.52 (0.436)
Investment ratio of GDP	0.04 (0.435)	0.05 (0.409)	0.02 (0.720)	0.04 (0.567)	0.06 (0.308)
Real interest rate (%)		0.00 (0.872)	0.00 (0.854)	−0.00 (0.256)	−0.00 (0.273)
Deposit money banks' assets to GDP (%)			−0.05** (0.028)	−0.03 (0.167)	−0.03 (0.203)
Inflation rate (%)				−0.16 (0.885)	−0.33 (0.767)
Chinn–Ito index				−0.02 (0.103)	−0.02 (0.135)
Domestic credit to private sector (% of GDP)				0.00 (0.127)	0.00 (0.166)
Urban population (% of total)				−0.05 (0.626)	−0.09 (0.399)
Constant	127.18 (0.108)	167.36* (0.065)	217.31** (0.026)	175.08 (0.165)	173.26 (0.178)
Country fixed-effect	YES	YES	YES	YES	YES
Year fixed-effect	YES	YES	YES	YES	YES
Observations	668	589	572	564	549
R-squared	0.26	0.28	0.28	0.30	0.30
Adj. R-squared	0.17	0.18	0.18	0.19	0.19

Dep = Dependent variable, GDP = gross domestic product, log = logarithm, TFP = total factor productivity.

Note: ***, **, * denote statistical significance at 1%, 5%, and 10%, respectively. Calculated p-values are shown in parentheses.

Source: Authors. See section 5.2.1.

specifications by within-estimator. The difference between models (1) to (4) is that we control different sets of control variables in the regression. In model (5), we add extra lag of the dependent variable based on model (4) to control for the persistence of the data. Those changes in model specifications have slight effects on the estimated magnitude and significance of the manufacturing employment share. Based on Tables 5.5 and 5.6, a 10% level increase in manufacturing employment share in the total economy is likely to lead to a 4% increase in gross private savings ratio, and a 2.5% increase in TFP growth. When we redo the regressions using absolute criterion classification, the results shown in Tables 5.7 and 5.8 reveal similar conclusions.

All these empirical results have confirmed our hypothesis on the underlying mechanisms of manufacturing development. As a matter of fact, many East Asian economies that promote industrialization are also accompanied by high saving ratios and rapid growth rates. Although culture and relative price differences also contribute to various levels of the saving ratio or even growth across economies, the emergence of the manufacturing sector could also lead to significant shifts by boosting the demand for capital, as well as increasing the investment return.

5.4 | Conclusion

In this chapter, we highlight the influences of manufacturing development for middle-income economies. To begin with, we investigate the substantial externalities of manufacturing sector development on other sectors during the middle-income stage. Moreover, we test the underlying mechanisms through which the manufacturing sector contributes to economic growth. We find that manufacturing development not only increases the incentive to save, but also promotes technological accumulation.

Table 5.7: Manufacturing Employment Share and Gross Private Savings Ratio: Absolute Criterion

Dep: Gross private savings ratio (GPSR)	(1)	(2)	(3)	(4)	(5)
Manufacturing employment share	0.56***	0.53***	0.51***	0.44***	0.37***
	(0.000)	(0.000)	(0.000)	(0.000)	(0.000)
GPSR, 1st lag	−0.01	−0.00	−0.01	−0.09	−0.17**
	(0.848)	(0.983)	(0.824)	(0.184)	(0.034)
GPSR, 2nd lag					0.06
					(0.117)
GPSR, 3rd lag	−0.55	−0.07	−1.99	2.82	0.12
	(0.932)	(0.991)	(0.764)	(0.718)	(0.988)
log GDP per capita, 1st lag	2.16	1.87	1.88	−3.78	4.69
	(0.739)	(0.778)	(0.780)	(0.654)	(0.689)
log GDP per capita, 2nd lag					−6.95
					(0.392)
log GDP per capita, 3rd lag	0.23*	0.27*	0.27*	0.44**	0.38*
	(0.088)	(0.063)	(0.081)	(0.029)	(0.082)
Inflation rate (%)	−0.01	−0.05*	−0.08**	0.07	0.06
	(0.122)	(0.072)	(0.013)	(0.252)	(0.275)
Chinn–Ito index	−0.09	−0.58	−0.89	−1.74	−1.98
	(0.924)	(0.590)	(0.427)	(0.155)	(0.107)
Deposit money banks' assets to GDP (%)	0.02	0.02	0.00	0.03	0.04
	(0.516)	(0.519)	(0.870)	(0.304)	(0.229)
Domestic credit to private sector (% of GDP)	−0.01	−0.02	−0.03*	−0.00	−0.00
	(0.294)	(0.105)	(0.080)	(0.778)	(0.798)
Real interest rate (%)		−0.05	−0.08**	0.10	0.09
		(0.109)	(0.021)	(0.234)	(0.300)
Dependency ratio (%)			0.30**	0.29	0.29
			(0.027)	(0.172)	(0.187)
Urban population (% of total)			0.13	0.52***	0.51**
			(0.359)	(0.009)	(0.019)
Public health and education expenditure to GDP (%)				−0.15	−0.04
				(0.578)	(0.883)
Constant	−8.80	−11.52	−28.91	−46.61	−33.64
	(0.566)	(0.487)	(0.126)	(0.267)	(0.478)
Country fixed-effect	YES	YES	YES	YES	YES
Year fixed-effect	YES	YES	YES	YES	YES
Observations	449	430	430	249	238
R-squared	0.88	0.88	0.89	0.94	0.94
Adj. R-squared	0.86	0.86	0.86	0.92	0.92

Dep = Dependent variable, GDP = gross domestic product, log = logarithm.

Notes: ***, **, * denote statistical significance at 1%, 5%, and 10%, respectively. Calculated p-values are shown in parentheses.

Source: Authors. See section 5.2.1.

Our empirical findings in this chapter not only have substantial policy implications but also provide a set of facts that may serve as a guide to the further development of economic growth theory. The most important policy implication drawn from our work is the necessary industrial policy for middle-income economies. Since the early 1980s, however, there has been a noticeable slowdown of industrial development in many developing countries, particularly in Latin America and sub-Saharan Africa. Over the past decade and a half, many African countries have suffered sustained deindustrialization of manufacturing capacity, and they remain the least industrialized in the world (Lall and Stewart 1996). It seems that governments in developing economies should come up with an effective strategy to prevent a country from premature deindustrialization (Rodrik 2016), especially in the era of globalization. When the manufacturing sector, the engine of growth for developing countries, weakens, aggregate productivity is likely to decline. Therefore, in our view, the poor performance of manufacturing and the relatively strong performance of services in some developing economies may not be a good sign for maintaining sustainable long-term economic growth.

Moreover, our empirical findings on sectoral differences between manufacturing and the services sector may also be of use for economic growth theory. Despite the prevalence of one-sector neoclassical theory (Barro and Sala-i-Martin 2004; Blanchard and Fischer 1989), many studies try to extend those basic growth models to multi-sector ones (Herrendorf, Rogerson, and Valentinyi 2013; Herrendorf and Valentinyi 2006; Zhang 2011) to investigate the theoretical effects of structural change and sectoral differences. However, in addition to the discussions on the existence and uniqueness of the equilibrium in the multi-sector model, how to incorporate different sectors and their interactions into the model remains the vital question. Our empirical findings on the unique characteristics of the manufacturing sector during the middle-income stage should shed some light on future economic modeling.

Table 5.8: Manufacturing Employment Share and Total Factor Productivity Growth: Absolute Criterion

Dep: TFP growth rate	(1)	(2)	(3)	(4)	(5)
Manufacturing employment share	0.22* (0.093)	0.23 (0.113)	0.25* (0.097)	0.30* (0.056)	0.36** (0.024)
TFP growth rate, 1st lag	0.18*** (0.000)	0.18*** (0.000)	0.17*** (0.001)	0.18*** (0.000)	0.15*** (0.004)
TFP growth rate, 2nd lag					0.01 (0.862)
log GDP per capita, 1st lag	−25.42*** (0.001)	−25.97*** (0.002)	−27.58*** (0.001)	−29.81*** (0.001)	−24.99*** (0.005)
log GDP per capita, 2nd lag	17.41** (0.020)	17.12** (0.032)	19.38** (0.021)	22.07*** (0.009)	−0.24 (0.985)
log GDP per capita, 3rd lag					19.13** (0.020)
log population	3.47 (0.525)	3.31 (0.573)	−0.05 (0.994)	3.40 (0.683)	6.52 (0.449)
Investment ratio of GDP	0.06 (0.303)	0.08 (0.172)	0.05 (0.395)	0.07 (0.255)	0.10 (0.117)
Real interest rate (%)		−0.00 (0.997)	−0.00 (0.989)	−0.00 (0.700)	−0.00 (0.179)
Deposit money banks' assets to GDP (%)			−0.05** (0.027)	−0.04 (0.124)	−0.02 (0.409)
Inflation rate (%)				0.83 (0.482)	1.01 (0.395)
Chinn–Ito index				−0.03* (0.053)	−0.03** (0.043)
Domestic credit to private sector (% of GDP)				0.00 (0.425)	0.00 (0.127)
Urban population (% of total)				−0.06 (0.619)	−0.15 (0.220)
Constant	10.12 (0.921)	18.75 (0.865)	71.20 (0.559)	10.77 (0.943)	−51.46 (0.742)
Country fixed-effect	YES	YES	YES	YES	YES
Year fixed-effect	YES	YES	YES	YES	YES
Observations	611	553	536	529	511
R-squared	0.28	0.29	0.30	0.32	0.33
Adj. R-squared	0.18	0.19	0.20	0.21	0.22

Dep = Dependent variable, GDP = gross domestic product, log = logarithm, TFP = total factor productivity.

Notes: ***, **, * denote statistical significance at 1%, 5%, and 10%, respectively. Calculated p-values are shown in parentheses.

Source: Authors. See Section 5.2.1.

References

Acemoglu, D., and V. Guerrier. 2008. Capital Deepening and Nonbalanced
Economic Growth. *Journal of Political Economy* 116(3): 467–498.

Acemoglu, D., S. Johnson, and J. A. Robinson. 2005. Institutions as a
Fundamental Cause of Long-Run Growth. In *The Handbook of Economic
Growth*, edited by P. Aghion and S. N. Durlauf. Amsterdam: Elsevier
North-Holland.

Acemoglu, D., S. Naidu, P. Restrepo, and J. A. Robinson. 2015. Democracy
Does Cause Growth. NBER Working Paper 20004. Cambridge, MA:
National Bureau of Economic Research.

Aghion, P., D. Comin, P. Howitt, and I. Tecu. 2016. When Does Domestic
Savings Matter for Economic Growth? *IMF Economic Review* 64(3):
381–407.

Amirapu, A., and A. Subramanian. 2015. Manufacturing or Services?
An Indian Illustration of a Development Dilemma. CGD Working Paper
409. Washington, DC: Center for Global Development.

Arellano, M., and S. Bond. 1991. Some Tests of Specification for Panel Data:
Monte Carlo Evidence and an Application to Employment Equations.
Review of Economic Studies 58(2): 277–297.

Arrow, K. 1962. The Economic Implications of Learning by Doing. *Review of
Economic Studies* 29: 155–173.

Attanasio, O. P., L. Picci, and A. E. Scorcu. 2000. Saving, Growth, and
Investment: A Macroeconomic Analysis Using a Panel of Countries.
The Review of Economics and Statistics 82(2): 182–211.

Barro, R. J. 1991. Economic Growth in a Cross Section of Countries.
The Quarterly Journal of Economics 106(2): 407–443.

Barro, R. J., and X. I. Sala-i-Martin. 2004. *Economic Growth, Second Edition*:
Cambridge, MA: The MIT Press.

Baumol, W. J. 1967. Macroeconomics of Unbalanced Growth: The Anatomy
of Urban Crisis. *The American Economic Review* 57(3): 415–426.

———. 2001. Paradox of the Services: Exploding Costs, Persistent Demand.
In *The Growth of Service Industries: The Paradox of Exploding Costs and
Persistent Demand,* edited by T. Ten-Raa and R. Schettkat. Cheltenham,
United Kingdom: Edwar Elgar.

Baumol, W. J., and W. G. Bowen. 1965. On the Performing Arts: The Anatomy of Their Economic Problems. *The American Economic Review* 55(1/2): 495–502.

Bernanke, B. S. 1984. Permanent Income, Liquidity, and Expenditure on Automobiles: Evidence from Panel Data. *Quarterly Journal of Economics* 99(3): 587–614.

Blanchard, O., and S. Fischer. 1989. *Lectures on Macroeconomics*: Cambridge, MA: The MIT Press.

Bluestone, B., and B. Harrison. 1982. *The Deindustrialization of America*. New York, NY: Basic Books.

Boucekkine, R., F. de Río, and O. Licandro. 2003. Embodied Technological Change, Learning-by-Doing and the Productivity Slowdown. *Scandinavian Journal of Economics* 105(1): 87–97.

Buera, F. J., and J. P. Kaboski. 2012. The Rise of the Service Economy. *American Economic Review* 102(6): 2540–2569.

Caselli, F., G. Esquivel, and F. Lefort. 1996. Reopening the Convergence Debate: A New Look at Cross-Country Growth Empirics. *Journal of Economic Growth* 1(3): 363–389.

Chakravarty, S., and A. Mitra. 2009. Is Industry Still the Engine of Growth? An Econometric Study of the Organized Sector Employment in India. *Journal of Policy Modeling* 31: 22–35.

Chenery, H., and H. Elkington. 1980. *Structural Change and Development Policy*. Oxford, United Kingdom: Oxford University Press.

Clark, C. 1940. *Conditions of Economic Progress*. London: Macmillan Publishers.

Cornwall, J. 1976. Diffusion, Convergence and Kaldor's Laws. *The Economic Journal* 86(342): 307–314.

Cruz, M. 2015. Premature De-industrialisation: Theory, Evidence and Policy Recommendations in the Mexican Case. *Cambridge Journal of Economics* 39: 113–137.

Dasgupta, S., and A. Singh. 2005. Will Services Be the New Engine of Indian Economic Growth? *Development and Change* 36(6): 1035–1057.

———. 2006. *Manufacturing, Services and Premature Deindustrialization in Developing Countries: A Kaldorian Analysis*. WIDER Working Paper 049. Helsinki: World Institute for Development Economic Research (UNU-WIDER).

Fagerberg, J., and B. Verspagen. 1999. Modern Capitalism in the 1970s and 1980s. In *Growth, Employment and Inflation*, edited by M. Setterfield. Basingstoke, United Kingdom: MacMillan.

Feldstein, M., and C. Horioka. 1980. Domestic Saving and International Capital Flows. *Economic Journal* 90(358): 314–329.

Fixler, D. J., and D. Siegel. 1999. Outsourcing and Productivity Growth in Services. *Structural Change and Economic Dynamics* 10(2): 177–194.

Friedman, M. 1957. *The Permanent Income Hypothesis: A Theory of the Consumption Function.* Newhaven, CT: Princeton University Press.

Fuchs, V. R. 1981. Economic Growth and the Rise of Service Employment. In *Towards an Explanation of Economic Growth*, edited by H. Giersch. Tubingen, Germany: J.C.B. Mohr (Paul Siebeck).

Gollin, D., R. Jedwab, and D. Vollrath. 2016. Urbanization With and Without Industrialization. *Journal of Economic Growth* 21: 35–70.

Greenwood, J., Z. Hercowitz, and P. Krusell. 1997. Long-Run Implications of Investment-Specific Technological Change. *The American Economic Review* 87(3): 342–362.

Greenwood, J., and A. Seshadri. 2005. Technological Progress and Economic Transformation. In *Handbook of Economic Growth, Vol. 1*, edited by P. Aghion and S. Durlauf. Amsterdam: Elsevier North-Holland.

Gregorio, J. D. 1992. Economic Growth in Latin America. *Journal of Development Economics* 39(1): 59–84.

Guerrieri, P., and V. Meliciani. 2005. Technology and International Competitiveness: The Interdependence between Manufacturing and Producer Services. *Structural Change and Economic Dynamics* 16(4): 489–502.

Hall, R. E. 1978. Stochastic Implications of the Life Cycle-Permanent Income Hypothesis: Theory and Evidence. *Journal of Political Economy* 85(6): 971–987.

Hall, R. E., and F. S. Mishkin. 1982. The Sensitivity of Consumption to Transitory Income: Estimates from Panel Data on Household. *Econometrica* 50(2): 461–481.

Hausmann, R., J. Hwang, and D. Rodrik. 2007. What You Export Matters. *Journal of Economic Growth* 12: 1–25.

Helpman, E., and G. M. Grossman. 1991. *Innovation and Growth in the Global Economy*. Cambridge, MA: The MIT Press.

Herrendorf, B., R. Rogerson, and A. Valentinyi. 2013. *Growth and Structural Transformation*. Handbook of Economic Growth.

Herrendorf, B., and A. Valentinyi. 2006. On the Stability of the Two-Sector Neoclassical Growth Model with Externalities. *Journal of Economic Dynamics and Control*, 30(8): 1339–1361.

Imbs, J., and R. Wacziarg. 2003. Stages of Diversification. *American Economic Review* 93(1): 63–86.

Jones, B. F., and B. A. Olken. 2005. Do Leaders Matter? National Leadership and Growth Since World War II. *The Quarterly Journal of Economics* 120(3): 835–864.

Jovanovic, B., and P. L. Rousseau. 2002. Moore's Law and Learning by Doing. *Review of Economic Dynamics* 5: 346–375.

Ju, J., J. Y. Lin, and Y. Wang. 2015. Endowment Structures, Industrial Dynamics, and Economic Growth. *Journal of Monetary Economics* 76: 244–263.

Kaldor, N. 1957. A Model of Economic Growth. *Economic Journal* 67(268): 591–624.

Kose, M. A., E. Prasad, K. Rogoff, and S.-J. Wei. 2009. Financial Globalization: A Reappraisal. *IMF Staff Papers* 56: 8–62.

Kuznets, S. 1957. Quantitative Aspects of the Economic Growth of Nations: II. Industrial Distribution of National Product and Labor Force. *Economic Development and Cultural Change* 5(4): 1–111.

Lall, S., and F. Stewart. 1996. Trade and Industrial Policy in Africa. *Development* 2: 64–67.

Lavopa, A., and A. Szirmai. 2014. *Structural Modernization and Development Traps: An Empirical Approach*. UNU–MERIT Working Papers ISSN 1871–9872. Maastricht, The Netherlands: The United Nations University–Maastricht Economic and Social Research Institute on Innovation and Technology.

Lavopa, A. M. 2015. Structural Transformation and Economic Development. Can Development Traps be Avoided? Maastricht University Doctoral Thesis.

Lee, K. Y. 2005. India in an Asian Renaissance. Keynote Speech by Minister
    Mentor Lee Kuan Yew at the Official Opening of the Lee Kuan Yew
    School of Public Policy. Singapore, Shangri-La Hotel, 4 April 2005.
    Singapore Government Press Release. http://www.nas.gov.sg/
    archivesonline/speeches/view-html?filename=2005112101.htm.

Lee, J.-W., and W. J. McKibbin. 2014. Service Sector Productivity and
    Economic Growth in Asia. ADBI Working Paper 490. Tokyo:
    Asian Development Bank Institute.

Loko, B., and M. A. Diouf. 2009. Revisiting the Determinants of Productivity
    Growth: What's New? IMF Working Paper 09/225. Washington, DC:
    International Monetary Fund.

Maroto-Sánchez, A., and J. R. Cuadrado-Roura. 2009. Is Growth of Services
    an Obstacle to Productivity Growth? A Comparative Analysis.
    Structural Change and Economic Dynamics 20: 254–265.

Mishel, L. R. 1989. The Late Great Debate on Deindustrialization. Challenge
    32(1): 35–43.

Modigliani, F. 1966. The Life Cycle Hypothesis of Saving, the Demand for
    Wealth and the Supply of Capital. Social Research 33(2): 160–217.

Naudé, W., and A. Szirmai. 2012. The Importance of Manufacturing in
    Economic Development: Past, Present and Future Perspectives.
    UNU–MERIT Working Papers ISSN 1871-9872. Maastricht,
    The Netherlands: The United Nations University–Maastricht Economic
    and Social Research Institute on Innovation and Technology.

Nickell, S. 1981. Biases in Dynamic Models with Fixed Effects. Econometrica
    49: 1417–1426.

Palma, J. G. 2005. Four Sources of Deindustrialization and a New Concept of the
    Dutch Disease: Stanford, CA: Stanford University Press.

Park, S.-H., and K. S. Chan. 1989. A Cross-Country Input–Output Analysis
    of Intersectoral Relationships between Manufacturing and Services and
    their Employment Implications. World Development 17(2): 199–212.

Pellegrini, G. 2007. The Baumol Gap Revisited. An Econometric Analysis
    of the Productivity Differential between U. K. Manufacturing and
    Service Firms, 1982–1999. Labor 7(2): 143–157.

Pesaran, M. H., and R. Smith. 1995. Estimating Long-Run Relationships from
    Dynamic Heterogeneous Panels. Journal of Econometrics 68(1): 79–113.

Phelps, E. S. 1962. The New View of Investment: A Neoclassical Analysis. *The Quarterly Journal of Economics* 76(4): 548–567.

Prasad, E. S., R. G. Rajan, and A. Subramanian. 2007. Foreign Capital and Economic Growth. *Brookings Papers on Economic Activity* 1: 153–230.

Pugno, M. 2006. The Service Paradox and Endogenous Economic Growth. *Structural Change and Economic Dynamics* 17: 99–115.

Rodrik, D. 2013. Unconditional Convergence in Manufacturing. *The Quarterly Journal of Economics* 128(1): 165–204.

———. 2016. Premature Deindustrialization. *Journal of Economic Growth* 21(1): 1–33.

Romer, P. M. 1986. Increasing Returns and Long-Run Growth. *Journal of Political Economy* 94(5): 1002–1037.

Rowthorn, R., and K. Coutts. 2004. De-industrialisation and the Balance of Payments in Advanced Economies. *Cambridge Journal of Economics* 28(5): 767–790.

Rowthorn, R., and R. Ramaswamy. 1999. Growth, Trade, and Deindustrialization. *IMF Staff Papers* 46(1): 18–41.

Rowthorn, R. E. 1987. *De-Industrialization Foreign Trade*: Cambridge, United Kingdom: Cambridge University Press.

Su, D., and Y. Yao. 2016. Manufacturing as the Key Engine of Economic Growth for Middle-Income Economies. ADBI Working Paper 573. Tokyo: Asian Development Bank Institute.

Szirmai, A. 2012. Industrialisation as an Engine of Growth in Developing Countries, 1950–2005. *Structural Change and Economic Dynamics 23*: 406–420.

Szirmai, A., and B. Verspagen. 2015. Manufacturing and Economic Growth in Developing Countries, 1950–2005. *Structural Change and Economic Dynamics* 34: 46–59.

Tregenna, F. 2009. Characterising Deindustrialisation: An Analysis of Changes in Manufacturing Employment and Output Internationally. *Cambridge Journal of Economics* 33: 433–466.

Zhang, J. S. 2011. The Analytical Solution of Balanced Growth of Non-linear Dynamic Multi-sector Economic Model. *Economic Modelling* 28: 410–421.

CHAPTER 6

Service Sector Growth and the Middle-Income Trap: The Case of the People's Republic of China

Yanrui Wu

6.1 | Introduction

Unprecedentedly high economic growth for several decades has earned the People's Republic of China (PRC) upper-middle-income status with per capita gross domestic product (GDP) exceeding $8,000 in 2016. However, this growth has been largely driven by capital accumulation and the expansion of export-oriented manufacturing (World Bank 2013). With the rising cost of labor and the continuing appreciation of the yuan, the PRC economy is at a crossroads, heading to a new path of growth. In particular, services have been identified as the key source of growth, as echoed in a keynote speech by the PRC's Premier Li Keqiang.[1] What role has the service sector played in the PRC's growth process? Will service growth help the PRC economy avoid the so-called middle-income trap and hence join the high-income country club in the coming years? These are some of the questions we explore in this chapter.

Studies of the PRC's service industry have been constrained by a lack of and inaccurate information. For a long time, PRC firms have played the role of multiple agencies. They are not only producers but also providers of services to their employees and their family members. Apart from productive activities,

---

[1] "Making the Service Sector the New Engine for Sustainable Economic and Social Development," Keynote speech at the 2nd China Beijing International Fair for Trade in Services and the Global Services Forum Beijing Summit, 29 May 2013.

for example, PRC firms under the old centrally planned economic system had to build and manage hospitals, schools, grocery shops, and so on. This has made it complicated to account for services in the PRC economy. During the pre-reform era, the PRC's system of national accounts followed Soviet practice. Large segments of the service sector such as services provided by firms were classified as "nonproductive" activities and hence excluded from the official service sector statistics. Though the situation has changed considerably since the introduction of economic reforms, the official statistical system is still subjected to the influence of the practice under the old regime. Over time, the PRC government has made major efforts to improve data collection and standardize the country's system of national accounts. For example, the first census of the service sector was conducted during 1991–1992 (NTICO 1995). This was followed by two nationwide economic censuses conducted in 2004 and 2008, respectively (NECO 2006, 2010). As a result, periodic revisions of the PRC's national accounts have been released. In particular, the service sector value added was revised upward by 16.8% following the country's first-ever national economic census in 2004. Some scholars argued that there are still errors in the official statistics (Xu and Ljungwall 2008; Zhang and Zhu 2015). While efforts have been made to check the sources and consistency of data used in this study, the correction of official statistics through rigorous exercises is beyond the scope of this study.[2] Readers should bear in mind this caveat when the conclusions of this chapter are interpreted.

The rest of the chapter begins with an investigation of the role of services in the PRC economy in Section 6.2. This is followed by a discussion of trade and foreign investment in the service industry in the PRC (Section 6.3). Section 6.4 examines the PRC's service economies from an international perspective. Subsequently, service sector growth and its implications for the PRC's avoidance of the middle-income trap are explored in Section 6.5. The final section concludes the chapter.

---

[2] For more general discussion about the quality of the PRC statistics, readers may refer to Wu (2000), Rawski (2001), and Holz (2014).

6.2 | The Role of Services in the PRC Economy

Since the launch of the economic reform program in 1978, the PRC has
undergone rapid industrialization. A casual traveler to the PRC can easily
observe the transformation of the PRC's society and the economy as a result
of recent industrialization. What is less visible is the equally rapid growth of the
country's service sector. Figure 6.1 shows the evolution of output shares in the
economy's three sectors—agriculture, industry, and services. The industrial
sector consists of manufacturing, construction, and utilities which together
account for about 40%–50% of the PRC's GDP. Starting at a low base, services
in the PRC surpassed agriculture in 1985 and overtook the industrial sector
in 2013. According to the latest statistics, the PRC's GDP grew by 6.7%
while services achieved a growth rate of 7.8% in 2016 (NBS 2017).

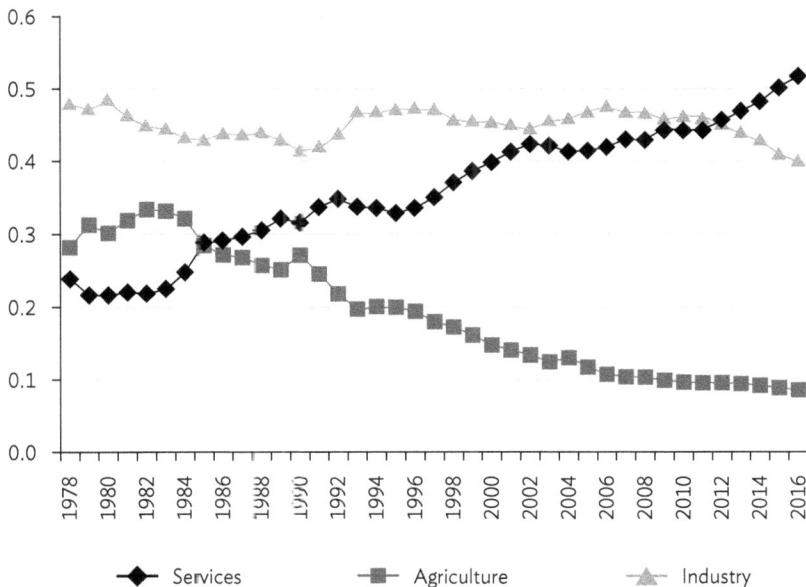

Figure 6.1: **GDP Shares in Three Sectors, 1978–2016 (Current Prices)**

GDP = gross domestic product.
Note: The values on the y-axis are ratios of sectoral GDP shares.
Source: Author's own calculation using data from National Bureau of Statistics (various years, 2017).

Figure 6.2: GDP Shares in Three Sectors, 1978–2016
(2010 Constant Prices)

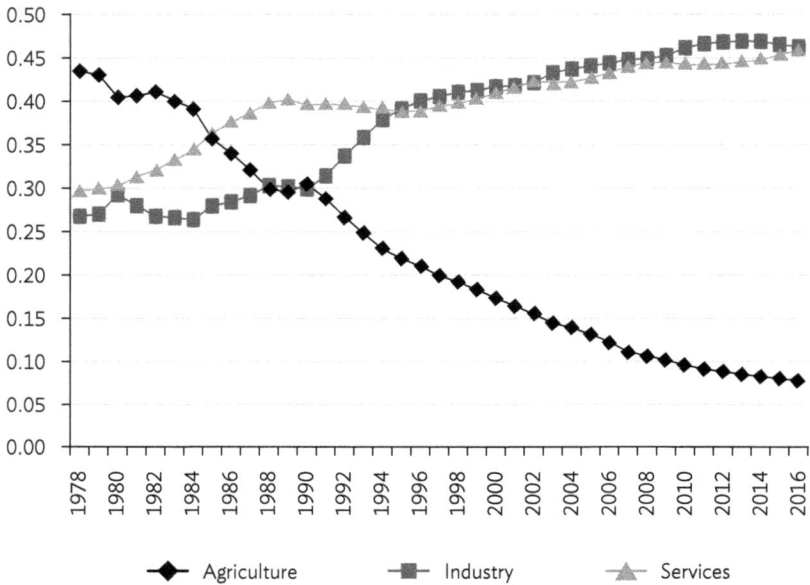

GDP = gross domestic product.

Note: The values on the y-axis are ratios of sectoral GDP shares.

Source: Author's own calculation using data from National Bureau of Statistics (various years, 2017).

Services accounted for 51.6% of the PRC's GDP in 2016. One may argue that service sector shares are inflated due to variations in price changes across the three sectors (Naughton 2016). This is true to some extent, as illustrated in Figure 6.2, where GDP shares are calculated at constant prices. However, the constant GDP shares imply that 53.3% of the PRC's incremental GDP in 2016 was generated by services (Figure 6.3). There is no doubt that the service sector is now the main source of growth in the PRC economy.

In terms of sectoral employment in recent decades, agriculture has seen a net outflow of labor to both the industrial sector and the service sector, though the agricultural employment share maintained its dominant position for about 2 decades (1991–2010) (Figure 6.4).

Figure 6.3: Incremental GDP Shares in Three Sectors, 1978–2016 (2010 Constant Prices)

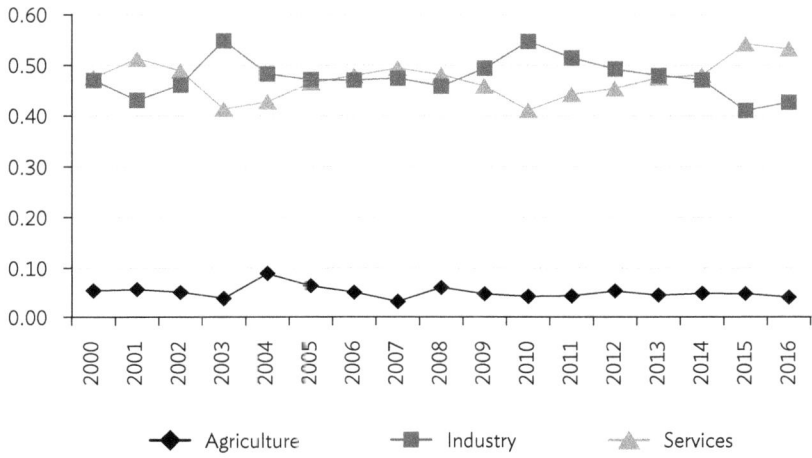

GDP = gross domestic product.

Note: The values on the y-axis are ratios of sectoral GDP shares.

Source: Author's own calculation using data from National Bureau of Statistics (various years, 2017).

Figure 6.4: Employment Shares by Sector, 1991–2015

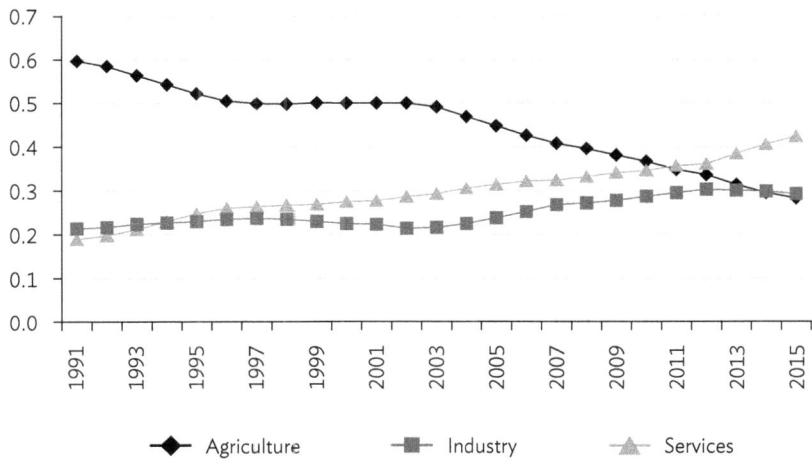

Note: The values on the y-axis are ratios of sectoral employment over the PRC's total employment.

Source: Author's own calculation using data from National Bureau of Statistics (various years).

Its recent peak was recorded in 2002 with an employment share of about 50% or 366 million employees. But these numbers are debatable. It is argued that agricultural employment may be substantially overestimated due to the existence of "phantom farmers" who live in rural areas and may actually be working in services (Rawski and Mead 1998; Cai 2004; Ghose 2005). If so, service sector employment may be underestimated. According to Figure 6.4, the industrial and service sectors have maintained steady growth in employment over time. Services overtook the industrial sector in 1994 and the agricultural sector in 2011. In 2014, the agricultural sector employment share (29.5%) fell below behind that of the industrial sector (29.9%) for the first time.

In 2013, for the first time, the PRC's industrial sector recorded negative growth of labor. Thus, the peak point for the PRC's industrial employment was reached in 2012 with a share of about 30%. This share is smaller, however, than the similar peak share of 36% observed in the Republic of Korea in 1991 (Park and Shin 2012). Services are now the only places in the PRC where net job growth is positive. This should continue to be the case for a long time as it is determined by the increasing demand for services in the economy (Ding and Xu 2015). It is also due to the difference in labor productivity between the three economic sectors (Figure 6.5). It is apparent that, due to higher labor productivity, the industrial and service sectors are still attractive to rural migrant workers. Thus, part of the employment growth in services is efficiency driven as rural migrant workers move from the low-efficiency farming sector to high-productivity services (Qin 2006). However, after continuous growth for over 3 decades, demand for labor in manufacturing is slowing if not stagnant. As a result, services have become the main receiving sector of rural migrant workers even though its labor productivity lags behind the industrial sector. In this sense, employment growth in services is also partly demand driven. This phenomenon has been widely discussed in the literature on the development of more advanced economies, where service employment grew fast even though manufacturing labor productivity was higher than service productivity (Baumol 1967; Fuchs 1968).

Figure 6.5: Labor Productivity in the PRC Economy, 1991–2015

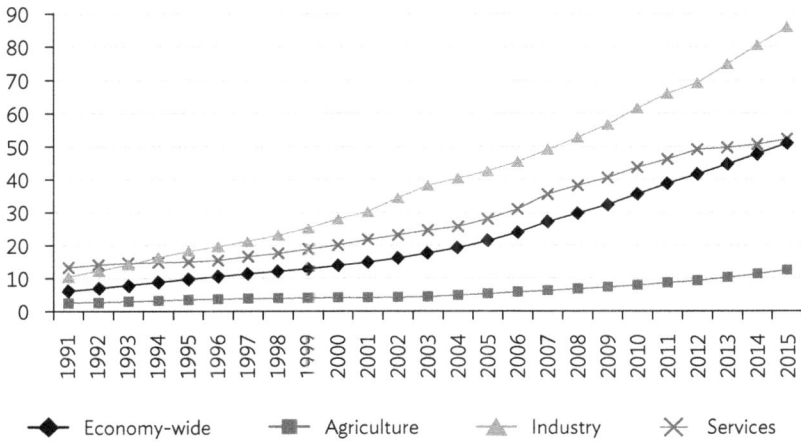

Note: The unit on the y-axis is CNY1,000 per head expressed in 2000 constant prices.

Source: Author's own calculation using data from National Bureau of Statistics (various issues).

There is, however, considerable variation across the regions in the PRC. The share of services over gross regional product (GRP) in 2015 ranged from the lowest of 38.8% in Guangxi and Jilin to the highest of 79.7% in Beijing (NBS, various issues). One possible explanation for the existence of regional disparity in services may be the spatial concentration of certain service activities such as finance, insurance, and real estate (Wang 2013). Mattoo (2003) argued that initial restrictions on the geographic scope of service liberalization after the PRC's accession to the World Trade Organization (WTO) might also encourage the agglomeration of economic activities in certain regions. These activities could be mainly related to new or modern services such as information, finance, and insurance services, which are tradable and more capital intensive.[3]

---

[3] In this chapter, services are classified into old or traditional services (social and personal services, hotels and restaurants, wholesale and retail, transport, education, health, and government services) and new or modern services (financial intermediation, information, and professional business services). It should be noted that this classification is not unique. For example, some authors put transport in the new service category (Ghani and O'Connell 2014) or transport, education, and health services in a third group (Eichengreen and Gupta 2013).

These services have also become the world's fastest growing component of international trade (Cattaneo et al. 2010). Thus, service sector development cannot be isolated from the highly globalized environment. Globalization also makes services and manufacturing become more and more interrelated (Rodriguez and Melikhova 2015; Yusuf 2015). As the PRC's manufacturing activities are concentrated in the more developed coastal areas, those areas are expected to attract more service activities.

In the PRC, two city economies, namely Beijing and Shanghai, and two small provinces, Hainan and Tibet Autonomous Region, have relatively more developed service sectors. Beijing (with a service sector GDP share of 79.7%) is unique because it is the nation's capital city and hosts numerous company headquarters, many top universities, and research centers in the PRC, and foreign embassies. Beijing's service sector share was also boosted by the relocation of Beijing's manufacturing activities to neighboring provinces, in particular before and after the Olympic Games of 2008. Shanghai's service sector share of 67.8% in 2015 is probably more representative of the PRC's cities. For example, Shenzhen's service sector share was 58.8% in 2015, which is not far behind Shanghai's.[4] Moreover, both Shanghai and Shenzhen have their own ports, which help them to maintain a sizable sector of manufacturing activities in their outskirts. Beijing is not a port city and its manufacturing sector is disappearing gradually. In addition, the PRC's city economies such as Beijing and Shanghai have no farming sector and hence have a relatively large service sector compared with other regional economies in the country. Hainan and Tibet Autonomous Region have a service share over 53% because these two regions are popular tourist destinations with very little manufacturing activity. It is interesting to observe that Tianjin, a city economy, has a service sector (GDP share: 52.2%), which is smaller than those in Shanghai and Beijing. One possible explanation is the geographic location of Tianjin, which is a port city and also the gateway to Beijing. Some of Beijing's manufacturing activities have been relocated

---

4   Shenzhen is a special economic zone and part of Guangdong province in terms of administrative governance.

to Tianjin recently. As a result, Tianjin has a relatively larger manufacturing sector than Beijing and Shanghai. Overall, most regions in the PRC have an underdeveloped service sector with a relatively small value-added share over GRP.

Over time, regional disparity seems to have increased. The standard deviation of regional shares of service sector value added over GRP increased from 3.55% in 1991 to 9.29% in 2013 and then fell to 8.79% in 2015 (Figure 6.6). However, if the three municipalities (Beijing, Shanghai, and Tianjin) are excluded from the sample, regional disparity has hardly changed for over 2 decades. The employment statistics show the same story. Thus, the three cities should be treated differently. In many existing studies, this factor has not been taken into account, which may lead to the conclusion of regional divergence in the PRC's service development or simply biased findings (Wang 2013; Ding and Xu 2015). Therefore, if the three city economies are excluded, there is no evidence of convergence or divergence in terms of service sector development across the regions in the PRC.

Figure 6.6: Standard Deviation of Regional Service Sector Value-Added Shares

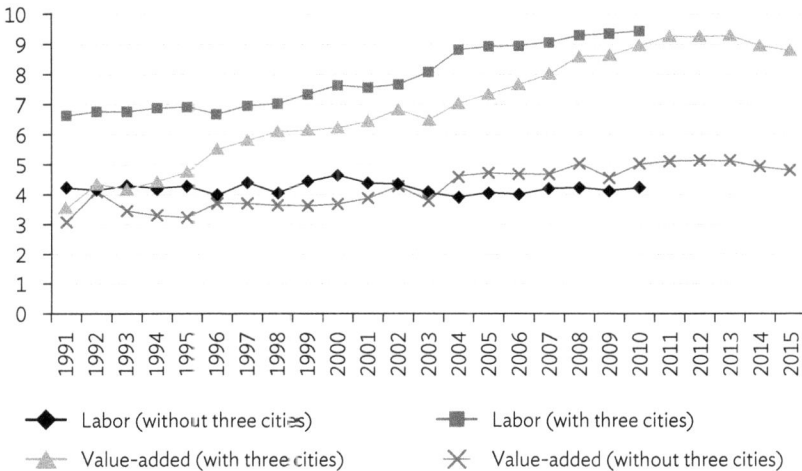

Source: Author.

6.3 | Trade and Foreign Investment in the PRC's Service Sector

The PRC's trade in services has followed the same trend of changes as merchandise trade (Figure 6.7). In particular, trade in services expanded dramatically from 2005 to 2015. A major trigger was probably the country's full commitment to WTO rules starting in 2006. The PRC became a WTO member in 2001 and after a 5-year period of transition, the PRC's commitment to the WTO was fully implemented in 2006. Since then, trade in services has grown faster than merchandise trade. In recent years, the PRC's imports of services in particular have seen very rapid growth.

Figure 6.7: Indexes of the People's Republic of China's Goods and Services Trade, 2005–2015

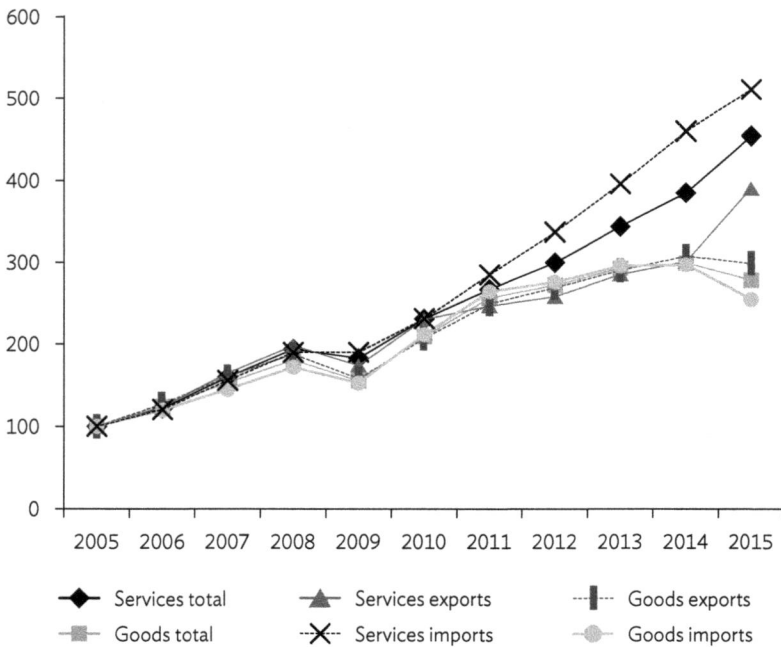

Note: The value of trade in 2005 was set to 100.

Source: Author's own estimates.

Several factors may explain this drastic change. First, the PRC's "approved destination status" policy has been quite successful at encouraging its citizens to travel overseas for leisure (Arita, la Croix, and Mak 2014). Second, the relaxation of foreign exchange controls has made it easy and popular for the PRC youth to study overseas. Students are the largest foreign student group in many developed countries such as the United States (US), Australia, and the United Kingdom. Finally, the PRC's policy of "go global" directed at the PRC's entrepreneurs and multinationals has triggered a wave of overseas mergers and acquisitions as well as investment by domestic firms. As a result, travel and transportation amounted to over 70% of the PRC's service imports in 2015 (NBS various issues).

As the world's largest merchandise exporter, the PRC was ranked only fifth in the world in terms of service export share (3.6%) behind the US (12.3%), the United Kingdom (5.7%), Germany (5.2%), and France (4.2%).[5] The country's service exports are comirated in turn by "other business," "travel," and "transport" services, which together accounted for about 82% of total service exports, as can be seen in Table 6.1.[6] Overall, the PRC is less competitive than India in computer and information services. In terms of financial services and royalties and license fees, the PRC is still far behind the US. These findings confirm that the PRC's comparative advantages lie in relatively low-end services, which are less knowledge and capital intensive (Tang, Zhang, and Findlay 2013). In contrast to merchandise trade, the PRC's service trade has been in deficit for nearly 2 decades, with a record deficit of about $160 billion in 2014 (NBS various issues). Though trade in services has grown rapidly, its share in total trade (both goods and services) has changed very little, moving from the peak level of 13.8% in 1997 to a trough of 9.8% in 2006 and to a new peak of 15.3% in 2015. These figures are well below the world average of about 20% (Chen and Whalley 2014).

---

5   These are based on 2012 service trade statistics reported by the United Nations (2015).
6   Tradable services are divided into 11 categories by the United Nations (2015). The ninth group, "other business" services, is further divided into three sub-categories—merchandise trade and other trade-related services (9.1), operational leasing services (9.2); and miscellaneous business, professional, and technical services (9.3).

Table 6.1: Service Export Shares (%) by Categories, 2013

Categories	PRC	India	Russian Federation	US
1. Transportation	18.3	11.5	31.2	13.0
2. Travel	25.1	12.5	18.2	25.8
3. Communications	0.8	1.5	2.6	2.1
4. Construction	5.2	0.8	8.9	0.4
5. Insurance	1.9	1.5	0.8	2.4
6. Financial	1.5	4.3	2.6	12.5
7. Computer and information	7.5	46.9	4.0	2.9
8. Royalties and license fees	0.4	0.3	1.1	19.2
9. Other business services	38.6	19.4	28.0	17.9
10. Personal, cultural, and recreational	0.1	0.8	1.2	0.1
11. Government, n.i.e.	0.6	0.3	1.5	3.7
World Service Export Share	3.6	2.7	1.1	12.3

n.i.e. = not identified elsewhere, PRC = People's Republic of China, US = United States.

Notes: The shares are calculated by drawing data from the service trade database of the United Nations (2015), which classifies tradable services into 11 categories as listed here. The "world service export share" is based on 2012 data as there are too many missing values in the 2013 database.

Source: Author's own estimates.

Apart from international trade, the PRC's service sector has also attracted considerable amounts of foreign investment. The amount of actually utilized foreign direct investment (FDI) in services increased from about $15 billion in 2005 to $81 billion in 2015 (NBS, various years and 2017). This is equivalent to an annual growth rate of about 19%. An important factor underlying this growth was the PRC's accession to the WTO in 2001 and its full commitment to the WTO agreement in 2006. The impact of WTO membership on FDI is evident in the changing shares of investment across the three economic sectors (Figure 6.8). In 2005, about 73.5% of the PRC's FDI was invested in the industrial sector. In 2011, services overtook the industrial sector and had the largest FDI share of the three sectors. By 2015, the service sector share

Figure 6.8: Sectoral Composition of Foreign Direct Investment in the People's Republic of China, 2005–2015 (%)

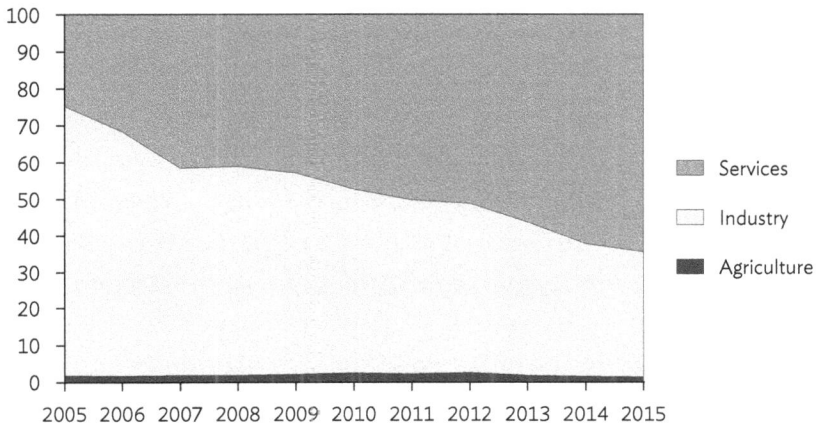

Source: Author's own estimates using data from National Bureau of Statistics (various years).

of the PRC's FDI had reached 64.4%. The leading areas include real estate ($29 billion), finance ($15 billion), retail and wholesale ($12 billion), leasing and business services ($10 billion), and transport ($4 billion) (NBS 2016). Scholars have criticized the dominance of FDI in the real estate sector and hence suggested further reforms to remove barriers to foreign providers and encourage diversification of investment (Yin 2011). In particular, there is relatively little foreign investment in new services.

In recent years, the PRC's service providers have also been actively engaged in offshore activities. Contrary to popular perception, the PRC's outward direct investment (ODI) is dominated by investment in services rather than mining (Table 6.2). Though the service sector share tends to fluctuate over time, it accounted for about 73% of the PRC's ODI in 2015. The leading sectors include leasing and business services, financial intermediation, and wholesale and retail trade. Interestingly, there has been a rising trend in the combined ODI shares of leasing and business services and financial intermediation which fall into the category of new services.

Table 6.2: The PRC's Offshore Direct Investment by Sector, 2007–2015

Sectors	2007	2008	2009	2010	2011	2012	2013	2014	2015
Total ODI ($ billion)	26.5	55.9	56.5	68.8	74.7	87.8	107.8	123.1	145.7
Sectoral shares (%)									
Agriculture	1.0	0.3	0.6	0.8	1.1	1.7	1.7	1.7	1.8
Mining	15.3	10.4	23.6	8.3	19.4	15.4	23.0	13.4	7.8
Industry	9.8	6.8	5.4	10.6	14.2	15.8	11.4	12.0	17.8
Services	73.8	82.5	70.4	80.3	65.4	67.1	64.0	72.9	72.7
Leasing and business services	21.2	38.8	36.2	44.0	34.3	30.5	25.1	29.9	24.8
Financial intermediation	6.3	25.1	15.5	12.5	8.1	11.5	14.0	12.9	16.6
Wholesale and retail trades	24.9	11.7	10.9	9.8	13.8	14.9	13.6	14.9	13.2
Real estate	3.4	0.6	1.7	2.3	2.6	2.3	3.7	5.4	1.9
Transport, storage, and post	15.3	4.8	3.7	8.2	3.4	3.4	3.1	3.4	5.4
Other services	2.7	1.5	2.5	3.4	3.1	4.7	4.6	6.5	10.8

ODI = offshore direct investment, PRC = People's Republic of China.

Source: Author's own estimates using data from National Bureau of Statistics (various years).

Accordingly, investment in traditional services such as wholesale and retail trade and transport has fallen. This trend reflects the tradability of new services. It may also echo the underdevelopment of new services in the PRC and hence providers in the PRC look for potential spillover effects of ODI projects into domestic services. Empirical research shows that the determinants of foreign investment in services are similar to those in manufacturing (Ramasamy and Yeung 2010; Yin, Ye, and Xu 2014). Thus, PRC service ODI may also have the client-following and market-seeking characteristics. Some service ODI is simply following the PRC's exporters and investors overseas. Other ODI may be just market-seeking, particularly in regions with ethnic communities. However, understanding the PRC's ODI is complicated due to the role of Hong Kong, China. In 2015, $89.8 billion of the PRC's total ODI (of $145.7 billion) was invested in Hong Kong, China, which nowadays produces nothing but services (NBS, various issues). Thus, the bulk of the PRC's service ODI is probably invested in the provision of services for the PRC economy. Then the PRC's ODI net of investment in Hong Kong, China is dominated by investment in mining and manufacturing. This is consistent with the PRC's comparative advantage in manufacturing rather than services, especially new services.

6.4 | The PRC's Service Sector in International Perspective

From an international perspective, it is well known that the PRC's service sector is underdeveloped compared with economies at a similar stage of development (Wu 2007; Rutkowski 2015). This is also confirmed by the latest data from the World Bank (2015). Figure 6.9 presents service sector value-added shares over GDP against per capita GDP (in international dollars) for selected economies. It is clear that the PRC is an outlier among the economies with income per capita within the range of $3,000–$20,000 at purchasing power parity (PPP) in 2013. The PRC falls well below the global trend line in Figure 6.8. Thus, there is great scope for the expansion of services in the economy. The PRC's policy makers have realized their neglect of services and have recently adopted economic policies to rebalance the country's economy and to exploit the potential of services as the new engine of growth. It has been argued that further reforms to boost services growth should cover the domestic financial market, the exchange rate regime, and the social security and health care systems (Ozyurt 2013). Nabar and Yan (2013) reckoned that credit and labor market frictions have impeded productivity growth in the PRC's service sector. Thus, reducing these frictions is essential for the transformation of the growth model of the economy.

Figure 6.9: Service Sector GDP Shares in 2013

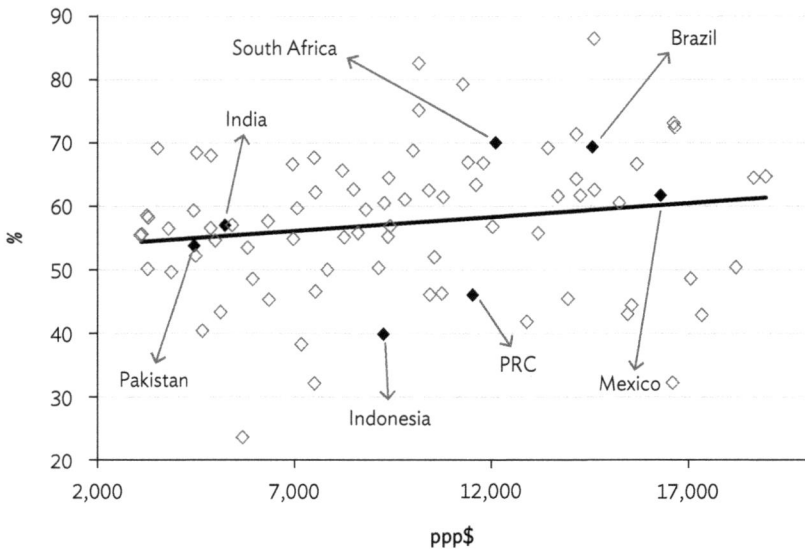

GDP = gross domestic product, ppp = purchasing power parity, PRC = People's Republic of China.
Source: Author's own work based on World Bank (2015).

At the sub-sector level, the PRC's service sector GDP is dominated by finance and insurance, wholesale and retail trades, real estate, and transport services (Table 6.3). The last three groups belong to the category of traditional services. In comparison with the US, the PRC's new service development is lagging behind (Table 6.3). In particular, the PRC's professional and business services are relatively small. New services are internationally tradable goods and hence are vital for service innovation and improvement in competitiveness and efficiency. The underdevelopment of the PRC's new services is also reflected in international trade. Ghani (2011) and Mukherjee (2015) discussed the contrasting development of information technology (IT) and IT-enabled service exports in the PRC and India. India has performed far better than the PRC, as shown in Table 6.1. In addition, the PRC's health, government, and social services are also lagging behind the developed world's.

Table 6.3: Composition of Services in the PRC, India, the Russian Federation, and the United States (%)

Subsectors	PRC	India	Russian Federation	US
New Services				
Finance and insurance	17.1	13.7	8.2	21.7
Information	4.7	11.8		5.0
Professional and business services	3.6	2.3		12.9
Subtotal	*25.4*	*27.8*	*8.2*	*39.6*
Old Services				
Accommodation and food services	4.5	2.5	1.7	3.0
Arts, entertainment, and recreation	1.5	0.8		1.1
Educational services	7.0	6.9	5.0	1.2
Government	9.7	10.5	11.2	14.8
Health care and social assistance	3.9	2.6	6.3	7.8
Real estate and rental and leasing	12.7	8.3	20.1[a]	14.1
Transportation and warehousing	10.6	11.4	14.2[b]	3.1
Wholesale and retail trades	21.3	26.0	30.5	12.8
Other services	3.5	3.2	2.7	2.4
Subtotal	*74.6*	*72.2*	*91.8*	*60.4*

PRC = People's Republic of China, US = United States.

[a] Including business services.

[b] Including "communications" services

Notes: Efforts were made to check the consistency of service data across countries. There is no doubt that further work can be done to improve service sector data collection in the world economies. The value-added shares are estimated by using statistics of the Russian Federation in 2013 (MED 2015), the PRC and the US in 2012 (NBS various issues; BEA 2015), and India in 2010 (Pais 2014).

Source: Author's own work.

A consequence of economic growth and rising income in a society is rapid urbanization (Noland, Park, and Estrada 2012). In the PRC, the process of urbanization has been slow due to the notorious household registration (*hukou*) system. However, service sector development has been even slower than the pace of urbanization. Figure 6.10 illustrates service sector GDP shares against urbanization in 85 countries with per capita GDP within the range of $3,000–$20,000 at PPP in 2013, including the PRC with per capita GDP of $11,525 at PPP (World Bank 2015). For a comparison, data for the PRC's 31 administrative regions are also plotted in the same chart. It is apparent that, with the exception of Beijing, Shanghai, and Tibet Autonomous Region, the PRC's regions are outliers which are located well below the trend line in Figure 6.10. The chart also shows that Beijing as the country's capital city has outperformed the world's average economies in terms of service sector development. Shanghai has just achieved the average performance. Tibet Autonomous Region is the third region with an average performance due to its low level of urbanization and an almost nonexistence of manufacturing activities. Thus, to catch up with the global trend, there is ample scope for service growth in the PRC, which is now in the process of rapid urbanization.

Figure 6.10: Service Sector GDP Shares versus Urbanization in 2013

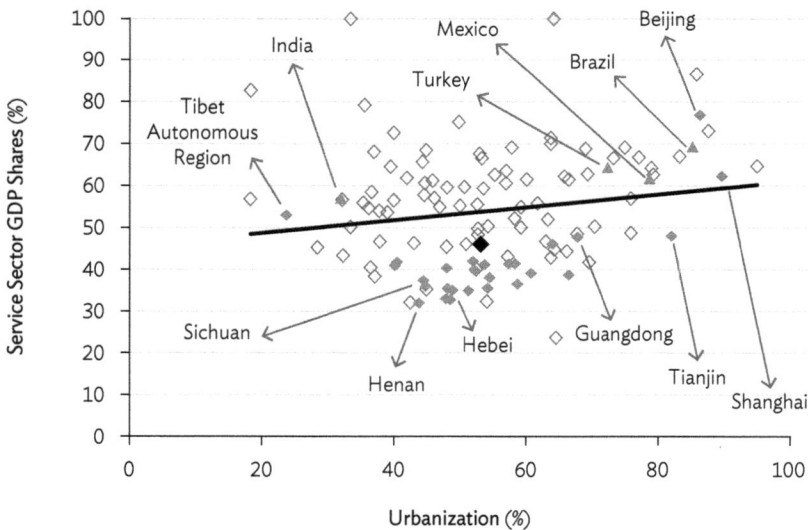

GDP = gross domestic product.

Note: The blank diamonds represent 85 countries with per capita income within the range of $3,000–$20,000 (PPP) in 2013 including the PRC. The solid diamonds represent regional economies.

Source: Author's own estimates using data from the World Bank (2015) and National Bureau of Statistics (various issues).

According to the World Bank (2013), by 2030, the PRC's urban residents would account for about two-thirds of the country's population. That means about 13 million additional urbanites in the PRC's cities each year. The new arrivals will lead to more demand for urban services, which will become an important source of service growth. Japan went through the same trajectory in the 1960s and 1970s (Wu 2016). In addition to demand factors, the PRC's service growth will also be productivity driven. Empirical evidence has shown that total factor productivity growth is more important in the service sector than that in the manufacturing sector (Wu 2015).

6.5 | Middle-Income Trap: Will Services Help the PRC Weather the Storm?

The middle-income trap concept refers to economies that reached middle-income status and then failed to move on to the high-income stage due to a sharp growth slowdown or prolonged stagnation. Since its first appearance in a World Bank report published in 2007, the middle-income trap concept has been controversial and hence triggered a lively debate in academic as well as policy making circles (Gill and Kharas 2007; Felipe, Kumar, and Galope 2014; Wu 2014). In the empirical literature, researchers have not reached consensus about the precise definition of "middle income." Nor is the duration of "staying in the middle" clearly defined. What is clear is that there is a large gap in growth between the trapped economies and those that graduated (i.e., joined the high-income group). Figure 6.11 demonstrates the evolution of per capita income over time for selected economies that are now classical examples of trapped and graduated middle-income economies (with per capita GDP of around $3,000). One of the characteristics of the trapped middle-income economies is that they have not reached per capita income of $10,000 after several decades. During the same time period, the graduated economies first exceeded the per capita income level of $10,000 and then further bypassed the level of $20,000. Interestingly, three Asian graduates (Japan, the Republic of Korea, and Singapore) took a much shorter course than other graduated economies to reach their "rich" status. In the case of the PRC, two projected scenarios with average growth rates of 6.5% (the PRC–1) and 4.0% (the PRC–2), respectively, are presented in Figure 6.11. It can be seen that, in both cases, the PRC would be on course to follow major graduated economies in East Asia such as Japan and the Republic of Korea to become one of the high-income economies by the year 2050.

Figure 6.11: Evolution of GDP per Capita in Selected Economies

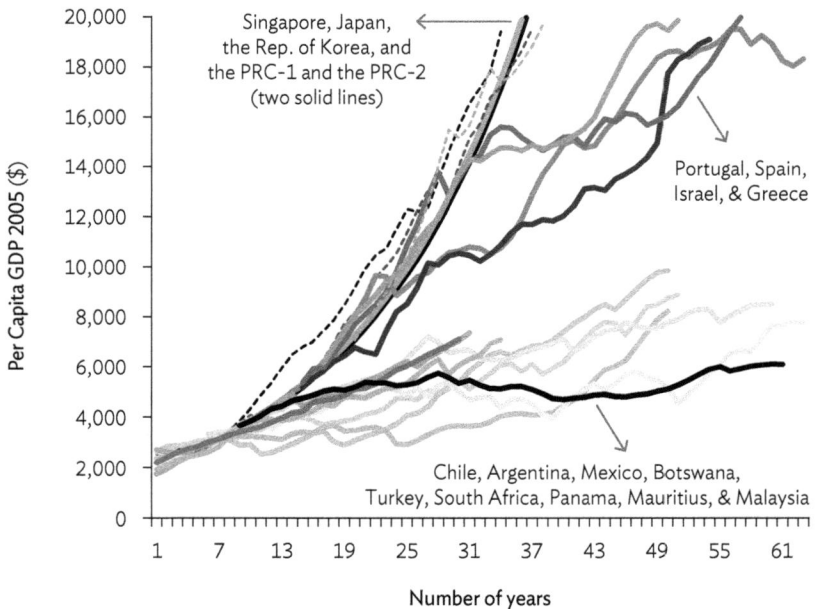

GDP = gross domestic product, PRC = People's Republic of China.
Note: The curves were drawn by using data from the World Bank (2015).
Source: Author's own estimates.

Have services played a role in helping economies escape from the middle-income trap? Figure 6.12 illustrates the growth trend of services in selected economies that are trapped in or graduated from the middle-income stage. At least four observations can be made. First, services grew steadily in graduated economies such as Japan, Portugal, and Spain.

Second, growth has been very volatile in some trapped economies, namely Argentina and Botswana. Third, the service sectors in some trapped economies started as a dominant economic sector. This may imply that the manufacturing sector was very small when these economies had just gained the status of middle-income economies. Examples include Chile, Mexico, and South Africa. Finally, the PRC has been a member of the middle-income economies group for about a decade. The country's service sector has been growing steadily. Its trajectory of growth seems to follow those of Japan and the Republic of Korea though it had a relatively low start. If this prediction is correct, it would be good news for the PRC.

Figure 6.12: **Evolution of Service Sector GDP Shares in Selected Economies**

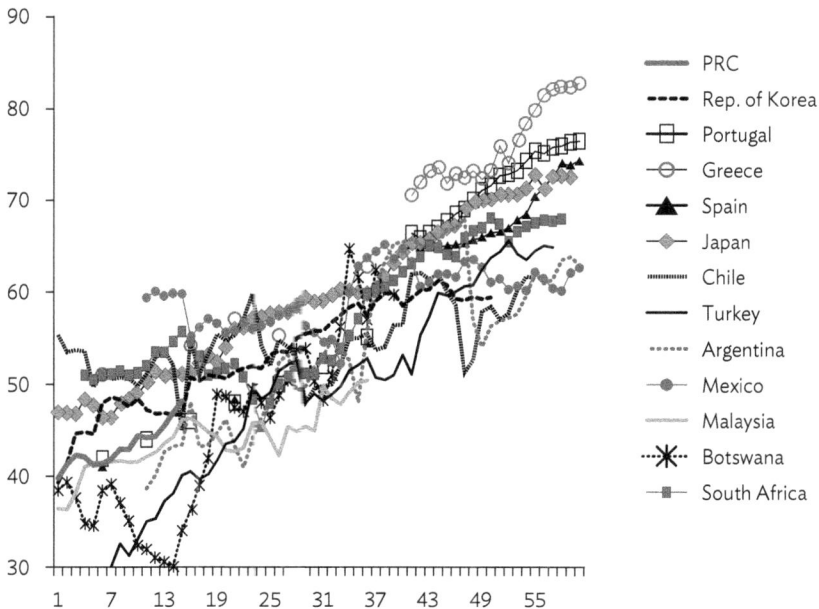

GDP = gross domestic product, PRC = People's Republic of China.

Note: The curves were drawn by using data from the World Bank (2015). All economies begin at the similar stage of development (middle-income status).

Source: Author's own work.

The pattern of service development can also be explained by using the concept of Eichengreen and Gupta (2013) who proposed a model of two-wave growth. The first wave occurs at the low- income stage and the second wave comes at the stage with relatively high per capita income or middle income. This explanation is also applicable to the service sector in the PRC. Recent growth in the PRC's services has gone through two waves. The first wave of service growth commenced immediately after the introduction of economic reforms, when rapid growth was recorded (Figure 6.13). The growth momentum in this period was partly due to the repression of services during the pre-reform period, which was gradually removed. The second wave of growth started after the PRC's commitments to WTO membership were fully implemented in 2006 and the country's GDP per capita was about $2,000. Many economies have gone through this process.

Figure 6.13: Two Waves of Service Growth in the PRC

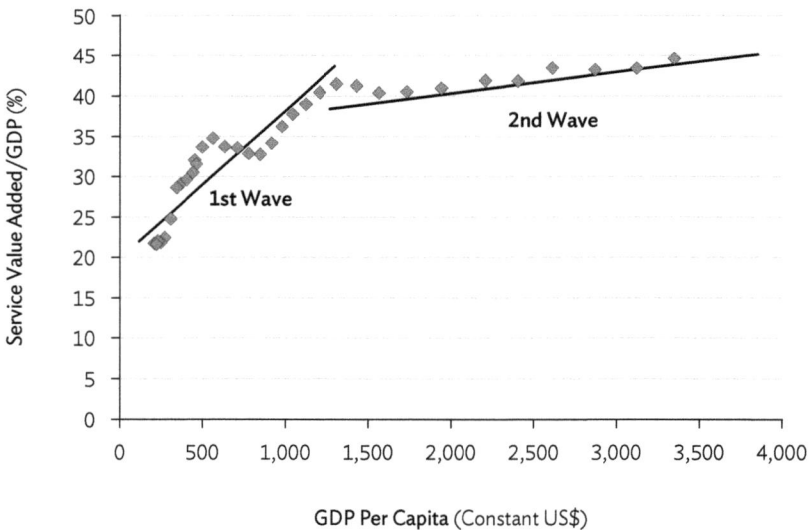

GDP = gross domestic product, PRC = People's Republic of China, US = United States.
Source: Author's own work using data from the World Bank (2015).

The duration of the second process could be very long and vary considerably between the economies. For example, it took 15 years for the service sector GDP share to increase from 40% to 50% in the Republic of Korea. The PRC's service sector has also been in this position for 15 years. In 2015, its GDP share exceeded 50% for the first time. However, this process lasted for 32 years in Malaysia, which may indicate the laggardness of structural transformation in these economies. The next level of service GDP share expansion from 50% to 60% lasts even longer. It lasted 23 years in Japan and 27 years in the Republic of Korea. If these are used as the criteria, the PRC's service development still has a long way to go. In short, the service sector has great potential for further growth and may help the economy avoid the middle-income trap.

In addition, the first wave of growth was led by traditional services. The second wave growth is still ongoing and mainly driven by new services, which are lagging behind, as discussed in Section 6.2. Apart from new services, there is also large growth potential associated with services in education, health, and social security in the PRC. Table 6.3 shows that these service subsectors amount to about 21% of total service value added or about 10% of the PRC's GDP in 2012. This figure is similar to what is recorded in Japan in the 1970s and in the Republic of Korea in the 1980s. By 2010, the combined share of these subsectors had doubled in Japan (Dorrucci, Pula, and Santabarbara 2013). The same can be expected to happen in the PRC as the country is actively introducing a universal social security system and promoting equal access to quality public services (World Bank 2013).

6.6 | Conclusion

The PRC's service sector has made substantial contributions to the country's productivity and GDP growth though it is underdeveloped compared with economies at a similar stage of development. As the PRC's economic growth path changes and the government adopts the right policies, the service sector in the country is well positioned to expand and modernize in the near future.

It will help rebalance the PRC's economy away from its heavy reliance on manufacturing and exporting. Services will therefore play an even more important role in the country's further economic growth and may help the economy escape the middle-income trap. To realize these goals, further economic reforms and competent government policies are needed.

International experience shows that trade in services may have a significant and positive effect on service productivity growth (Park and Shin 2012). The PRC's trade in services is expanding but still lagging behind the world's major economies. Further service liberalization would boost trade and make services more attractive to foreign investors. In particular, reforms should aim to remove barriers to trade and foreign investment in new services. Foreign participation would bring productivity gains in services and will be helpful, therefore, for general industrial transformation and upgrading. Moreover, even in traditional services such as transport, education, and health, further reforms would allow for easy entry and hence boost the role of private providers. These sectors are currently dominated by the state with an ownership share exceeding 70% (Rutkowski 2015). Greater private participation could improve efficiency and create more jobs.

The PRC's pace of urbanization has been hindered by the existence of the stringent *hukou* system. Though rural–urban mobility is less constrained nowadays, rural–urban divides still exist due to many other factors such as fragmented social security services provided by various governments and their agencies. Reforms to introduce a portable social security system would accelerate urbanization and create demand for services in urban areas. Rising service demand would boost economic growth and create more jobs. This service-led growth would be the new mode of growth and could reshape the PRC's economy in the coming decades.

References

Arita, S., S. la Croix, and J. Mak. 2014. Effect of Approved Destination Status on Mainland Chinese Travel Abroad. *Asian Economic Journal* 28(3): 217–237.

Baumol, W. J. 1967. Macroeconomics of Unbalanced Growth: The Anatomy of Urban Crisis. *American Economic Review* 57(3): 415–426.

Bureau of Economic Analysis (BEA). 2015. *Online Database* prepared by the Industry Economic Accounts Directorate, BEA, US Department of Commerce. www.bea.gov.

Cai, F. 2004. The Consistency of China's Statistics on Employment: Stylized Facts and Implications for Public Policies. *Chinese Economy* 37(5): 74–89.

Cattaneo, O., M. Engman, S. Sáez, and R. M. Stern. 2010. Assessing the Potential of Services Trade in Developing Countries: An Overview. In *International Trade in Services: New Trends and Opportunities for Developing Countries*, edited by O. Cattaneo, M. Engman, S. Sáez, and R. M. Stern. Washington, DC: The World Bank.

Chen, H., and J. Whalley 2014. China's Service Trade. *Journal of Economic Survey* 28(4): 746–774.

Ding, S., and S. Xu. 2015. Will the Service Sector Promote China's Long-Term Employment Growth. *China Economist* 10(1): 14–25.

Dorrucci, E., G. Pula, and D. Santabarbara. 2013. China's Economic Growth and Rebalancing. *Occasional Paper Series 142*. Frankfurt, Germany: European Central Bank.

Eichengreen, B., and P. Gupta. 2013. The Two Waves of Service-Sector Growth. *Oxford Economic Papers* 65(1): 96–123.

Felipe, J., U. Kumar, and R. Galope. 2014. Middle-Income Transitions: Trap or Myth? ADB Economics Working Paper 421. Manila: Asian Development Bank Institute.

Fuchs, V. R. 1968. *The Service Economy*. Cambridge, MA: National Bureau of Economic Research.

Ghani, E. 2011. The Service Revolution. Paper presented at ILO conference. Geneva.

Ghani, E., and S. D. O'Connell. 2014. Ethiopia's Growth Surge: The Role of Services. Unpublished manuscript.

Ghose, A. K. 2005. Employment in China: Recent Trends and Future Challenges. Employment Strategy Paper 2005/14. Employment Analysis Unit, Employment Strategy Department, International Labour Organization.

Gill, I., and H. Kharas. 2007. *An East Asian Renaissance: Ideas for Economic Growth*. Washington, DC: The World Bank.

Holz, C. A. 2014. The Quality of China's GDP Statistics. *China Economic Review* 30: 309–338.

Mattoo, A. 2003. China's Accession to the WTO: The Services Dimension. *Journal of International Economic Law* 6(2): 299–339.

MED. 2015. Production of GDP. Online database from the Federal Web Portal for Small and Medium-Sized Enterprises, Ministry of Economic Development of the Russian Federation (http://en.smb.gov.ru/analytic/gdp/).

Mukherjee, A. 2015. Services Sector in India: Trends, Issues and Way Forward. Unpublished manuscript.

Nabar, M., and K. Yan. 2013. Sector-Level Productivity, Structural Change, and Rebalancing in China. IMF Working Paper WP/13/240. Washington, DC: International Monetary Fund.

National Bureau of Statistics (NBS). 2017. *Preliminary Accounts of GDP for the 4th Quarter and 2016* online report released by the NBS and accessed on 21 January 2017. http://www.stats.gov.cn/tjsj/zxfb/201701/t20170120_1456385.html.

———. various years. *China Statistical Yearbook* compiled and published annually by NBS. Beijing: China Statistics Press.

National Economic Census Office (NECO). 2006. *China Economic Census Yearbook 2004*, compiled by NECO, the State Council. Beijing: China Statistics Press.

National Tertiary Industry Census Office (NTICO). 1995. *Zhongguo Shou Ci Di San Chan Ye Pu Cha Zi Liao, 1991–1992* (Statistics of the First Census on the Tertiary Industry in China 1991–1992), compiled by the National Tertiary Industry Census Office (Quan guo di san chan

ye pu cha ban gong shi bian), Beijing: Zhongguo tong ji chu ban she
(China Statistics Press).

Naughton, B. 2016. Restructuring and Reform: China 2016. In *Structural
Change in China: Implications for Australia and the World,* edited by
I. Day and J. Simon. Conference Proceedings, Reserve Bank of Australia,
Sydney.

NECO. 2010. *China Economic Census Yearbook 2008*, compiled by NECO,
the State Council. Beijing: China Statistics Press.

Noland, M., D. Park, and G. B. Estrada. 2012. Developing the Service Sector
as Engine of Growth for Asia: An Overview. ADB Economics
Working Paper 320. Manila: Asian Development Bank.

Ozyurt, S. 2013. Currency Undervaluation and Economic Rebalancing towards
Services: Is China an Exception? *China and World Economy* 21(1): 47–63.

Pais, J. 2014. Growth and Structure of the Services Sector in India. ISID
Working Paper 160. New Delhi: Institute for Studies in Industrial
Development.

Park, D., and K. Shin. 2012. The Service Sector in Asia: Is It an Engine
of Growth? ADB Economics Working Paper 322. Manila:
Asian Development Bank.

Qin, D. 2006. Is China's Growing Service Sector Leading to Cost Disease?
Structural Change and Economic Dynamics 17(3): 267–87.

Ramasamy, B., and M. Yeung. 2010. The Determinants of Foreign Direct
Investment in Services. *The World Economy* 33(4): 573–596.

Rawski, T. G. 2001. What Is Happening to China's GDP Statistics?
China Economic Review 12(4): 347–354.

Rawski, T. G., and R. W. Mead. 1998. On the Trail of China's Phantom
Farmers. *World Development* 26(5): 767–781.

Rodriguez, M., and Y. Melikhova. 2015. Services in Russia: Past, Present and
Future. Unpublished manuscript.

Rutkowski, R. 2015. Service Sector Reform in China. Policy Brief 15-2.
Washington, DC: Peterson Institute for International Economics.

Tang, Y., Y. Zhang, and C. Findlay. 2013. What Explains China's Rising Trade
in Services? Empirical Analysis with a Modified Gravity Model and
Panel Data. *Chinese Economy* 46(6): 7–31.

United Nations, Statistics Division. 2015. *UN Service Trade Statistics Database.* http://unstats.un.org/unsd/default.htm.

Wang, E. 2013. The Service Sector in the Chinese Economy: A Geographic Appraisal. *Eurasian Geography and Economics* 50(3): 275–300.

World Bank. 2013. *China 2030: Building a Modern Harmonious and Creative Society.* Report prepared by the World Bank and Development Research Centre of the State Council, Beijing.

———. 2015. *World Development Indicators.* http://data.worldbank.org/products/wdi.

Wu, H. X. 2000. China's GDP Level and Growth Performance: Alternative Estimates and the Implications. *Review of Income and Wealth* 46(4): 475–499.

Wu, Y. 2007. Service Sector Growth in China and India: A Comparison. *China: An International Journal* 5(1): 137–154.

———. 2014. Productivity, Economic Growth and the Middle Income Trap: Implications for China. *Frontiers of Economics in China* 9(3): 460–483.

———. 2015. China's Services Sector: The New Engine of Economic Growth. *Eurasian Geography and Economics* 56(6): 618–634.

———. 2016. Discussant for "Restructuring and Reform: China 2016." In *Structural Change in China: Implications for Australia and the World,* edited by I. Day and J. Simon. Conference Proceedings, Reserve Bank of Australia, Sydney.

Xu, D., and C. Ljungwall. 2008. What Is the Real Size of China's Economy? *China Economic Journal* 1(1): 97–105.

Yin, F. 2011. Foreign Direct Investment in China's Service Industry: Effects and Determinants. *China: An International Journal* 9(1), 144–163.

Yin, F., M. Ye, and L. Xu. 2014. Location Determinants of Foreign Direct Investment in Services Evidence from Chinese Provincial-level Data. ARC Working Paper 64. London: Asia Research Centre, London School of Economics.

Yusuf, S. 2015. Growing with Services. Unpublished manuscript.

Zhang, J., and T. Zhu. 2015. Re-Estimating China's Underestimated Consumption. *Comparative Economic Studies* 57: 55–74.

CHAPTER 7

Globalization, Structural Change, and Interregional Productivity Growth in the Emerging Economies

Jagannath Mallick

7.1 | Introduction

There is a burning debate among academics and policy makers on the issue of the middle-income trap (MIT) of an economy. Economic structure and income inequality at the regional and individual levels are established as two of the factors of the middle-income trap of an economy (Aiyar et al. 2013; Egawa 2013; Islam 2015). Globalization and economic integration have affected emerging economies in various ways. They have facilitated the transfer of technology, contributed to the efficiencies in production, and also substantially increased foreign direct investment (FDI) inflows and trade. The inflow of FDI brings advanced technology and modern management skills to host economies, which enhances labor productivity directly as input to the production function. In addition, it may affect the human capital, infrastructure, domestic firms, etc., which in turn contribute to the productivity growth also (Hale and Long 2007). Further, certain studies establish the fact that globalization increases income inequalities within countries through interregional competition (Candelaria, Daly, and Hale 2013; Ezcurra and Rodríquez-Pose 2013; Wan, Lu, and Chen 2007).[1]

---

[1] The persistence of regional imbalances in economic growth and development in the context of the People's Republic of China (PRC) and India is a hot debate (Li and Wei 2010; Mallick 2015b, 2014, 2013a, 2013b).

Furthermore, FDI is also expected to have an endogenous relationship with productivity growth (Li and Liu 2005).

The disproportionate nature of the economic structure is one of the reasons for an MIT. For instance, there is a significant concentration of employment in the agriculture sector, a low-productivity sector in emerging and developing countries. The agriculture sector's share of income is substantially low compared with that of employment. This has led to highly heterogeneous labor productivity across various activities, which results in low aggregate labor productivity in these countries. The differences in factor returns across various activities may lead to a reallocation of factors or structural change, which may boost overall productivity growth (Lewis 1954; Kuznets 1979; Syrquin 1984). The reallocation of labor from low- to high-productivity activities benefits growth (Lewis 1954), which is referred to as the "growth bonus" (Temple 2001). Therefore, structural change should be seen as a major source of labor productivity growth (LPG) and hence economic growth. Further, there is a high variation in labor productivity across the regions in the emerging economies. There is also high variation in labor productivity across the sectors in the low-income regions in the emerging economies. Such a productivity gap may cause the reallocation of labor from the low- to the high-productivity sector within the region. Therefore, the underdeveloped or low-income regions should gain more from the structural change than the developed regions, which helps to reduce the imbalances. This reallocation may cause convergence, assuming poor regions have relatively more labor in low-productivity sectors such as agriculture (Abramovitz 1986).

The relevance of the issues of structural change and interregional productivity growth in the emerging economies is largely due to (i) these countries' rising international trade and FDI inflows; (ii) advancement of technologies that have reduced production costs; (iii) the changing federalism structure from cooperative to competitive; and (iv) the persistence of interregional income inequalities within a country. The importance of the issue of regional income disparities in a country is highlighted in Ezcurra and Rodríquez-Pose (2013). However, the existing studies on this issue such as McMillan and

Rodrik (2011), Havlik (2005), Mallick (2017), Mallick (2015a), Fukao and Yuan (2012), and Brandt, Hsien, and Zhu (2008) are mainly focused on the national level. The structural transformation occurs not only across the broad sectors, but also across the subsectors. Nevertheless, more disaggregated-level study at the regional level s a challenging task in the context of the emerging economies, due to unavailability of data.

This is an empirical question as to whether structural change has been important for disparity in LPG. The main purpose of this chapter is to examine the patterns of economic structure between three broad sectors, and to measure the effects of structural change on the disparity in LPG across regions in India and the People's Republic of China (PRC). It is important to know whether, and to what extent, the reallocation of employment from relatively low- to high-productivity sectors has an effect on interregional LPG. If poor regions benefit more, then the policies targeted at facilitating structural change may help to reduce regional disparities and to reduce poverty. As India and the PRC are middle-income countries (MICs), it is important to reduce the regional disparity to avoid the middle-income trap (Egawa 2013; ADB 2011; Eichengreen, Park, and Shin 2011).

The issue is crucial for countries like India and the PRC due to its wider policy implications. The patterns of employment structure will help us to understand the process of structural change. The decomposition of LPG will suggest the role of structural change in the d sparity of LPG and hence economic growth. However, there is a dearth of studies that compare the issues of structural change and interregional productivity growth at the regional level in India and the PRC. These are the two largest emerging economies and they have been broadly following similar patterns of growth and interregional disparity since the initiation of substantial economic reform measures. Further, the structural changes are expected to play a larger role in reducing imbalances in interregional productivity growth and economic growth. Hence, a comparative study of the experience of India and the PRC during the period of globalization will be useful for policy makers for framing policies to achieve higher national economic growth and development, by reducing interregional inequalities and poverty (Hasan, Lamba, and Gupta 2013). Therefore, the present study attempts to strengthen the existing literature from several points of view in the context of regions in India and the PRC. First, the study decomposes the employment growth to understand the process of structural change. Second, the study measures the contribution of the effect of structural change to overall LPG. Third, the study empirically evaluates the effect of same on LPG by controlling the effects of economic globalization represented by FDI, and by taking into account the spatial interactions. Fourth, the study examines the interaction effect of FDI with physical investment and human capital. Finally, the study provides policy implications for reducing regional disparities in productivity growth and achieving higher regional and national economic growth.

7.2 | Data and Empirical Approaches

7.2.1 Data

The study uses annual data at the state level for India and provincial level in the PRC from 1993 to 2010. The study follows a three-sector classification of the economy: primary, secondary, and tertiary sectors. There are no ready-made data on state-level sectoral employment in India. The study uses the quinquennial surveys of the National Sample Survey (NSS) to estimate the sectoral-level employment data. The estimation of state-wise employment is described in Appendix A. The gross state domestic product (GSDP) at the base year of 2004–2005 is taken from the Central Statistical Organization (CSO) for India. The sectoral-level provincial data on labor and income in the PRC are taken from the National Bureau of Statistics of China (NBSC). The estimates of labor at the regional level in both countries are controlled by the national aggregate data from World KLEMS, which is a reliable and internationally comparable data source.

The data on other variables used in the empirical analysis are mainly sourced from the NBSC (for the PRC) and the CSO, annual reports of the University Grant Commission, and Secretariat of Industrial Assistance (SIA) (for India).

The data on investment at the state level are not available in India; their detailed limitations are discussed in Mallick (2012; 2013a; 2013b; 2014). This chapter estimates the same based on the conventional theoretical propositions by using national-level sectoral investment data, which are explained in Appendix A. The detailed variables, measurement, and data sources of the variables included in the empirical analysis are described in Table A7.1.

7.2.2 Decomposition of Employment Growth

Shift-share analysis is used to decompose the regional economic structure into various effects. This method has been employed since the early 1960s (Ashby 1970; Dunn 1960; Fuchs 1959; Perloff et al. 1960). In recent years, shift-share analysis and various transformations of the tool have been extensively employed in regional economic literature (Herzog and Olsen 1997). The classical shift-share equation is designed to decompose the growth of a regional variable into three effects. Given the variable by sector across regions in an economy, the change in employment (d_{ij}) between two points of time in an individual sector "i" for region "j" can be divided into national growth effect (g_{ij}), industry mix effect (m_{ij}), and competitive effect (c_{ij}). This indicates that each region's growth can be divided into components due to the achievement of national growth, and the residuals, which is known as the net-shift effect (Herzog and Olsen 1997). This can be expressed as below.

$$d_{ij} = g_{ij} + m_{ij} + c_{ij} \tag{1}$$

$$d_{ij} = I^t_{ij} - I^{t-1}_{ij} \tag{2}$$

$$g_{ij} = I^{t-1}_{ij} * G \tag{3}$$

$$m_{ij} = I^{t-1}_{ij}(G_i - G) \tag{4}$$

$$c_{ij} = I^{t-1}_{ij}(G_{ij} - G_i) \tag{5}$$

where l^t_{ij} and l^{t-1}_{ij} are the employment in sector 'i' (I = 1, 2, 3) for region 'j' in time period 't' and 't-1', respectively. G, G_i and g_{ij} are the national total growth rate, national sectoral growth rate, and regional sectoral growth rate, respectively. The national growth effect across the region will be positive (negative) if the national growth is positive (negative). Similarly, the industry mix effect of a sector is positive (negative) in all regions if national employment in that sector grows faster (slower) than the national total employment. The competitive position for sector 'i' in 'j' region will be positive (or negative) depending on whether regional employment growth in this sector is faster (or slower) than employment growth in the same sector at the national level. In addition, a positive (or negative) competitive position of a sector indicates that a region's share of national employment in that sector is increasing (or decreasing).

7.2.3 Decomposition of Labor Productivity Growth

The contribution of the reallocation effect of labor to interregional LPG is measured by using shift-share analysis. The labor reallocation effect approach to measure structural change has been widely used in several empirical studies (De Vries et al. 2012; Havlik 2005; McMillan and Rodrik 2011), due to its advantage of capturing the technological intensity of sectors (Syrquin 1988). The method is explained as follows:

If V_t and L_t are the total value added and employment at period 't' for a region, labor productivity at time t (LP_t) may be defined as follows:

$$LP_t = \frac{V}{L} = \frac{v^1_t + v^2_t + v^3_t}{L} = \frac{l^1_t * \left(v^1_t / l^1_t\right)}{L} + \frac{l^2_t * \left(v^2_t / l^2_t\right)}{L}$$
$$+ \frac{l^3_t * \left(v^3_t / l^3_t\right)}{L} = \sum_{i=1}^{i=3} s^i_t * lp^i_t \tag{6}$$

where $s^i_t = \frac{l^i_t}{L_t}$ is the share of industry i in total employment in time period t, lp^i_t is the labor productivity of industry i in time period t, i = 1,2,3, and t = 1994, 1995, ..., 2010.

The change in LP between the two points of time t and t-1 can be written as

$$dLP_t = \sum \left(s_{t-1}^i * dlp_t^i \right) + \sum \left(lp_t^i * ds_t^i \right) + \sum \left(ds_t^i * dlp_t^i \right)$$

Thus, the change in the aggregate level of labor productivity can be expressed as:

$$LP_t - LP_{t-1} = \sum_{i=1}^{3} \left(lp_t^i - lp_{t-1}^i \right) * s_{t-1}^i + \sum_{i=1}^{3} \left(s_t^i - s_{t-1}^i \right) * lp_t^i +$$
$$\sum_{i=1}^{3} \left(lp_t^i - lp_{t-1}^i \right) * \left(s_t^i - s_{t-1}^i \right)$$

(7)

Equation (7) can be modified to reflect growth rates by dividing LP_{t-1} on both sides.

$$\frac{LP_t - LP_{t-1}}{LP_{t-1}} = \frac{\sum_{i=1}^{3} \left(lp_t^i - lp_{t-1}^i \right) + s_{t-1}^i}{LP_{t-1}} + \frac{\sum_{i=1}^{3} \left(s_t^i - s_{t-1}^i \right) * lp_t^i}{LP_{t-1}}$$
$$+ \frac{\sum_{i=1}^{3} \left(lp_t^i - lp_{t-1}^i \right) + \left(lp_t^i - lp_{t-1}^i \right)}{LP_{t-1}}$$

(8)

Equation (8) suggests that aggregate productivity growth can be decomposed into three parts. The first term on the right side of the equation is called "intra-sectoral effect" or "within effect" (WE); this measures the change in the magnitude of LPG due to the change in productivity. The other two components are called "inter-sectoral effect" or "between effect" (BE) and "dynamic sectoral effect" (DSE), respectively. A positive BE value implies that labor is shifting from lower- to higher-productivity sectors, which adds to the overall productivity growth. In contrast, a negative BE value suggests that labor is shifting from higher- to lower-productivity sectors. The DSE is the interaction between the changes in sectoral productivity and changes in the employment share in the sectors. A positive DSE value indicates that changes in sectoral productivity and in employment share are either both negative or both positive. A negative DSE value suggests that one of the two changes is negative while the other is positive. This indicates that productivity may decline when employment expands or increase when employment decreases.

7.2.4 Empirical Specifications

The study focuses on the impact of structural change on interregional LPG by taking into account the spatial correlation among the regions in India and the PRC. The control variables in the empirical analysis have been selected on the basis of existing studies on the determinants of productivity growth, and include FDI to represent economic globalization (Blomstrom and Kokko 1998; Globerman and Ries 1994; Baldwin and Dhaliwal 2001; Rao and Tang 2005; Baldwin and Gu 2005; Driffield and Munday 2002); human capital (Schultz 1975; Welch 1970; Romer 1990; Benhabib and Speigel 1992; Apergis, Economidou, and Filippidis 2008; Lucas 1988; Kremer and Thompson 1993), and physical capital formation (Zhang 2002; Biggeri 2003; Zhang and Zhang 2003).

The empirical analysis includes 20 major states and 30 provinces for India and the PRC, respectively, over the period from 1993–1994 to 2010–2011. The study analyzes in a panel data framework, as it controls the individual heterogeneity of the regions and has a greater degree of freedom and efficiency (Baltagi 2001). A panel data equation can be written as follows:

$$Y_{it} = \partial + \beta * EX_{it} + \mu_i + \varepsilon_{it} \tag{9}$$

where i = 1, 2, ... n (n = 20 for India and n = 30 for the PRC) and t = 1994–1995, 1995–1996, ..., 2010–2011. Y_{it} is the LPG and EX_{it} is the vector of explanatory variables. In the panel data method, the error term is a composite residual consisting of time-invariant individual-specific (states/provinces) components μ_i that capture various characteristics of the region, which are not observable, but have a significant impact on the LPG, and a disturbance term ε_{it}, which satisfies the classical linear regression model assumptions. In other words, ε_{it} and μ_i are independent for each i over all t, and there is no autocorrelation in the ε_{it}.

Some of the explanatory variables such as FDI, structural change, and investment may be endogenously related to the LPG. These problems can be tackled through a dynamic panel model by adopting the approach of the

generalized method of moments (GMM) estimator. The dynamic panel
GMM has been widely employed in the empirical literature on development
economics due to its advantages.[2] This methodology is designed to take
into account the following: (i) the time series dimension of the data,
(ii) unobserved individual specific effects, (iii) inclusion of the lagged
dependent variables as the explanatory variables, and (iv) the endogenous
relationship of explanatory variables. The dynamic representation of the panel
data equation (10) is as follows:

$$Y_{it} = \alpha Y_{it-1} + \delta X_{it} + \lambda Z_{it} + \mu_i + \varepsilon_{it} \qquad (10)$$

where Y_{it-1} is a 1-year lag of LPG, X_{it} is the vector of strictly exogenous
variables, and Z_{it} is the vector of predetermined and endogenous variables,[3]
and where α, δ, and λ are the parameters. The presence of the lagged
dependent variable as one of the explanatory variables makes the relationship
dynamic. There are two approaches to estimating the dynamic panel
data: difference GMM and system GMM. In difference GMM, the lagged
values of the explanatory variables are used as the instruments. There are
statistical problems in the difference GMM when the first differences of the
regressors are persistent, which makes the lagged levels of Z and X weak
instruments. The use of weak instruments increases the variance of the
coefficient, which becomes biased in small samples. To reduce the potential
bias and inaccuracy associated with the use of the DIFF–GMM estimator,
Arellano and Bover (1995) and Blundell and Bond (1998) developed a
system of regressions in differences and levels.[4] The lagged levels of the
explanatory variables are the instruments in the regression in differences,
and the lagged differences of explanatory variables are the instruments
in the regression in levels. However, the validity of the moment conditions

---

[2]   The GMM estimator is good at exploiting the time series variation in the data, accounting for
       unobserved individual specific effects, and therefore providing better control for endogeneity of
       all the explanatory variables (Beck, Levine, and Loayza 2000).
[3]   Predetermined variables and endogenous variables are assumed to be correlated with only past
       errors, and both past and present errors, respectively.
[4]   For a detailed explanation of the GMM estimator, see Green (2006), Wooldridge (2002, Chapter 8
       and Chapter 14), and Roodman (2009).

decides the consistency of the GMM estimator. There are two specification tests based on Arellano and Bond (1991), Arellano and Bover (1995), and Blundell and Bond (1998) to judge the validity of the instruments, and hence the consistency of the GMM estimator: first, Hansen's test of overidentifying restrictions, which verifies the joint null hypothesis, that the instruments are valid instruments; second, the Arellano–Bond test, which tests the hypothesis of no second-order serial correlation in the error term.

Spatial Effects in Dynamic Panel Data

The panel data do not capture the spatial interaction or correlation among the regions as in Fukumi, Mallick, and Furuta (2017), which analyses the impact of electricity tariff on the productivity of the manufacturing firms across the Indian states. The sign of spatial correlation is issue-specific. For instance, in the context of productivity growth or overall economic growth, the spatial correlation is expected to have a positive effect. However, in some cases, for instance the location of investment, the correlation could be negative or positive. The location of investment in one region may affect its neighboring regions positively due to the effects of the agglomeration effect or spillover. This relation may be negative, on the other hand, because the relatively strong business environment of a region reduces the location of investment in its neighboring regions. These kinds of relations (or spatial interaction effects) can be controlled through spatial dependence models. According to Anselin and Bera (1998), the spatial dependence can be taken into account by the spatial autoregressive (SAR) model, where a spatial lag of the dependent variable is included as one of the explanatory variables on the right-hand side of the equation. The panel representation of the spatial lag model can be specified as follows:

$$Y_{it} = \alpha + \rho \sum_{j=1}^{n} w_{ij} Y_{it} + \beta X_{it} + \mu_i + \varepsilon_{it}. \tag{11}$$

where $\sum_{j=1}^{n} w_{ij}$ is the classical weight matrix,[5] which is a row-standardized matrix of spatial weights describing the structure and intensity of spatial effects.

---

[5] In this chapter, the weight matrix is based on the classical binary connectivity matrix, which assumes a value of 1 if the two regions share a common border and zero otherwise.

ρ is the spatial autoregressive coefficient, which is the parameter of the spatially lagged dependent variable that captures the spatial interaction effect. This indicates the extent to which the LPG in one region is determined by the behavior of its neighborhood, after controlling for the important factors of LPG. The sign of the value of the ρ parameter indicates the sign of the spatial autocorrelation. The error term ε_{it} is again assumed to be normally distributed and independent of the explanatory variables and spatially lagged dependent variable, under the assumption that all spatial dependence effects are captured by the lagged term. In other words, ε_{it} is the classical zero mean error term assumed to be independent under the hypothesis that all spatial dependence effects are captured by the spatially lagged variable term. Equation (11) is known as the "fixed-effect lag model." Corresponding to the dynamic panel GMM estimator in equation (10), the dynamic spatial panel lag model can be specified as follows (Baltagi, Fingleton, and Pirotte 2014):

$$Y_{it} = \alpha Y_{it-1} + \rho \sum_{j=1}^{n} w_{ij} Y_{it} + \delta X_{it} + \lambda Z_{it} + \mu_i + \varepsilon_{it}. \tag{12}$$

This model can also be estimated by the difference GMM and system GMM approaches like the nonspatial dynamic panel data model.

7.3 | Structural Change in India and the PRC

The economic structure of India and the PRC has been changing with the pace of economic reform measures. India introduced comprehensive economic reform measures in 1991. The structure of employment and income in the three broad sectors is presented in Figure 7.1 for India. India's economy was predominated by primary sector activities, with 65% of the employment and 31% of total value added in 1993. However, this sector's share in employment had come down to 53% and in value added to 17% in 2010. Further, the employment share of the secondary sector was 14% in 1993; this increased to 18% in 2010. This sector's share in value added increased from 25% in 1993 to 27% in 2010. The employment share of the service sector increased from 21% in 1993 to 29% in 2010.

Figure 7.1: Economic Structure in India

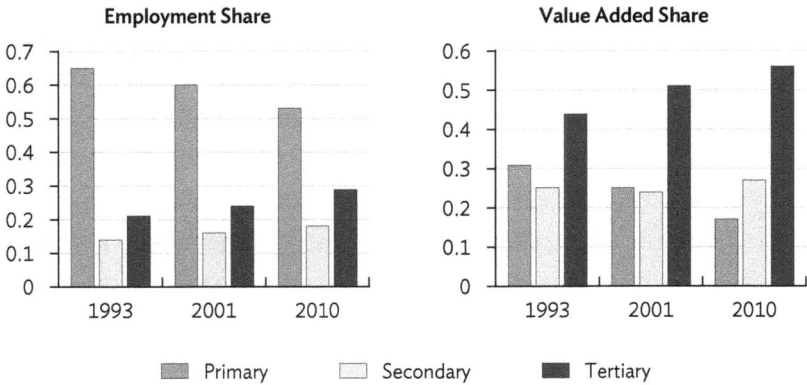

Source: World KLEMS.

During the same time span, the share of value added increased from 44% to 56%. Although the service sector has been the driver of India's economic growth, the absorption of labor in this sector has not kept pace with its growth in value added. There is a disproportionate concentration of employment with respect to the value added across the three sectors, which leads to a substantial gap in labor productivity across sectors.

As seen in Figure 7.2, the intent and speed of structural change in the PRC's economy exceeded that seen in India. Like India, the PRC was a predominantly agrarian economy in which the primary sector accounted for 53% of the employment and 25% of total value added in 1993. After reform measures were introduced in 1978, the PRC experienced a rapid and widespread industrialization and tertiarization. By 2010, the primary sector's share of employment had declined to 34%, and that of income to 15%. In contrast, the secondary sector's share increased from 23% in 1993 to 27% in 2010, and that of income increased from 41% in 1993 to 45% in 2010. The service sector's share increased from 24% in 1993 to 39% in 2010 and that of income increased from 34% in 1993 to 40% in 2010.

Figure 7.2: Economic Structure in the People's Republic of China

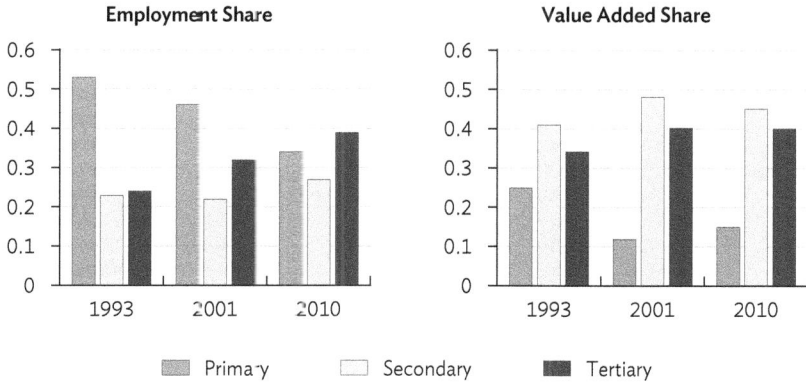

Source: World KLEMS.

The PRC, as a planned socialist country, had given priority to agriculture and industry over the tertiary sector. As a result, the service sector's share in value added is lower than that of other market economies with an identical level of development to India. There is a high gap in labor productivity between the sectors, as in India.

However, the economic structure in terms of employment is found to be different across the regions within both the PRC and India. All the regions are categorized into three groups: high-income (HI), middle-income (MI), and low-income (LI) regions, based on the per capita income in 2010–2011. The employment structure across the states in India is presented in Figure 7.3. This shows that the primary sector's share of employment was larger than that of the other two sectors in LI regions in 1993 and 2010. This was also larger than the primary sector's employment share in MI and HI regions. There was a significant shift in employment from the primary sector to nonprimary sector in all the LI regions between 1993 and 2010 (Figure A7.1). Similarly, the primary sector had a higher share of employment in LI regions than in MI and HI regions. The shift in employment from the primary to the nonprimary sector was higher in LI regions than in MI and Hi regions (Figure A7.1).

Figure 7.3: Employment Structure in 1993 and 2010 in the States in India (major 20) (%)

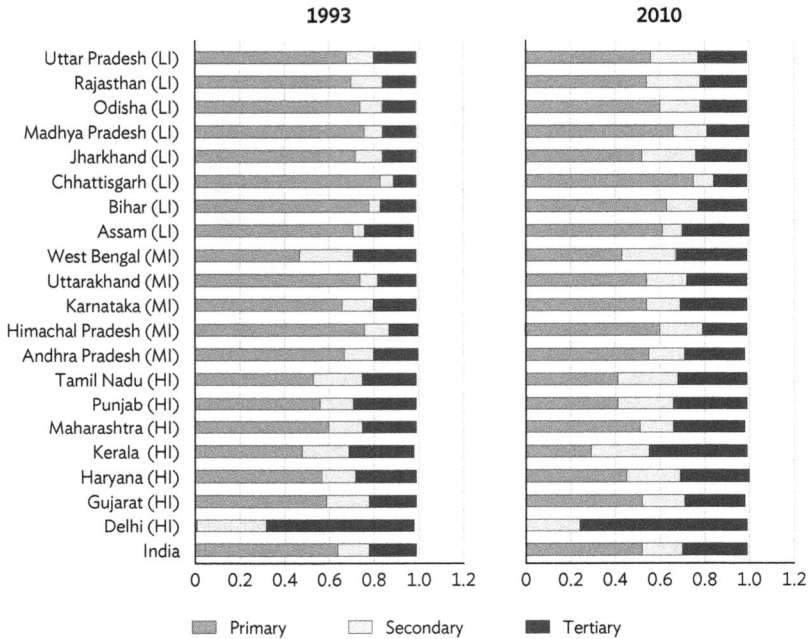

HI = high income, LI = low income, MI = middle income.
Source: Author's calculation.

In sum, the pattern of change in employment share and income share at the national level confirms that the activities have shifted from the primary to the secondary and tertiary sector in both countries. However, as of 2010 about 53% of labor is still concentrated in the primary sector in India, and about 34% in the PRC. This suggests that there is a gap in labor productivity across sectors in both countries. The regional patterns of employment structure suggest that a higher share of employment is shifted from the primary sector to the nonprimary sector in LI regions than in the MI and HI regions in both countries. However, the LI regions are still left with a significant primary sector employment share. To transfer this unproductive labor, both countries need appropriate economic reform measures at both regional and national levels.

Figure 7.4: **Employment Structure in 1993 and 2010 in the Provinces of the PRC (%)**

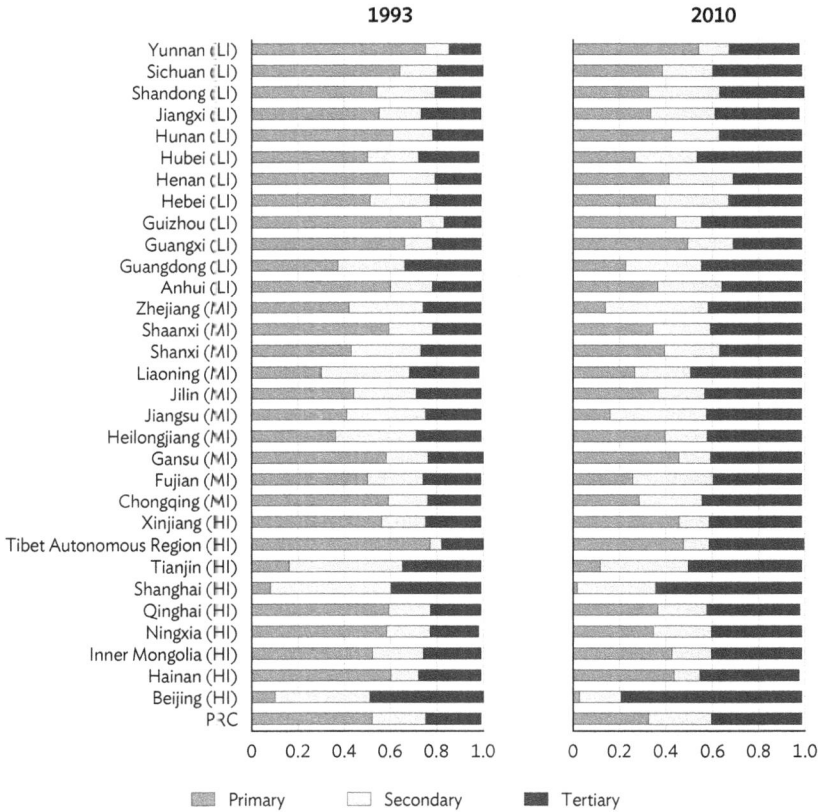

HI = high income, LI = low income, MI = middle income, PRC = People's Republic of China.

Source: Author's calculation.

Further, India's economic growth strategy is driven by only the service sector, and its manufacturing sector should be made competitive. Services are more skill-intensive than manufacturing activities, and hence they create fewer jobs. India now needs to develop the manufacturing sector, which will absorb millions of additional labor. The PRC, on the other hand, needs to develop service activities and go up the value chain, from less skill-intensive to more skill-intensive, which will enable it to avoid the middle-income trap.

It is impossible for it to avoid the middle-income trap if it is manufacturing-centric. Hence, there is enough room for India to use manufacturing as a growth escalator, and for the PRC to tap into services as a growth escalator. Various skill development and training programs should be provided in the low-income region, which would help the unproductive agricultural sector's labor to move to productive industrial and service activities.

7.4 | Decomposition of Interregional Employment Growth

A shift-share analysis of employment change between 1993 and 2010 is undertaken to understand the pattern of the economic structure across the regions revealed in the above section. The shift-share analysis provides some interesting findings across three groups of states in India in Figure 7.5 (Table A7.2 for all states). The national total employment growth is positive, for which the national growth effect (NGE) is positive in the three sectors across all the regions. The industry mix effect (IME) of the secondary and tertiary sector is positive, and that of the primary sector is negative across the three regions. This means the national employment in the primary sector has grown more slowly than the national total employment, which results in a negative industry mix effect across the three regions. However, the magnitude of negative IME of the primary sector in the LI region is higher than that in the MI and HI regions.

The competitive effect (CE) of each of the three sectors is negative in both HI and MI regions. This means that employment in these sectors has grown more slowly than at the national sectoral level of employment in HI and MI regions. However, LI states have a positive competitive effect on each of the three sectors. This indicates that the employment in each of the three sectors in LI states has grown faster than the national sectoral-level employment growth. The competitive effect of the industrial sector is higher than in the other two sectors in LI regions. This indicates that the industrial sector is more advantageous than the other two sectors in LI regions.

Figure 7.5: Decomposition of Employment Change
in Indian States ('000)

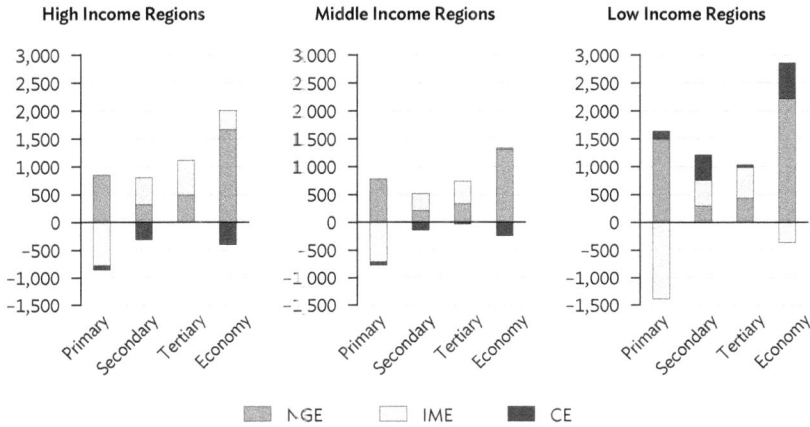

CE = competitive effect, IME = industry mix effect, NGE = national growth effect.
Note: The figures are in terms of annual averages.
Source: Author's calculation.

Such a nature of growth of employment leads to significant structural change
in terms of sectoral composition of labor among the Indian states as revealed
in Figure 7.3 and Figure A7.1.

The overall change in total (economy) employment in LI states is higher than
in the HI and MI states. The NGE effect is dominant in the change in total
employment across all three regions. The IME effect is positive in HI states,
and the CE effect is positive in both MI and HI states. In LI states, though the
CE is positive, the IME is negative in the change in total employment due to a
stronger negative effect of its primary sector.

The shift-share results for the three groups of provinces of the PRC are provided
in Figure 7.6 (Table A7.4 for all the provinces). Like India, the NGE is positive
across all the sectors in all three regions. The IME is negative in the primary
sector and positive in the secondary and tertiary sectors in all three regions.

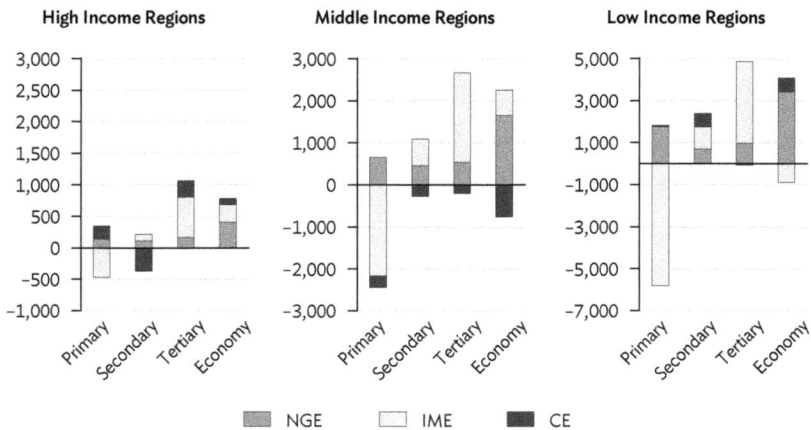

Figure 7.6: Decomposition of Employment Change in the People's Republic of China's Provinces ('000)

CE = competitive effect, IME = industry mix effect, NGE = national growth effect.

Note: The figures are in terms of annual averages.

Source: Author's calculation.

There is stronger negative IME of the primary sector and positive IME of the tertiary sector in both LI and MI regions than in HI regions. This means that there is a strong disadvantage of the primary sector and advantage of the secondary sector in both MI and LI regions.

The competitive effects of the primary and tertiary sectors are positive, and that of the secondary sector is negative in HI regions, while the competitive effects of all three sectors are negative in MI regions. The competitive effect is positive only in the primary sector in LI regions. This nature of change in employment across the regions leads to a significant change in the composition of employment as observed in Figures 7.4 and A7.1.

The magnitude of the change in total employment in MI and LI regions is higher than in the HI regions in the PRC. The national growth effect significantly contributes to the total change in employment in both MI and LI regions.

The other contributors to this change are the industry mix effect for the MI regions and competitive effects for the LI regions in the PRC. However, the negative competitive effect causes the change in total employment in MI regions to be lower than that in LI regions in the PRC. Hence, the magnitude of the change in total employment in LI regions is higher than that in MI and HI regions in both countries. By and large, the labor reallocates from the primary sector to both secondary and tertiary sectors fairly in LI regions in India. While a major proportion of employment reallocates to the service sector, the rest reallocates to the secondary sector in the LI regions in the PRC.

7.5 | Structural Change and Interregional Productivity Growth

The LPG is decomposed into WE, BE, and DSE in the states in India and provinces in the PRC. The results for the three groups of Indian states are presented in Figure 7.7 (Table A7.4 for all states). This confirms that there is a disparity in the sectoral productivity growth across the Indian states during this period of study. The average growth rate of sectoral productivity in HI states is 6.47%, which indicates that sectoral productivity growth has grown at an average rate of 6.47% in the HI states, while the sectoral productivity in MI states and LI states has grown at a lower rate than in HI states. Also, the sectoral productivity growth is the major component of LPG. Hence, the disparity in sectoral productivity growth leads to a disparity in LPG across the Indian states.

As regards structural change effects, their contribution in LI states is higher than that in MI and HI states. As discussed above, a higher magnitude of shifting of the labor force from primary to other activities causes the structural change effect to be higher than that of MI states and HI states in India. Hence this nature of shifting of the labor force and contribution of the structural change effect to LPG may reduce the disparity in LPG across the Indian states.

Figure 7.7: **Structural Change Effect and Interregional Labor Productivity Growth in India (%)**

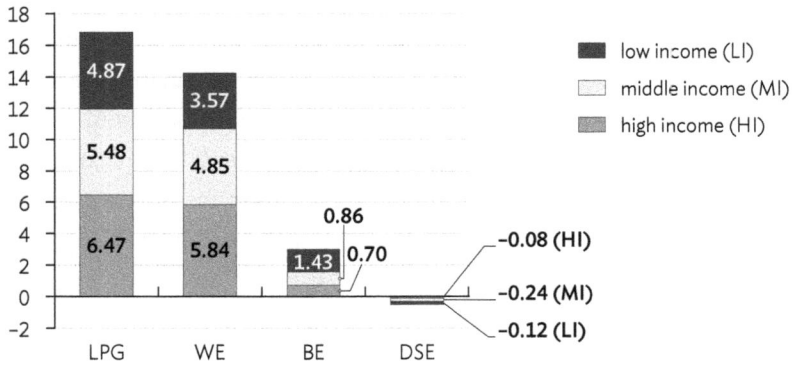

BE = between effect, DSE = dynamic sectoral effect, LPG = labor productivity growth, WE = within effect.
Note: The figures are in terms of annual averages.
Source: Author's calculation.

Similarly, all the provinces of the PRC are grouped into HI, MI, and LI regions. The decomposition results indicate that many of the LI regions contribute to LPG through the structural change effect (Table A7.5 for all provinces). Figure 7.7 also shows that the average structural change effect in LI regions is higher than that in MI and HI regions as in India, which follows the predictions by Lewis (1954), Kuznets (1979), and Syrquin (1984).

Further, the decomposition results confirm that there is differentiation in LPG across the three regions in both countries during this study period. According to Figure 7.7, the average LPG in LI states, MI states, and HI states in India is 4.87%, 5.48%, and 6.47%, respectively. In the case of the PRC, the labor productivity in MI regions and HI regions has grown almost at the same rate, while the LPG in LI regions is lower than that in MI and HI provinces as in India. Further, the coefficient of variation of the labor productivity across all the states and provinces in both countries has been growing (Table A7.6), which confirms the existence of high disparity in productivity across the regions.

7.6 | Empirical Results

The impact of the structural change effect on interregional LPG between 1993 and 2010 has been examined by using the dynamic spatial panel data methods.

The functional specification for the empirical analysis is

$$LPG = f(SC, \text{human capital, FDI, physical investment}) \tag{13}$$

where SC is the structural change that comprises BE and DSE. The LPG equation 13 is expected to be dynamic in nature as it may depend on the previous years' labor productivity growth, which may suggest whether the LPG is diverging or converging across the regions. Further, as explained before, higher wages are induced by higher LPG, which determines the reallocation of labor from lower- to higher-productivity activities. Hence, SC is expected to have an endogenous relationship. Similarly, FDI is also expected to have simultaneous relations with LPG as is shown by Zhang (2002) and Zhang and Zhang (2003) in the context of the PRC's provinces, because the multinational enterprises look for investment in the regions with higher labor productivity or LPG to minimize their cost of production. Further, physical investment is also expected to have endogenous relations with LPG across the regions in an economy. This nature of the relationship of these three independent variables in equation 13 can be addressed by the dynamic panel data model. As the present study focuses on capturing the spatial correlations, the dynamic spatial panel lag method is most appropriate. This section focuses on results from the spatial dynamic panel GMM estimations. The econometric literature suggests that the system GMM provides more consistent and efficient estimates than the difference GMM. Hence, the results from a dynamic spatial panel lag model using the system GMM estimator are presented in Table 7.1 for India and Table 7.2 for the PRC.

Table 7.1: Structural Change Effect on Interregional Labor Productivity Growth (India)

Independent Variables	Model 1	Model 2	Model 3	Model 4
L.LPG	−0.12 (0.03)[a]	−0.12 (0.03)[a]	−0.11 (0.03)[a]	−0.11 (0.03)[a]
SC	0.36 (0.16)[b]	0.39 (0.15)[b]	0.33 (0.16)[b]	0.38 (0.15)[b]
Human capital	0.38 (0.17)[b]	0.42 (0.17)[b]	0.40 (0.16)[b]	0.43 (0.16)[b]
FDI	0.19 (0.10)[c]	0.16 (0.10)[c]	0.92 (0.43)[b]	0.82 (0.43)[b]
Investment	0.14 (0.01)[a]	0.14 (0.01)[a]	0.14 (0.01)[a]	0.14 (0.01)[a]
FDI*Investment		0.01 (0.005)[b]		0.01 (0.005)[c]
FDI*Human capital			0.64 (0.36)[c]	0.57 (0.35)[c]
Spatial Autocorrelation Coefficient	0.11 (0.01)[a]	0.11 (0.01)[a]	0.11 (0.01)[a]	0.11 (0.01)[a]
Observations	320	320	320	320
States	20	20	20	20
Wald test	754[a]	779[a]	766[a]	795[a]
F test	126[a]	111[a]	109[a]	99[a]
(Buse 1973) R2	0.71	0.71	0.71	0.72
(Buse 1973) R2 Adj	0.70	0.71	0.70	0.71
Raw Moments R2	0.70	0.71	0.71	0.71
Raw Moments R2 Adj	0.70	0.70	0.70	0.70
Log Likelihood Function	−937	−936	−935	−934
Sargan Over Identification LM Test	421	440	435	451

FDI = foreign direct investment, LPG = labor productivity growth, SC = structural change.

[a] Statistical significance at 1%.

[b] Statistical significance at 5%.

[c] Statistical significance at 10%.

Source: Author's estimation.

The results of four sets of regressions for each of the countries are provided. The first specification uses structural change and three control variables as in equation 13. The second, third, and fourth specifications use the first interaction term, the second interaction term, and both interaction terms, respectively. The first interaction term is the interaction between FDI and

domestic physical investment. There could be correlation between them.
If the correlation is positive (negative), it suggests a crowding-in (crowding-out) relation between FDI and the domestic physical investment. The impact
of FDI is more than the domestic investment in the developing countries as
argued by Graham and Krugman (1991). It is expected that a foreign firm
will enjoy lower costs and higher productive efficiency than its domestic
counterparts in the host country. The higher efficiency of FDI would be
the result of the combination of advanced management skills and modern
technologies, where the advanced technologies are transferred to developing
countries mainly through FDI. The second term is the interaction between
the FDI and human capital. As argued in the literature, human capital is a
crucial factor of inflows of FDI across the regions within an economy. Hence,
to avoid multicollinearity problems the inclusion of these interaction effects
is necessary. As can be seen, the inclusion of these interaction effects has
contributed to explaining the variation in LPG as reflected by the value of the
log likelihood function in both countries.

The results in Table 7.1 provide interesting findings regarding India. First,
the autocorrelation coefficients for the spatial effects are found to be
significant for all four models. This indicates that the states surrounded by
higher-productivity growth regions are influenced positively. This is due
to the spillover effect of knowledge, technological diffusion, interregional
trade, migration, and capital movement, etc., which are not captured in this
specification. Second, the structural change effect is found to be significant
in all the models with a positive sign. This indicates the significance of the
structural change effect for boosting interregional LPG.

Third, the study includes FDI, human capital, and physical investment as
the possible factors in explaining productivity growth. The coefficients of all
these control variables are statistically significant with a positive sign in all
four models. This suggests that FDI, human capital, and physical investment
are the important factors for the variation in LPG across the Indian states
during this study period. The findings of this study corroborate several earlier
findings in the context of India (Goldar, Renganathan, and Banga 2004;

Kathuria, Raj, and Sen 2013; Siddharthan and Lal 2004) that FDI positively affects interregional productivity growth. The inflow of FDI has boosted productivity growth by bringing new advanced technologies and management skills to India. Further, Kathuria, Raj, and Sen (2013) also provided evidence to show that human capital is a crucial factor for productivity growth in the context of India. In a recent study by Mallick and Pavel (2018) found significant impact of FDI on regional income growth in an advanced country like the Czech Republic. Productivity growth has a significant relationship with the quality of human capital, through the technological competence of the workforce. One and the same technology can be applied in two different firms, but the output would vary with respect to the skill or human capital of the labor force employed in these firms. Hence the nature of human capital is also crucial to productivity growth (Apergis, Economidou, and Filippidis 2008; Benhabib and Speigel 1992; Romer 1990; Schultz 1975; Welch 1970). Further, other studies—with a somewhat different focus—have also found that FDI, human capital, and physical capital are crucial for the variation in economic growth across the Indian states (Mallick 2012; 2014).

Although both FDI and physical investment are statistically significant in all the models, the differences that are found in the value of coefficients constitute one of the crucial findings of this study. For instance, the values of coefficients of FDI and investment in Model 4 are 0.82 and 0.14, respectively. This indicates that a 1% increase in the share of FDI in GDP leads to a 0.82% increase in LPG, and a 1% increase in the share of physical investment in GDP leads to an increase in LPG of 0.14%. It can be inferred, therefore, that FDI encourages the boosting of productivity growth more than physical investment. This could be due to the direct role that multinational enterprises have in the production process of local firms through both forward and backward linkage effects. Multinationals try to increase their profit by increasing the efficiency of local firms through importing their capital, advanced technologies, marketing, and managerial skills (Baldwin and Dhaliwal 2001; Baldwin and Gu 2005; Blomstrom and Kokko 1998; Globerman and Ries 1994; Rao and Tang 2005). The findings corroborate those of Mallick (2012) in the Indian states.

Fourth, it is important to note that the 1-year lag of labor productivity growth is statistically significant, and negative for India. This suggests that LPG is converging across the Indian states with conditioning of the spatial correlations, structural change effects, FDI, physical investment, and human capital during this study period.

Fifth, the interaction effects are also statistically significant in all the models in the context of India. The coefficient of the interaction effect between FDI and investment is positive, which shows that FDI is also contributing to productivity growth indirectly by crowding in the domestic investment across the Indian states during this study period.[6] The positive coefficient of the interaction effect of FDI and human capital indicates that they have positive relationships during the study period. It is worth noting that Borenzstein, Gregorio, and Lee (1995) provided evidence to confirm that the interaction effects of FDI with domestic investment and human capital on the national economic growth are positive in the context of developing countries. Further, other studies with a somewhat different focus have also found an interaction effect between foreign financing and the level of human capital on economic growth. Cohen (1992) found a positive interaction between human capital and the overall access to foreign financing of developing countries. The findings of this study may in fact provide a rationale for his finding, at least as far as the FDI component of foreign financing is concerned. Romer (1993) found a positive effect of the interaction between secondary school enrollment and machinery imports on economic growth. While imports of machinery and equipment may be one channel for the international transmission of technological advances, FDI probably has an even larger role, as it also allows the transmission of knowledge on business practices, management techniques, etc.

There are some different stories to tell about the disparity in productivity growth across the PRC's provinces from the results in Table 7.2.

---

[6] FDI can influence an economy through four channels: job creation, trade expansion, technology improvement, and economic growth promotion through capital accumulation and factors of production.

Table 7.2: Structural Change Effect on Interregional Labor Productivity Growth (PRC)

Independent Variables	Model 5	Model 6	Model 7	Model 8
L.LPG	0.05 (0.04)	0.06 (0.04)	0.03 (0.04)	0.04 (0.04)
SC	0.28 (0.14)[b]	0.32 (0.15)[b]	0.27 (0.14)[b]	0.29 (0.14)[b]
Human Capital	0.08 (0.01)[a]	0.09 (0.01)[a]	0.09 (0.01)[a]	0.10 (0.01)[a]
FDI	0.04 (0.05)	0.23 (0.24)	1.77 (0.7)[b]	1.69 (0.69)[b]
Investment	0.18 (0.01)[a]	0.17 (0.02)[a]	0.17 (0.17)[a]	0.17 (0.02)[a]
FDI*Investment		0.004 (0.005)		0.01 (0.005)
FDI*Human capital			0.02 (0.01)[b]	0.02 (0.01)[b]
Spatial Autocorrelation Coefficient	0.14 (0.01)[a]	0.14 (0.01)[a]	0.14 (0.01)[a]	0.14 (0.01)[a]
Observations	480	480	480	480
Provinces	30	30	30	30
Wald test	227[a]	283[a]	296[a]	344[a]
F test	38[a]	40[a]	42[a]	43[a]
(Buse 1973) R2	0.32	0.37	0.39	0.42
(Buse 1973) R2 Adj	0.32	0.37	0.38	0.41
Raw Moments R2	0.89	0.89	0.89	0.89
Raw Moments R2 Adj	0.89	0.89	0.89	0.89
Log Likelihood Function	−1,294	−1,294	−1,293	−1,292
Sargan Over Identification LM Test	504	529	527	550

FDI = foreign direct investment, LPG = labor productivity growth, PRC = People's Republic of China, SC = structural change.

[a] Statistical significance at 1%.

[b] Statistical significance at 5%.

Source: Author's estimation.

The results do not suggest the presence of conditional convergence or divergence of LPG across the provinces, unlike India. FDI is found to be significant after controlling for interaction effect with the human capital in Model 7 and Model 8. The inflow of FDI has boosted productivity

growth by bringing new advanced technologies and managerial skills to
the PRC's provinces. This finding is consistent with Biggeri (2003), Zhang
and Zhang (2003), Li and Wei (2010), and Xu, Lai, and Qi (2008) for the
PRC in establishing a positive impact of FDI on productivity growth across
provinces. The coefficients of human capital are found to be strongly
statistically significant in all the models. Studies such as Zhang (2002), Xu,
Lai, and Qi (2008), and Wei and Hao (2011) at the provincial level in the
PRC also provide evidence to show that human capital is a crucial factor for
productivity growth. Further, visible differences are seen in the magnitude of
coefficients of human capital between India and the PRC with respect to the
differences in the measurement of human capital. In the case of India, human
capital is represented by enrollment in higher educational institutions, while
it is measured by the literacy rate by the age of 15 and above for the PRC.
This finding provides an important message from this analysis that a higher
level of education has a larger effect on productivity growth, as deduced by
Lucas (1988) and Kremer and Thompson (1993).

The coefficient of physical investment is found to be positive and statistically
significant in all the models. This corroborates Zhang (2002), Biggeri (2003),
and Zhang and Zhang (2003) at the provincial level in the PRC. However,
the interaction effect between FDI and physical investment is not significant.
This is a hotly debated issue in the context of the PRC. Many scholars believe
that there exists an FDI crowding-out effect on PRC's domestic investment
(Huang 2003; Buckley, Clegg, and Wang 2002) due to the PRC's high
saving rates and preferential policies to FDI. Therefore, they argue that FDI's
contribution to capital accumulation is limited and FDI promotes the PRC's
economic growth mainly through factors of production. However, some
other studies were not able to find any definite proof of FDI crowding out
domestic investment in the PRC (Agosin and Machado 2005; Wang and
Li 2004). Further, the positive relationship between FDI and human capital
is established through the positive and statistical significance of their
coefficients in Models 7 and 8.

7.7 | Conclusions and Policy Implications

This chapter provides an explanation for the growing regional income inequality in emerging economies, with special emphasis on the impact of the structural change effect on LPG by using a recently developed methodology in the context of India and the PRC during the period 1993–2010. I have taken into account the spatial interaction effects among the regions, which has not been considered in previous studies of the related topics. This allows me to take into consideration the role played by a number of dimensions that flow or spill over from one region to its neighbors within a country.

The descriptive analysis shows that the economy as a whole and the activities in terms of reallocation of labor are shifting away from the primary sector to the secondary and service sectors in both countries. Although a higher proportion of unproductive labor force is concentrated in the LI region's primary sector, a substantially greater number of employment reallocates from the primary sector to the nonprimary sector in the LI region than in the HI and MI regions in both countries, which results in a higher contribution of the structural change effect to LPG in the low-income regions than in the MI and HI regions. This trend is helpful for reducing regional imbalances in LPG and hence income inequalities, which in turn helps in avoiding the middle-income trap (Egawa 2013).

The GMM system results from the dynamic spatial panel data show a positive association between the structural change effect and the interregional LPG in each country by controlling for physical investment, human capital, and FDI as representative of the degree of economic globalization in both countries. This conclusion still holds when the interaction terms are used as additional control variables to avoid the possible multicollinearity relations of FDI with physical investment and with human capital in the estimation. Hence, the structural change effect is crucial in reducing the regional imbalances, as it significantly explains the interregional LPG, where a higher contribution is achieved by the LI regions than the MI and HI regions.

Further, the findings show that neighborhood relations are significant in explaining the interregional LPG in both countries. That means a higher LPG in one region drives LPG in its neighboring regions.

The empirical analysis establishes that FDI is significant, where FDI broadly represents the degree of economic globalization. Based on the results of the study, regions with a greater degree of economic globalization or integration with the rest of the world, everything else being equal, have higher LPG. This is potentially important, since the level of international market integration in many emerging economies still has large potential to grow. The results of this chapter provide an additional contribution to the debate by emphasizing the impact of economic globalization and integration on interregional LPG, and hence income inequality within a country. However, one of the limitations of the study is that only FDI is used to represent the degree of economic globalization without considering international trade.[7]

The rising regional inequality in LPG leads to regional income inequalities and presents huge challenges to social and economic stability, which may push India and the PRC into the middle-income trap. The empirical results of the study provide the following policy implications for reducing regional disparities:

- The findings show that human capital is significant in explaining the interregional LPG in both countries. Hence, to ensure and achieve higher labor productivity, the relevant policies related to knowledge must be pursued with a view to providing incentive and encouraging investments in human capital, technology, and innovations in the entire country. A special consideration should be given to encouraging and promoting them in the lagging regions.
- Further, globalization will lead to higher regional inequality in India and the PRC unless concerted efforts are devoted to promoting FDI flows and trade in the lagging regions. The FDI inflow brings advanced technology and expertise from the country of origin and helps in enhancing labor

---

[7]   Due to the unavailability of data on trade at the state level in India, the study is restricted to the use of only FDI to represent the degree of economic globalization and integration.

productivity in the hosting regions. The formulation of more and more outward-oriented policies would further enhance productivity. Hence, special promotional policies should be designed to encourage FDI flows and trade in the lagging regions as they are in a disadvantageous position with respect to market potential and location considerations. A converging trend in these will help in reducing regional inequalities.

- With regard to the lagging regions, the incentive policies for the promotion of FDI and human capital should be redesigned by coordinating governments at both local and national levels.

- Also, the equalization of domestic capital across regions will reduce regional inequality. To narrow down the gaps in capital possession, it is necessary, though difficult, to break the vicious circle existing in capital formation. This calls for the development of a financial market, especially in poor rural areas. Again, policy support for investment in poorer regions is needed in terms of tax concessions and bank lending.

- In addition to the direct policy measures aimed at boosting LPG, further policy measures should be taken to increase the contributions due to the reallocation of the labor effect. A larger proportion of the unproductive labor force of the lagging regions is concentrated in the agricultural sector, which is mainly in rural areas. However, there are certain restrictions on migration in some of the emerging economies, for instance the *hukou* system in the PRC. Hence, restrictions on migration with regard to both location and sector should be lifted and rural–urban migration encouraged, which will transfer the labor force from low- to high-productivity activities. Labor mobility can be facilitated through the establishment of various labor market institutions.

Structural change not only increases productivity growth, it also reduces poverty by pushing up the wage rate in the agricultural sector (Hasan, Lamba, and Gupta 2013). A huge proportion of workers is concentrated mainly in the agricultural sector in the low-income regions. The reallocation of labor from agriculture to nonagriculture increases the wage rate of the laborers who move to the nonagricultural sector, and also those who remain working in the agricultural sector.

International trade and infrastructure are also crucial for promoting both domestic and foreign investment, and hence LPG. Therefore, integrated domestic markets should be promoted by removing interregional trade barriers in the lagging regions. Further, financial assistance and administrative help should be provided to develop public infrastructure such as highways and telecommunication networks in the lagging regions.

References

Abramovitz, M. 1986. Catching Up, Forging Ahead and Falling Behind. *Journal of Economic History* 46(2): 385–406.

Agosin, M. R., and R. Machado. 2005. Foreign Investment in Developing Countries: Does it Crowd in Domestic Investment? *Oxford Development Studies* 33(2): 149–162.

Aiyar, S., R. Duval, D. Puy, Y Wu, and L. Zhang. 2013. Growth Slowdowns and the Middle-Income Trap. IMF Working Paper 13/71. Washington, DC: International Monetary Fund.

Anselin L., and A. K Bera. 1998. Spatial Dependence in Linear Regression Models with an Introduction to Spatial Econometrics. In *Handbook of Applied Economic Statistics*, edited by A. Hullah and D. E. A. Gelis. New York, NY: Marcel Deker.

Apergis, N., C. Economidou, and I. Filippidis. 2008. Innovation Technology Transfer and Labor Productivity Linkages: Evidence from a Panel of Manufacturing Industries. *Review of World Economics* 144(3): 491–508.

Arellano, M., and S. Bond. 1991. Some Tests of Specification for Panel Data: Monte Carlo Evidence and an Application to Employment Equations. *Review of Economic Studies* 58(2): 277–297.

Arellano, M., and O Bover. 1995. Another Look at the Instrumental-Variable Estimation of Error: Components Models. *Journal of Econometrics* 68(1): 29–51.

Ashby, L. D. 1970. Changes in Regional Industrial Structure: A Comment. *Urban Studies* I(3): 298–304.

Asian Development Bank (ADB). 2011. *Asia 2050: Realizing the Asian Century*. Manila: ADB.

Baldwin, J. R., and N. Dhaliwal. 2001. *Heterogeneity in Labour Productivity Growth in Manufacturing: Differences between Domestic and Foreign-Controlled Establishments*. Productivity Growth in Canada. Ottawa: Statistics Canada.

Baldwin, J. R., and W. Gu. 2005. *Global Links: Multinationals, Foreign Ownership and Productivity Growth in Canadian Manufacturing*. Statistics Canada, Micro Economic Studies and Analysis Division, Ottawa, Canada.

Baltagi, B. H. 2001. *Econometric Analysis of Panel Data*. Hoboken, NJ: John Wiley & Sons.

Baltagi, B. H., B. Fingleton, and A. Pirotte. 2014. Estimating and Forecasting with a Dynamic Spatial Panel Data Model. *Oxford Bulletin of Economics and Statistics* 76(1): 112–138.

Beck, T., R. Levine, and N. Loayza. 2000. Financial Development and the Sources of Growth. *Journal of Financial Economics* 58 (1–2): 261–300.

Benhabib, J., and M. M. Speigel. 1992. *The Role of Human Capital in Economic Development: Evidence from Aggregate Cross-Country and Regional US Data*. New York, NY: Department of Economics, New York University.

Biggeri, M. 2003. Key Factors of Recent Chinese Provincial Economic Growth. *Journal of Chinese Economics and Business Studies* 1: 159–183.

Blomstrom, M., and A. Kokko. 1998. Multinational Corporations and Spillovers. *Journal of Economic Surveys* 12(3): 247–277.

Blundell, R., and S. Bond. 1998. Initial Conditions and Moment Restrictions in Dynamic Panel Data Models. *Journal of Econometrics* 87(1): 115–143.

Borenzstein, E., J. Gregorio, and J. Lee. 1995. How Does Foreign Direct Investment Affect Economic Growth? NBER Working Paper 5057. Cambridge, MA: National Bureau of Economic Research.

Brandt, L., C. Hsieh, and X. Zhu. 2008. Growth and Structural Transformation in China. In *China's Great Economic Transformation*, edited by L. Brandt and T. Rawski. Cambridge, United Kingdom: Cambridge University Press.

Buckley, P. J., J. Clegg, and C. Wang. 2002. The Impact of Inward of FDI
    on the Performance of Chinese Manufacturing Firms. *Journal of
    International Business Studies* 33(4): 637–655.

Candelaria, C., M. Daly, and G Hale. 2013. Persistence of Regional Inequality
    in China. Working Paper 2013-06. San Francisco, CA: Federal Reserve
    Bank of San Francisco.

Cohen, D. 1992. Foreign Finance and Economic Growth: An Empirical
    Analysis. In *Capital Mobility*, edited by L. Leiderman and A. Razin.
    Washington, DC and New York, NY: CEPR and Cambridge
    University Press.

De Vries, G. J., A. A. Erumban, M. P. Timmer, I. Voskoboynikov, and
    H. X. Wu. 2012. Deconstructing the BRICs: Structural Transformation
    and Aggregate Productivity Growth. *Journal of Comparative Economics*
    40: 211–227.

Driffield, N., and M. Munday. 2002. Foreign Direct Investment,
    Transactions Linkages and the Performance of the Domestic Sector.
    International Journal of the Economics of Business 9(3): 335–351.

Dunn, E. S., Jr. 1960. A Statistical and Analytical Technique for Regional
    Analysis. *Papers and Proceedings of the Regional Science Association*
    VI(1960): 97–112.

Egawa, A. 2013. Will Income Inequality Cause a Middle-income Trap in Asia?
    Bruegel Working Paper 2013/06. Brussels: Bruegel.

Eichengreen, B., P. D. Park, and K. Shin. 2011. When Fast Growing Economies
    Slow Down: International Evidence and Implication for China.
    NBER Working Paper 16919. Cambridge, MA: National Bureau of
    Economic Research.

Ezcurra, R., and A. Rodríquez-Pose. 2013. Does Economic Globalization
    Affect Regional Inequality? A Cross-country Analysis. *World Development*
    52: 92–103.

Fuchs, V. R. 1959. Changes in the Location of US Manufacturing since 1929.
    Journal of Regional Science 1(2): 1–17.

Fukao K., and T. Yuan. 2012. China's Economic Growth, Structural Change
    and the Lewisian Turning Point. *Hitotsubashi Journal of Economics* 53(2):
    147–176.

Fukumi, A., J. Mallick, and M. Furuta. 2017. Power Tariff Policy and Manufacturing Sector Productivity in India. Discussion Paper No. 99. Institute for Policy Analysis and Social Innovation, University of Hogo, Kobe, Japan.

Globerman, S., and J. Ries, 1994. The Economic Performance of Foreign Affiliates in Canada. *Canadian Journal of Economics* 27: 143–156.

Goldar, B. N., V. S. Renganathan, and R. Banga. 2004. Ownership and Efficiency in Engineering Firms: 1990–91 to 1999–2000. *Economic and Political Weekly* 31 January: 441–447.

Graham, E., and P. Krugman. 1991. *Foreign Direct Investment in the United States*. Washington, DC: Institute for International Economics.

Greene, W. H. 2006. *Econometric Analysis*, 5th ed. Upper Saddle River, NJ: Prentice Hall.

Hale, G., and C. Long. 2007. Is There Evidence of FDI Spillover on Chinese Firms' Productivity and Innovation? Yale University Economic Growth Center Discussion Paper 934. Newhaven, CT: Yale University.

Hasan, R., S. Lamba, and A. S. Gupta. 2013. Growth, Structural Change, and Poverty Reduction: Evidence from India. ADB South Asia Working Paper Series 22 (November). Manila: ADB.

Havlik, P. 2005. Structural Change, Productivity and Employment in the New EU Member States. WIIW Research Report 313. Vienna: Vienna Institute for International Economic Studies.

Herzog, H., Jr., and R. Olsen. 1997. Shift-Share Analysis Revisited: The Allocation Effect and the Stability of Regional Structure. *Journal of Regional Science* 17(December): 441–454.

Huang, Y., ed. 2003. *Selling China: Foreign Direct Investment During the Reform Era*. New York, NY: Cambridge University Press.

Islam, S. N. 2015. Will Inequality Lead China to the Middle Income Trap? DESA Working Paper 142. New York, NY: United Nations Department of Economic and Social Affairs.

Kathuria, V., S. R. Raj, and K. Sen. 2013. Impact of Human Capital on Manufacturing Productivity Growth in India. In *Human Capital and Development: The Indian Experience,* 2nd ed., edited by N. Siddharthan and K. Narayanan. New Delhi: Springer.

Kremer, M., and J. Thompson. 1993. Why Isn't Convergence Instantaneous? Mimeo. Harvard University.

Kuznets, S. 1979. Growth and Structural Shifts. In http://catalogue. nla.gov.au/Record/999370, edited by W. Galenson. Ithaca, NY: Cornell University Press.

Lewis, W. A. 1954. Economic Development with Unlimited Supplies of Labour. *The Manchester School* 22: 139–191.

Li, X., and X. Liu. 2005. Foreign Direct Investment and Economic Growth: An Increasingly Endogenous Relationship. *World Development* 33(3): 393–407.

Li, Y., and Y. H. D. Wei. 2010. The Spatial-Temporal Hierarchy of Regional Inequality of China. *Applied Geography* 30: 303–316.

Lucas, R. 1988. On the Mechanics of Economic Development. *Journal of Monetary Economics* 22: 3–42.

Mallick, J. 2012. Private Investment in ICT Sector of Indian States. *Indian Economic Review* 47(1): 33–56.

———. 2013a. Private Investment in India: Regional Patterns and Determinant. *Annals of Regional Science* 51(2): 515–536.

———. 2013b. Public Expenditure, Private Investment and States Income in India. *Journal of Developing Areas* 47(1): 181–205.

———. 2014. Regional Convergence of Economic Growth during Post-Reform Period in India. *The Singapore Economic Review* 59(2): 1450012-1–1450012-18.

———. 2015a. Globalisation, Structural Change and Productivity Growth in the Emerging Countries. *Indian Economic Review* 50(2): 181–216.

———. 2015b. Private Investment and Income Disparity Across Indian States: Ideas for India. London School of Economics, International Growth Center. http://www.ideasforindia.in/article. aspx?article_id=1459. 3 June.

———. 2017. Structural Change and Productivity Growth in the Emerging Countries. ADBI Working Paper 656. Tokyo: ADB Institute.

Mallick J., and Z. Pavel. 2018. FDI and Regional Income Disparity in the Czech Republic. *Scientific Papers of the University of Pardubice* (SciPap), Series D Faculty of Economics and Administration, 26(43 [2]): 159–171.

McMillan, M., and D. Rodrik. 2011. Globalization, Structural Change, and Productivity Growth. NBER Working Paper 17143. Cambridge, MA: National Bureau of Economic Research.

Perloff, H. S., E. S. Dunn, Jr., E. E. Lampard, and R. F. Muth. 1960. *Regions, Resources and Economic Growth*. Baltimore, MD: The Johns Hopkins University Press.

Rao, S., and J. Tang. 2005. Foreign Ownership and Total Factor Productivity. In *Governance, Multinationals and Growth*, edited by L. Eden and W. Dobson. Cheltenham, United Kingdom and Northampton, MA: Edward Elgar.

Romer, P. 1993. Idea Gaps and Object Gaps in Economic Development. *Journal of Monetary Economics* 32: 543–573.

Romer, P. M. 1990. Endogenous Technical Change. *Journal of Political Economy* 98(2), Part 2: S71–102.

Roodman, D. 2009. How to do Xtrabond2: An Introduction to Difference and System GMM in Stata. *Stata J* 9(1): 80–136.

Schultz, T. W. 1975. The Value of the Ability to Deal with Disequilibrium. *Journal of Economic Literature* 13: 827–846.

Siddharthan, N. S., and K. Lal. 2004. Liberalisation, MNE and Productivity of Indian Enterprises. *Economic and Political Weekly*, 13 January: 448–452.

Sivasubramonian, S. 2004. *The Sources of Economic Growth in India: 1950–51 to 1999–2000*. New Delhi: Oxford University Press.

Syrquin, M. 1984. Resource Reallocation and Productivity Growth. In *Economic Structure and Performance,* edited by M. Syrquin, L. Taylor, and L. E. Westphal. New York, NY: Academic Press.

———. 1988. Patterns of Structural Change. In *Handbook of Development Economics,* Vol. I, edited by H. Chenery and T. N. Srinivasan. Amsterdam: Elsevier, North-Holland.

Temple J. 2001. Structural Change and Europe's Golden Age. CEPR Discussion Paper 2861 (June). London: Centre for Economic Policy Research.

Visaria, P. 2002. Workforce and Employment in India, 1961–94. In *National Income Accounts and Data Systems*, edited by B. S. Minhas. New Delhi: Oxford University Press.

Wan, G. H., M. Lu, and Z. Chen. 2007. Globalization and Regional Inequality: Evidence from within China. *Review of Income and Wealth* 53(1): 35–59.

Wang, Z., and Z. Li. 2004. Re-examine the Crowd in or Crowd Out Effects of FDI on Domestic Investment. *Statistical Research* July: 37–43.

Wei, Z., and R. Hao. 2011. The Role of Human Capital in China's Total Factor Productivity Growth: A Cross-province Analysis. *The Developing Economies* 49(1): 1–35.

Welch, F. 1970. Education and Production. *Journal of Political Economy* 7(8): 35–59.

Wooldridge, J. M. 2002. *Econometric Analysis of Cross Section and Panel Data.* Cambridge: MIT Press.

Xu, H., M. Lai, and P. Qi. 2008. Openness, Human Capital and Total Factor Productivity Evidence from China. *Journal of Chinese Economic and Business Studies* 6(3): 279–289.

Zhang, X., and K. Zhang. 2003. How Does Globalization Affect Regional Inequality Within a Developing Country? Evidence from China. *The Journal of Development Studies* 39: 47–67.

Zhang, Z. Y. 2002. Productivity and Economic Growth: An Empirical Assessment of the Contribution of FDI to the Chinese Economy. *Journal of Economic Development* 27(2): 81–94.

APPENDIX A

Measurement of State-Wise Employment in India

Data for employment at the state level are available from three main sources: census studies, undertaken every 10 years; reports from the National Sample Survey Organization (NSSO); and annual employment figures of the registered manufacturing sector from the Annual Survey of Industries (ASI). The NSSO provides data on average person-days employed only for usually occupied workers, as per the data collected through the daily status approach. However, these data include self-employed and unpaid family workers. The reports also provide worker population ratios (WPRs) by using three approaches, whereas WPRs by using only the usual status approach (or activities of the previous year) are comparable with census results (Sivasubramonian 2004; Visaria 2002). Hence, the study estimates the number of workers by multiplying the WPR by the usual status approach with the estimates of the mid-year population in the respective years.

The study uses five survey reports from the NSSO in the years 1993–1994 (50th round), 1999–2000 (55th round), 2005–2006 (62nd round), 2009–2010 (66th round), and 2011–2012 (68th round). Based on these estimates, the state-wise share of total employment in the three broad sectors has been calculated, which are also used to obtain the inter-period shares through the interpolation method. Then, for international comparisons, these estimated annual shares are used to distribute the three broad sectoral annual employed persons at the national level from World KLEMS data.[1]

---

[1] World KLEMS provides data for India between 1980 and 2008. Hence the study uses the growth rate of employment in three broad sectors from the "GGDC 10-sector database" to extend the series for 2009 and 2010.

Table A7: Estimation of State-Wise Employment (Persons in '000)

NSSO Round	Year	Nature	Remarks
68th	2011–2012	(1) Distribution of employment within 21 industries for 35 states/U.T. (2) WPR by gender and location (3) projected population by gender and location as of 1 January 2012	WPR is multiplied by the projected population to obtain the estimated employed persons. Then, the industry-wise distribution series is used to obtain the employed persons by states for 21 broad sectors
66th	2009–2010	(1) Distribution of employment within 9 industries for 35 states/U.T. (2) WPR by gender and location (3) projected population by gender and location as of 1 January 2010	WPR is multiplied by the projected population to obtain the estimated employed persons. Then, the industry-wide distribution series is used to obtain the employed persons by states for 9 broad sectors
61st	2004–2005	(1) Distribution of employment within 9 industries for 35 states/U.T. (2) WPR by location (3) projected population by location as of 1 January 2005	'do'
55th	1999–2000	Distribution of employment within 9 industries for 32 states/U.T., and the estimated employed persons	'do'
50th	1993–1994	Distribution of employment within 9 industries for 32 states/U.T., and the estimated employed persons	'do'

NSSO = National Sample Survey Organization, U.T. = Union Territories, WPR = worker population ratios.
Source: Author.

Measurement of State-Wise Capital Stock in India

State-level data on physical capital stock are not available in the public domain
in India (Mallick 2014, 2013a, 2013b, 2012). The National Accounts Statistics
(NAS) of the Central Statistical Organization (CSO) provides annual data on
capital stock at the sectoral level in India. I have made use of these all-India data
to generate state-level capital stock across sectors. The estimation is based on
the assumption that the sectoral capital-output ratio remains the same for all

the states in India in each year. The characteristics of the sector are taken into account by using 17 sectoral classifications: (1) agriculture; (2) forestry and logging; (3) fishing; (4) mining and quarrying; (5.a) manufacturing registered; (5.b) manufacturing unregistered; (6) construction; (7) electricity, gas, and water supply; (8.a) railways; (8.b) transport by other means; (8.c) storage; (8.d) communication; (9) trade, hotels, and restaurants; (10) banking and insurance; (11) real estate, ownership of dwellings, and business services; (12) public administration and defense; (13) other services. I have obtained the national sectoral-level income and capital stock data at 2004–05 prices from the NAS for the years 1993–2010. I then calculated the capital-income ratios for all the above 17 sectors in all the years at the national level, and applied these sectoral ratios with the sectoral-level state income from the CSO to estimate the state-level net capital stock in all years across the 17 sectors. The aggregate of all 17 sectors' net capital stock is considered as the total net capital stock of a state. The state-level investment is calculated as the net addition of capital stock during a year.

Table A7.1: Data and Variables

Variables	Measurement	Sources	
		India	PRC
Structural Change (SC)	BE+DSE	Estimated	Estimated
Investment	Percentage of investment in income	Investment is the net addition of capital stock. The measurement of capital stock is detailed in Appendix A.	Investment data are sourced from the NBSC, and are converted to constant prices by the regional income deflator
Human capital	The ratio of educated people to the total population	(The ratio of enrollment of students in higher education to the total population). Annual reports of University Grant Commissioner of India	(The percentage of literate people aged 15 and over) NBSC
FDI	Percentage of FDI in income	Secretariat of Industrial Assistance (SIA)	NBSC

BE = between effect, DSE = dynamic sectoral effect, FDI = foreign direct investment, NBSC = National Bureau of Statistics of China, PRC = People's Republic of China.

Source: Author.

Table A7.2: Decomposition of Regional Employment Change ('000') in Indian States (major 20)

States	Primary			Secondary			Tertiary			Income Level
	NGE	IME	CE	NGE	IME	CE	NGE	IME	CE	
Delhi	1.0	-0.8	-4.9	16.3	24.5	-24.3	37.6	47.9	21.7	HI
Gujarat	170.8	-154.5	97.3	48.8	75.6	-55.8	66.4	84.0	10.5	HI
Haryana	52.5	-49.1	22.4	18.6	31.0	19.1	29.0	36.7	-6.7	HI
Kerala	61.2	-55.1	-117.0	36.5	55.9	-43.2	58.2	72.9	-0.1	HI
Maharashtra	316.0	-287.4	124.3	83.7	128.8	-104	153.9	193.4	50.7	HI
Punjab	63.4	-57.5	-14.2	22.3	36.3	23.6	36.7	45.7	-10.1	HI
Tamil Nadu	186.4	-165.2	-182.0	88.6	132.5	-117	105.6	131.3	-79.4	HI
Andhra Pradesh	312.7	-278.7	-148.0	66.8	103.2	-53.8	117.9	146.3	-41.5	MI
Himachal Pradesh	27.4	-24.9	-14.1	6.0	9.7	3.2	6.4	8.1	4.1	MI
Karnataka	203.5	-183.6	-37.2	41.7	63.4	-48.7	70.1	89.1	46.3	MI
Uttarakhand	28.7	-26.4	-8.4	4.6	7.7	13.6	8.5	10.8	12.5	MI
West Bengal	185.0	-169.1	121.9	82.0	123.4	-78.5	113.6	145.3	-51.7	MI
Assam	75.6	-71.9	36.4	7.4	11.6	10.1	33.2	40.2	8.8	LI
Bihar	206.5	-192.9	19.8	19.9	34.7	103.8	50.8	68.6	47.5	LI
Chhattisgarh	97.3	-92.1	26.8	9.4	15.3	2.1	15.7	20.3	3.8	LI
Jharkhand	77.1	-71.2	-51.3	17.6	29.9	39.5	19.6	26.5	22.1	LI
Manipur	5.8	-5.3	-1.7	1.2	1.8	1.5	2.4	3.2	-1.3	LI
Odisha	137.9	-124.3	-38.7	29.1	47.2	13.8	35.4	44.6	3.9	LI
Rajasthan	191.9	-176.2	-42.4	48.8	79.8	68.0	51.2	66.3	24.6	LI
Uttar Pradesh	461.6	-426.0	116.0	115.9	188.2	143.0	163.1	204.3	-71.5	LI

CE = competitive effect, HI = high income, ME = industry mix effect, LI = low income, MI = middle income, NGE = national growth effect.

Note: The figures in the table are in terms of annual averages.

Source: Author's calculation.

Table A7.3: Decomposition of Regional Employment Change ('000) in the PRC's Provinces

States	Primary			Secondary			Tertiary			Income Level
	NGE	IME	CE	NGE	IME	CE	NGE	IME	CE	
Beijing	5	−18	3	21	21	−70	41	160	275	HI
Hainan	16	−57	34	3	4	−3	10	39	8	HI
Inner Mongolia	43	−150	80	17	14	−68	28	111	−35	HI
Ningxia	12	−40	6	5	7	7	6	26	10	HI
Qinghai	11	−36	6	3	6	2	6	25	9	HI
Shanghai	6	−18	−15	30	30	−136	33	129	12	HI
Tianjin	6	−22	4	17	15	−74	16	65	−38	HI
Tibet Autonomous Region	7	−24	12	1	2	6	3	11	18	HI
Xinjiang	31	−108	80	10	9	−36	19	75	3	HI
Chongqing	72	−225	−167	26	46	55	45	179	15	MI
Fujian	60	−197	−28	38	71	119	46	184	3	MI
Gansu	56	−197	116	16	17	−49	31	123	−6	MI
Heilongjiang	56	−202	223	37	25	−242	46	184	−101	MI
Jiangsu	113	−337	−339	110	179	94	100	398	71	MI
Jilin	43	−143	27	23	16	−120	34	137	−100	MI
Liaoning	53	−186	119	53	42	−298	65	259	−93	MI
Shaanxi	80	−264	−33	29	34	−13	45	184	−66	MI
Shanxi	51	−174	68	35	35	−118	40	158	−56	MI
Zhejiang	81	−241	−264	84	171	294	82	328	130	MI
Anhui	152	−494	−80	53	92	128	77	311	−38	LI
Guangdong	118	−411	242	99	172	199	130	513	114	LI
Guangxi	125	−420	147	26	46	102	60	248	−145	LI
Guizhou	107	−353	15	17	24	−2	44	175	234	LI
Hebei	131	−434	−11	81	105	−58	80	320	−188	LI
Henan	242	−834	283	91	141	163	103	406	−56	LI
Hubei	99	−317	−190	48	56	20	80	320	6	LI
Hunan	164	−544	14	50	68	−9	85	338	−67	LI
Jiangxi	84	−270	−85	32	60	55	58	234	−145	LI
Shandong	190	−607	−123	107	167	3	109	433	81	LI
Sichuan	214	−677	−330	64	96	22	108	434	8	LI
Yunnan	133	−456	186	20	27	30	38	152	136	LI

CE = competitive effect, HI = high income, IME = industry mix effect, LI = low income, MI = middle income, NGE = national growth effect, PRC = People's Republic of China.

Note: The figures in the table are in terms of annual averages.

Source: Author's calculation.

Table A7.4: Decomposition of Labor Productivity Growth in Indian States (major 20)

States	WE	BE	DSE	Income Level
Delhi	5.73	0.25	−0.03	HI
Gujarat	6.40	0.64	−0.11	HI
Haryana	5.12	0.75	−0.01	HI
Kerala	5.20	0.98	0.05	HI
Maharashtra	4.95	0.88	0.02	HI
Punjab	3.34	0.56	0.02	HI
Tamil Nadu	6.31	1.01	0.05	HI
Andhra Pradesh	5.65	0.94	0.00	MI
Himachal Pradesh	4.64	1.84	0.06	MI
Karnataka	4.83	1.22	0.04	MI
Uttarakhand	3.09	0.70	−0.01	MI
West Bengal	4.69	0.30	−0.02	MI
Assam	1.65	0.88	−0.18	LI
Bihar	3.87	1.55	−0.12	LI
Chhattisgarh	3.93	1.25	0.06	LI
Jharkhand	2.94	2.25	−0.37	LI
Madhya Pradesh	3.23	1.09	0.02	LI
Odisha	4.27	1.26	0.03	LI
Rajasthan	4.92	1.31	0.01	LI
Uttar Pradesh	5.26	2.22	0.13	LI
India	4.56	0.96	0.05	HI

BE = between effect, DSE = dynamic sectoral effect, HI = high income, LI = low income, MI = middle income, WE = within effect.

Note: The figures in this table are n terms of annual averages.

Source: Author's calculation.

Table A7.5: Decomposition of Interregional Labor Productivity Growth in the PRC's Provinces

Provinces	WE	BE	DSE	Income Level
Beijing	8.77	0.45	−0.16	HI
Hainan	5.98	0.12	−0.02	HI
Inner Mongolia	10.27	0.18	−0.11	HI
Ningxia	9.97	1.52	−0.02	HI
Qinghai	8.65	1.30	−0.01	HI
Shanghai	9.74	0.23	−0.18	HI
Tianjin	11.58	0.03	−0.07	HI
Tibet Autonomous Region	4.31	2.70	−0.13	HI
Xinjiang	9.82	0.17	−0.12	HI
Anhui	7.97	1.19	0.02	LI
Guangdong	7.20	0.73	−0.03	LI
Guangxi	7.51	1.17	−0.33	LI
Guizhou	7.83	1.47	−0.12	LI
Hebei	9.47	0.79	−0.06	LI
Henan	8.59	1.09	−0.01	LI
Hubei	9.09	0.72	−0.11	LI
Hunan	9.38	0.89	0.02	LI
Jiangxi	9.80	0.82	−0.04	LI
Shandong	8.65	1.16	0.03	LI
Sichuan	8.57	1.17	0.03	LI
Yunnan	6.82	1.87	0.00	LI
Chongqing	8.63	1.59	0.05	MI
Fujian	7.48	1.10	−0.16	MI
Gansu	9.36	0.41	−0.03	MI
Heilongjiang	10.72	−0.86	−0.35	MI
Jiangsu	8.45	0.98	−0.01	MI
Jilin	10.84	−0.02	−0.16	MI
Liaoning	9.79	−0.25	−0.19	MI
Shaanxi	9.75	1.35	0.00	MI
Shanxi	11.03	0.40	−0.03	MI
Zhejiang	7.69	1.26	0.04	MI
All	8.59	0.98	0.04	

BE = between effect, DSE = dynamic sectoral effect, HI = high income, LI = low income, MI = middle income, PRC = People's Republic of China, WE = within effect.

Note: The figures are in terms of annual averages.

Source: Author's calculation.

Table A7.6: Coefficient of Variations in Labor Productivity

Country	1993–1994	2010–2011
India	47	62
PRC	57	58

PRC = People's Republic of China.

Note: The coefficient of variations across all the regions in India and the PRC.

Source: Author's calculation.

Figure A7.1: Change in Regional Employment Structure

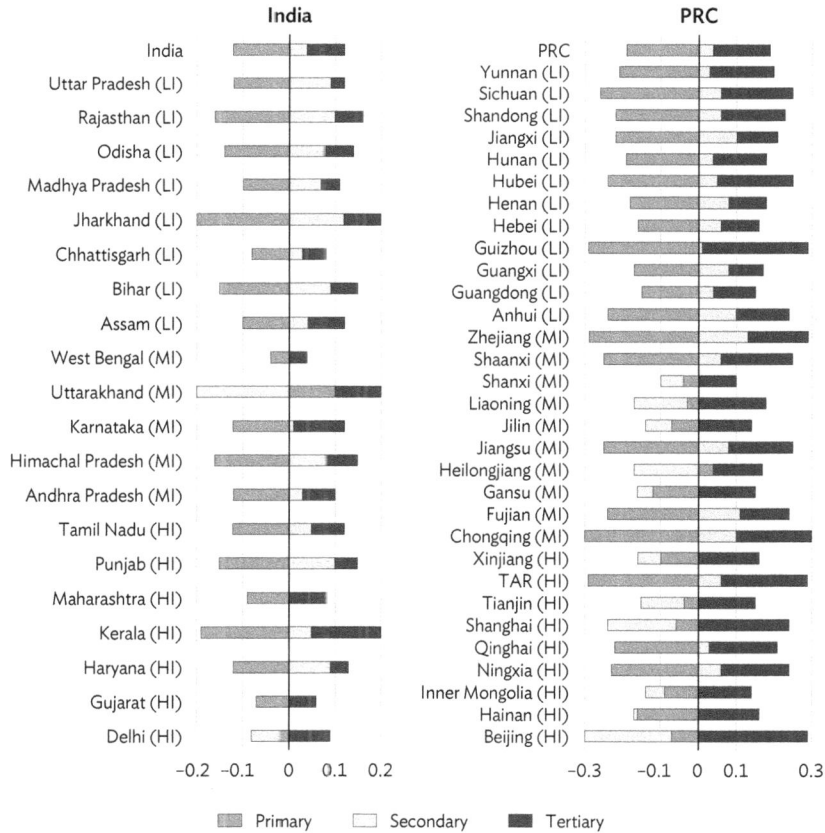

HI = high income, LI = low income, MI = middle income, PRC = People's Republic of China, TAR = Tibet Autonomous Region.

Source: Author's calculation.

CHAPTER 8

Housing Prices and Investment: An Assessment of the Inland-Favoring Land Supply Policies in the People's Republic of China

Libin Han and Ming Lu

8.1 | Introduction

In recent years, the People's Republic of China (PRC) has faced a decline in economic growth and investment. The gross domestic product (GDP) growth rate declined from 9.2% in 2009 to 7.3% in 2014. The total fixed asset investment rate also decreased, from 30.0% in 2009 to 14.7% in 2014.[1] Since 2003, housing prices have continued to rise quickly, especially in coastal areas (Liang, Lu, and Zhang 2016). Since 2003, the PRC's central government has allocated more construction land-use quotas to inland provinces,[2] for the purpose of balancing the growth gap between coastal and inland regions (Lu and Xiang 2016). This change in policy has also limited the land supply and led to faster housing price growth in coastal regions (Liang, Lu, and Zhang 2016).

These observations inspired two interlinked questions that are addressed in this chapter. "What is the role of inland-favoring land supply policy?" and

---

[1] The data are from the website of the National Bureau of Statistics of China. http://data.stats.gov. cn/ks.htm?cn=C01.

[2] In this chapter, inland provinces refer to central and western provinces, including all non-coastal provinces and Guangxi. Beijing is included in the coastal area.

"How do housing prices affect investment?" However, there are no existing
studies addressing how the change in land supply policy has affected
investment by affecting housing prices.

To answer these two questions, the cities were first divided into two groups:
the cities in which the share of national land supply increased, and those in
which the share of national land supply decreased. Many coastal cities had
faced limitations in land supply after 2003. The cities in which the land supply
share decreased showed faster increases in housing prices after 2003 than
other cities did.

Then we assume that the land policy may affect the firms' investment
through two channels. The first channel is a collateral effect. The rising
housing prices appreciated the value of fixed assets like housing and
factories, which could be the collateral when firms borrow. Firms may get
more loans because of the appreciation in collateral value. This channel has
a positive effect on investment by firms. The second channel is called the
crowding-out effect. The rising housing prices would crowd out investments
in fixed capital by non-real estate firms, while attracting more investment
in real estate. The crowding-out effect has negatively affected firms' overall
investment. The net effect of housing prices on the investment rate was found
to be negative.

Our chapter relates to several strands of literature. In recent years, there has
been a growing literature on the effect of the real estate market on investment.
These articles focused on the role of the collateral channel of housing prices in
firm behavior. Chaney, Sraer, and Thesmar (2012) showed that, through the
collateral channel, shocks to the value of real estate can have a large impact
on aggregate investment. From 1993 to 2007, a representative United States
corporation invested $0.06 of each $1 of its collateral. Firms change their
debt structure considerably in response to collateral value appreciation
(Cvijanović 2014). By providing collateral, housing prices render bank loans
more readily available to small businesses, which increases employment
(Adelino, Schoar, and Severino 2013; Charles, Hurst, and Notowidigdo 2013;

Chaney, Sraer, and Thesmar 2013). However, the collapse of the real estate market has had a large impact on investment by firms. Gan (2007) examined the shock to collateral value caused by the collapse of the land market in Japan in the 1990s. Results showed that for every 10% drop in collateral value, the average investment rate of firms dropped by about 0.8 percentage points. However, studies about the effect of collateral performed using data from the PRC have been inconclusive (Wu, Gyourko, and Deng 2015; Luo and Zhou 2013; Chen, Wang, and Liu 2015). Our study shows the existence of the collateral effect and provides new evidence about the effect of housing prices on firms' investment.

In addition to the collateral channel, housing prices may also have a negative spillover effect on investment. One reason for this may be that an increase in housing prices attracts more bank loans to ordinary households and fewer to firms. Firms themselves also tend to invest more in real estate, preferring it to fixed capital for production. A study of United States bank loans from 1988 to 2006 showed that, on average, one standard deviation increase in housing prices leads to a 3.4% drop in firms' investment, especially for small and financially constrained firms (Chakraborty, Goldstein, and MacKinlay forthcoming). Rong and Wang (2014) found that the housing price boom increased the probability of non-real estate firms entering the real estate market and hindered innovation. The greater the investment in the real estate market, the less productive investment was in manufacturing (Luo and Zhang 2015).

Unlike in the existing literature, here, the exogenous shock from the change in land policy in the PRC was used to study the effect of housing prices. Since 2003, the PRC's central government has allocated more construction land-use quotas to inland cities than elsewhere. This change from the previous policy of focusing on coastal areas has led to a divergence in housing prices between inland and coastal cities. This has provided a quasi-natural experiment that can be used to identify the effect of housing prices in different cities. The current work takes into account the collateral effect and crowding-out effect together, indicating that the crowding-out effect is the dominant channel. In other words, the rising housing prices have a net reducing effect on productive investment by manufacturing firms.

The current work is also related to regional development policy. Many papers
have discussed the decline of the PRC's total factor productivity (TFP) growth
(Wu 2013; Lu and Xiang 2016). The regional development policy, which
allocates more production factors, such as capital, land-use quotas, and fiscal
transfers, to the less productive regions, is found to be one important cause
of the decline in the PRC's TFP growth (Lu and Xiang 2016). Our research
provides new evidence of the unexpected consequences of regional
development policy We show that the land supply restriction on coastal and
large cities results in a decline in manufacturing investment. In other words,
the policy helping lagged regions by restricting the more developed regions
may lead to a loss in growth.

The rest of the chapter is organized as follows. Section 8.2 provides
the background of the land policy. Section 8.3 describes the empirical
strategy and data. Section 8.4 gives the main results. Section 8.5 shows an
examination of the channels. Section 8.6 presents our conclusion.

8.2 | Land Policy Background

8.2.1 Construction Land-Use Quota System in the PRC

In this chapter, the term land use refers to construction land use, mainly
for urban development. In the PRC, the government has strict regulations
regarding construction land use. According to the Land Administrative
Law (2006), construction land use must be in accordance with the central
government's overal plan and annual management plan.

Every year, the central government formulates an annual land-use plan,
which distributes the incremental construction land-use quotas to provincial
governments. Then the provincial governments allocate the quotas to the
next lower levels of government. To prevent encroachment onto agricultural
land, these quotas must be followed precisely. If a local government were
found to have exceeded its construction land-use quotas, its quota for the

subsequent year would be cut. In the medium term, the government produces its "Outline of the National Overall Plan of Land Use," which outlines the construction land quotas for the next 15 years. Local governments must follow the limits on construction land quotas stipulated in the plan.

The top-down construction land-use system has an information asymmetry problem. Even if the local governments have more information regarding the demands of local land use, they do not have the right to make decisions regarding land-use quotas, which are under the control of the central government.

8.2.2 Changes in Land Supply Policy After 2003

The PRC's central government has used a strict land management system to manipulate the land supply for macroeconomic regulation. The distribution of construction land-use quotas has been a particularly important policy tool to support local development in less developed regions. The regional distribution of land supply experienced a sharp turning point in 2003. Since 2003, the central government has strengthened land-use administration, and changed the land supply trend between regions. As shown in Figure 8.1, before 2003, the share of inland land supply decreased annually, but after 2003, the share of inland land supply increased from less than 30% to more than 50% during 2003–2013 period. This indicates that the coastal provinces have been more restricted in construction land supply after 2003. This trend is predicted to continue, according to "China's National New-type Urbanization Plan (2014–2020)" and the "13th Five-Year Plan for Land and Resources." In these two development plans, the central government clearly pointed out that the construction land supply would continue to be biased toward the inland provinces. This is not because the coastal region had no land available for urban use but because their land supply share has decreased since 2003. Even the most populous city, Shanghai, still reserves almost one-third of its land for agricultural use.

Figure 8.1: Inland Areas' Share of the Total Land Supply

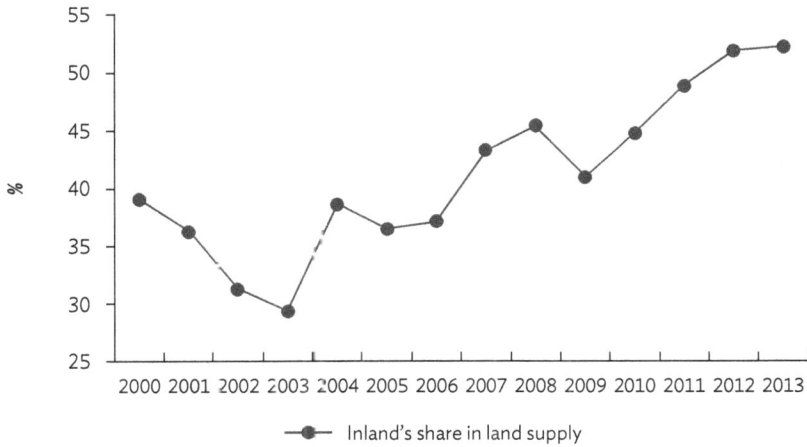

Source: *China Land and Resources Statistical Yearbook* (China Geological Press), various years.

8.3 | Data and Empirical Strategy

8.3.1 Data

The data used here are from two main sources. The firm-level data are from the PRC's industrial enterprises database. The firm-level investment rate was calculating using these data.[3] Outliers were excluded.[4] Eight capital-intensive industries directly related to natural resources or public utilities, were dropped. These included mining and washing of coal, extraction of petroleum and natural gas, mining and processing of ferrous metal ores, mining and processing

---

[3] Nie, Jiang, and Yang (2012) and Brandt, Biesebrocek, and Zhang (2014) discussed the data quality of the PRC's industrial enterprise database to process the data.

[4] The outliers that were excluded include businesses that are no longer extant; businesses with primary income below CNY5,000,000; businesses with fewer than eight employees; firms older than 100 years or in the planning stage; and firms for which any of the key variables such as firm age, number of employees, total assets, investments, and wages were less than or equal to zero. Samples whose key variables such as investment, age, profit, cash, or leverage are missing were also excluded. Then the top and bottom 1% observations of investment were excluded.

of nonferrous metal ores, mining and processing of nonmetal ores, production and supply of electric power and heat power, production and supply of water, and production and supply of gas. Firm observations that had been in the database fewer than 2 years in succession were excluded. And we removed the firm observations, which did not appear in the database during 2003–2004. The National Bureau of Statistics of China's enterprise data from 2001 to 2006 were used in this chapter as land supply data. The listed company data were used to check the crowding-out channel because data from the National Bureau of Statistics of China did does not include information regarding firms' collateral value.

Another source of data is city-level data, which is from three statistical yearbooks for various years: *China City Statistical Yearbook and China Regional Economic Statistical Yearbook* published by China Statistics Press; and *China Land and Resources Statistical Yearbook* published by China Geological Press. Housing price is a key variable. Prefecture city-level housing prices are not publicly available, so we calculated housing prices using housing sales divided by sold housing area. The data are from *China Regional Economic Statistical Yearbook*. This means that housing prices for 286 cities were available from 2001 to 2006. The total area of the land supply was another key variable. This information was taken from *China Land and Resources Statistical Yearbook*. The land supply area is land transfer data, which includes bids, auctions, and listing methods to transfer construction land. After 2003, construction land-use quotas were available at the provincial level but not the city level. As checked by Liang, Lu, and Zhang (2016), the provincial-level land supply aggregated from these city-level data were closely correlated with provincial level land-use quota, for which the information was publicly available.

8.3.2 Empirical Strategy

To address the two main issues that are the subject of this work, it was necessary to assess the change of the construction land supply share at the city level. It was also necessary to show the exogeneity of the land supply share change to local governments after 2003.

For the first step, equation (1) was used to calculate the changes in land supply share. The data period was 2001–2006. The third general land plan started in 2006, so our work focused on the second general land plan period. $landtrans_{it}$ is the national land transfer in year t. $landtrans_{it}$ denotes the land transfers area of city i in year t. Then equation (2) was used to divide the cities into two groups according to the change in the share of the land supply from 2001–2003 and 2004–2006. $land\_dec$ takes 1 if city i's share of the land supply decreased after 2003. Otherwise, it was 0. In other words, if $land\_dec$ is 1, the land supply was relatively limited in these cities after 2003.

$$\Delta land\_ratio_i = \frac{\sum\limits_{t=2001}^{2003} landtrans_{it}}{\sum\limits_{t=2001}^{2003} \sum\limits_{i=1}^{197} landtrans_{it}} - \frac{\sum\limits_{t=2004}^{2006} landtrans_{it}}{\sum\limits_{t=2004}^{2006} \sum\limits_{i=1}^{197} landtrans_{it}} \quad (1)$$

$$land\_dec_i = \begin{cases} = 1, \; if \; \Delta land\_ratio_i < 0 \\ = 0, \; if \; \Delta land\_ratio_i > 0 \end{cases} \quad (2)$$

There is one important reason why land supply share rather than land supply area was used here. Land-use quotas are set by the central government. If the overall land-use quotas were reduced, the share of land supply at city level is a better index of any changes in the inland-favoring land policy than the overall supply.

The sample for adjacent cities was used to control for unobservable variables. First the cities in which the land supply share had decreased were identified, and then adjacent cities in which the land supply share increased after 2003 were identified. Figure 8.2 presents these cities as used in our study. The black cities experienced a decrease in land supply share after 2003. The gray and light gray areas are cities in which the land supply share increased after 2003. The white areas are those for which no data were available. The gray areas are adjacent cities in which there was an increase in land supply after 2003 and the black areas are cities in which there was a decrease.

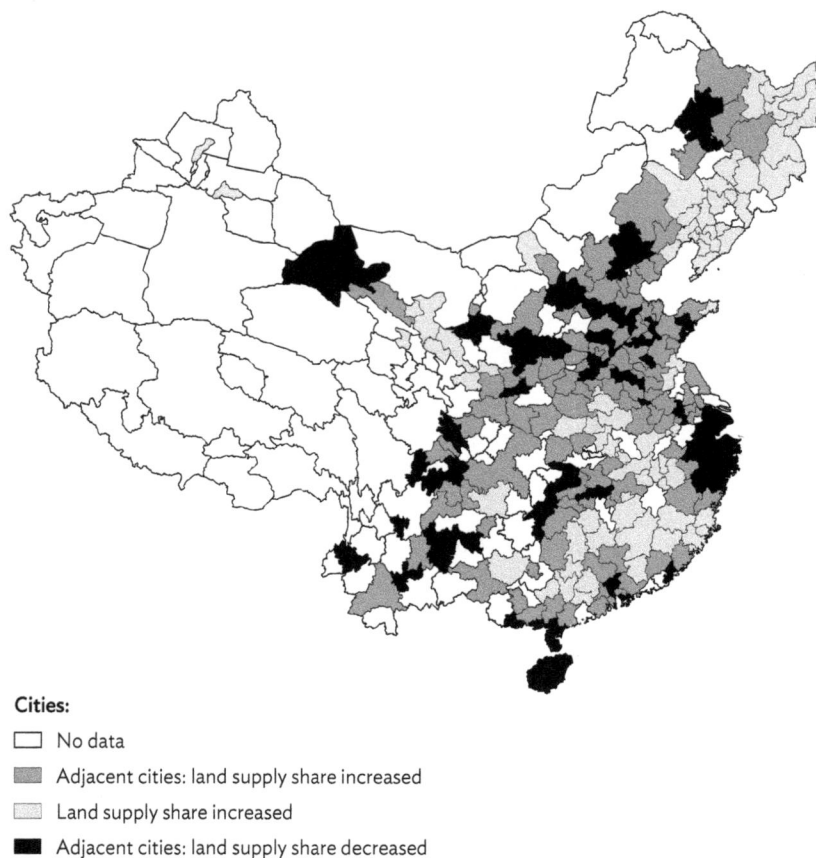

Figure 8.2: Changes in the Land Supply Share after 2003

Cities:
☐ No data
▨ Adjacent cities: land supply share increased
▨ Land supply share increased
■ Adjacent cities: land supply share decreased

Source: Authors.

Table 8.1 shows the characteristics of sample cities. They account for 68.8% of all the prefecture-level cities. Here, 32% of the cities that saw increases in land supply share after 2003 were coastal, and 45.7% of the cities saw a decrease in land supply share. Most of the cities in which land supply shares increased are located over 500 kilometers from the nearest major seaports—Hongkong, China; Shanghai; and Tianjin. In other words, the coastal cities are more likely to have restricted land supplies after 2003.

Table 8.1: Cities in which the Land Supply Share
Increased or Decreased

	Number of cities (1)	Coastal cities (2)	Inland cities (3)	Share of coastal cities (2)/(1)	Number of cities (distance to nearest three major seaports >500 kilometer) (4)
Land supply share increased	127	41	86	32.0%	70
Land supply share decreased	70	32	38	45.7%	35

Source: Authors.

The land supply between the two groups diverged after 2003, as shown in Figure 8.3. The land supply increased in both groups before 2003, showing a parallel trend. However, after 2003, the land supply area of cities in which the land supply share increased is growing more quickly than in those in which the land supply share decreased.

Figure 8.3: Land Supply Area among Cities

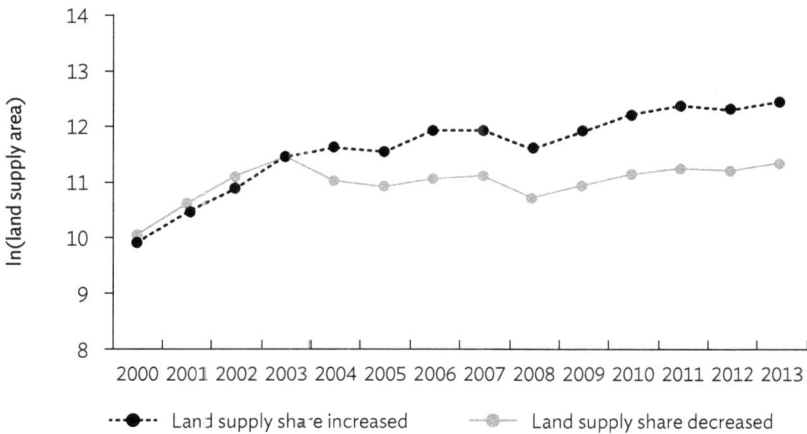

Sources: China Land and Resources Statistical Yearbook (China Geological Press), various years. Author's calculations.

To formally confirm that the diverging trend was exogenous to city governments, the variables from 2003 were used to explain the change in land supply share after 2003. The dependent variable is binary: This value is 1 if a city's land supply share decreased after 2003; otherwise it was 0. Because we focus on whether the land supply share changed, not on whether the magnitude of land supply share changed, we use the binary variable, not the percentage increase or decrease, as the dependent variable. Therefore, a probit model is estimated to identity the factors that affect the land supply share. Table 8.2 shows the results of the probit model regression. Columns 1 and 3 show the effect of geographic location. The coefficient of Coast is significant, indicating that the coastal cities were more likely to have a restricted land supply after 2003.

Table 8.2: **Whether Land Supply Share Decreased after 2003 (yes = 1)**

	(1)	(2)	(3)	(4)
Land_share_2003		137.1*** (33.87)		130.9*** (36.54)
Coast	2.095*** (0.592)	1.105 (0.698)	1.848*** (0.662)	1.181 (0.736)
Population density			0.172 (0.127)	0.148 (0.129)
Land productivity			0.680 (1.415)	0.180 (1.478)
Industry structure			-0.00261 (0.212)	-0.0707 (0.213)
Ln per capita GDP			0.565** (0.224)	0.240 (0.240)
Land fiscal			-0.00487 (0.0557)	-0.0426 (0.0677)
Constant	-1.187*** (0.396)	-1.524*** (0.410)	-6.872*** (2.309)	-3.951 (2.445)
Province Dummy	Y	Y	Y	Y
Observations	215	215	215	215

GDP = gross domestic product.
Notes: Significance levels: *** 0.01; ** 0.05; * 0.1. Standard errors clustered at city level in parentheses.
Source: Authors.

Columns 2 and 4 show that when land supply share in 2003 is added, the coefficient of Coast becomes insignificant. The higher a city's land supply share in 2003, the more likely it would be to have a restricted land supply after 2003. The coefficient for coastal cities is not significant in Columns 2 and 4 because the coastal cities had had a higher share of land supply share, but they became more restricted after 2003. For local governments, the land resources are important to economic development. Thus, changes in the land supply share are not manipulated by the local government because almost none of the demand-side variables, such as land finance, per capita GDP, industrial structure, land-use productivity, or population density are significant.[5] Nevertheless, when land supply share is not controlled in regression 3, GDP per capita has a positive sign, while population density is also marginally significant. This means that cities where the demand for construction land was stronger faced greater probabilities of land supply restriction after 2003 As shown in Table 8.2, this can only be explained by the exogenous change in land supply policy. Thus, we are confident that the divergence between the two groups after 2003 represents the changes in exogenous land supply policy of the central government. We also use the percentage of land supply share change as the dependent variable—the result is robust (we do not report this result in the chapter).

8.4 | Empirical Model and Main Estimation Results

8.4.1 Empirical Model

The regression models used to estimate values in this chapter are shown below:

$$\text{Lnhp} = \alpha_0 + \alpha_1 * \text{Land\_dec}_i \times \text{After}_{2003} + \alpha_2 * \text{Land\_dec}_i + \alpha_3 \text{After}_{2003} \qquad (2)$$
$$+ \delta X_{it} + \lambda_t + \varepsilon_t$$

[5] Population density is measured by populations/area of *shixiaqu* (the urban area); land productivity is defined as GDP/build-up area; industry structure is a ratio of the value of third industry divided by the value of second industry; per capita GDP refers to that in *shixiaqu*. "Land fiscal" is the ratio of land transfer revenues to budget revenues.

Here, hp is housing price; Land_dec$_i$ denotes the dummy for cities in which the land supply share decreased after 2003; the interaction term, Land_dec$_i$ × After$_{2003}$, refers to the effect of decreased land supply share after 2003; After$_{2003}$ is a time dummy for the period after 2003. X_{it} is a vector to control for city i's characteristics in year t, including per capita GDP, industrial structure, and employment density. Among them, the per capita GDP data were for a city's urban area (*shixiaqu*), and the industrial structure was the ratio of the third industrial output value to the second industry output. λ_t and ε_{it} are time fixed effects and random term, respectively.

$$\text{Ln}\frac{\text{Invest}_{jit}}{\text{Asset}_{jit-1}} = \beta_0 + \beta_1 * \text{Land\_dec}_i \times \text{After}_{2003} + \beta_2 * \text{Land\_dec}_i \qquad (3)$$
$$+ \beta_3 \text{After}_{2003} + \delta Z_{jit} + \lambda_t + \mu_j + v_{jit}$$

Here, Invest$_{jit}$ is a measurement for investment of firm j, city i in year t; Z_{jit} denotes firm-level characteristics.[6] μ_j and v_{jit} are firm-level fixed effects and random term, respectively. β_1 is the estimate of the effect of land supply change on investment.

$$\text{Ln}\frac{\text{Invest}_{jit}}{\text{Asset}_{jit-1}} = \gamma_0 + \gamma_1 * \text{Land\_dec}_i \times \text{After}_{2003} + \gamma_2 * \text{Land\_dec}_i \qquad (4)$$
$$+ \gamma_3 \text{After}_{2003} + \gamma_4 \text{Lnhp} + \delta X_{jit} + \lambda_t + \mu_j + v_{jit}$$

Here, Lnhp is inserted into the right-hand side of the equation. γ_4 represents the effect of housing price on investment. The change from β_1 to γ_1 represents the effect of land supply policy through housing price, while γ_1 is the remaining effect of land supply change on investment through other unobserved channels.

8.4.2　Effect of Changes in Land Supply Policy on Housing Prices

Housing price is an important intermediate variable through which the land supply policy influences investment. If a city's land supply is restricted, the housing price would increase faster compared with cities in which the

---

[6]　The firm-level control variables included ownership (SOE=1), profit_ratio (profit/asset), leverage (debt/asset), and cash/asset of the previous year.

land supply share increased. After 2003, the inland-favoring land supply caused housing prices to diverge between cities in which the land supply share increased and in those in which the land supply share decreased. Table 8.3 reports how the changes in land supply policy after 2003 influenced city housing prices. The coefficient of Land_dec×After2003 in columns (1) and (2) was significant. Even if it is possible to control for the interaction between province and year dummies, this coefficient remained significant.

Table 8.3: Land Supply Policy and Housing Price

Dep. Var: Lnhp	(1)	(2)		(3)	(4)
After$_{2003}$	0.376*** (0.0342)	0.367*** (0.0397)	Land_dec × Year$_{2002}$	0.0184 (0.0396)	0.0185 (0.0406)
Land_dec$_i$ × After$_{2003}$	0.0526* (0.0282)	0.0545* (0.0287)	Land_dec × Year$_{2003}$	0.0471 (0.0413)	0.0530 (0.0427)
Ln per capita GDP	0.0978* (0.0504)	0.120* (0.0612)	Land_dec × Year$_{2004}$	0.0790* (0.0472)	0.0820* (0.0487)
Industry structure	−0.0420 (0.0374)	−0.0401 (0.0405)	Land_dec × Year$_{2005}$	0.0725* (0.0413)	0.0783* (0.0423)
Ln population density	0.00168 (0.0289)	0.00412 (0.0310)	Land_dec × Year$_{2006}$	0.0749* (0.0436)	0.0779* (0.0449)
Ln per capita road area	0.0227 (0.0251)	0.0173 (0.0260)	Ln per capita GDP	0.0994** (0.0504)	0.122** (0.0609)
Ln per capita green areas	−0.00714 (0.0156)	−0.00967 (0.0168)	Industry structure	−0.0407 (0.0375)	−0.0385 (0.0405)
			Ln population density	0.000106 (0.0287)	0.00250 (0.0307)
			Ln per capita road areas	0.0244 (0.0250)	0.0191 (0.0258)
			Ln per capita green areas	−0.00614 (0.0157)	−0.00876 (0.0169)
Year effect	Y	Y	Year effect	Y	Y
Province time trend	N	Y	Province time trend	N	Y
Observations	1,114	1,030	Observations	1,114	1,030
R-squared	0.691	0.691	R-squared	0.692	0.692
Number of city	197	183	Number of city	197	183

GDP = gross domestic product.
Notes: Significance levels: *** 0.01; ** 0.05; * 0.1. Standard errors clustered at city level in parentheses.
Source: Authors.

We expect that the housing price would have diverged after 2003, because the land supply diverged between the two groups in which the land supply share increased or decreased. Table 8.3 indicates that housing prices in cities in which the land supply was constrained were higher than in those in cities in which the land supply share had increased after 2003. Models (3) and (4) control for the interaction terms of Land_dec and each year with and without the interaction terms between provinces and year dummies. The cities in which land supply was restricted after 2003 saw significantly higher housing prices only after 2003. In other words, it is here concluded that the shock from land supply policy has caused housing prices in these two groups of cities to diverge.

8.4.3 Effect of Housing Prices on Investment

Next, firms' investment rates served as the dependent variable. It was defined as investment in fixed assets divided by the total assets of the previous year. Because the capital stock has many negative values, the total assets, rather than the capital stock, were used. The first column of Table 8.4 shows that the shock of the construction land supply policy had only a marginally significant effect on investment. Column 2 shows housing prices had a significant effect on firms' investment rate. On average, a 10% increase of housing prices led to a drop of about 0.137% in investment rate. As shown in column 3, the effect of housing prices was still significant after controlling for land_dec×after2003. Although the coefficient of Land_dec×after2003 is not significant, its magnitude was reduced by half from (1) to (3). This means the land supply policy has a weak effect on firms' investments, exerted through changes in housing prices. However, Table 8.5 shows the net effect of housing prices on investment rate to be negative.

In previous analyses, two groups of cities in which the land supply share decreased or increased were compared. Even if the adjacent samples were used to control unobservable variables to facilitate the comparability of the two groups, the control group may also be affected by the policy.

Table 8.4: Land Policy, Housing Price, and Investment Rate

Dep. Var: $\text{Ln}\dfrac{\text{Invest}_{jit}}{\text{Asset}_{jit}}$	(1)	(2)	(3)
Land_dec$_i$ × After$_{2003}$	−0.00238 (0.00221)		−0.00108 (0.00230)
Lnhp		−0.0137*** (0.00450)	−0.0133*** (0.00454)
After$_{2003}$	−0.0273 (0.0198)		−0.0233 (0.0194)
Ownership	−0.00657*** (0.00136)	−0.00655*** (0.00138)	−0.00653*** (0.00138)
Profit_ratio	−0.246*** (0.0390)	−0.247*** (0.0389)	−0.247*** (0.0389)
Leverage	−0.0367*** (0.00512)	−0.0367*** (0.00512)	−0.0367*** (0.00512)
Cash/Asset$_{t-1}$	0.250*** (0.0360)	0.250*** (0.0360)	0.250*** (0.0360)
Ln industry structure	−0.00756 (0.00497)	−0.00906* (0.00481)	−0.00868* (0.00474)
Ln per capita GDP	−0.000779 (0.00440)	0.00201 (0.00440)	0.00220 (0.00443)
Ln industry_structure$_{2001}$ × After$_{2003}$	1.97e-05 (0.00283)	−0.00213 (0.00310)	−0.00180 (0.00290)
Ln per capita GDP$_{2001}$ × After$_{2003}$	0.000482 (0.00193)	0.000271 (0.00165)	0.000638 (0.00188)
Constant	0.0506 (0.0462)	0.125** (0.0495)	0.120** (0.0503)
Year FE	Y	Y	Y
Industry time trend	Y	Y	Y
Firm FE	Y	Y	Y
Observations	387,920	387,920	387,920
R-squared	0.037	0.037	0.037
Number of Firms	104,700	104,700	104,700

GDP = gross domestic product.

Notes: Significance levels: *** 0.01; ** 0 05; * 0.1. Standard errors clustered at city level in parentheses.

Source: Authors.

To alleviate this concern, one control group was established to confirm whether the previous results were robust. Unfortunately, there can be no true control group for the land supply policy shock because every city in the PRC was affected by the change in policy in 2003. It is here assumed that the cities in which the effects of the change in land policy were weak would be sufficient to serve as an approximate control group. Cities for which the absolute value of $\Delta land\_ratio_i$ was in the lowest 25% quantile were considered suitable. It is here assumed that those cities were not affected by the land policy shock, because their land supply share changed only slightly. Table 8.5 reports the robustness of the effects of housing prices on investment rate. As in earlier analyses, after controlling for housing prices, the direct effect of the change in land supply share change becomes insignificant for columns (1) to (3). It remains significant, though smaller, for columns (4) to (6).

Table 8.5: Land Policy, Housing Prices, and Investment Rate by Group

	Group in which the land supply share decreased and control group (Land_dec=1, if share decrease)			Group in which the land supply share increased and control group (Land_dec=1, if share increase)		
	(1)	(2)	(3)	(4)	(5)	(6)
Land_dec×After2003	-0.00712* (0.00387)		-0.00370 (0.00368)	-0.00856** (0.00396)		-0.00787** (0.00394)
Lnhp		-0.0236*** (0.00541)	-0.0232*** (0.00536)		-0.0118** (0.00481)	-0.0111** (0.00478)
After2003			-0.00662 (0.0189)			-0.0224 (0.0389)
Firm level control variables	Y	Y	Y	Y	Y	Y
City level control variables	Y	Y	Y	Y	Y	Y
Year FE	Y	Y	Y	Y	Y	Y
Industry time trend	Y	Y	Y	Y	Y	Y
Firm FE	Y	Y	Y	Y	Y	Y
Observations	223,634	223,634	223,634	189,112	189,112	189,112
R-squared	0.039	0.039	0.039	0.037	0.036	0.036

Notes: Significance levels: *** 0.01; ** 0.05; * 0.1. Standard errors clustered at city level in parentheses.
Source: Authors.

8.5 | Channels from Housing Price to Investment

In this section, the channels through which housing prices may affect
firms' investment were evaluated, and two of them were empirically tested.
The collateral effect improves the firms' ability to receive loans for investment,
while the crowding-out effect attracts more investment into the real estate
market and reduces fixed capital investment. The net effect of housing price
on investment depends on the relative power of these two channels.

8.5.1 Effect of Collateral

The collateral effect means that the rising housing prices increase the overall
value of the firms' holdings in houses and other buildings, which can be used
as collateral when borrowing. Rising values of collateral can reduce the firm's
financial constraints, enabling it to borrow more for investment. The enterprise
data of the National Bureau of Statistics of China do not provide the firms'
collateral value. So we use the listed companies' data during 2003–2007
instead to check the channel. The collateral value was calculated as follows:

$$\text{RE\_value}_{it} = \left(\text{RE\_value}_{2003} \times \prod_{t=2003}^{t-1}\left[1 + HPI_{jt}\right]\right)\Big/Asset_{t-1},$$

where RE_value_{2003} is the market value of real estate assets in the beginning
of 2003. HPI_{jt} indicates the rate of growth in real estate price of each given city
in year t. RE_value_{it} represents the changes in real estate assets in market value
over time at the beginning of 2003. It is here assumed that a firm's real estate
assets are located in the same city as its headquarters.

Table 8.6 reports the regression results for the collateral effect. Columns 1
and 2 are the full sample regression. After controlling for other variables
that influence investment, the value of collateral was found to have a
positive effect on the rate of firms' investments. On average, a 10% increase
in collateral value was associated with a corresponding increase in the
investment rate of 0.974%. Column 2 shows that after controlling for the
collateral effect, the coefficient of housing price became significantly negative.

Columns 3–6 show regressions for different groups of cities. The results showed the collateral effect to be significant in both groups. In the cities in which the land supply share decreased, the housing price had a negative effect on firms' investment rate.

Table 8.6: Effects of Collateral on Investment

Dep. Var: $\text{Ln}\dfrac{\text{Invest}_{jit}}{\text{Asset}_{jit-1}}$	All		Land supply share decreased		Land supply share increased	
	(1)	(2)	(3)	(4)	(5)	(6)
Lnhp	−0.0134	−0.0307*	−0.0515*	−0.0659**	0.0139	−0.0105
	(0.0172)	(0.0178)	(0.0271)	(0.0276)	(0.0228)	(0.0241)
RE_value		0.0974***		0.0846**		0.138***
		(0.0268)		(0.0329)		(0.0469)
Cash	0.0178***	0.0174***	0.0185***	0.0186***	0.0156**	0.0138*
	(0.00430)	(0.00429)	(0.00546)	(0.00544)	(0.00701)	(0.00701)
Tobin_Q	0.0339***	0.0288***	0.0215	0.0179	0.0429***	0.0347**
	(0.00999)	(0.0101)	(0+.0145)	(0.0146)	(0.0138)	(0.0140)
Leverage	−0.0821***	−0.0838***	−0.0598**	−0.0575**	−0.109***	−0.120***
	(0.0188)	(0.0187)	(0.0255)	(0.0254)	(0.0281)	(0.0282)
Lnsale	0.0113***	0.0159***	0.0113**	0.0159***	0.0101*	0.0156***
	(0.00399)	(0.00418)	(0.00571)	(0.00597)	(0.00562)	(0.00589)
Constant	−0.0903	−0.0607	0.229	0.237	−0.271	−0.207
	(0.159)	(0.159)	(0.253)	(0.253)	(0.205)	(0.205)
Year FE	Y	Y	Y	Y	Y	Y
Firm FE	Y	Y	Y	Y	Y	Y
Observations	2,140	2,140	1,203	1,203	937	937
R-squared	0.085	0.092	0.102	0.109	0.077	0.088
Number of firms	455	455	254	254	201	201

Notes: Significance levels: *** 0.01; ** 0.05; * 0.1. Standard errors clustered at city level in parentheses.
Source: Authors.

Table 8.6 only shows the correlation between collateral values and investment rate. If the value of collateral appreciates, the firms did not take out mortgage loans on mortgage, the increase in investment does not mean that it is caused by collateral appreciation. However, if firms borrow more when the value of collateral increases, the collateral–investment relationship is more likely to be causal. Table 8.7 shows the results of the investigation of whether bank loan increases with collateral value. Regression results showed a 1% increase in the average collateral value to be associated with 0.09% more loans. The positive relationship holds for both groups of samples. The control variables such as $Cash/Asset_{t-1}$, Tobin_Q (stock value/asset), lnsale (total sales income) and leverage (debt/asset), all had significant effects on the investment rate.

Table 8.7: Effect of Collateral on Loans

Dep. Var: $Ln\left(\dfrac{Loan_t}{Asset_{t-1}}\right)$	All		Land supply share decreased		Land supply share increased	
	(1)	(2)	(3)	(4)	(5)	(6)
Lnhp	0.0238 (0.0192)	0.00659 (0.0198)	-5.59e-06 (0.0306)	-0.0142 (0.0312)	0.0462* (0.0249)	0.0195 (0.0264)
RE_value		0.0973*** (0.0298)		0.0815** (0.0368)		0.153*** (0.0515)
Cash	-0.0571*** (0.00475)	-0.0576*** (0.00474)	-0.0505*** (0.00613)	-0.0505*** (0.00612)	-0.0684*** (0.00756)	-0.0708*** (0.00756)
Tobin_Q	0.0390*** (0.0111)	0.0337*** (0.0112)	0.0316* (0.0163)	0.0282* (0.0164)	0.0468*** (0.0152)	0.0370** (0.0154)
Leverage	-0.119*** (0.0210)	-0.121*** (0.0210)	-0.105*** (0.0288)	-0.103*** (0.0287)	-0.142*** (0.0311)	-0.154*** (0.0312)
Lnsale	0.0175*** (0.00468)	0.0225*** (0.00490)	0.0210*** (0.00638)	0.0255*** (0.00668)	0.0115* (0.00692)	0.0184** (0.00726)
Constant	-0.496*** (0.181)	-0.474*** (0.181)	-0.378 (0.286)	-0.368 (0.285)	-0.531** (0.235)	-0.480** (0.234)
Year FE	Y	Y	Y	Y	Y	Y
Firm FE	Y	Y	Y	Y	Y	Y
Observations	2,133	2,133	1,197	1,197	936	936
R-squared	0.137	0.142	0.124	0.129	0.166	0.176
Number of Firms	454	454	253	253	201	201

Notes: Significance levels: *** 0.01; ** 0.05; * 0.1. Standard errors clustered at city level in parentheses.
Source: Authors.

8.5.2 Crowding-Out Effect

Unfortunately, no city-level data regarding the profits or profitability of the real estate industry were available, so city-level of real estate investment served as the independent variable to test the crowding-out effect. Inv_hp denotes the investment of residential buildings in city i (shixiaqu). The *China City Statistical Yearbook* reports the investment of residential buildings every year.

Table 8.8: **Crowding-Out Effect on Productive Investment**

Dep. Var: $Ln\left(\dfrac{I_t}{Asset_{t-1}}\right)$	All		Land supply share decreased		Land supply share increased	
	2001–2003	2004–2006	2001–2003	2004–2006	2001–2003	2004–2006
	(1)	(2)	(3)	(4)	(5)	(6)
Ln Inv_hp	-0.00852	-0.0232***	-0.0152	-0.0235*	-0.00987	-0.0190**
	(0.00813)	(0.00683)	(0.0149)	(0.0120)	(0.0116)	(0.00900)
Profit_ratio	-0.186***	-0.210***	-0.240***	-0.193***	-0.154***	-0.230***
	(0.0346)	(0.0405)	(0.0639)	(0.0659)	(0.0378)	(0.0260)
Cash/$Asset_{t-1}$	-3.35e-05*	1.88e-07	0.247***	0.203***	0.201***	0.217***
	(1.73e-05)	(8.12e-06)	(0.0576)	(0.0592)	(0.0417)	(0.0295)
Ln Industry structure	0.223***	0.210***	-0.0536	-0.00189	-0.00911	-0.0162
	(0.0347)	(0.0350)	(0.0645)	(0.0264)	(0.0310)	(0.0127)
Ln Employment/area	-0.0163	-0.00953	-3.54e-06	-9.91e-05	2.26e-05	-0.000158***
	(0.0283)	(0.0116)	(5.20e-05)	(8.37e-05)	(4.10e-05)	(5.87e-05)
Land price	-1.31e-06	-0.000111**	-3.77e-05	2.46e-06	-2.17e-05	-8.04e-06
	(2.35e-05)	(5.61e-05)	(2.74e-05)	(8.53e-06)	(1.66e-05)	(1.85e-05)
Constant	0.0598	0.357***	0.282	0.367*	0.0864	0.324**
	(0.115)	(0.120)	(0.231)	(0.205)	(0.143)	(0.147)
Year FE	Y	Y	Y	Y	Y	Y
Industry FE	Y	Y	Y	Y	Y	Y
Observations	136,181	326,040	78,526	193,218	57,655	132,822
R-squared	0.014	0.021	0.017	0.021	0.012	0.023
Number of Firms	77,075	146,390	44,488	85,268	32,587	61,122

Notes: Significance levels: *** 0.01; ** 0.05; * 0.1. Standard errors clustered at city level in parentheses.
Source: Authors.

The dependent variable is firm-level ratio of productive investment to fixed assets. As shown in Table 8.8, before 2003, investment in real estate had no significant effects or the productive investment. However, after 2003, the coefficients in both groups become significantly negative. On average, every 10% increase in real estate investment brought down firms' investment rates by about 0.2%. After 2003, in both groups of cities, real estate investment crowded out the firms' productive investment. In the data examined here, the correlation between real estate investment and housing price was as high as 0.7215 after control ing for year fixed effects. The significant negative effect of housing investment on productive investment may be interpreted as higher housing prices attracting more investment into the real estate market while crowding out productive investment in manufacturing.

8.6 | Conclusions

The manner in which housing prices affect investment has significant implications for the asset and capital market. This has become very important for the PRC, which is experiencing fast increases in housing prices accompanied by a declining investment rate.

In this chapter, micro data were used to investigate the role of land supply policy in the relationship between housing prices and firm-level investment. Empirical evidence showed that the shock of the change in land policy in 2003 had a significant impact on housing prices. Housing prices were found to rise faster in the cities in which land supply share decreased after 2003. The investment rate declined when housing prices rose. On one hand, the value of collateral appreciated because the increase in housing prices helps firms secure loans. On the other hand, rising housing prices also attract more real estate market investment, crowding out productive investment in manufacturing. When the crowding-out effect dominates, as seen in the PRC, there is less real growth in manufacturing.

Our study also highlights one unexpected result of the PRC's regional development policy. When the land supply is manipulated by the PRC central government to limit the growth of the coastal region in favor of regional development, housing prices rise faster near the coast than inland. The housing prices, and accordingly the land prices, have directly raised costs of production. The housing prices also raised living costs, and this spills over into wages (Liang, Lu, and Zhang 2016). Nevertheless, housing prices also crowded out productive investment. All these results may hurt firms' competitiveness and the sustainability of growth. Thus, at least for the PRC's economy, a more efficient land market, rather than the current one manipulated by the government, should be developed to allow the land supply to change in response to demand, so that the negative consequences of the fast-rising housing prices can be mitigated.

Of course, our study has some shortcomings that should be improved in our future work. First, after 2007 the land supply in different regions diverged further, but, being constrained by the firm-level data, we only used the 2001–2007 data. Therefore, the effect of housing prices on investment rate may be underestimated. Second, our identification of land policy change just captured one exogenous shock on housing prices between 2001–2003 and 2004–2006. However, the estimation of the effects of housing prices on investment may still suffer from missing variable bias.

References

Adelino, M., A. Schoar, and F. Severino. 2015. Housing Prices, Collateral, and Self-Employment. *Journal of Financial Economics* 117(2): 288–306.

Brandt, L., J. V. Biesebrocek, and Y. Zhang. 2014. Challenges of Working with Chinese NBS Firm-level Data. *China Economic Review* 30(12): 339–351.

Chakraborty, I., I. Goldstein, and A. MacKinlay. Forthcoming. Housing Price Booms and Crowding-Out Effects in Bank Lending. *Review of Financial Studies.* http://papers.ssrn.com/sol3/papers.cfm?abstract_id=2246214.

Chaney, T., D. Sraer, and D. Thesma r. 2012. The Collateral Channel: How Real Estate Shocks Affect Corporate Investment. *American Economic Review* 102(6): 2381–2409.

Charles, K. K., E. Hurst, and M. J. Notowidigdo. 2013. Manufacturing Decline,
Housing Booms, and Non-Employment. NBER Working Paper 18949.
Cambridge, MA: National Bureau of Economic Research.

Chen, P., C. Wang, and Y. Liu. 2015. Real Estate Prices and Firm Borrowings:
Micro Evidence from China. *China Economic Review* 36(12): 296–308.

Cvijanović, D. 2014. Real Estate Prices and Firm Capital Structure.
Review of Financial Studies 27(9): 2690–2735.

Gan, J. 2007. Collateral, Debt Capacity, and Corporate Investment: Evidence
from a Natural Experiment. *Journal of Financial Economics* 88(3): 709–734.

Liang, W., M. Lu, and H. Zhang. 2016. Housing Prices Raise Wages:
Estimating the Unexpected Effects of Land Supply Regulation in China.
Journal of Housing Economics 33(9): 70–81.

Lu, M., and K. Xiang. 2016. Great Turning: How Has Chinese Economy Been
Trapped in an Efficiency-and-Balance Tradeoff? *Asian Economic Papers*
15(1): 25–50.

Luo, S., and Y. Zhou. 2013. Do Housing Price Affect Corporate Investment?
Theoretical and Empirical Analysis (in Chinese). *Chinese Journal of
Finance and Economics* 39(8): 133–144.

Luo, Z., and C. C. Zhang. 2015. Credit Expansion, Real Estate Investment
and the Efficiency of Resource Allocation in Industry (in Chinese).
Journal of Financial Research 7: 60–75.

Nie, H., T. Jiang, and R. Yang. 2012. A Review and Reflection on the Use
and Abuse of Chinese Industrial Enterprises Database (in Chinese).
The Journal of World Economy 37(5): 1–13.

Rong, Z., and W. Wang. 2014. Housing Boom and Firms' Entry to Real Estate:
Evidence from Listed Non-Real Estate Firms in China (in Chinese).
Journal of Financial Research 4: 158–173.

Wang, W., and R. Zhao. 2014. Housing Boom and Firm Innovation: Evidence
from Industrial Firms in China (in Chinese). *China Economic Quarterly*
13(2): 465–490.

Wu, H. X. 2013. Measuring and Interpreting Total Factor Productivity in
Chinese Industry (in Chinese). *Comparative Studies*, 69(December).
http://magazine.caixin.com/2013/cs_69/.

Wu, J., J. Gyourko, and Y. Deng. 2015. Real Estate Collateral Value and
Investment: The Case of China. *Journal of Urban Economics* 86(3): 43–53.

CHAPTER 9

Inequality, Aging, and the Middle-Income Trap

Chen Wang and Jiajun Lan

9.1 | Introduction

Generally speaking, when an economy reaches middle-income level, the unemployed and underemployed rural labor force pool is drained. Thus, both rural and urban wages begin to rise, eroding competitiveness. Meanwhile, it becomes more difficult to imitate foreign technologies, and capital accumulation starts to slow due to decreasing returns. More importantly, as discussed further below, middle-income countries usually face the challenges of high inequality and fast aging. These are some of the reasons why many economies become stagnant after achieving middle-income status. This phenomenon was termed the middle-income trap (MIT) by Gill, Kharas, and Bhattasali (2007).

According to the World Bank (2012), among the 101 middle-income countries in 1960, only 13 had stepped out of the MIT by 2008. In particular, most Latin American countries have been trapped in the MIT for several decades (Gill, Kharas, and Bhattasali 2007). Recently, emerging economies have faced significant growth slowdowns (World Bank 2017). Most notably, the People's Republic of China reached a peak growth rate of 14.2% in 2007 and since then has experienced successive reductions in the growth rate— e.g., from 7.3% in 2014 to 6.9% in 2015 to 6.7% in 2016.

The concept of middle income can be defined in absolute or relative terms. The former specifies a range of absolute income level. For example, Spence (2011) considered $5,000–$10,000 per capita income as the range where transition to high income becomes problematic. According to Felipe, Abdon, and Kumar (2012), the range is $2,000–$11,750 per capita gross national income (GNI) (measured at constant 1990 United States [US] dollar). The World Bank and Aiyar et al. (2013) applied the threshold of $1,045–$12,736 per capita GNI (measured at constant 2014 US dollar). On the other hand, middle income can be defined relative to the per capita income in the US. For instance, the World Bank (2012) used 5%–45% of the US per capita income as the relative range. Woo et al. (2012) used a more stringent range of 20%–55% of US per capita income. The range applied by Robertson and Ye (2015) is 8%–38% of US per capita gross domestic product (GDP).

To define the MIT, the next question is how many years can an economy stay within the middle-income range before it is labeled a MIT country. The critical number is 49, as used by Agenor, Canuto, and Jelenic (2012); Aiyar et al. (2013); Bulman, Eden, and Nguyen (2017); and the World Bank (2012). This is just 1 year shorter than Woo et al. (2012) suggested. Felipe, Abdon, and Kumar (2012) applied the number 42.

Regarding determinants of the MIT, Vivarelli (2014) listed capability building, structural change, innovation, and entrepreneurship. Eichengreen, Park, and Shin (2012, 2014) found that growth slowdowns are less likely in countries where the population has a relatively high level of secondary and tertiary education and where high technology products account for a relatively large share of exports, which essentially correlates with innovation and capacity or human capital stock.

Two drivers of the MIT that are unique to middle-income countries are high inequality and aging (see ADB 2011; Egawa 2013). The well-known Kuznets (1955) hypothesis dictates that middle-income countries are likely to face rising and high inequality. Lambert (1994) suggests that migration brought by industrialization in urban areas causes rapid urbanization and income inequality. As summarized by Wan, Lu, and Chen (2006), there are many channels through which rising inequality can harm growth.

First, under an imperfect capital market, high levels of inequality imply that more people face credit constraints. This adversely affects investment in human or physical capital (Fishman and Simhon 2002; Galor and Zeira 1993). Second, worsening income distribution may lead to rises in the fertility rate among the poor, causing less investment in education (De la Croix and Doepke 2004). Third, large income disparity means weaker domestic demand, as the poor have much higher marginal propensity to consume. Fourth, growing inequality increases redistributive tax pressures, deterring investment incentives (Alesina and Rodrik 1994; Benabou 1996; Persson and Tabellini 1994). Finally, as is commonly acknowledged, high inequality may lead to a more unstable sociopolitical environment for economic activities (Benhabib and Rustichini 1996).

On the other hand, aging represents another typical challenge faced by many middle-income countries. The economics of demography (Becker 1991) dictate that fertility usually declines as an economy grows. This is because economic development is typically accompanied by structural transformation from an agriculture-based to a manufacturing-based economy, where more and more of the population moves to cities. Women who live in urban areas have more schooling and employment opportunities than rural women. Consequently, urban women react by working more, marrying later, and having fewer children. Also, the cost of raising children becomes high as an economy develops and becomes urbanized. These are some of the reasons why middle-income countries typically face slow population growth, resulting in aging. For example, in Viet Nam, the fertility rate has declined significantly from a level of 5.4 in the 1980s to 1.8 in 2010 (World Bank 2012). In rich cities such as Shanghai in the People's Republic of China, the birth rate has fallen below the population replacement rate.

Aging affects growth through a number of channels. An aging population implies less labor input (the supply side problem), fewer savings (the investment problem), and sluggish consumption (the demand problem). Bulman, Eden, and Nguyen (2017) considered both the level of inequality and its changes, as well as aging in modeling the MIT. They found that countries that "escaped" the middle-income trap have greater equality and lower age dependency ratios, and escapees at all middle-income levels are also less likely to see increases in inequality and decreases in the age dependency ratio (i.e., the so-called "demographic dividend").

Despite the huge interest in and significance of the MIT issue, analytical research is lagging. In particular, more research is needed to pin down factors that contribute to the MIT. As a matter of fact, how to construct or quantify the concept of the MIT is the very foundation of any analytical work. The construction of MIT indicators will facilitate modeling work on the determinants or impacts of the MIT. This chapter will propose such indicators and then use them to explore the determinants, focusing on the roles of inequality and aging. These two drivers are unique to most middle-income countries.

The plan of this chapter is as follows. Section 9.2 develops the analytical framework where indicators of the MIT will be proposed, and presents stylized facts, demonstrating the prevalence of the MIT under both the relative and absolute definitions. Section 9.3 discusses empirical results, only using the relative definition, as we believe it makes more sense than the absolute alternative. Finally, section 9.4 concludes.

9.2 | Middle-Income Trap Indicators

As previously discussed, there are two definitions of middle income. Thus, two indicators measuring the probabilities that a country may escape the middle-income trap will be proposed. They are denoted P_A and P_R, corresponding to the absolute and relative definitions of MIT, respectively. We start with P_A. The middle-income range is set as \$2,000–\$15,000 (at 2010 constant US dollar) and the threshold number of years is 50. In this case, a country is stuck in the MIT if it takes more than 50 years to reach the upper bound of \$15,000 after reaching the lower bound of the middle-income range (\$2,000 GDP per capita). For each year after entering the middle-income range, the possibility P_A of escaping the MIT can be defined as:

$$P_A = \begin{cases} R_g/E_g & \text{if} & 0 < R_g < E_g \\ 1 & \text{if} & R_g \geq E_g \\ 0 & \text{if} & R_g \leq 0 \end{cases} \tag{1}$$

where R_g represents actual GDP growth rate and E_g represents the expected GDP growth rate that is required to escape the MIT. The latter, for each year, can be solved for by using $GDP_i * (1 + E_g)^{50-i} = 15{,}000$, where i denotes the i-th year of the country after entering the middle-income range.

The relative measure P_R can be constructed similarly. In this chapter, we use 5%–45% of US GDP per capita as the range of middle income. The threshold number of years is still 50. In this case, an economy must on average improve its relative income by 0.8% per year or more to escape the MIT. For the first year after entering the middle-income range, the probability of jumping out of the MIT can be defined as the actual improvement divided by 0.8%. If the computed ratio is negative, the probability is set to be 0; if the computed ratio is greater than 1, it is set to be 1. For the second year, the denominator is adjusted depending on the actual improvement in the first year. Suppose the actual improvement was h%, so the relative income of the first year is 5+h%. The denominator is to be recalculated as (45% − first year relative income)/50. For other years, the denominator is simply (45% − previous year relative income)/(50 − years elapsed).

Our data sample covers the years 1960–2015. If an economy already surpassed the lower threshold of the middle-income range in 1960, we use the average GDP growth rate over 1960–1975 to make inferences about the number of years it had middle-income status before 1960. Table 9.1 presents the definitions and data sources of variables and Table 9.2 reports the summary statistics. The list of countries is presented in the Appendix (Tables A9.1 and A9.2).

Table 9.1: Variable Definitions and Data Sources

Variable	Definition	Data Sources
Gini	Gini coefficient	WIID; SWIID etc.
P_RGDP	The probability of jumping out of the MIT (relative definition), based on GDP	WDI
P_RGNI	The probability of jumping out of the MIT (relative definition), based on GNI	WDI
Pop65	Population ages 65 and above (% of total)	WDI
Inv	Gross capital formation (% of GDP)	WDI
LFP	Labor force participation rate (% of total population ages 15–64)	WDI
TFP_gr	TFP growth rate	PWT
Trade	Trade (% of GDP)	WDI
GDP_indu	Industry, value added (% of GDP)	WDI
ln(Inf)	Inflation rate, consumer prices (log, annual %)	WDI
HC	Human capital index	PWT

GDP = gross domestic product, GNI = gross national income, MIT = middle-income trap, PWT = Penn World Table, SWIID = Standardized World Income Inequality Database, TFP = total factor productivity, WDI = World Development Indicators, WIID = World Income Inequality Database.

Sources: World Bank. World Development Indicators; Penn World Table (Feenstra, Inklaar, and Timmer 2015); UNU–WIDER. World Income Inequality Database (WIID3.4); Standardized World Income Inequality Database.

Table 9.3 lists countries that have fallen into the MIT according to the absolute definition. Among the 199 countries, 80 countries have fallen into the MIT, with most MIT countries in Africa (16), followed by 15 countries in North America, 15 Asian countries, 11 South American countries, 14 European countries, and 9 countries in Oceania. Categorized by income level, most MIT countries are lower middle-income and upper middle-income countries. The former group includes 20 countries while the latter group includes 53 countries. Only seven high-income countries have fallen back into the MIT.

Table 9.2: **Descriptive Statistics of Variables**

Variable	Obs	Mean	Std. Dev.	Min	Max
Gini	8,068	0.378	0.056	0.209	0.675
P_RGDP	2,740	0.081	0.245	0	1
P_RGNI	2,472	0.218	0.388	0	1
Pop65	8,007	6.577	4.488	1.011	23.587
Inv	6,291	22.642	9.564	-13.405	219.069
LFP	3,584	68.125	9.971	41.000	91.500
TFP_gr	4,745	0.005	0.053	-0.657	0.812
Trade	6,569	74.277	50.971	0	504.884
GDP_indu	5,329	29.191	12.046	2.531	96.736
ln(Inf)	5,972	1.797	1.416	-7.393	10.103
HC	6,263	2.066	0.734	1.007	3.734

Max = maximum, Min = minimum, Obs = observation, Std.Dev. = standard deviation.

Source: World Bank. World Development Indicators; Penn World Table (Feenstra, Inklaar, and Timmer 2015); UNU–WIDER. World Income Inequality Database (WIID3.4); Standardized World Income Inequality Database.

Table 9.3: **Countries that Have Fallen into the Middle-Income Trap**
(absolute definition, by continent)

Asia	Europe	North America	South America	Africa	Oceania
Azerbaijan	Albania	Antigua and Barbuda	Argentina	Algeria	Fiji
Georgia	Belarus	Belize	Brazil	Angola	Kiribati
Indonesia	Bosnia and	Costa Rica	Chile	Botswana	Marshall Islands
Iran	Herzegovina	Cuba	Colombia	Congo	Micronesia
Iraq	Bulgaria	Dominica	Ecuador	Cote d'Ivoire	Palau
Jordan	Croatia	Dominican Republic	Guyana	Egypt	Samoa
Kazakhstan	Hungary	El Salvador	Paraguay	Gabon	Tonga
Lebanon	Kosovo	Grenada	Peru	Libya	Tuvalu
Malaysia	Latvia	Guatemala	Suriname	Mauritius	Vanuatu
Maldives	Macedonia	Jamaica	Uruguay	Morocco	
Mongolia	Montenegro	Mexico	Venezuela	Namibia	
Thailand	Romania	Nicaragua		Nigeria	
Turkey	Russian	Panama		Seychelles	
Turkmenistan	Federation	St. Lucia		South Africa	
West Bank	Serbia	St. Vincent and the		Swaziland	
and Gaza	Ukraine	Grenadines		Tunisia	

Source: World Bank. World Development Indicators.

Table 9.4: Countries that Have Fallen into the MIT
(absolute definition, by income level)

Lower-Middle Income	Upper-Middle Income		High Income
Congo	Albania	Lebanon	Antigua and Barbuda
Cote d'Ivoire	Algeria	Libya	Chile
Egypt	Angola	Macedonia	Croatia
El Salvador	Argentina	Malaysia	Hungary
Guatemala	Azerbaijan	Maldives	Latvia
Indonesia	Belarus	Marshall Islands	Seychelles
Kiribati	Belize	Mauritius	Uruguay
Kosovo	Bosnia and Herzegovina	Mexico	
Micronesia	Botswana	Montenegro	
Mongolia	Brazil	Namibia	
Morocco	Bulgaria	Palau	
Nicaragua	Colombia	Panama	
Nigeria	Costa Rica	Paraguay	
Samoa	Cuba	Peru	
Swaziland	Dominica	Romania	
Tonga	Dominican Republic	Russian Federation	
Tunisia	Ecuador	Serbia	
Ukraine	Fiji	South Africa	
Vanuatu	Gabon	St. Lucia	
West Bank and Gaza	Georgia	St. Vincent and	
	Grenada	the Grenadines	
	Guyana	Suriname	
	Iran	Thailand	
	Iraq	Turkey	
	Jamaica	Turkmenistan	
	Jordan	Tuvalu	
	Kazakhstan	Venezuela	

Source: World Bank. World Development Indicators.

Under the relative definition, 88 countries have fallen into the MIT, as shown in Table 9.5. Different from the results using the absolute definition, Europe hosts most MIT countries (20) here, followed by 18 North American countries, 16 Asian countries, 15 African countries, 11 South American countries, and 8 countries in Oceania. In addition, four high-income countries have dropped back and are trapped in the MIT: Chile, the Seychelles, Trinidad and Tobago, and Uruguay. Similar to earlier results, as shown in Table 9.6, most MIT countries are from the upper middle-income group (53). It seems that the real hurdle to escaping the MIT is stagnant growth after reaching upper middle-income status.

Table 9.5: Countries that Have Fallen into the MIT
(relative definition, by continent)

Asia	Europe	North America	South America	Africa	Oceania
Azerbaijan	Albania	Antigua and Barbuda	Argentina	Algeria	Fiji
Georgia	Belarus	Barbados	Brazil	Angola	Marshall
Indonesia	Bosnia and	Belize	Chile	Botswana	Islands
Iran	Herzegovina	Costa Rica	Colombia	Congo	Micronesia
Iraq	Bulgaria	Cuba	Ecuador	Cote d'Ivoire	Palau
Jordan	Croatia	Dominica	Guyana	Gabon	Samoa
Kazakhstan	Czech Republic	Dominican Republic	Paraguay	Libya	Tonga
Lebanon	Estonia	El Salvador	Peru	Mauritius	Tuvalu
Malaysia	Hungary	Grenada	Suriname	Morocco	Vanuatu
Maldives	Kosovo	Guatemala	Uruguay	Namibia	
Mongolia	Latvia	Jamaica	Venezuela	Nigeria	
Oman	Lithuania	Mexico		Seychelles	
Thailand	Macedonia	Nicaragua		South Africa	
Turkey	Montenegro	Panama		Swaziland	
Turkmenistan	Poland	St. Kitts and Nevis		Tunisia	
West Bank	Portugal	St. Lucia			
and Gaza	Romania	St. Vincent and			
	Russian	the Grenadines			
	Federation	Trinidad and Tobago			
	Serbia				
	Slovak Republic				
	Ukraine				

MIT = middle-income trap.

Source: World Bank. World Development Indicators.

9.3 | Empirical Analysis

In essence, the concept of the MIT means growth slowdown. Thus, growth theory can guide the analytical framework and modeling exercise. In reality, the most important and natural questions in the minds of policy makers and other stakeholders are: what is the probability that a middle-income country will fall into the MIT? And what are the impacts of various factors affecting this probability? To answer these questions, we replace the usual growth rate by the probability (denoted by P) of an economy falling into the MIT in a growth model:

$$P = f(Ine, Aging, X) + u \tag{2}$$

where u is a composite error term consisting of country and year fixed effects and the usual white noise; *Ine* is an inequality indicator; *Aging* is an aging indicator; and X represents a vector of control variables. Based on economic growth theory, two classic variables are included—gross capital formation (percentage of GDP) and the labor force participation rate (percentage of total population aged 15–64).

Following Eichengreen, Park, and Shin (2012), an important control variable is total factor productivity (TFP). The authors asserted that 85% of economic growth slowdown is due to TFP and only 15% due to capital accumulation. Similar results were found by Daude and Fernandez–Arias (2010) using data from Latin American and Caribbean countries. We use the TFP growth rate from Penn World Table 9.1. Needless to say, international trade is one of the most crucial determinants of growth. Lewis (1980) viewed trade as the engine of growth. This variable will be indicated by the ratio of total trade to GDP from the World Bank's World Development Indicators (WDI).

Structural transformation is another driver of development. As pointed out by Kuznets (1955, 1963), Lewis (1955), Rostow (1959), and Kaldor (1967), during the initial stages of development, poor countries can grow by reallocating labor from low- productivity agriculture to high-productivity manufacturing. We use the GDP share of the manufacturing sector and its square to account for structural transformation. Moreover, the inflation rate or consumer price index is included to control macroeconomic stability.

Before discussing empirical modeling results, some preliminary data analysis of our key independent variables will be presented. Figure 9.1 demonstrates that the mid-1980s was a crucial period. Before then, inequalities shared a similar trend irrespective of group of countries. After then, middle-income countries have tended to experience fast rises in income inequality and income inequality in high-income countries has remained more or less stable.

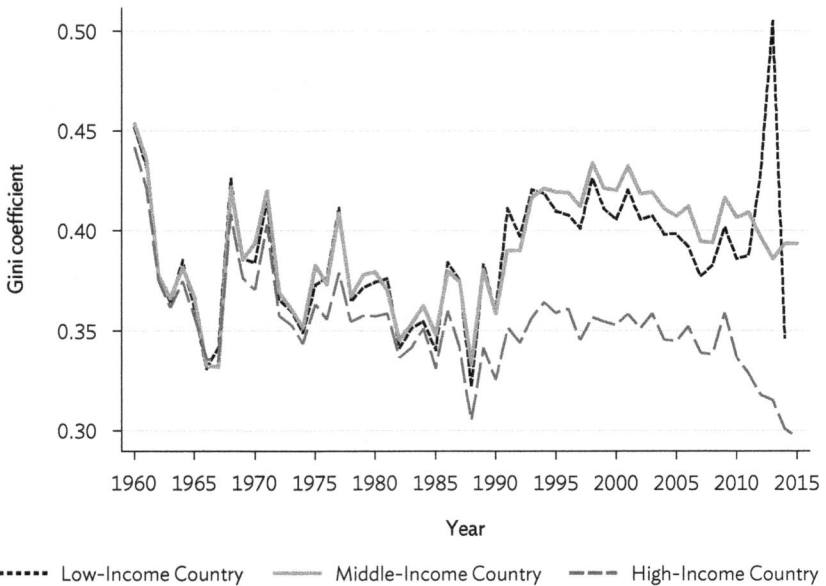

Figure 9.1: Income Inequality, by Country Groups

Sources: UNU–WIDER. World Income Inequality Database (WIID3.4); Standardized World Income Inequality Database; POVCAL; LIS.

Regarding aging, Figure 9.2 confirms that the proportion of the population aged 65 and above is much higher in middle-income countries than in low-income countries, although it is lower than that in developed or already aged high-income countries. Note that the slope of the curve in Figure 9.2 is almost flat for low-income economies and steepest for developed countries, with middle-income countries in between.

How is aging related to GDP? Figure 9.3 plots per capita GDP (in logarithm) against total fertility rate. It clearly shows a negative correlation. This negative correlation remains strong when crude birth rate is used instead of fertility rate, as shown in Figure 9.4.

Figure 9.2: Aging, by Country Groups

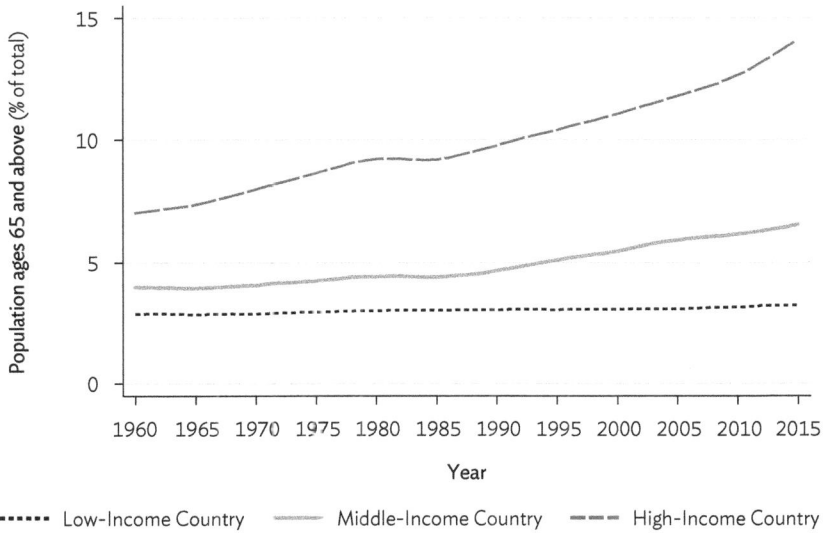

Source: World Bank. World Development Indicators.

Figure 9.3: Total Fertility Rate and GDP per Capita

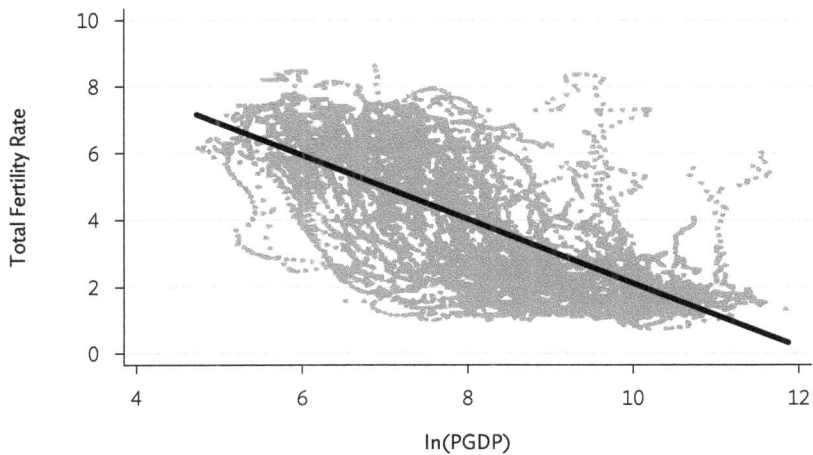

GDP = gross domestic product.
Note: 1960–2015, 217 countries and regions, data from WDI.
Source: World Bank. World Development Indicators.

Figure 9.4: Crude Birth Rate and GDP per Capita

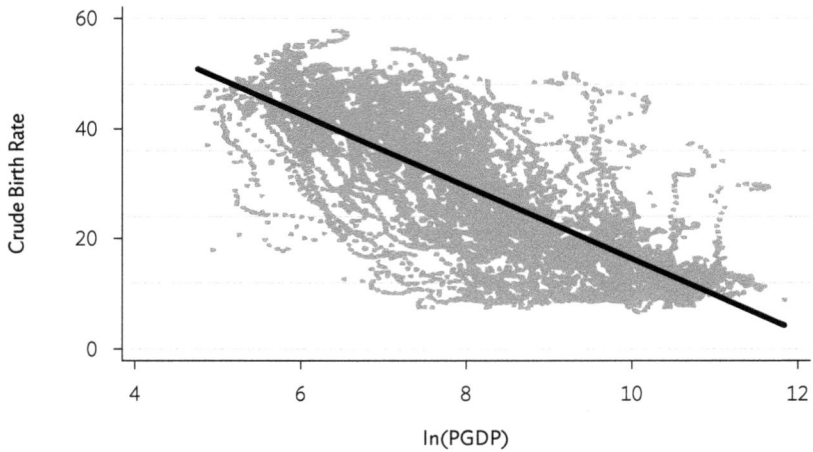

GDP = gross domestic product.

Note: 1960–2015, 217 countries and regions, data from WDI.

Source: World Bank. World Development Indicators.

As mentioned above, the modeling exercise will be conducted using the relative definition of the MIT only, as the absolute definition makes less sense to us. Table 9.7 reports our baseline results, with both year and country fixed effects controlled for Models 3–7. In Table 9.7, the first column includes only the inequality indicator and in the second column both inequality and aging are considered. Other control variables are added in subsequent columns. The results demonstrate that inequality is negatively and significantly correlated with the likelihood of escaping the MIT. For every unit of reduction in the Gini index, the probability of falling into the MIT drops by 20%–30%, which is surprisingly high. Similarly, aging is a significant driver of the MIT. For every 10% decrease in the proportion of aged population, the likelihood of avoiding the MIT rises by 0.5%, which is economically much less important than the impact of income distribution. Consistent with earlier studies, the beneficial impact of TFP is quite pronounced, along with investment and industrialization. Trade has positive coefficient estimates but they are insignificant.

Table 9.7: Baseline Results

Variables	(1) P_R GDP	(2) P_R GDP	(3) P_R GDP	(4) P_R GDP	(5) P_R GDP	(6) P_R GDP	(7) P_R GDP
Gini	-0.258** (0.0972)	-0.229** (0.0917)	0.108 (0.113)	-0.262* (0.130)	-0.260* (0.128)	-0.295** (0.124)	-0.335** (0.135)
Pop65		0.000756 (0.00191)	-0.0135** (0.00539)	-0.0472*** (0.0146)	-0.0511*** (0.0158)	-0.0579*** (0.0185)	-0.0589*** (0.0198)
Inv				0.00563*** (0.00111)	0.00564*** (0.00111)	0.00632*** (0.00115)	0.00659*** (0.00125)
LFP				-0.00176 (0.00148)	-0.00184 (0.00146)	0.000259 (0.00184)	0.000796 (0.00191)
TFP_gr				0.618*** (0.199)	0.617*** (0.196)	0.839*** (0.208)	0.840*** (0.227)
Trade					0.000333 (0.000281)	0.000361 (0.000298)	0.000328 (0.000318)
GDP_indu						-0.0227*** (0.00644)	-0.0242*** (0.00705)
(GDP_indu)^2						0.000270*** (7.72e-05)	0.000292*** (8.69e-05)
ln(Inf)							0.000599 (0.00591)
Constant	0.183*** (0.0407)	0.165*** (0.0407)	0.0633 (0.0825)	0.585** (0.231)	0.596** (0.231)	0 (0)	0.971*** (0.291)
Country	N	N	Y	Y	Y	Y	Y
Year	N	N	Y	Y	Y	Y	Y
Observations	2,740	2,717	2,717	1,045	1,045	994	976
Adjust R-squared	0.005	0.004	0.585	0.715	0.715	0.713	0.713
Within R-squared			0.065	0.163	0.164	0.187	0.192
Number of groups	107	105	105	57	57	56	56

GDP = gross domestic product.

Notes: Standard errors in parentheses. *** p<0.01, ** p<0.05, * p<0.1.

Sources: World Bank. World Development Indicators; Penn World Table (Feenstra, Inklaar, and Timmer 2015); UNU–WIDER: World Income Inequality Database (WIID3.4); Standardized World Income Inequality Database.

The baseline results are obtained using GDP per capita as the welfare measure. To check the robustness of the baseline results, we use GNI instead. The modeling outputs can be found in Table 9.8. It is clear that the earlier finding on the inequality impact appears robust. However, the aging variable becomes insignificant, although in two thirds of the cases the coefficients are still negative. Remember that the impact of aging on the MIT is quite minor in any case.

Table 9.8: Robustness Checks: Relative Jump Probability Based on GNI

Variables	(1) P_RGNI	(2) P_RGNI	(3) P_RGNI	(4) P_RGNI	(5) P_RGNI	(6) P_RGNI	(7) P_RGNI
Gini	-1.159*** (0.240)	-1.045*** (0.209)	0.600*** (0.206)	-0.446** (0.216)	-0.439* (0.227)	-0.343* (0.193)	-0.386* (0.221)
Pop65		0.00391 (0.00453)	-0.00276 (0.00904)	-0.00387 (0.0147)	0.0121 (0.0148)	-0.0177 (0.0151)	-0.0217 (0.0174)
Inv				0.00917*** (0.00169)	0.00886*** (0.00178)	0.0110*** (0.00172)	0.0110*** (0.00160)
LFP				0.00640 (0.00426)	0.00670 (0.00419)	0.00544 (0.00463)	0.00582 (0.00449)
TFP_gr				0.795*** (0.272)	0.812*** (0.267)	0.736*** (0.244)	0.710** (0.275)
Trade					-0.00150* (0.000836)	-0.000521 (0.000765)	-0.000355 (0.000859)
GDP_indu						-0.0161 (0.0122)	-0.0138 (0.0116)
(GDP_indu)^2						0.000124 (0.000163)	9.45e-05 (0.000154)
ln(Inf)							-0.0119* (0.00636)
Constant	0.676*** (0.109)	0.601*** (0.101)	-0.475*** (0.159)	-0.435 (0.375)	0 (0)	0 (0)	0.103 (0.339)
Country	N	N	Y	Y	Y	Y	Y
Year	N	N	Y	Y	Y	Y	Y
Observations	2,359	2,336	2,336	956	956	923	906
Adjust R-squared	0.034	0.034	0.535	0.635	0.638	0.642	0.643
Within R-squared			0.219	0.209	0.215	0.222	0.224
Number of groups	105	103	103	62	62	61	60

GNI = gross national income.

Notes: Standard errors in parentheses. *** $p<0.01$, ** $p<0.05$, * $p<0.1$.

Source: World Bank. World Development Indicators; Penn World Table (Feenstra, Inklaar, and Timmer 2015); UNU-WIDER: World Income Inequality Database (WIID3.4); Standardized World Income Inequality Database.

Table 9.9: Robustness Checks: Different Orders of Autocorrelation

Variables	(1) L.2	(2) L.3	(3) L.4	(4) L.5	(5) L.10
Gini	−0.335**	−0.335**	−0.335**	−0.335**	−0.335***
	(0.152)	(0.141)	(0.138)	(0.128)	(0.111)
Pop65	−0.0589***	−0.0589***	−0.0589***	−0.0589***	−0.0589***
	(0.0202)	(0.0200)	(0.0193)	(0.0185)	(0.0183)
Inv	0.00659***	0.00659***	0.00659***	0.00659***	0.00659***
	(0.00134)	(0.00136)	(0.00133)	(0.00128)	(0.00102)
LFP	0.000796	0.000796	0.000796	0.000796	0.000796
	(0.00215)	(0.00219)	(0.00224)	(0.00222)	(0.00222)
TFP_gr	0.840***	0.840***	0.840***	0.840**	0.840**
	(0.257)	(0.280)	(0.294)	(0.302)	(0.302)
Trade	0.000328	0.000328	0.000328	0.000328	0.000328
	(0.000327)	(0.000320)	(0.000301)	(0.000281)	(0.000248)
GDP_indu	−0.0242***	−0.0242***	−0.0242***	−0.0242***	−0.0242***
	(0.00686)	(0.00683)	(0.00661)	(0.00671)	(0.00650)
(GDP_indu)^2	0.000292***	0.000292***	0.000292***	0.000292***	0.000292***
	(8.03e-05)	(7.72e-05)	(7.26e-05)	(7.41e-05)	(6.92e-05)
ln(Inf)	0.000599	0.000599	0.000599	0.000599	0.000599
	(0.00584)	(0.00565)	(0.00567)	(0.00565)	(0.00386)
Constant	0.971***	0.971***	0.971***	0.971***	0.971***
	(0.294)	(0.280)	(0.268)	(0.250)	(0.208)
Country	Y	Y	Y	Y	Y
Year	Y	Y	Y	Y	Y
Observations	976	976	976	976	976
Adjust R-squared	0.643	0.643	0.643	0.643	0.643
Within R-squared	0.192	0.192	0.192	0.192	0.192
Number of groups	56	56	56	56	56

Notes: Standard errors in parentheses. *** $p < 0.01$, ** $p < 0.05$, * $p < 0.1$.

Sources: World Bank. World Development Indicators; Penn World Table (Feenstra, Inklaar, and Timmer 2015); UNU-WIDER: World Income Inequality Database (WIID3.4); Standardized World Income Inequality Database.

Since the models are estimated using Driscoll–Kraay standard errors (Driscoll and Kraay 1998), the order of autocorrelation is set to be 1. For robustness checks, we set the order of autocorrelation to 2, 3, 4, 5, and 10, respectively. The results as tabulated in Table 9.9 are quite consistent with our baseline findings and they are robust to different orders of autocorrelation. It is useful to note that the magnitudes of the estimates for our key independent variable are remarkably stable, confirming the reliability of our conclusions.

Table 9.10: Robustness Checks: Gini Growth Rate

Variables	(1) P_RGDP	(2) P_RGDP	(3) P_RGDP	(4) P_RGDP	(5) P_RGDP	(6) P_RGDP	(7) P_RGDP
Gini	0.00527 (0.0378)	−0.00593 (0.0357)	−0.0497* (0.0249)	−0.105* (0.0525)	−0.105* (0.0524)	−0.105* (0 0567)	−0.103[a] (0.0607)
Pop65		0.00250 (0.00196)	−0.0165*** (0.00505)	−0.0467*** (0.0144)	−0.0512*** (0.0157)	−0.0575*** (0 0185)	−0.0581*** (0.0197)
Inv				0.00548*** (0.00114)	0.00549*** (0.00114)	0.00617*** (0.00119)	0.00636*** (0.00130)
LFP				−0.00137 (0.00150)	−0.00144 (0.00148)	0.000517 (0.00190)	0.00102 (0.00197)
TFP_gr				0.621*** (0.197)	0.619*** (0.194)	0.839*** (0.206)	0.840*** (0.226)
Trade					0.000380 (0.000294)	0.000418 (0.000309)	0.000399 (0.000332)
GDP_indu						−0.0227*** (0.00635)	−0.0241*** (0.00692)
(GDP_indu)^2						0.000272*** (7.62e-05)	0.000293*** (8.52e-05)
ln(Inf)							0.000561 (0.00590)
Constant	0.0786*** (0.00612)	0.0611*** (0.0122)	0.141** (0.0540)	0.455** (0.192)	0.467** (0.191)	0 (0)	0 (0)
Country	N	N	Y	Y	Y	Y	Y
Year	N	N	Y	Y	Y	Y	Y
Observations	2,661	2,641	2,641	1,038	1,038	987	970
Adjust R-squared	0.240	0.239	0.604	0.715	0.715	0.713	0.713
Within R-squared			0.055	0.163	0.164	0.187	0.191
Number of groups	100	99	99	57	57	56	56

GDP = gross domestic product.

Notes: Standard errors in parentheses. *** p<0.01, ** p<0.05, * p<0.1.

[a] marginally significant P = 0.105.

Sources: World Bank. World Development Indicators; Penn World Table (Feenstra, Inklaar, and Timmer 2015); UNU-WIDER: World Income Inequality Database (WIID3.4); Standardized World Income Inequality Database.

Bulman, Eden, and Nguyen (2017) pointed out that larger increases in income inequality are associated with slower growth. To examine if rises in inequality, rather than the actual level of inequality, really matter, we replace the Gini observations with the changes and repeat the baseline estimations. The results of Table 9.10 are in line with Bulman, Eden, and Nguyen (2017), in the sense that worsening income distribution does erode the probability of escaping the MIT, although the level of statistical significance is not high.

Table 9.11: Robustness Checks: Missing Variable—Education (PWT Human Capital Index)

Variables	(1) P$_R$ GDP	(2) P$_R$ GDP	(3) P$_R$ GDP	(4) P$_R$ GDP	(5) P$_R$ GDP	(6) P$_R$ GDP	(7) P$_R$ GDP
Gini	−0.138 (0.0829)	−0.145* (0.0827)	0.0701 (0.133)	−0.269** (0.129)	−0.267** (0.127)	−0.299** (0.124)	−0.342** (0.136)
Pop65		−0.000445 (0.00347)	−0.0172*** (0.00604)	−0.0467*** (0.0145)	−0.0503*** (0.0156)	−0.0571*** (0.0183)	−0.0583*** (0.0196)
Human capital index	0.0151* (0.00815)	0.0172 (0.0185)	−0.177*** (0.0564)	−0.0801 (0.0647)	−0.0742 (0.0632)	−0.0655 (0.0541)	−0.0704 (0.0599)
Inv				0.00556*** (0.00111)	0.00557*** (0.00110)	0.00625*** (0.00115)	0.00652*** (0.00125)
LFP				−0.00185 (0.00145)	−0.00191 (0.00144)	0.000162 (0.00186)	0.000726 (0.00194)
TFP_gr				0.623*** (0.198)	0.622*** (0.195)	0.845*** (0.206)	0.843*** (0.225)
Trade					0.000302 (0.000267)	0.000334 (0.000282)	0.000307 (0.000304)
GDP_indu						−0.0223*** (0.00591)	−0.0236*** (0.00634)
(GDP_indu)^2						0.000265*** (7.11e-05)	0.000285*** (7.87e-05)
ln(Inf)							0.000315 (0.00598)
Constant	0.0998** (0.0405)	0.101** (0.0388)	0.599*** (0.198)	0.818** (0.303)	0.810** (0.298)	1.143*** (0.361)	1.163*** (0.389)
Country	N	N	Y	Y	Y	Y	Y
Year	N	N	Y	Y	Y	Y	Y
Observations	2,357	2,357	2,357	1,045	1,045	994	976
Adjust R-squared	0.003	0.003	0.584	0.715	0.715	0.713	0.713
Within R-squared			0.089	0.164	0.165	0.188	0.193
Number of groups	80	80	80	57	57	56	56

PWT = Penn World Table.

Notes: Standard errors in parentheses. *** p<0.01, ** p<0.05, * p<0.1.

[a] marginally significant P = 0.105.

Sources: World Bank. World Development Indicators; Penn World Table (Feenstra, Inklaar, and Timmer 2015); UNU-WIDER: World Income Inequality Database (WIID3.4); Standardized World Income Inequality Database.

Other estimation results are consistent with expectations, or with those in the baseline estimations.

Recall that both Eichengreen, Park, and Shin (2014) and Jimenez, Nguyen, and Patrinos (2012) stressed the importance of human capital, which has not been considered so far in model estimation. Adding the human capital index of Penn World Table (PWT) into the baseline model does not alter our previous findings regarding the impacts of income distribution or aging. Interestingly, the human capital variable turns out to be insignificant once control variables are added (see Table 9.11). One possible reason may lie in the fact that it is highly correlated with TFP. In other words, the impact of human capital on growth goes through the productivity channel.

Two other results are worth noting. Industrialization is found to exert a nonlinear impact on the MIT. The probability of escaping the MIT displays a U-pattern as industrialization proceeds. Another finding relates to the variable of inflation, which is not significant in any of the models. As is commonly practiced, inflation is a proxy indicating macroeconomic stability. These counterintuitive results deserve further research efforts.

9.4 | Summary and Conclusions

Many countries are concerned about the possibility of falling into the middle-income trap (MIT), not only those that have been experiencing stagnant growth, but also emerging economies. The emergence of the recent de-globalization wave reinforces such a concern. Even the PRC is confronted with the MIT challenge. On the other hand, carefully constructed indicators for rigorously analyzing the MIT issue are lacking or largely absent.

This chapter contributes to the literature and policy debate by proposing a simple but intuitively appealing technique which can be used to estimate the probability of an economy escaping the MIT, irrespective of how the MIT is defined (in the absolute sense or the relative sense).

This probability is then regressed on inequality and aging indicators, along with control variables. These two key independent variables are unique to middle-income countries.

Several robust results or findings are worth reiterating. First, both the level of and the change in inequality (indicated by the Gini index) are important drivers of the MIT, with surprisingly large impacts. This helps substantiate the conventional perception that Latin American countries are trapped in the MIT largely due to their high and lasting income inequality. Secondly, relative to income distribution, aging is found to be much less important in terms of both magnitude and statistical significance. This does not necessarily mean that aging is not correlated with growth. Rather, it may imply that the issue of aging can be addressed before a country reaches high-income status and becomes an aged society. It is questionable if the same can be said about income disparity. Third, TFP growth and structural transformation are fundamental drivers for an economy to escape the MIT. However, earlier industrialization may not generate the expected impact on growth, perhaps depending on development strategies related to openness, urbanization, and so on. Finally, the accumulation of human capital may not be useful unless it helps promote innovation and productivity growth.

The policy messages from this chapter are quite profound. Fighting inequality and improving income distribution are a must if a country does not wish to fall into the MIT, while the issue of aging is secondary. For many countries—particularly the lower middle-income countries—rural–urban disparity constitutes the largest component of national inequality and can be reduced through well-managed urbanization, which simultaneously helps promote innovation and productivity growth. In short, successful urbanization could be the single most important force driving developing countries out of the MIT.

References

Agenor, P. R., O. Canuto, and M. Jelenic. 2012. Avoiding Middle-Income
Growth Traps. *Economic Premise, Poverty Reduction and Economic
Management Network (PREM)* Nr. 98. Washington, DC: The World Bank.

Aiyar, S., R. Duval, D. Puy, Y. Wu, and L. Zhang. 2013. Growth Slowdowns
and the Middle-Income Trap. IMF Working Paper WP/13/71.
Washington, DC: International Monetary Fund.

Alesina, A., and D. Rodrik. 1994. Distributive Politics and Economic Growth.
Quarterly Journal of Economics 109(2): 465–490.

Asian Development Bank. 2011. *Asia 2050: Realizing the Asian Century.*
Manila, Vivek Mehra for SAGE Publications India.

Becker, G. S. 1991. *A Treatise on the Family.* Cambridge, MA: Harvard
University Press.

Benabou, R. 1996. Inequality and Growth. In *NBER Macroeconomics Manual,*
edited by B. S. Bernanke and J. J. Rotemberg. Cambridge, MA: MIT Press.

Benhabib, J., and A. Rustichini. 1996. Social Conflict and Growth. *Journal of
Economic Growth* 1(1): 129–146.

Bulman, D., M. Eden, and H. Nguyen. 2017. Transitioning from Low-Income
Growth to High-Income Growth: Is There a Middle-Income Trap?
Journal of the Asia Pacific Economy 22(1): 5–28.

Daude, C., and E. Fernandez–Arias. 2010. *On the Role of Productivity and
Factor Accumulation in Economic Development in Latin America and
the Caribbean.* Washington, DC: Inter-American Development Bank.

De La Croix, D., and M. Doepke. 2004. Inequality and Growth: Why Differential
Fertility Matters. *American Economic Review* 93(4): 1091–1113.

Driscoll, J. C., and A. C. Kraay. 1998. Consistent Covariance Matrix Estimation
with Spatially Dependent Panel Data. *Review of Economics and Statistics*
80: 549–560.

Egawa, A. 2013. Will Income Inequality Cause a Middle-income Trap in Asia?
Bruegel Working Paper 2013/06. Brussels: Bruegel.

Eichengreen, B., D. Park, and K. Shin. 2012. When Fast-Growing Economies
Slow Down: International Evidence and Implications for China.
Asian Economic Papers 11(1): 42–87.

———. 2014. Growth Slowdowns Redux. *Japan and the World Economy* 32: 65–84.

Feenstra, R. C., R. Inklaar, and M. P. Timmer. 2015. The Next Generation of the Penn World Table. *American Economic Review* 105(10): 3150–3182.

Felipe, J., A. Abdon, and U. Kumar. 2012. Tracking the Middle-income Trap: What Is It, Who Is in It, and Why? Levy Economics Institute of Bard College Working Paper 715. Annandale-on-Hudson, NY: Levy Economics Institute.

Fishman, A., and A. Simhon. 2002. The Division of Labor, Inequality and Growth. *Journal of Economic Growth* 7: 117–136.

Galor, O., and J. Zeira. 1993. Income Distribution and Macroeconomics. *Review of Economic Studies* 60: 35–52.

Gill, I. S., H. J. Kharas, and D. Bhattasali. 2007. *An East Asian Renaissance: Ideas for Economic Growth*. Washington, DC: World Bank.

Jimenez, E., V. Nguyen, and H. A. Patrinos. 2012. Stuck in the Middle? Human Capital Development and Economic Growth in Malaysia and Thailand. World Bank Policy Research Working Paper 6283. Washington, DC: The World Bank.

Kaldor, N. 1967. *Strategic Factors in Economic Development*. New York, NY: Cornell University Press.

Kuznets, S. 1955. Economic Growth and Income Inequality. *American Economic Review* 45(1): 1–28.

———. 1963. Quantitative Aspects of the Economic Growth of Nations: Distribution of Income by Size. *Economic Development and Cultural Change* 11(2): 1–79.

Lambert, P. J. 1994. Redistribution through Income Tax. In *Models and Measurement of Welfare and Inequality*, edited by W. Eichhorn. Berlin/Heidelberg, Germany: Springer Verlag.

Lewis, A. 1955. *The Theory of Economic Growth*. Homewood, IL: Irwin.

Lewis, W. A. 1980. The Slowing Down of the Engine of Growth. *American Economic Review* 70(4): 555–564.

Persson, T., and G. Tabellini. 1994. Is Inequality Harmful for Growth? Theory and Evidence. *American Economic Review* 84: 600–621.

Robertson, P. E., and L. Ye. 2015. On the Existence of a Middle-Income Trap. University of Western Australia Working Paper 13/12. Perth, Australia: University of Western Australia.

Rostow, W. W. 1959. The Stages of Economic Growth. *Economic History Review* 12: 1–16.

Spence, M. 2011. *The Next Convergence. The Future of Economic Growth in a Multispeed World.* New York, NY: Farrar Strauss and Giroux.

Vivarelli, M. 2014. Structural Change and Innovation as Exit Strategies from the Middle Income Trap. IZA Discussion Paper 8148. Bonn, Germany: Institute of Labor Economics.

Wan, G., M. Lu, and Z. Chen. 2006. The Inequality–Growth Nexus in the Short and Long Run: Empirical Evidence from China. *Journal of Comparative Economics* 34(4): 654–667.

Woo, W. T., M. Lu, J. S. Sachs, and Z. Chen. 2012. *A New Economic Growth Engine for China: Escaping the Middle-income Trap by Not Doing More of the Same.* Singapore: World Scientific Publishing Company and London: Imperial College Press.

World Bank. 2012. *China 2030: Building a Modern, Harmonious, and Creative High-Income Society.* Washington, DC: World Bank.

———. 2017. *Global Economic Prospects 2017: Weak Investment in Uncertain Times.* Washington, DC: World Bank.

Table A9.1: List of Countries (by continent)

ASIA		
Afghanistan	Israel	Pakistan
Armenia	Japan	Philippines
Azerbaijan	Jordan	Qatar
Bahrain	Kazakhstan	Saudi Arabia
Bangladesh	Republic of Korea	Singapore
Bhutan	Kuwait	Sri Lanka
Brunei Darussalam	Kyrgyz Republic	Tajikistan
Cambodia	Lao People's Democratic Republic	Thailand
People's Republic of China	Lebanon	Timor-Leste
Cyprus	Macau, China	Turkey
Georgia	Malaysia	Turkmenistan
Hong Kong, China	Maldives	United Arab Emirates
India	Mongolia	Uzbekistan
Indonesia	Myanmar	Viet Nam
Iran	Nepal	West Bank and Gaza
Iraq	Oman	Yemen

EUROPE		
Albania	Greece	Montenegro
Andorra	Hungary	Netherlands
Austria	Iceland	Norway
Belarus	Ireland	Poland
Belgium	Isle of Man	Portugal
Bosnia and Herzegovina	Italy	Romania
Bulgaria	Kosovo	Russian Federation
Croatia	Latvia	Serbia
Czech Republic	Liechtenstein	Slovak Republic
Denmark	Lithuania	Slovenia
Estonia	Luxembourg	Spain
Faroe Islands	Macedonia	Sweden
Finland	Malta	Switzerland
France	Moldova	Ukraine
Germany	Monaco	United Kingdom

continued next page

Table A9.1 *Continued*

NORTH AMERICA		
Antigua and Barbuda	Dominica	Mexico
Aruba	Dominican Republic	Nicaragua
The Bahamas	El Salvador	Panama
Barbados	Greenland	Puerto Rico
Belize	Grenada	St. Kitts and Nevis
Bermuda	Guatemala	St. Lucia
Canada	Haiti	St. Vincent and the Grenadines
Costa Rica	Honduras	Trinidad and Tobago
Cuba	Jamaica	United States

SOUTH AMERICA		
Argentina	Colombia	Peru
Bolivia	Ecuador	Suriname
Brazil	Guyana	Uruguay
Chile	Paraguay	Venezuela

AFRICA		
Algeria	Ethiopia	Nigeria
Angola	Gambia	Rwanda
Benin	Ghana	Sao Tome and Principe
Botswana	Guinea	Senegal
Burkina Faso	Guinea-Bissau	Seychelles
Burundi	Kenya	Sierra Leone
Cabo Verde	Lesotho	South Africa
Cameroon	Liberia	South Sudan
Central African Republic	Libya	Sudan
Chad	Madagascar	Swaziland
Comoros	Malawi	Tanzania
Dem. Rep. Congo	Mali	Togo
Congo	Mauritania	Tunisia
Cote d'Ivoire	Mauritius	Uganda
Djibouti	Morocco	Zambia
Egypt	Mozambique	Zimbabwe
Equatorial Guinea	Namibia	Gabon
Eritrea	Niger	

OCEANIA		
Australia	Nauru	Solomon Islands
Fiji	New Zealand	Tonga
Kiribati	Palau	Tuvalu
Marshall Islands	Papua New Guinea	Vanuatu
Micronesia	Samoa	

Table A9.2: List of Countries (by income level)

LOW INCOME

Afghanistan	Gambia	Niger
Benin	Guinea	Rwanda
Burkina Faso	Guinea-Bissau	Senegal
Burundi	Haiti	Sierra Leone
Central African Republic	Liberia	South Sudan
Chad	Madagascar	Tanzania
Comoros	Malawi	Togo
Dem. Rep. Congo	Mali	Uganda
Eritrea	Mozambique	Zimbabwe
Ethiopia	Nepal	

LOWER-MIDDLE INCOME

Armenia	Kenya	Samoa
Bangladesh	Kiribati	Sao Tome and Principe
Bhutan	Kosovo	Solomon Islands
Bolivia	Kyrgyz Republic	Sri Lanka
Cabo Verde	Lao People's Democratic	Sudan
Cambodia	Republic	Swaziland
Cameroon	Lesotho	Tajikistan
Congo	Mauritania	Timor-Leste
Cote d'Ivoire	Micronesia	Tonga
Djibouti	Moldova	Tunisia
Egypt	Mongolia	Ukraine
El Salvador	Morocco	Uzbekistan
Ghana	Myanmar	Vanuatu
Guatemala	Nicaragua	Viet Nam
Honduras	Nigeria	West Bank and Gaza
India	Pakistan	Yemen
Indonesia	Papua New Guinea	Zambia
	Philippines	

continued next page

Table A9.2 *Continued*

UPPER-MIDDLE INCOME		
Albania	Fiji	Palau
Algeria	Georgia	Panama
Angola	Grenada	Paraguay
Argentina	Guyana	Peru
Azerbaijan	Iran	Romania
Belarus	Iraq	Russian Federation
Belize	Jamaica	Serbia
Bosnia and Herzegovina	Jordan	South Africa
Botswana	Kazakhstan	St. Lucia
Brazil	Lebanon	St. Vincent and the Grenadines
Bulgaria	Libya	Suriname
People's Republic of China	Macedonia	Thailand
Colombia	Malaysia	Turkey
Costa Rica	Maldives	Turkmenistan
Cuba	Marshall Islands	Tuvalu
Dominica	Mauritius	Venezuela
Dominican Republic	Mexico	Gabon
Ecuador	Montenegro	
Equatorial Guinea	Namibia	

HIGH INCOME		
Andorra	Greece	Norway
Antigua and Barbuda	Greenland	Oman
Aruba	Hong Kong, China	Poland
Australia	Hungary	Portugal
Austria	Iceland	Puerto Rico
The Bahamas	Ireland	Qatar
Bahrain	Isle of Man	Saudi Arabia
Barbados	Israel	Seychelles
Belgium	Italy	Singapore
Bermuda	Japan	Slovak Republic
Brunei Darussalam	Republic of Korea	Slovenia
Canada	Kuwait	Spain
Chile	Latvia	St. Kitts and Nevis
Croatia	Liechtenstein	Sweden
Cyprus	Lithuania	Switzerland
Czech Republic	Luxembourg	Trinidad and Tobago
Denmark	Macau, China	United Arab Emirates
Estonia	Malta	United Kingdom
Faroe Islands	Monaco	United States
Finland	Nauru	Uruguay
France	The Netherlands	
Germany	New Zealand	

CHAPTER 10

Distortions, Growth Catch-Up, and Sustainable Growth

Xiaojing Zhang, Cheng Li, and Yu Li

10.1 | Introduction

The question of whether rapid economic growth is necessarily followed by slowdown and stagnation has been at the center of recent academic debate (Eichengreen, Park, and Shin 2011; Pritchett and Summers 2014). It can be further divided into some sub-questions, including what are the driving forces of rapid growth?, what are the changing roles played by market reforms, factor accumulations (especially investment and labor force) and government behavior in the course of development?; and what are the key factors to achieve sustainable development? Undoubtedly, these questions sorely need answering in the case of present-day People's Republic of China (PRC), which is challenged by economic slowdown and socioeconomic structural transformations. This chapter attempts to shed some light on this issue by focusing on "distortion," a factor of both theoretical and practical importance.

From a theoretical perspective, a "distortion" refers to a departure from the perfect competitive equilibrium with no externalities in which resources have been optimally allocated so that each economic agent maximizes her own welfare. It is usually caused by market imperfection. In the above sense, distortion is pervasive in economies of all income levels, but their characteristics, extents, types, forms, and impacts on socioeconomic development differ substantially across countries.

In particular, in terms of their causes, distortions can be divided into two categories. The first is "endogenous distortion," caused by market imperfection and underdevelopment. The second is "policy-imposed distortion," caused by government policies and interventions. The latter is often founded upon or even on the pretext of the former (Bhagwati 1969).

There are, in theory, two extreme types of distortions: The "night-watchman state" where an economy functions under the "laissez-faire" principle with minimal distortions, and the "paternalist state" where the system of welfare covers citizen from "cradle to grave," which are commonly considered as two extreme types. Most countries, if not all, lie in between them.

Judged from the forms, there are more indirect and highly institutionalized distortions, with the aim of adjusting market failure and of providing public services of positive externality, such as elementary education, environmental protection, and basic research. Some are more direct and of administrative color, with governments directly involved in economic constructions and industrial development—usually through state-owned enterprises and selective industrial policies. It should be stressed that direct distortions are often associated with strategies of catching-up. The latter could, however, backfire in practice, especially when national conditions and factors related to the development phase are disregarded.

Judged by impact on economic performance, distortions differ in many aspects across different countries. Generally speaking, at the early stage of development, facing domestic institutional imperfection and heated competition from abroad, intensive distortions, especially selective industrial policies and development strategies, can be used for mobilizing resources, accumulating capital, and protecting "infant industries." Nevertheless, as an economy becomes more mature in terms of both industrial structure and market institutions, distortions' adverse effects on the economy begin to manifest themselves. In particular, through rent seeking by the government sector, distortions may change the incentives and behavior of private economic agents, thereby hindering innovation and long-term growth.

In summary, the question of what the "necessary" distortions are in the context of growth catch-up remains up for discussion.[1] To a large extent, it pertains to the choice of the PRC's development path in the future. Without a solid theoretical understanding of distortion, there is a risk that reforms will falter or be blindly pursued, thus trapping the PRC at the middle-income level.

This chapter attempts to provide a comprehensive perspective on the relationship between distortions and economic performance, and to discuss the policy implications of distortions for the PRC's reforms and sustainable development. The rest of the chapter is organized as follows. Section 10.2 reviews the recent literature on distortions. Section 10.3 discusses the favorable distortions and their applicable conditions. Section 10.4 provides evidence from international experiences for the impact of distortions on economic performance. Section 10.5 turns to the PRC's case, with an emphasis on the marketization process of the PRC regions. The last section concludes the chapter and provides policy discussions.

10.2 | Literature Review

Regarding the academic literature, distortion as a research topic was first proposed by Bhagwati (1969), in which he generalized the theory of distortions (mostly in trade) and welfare and proposed a conceptual distinction between "endogenous" distortions and "policy-imposed" distortions.

Since then, distortions have received attention, but mainly the experiences of developing countries, including taxation, state-owned enterprises, administrative monopoly, trade and industrial policies, financial repression, exchange rate management, and government regulations. In particular,

---

[1] For economic latecomers, "catch-up" constitutes an eternal theme, and distortions aimed at catching up are pervasive: for instance, Japan massively stimulated her economy regardless of the fact that potential growth had been slowed down in the 1960s. This distortion caused serious economic bubbles and resulted in the so-called "lost two decades." In some Latin American countries, responding to rising populism, social welfare systems appeared to be excessively developed regardless of economic conditions, leading to stagnation and social unrest.

the economics of development and institutional economics have provided intensive theoretical analysis and policy discussions on economic take-off, and development strategies in developing countries, such as McKinnon (1973), Sah and Stiglitz (1987), Grossman and Helpman (1994), Parker (1995), Shleifer and Vishny (1998), Hall and Jones (1999), Qian (2000), Gordon and Li (2009), and Acemoglu and Robinson (2012). Relatively speaking, thanks to matured market systems, endogenous distortions are less pervasive in advanced economies, where they mainly relate to taxation and discretionary government stabilizing policies as documented in Judd (1985), Chamley (1986), Lucas (1990), and Easterly (1993).

More interestingly, as the PRC reaches the middle-income level, its economic structures, comparative advantages, sources, and path of long-term growth have all changed substantially. Thus, the relationship between government and market in general, and the mixed impact of distortions on the economy in particular, have been at the center of recent academic discussions, including Parker (1995), Young (2000), Lin (2003), Zhu, Jin, and Luo (2005), Zhang (2008), Zhang (2005), Hsieh and Klenow (2009), Zhang and Cheng (2010), Li and Lin (2011), Song, Storesletten, and Zilibotti (2011), Yan and Hu (2013), and Qian (2016). The topics of interest include factor price distortions, taxation distortions, financial repression, fragmentation of domestic markets, and distortions regarding openness. Recently, Yang (2016) further stressed that mitigating the distortions regarding factor allocation is the key to structural reforms in today's PRC.

It should be emphasized that although some studies do not directly address "distortions," they focus on some highly relevant questions, especially the aforementioned "policy-imposed" distortions. Indeed, the very nature of the distortion should be understood in the context of the government–market relationship and the role of government in development.

From this angle, early literature on structuralist economics of development focuses on market imperfection in developing countries, and claims that the hand of government can help repair the deficiencies of the market.

In other words, because of the presence of "endogenous distortions" (including market rigidity, hysteresis, shortage oversupply, inelasticity of supply and demand, undershooting, etc.), the government needs to proactively intervene in the functioning of markets through distorting policies and measures, including forced savings, "big-push," industry selection, and import substitution. Despite their positive effects in some areas, the focus on the government interventions leads to various problems, and thus it is replaced by neoclassical economics of development, which emphasizes the forces of markets and the importance of price mechanisms. In fact, the story is more complex in practice than in theory. Although some East Asian economies (such as Japan and the Republic of Korea) avoided the "middle income trap," largely thanks to the efforts of government, some followers, such as Malaysia and Indonesia, seem to have become trapped at the middle-income level in the aftermath of the Asian financial crisis in the late 1990s. Later on, intensive discussions and hot debates emerged around the so-called "Washington Consensus" versus the "Beijing Consensus." The underlying question of those concerns is once again that of the relationship between government and market. Of course, the topic became even more relevant in the wake of the 2008 crisis and a growing body of literature has emerged since then.

In his theoretical framework labeled New Structural Economics, Lin (2014) stressed that an economy should specialize according to its comparative advantages and this path of development cannot be reached through a laissez-faire market mechanism and, thus, the efforts of government are needed. Since comparative advantages are mainly based on factor endowment (including capital, labor force, and natural resources), the changes in the latter can also cause the changes in comparative advantages. Indeed, to exploit the comparative advantages, both markets and government are indispensable. In this regard, two cases can be considered: (1) If the government gives priority to the development of the industry of no comparative and competitive advantages, the enterprises in this industry will need protection (i.e., a distortion) because of their lack of viability; (2) If the industry has comparative advantages, the enterprises involved will have high international competitive ability thanks to their viability, thereby improving their capital accumulations. As Lin argued, government should proactively improve the industrial upgrading and technical innovations through "growth identification" and "facilitation." In essence, the New Structural Economics developed by Lin attempts to strike a balance between government and market. It seems that the former has been overemphasized by early structural development economics and the latter by the Washington consensus.

In criticizing the traditional theory of comparative advantages, Stiglitz and Bruce (2017) emphasized the importance of learning. He argued that in the traditional theoretical framework, comparative advantage relies on the assumption that knowledge is publicly available and its focus is on factor endowment (such as the capital–labor ratio). Nevertheless, since capital is mobile across countries, capital endowment seems to be unhelpful for understanding static comparative advantage. Instead, comparative advantage is mainly determined by immobile factors, such as knowledge, labor, and institutions. The most important of these is learning ability at the level of society. Given the fact that the market seems to be inefficient in producing and spreading knowledge, governments, especially those in developing countries, need to play a proactive role in improving learning ability.

From a broader perspective, Bardhan (2016) addressed the roles of government and their complexity. He argues that because of the comprehensiveness of the goals of development and the multidimensionality of government functions, along with coordination failure and the difficulty of collective action, the role of government needs redefining. From both historical and logical perspectives, Bardhan related stages of development and government's roles. Jia (2011) and Wen (2016) also stressed the following fact: government interventions played an important and even indispensable role in the success of the early industrialized countries.

Fukuyama (2012, 2015) stressed the importance of "state capacity," and thus provided an argument in support of strong government. He claimed that the prosperity of a country needs state capacity, accountable government (democracy), and rule of law. According to Fukuyama, the United States is suffering from weak state capacity, but enjoys accountable government, and rule of law; in contrast, the PRC has strong state capacity, but with weak or immature accountable government and rule of law. Besley and Persson (2009) also documented that the experiences of advanced economies show that taxation and contract enforcement, as two important elements of state capacity, constitute necessary preconditions for prosperity. Nevertheless, it should be noted that there is no standard definition for the term "state capacity." Loosely speaking, in our view, it includes market support (property rights delimitation and protection, contract enforcement, market rules), resources allocation (such as taxation), and adjusting social relationships.

Acemoglu, García–Jimeno, and Robinson (2015) also argued that the state capacity is a crucial explanatory factor for both the Asian miracle and the mediocre growth performances of many African and South American countries. This claim is further supported by cross-country data (Gennaioli and Rainer 2007) and subnational data (Michalopoulos and Papaioannou 2013; Bandyopadhyay and Green 2012). It is noteworthy that the importance of state capacity is by no means unconditional. It should be constrained by accountable government and rule of law. Without those two constraints, a strong government might turn into its opposite—the Leviathan, or grabbing-hand government. Thus, a strong government should also be a limited government.

Historically, there has been a rise and fall in the government's role in economic development. In particular, during economic booms, it is not uncommon that their role is either ignored, or considered as an impediment to prosperity. In contrast, during crisis their role is often overemphasized. The 2008 crisis is not an exception. Indeed, in the wake of this event, a growing body of literature focusing on the (mainly positive) role of government emerged. In this regard, four points should be made: (1) Government, as a last resort, is able to tackle a crisis and mitigate various shocks, through stabilizing policies such as debt-transmission from the private sector to the public sector, especially in advanced economies; (2) Government helps with innovation (for example, Mazzucato [2013] showed that government in advanced countries actually plays a crucial role in innovation through industrial policies); (3) Government, as a venture capitalist, can also fill the gap between public and private investment; (4) Government can not only make up for market deficiency, but proactively create the market as well. This argument is in sharp contrast with some in neoclassical economics,[2] and thus has led to some criticism (Mingardi 2015).

It should be stressed that government interventions and distortions are not interchangeable. In other words, not all government intervention is seen as distortion. More rigorously, distortions can be defined as government intervention that leads to the deviation from optimal allocation of resources. In this spirit, the "market-augmenting government" of Olson (2000) and the "market-enhancing government" of Aoki, Murdock, and Okuno-Fujiwara (1997) should not be considered as distortions. According to Olson, the success of economic development should be based on two conditions: One is the clear delimitation of rights, another is the protection of the economy from extortion and abuse of public power. The "market-augmenting" government is indeed defined by these conditions, which, in much the same spirit of "state capacity," imply that the government should play a role in market creation and function. When discussing government in East Asian economies, Aoki and others proposed the concept of "market-enhancing." He argued that because government failure is not less pervasive than market failure in economic activities, various industrial and social organizations, such as associations of enterprises, trade unions, financial intermediaries, and chambers of commerce, can contribute to addressing these two kinds of failure. Thus, government should also foster the development of these organizations and build institutional frameworks to coordinate with them. To judge whether a government intervention is a kind of distortion, therefore, the key criterion is whether this intervention can reinforce the market mechanism.

---

[2]   In neoclassical economics, industrial policies are usually considered as distortions and government interventions often leading to government failure.

To sum up, like government, distortions play mixed roles in development, which depend on a number of socioeconomic characteristics and institutional factors. Given such complexity, it is very important to investigate, from both theoretical and empirical perspectives, the interaction between distortions and development.

10.3 | How Are Favorable Distortions Possible?

This chapter mainly addresses distortions in developing countries, which usually experience two kinds of mutually reinforcing distortions—"endogenous distortions" and "policy-imposed distortions."[3] In this chapter, we pay more attention to the latter, which it is believed can contribute to economic takeoff and catch up.

In neoclassical economics, catch-up of developing countries is a natural process thanks to "convergence."[4] In practice, however, convergence is often conditional and, indeed, the gap between developed and developing countries in many cases is getting bigger. In some East Asian economies including Japan; the Republic of Korea; Singapore; and Taipei,China, government interventions are sometimes considered to be a contributing factor to their impressive growth performance (World Bank 1993). In addition to the East Asian economies, strong government interventions (such as tariff barriers, exploitation of colonies and overseas markets, and infant industry protection) can be found in many developed countries during their early industrialization process.[5] Although these government interventions are often distorting

---

[3] For example, the domestic market is generally fragmented by nature in many developing countries. Nevertheless, it is not uncommon that local governments establish further artificial/institutional barriers (such as in the PRC) for the sake of catch-up and interregional competition.

[4] For example, Rodrick (2006) discussed the unconditional convergence in manufacturing.

[5] For example, in the 16th and 18th centuries, the United Kingdom made proactive policy interventions to develop its overseas textile markets, cotton supply chain, and trade network through, for example, the quasi state-owned East India Company. As argued in Wen (2016), it was these policy efforts, rather than Glorious Revolution and Constitutional Monarchy, which triggered the first wave of the Industrial Revolution. Almost without exception, other western countries, such as the United States, France, Germany, the Soviet Union, and Japan, all followed, at least in some aspects, the mode of the United Kingdom, and achieved prosperity.

in the light of neoclassical economics, their positive impact on economic development may generally surpass their negative impact, and thus they can be considered as "favorable" distortions.

How are the favorable distortions possible? What are their preconditions? What are the logic and mechanism underlying them? In what follows, we provide four arguments regarding those questions—advantage of backwardness, second-best principle, coordination failure, and political economy perspective.

10.3.1 Advantage of Backwardness

Gerschenkron (1962) firstly dealt with "economic backwardness" and pointed out that a country such as the Soviet Union was backward relative to Britain when it embarked on industrialization, and did not go through the same stages. His theory predicts that the more "economically backward" a country is, the more we will see, for example, more rapid rates of industrial growth and a more active role for the government and large banks in supplying capital and entrepreneurship.

A developing economy can also be at an advantage because of its relative backwardness—in that it can borrow technologies, business models, and marketing procedures from more advanced economies; and in that imitation may be easier and faster than original innovation on which the leading economies have to rely. However, when the advantage of backwardness gradually narrows and the uncertainty of frontier innovation increases, the government will find it more difficult to collect enough information and make correct decisions. The "government-picking-the-winner" model turns out to be a failure. That is why, as economies move to higher incomes and rely more on innovation as the engine of growth, the government intervention as a major form of distortion will amplify its adverse effects on the economy. Therefore, mitigating distortions and letting the market play a decisive role in resource allocation are key to sustainable development and therefore also key to avoiding the middle-income trap.

10.3.2 Second-Best Principle

Another factor of interest is the "second-best principle." The second-best principle (Lipsey and Lancaster 1956) implies that if it is not feasible to remove a particular market distortion, introducing a second (or more) market distortion(s) may partially counteract the first, and lead to a more efficient outcome. In this regard, the argument put forward by Qian (2016) is of direct relevance to the topic of this chapter. As he pointed out, some favorable distortions are possible given the "second-best principle". Contrary to the "first-best principle," claiming that a distortion must lead to a decline in efficiency, the "second-best principle" means that in the presence of multiple distortions, the reduction of one distortion does not necessarily increase efficiency, and the addition of another distortion does not necessarily decrease efficiency.

Arguably, "rent-seeking" behavior, which is often caused by government regulations, industrial policies, and development strategies, may improve the marketization process in the presence of institutional barriers. Nevertheless, in the early stage of development and industrialization, both entrepreneurship and capital are scarce resources. In this context, investments, learning, and innovations may be encouraged by rent-seeking behavior—as long as the latter is consistent with the principle of market-oriented reform. As both government regulations and institutional barriers on the one hand, and rent-seeking behavior on the other, can be seen as distortions, in this sense a distortion can be used to tackle another. In recent years, this logic has been discussed in the literature on government behavior (Bardhan 2016).

Obviously, the PRC's reform proceeds in the presence of many distortions, especially the inherent "original sin" distortions (such as underdevelopment of market system and inadequate protection of property rights), so it needs to be "adjusted" by distortion of other kinds, such as active government intervention. For instance, when property rights are secured, the efficiency of private enterprise is generally high, and other forms of ownership of enterprises, due mainly to the principal–agent problem, will cause distortions.

But if property rights are insecure because of imperfect rule of law, then privately owned firms will need to pay to secure protection for their property. Therefore, in this context the reform is likely to choose one distortion to deal with another, such as the use of local government power to protect property rights against a higher level of government, which may improve efficiency. In this sense, some distortions may be reasonable and necessary. But despite their favorable effects under some circumstances, distortions as transitional institutional arrangements in line with the second-best principle may incur high costs, and even become significant barriers to further deepening reforms as an economy enters a higher stage of maturity.

10.3.3 Coordination Failure

Generally speaking, different types of governance should be consistent with different goals of the organization. At different stages of development, an economy may suffer from various kinds of coordination failure, and in this context, government (or the state), market, community, and so forth all can play a role as "coordinator" (either complementary or contradictory) in dealing with this challenge. Clearly, the applicability of the coordination mechanism or arrangement highly depends on the socioeconomic environments and thus, to avoid a simplistic and a historical perspective, one should emphasize that there is no universal and optimal model for this.

In theory, the market may be an outstanding coordinator of noncooperative interactions,[6] inefficient governance, and performance incentives. However, if the residual claim and control are misallocated, and the long-run investment decisions have important strategic complementarity, the market as a coordinator ceases to be efficient. In particular, the poor tend to be more affected by imperfections and inadequacy of credit and insurance

---

[6] In noncooperative interactions, economic agents make their decisions individually, without looking at those of others in the context.

markets, which discourages productive investments, innovations, and human resources development. In this context, noncooperative interactions tend to be inefficient and therefore coordination and selective incentives by the government are needed to stimulate cooperative actions among market agents.

Market failure in coordination provides the basis for government intervention. In spite of a different focus, this argument is in the same spirit as the aforementioned "second-best principle." In some areas and socioeconomic environments (such as underdeveloped markets), the hand of government is indispensable to deal with market failure. Therefore, in addition to the role of night watchman and protector of property rights, government may play a multiple role as coordinator, guide, and stimulator, especially in the context of structural changes and an uncertain development path. As a matter of fact, development and transition countries appear to encounter more challenges from coordination failure and thus government should be associated with proper capacity in mobilizing resources, making decisions, regulating markets, enforcing laws, and collecting and treating information. Ideally, government should remain neutral regarding specific interests, and be subjected to institutional balance and checks to avoid abuse of government power. But although government interventions aim to tackle market failure, they may also be subject to malfunction and imperfection themselves. For example, although industrial policies regained their popularity in the wake of the 2008 financial crisis, the adverse effects of the government-picking-the-winner model (such as rent-seeking behavior) have become more evident. It implies that when intervening in the market, government should tackle both coordination failure and its own deficiency. Obviously, in practice it is extremely hard to do so, especially to succeed in striking a balance between market mechanism and policy distortions. That just shows that favorable distortions, which are not always easy to see, are indeed only possible under certain strict conditions.

10.3.4 Perspective of Political Economy

Distortion is mostly defined from an economics perspective and thus examined with reference to market equilibrium. If taking the somewhat broader perspective of political economy, which may take account of aspects beyond economics such as national security, geopolitical or ideological factors, and so forth, some distortions could be taken as normal or favorable. For instance, the success of the *"two bombs, one satellite"* program in the PRC before market reforms and opening up is highly praised in the "Beijing Consensus," but apparently conflicts with the narrowly defined principle of comparative advantage or cost–benefit analysis. Another example is to sacrifice the interests of farmers to give priority to the development of heavy industry (also from the experience of the PRC). These examples indicate that whether a policy is favorable or not depends on which benchmark or position is chosen.[7]

10.4 | International Evidence

10.4.1 Descriptive Analysis

Our analysis of international experiences is based on a sample of 50 countries of different income levels. It includes major economies in various continents and at different stages of development. Notably, given the fact that the aggregation of the 50 countries under consideration accounts for 80%, and 90%, of world population and GDP, respectively, this sample is highly representative. Moreover, this representative sample will also help to tackle the potential bias due to extremely small economies.

---

[7] It should be noted that if arbitrarily changing the criterion of judgment, the distortions will become undefined. In this chapter, unless otherwise stated, by distortion we mean departure from the optimal allocation of economic resources.

Table 10.1: Countries in the Sample

High Income (24 countries)	Upper Middle Income (15 countries)	Lower Middle Income (11 countries)
Argentina, **Australia**, Austria, Belgium, **Canada**, Chile, **France**, **Germany**, Israel, **Italy**, **Japan**, **Republic of Korea**, Netherlands, New Zealand, Norway, Poland, **Saudi Arabia**, Singapore, Spain, Sweden, Switzerland, United Arab Emirates, **United Kingdom**, **United States**	Algeria, Angola, **Brazil**, **People's Republic of China**, Colombia, Ecuador, Iran, Kazakhstan, **Mexico**, Peru, **Russian Federation**, **South Africa**, Thailand, **Turkey**, Venezuela	Bangladesh, Egypt, **India**, **Indonesia**, Kenya, Malaysia, Morocco, Nigeria, Pakistan, Philippines, Viet Nam

Notes: 1. Income levels are defined according to World Bank standards applied to 2016 data.
2. Country names in bold stand for G20 group members.
Source: Authors.

Regarding the measure of economic distortions, we rely on the Index of Economic Freedom (IEF for short; overall index), which is jointly published by the Heritage Foundation and the Wall Street Journal. As a commonly used indicator of economic freedom, or, accordingly, an opposite indicator of distortions, the overall IEF is composed of 10 sub-indexes, including "property rights," "freedom from corruption," "fiscal freedom," "government spending," "business freedom," "labor freedom," "monetary freedom," "trade freedom," "investment freedom," and "financial freedom." All the sub-indexes are valued from 0 (least free) to 100 (most free).[8] Thanks to its broad coverage of a number of dimensions of market functioning and economic activities, it is believed that the IEF can serve as a good indicator for the multifaceted distortions we discussed above.

Intuitively, there may exist a positive correlation between *Freedom* and income level. As shown in Figure 10.1, high-income countries are generally associated with freer economic systems, and, by contrast, middle-income

---

[8]   For details on IEF, see http://www.heritage.org/index/book/methodology.

countries tend to suffer from more market distortions. Surprisingly, when regressing *Freedom* on GDP per capita, the R squared is as high as 0.51, indicating that *Freedom* alone can explain a significant part of income level differences across the countries in the sample.

Figure 10.1: Economic Freedom and Income Level

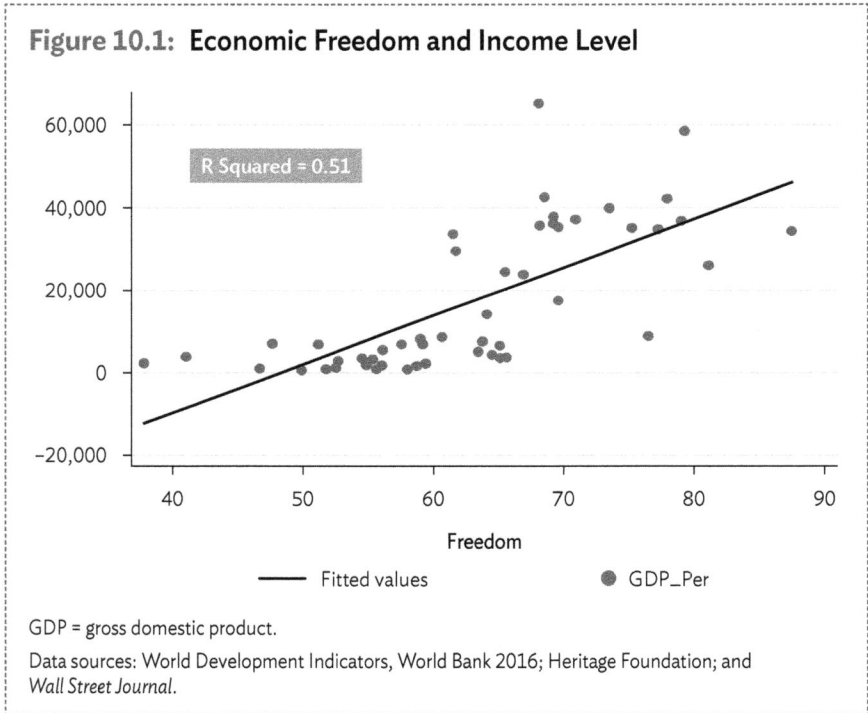

GDP = gross domestic product.
Data sources: World Development Indicators, World Bank 2016; Heritage Foundation; and *Wall Street Journal*.

10.4.2 Econometric Investigation

With the above theoretical discussions in mind, we next empirically investigate the impact of distortions on the growth of total factor productivity (TFP), which is believed to be a crucial, if not the only, engine of long-term economic growth.[9] For this purpose, we draw on the TFP estimates offered by the

---

[9]   It is worth noting that, as shown in Eichengreen, Park, and Shin (2011), the TFP growth slowdown could explain about 85% of the recent slowdown in economic growth.

Conference Board.[10] Specifically, we regress the following equation with the help of a panel data set, which is composed of the above 50 countries over the period of 1995–2014. The empirical model can be written as follows:

$$TFP_{it} = \beta_1 Freedom + \beta_1 \sum_{l=1}^{k} CV_{itl} + \alpha_i + \mu_t + \varepsilon_{it}, \tag{1}$$

where CV refers to a set of control variables that have potential impact on TFP growth: GDP growth (denoted as $GDPGrowth$), Openness, which is measured by two variables: the exports of goods and services (as a percentage of GDP; denoted as $TradeOpen$), and the Chinn–Ito Index of capital account openness (denoted as $KaOpen$; see Chinn and Ito 2008). Year dummies are also added to control for the potential common (especially worldwide) shocks to TFP growth in the sampled countries.

The regressions are first conducted on the full sample. As shown in columns (1) and (2) of Table 10.2, we identify a significant negative impact of economic freedom on TFP growth, regardless of the different control variables. Among the latter, both GDP growth and trade openness have significantly positive coefficients, which are in line with expectations: in principle, TFP growth is a residual of gross domestic product (GDP) growth after adjusting the growth of capital and labor input, thus the two variables should be positively correlated; the engagement in foreign trade may also contribute to TFP, mainly through the benefits from industrial specification and spillover of technology. However, the impact of capital account opening up on TFP appears to be insignificant.

Next, we introduce the *Indicator of Quality of Government* (denoted as QOG) given by *International Country Risk Guide* (see Dahlberg et al. 2016). It is a composite index measuring "corruption," "law and order," and "bureaucracy quality." Since higher values of this variable indicate higher quality of government, its expected sign is positive. As can be seen from column (3),

---

[10]   The Conference Board. 2016. The Conference Board Total Economy Database™, November 2016. http://www.conference-board.org/data/economydatabase/.

Freedom is associated with a negative coefficient, and *QOG* positive. However, both coefficients are insignificantly different from zero. We conjecture that there are two reasons for these results: the first is the multicollinearity between *Freedom* and *QOG*; the second is the relatively low variability in the *QOG* data.

Table 10.2: Total Factor Productivity Growth and Economic Freedom (1995–2014)

Models / Variables	(1)	(2)	(3)	(4)	(5)	(6)	(7)
Samples	All	All	All	All	Lower middle income	Upper middle income	High income
Freedom	−0.0282 (0.0160)*	−0.0316 (0.0170)*	−0.0267 (0.0174)	−0.3407 (0.1057)***	−0.1410 (0.0535)***	−0.0714 (0.0247)***	0.0506 (0.0169)***
Freedom_sq	–	–	–	0.0027 (0.0009)***	–	–	–
GDPGrowth	0.6041 (0.0202)***	0.6041 (0.0203)***	0.6089 (0.0205)***	0.6100 (0.0202)***	0.3981 (0.0529)***	0.7774 (0.0319)***	0.6065 (0.0266)***
TradeOpen	0.0382 (0.0086)***	0.0376 (0.0087)***	0.0386 (0.0087)***	0.0434 (0.0087)***	0.0200 (0.0203)	0.0793 (0.0229)***	0.0268 (0.0089)***
KaOpen	–	0.2459 (0.4193)	0.1377 (0.4221)	–	–	–	–
QOG	–	–	0.9374 (1.1708)	0.8265 (1.1586)	–	–	–
Year dummies	Yes	Yes	Yes	Yes	Yes	Yes	Yes
Hausman Chi(2) Statistics	93.05 ***	80.40***	72.09***	85.90***	17.81 ***	50.40 ***	37.38 ***
Observations	972	971	970	971	220	284	468
R^2 (within)	0.6313	0.6309	0.6330	0.6372	0.4242	0.8092	0.7221

Notes: 1. Standard errors in parentheses, with ***, **, * denoting 1%, 5%, and 10% level of significance, respectively. Moreover, given the relatively small size of our sample, bootstrap standard errors are also considered, whereas the statistical significance of the variables remains essentially the same.

2. All regressions above include a constant.

3. According to Hausman test results, fixed-effect models are applied to all regressions in the table.

Source: Authors.

Furthermore, it is also possible that economic freedom and TFP growth are correlated in a nonlinear way. With this query in mind, we incorporate the squared freedom index into regressions. As can be seen from column (4), *Freedom* and it quadratic term, denoted as *Freedom_sq*, have significant coefficients with opposite signs: negative for *Freedom*, and positive for *Freedom_sq*. The results imply that in case of a low level of economic freedom, market distortions may spur TFP growth. However, as the economic system becomes more mature and freer, distortions turn out to hinder TFP growth. According to the estimates, the inflection point of the freedom index is around 63, roughly equal to those of France and Saudi Arabia in 2014.

Finally, as argued in the Introduction, the distortions–TFP growth relationship may also vary among countries at different stages of development. To test this conjecture, we next conduct regressions for each group of countries by income level—"lower middle income," "upper middle income," and "high income." As shown in columns (5) to (7), although the coefficients of freedom remain significant among the three subsamples, their signs are negative for the first two cohorts and positive for the third one. In addition, the negative coefficient of *Freedom* in the upper-middle-income group is greater (namely with a smaller absolute value) than that in the lower-middle-income group. Arguably, these results support our conjecture that market distortions will contribute to TFP growth in the early stages of development, and as the economy expands this positive impact of distortions will fade away and even change its sign.

10.5 | Evidence from the PRC

This section turns to the experiences of the PRC since the reform and opening up in 1978. Specifically, with the help of panel analysis, we explore the relationship between the PRC's policy distortions, measured by the Marketization Index, and the province-level (or equivalent region) TFP growth.

10.5.1 Distortions Measured by Marketization Index

As a commonly used indicator of market development or distortions, the provincial Marketization Index (MI) is compiled by the National Economic Research Institute (NERI). It is a composite measure of the PRC's marketization process in five dimensions: government–market relations, development of nonstate economy, development of product market, development of factors market, and development of intermediary and legal environment. The MI and all of its components are measured on a scale from 0–10. A province scores a higher MI when it stays in a leading position compared with other provinces in its progress toward market economy and suffered fewer distortions compared with lower MI provinces. Here we use some statistical charts to explain the basic facts and characteristics of the PRC's marketization process in 1997–2014.

First, the PRC's marketization in general moves forward, while its speed varies between different periods. The PRC's MI continued to rise during 1997–2014 (the only exception is 2010, slightly down by 1.36%), indicating that the PRC's market–oriented reform has been effectively pursued. Overall, the growth rate of MI varies widely between different periods: (1) from 1999 to 2004, the MI increased rapidly, probably due to the PRC's accession to the World Trade Organization (WTO); (2) from 2005 to 2010, the MI continued to rise, but the growth rate gradually slowed; and (3) from 2011 to 2014, growth of the MI picked up and the average annual grow rate was about 5%.

As illustrated in Figure 10.2, the variation of the MI between provinces expanded after 2008, and its distribution is roughly consistent with the level of regional economic development—the eastern region as a whole had the highest MI, followed by the central region, and then the western region, which had the lowest score.

Figure 10.2: **Mean Value of Marketization Index by Region (1997–2014)**

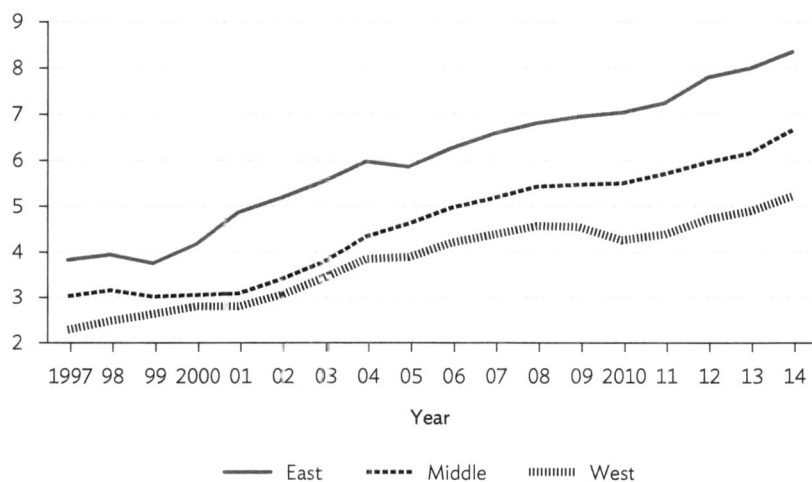

Sources: Fan, Wang, and Zhang (2001) and Fan, Wang, and Zhu (2003); National Economic Research Institute.

Furthermore, each MI dimension follows a different trend.[11] Most dimensions of the MI showed an upward trend in most periods (Figure 10.3). The dimension with a clear downward trend is government–market relations. In 2006–2013, the government–market relations dimension fell from 7.18 to 5.70, and rose slightly to 6.02 in 2014. The government–market relations dimension consists of three indicators: the proportion of resources allocated by the market, the government intervention in the enterprise, and the government size. The three indicators fell by 1.33, 0.77, and 1.53 points, respectively, indicating that since the financial crisis of 2008, the government of the PRC has strengthened its power in the resources allocation and expanded its size.

---

[11] Since the 1997–2009 MI is based on the year 1997 and the 2008–2014 MI is based on 2008, the indexes for these two periods cannot be compared directly. Therefore, we choose 2014 as the benchmark and adjust the 1997–2008 MI by calculating the growth rate of the MI.

Figure 10.3: Changing Scores of the Five Marketization Index Dimensions (1997–2014)

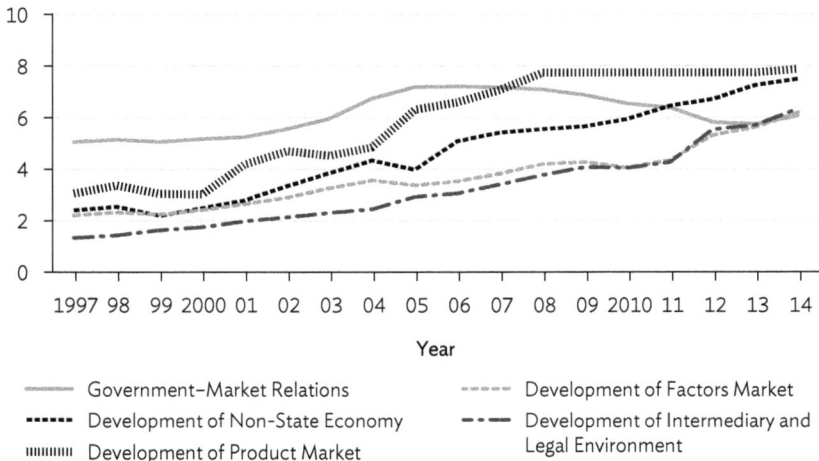

Government–Market Relations
Development of Non-State Economy
Development of Product Market
Development of Factors Market
Development of Intermediary and Legal Environment

Sources: Fan, Wang, and Zhang (2001) and Fan, Wang, and Zhu (2003); National Economic Research Institute.

10.5.2 Provincial Total Factor Productivity Growth in the PRC

As suggested in some research, compared with the developed countries, the contribution of the PRC's TFP to economic growth has yet to be further improved. For instance, Brandt and Zhu (2010) decomposed the PRC's economic growth since the reform and opening-up policy in 1978, and found the contribution of TFP to economic growth in the PRC was 62% in 1978–1988, 48% in 1988–1998, and 47% in 1998–2008, with a gradually declining tendency. In this section, we count TFP for the PRC's provinces from 1978 to 2015 by using the Solow growth calculation method. Since the Solow model is the most widely used method for calculating TFP, our improvement is mainly about the estimation of production factor inputs. Based on TFP growth, we can identify the main driving force of the PRC's economic growth and judge whether the PRC economy has entered the efficiency-driven stage.

Equation of Total Factor Productivity Calculation

The production function is characterized as a Cobb–Douglas production function:

$$Y = AK^{\alpha}(L*H)^{(1-\alpha)},\tag{2}$$

A is TFP, α is the capital output elasticity, $(1-\alpha)$ is the human capital output elasticity. Deriving the derivative of time t, equation (1) changes to

$$\dot{A} = \dot{Y} - \alpha\dot{K} - (1-\alpha)\dot{L}\dot{H}\tag{3}$$

Furthermore, we use the Hodrick–Prescott (HP) filtering method to remove the stochastic perturbation factor ε_t of $\dot{A}$, and finally estimate the growth rate of the TFP, $\hat{A}$.

Input accounting

(1) Physical capital

The widely used method for estimating the physical capital stock is the perpetual inventory method initiated by Goldsmith (1951):

$$K_t = K_{t-1}(1 - \delta_t) + I_t.$$

To use this method, four parameters need to be determined: the capital stock in the base period K; investment in every period I; capital price index i; and depreciation rate δ. First, learning from Young (2000), we set 1952 as the base period, and multiply the investment in fixed assets in 1952 by 10 to obtain the capital stock for that year. Second, we use the capital formation in every year as the investment increment. Third, for the capital price index, in 1952–1990, we use the retail price index as a proxy for it; and in 1991–2015, we use the price deflator of fixed asset investment to deflate the value of capital stock. Fourth, the depreciation rate from 1952 to 1977 was calculated to be 5%, and it increased by 0.1% from 1978. This approach is adopted from Wang, Fan, and Liu (2009).

(2) Human capital

According to the Solow model, the human capital could be defined as the product of the number of workers (L) and the average number of years of education (H) of labor. The number of labor (L) could be obtained from the China Statistical Yearbook. The average education year (H) could be calculated based on the census data of 1982, 1990, 2000, 2005, and 2010.

(3) Capital output elasticity

Chen et al. (1988), Chow and Li (2002), and Lu and Cai (2016) used the aggregate production function to estimate the capital output elasticity. Bai and Zhang (2015) argued that the share of capital income from the aggregate production function is constant, but this is inconsistent with the PRC's reality (also see Perkins and Rawski 2008). Therefore, we use the income approach to calculate the capital income share of each province as a capital output elasticity. The calculation formula is as follows:

$$\alpha_{it} = \frac{\text{Depreciation of fixed assets}_{it} + \text{Operating surplus}_{it}}{\text{Laborers' remuneration}_{it} + \text{Depreciation of fixed assets}_{it} + \text{Operating surplus}_{it}} \quad (4)$$

(4) Statistics of Total Factor Productivity

Following the above method, we estimate the PRC's provincial TFP growth.[12] The statistics for the variables are shown in Table 10.3:

Table 10.3: Descriptive Statistics

Variable	Observation	Mean	St.d	Minimum	Maximum
GDP (billion yuan)	1,064	146.65	227.22	1.30	1,782.79
Physical Capital (billion yuan)	1,064	280.16	448.22	3.48	3,438.21
Human Capital (million person*year)	1,064	219.73	148.02	12.50	812.43
Income Share of Capital (%)	1,064	0.42	0.09	0.21	0.73
TFP	1,064	0.47	0.28	0.10	1.95
TFP Growth	1,064	0.042	0.028	−0.15	0.15

GDP = gross domestic product, St.d = standard deviation, TFP = total factor productivity.
Source: Authors.

---

[12]   Since there are too many missing values for Chongqing, Hainan, and Tibet Autonomous Region, we exclude these three regions and calculate TFP growth using data of 28 provinces.

Figure 10.4: Total Factor Productivity in the East/Middle/West Regions (1978–2015)

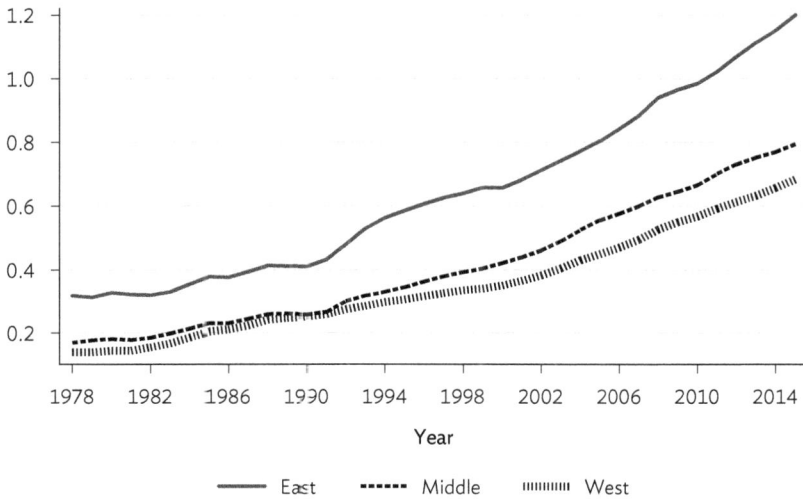

Source: Authors and National Bureau of Statistics (various years).

Figure 10.4 presents the TFP in the three regions[13] of the PRC. In 1978–2015, TFP steadily increased in each region but at a different pace: TFP in the eastern region is significantly faster than in the central and western regions. The gap of TFP between central and western regions gradually increased.

TFP growth of each region is shown in Figure 10.5. In most years from 1978 to 2015, the PRC's eastern, central, and western regions saw positive TFP growth, but the growth rate fluctuated greatly in different years. In the 1980s and 1990s, TFP growth showed a tendency to first increase and then decrease. From 2000, the TFP growth trend stabilized, and after 2010 it significantly declined.

---

13   The eastern region includes Beijing, Tianjin, Hebei, Liaoning, Shanghai, Jiangsu, Zhejiang, Fujian, Shandong, and Guangdong. The central region includes Shanxi, Jilin, Heilongjiang, Anhui, Jiangxi, Henan, Hubei, and Hunan. The western region includes Inner Mongolia, Guangxi, Sichuan, Guizhou, Yunnan, Shaanxi, Gansu. Qinghai, Ningxia, and Xinjiang.

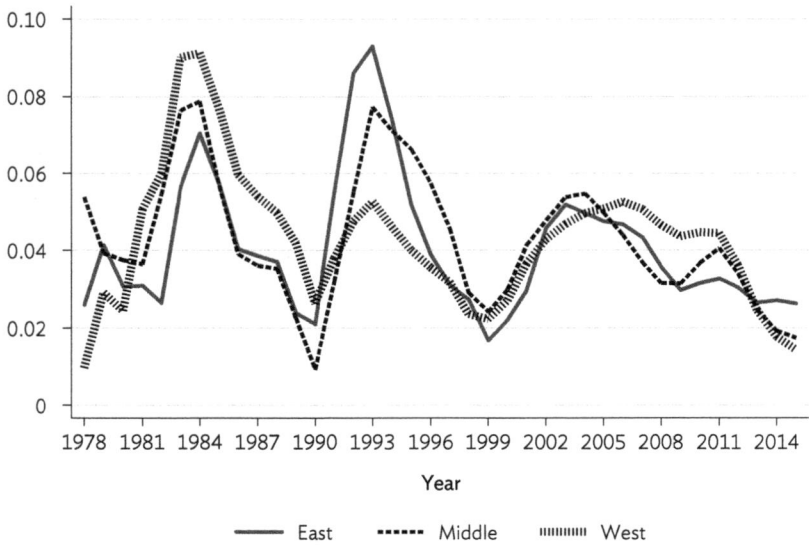

Figure 10.5: Total Factor Productivity Growth in the East/Middle/West Regions (1978–2015)

Source: Authors and National Bureau of Statistics (various years).

10.5.3 Empirical Model

In this section, we establish a panel regression model to further investigate the long-term quantitative contributions of marketization to total provincial TFP.[14]

We construct the following empirical regression model.

$$TFP_{it} = c + \beta_1 MI_{i,t} + \beta_l \sum_{l=1}^{k} CV_{itl} + \alpha_i + \mu_t + \varepsilon_{i,t} \tag{6}$$

The subscripts i and t represent the provinces and years. The explanatory variable TFP of the regression model is set as the TFP growth rate of the province i in year t. The core explanatory variable $MI_{i,t}$ is the Marketization

---

[14]   Due to the serious lack of data in Chongqing, Hainan, and Tibet Autonomous Region, we excluded these three regions and obtained a full sample of 28 provinces.

Index (MI) of province i in year t. The fixed effect α_i eliminates all the variations among provinces that do not change over time, while the time-fixed effect μ_t removes all time-level disturbances that do not vary with the province. $\varepsilon_{i,t}$ represents the residual term of the regression model.

We focus on the estimated coefficients β_1 of the independent variable $MI_{i,t}$. The economic connotation of the coefficient β_1 is interpreted as the average effect of the MI on the dependent variable, that is, the influence of the MI on the TFP growth rate.

Other control variables of the regression include: (1) GDP per capita, which is used to control the levels of economic development; (2) government size, which is defined as government expenditure as a proportion of GDP; (3) openness, which is defined as the export share of GDP; and (4) investment rate, which is defined as the share of capital formation in GDP.

Regarding sample grouping, most of the provinces in the PRC were in the upper-middle-income group and the lower-middle-income group from 1997 to 2014.[15] Therefore, the subsample regressions are only for the lower-middle-income and the upper-middle-income group. The remaining empirical strategies are consistent with the international evidence section.

10.5.4 Regression Results

Table 10.4 demonstrates the regression results of equation (6). Columns (1)–(4) of Table 10.6 show the regression results for fixed effect using the full sample, and columns (5)–(6) show the subsample regression results. In columns (1)–(3), the MI has no significant effect on TFP growth. In column (4), both of MI's primary and secondary terms are significant, which confirms the nonlinear relationship between distortion and economic growth: that is, the impact of MI on TFP growth first declines and then increases.

---

[15]   There are only 17 observations in the high-income group.

Table 10.4: **Total Factor Productivity Growth and the PRC Marketization Index (1997–2014)**

Variable \ Model	(1)	(2)	(3)	(4)	(5)	(6)
Sample	All	All	All	All	Lower Middle Income	Upper Middle Income
MI	0.00123 (0.000976)	−0.000404 (0.000902)	−0.000261 (0.000937)	−0.00704 (0.00199)***	0.000608 (0.00176)	0.00400 (0.00160)**
MI_sq	–	–	–	0.000420 (0.00011)***	–	–
GDPPC	−0.0000172 (0.00000431)***	−0.0000241 (0.00000398)***	−0.0000235 (0.00000409)***	−0.0000323 (0.00000463)***	−0.00000191 (0.0000217)	0.00000347 (0.00000954)
TradeOpen	0.0465 (0.00947)***	0.0334 (0.00870)***	0.0327 (0.00880)***	0.0329 (0.00867)***	0.0275 (0.0194)	0.0568 (0.0151)***
InvRatio		−0.0651 (0.00659)***	−0.0656 (0.00665)***	−0.0581 (0.00684)***	−0.0959 (0.0115)***	−0.0587 (0.0110)***
GovSize			0.0116 (0.0205)	0.00967 (0.0202)		
Year Dummies	Yes	Yes	Yes	Yes	Yes	Yes
No. Observations	504	504	504	504	242	157
R² (within)	0.4643	0.5589	0.6330	0.6372	0.4242	0.8092

PRC = People's Republic of China, TFP = factor productivity.

Notes: 1. Standard errors in parentheses, with ***, **, * denoting 1%, 5%, and 10% level of significance, respectively.

   2. All regressions above include a constant.

   3. According to Hausman test results, fixed-effect models are applied to all regressions in the table.

Source: Authors.

The inflection point is 8.38, which corresponds to the market-wide level of the whole country in 2013–2014. Columns (5) and (6) show that the MI has a significant effect on the growth rate of TFP in the upper-middle-income group, but not in the lower-middle-income group. For the upper-middle-income group, MI increases by 1 point and the growth of TFP increases by 0.4% on average.

For other control variables, GDP per capita (*GDPPC*) has a negative effect on TFP growth, indicating that provinces with a high development level might lose the late-mover advantage and have more difficulty in promoting TFP growth.

Trade openness (*TradeOpen*) has significantly positive coefficients, which is in line with the international evidence. The investment rate (*InvRatio*) has negative effects on TFP growth in every column, and it has a greater negative effect on the lower-middle-income group. This indicates that there are large numbers of inefficient investments in the PRC, and the growth driven by low-efficiency investments is not conducive to TFP growth, confirming the views of Woo (1998), and Bai and Zhang (2015).

The evidence from the PRC is generally consistent with international experience. But it also has its own characteristics. Both the evidence from the PRC and international experience confirm the nonlinear relationship of distortion for TFP growth. With the development of the economy, the promotion of marketization on the growth of TFP will first decline and then rise, that is, the effect of distortion on the growth of TFP will rise first and then decline. In the international experience, however, the suppression effect of distortions occurs in the high-income group; while in the PRC, the suppression effect of distortions occurs in the upper-income group. Since the PRC has too few samples in high-income groups, we cannot obtain the regression results of high-income groups. However, combining international experience with the PRC experience, we can see that as more provinces enter the upper-middle-income and high-income stage, the negative effects of distortions on TFP growth will further manifest themselves.

10.5.5 Robustness Analysis

To check the robustness of the previous findings, we use the sub-indexes of MI as alternative measures for policy distortions. To investigate the nonlinear relationship between distortions and TFP growth, we also divide the sample period into two sub-samples: lower-middle-income group and higher-middle-income group. Other control variables remain unchanged. The results are shown in Table 10.5.[16]

---

[16] The MI includes five sub-indications, while the official departments did not publish the original data in 2009–2013 and as a sub-index of MI, Development of Product Market did not change during this period (Wang 2016). Therefore, in the robustness analysis, we do not take it into account.

Table 10.5: Total Factor Productivity Growth and the State-Owned Economy (1997–2014)

Model Variable	(1)	(2)	(3)	(4)	(5)	(6)	(7)	(8)
Sample	Lower Middle Income				Upper Middle Income			
MI1	−0.00196 (0.00118)*				0.00290 (0.00163)*			
MI2		0.00292 (0.0011)***				−0.00106 (0.00109)		
MI4			−0.00114 (0.00107)				0.00154 (0.00076)**	
MI5				0.00165 (0.00084)*				0.000488 (0.00027)*
GDPPP	−0.0000028 (0.000021)	−0.0000203 (0.000023)	0.000000 (0.000021)	−0.000013 (0.00002)	0.0000065 (0.000009)	0.0000036 (0.00001)	0.0000001 (0.00001)	0.0000037 (0.000009)
TradeOpen	0.0300 (0.0192)	0.0320 (0.0191)*	0.0304 (0.0194)	0.0211 (0.0194)	0.0537 (0.0153)***	0.0463 (0.0150)***	0.0577 (0.0155)***	0.0501 (0.0149)***
InvRatio	−0.0936 (0.0113)***	−0.0953 (0.0112)***	−0.0918 (0.0118)***	−0.0933 (0.0113)***	−0.0657 (0.0111)***	−0.0615 (0.0113)***	−0.0664 (0.0111)***	−0.0600 (0.0111)***
Year Dummies	Yes	Yes	Yes	Yes	Yes	Yes	Yes	Yes
No.Observations	242	242	242	242	157	157	157	157
R2 (within)	0.6034	0.6059	0.6002	0.6057	0.796	0.7650	0.7707	0.7700

Notes: 1. Standard errors in parentheses, with ***, **, * denoting 1%, 5%, and 10% level of significance, respectively.

      2. All regressions above include a constant.

Source: Authors.

The Government–Market Relations (MI1) have a significant negative effect on TFP growth in the lower-middle-income group, and a significantly positive effect in the upper-middle-income group.

The Development of Non-State Economic (MI2) promoted TFP growth in the lower-middle-income group, but not in the upper-middle-income group. The reason may be that after undergoing a large-scale reform of state-owned enterprises, the PRC economy has formed a vertical structure. Upstream industries (such as energy, finance, and telecommunications) are still occupied by state-owned enterprises, and most downstream industries (such as consumer goods, manufacturing, and consumer services such as hotel and entertainment industries) have been dominated by private economy (Li, Liu, and Wang 2014). With the PRC's accession to the WTO, both downstream industry and upstream industry have greatly improved. Therefore, in the upper-middle-income group, the state-owned economy and the non-state-owned economy are equally important for improving TFP growth. The relative share of the non-state-owned economy in the overall economy has no significant effect on TFP growth.

The Development of Factors Market (MI4) has no significant effect on TFP growth in the lower-middle-income group, and a significant positive effect on TFP in the upper-middle-income group. The report of the 19th National Congress of CPC pointed out that economic system reform must focus on improving the property rights system and the market-oriented allocation of factors. Further improving the allocation efficiency of factor market is an important guarantee for the sustainable development of the economy.

Finally, the Development of Intermediary and Legal Environment (MI5) has a significant positive impact on TFP growth in both of the lower-middle-income group and the upper-middle-income group. The regression results for other variables are consistent with those in Table 10.4.

10.6 | Concluding Remarks and Policy Implications

Our empirical results based on international experiences show that distortions can hinder the engine of long-term growth—measured by the TFP—in high-income economies. By contrast, distortions may help middle-income economies to achieve faster TFP growth under certain conditions.

Empirical study of the PRC's provinces generally shows that marketization significantly promoted the growth of the PRC's TFP during the period 1997–2014. That is to say, distortions had significant negative effects on the PRC's TFP growth during this period. However, in the early stage of development (1978–1991), distortions played a significantly positive role in TFP growth.

Overall, despite some slight differences, the main findings from international and the PRC's experience seem basically consistent, so that we can conclude that in the early stage of development appropriate distortions can help break through the poverty trap. But as the economy climbs to a higher-income level, the adverse effects of distortions become more and more significant and eventually hinder sustainable growth.

Our findings have important implications for the PRC's policy making. First, the transition from middle-income to high-income economy is also a process of mitigating market distortions. Although the latter might have contributed to the PRC's economic takeoff and growth catch-up in the past, serious problems due to distorting market systems have been created and become substantial impediments to reform and development in the future. In view of this, to avoid the so-called middle-income trap, and to achieve sustainable development, the key is to promote market-oriented reforms and, in particular, reduce inappropriate government interventions and institutional distortions.[17]

Second, it by no means implies that the economy can function well without government. From a theoretical standpoint, government services and distortions differ in many important ways. In particular, an efficient government with appropriate "state capacity" is indispensable in a modern market-based economy. As a matter of fact, it is not uncommon that in advanced economies with mature market systems, government also plays a proactive role in many socioeconomic dimensions, especially in encouraging innovation. In other words, the distortions per se can be viewed as the situation in which government does not assume its role properly. What should be done to let the government play a "better" role in a market economy context as stated in the Third Plenary Session of the 18th CPC Central Committee? In our view, instead of "replacing" market mechanism, government should play a proactive role in the "market-reinforcing" process.

---

[17] See *Renmin Ribao (People's Daily)*. 2016. Seven Questions on Supply-side Structural Reforms: Authoritative Insider's View on Current Economic Situation. 4 January.

In other words, various government interventions should only be judged by their contributions to market-oriented reforms, especially to helping the market play a decisive role in resource allocation.

Third, with clear objectives of economic reforms, "favorable distortions" should be subjected to strict constraints. Although "favorable distortion" is indeed often taken as a supportive argument for keeping distortion and the important role of government in the economy, the relationship between distortion and economic performance is complex, especially nonlinear. In particular, favorable distortion substantially depends on various socioeconomic conditions related to stage of development. If these conditions are not met, distortions will hamper development. For instance, the advantage of backwardness, second-best principle, and coordination failure all have their theoretical preconditions, and, generally speaking, are appropriate for developing countries who have immature market systems, serious structural problems, and challenges regarding "takeoff" and "transition." Since those countries, including the PRC, enter into a higher level of development with an improved institutional environment, the so-called favorable distortions will become less plausible. For this reason, the PRC's policy makers should take a clear stand to reduce distortions, and to let the market play a decisive role in resource allocation. Otherwise, in the name of "growth catch-up," the policy-imposed distortion will occur frequently, and the direction of market-oriented reform will become blurred and swing. Mitigating unfavorable distortions is largely a process of exploring the favorable borderline between government and market, which constitutes a major challenge for all economies.

References

Acemoglu, D., and J. Robinson. 2012. *Why Nations Fail? The Origins of Power, Prosperity, and Poverty.* New York, NY: Crown Business.

Acemoglu, D., C. García-Jimeno, and J. Robinson. 2015. State Capacity and Economic Development: A Network Approach. *American Economic Review* 105(8): 2364–2409.

Aoki, M., K. Murdock, and M. Okuno-Fujiwara. 1997. Beyond the East Asian Miracle: Introducing the Market Enhancing View. In *The Role of Government in East Asian Economic Development: Comparative Institutional Analysis*, edited by M. Aoki, M. Okuno-Fujiwara, and H. Kim. Oxford, United Kingdom: Oxford University Press.

Bai, C., and Q. Zhang. 2015. China's Productivity Estimate and Its Wave Decomposition. *The Journal of World Economy (Shi Jie Jing JI)* 12: 3–28.

Bandyopadhyay, S., and E. D. Green. 2012. Pre-Colonial Political Centralization and Contemporary Development in Uganda. Paper presented at the American Political Science Association Annual Meeting. New Orleans, LA.

Bardhan, P. 2016. State and Development: The Need for a Reappraisal of the Current Literature. *Journal of Economic Literature* 54(3): 862–892.

Besley, T., and T. Persson. 2009. The Origins of State Capacity: Property Rights, Taxation, and Politics. *American Economic Review* 99(4): 1218–1244.

Bhagwati, J. N. 1969. The Generalized Theory of Distortions and Welfare. MIT Working Paper 39. Cambridge, MA: Massachusetts Institute of Technology, Department of Economics.

Brandt, L., and X. D. Zhu. 2010. Accounting for China's Growth. *SSRN Scholarly Paper* ID 1556552. Rochester, NY. Social Science Research Network.

Chamley, C. 1986. Optimal Taxation of Capital Income Taxation in General Equilibrium with Infinite Lives. *Econometrica* 54: 607–622.

Chen, K., H. C. Wang, Y. X. Zheng, G. H. Jefferson, and T. G. Rawski. 1988. Productivity Change in Chinese Industry: 1953-1985. *Journal of Comparative Economics* 12(4): 570–591.

Chinn, M. D., and H. Ito. 2008. A New Measure of Financial Openness. *Journal of Comparative Policy Analysis* 10(3): 309–322.

Dahlberg, S., S. Holmberg, B. Rothstein, A. Khomenko, and R. Svensson. 2016. *The Quality of Government Basic Dataset 2016: Codebook*. Gothenburg, Sweden: The Quality of Government Institute, University of Gothenburg.

Easterly, W. 1993. How Much Do Distortions Affect Growth? *Journal of Monetary Economics* 32(2): 187–212.

Eichengreen, B., D. Park, and K. Shin. 2011. When Fast Growing Economies Slow Down: International Evidence and Implications for China. NBER Working Paper 16919. Cambridge, MA: National Bureau of Economic Research.

Fan, G., X. Wang, and L. Zhang. 2001. *NERI Index of Marketization of China by Province*. Beijing: Economic Science Press.

Fan, G., X. Wang, and H. Zhu 2003. *NERI Index of Marketization of China by Province*. Beijing: Economic Science Press.

Fukuyama, F. 2012. *The Origins of Political Order*. Guilin, PRC: Guangxi Normal University Press.

———. 2015. *Political Order and Political Decay: From the Industrial Revolution to the Globalization of Democracy*. Guilin, PRC: Guangxi Normal University Press.

Gennaioli, N., and I. Rainer. 2007. The Modern Impact of Precolonial Centralization in Africa. *Journal of Economic Growth* 12(3): 185–234.

Gerschenkron, A. 1962. *Economic Backwardness in Historical Perspective*. Cambridge, MA: Belknap Press.

Goldsmith, R. W. 1951. A Perpetual Inventory of National Wealth. *NBER Book Series Studies in Income and Wealth* 14: 5–61.

Gordon, R., and W. Li. 2009. Tax Structure in Developing Countries: Many Puzzles and a Possible Explanation. *Journal of Public Economics* 93(7/8): 855–366.

Grossman, G., and E. Helpman. 1994. Protection for Sale. *American Economic Review* 84: 833–850.

Hall, R. E., and C. J. Jones. 1999. Why do Some Countries Produce so Much More Output per Worker than Others? *Quarterly Journal of Economics* 114(1): 83–116.

Hsieh, C. T., and P. J. Klenow. 2009. Misallocation and Manufacturing TFP in China and India. *Quarterly Journal of Economics* 124(4): 1403–1448.

Jia, G. 2011. *The American School: The National Economic Theory that Fostered the Economic Rise of the United States*. Beijing, PRC: Social Sciences in China Press.

Judd, K. 1985. Redistributive Taxation in a Simple Perfect Foresight Model. *Journal of Public Economics* 28: 59–83.

Li, F., and Y. Lin. 2011. Development Strategy, Viability and Institutional Distortions in Developing Countries. *Nankai Economics Studies (Nan Kai Jing Ji Yan Jiu)* 5: 3–19.

Li, X., X. Liu, and Y. Wang. 2014. A Model of China's Economic Growth. *China Journal of Economics* 1(4): 1–48.

Lin, J. Y. 2003. Development Strategy, Viability and Economic Convergence. *Economic Development and Cultural Change* 53(2): 277–308.

———. 2014. *New Structural Economics: A Framework for Rethinking Development and Policy.* Beijing: Beijing University Press.

Lipsey, R. G., and K. Lancaster. 1956. The General Theory of Second Best. *Review of Economic Studies* 24 (1): 11–32.

Lucas, R. 1990. Supply Side Economies: An Analytic Review. *Oxford Economic Papers* 42(2): 293–316.

Lu, Y., and F. Cai. 2016. From Demographic Dividends to Reform Dividends: Simulations Based on China's Potential Growth Rate. *The Journal of World Economy (Shi Jie Jing JI)* 3: 3–23.

Mazzucato, M. 2013. Financing Innovation: Creative Destruction vs. Destructive Creation. *Industrial and Corporate Change* 22(4): 851–867.

McKinnon, R. 1973. *Money and Capital in Economic Development.* Washington, DC: Brookings Institution.

Michalopoulos, S., and E. Papaioannou. 2013. Pre-Colonial Ethnic Institutions and Contemporary African Development. *Econometrica* 81(1): 113–152.

Mingardi, A. 2015. A Critique of Mazzucato's Entrepreneurial State. *Cato Journal,* 35(Fall): 603–625.

National Bureau of Statistics of China (NBSC) (various issues). *China Statistical Yearbook.* Beijing: China Statistics Press.

Olson, M. 2000. *Power and Prosperity: Outgrowing Communist and Capitalist Dictatorships.* New York, NY: Basic Books.

Parker, E. 1995. Shadow Factor Price Convergence and the Response of Chinese State-owned Construction Enterprises to Reform. *Journal of Comparative Economics* 21(1): 54–81.

Perkins, D. H., and T. G. Rawski. 2008. Forecasting China's Economic Growth to 2025. In *China's Great Economic Transformation,* edited by L. Brandt and T. G. Rawski. Cambridge, MA: Cambridge University Press.

Pritchett, L., and L. Summers 2014. Asiaphoria Meets Regression to the Mean. NBER Working Paper 20573. Cambridge, MA: National Bureau of Economic Research.

Qian, Y. 2000. The Process of China's Market Transition (1978–1998): The Evolutionary, Historical, and Comparative Perspectives. *Journal of Institutional and Theoretical Economics* 156(1): 151–171.

———. 2016. Speech at the award ceremony of the *China Economics Prize* in Beijing. 4 December.

Rodrik, D. 2006. Goodbye Washington Consensus, Hello Washington Confusion: A Review of the World Bank's Economic Growth in the 1990s: Learning from a Decade of Reform. *Journal of Economic Literature* 44(December): 973–987.

Sah, R. K., and J. E. Stiglitz. 1987. The Taxation and Pricing of Agricultural and Industrial Goods in Developing Countries. In *The Theory of Taxation for Developing Countries*, edited by D. Newbery and N. Stern. New York, NY: Oxford University Press and The World Bank.

Shleifer, A., and R. Vishny. 1998. *The Grabbing Hand: Government Pathologies and Their Cures*. Cambridge, MA: Harvard University Press.

Song, Z., K. Storesletten, and F. Zilibotti. 2011. Growing like China. *American Economic Review* 101: 202–241.

Stiglitz, J. E., and G. Bruce. 2017. *Creating a Learning Society: A New Approach to Growth, Development, and Social Progress.* Beijing: Citic Press.

Wang, X., G. Fan, and P. Liu. 2009. Transformation of Growth Pattern and Growth Sustainability in China. *Economic Research Journal (Jing Ji Yan Jiu)* 1(1): 0–14.

Wang, X., G. Fan, and J. Yu. 2017. *NERI Index of Marketization of China by Province.* Beijing, PRC: Economic Science Press.

Wen, Y. 2016. *Great Industrial Revolution.* Beijing: Tsinghua University Press.

Woo, W. T. 1998. China's TFP: The Primary Role of Re-allocation of Labor from the Agricultural Sector. *Economic Research Journal (Jing Ji Yan Jiu)* 3(3): 31–39.

World Bank. 1993. *The East Asian Miracle: Economic Growth and Public Policy: Main Report.* New York: Oxford University Press.

Yan, C., and Z. Hu. 2013. Innovation Driven, Tax Distortion and Long-run Growth. *Economic Research Journal (Jing Ji Yan Jiu)* 12: 55–67.

Yang, W. 2016. The Structural Reform on the Supply Side Does Not Deny the Expansion of Domestic Demand. *China Economic & Trade Herald (Zhong Guo Jing Mao Dao Kan)* (1).

Young, A. 2000. The Razor's Edge: Distortions and Incremental Reform in the People's Republic of China. NBER Working Paper 7828. Cambridge, MA: National Bureau of Economic Research. http://www.nber.org/papers/w7828.

Zhang, S., and L. Cheng. 2010. Factor Price Distortion and Wealth Transfer in China's Economic Transition. *The Journal of World Economy (Shi Jie Jing Ji)* (10): 3–24.

Zhang, X., 2005. International Capital Flows, Economic Distortions and Macroeconomic Stability. *Economic Research Journal (Jing Ji Yan Jiu)* (4): 4–16.

Zhang, Y. W. 2008. Eliminating Policy-induced Distortions and Constructing Opening Economic System. *Academic Monthly (Xue Shu Yue Kan)* (1): 60–69.

Zhu, X., X. Jin, and D. Luo. 2005. Market Segmentation and the Expansion of China's Export. *Economic Research Journal (Jing Ji Yan Jiu)* (1): 68–76.

CHAPTER 11

Why Geographic Dispersion Before Its Time: Industrial Policy and Economic Geography in the People's Republic of China

Yiyun Wu and Xiwei Zhu

11.1 | Introduction

The People's Republic of China (PRC) experienced convergence of provincial industrial structures with the inverse process of specialization between urban and rural areas at the very beginning of its market-oriented economic reform in the mid-1980s. This phenomenon was termed a "skewed pyramid" to warn against unbalanced development (Ma 1989). Twenty years later, however, geographic concentration and industrial specialization in the PRC, which had increased rapidly and continuously since the late 1980s, began to decline. What caused the PRC's recent geographic manufacturing dispersion? This chapter investigates the evolution of the PRC's economic geography and concludes that the spatial dispersion of manufacturing firms and more severe industrial isomorphism among provinces are closely related to the local governments' development policies. The underlying mechanism is quite simple: to be able to apply for special privileges from the central government, local governments have a strong incentive to mimic the former's industrial policies when setting up their own.

There are many papers focusing on whether geographic concentration and industrial specialization in the European Union (EU) and the United States (US) change as per the predictions of New Economic

Geography (Krugman 1991a; Kim 1995; Ellison and Glaeser 1997; Amiti 1999; Midelfart-Knarviket et al. 2002). As for the PRC, although Young (2000) previously inspired researchers' interests in the reshaping process of its post-reform economic geography, not much empirical work emerged until high-quality statistical data became available in the past few decades (Wen 2004; Bai et al. 2004; Fan 2004, 2008; Lu and Tao 2006, 2007, 2009; Huang and Li 2006). Compared with the market-oriented evolution of the EU and the US, the PRC's evolving geographic manufacturing distribution is triggered not only by agglomeration and dispersion forces suggested in Wen (2004), but also by local protectionism and market segmentation stemming from fiscal decentralization (Young 2000). Bai et al. (2004), Lu and Tao (2007), and Lu and Tao (2009) have shown that industries with higher after-tax profit and share of state ownership have less geographic concentration, thus supporting their hypothesis that local protectionism hinders geographic concentration. Jin, Chen, and Lu (2006) also showed that government interventions impede the PRC's industrial agglomeration. In short, local government acts as a troublemaker that distorts the spatial reallocation of industrial activities and causes inefficiency. Meanwhile, large empirical studies also support that market-oriented activities are the main determinants reshaping the PRC's economic geography and its manufacturing industries' agglomeration in the coastal region during 1985–2004 (Wen 2004; Bai et al. 2004; Jin, Chen, and Lu 2006; Lu and Tao 2006, 2007, 2009; Fan 2004, 2008; Luo and Cao 2005; Wang and Wei 2007). Due to data availability, previous studies could only explore the spatial redistribution of manufacturing industries from 1978 to 2005. Lack of further empirical work brings two obvious limitations for understanding the whole story. First, it is impossible to fully evaluate the central government's regional development strategies since 2000 (such as the Western Development Drive, Revitalization of Northeast PRC, and Rise of Central PRC). Second, local government is always considered a self-interested troublemaker that undermines spatial efficiency. But local government's reaction is rational under the specifically vested interest pattern; thus, perhaps the central government should also bear some responsibility for the distortion.

Empirical works on the EU and the US (Kim 1995; Midelfart–Knarvik et al.
2000; Aiginger and Davies 2004) indicate that, in the long term, geographic
concentration of manufacturing industries experiences a bell-shaped curve
during the process of regional integration. If this is a common rule, it is
important to answer which position on the curve the PRC is on right now.
Meanwhile, if geographic concentration of manufacturing industries has
ceased its uptrend, it is unfair to blame local governments for the spatial
distortion. However, Lu and Tao (2007) revealed that, compared with
the US and other economies, the PRC's four-digit-level manufacturing
industries are far much less geographically concentrated. Thus, if geographic
concentration in the PRC has already started decreasing as Fan and Li (2011)
and Wang et al. (2010) showed, it would be interesting to see which forces
determine the change: market forces or local government inventions.

Few papers have evaluated the active role local government might play during
industrial development and upgrading, which is actually highly stressed by
the new structural economics (Lin 2012). In reality, it is common for the
PRC local governments to leverage development planning and preferential
policies to widely affect some specific industries, which is a main influencing
factor. Song and Wang (2013) were the first to use local government 5-year
plans to study the relation between preferential industrial policy and local
productivity. By contrast, this chapter pays particular attention to the role of
local government 5-year plans in determining provincial industrial structure,
and aims to explain the PRC's evolving economic geography.

In this chapter, we constructed a panel data of 37 two-digit industries
in 31 PRC provinces over the period 1999–2010 based on national and
provincial statistical yearbooks, which enables focusing on geographic
concentration and industrial specialization over a longer and more recent
time period than the relevant literature. The findings show that nonmarket
forces significantly affect the spatial distribution of economic activities
and support our hypotheses about the intervention of local governments
through preferential policies. Although local governments directly cause
lower spatial concentration and more highly assimilated regional industrial

structures, the central government should be blamed for inducing them to carry out similar industrial plans. The rest of the chapter is organized as follows. In Section 11.2, we discuss data source and indexes of geographic concentration and industrial specialization. Section 11.3 provides stylized facts of recent PRC geographic concentration and industrial specialization. Section 11.4 proposes theoretical hypotheses for testing. Section 11.5 presents econometric testing of the hypotheses and assesses robustness of the results. Section 11.6 concludes.

11.2 | Data and Measurement

11.2.1 Data

The existing literature usually uses two major sets of industrial statistics. The first is those published by the National Bureau of Statistics, such as *China Industry Economy Statistical Yearbook, China Statistical Yearbook,* or *China Economic Census Yearbook.* Though published statistical yearbooks are easily accessible, the coverage is often limited. The second is unpublished statistics, such as data from the *Annual Survey of Industrial Firms* (ASIF) conducted by the PRC's National Bureau of Statistics. Unpublished statistics sometimes provide a wider range of details, such as firm-level data. However, they are hard to access, which prevents most researchers from performing repeat studies. In addition, common data problems like gaps or typos, or lack of checking methods also undermine research.[1]

---

[1]   For example, *China Statistical Yearbook* (2006) reported that there were 271,835 industrial enterprises above designated size and 251,499 manufacturing enterprises above designated size in 2005. However, Lu and Tao (2009) claimed the data to be 265,739 and 246,379, less by 6,096 and 5,120, respectively. More detailed discussions about the potential problems in ASIF see Nie, Jiang, and Yang (2012).

In this chapter we construct a panel data of 37 two-digit industries (recycling and mining of other ores are excluded because of missing data) in 31 PRC provinces (including provinces, autonomous regions, and municipalities; hereafter, provinces) for the period from 1999 to 2010.[2] In general, gross output value, value added, and employment data are the most popular variables used to construct economic geography indexes. We agree with Bai et al. (2004) about redundant personnel where employment data may suffer from the surplus labor problem particularly prevalent in state-owned enterprises and lead to biased measurement. We also agree with Wen's 2004 opinion about gross output value and value added when constructing spatial Gini coefficients. Besides, as Krugman and Venables (1995) and Venables (1996) argued, the availability of intermediate input also influences firms' selection of location. Taking all these into consideration, this paper uses gross output value to calculate industrial geographic distribution.

To ensure comparability over time, we adjust gross output in terms of ex-factory price indexes of industrial products by sector from *China Urban Life and Price Yearbook* (2011), using 2003 as the base year.[3] All data are from *China Industry Economy Statistical Yearbook, China Statistical Yearbook, China Economic Census Yearbook,* and provincial statistical yearbooks. The discrepancy between the aggregated gross domestic product (GDP) of provinces and national GDP is often used to question the reliability of PRC statistics; however, it is found that the industrial statistics from provincial and national yearbooks are highly consistent.[4]

---

[2] The selection of the period from 1999 to 2010 is based on two reasons: first, since current studies have fully discussed the evolution of economic geography in the PRC from the 1980s to 2003, this chapter focuses on new trends since 2004; second, the statistic criteria saw major revisions in 1998 and 2010, respectively, making it inappropriate to compare data before and around 1998 or 2010. More detailed explanations of data sources and collection can be found in Appendix 1.

[3] Since *China Urban Life and Price Yearbook* lacks the price index of the agricultural products and byproducts processing industry, the printing industry, and ordinary machinery manufacturing industry before 2002, in this chapter we replace the relevant data by indexes of food manufacturing industry, paper and paper products industry, and, for special purposes, the equipment manufacturing industry of that year.

[4] See Appendix 1 for details.

11.2.2 Measurement

There are two aspects of structural change when dealing with economic geography: geographic concentration and industrial specialization. In previous studies, the Herfindahl–Hirschman Index, Hoover (GINI) coefficient, EG Index, Spatial Dispersion Index, and Entropy Index were mostly used to measure geographic concentration and industrial specialization. Considering the pros and cons of the above indexes,[5] we choose a comprehensive measurement that employs the geographic concentration Entropy index and industrial specialization Entropy index proposed by Aiginger and Davies (2004) as the major measuring indices. Second, the Krugman Index (Krugman, 1991a) is introduced to reflect the difference of industry composition among provinces and its shifts. Finally, in line with previous studies and to test the robustness of the study, the Hoover coefficient is also employed to calculate the PRC's geographic concentration and industrial specialization.

For convenience, x_{ir} represents the output of industry i in province r, where i stands for a given industry ($i = 1, 2, ..., I$) and r stands for a given province ($r = 1, 2, ..., R$). $x_{i.}$ represents gross output of industry i, $x_{.,r}$ for gross industry output in province r, and $x_{.,.}$ for gross PRC industrial output. $w_r \equiv x_{.,r}/x_{.,.}$ stands for the share of gross industry output in province r and $v_i \equiv x_{i.}/x_{.,.}$ stands for the share of gross output of industry i.

11.2.2.1 Entropy Index

As proposed by Aiginger and Davies (2004), the Entropy index of geographic concentration is defined as $CONC_i \equiv -\Sigma_r (x_{ir}/x_{i.}) \ln(x_{ir}/x_{i.})$. If a given industry i has equal output in all r provinces, $CONC_i = \ln R$. Alternatively, if its output is completely from one province, $CONC_i = 0$. Generally, $CONC_i$ increases the more evenly the industry i spreads its output across provinces;

---

[5] We will not go into details about the pros and cons of different indexes. See Cowell (1995) and Palan (2010).

it is therefore an inverse measure of concentration. The Entropy index of industrial specialization is defined as $SPEC_r \equiv -\Sigma_i(x_{ir}/x_{.r})\ln(x_{ir}/x_{.r})$. Analogous to $CONC_i$, $SPEC_r$ is an inverse measure of specialization which must lie between $[0, lnI]$. To capture average levels of specialization and concentration of industries in a country, Aiginger and Davies (2004) further proposed TYPSPEC and TYPCONC, defined as weighted averages with the weights being, respectively, the province (w_r) and industry (v_i) shares of gross output. Thus, $TYPSPEC \equiv \Sigma_r w_r \cdot SPEC_r$ and $TYPCONC \equiv \Sigma_i v_i \cdot CONC_i$.

11.2.2.2 Krugman Index

In Krugman (1991a), the structural difference of industries between two provinces is defined as $k_{r,r'} \equiv \Sigma_i |x_{ir}/x_{.r} - x_{ir'}/x_{.r'}|$, where $k_{r,r'}$ lies between $[0, 2]$. The more specialized the industries in province r and r', the closer $k_{r,r'}$ is to 2; in contrast, $k_{r,r'} = 0$ if the two provinces are completely symmetric.

11.2.2.3 Hoover Coefficient

The Hoover coefficient (Hoover 1936) can measure geographic concentration of a given industry i (Hoover coefficient of industry) and specialization of a given province r (Hoover coefficient of localization). Take the Hoover coefficient of industry as an example: first, calculate the location quotient for industry i for all regions, where $LQ_{ir} \equiv (x_{ir}/x_{.r})/(x_{.r}/x_{..})$. Then rank the location quotients in descending order and calculate the cumulative percentage of output in industry i over regions (y-axis). Finally, calculate the cumulative percentage of output in total over regions (x-axis). The concentration curve of industry i is thus formed. The coefficient of industry is defined as the area between the 45-degree line and the concentration curve divided by the entire triangular area. The localization curve is analogously constructed. By definition, both Hoover coefficients lie between $[0, 1]$. When the coefficient increases, the level of geographic concentration or industry specialization improves.

11.3 | The Evolution of Economic Geography in the PRC: Stylized Facts

11.3.1 Geographic Concentration

As described in Section 11.2, the average geographic concentration (*TYPCONC*) is calculated using output data for the 37 two-digit industries over the period 1999–2010. The time trend of *TYPCONC* is showed in Figure 11.1 (see Appendix 2 for $CONC_i$ by industry). From 1999 to 2010, the geographic concentration of industries first increased and then decreased. In 1999, the value of *TYPCONC* was 2.7242; from then on, it went down steadily to 2.6123 in 2005, showing that the concentration level constantly rose during this period, which is consistent with most of the previous studies (e.g., Bai et al. 2004; Wen 2004; Luo and Cao 2005; Lu and Tao 2006). However, after 2005, *TYPCONC* increased steadily to 2.6867 in 2010, which reflects a declining concentration level.

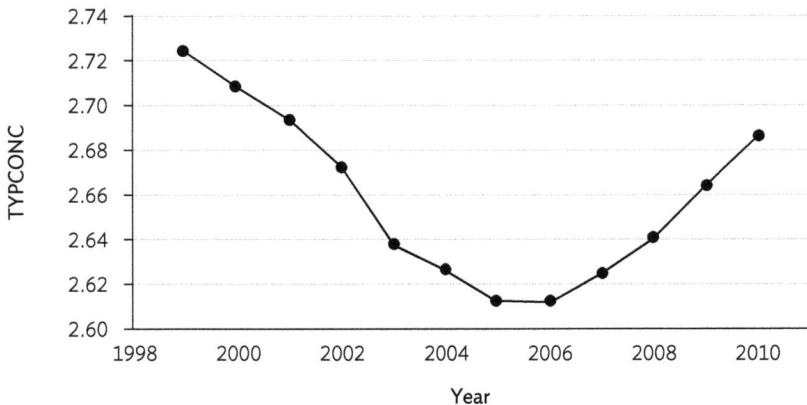

Figure 11.1: **Geographic Concentration over Time**

Source: Authors' calculations.

Figure 11.2: Concentration over Time by Sector

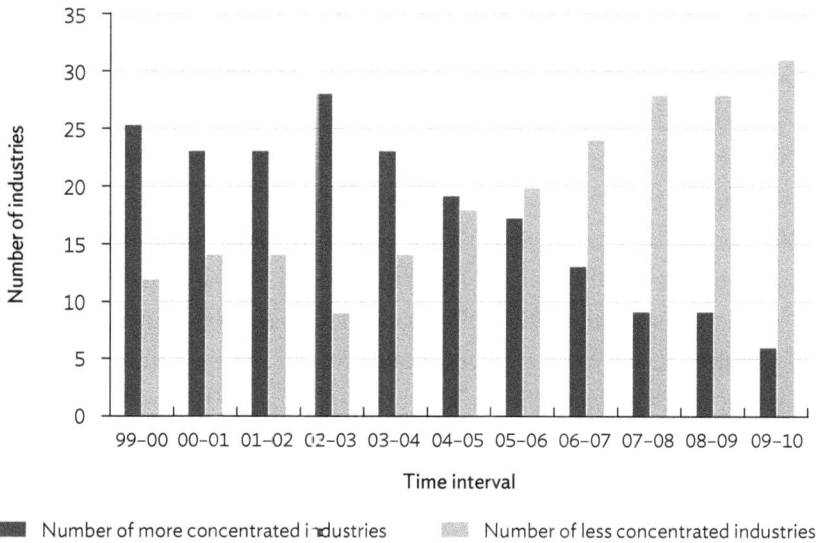

Number of more concentrated industries   Number of less concentrated industries

Source: Authors' calculations.

By definition, *TYPCONC* is the weighted average of industrial concentration, with the weights being shares of gross output. When looking into industries, from 1999 to 2005, communication equipment, computers, and other electronics contributed most to the growth of *TYPCONC*; from 2005 to 2010, transport equipment made the largest contribution to its descent. To overcome the influence from those heavily weighted industries, we further probed the change of each industry in neighboring years from 1999 to 2010, as shown in Figure 11.2. Since 2002, more and more industries started to get dispersed; then, until 2005, more decreasing industries were actually found than increasing ones. In detail, from 1999 to 2005, there were only 7 industries whose concentration decreased, while from 2005 to 2010, there were as many as 31 industries that became more dispersed rather than concentrated.

To test the robustness and compare the results with previous studies, we calculated the Hoover coefficient of localization of 37 industries over the period of 1999–2010.[6] Similar to the trend of *TYPCONC*, before 2005, the Hoover coefficient of localization did increase by 4.72% (by simple average) or 1.85% (by weighted average), whereas after 2005 it decreased by 1.26% (by simple average) or 5.44% (by weighted average). Furthermore, to trace the time line, we drew the concentration curve of PRC industries from 1985 to 2010 on the basis of Bai et al.'s 2004 data based on 32 industries in 29 provinces from 1985 to 1997 (see Figure 11.3).[7] It can be easily seen in the figure that, since the 1980s, the spatial distribution of industries in the PRC initially became more and more concentrated and then subsequently dispersed, which enriches the findings by Wang et al. (2010), and Fan and Li (2011). The results persist even if we focus only on manufacturing.

11.3.2 Industrial Specialization and Isomorphism

Table 11.1 reports the relative rate of change on industrial specialization from 1999 to 2010, including the Entropy index of the 31 provincial-level divisions (*SPEC_p*), the rate on *TYPSPEC*, and the Hoover coefficient of specialization (by simple average and weighted average). The table shows that the average specialization level also takes a bell-shaped curve within the past 12 years.

---

[6]   Due to length limit, Appendix 2 did not report the Hoover coefficient of each industry. Interested readers can contact us for the data. Since the Hoover coefficient of localization and the Entropy index are different in design, the results of the geographic concentration of a given industry are not exactly the same; however, the general trend judged from the two indexes is the same.

[7]   Note that data used in Bai et al. (2004) have slightly different statistic criteria from this chapter. In addition, they incorporate 32 industries and merge Hainan with Guangdong, and Chongqing with Sichuan, which are also different from here. Though these differences make a gap between data before and after 1998, the general trend of industrial geographic concentration in the PRC remains the same. Similarly, according to Lu and Tao's 2006 results of the Hoover coefficient of localization based on the output of two-digit provincial manufacturing industries, we can have the changing curve of manufacturing geography from 1985 to 2003, which also takes the trend of a bell-shaped concentration curve.

Figure 11.3: Time Trend of Average Hoover Coefficient of Localization

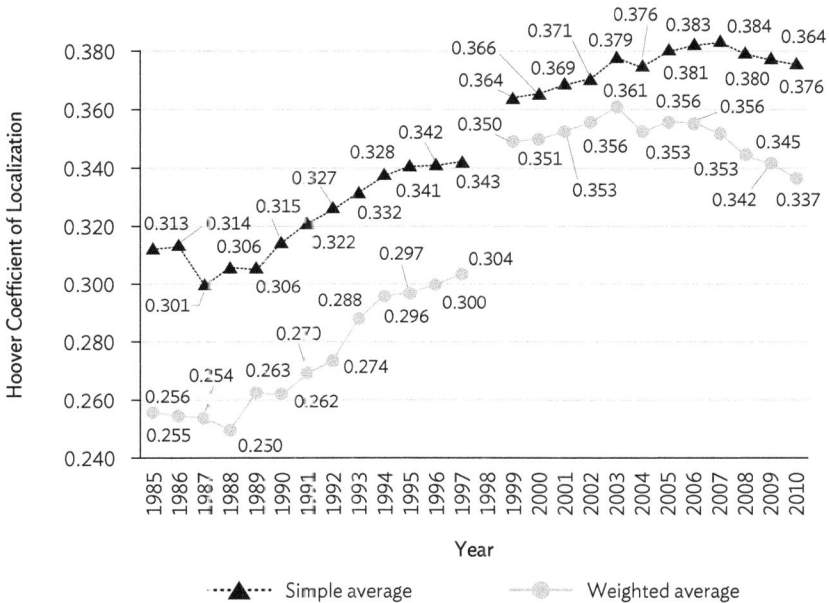

Source: The Hoover coefficient of localization during 1985–1997 is from Figure 1 of Bai et al. (2004), and after 1999 is calculated by the authors.

Twenty-two provinces experienced an increase in specialization from 1999 to 2005, resulting in a decrease in *TYPSPEC* to 2005 of 3.98%; in contrast, after 2005, only 10 provinces had an increase in specialization, resulting in an increase of 0.53%. The change of Hoover coefficient confirms the trend shown by *TYPSPEC*, which is also a bell-shaped curve, with 2005 as a turning point (see also Figure 11.4).[8]

---

[8] Although the results based on the Entropy index and the Hoover coefficient are not exactly the same, their conclusion of the changing trend of industrial specialization in the PRC at the two phases (from 1995 to 2005 and from 2005 to 2010) is the same. Technically speaking, the Entropy index is more sensitive to underdeveloped regions and the Hoover coefficient to developed regions.

Table 11.1: Relative Rate of Change on Industrial Specialization (SPEC$_r$) from 1999 to 2010 (%)

Province	99–10	99–05	05–10	Province	99–10	99–05	05–10
Shanghai	−14.81	−9.30	−6.08	Fujian	−1.06	−3.06	2.06
Guangdong	−12.74	−12.69	−0.06	Guizhou	−0.96	−2.81	1.90
Tibet Autonomous Region	−10.55	−13.68	3.63	Shaanxi	−0.45	−0.43	−0.02
Hainan	−10.26	−5.95	−4.59	Henan	0.21	−0.92	1.15
Beijing	−8.23	−7.93	−0.32	Jiangxi	0.47	0.37	0.09
Jiangsu	−8.12	−6.25	−1.99	Ningxia	0.83	−0.82	1.66
Hebei	−8.04	−9.35	1.44	Hunan	2.44	1.71	0.72
Chongqing	−7.32	−8.87	1.70	Liaoning	2.70	0.44	2.25
Tianjin	−6.95	−10.73	4.24	Sichuan	3.52	1.02	2.48
Hubei	−6.77	−6.08	−0.73	Inner Mongolia	8.14	2.29	5.71
Jilin	−5.23	−8.89	4.01	Yunnan	8.63	3.14	5.32
Shanxi	−4.26	−6.46	2.35	Qinghai	11.65	4.52	6.83
Guangxi	−3.58	−6.49	3.11	Xinjiang	28.64	11.61	15.26
Anhui	−2.83	−2.31	−0.54	Heilongjiang	31.20	20.16	9.19
Shandong	−2.53	−0.97	−1.57	TYPSPEC	−3.47	−3.98	0.53
Zhejiang	−1.68	−1.01	−0.67	HOOVER-a	−0.45	5.19	−5.36
Gansu	−1.45	−7.77	6.86	HOOVER-b	−3.78	2.45	−6.07

Note: HOOVER-a and HOOVER-b refer to simple average and weighted average Hoover coefficient of specialization. For full time series, see Appendix 3.

Source: Authors' calculations.

Since SPEC$_r$ only measures the change of industry structure within one single province, it is natural to introduce the Krugman Index (KI) to check what happens simultaneously between provinces. As shown in Figure 11.5, from 1999 to 2010, the interprovincial KI decreased by 2.23% in simple average and by 5.09% in weighted average. Thus, provincial industrial structure in the PRC converged in general from 1999 to 2010. To further confirm the facts, we divided the 31 provinces into four economic regions whose boundary line is set by the National Bureau of Statistics, namely the East Region

Figure 11.4: Regional Specialization over Time

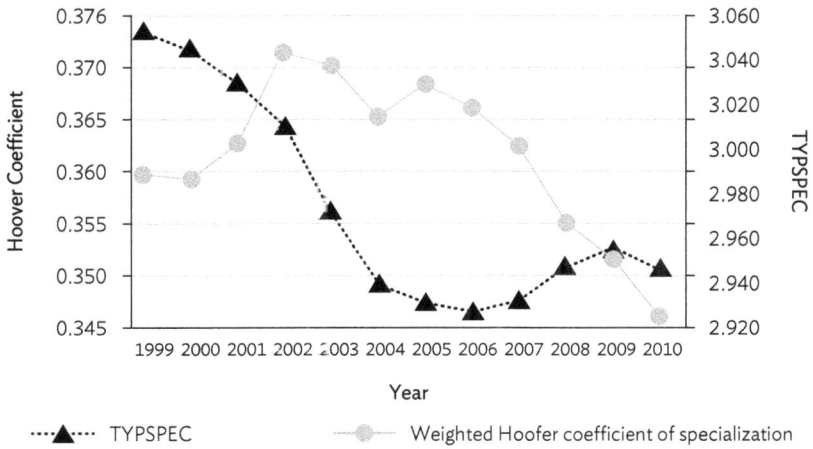

Source: Authors' calculations.

Figure 11.5: Krugman Index over Time

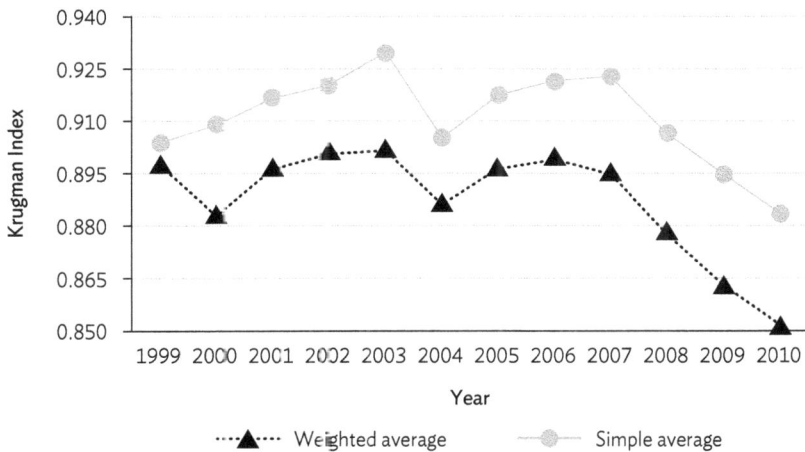

Source: Authors' calculations.

(including 11 provinces), the Central Region (including 6 provinces), the West Region (including 12 provinces), and the Northeast Region (including 3 provinces). Table 11.2 reports the results of interprovincial and interregional KI. From 1999 to 2010, specialization of the whole country declined sharply, resulting in much more uniform industrial structure across regions. Besides, the similarity of provincial industrial structure is much more severe within the East and the Central Region, than within the West and Northeast Regions. Finally, the similarity of provincial industrial structure within the East and the Central Region is easing, whereas that within and between the Central and the Northeast Region is getting more severe, resulting in a decreasing specialization of the country as a whole.

Table 11.2: Interprovincial Krugman Index and Its Relative Rate of Change from 1999 to 2010

	E-E	E-C	E-W	E-N	C-C	C-W	C-N	W-W	W-N	N-N	National
1999	0.6256	0.7471	0.9577	0.9280	0.5865	0.7828	0.8424	0.9188	0.9097	0.9405	0.8979
2010	0.6395	0.7280	0.9057	0.8081	0.6034	0.6836	0.7228	0.7874	0.7848	0.8551	0.8521
Change Rate (%)	2.23	–2.56	–5.44	–12.91	2.87	–12.67	–14.20	–14.30	–13.73	–9.09	–5.09

Notes: E means East Region, C means Central Region, W means West Region, and N for Northeast Region; so that E-E refers to the weighted average Krugman Index of provinces from within the East Region; and E-C refers to the weighted average Krugman Index of provinces from the East Region and the Central Region; and it is similar to read the rest notations.

Source: Authors' calculations.

In summary, two stylized facts of the PRC's economic geography can be concluded as follows: first, 2005 marked the ending of 20 years' increase in the geographic concentration following the economic reform and opening; after 2005, geographic concentration of industries starts to decrease. Second, industrial specialization also adopts a bell-shaped path and the provincial industrial structure is converging as a whole. Based on the above findings, we compare the results with theory and international experiences in the following section to see whether the case of the PRC follows the common evolution path or explores a new way with unique characteristics.

11.4 | Economic Geography in the PRC: Comparison and Hypotheses

11.4.1 Theoretical and Economic Background

The geographic distribution of economic activities is one of the key factors that affect efficiency. Generally speaking, increased industrial specialization is beneficial in terms of exploiting regional advantages and improving productivity. However, the overall benefit of increasing geographic concentration is ambiguous. On the one hand, higher concentration makes it possible to utilize external and scale economies; on the other hand, it enlarges the welfare gap between the core and the periphery. In Krugman's two-region two-sector model (1991a, 1991b), decreasing transportation costs always cause an increase in geographic concentration and industrial specialization. Thus these are sometimes viewed as two sides of a coin. In contrast, when there are more than two regions, Fujita, Krugman, and Venables (1999) found that concentration and specialization could change in the opposite direction when transportation costs decrease. More generally, Rossi-Hansberg (2005) and Aiginger and Rossi-Hansberg (2006) concluded that when transportation costs decrease, industrial specialization could increase while geographic concentration would decrease correspondingly. Therefore, in multi-region models, geographic concentration may follow a bell-shaped path and industrial specialization keeps increasing as transportation costs decrease.

In reality, the actual transportation costs of manufactured goods during the 20th century decreased by more than 90% (Glaeser and Kohlhase 2004). Meanwhile, Kim (1995) and Krugman (1991a) showed that the geographic concentration of manufacturing industries in the US reached its peak in the 1930s, after which it started to descend steadily. Midelfart-Knarvik et al. (2000) extended the time period and showed the degree to which US manufacturing geographic concentration continued to decrease in the 1990s. Henley (1994) discovered that in the 1980s the geographic concentration of United Kingdom manufacturing industries stopped increasing and industrial activities become more geographically dispersed.

Similarly, the *TYPCONC* and Hoover coefficient time line seems to indicate that geographic concentration in the PRC is "copying" the experiences of the US and the EU and has already turned from the increasing phase to the decreasing phase. However, it has been verified and widely known that the level of geographic concentration in the PRC is much lower compared with those of the US and European economies (Lu and Tao 2009). So why is the turning point in the PRC arriving before its time? As for the change of industrial specialization in the empirical studies on regional economic integration, Aiginger and Rossi-Hansberg (2006) argued that from 1987 to 1996 the industrial GINI coefficient of 50 states in the US increased by 2.3%, meaning the level of industrial specialization increased prominently when geographic concentration decreased. Both Amiti's 1999 study and Brülhart's 1998 study on European integration found that the resulting geographic concentration and industrial specialization increased in the 1970s and 1980s. Along with the Single Market Program since 1992, the geographic concentration of EU countries started to show a tendency for decentralization (Brülhart and Traeger 2005), while the industrial specialization continued to increase (Aiginer and Davies 2004; Aiginer and Rossi-Hansberg 2006). Another confusing problem is that, contrary to geographic concentration, the PRC's industrial specialization did not "copy" the changing trend of the US and EU economies. As indicated by the results of *TYPSPEC* and the interprovincial Krugman Index, PRC industrial and interprovincial specialization tended to decrease in recent years, which contradicts the pattern that every region needs to exploit its comparative advantages to accelerate economic development.

11.4.2 Hypotheses

As indicated in Sections 11.3 and 11.4.1, it seems that, in terms of economic geography, the PRC takes a road different from developed economies, which are not well predicted by New Economic Geography. Though previous studies have explained the PRC phenomenon from the perspective of local protectionism, which is helpful in understanding the lower level of geographic concentration in industries with higher after-tax profit margins or state-owned shares (e.g., Bai et al. 2004; Lu and Tao 2007; Huang and Li 2006), it still cannot explain why the PRC's geographic concentration and industrial specialization presents a downward trend in the process of its entering the World Trade Organization and integrating its domestic market. In fact, provincial governments could affect the speed of local industrial development through "passively defensive" protection; in addition, local officials' promotion competition (Zhou, 2004, 2007) gives them strong incentives to achieve better performance via active involvement in industry and economic development through preferential industrial policies. For instance, Xu, Wang, and Shu (2007) observed that an interprovince governor transfer program would increase the speed of economic development for lagging provinces. And economic development is usually achieved by vigorous development of the secondary industry pushed by the government. Song and Wang (2013) further proved that local governments' key industrial policies conceived in 5-year plans indeed increased these industries' productivity.

In the PRC, the *Five-Year Plan for National Economic and Social Development* (henceforth, 5-year plan) is one of the most significant means by which governments could reallocate resources. One of the reasons local governments favor 5-year plans is that officials could make use of the "visible hands" to intervene in the development of local industries, thus completing the task of economic performance needed for their personal promotion. More importantly, when local plans base themselves on the central government's 5-year plan and special plans for industrial development, it is advantageous for local government to apply for affiliated support (e.g., tax privileges for high-tech industry, strategic promotion policy for emerging industry, etc.). In this way, the provinces can acquire extra resources for local development, which also to some extent lead to "similarity" or "homogeneity" of industrial policies across the provinces. To obtain a clearer view, we collated data from the 10th to 11th national and provincial 5-year plans and classified the industries into two categories (at the two-digit industry level according to the National Bureau of Statistics): policy-oriented industries, and other industries. The policy-oriented industries refer to those termed "pillar industry," "advancing industry," "promising industry," "priority industry," "breakthrough industry," or described with verbs like "to enlarge and strengthen," "to prioritize," "to develop," "to accelerate," "to expand," or "to cultivate" when reviewing its 5-year plans. The remaining industries are "other (non-preferred) industries", which are either not mentioned in the plans, or whose prospects are described as "to rationally develop," "to relatively control," "to optimize and adjust," "to transform," "to reduce scale," "to gradually eliminate," "to limit," or "to orderly transfer" in 5-year plans.[9] Then, for further investigation, we introduce a dummy variable to represent "policy-oriented industries" (=1) and "other industries" (=0) in each 5-year plan. When we look into the 11th 5-year plan, it can be easily seen that those listed in the central government's 11th 5-year plan as policy-oriented industries on average are also thus chosen by as many as 20 provinces; those that do not appear in the central government's favorite list would, on average, only appear in nine provinces' lists as policy-oriented industries.[10] To measure policy similarity between the central government and the local governments, we calculate the Jaccard coefficient of similarity. The results are presented in Table 11.3.[11]

---

[9]   In some provinces' 5-year plans, the industries are usually named by collective terms of several industries (such as high-tech industry, information industry), by industrial sectors (such as chemistry industry) or by representative products in the industry. We looked into those provinces' 5-year plans and unified their terms at two-digit industry levels by referring to standard of classification published by National Bureau of Statistics (NBS) and provincial bureau of statistics, including *Product Classification for Statistics* (China Statistics Press 2010), *Classification of Strategic Emerging Industry* (2012), *Product Classification of New Materials, Classification of High-tech (Manufacturing) Industry* (2013), *Classification of High-tech Industry for Statistics* (NBS [2002] No. 33), *Interim Provisions for Classification of Information Industry for Statistics* and *Classification of Environment Protection*. For details, one may refer to the website of NBS, http://www.stats.gov. cn/tjsj/tjbz/. Note that Song and Wang (2013) used a different approach in defining industries: they regarded all the manufacturing mentioned in 30 provinces' 5-year plans as major industries, following the classification of industry code in National Economy (GB/T4754-2002) and ignored new material and new resource industries. Therefore, their numbers of policy-oriented industries are different from here.

[10]   Although Song and Wang (2013) adopted a different approach, their results also indicated that there were many major industries overlapping in provincial and national 5-year plans.

[11]   Given two objects, A and B, each with n binary attributes (either 1 or 0). Thus, there are four different kinds of combination of attributes for A and B, specified as M11, M01, M10 and M00 with M11+M01+M10+M00=n. The Jaccard similarity coefficient, J, is defined as J =M11/ (M01+M10+M11). Clearly J lies in [0, 1] and J =1 if A is the same as B. For comparison of two provinces (inter-temporal comparison of single province), we calculate the J directly. For comparison of two regions, e.g., eastern and western area, we first calculate the Jaccard coefficient of any province-pairs (one from the eastern area and the other from the western area), and then use simple average-term to represent similarity between regions.

Table 11.3: Jaccard Coefficient of Similarity of Preferential Industries in the 10th and 11th Five-Year Plans

Area	10th	11th	Inter-temporal	Area	10th	11th	Area	10th	11th
E-E	0.508	0.492	0.571	E-C	0.475	0.498	E-CG	0.464	0.432
C-C	0.479	0.653	0.570	E-W	0.309	0.346	C-CG	0.389	0.570
W-W	0.357	0.466	0.535	E-N	0.442	0.470	W-CG	0.318	0.481
N-N	0.406	0.620	0.597	C-W	0.345	0.508	N-CG	0.478	0.589
National	0.378	0.464	0.559	C-N	0.419	0.603	LG-CG	0.394	0.493
–	–	–	–	W-N	0.270	0.511	–	–	–

Notes: E for East Region, C for Central Region, W for West Region and N for Northeast Region, CG for central government and LG for local government, 10th and 11th for the 10th and 11th 5-year plan; so that E-E refers to the simple average of Jaccard coefficient of similarity among east provinces, and it is similar for the rest notations. Besides, "inter-temporal" refers to the simple average of Jaccard coefficient of similarity between the 10th and 11th 5-year plan of the same province.

Source: Authors' calculations.

From Table 11.3, we can see first that in the horizontal comparison across provinces, except those within the east region, the Jaccard coefficients of the central, west, and northeast regions, and the inter-provinces between any two different regions all increased, resulting in within-province Jaccard coefficients for the nation as a whole ranging from 0.378 (the 10th 5-year plan) to 0.464 (the 11th 5-year plan). In other words, the industrial policies within provinces in the central, west, and northeast regions and across regions become increasingly similar, whereas their policies became much more similar to those of the east provinces. Second, in cross-time comparison, the inter-temporal Jaccard coefficient of all provinces between the 11th 5-year plan and the 10th 5-year plan is 0.559. Only the coefficient of the west provinces is below the average level. This indicates that when all provinces' industrial policies become more similar to that of the east provinces, the policy of the west provinces deviates most from their past policies. Last, in terms of the relativity between the industrial policies of the central government and local governments, the Jaccard coefficient in the 10th 5-year plan is 0.394, while in the 11th 5-year plan it increases to 0.493. On the one hand, it indicates a high similarity between the industrial policies of the central government and local governments; on the other hand, it also shows that the level of similarity is even higher in the 11th 5-year plan. Notably, the east provinces are again special among all the four areas. The Jaccard coefficient is lower in the 11th 5-year plan than that in the 10th 5-year plan. That is to say, though all provinces follow the central government in making their own industrial policies, leading to a higher similarity among the industrial policies of all provinces, the east provinces keep themselves relatively independent and are good at adapting to their own conditions.

There is little doubt that once an industry is listed as policy-oriented in the 5-year plan of a province, it receives more support, such as priority in construction land allocation, special provincial development funds, convenience in clearance of imported equipment and parts, deduction of research fees, double amortization in the cost of intangible assets, priority in raw materials and electricity supply, and professional training for certain industries. Therefore, it is speculated in this chapter that those measures may allow favorite industries to expand rapidly in the valid period of the 5-year plan, and would consequently influence the spatial distribution of economic activities. On the basis of the previous discussion, we propose two hypotheses:

Hypothesis 1: for a given industry i in province r, if it is listed as policy-oriented in the local 5-year plan, then, during the valid period of the plan, its gross output share r would increase faster.

Hypothesis 2: for a given industry i in province r, if it is listed as policy-oriented in the local 5-year plan, then, during the valid period of the plan, its gross output share i would also increase faster.

If the above two hypotheses can be verified by the empirical study, it means that local government industrial policies do influence the distribution of economic geography. Due to the higher similarity in industrial policy among provinces from the 10th to the 11th 5-year plan, it could explain the changes in the PRC's recent geographic concentration and industrial specialization.

11.5 | Industrial Policy and Economic Geography: Empirical Analysis

To test the above two hypotheses, the national- and provincial-level 10th and 11th 5-year plans are used and a dummy variable $plan_{irn}$ (where 1 represents policy-oriented industries, and 0 others) is introduced to stand for the policy support that industry i faces in the nth 5-year plan of province r. Around 1998, the industrial statistic criteria experienced a major amendment. Thus, to ensure comparability, we only focus on the 10th 5-year plan (valid during 2001 to 2005) and the 11th 5-year plan (valid during 2006 to 2010) to evaluate the effect of industrial policy on economic geography.

11.5.1 Methodology

First, we will test whether economic geography changes as a result of policy intervention based on the 11th provincial 5-year plan. Let p_{ir} stand for industry i's output from the gross output of province r, and s_{ir} stand for industry i's output from the gross output nationwide. The basic regression model is defined as follows:

$$\Delta_{ir} = \alpha + \beta\, plan_{ir} + \Sigma_j \delta_j C_{irj} + \varepsilon_{ir} \tag{1}$$

where dependent variable Δ_{ir} is the change of industry i in the valid period of the 11th 5-year plan of province r. Two alternative variables are used here, i.e., Δp_{ir}, which is the change of p_{ir}, and Δs_{ir}, which is the change of s_{ir}. The variable Δp_{ir} reflects the industrial structure change within province r and Δs_{ir} catches the geographic change within industry i, defined as $\Delta p_{ir} = p_{ir2010} - p_{ir2005}$ and $\Delta s_{ir} = s_{ir2010} - s_{ir2005}$, respectively. The policy explanatory variable $plan_{ir}$ is the chapter's core, the coefficient of which is expected to be positive by the hypotheses in Section 11.4. C_{irj} is a group of control variables, measuring the influence of non-policy factors. ε_{ir} is a random error term with constant variance. When Δp_{ir} is the dependent variable, the main control variables include $firm_{ir}$, that is, the number of firms in the same industry in province r, and its quadratic term sfm_{ir}, which are respectively the proxy variables for

Marshall Externality (e.g., labor market pooling, specialized supply, and knowledge spillovers) and competitive effect. According to the New Economic Geography, the estimated coefficient of Marshall Externality ($firm_{ir}$) is expected to be positive, while the estimated coefficient of competitive effect (sfm_{ir}) is negative. In addition, p_{ir} is used to control the initial level of industry i in province r before implementing the 11th 5-year plan, and another set of dummy variables ID_i to control industry-specific characteristics. All control variables use lagged value to avoid possible reverse causality. When Δs_{ir} is the dependent variable, we follow Midelfart-Knarvik et al. (2000), in which the logarithmic value of regional population, $lnpop_r$, controls the regional specific characteristics, or use the logarithmic value of regional output, $lngdp_r$, as an alternative. The estimated coefficients of these two variables are expected to be positive. Meanwhile, the quadratic term of the total number of firms in industry i, $isfm_i$, is used to measure the competitive effect, and the improvement of transport infrastructures locally ($trans$) or regionally ($ntrans$) to measure the change of transportation costs, the estimated coefficients of which are negative and positive, respectively, according to New Economic Geography. Last, due to data availability, we follow Wooldridge (2004: 300) to deal with the omitted variables problem, where the lagged dependent variables are used in the cross-sectional regression model as a proxy to control the effect from other industrial development factors. For a detailed definition of variables, methodology of construction, and summary statistics, see Appendix 4.

11.5.2 Results

It needs to be pointed out that though such endogeneity problems as omitted variables and reverse causality have been addressed by lagged dependent and control variables in the model, they may still exist between the policy variable, $plan_{ir}$, and its dependent variable Δp_{ir}, since there is possibility of self-selection. That is to say, industry i is selected as policy-oriented in province r because the local government would cart its industrial policy to that of the central government's, resulting in a deviation from its comparative advantage and causing correlation between $plan_{ir}$ and ε_{ir}, which makes the ordinary least squares (OLS) result unreliable. To accommodate this, we introduce two other variables: *cplan* and *rplan*, representing the central government's industrial policy in the national 11th 5-year plan and its long-term strategies for regional development, respectively. Both are used as instrumental variables in two-stage least squares regression (2SLS). As mentioned above, local governments tend to refer to the central government's 5-year plan in making their own industrial policies, through which they can acquire extra resources for development. Generally speaking, the prioritized industries in the central government's plan are significant references for the local governments to choose their own policy-oriented industries,[12] thus leading to a high similarity in pillar or major industries across provinces. Meanwhile, for those provinces that are included in the central government's regional development program, the development strategies of the central government are also very influential. For example, the document entitled *Some Opinions on Promoting the Further Development of Western China by the State Council* emphasizes that provinces in the west region should cultivate industries with local advantages and establish a major area for national energy and mineral resources. Obviously, those instructive ideas will affect the choice of preferential industries by the provincial governments in the west region. Therefore, local governments' 11th 5-year plan ($plan_{ir}$) highly correlates with the central government's 11th 5-year plan (*cplan*) and its strategies for regional development (*rplan*). It needs to be emphasized that the central government's policies would influence the prioritized industry as a whole, though they cannot determine the development of a specific industry in every province, which means they can influence $\Sigma_i \Delta p_{ir}$ but not Δp_{ir}. Maximum likelihood estimation (MLE) and generalized method of moments (GMM) estimation are used to accommodate the problem of weak instrumental variables and heteroskedasticity caused by provincial and industrial differences.[13]

---

[12] For instance, when one of the prioritized industries had its name changed from "high and new industry" to "high-tech industry" in the central government's 11th 5-year plan, 21 provinces adopted the new name in their 11th 5-year plan instantly.

[13] However, when Δs_{ir} is the dependent variable, the local policy variable does not suffer from endogeneity problems. It is further proved by the close parameters estimated by OLS and fixed effects model estimation.

Table 11.4 reports the results with Δp_{ir} as the dependent variable. By regression Eq. (1), the OLS estimation (column 1 of Table 11.5) shows that the regression coefficient of $plan_{ir}$ is 0.745 with significant level below 1%. This means that local industrial policy does accelerate the development pace of policy-oriented industries. To improve efficiency of the estimates and control for the self-selection problem, the 2SLS model (column 2 of Table 11.5) uses cplan and rplan as the instrumental variables for $plan_{ir}$. In the first-stage regression, the robust F-statistic is 81.81, and the p-values of both regression coefficients are less than 0.01, indicating that cplan and rplan can effectively explain $plan_{ir}$. In addition, the p-values of the over-identification test and the Durbin–Wu–Hausman (DWH) test are 0.69 and 0.05, respectively, which means the instrumental variables are effective. The estimated regression coefficient of $plan_{ir}$ is positive (1.445) and significant, showing that being listed as a policy-oriented industry does grant extra advantages over other industries in the same province.

Meanwhile, the fact that OLS estimator of $plan_{ir}$ is less than that of 2SLS verifies our conjecture about local government choosing its policy-oriented industry to cart that of the central government's preference, resulting in underestimation by OLS regression. In addition, the results also show that when the number of firms ($firm_{ir}$) in one industry increases, the Marshall's externality benefits its development on one hand; on the other hand, the competition among firms also increases. The competitive effect is confirmed by the negative estimated coefficient of sfm_{ir} as the theory of New Economic Geography predicts. Though it is believed, according to the results of the first stage regression, that there is no serious weak instrument bias, Limited Information Maximum Likelihood (LIML) regression is introduced as a precautionary measure. As shown by the results in column 3 of Table 11.5, the estimators by 2SLS and LIML regression are quite close, which confirms there are no weak instrumental variables. Considering scale differences across the provinces and industries, columns 4 to 6 use GMM estimation, which is more effective in the presence of heteroskedasticity. The results are also close to that of 2SLS estimation. In column 5, the lagged dependent variable Δp_{irL} is replaced with lagged industrial development speed ar_{ir-L6} to catch the influence

Table 11.4: Impacts of Preferential Industry Policy on Industrial Specialization (Δp_{ir} as dependent variable)

	(1) OLS	(2) SLS	(3) LIML	(4) GMM	(5) GMM	(6) GMM
$plan_{ir}$	0.745*** (0.105)	1.445*** (0.331)	1.446*** (0.331)	1.477*** (0.321)	1.403*** (0.318)	1.451*** (0.359)
$firm_{ir}$	0.216*** (0.052)	0.167*** (0.048)	0.167*** (0.048)	0.170*** (0.048)	0.192*** (0.051)	0.167*** (0.048)
sfm_{ir}	-0.010*** (0.003)	-0.008** (0.003)	-0.008** (0.003)	-0.009** (0.0.03)	-0.010*** (0.003)	-0.008 (0.048)
Δp_{irL}	0.202*** (0.054)	0.204*** (0.053)	0.204*** (0.053)	0.201*** (0.052)		0.200*** (0.054)
ar_{ir-L6}					0.229** (0.318)	
p_{ir03}	-0.216*** (0.031)	-0.244*** (0.036)	-0.244*** (0.036)	-0.245*** (0.036)	-0.216*** (0.041)	-0.229*** (0.037)
scl_{ir04}						0.339 (0.224)
Constant	-0.345*** (0.147)	-0.336** (0.149)	-0.336** (0.149)	-0.346** (0.147)	-0.614*** (0.184)	-0.647** (0.263)
Industry dummy	Yes	Yes	Yes	Yes	Yes	Yes
N. of Obs.	1,144	1,144	1,144	1,144	1,107	921
R^2	0.270	0.236	0.236	0.232	0.187	0.258
F-statistic/Wald chi2	18.43	112.65	112.63	115.31	83.08	120.82
Over-identification		0.164 0.6859		0.164 0.6859	0.087 0.7676	0.075 0.7835
DWH		3.928 0.0475				
GMM C statistic chi2				5.116 0.0237	4.05134 0.0441	3.546 0.0597
Robust F-Statistic of the first stage		81.8065 0.0000	81.8065 0.0000	81.8065 0.0000	90.869 0.0000	62.6305 0.0000

GMM = generalized method of moments, LIML = limited information maximum likelihood, N. of Obs. = number of observations, OLS = ordinary least squares, SLS = two-steps least squares.

Notes: 1. Robust standard errors are in parentheses, with the P-value below.

2. *, **, and *** stand for significant at 10%, 5%, and 1%.

3. Due to lack of data, regression (6) does not include Beijing, Tianjin, Shanghai, Henan, and Hunan.

Source: Authors.

Table 11.5: **Impacts of Preferential Industry Policy on Geographic Concentration (Δs_{ir} as dependent variable)**

	(1) OLS	(2) SLS	(3) LIML	(4) GMM	(5) GMM	(6) GMM
$plan_{ir}$	0.384*** (0.090)	0.398*** (0.091)	0.370*** (0.085)	0.358*** (0.083)	0.393*** (0.088)	0.392*** (0.089)
Δs_{irL}	0.330** (0.157)			0.329** (0.161)	0.329** (0.161)	0.341** (0.157)
$lnpop_r$	0.280*** (0.041)	0.330*** (0.046)				
$lngdp_r$			0.190*** (0.052)	0.183*** (0.046)	0.183*** (0.045)	0.183*** (0.046)
ar_{ir-L3}		0.093 (0.076)	0.113 (0.074)			
$Rplan$	0.274** (0.108)	0.305*** (0.114)	0.574*** (0.111)	0.442*** (0.118)	0.442*** (0.118)	0.507*** (0.107)
$trans_r$				0.092* (0.055)	0.092* (0.055)	
$ntrans_r$			1.593** (0.738)			1.172* (0.701)
s_{ir03}	−0.115*** (0.024)	−0.118*** (0.024)	−0.117*** (0.025)	−0.115*** (0.024)	−0.115*** (0.024)	−0.116*** (0.024)
$isfm_i$	−0.133 (0.086)	−0.133 (0.089)			−0.136 (0.086)	−0.135 (0.086)
_cons	−2.202*** (0.290)	−2.652*** (0.315)	−0.201* (0.103)	−1.833*** (0.376)	−1.785*** (0.378)	−1.882 (0.371)
N. of Obs.	1,147	1,110	1,110	1,147	1,147	1,147
F-Statistic	27.88	27.18	25.32	24.78	22.26	22.84
R-squared	0.2182	0.2035	0.1961	0.2136	0.2150	0.2142

GMM = generalized method of moments, LIML = limited information maximum like ihood,
N. of Obs. = number of observations, OLS = ordinary least squares, SLS = two-steps least squares.

Notes: 1. Robust standard errors are in parentheses, with P-value below.

2. *, **, and *** stand for significant at 10%, 5%, and 1%.

Source: Authors.

of other economic trend factors. The results indicate that factors such as techniques and human resources promoting fast development could have a long-term influence on industry. Column 6 further considers the influence of firm scale (scl_{ir04}). However, the results of $plan_{ir}$ are not influenced when introducing firm scale. The estimated coefficient of scl_{ir04} indicates that when the proportion of small business increases by 1%, the share of industrial output in that region would increase by 0.3%. This result to some extent supports Rosenthal and Strange's (2010) conclusion of the positive relationship between small business and industry vitality.

Table 11.5 reports the results with Δs_{ir} as the dependent variable. Estimated coefficients of $plan_{i}$ are significant and around 0.4 (columns 1–8 in Table 11.5). It means that once listed as policy-oriented, the output share of industry i in province r out of the gross output of industry i as a whole would increase. However, when comparing the results in Tables 11.4 and 11.5, we can see that provincial plans' influence on industrial structure (around 1.4) is much stronger than on economic geography (around 0.4). This sounds reasonable since provincial industry policy would have larger influence inside a province rather than between provinces. In addition, the regression coefficients of $lnpop_{r}$ and $lngdp_{i}$ are both positive and significant as expected, which means local demands have a positive effect on the geographic concentration of the industry. Furthermore, as shown by the estimated coefficient of $rplan$, the central government's regional development strategies accelerate the proportional increase in the middle-west and northeast provinces. Thus, regional development strategies have a balancing effect on forerunners and followers. The regression coefficient of independent variables $trans_{r}$ and $ntrans_{r}$ measuring the improvement of transportation infrastructures locally or among regions are both positive, which indicates that the decrease of transportation costs is still helpful for the increase of geographic concentration. Last, the lagged dependent variable Δs_{irL}, or the coefficient of lagged development speed ar_{ir-L3}, are positive and, in most cases, significant, which means that historical factors also influence geographic concentration.

11.5.3 Panel Regression: Further Test

Section 5.2 shows that provincial industrial policy explains the economic geography changes during the valid period of the 11th 5-year plan (2006–2010). In this section, we will extend the time period under study to the valid period of both the 10th and 11th 5-year plan (2001–2010) with a panel model. Compared with the former, due to a major amendment to the industrial statistical criteria in 1998, we have fewer variables that could be used to analyze the changes during 2001–2010. However, there are also some advantages. As is known, omitted variables bias is a common problem in empirical studies. When the omitted variables are unobservable and unchanging individual differences, panel data offer another tool for eliminating the bias. Therefore, a two-period panel data constructed in this section could further test the robustness of the results. The panel model is set as follows:

$$\Delta_{irn} = \beta_0 + \beta_1\,plan_{irn} + \Sigma_j\delta_jC_{irnj} + \alpha_i + \gamma_r + \varepsilon_{irn} \tag{2}$$

where Δ_{irn} is the change of industry i in province r during the valid period of the nth 5-year plan. Two dependent variables Δp_{irn} and Δs_{irn} are used as in Section 5.1. Here, Δp_{irn} is the change of p_{ir}, defined as $\Delta p_{irn} = p_{irt} - p_{irt-5}$, and Δs_{irn} is the change of s_{ir}, defined as $\Delta s_{irn} = s_{irt} - s_{irt-5}$, with t as the last year of the valid period of the nth 5-year plan in both equations. The dummy variable of industrial policy $plan_{irn}$ measures the provincial policy faced by industry i during the valid period of the nth 5-year plan, with 1 being policy-oriented and 0 the others. As predicted by Hypothesis 1 and Hypothesis 2, the estimated coefficient of $plan_{irn}$ is positive, with α_i being a set of time-invariant characteristics of industry i, γ_r being a set of time-invariant characteristics of region r, and ε_{irn} being the random error. In addition, C_{irnj} is a group of variables controlling the influence of non-policy factors. When Δp_{irn} is the dependent variable, the main control variables include the lagged value of industry i's initial scale x_{irmL} in province r and the lagged value of numbers of firms in the industry fm_{irmL}. Considering the possible self-selection problem, the central government's nth 5-year plan $cplan_n$ and its regional development strategies $rplan_n$ are used again as two instrumental variables for local government's preferential industrial policies. When Δs_{irn} is the dependent variable, the control variables include s_{irnL}, the lagged value of industry i's initial scale in province r, and $trans_{rn}$, the improvement of transport infrastructures in implementing the nth 5-year plan.

Table 11.6: Impacts of Preferential Industry Policy on Industrial Specialization (Δp_{irn} as dependent variable)

	(1) FEM	(2) FEM	(3) IV-FEM (GMM)	(4) IV-FEM (LIML)	(5) IV-FEM (GMM)	(6) IV-FEM (LIML)
$plan_{irn}$	0.333** (0.136)	0.268** (0.131)	1.182* (0.666)	1.176* (0.712)	1.292* (0.683)	1.286* (0.732)
x_{irnL}					-0.273*** (0.048)	-0.267*** (0.049)
x_{irnL2}	-0.340*** (0.061)	-0.350*** (0.067)	-0.351*** (0.063)	-0.343*** (0.062)		
fm_{irnL}	0.172*** (0.041)	0.164*** (0.041)	0.177*** (0.043)	0.177*** (0.043)	0.170*** (0.042)	0.170*** (0.420)
Obs.	2,254	2,254	2,214	2,214	2,214	2,214
F test	12.22	8.30	10.91	10.99	10.30	10.30
Kleibergen–Paap Chi-sq (2) (Under-identification test)			22.83 0.0000	22.83 0.0000	22.85 0.0000	22.845 0.0000
Hansen J statistic (over-identification test)			1.490 0.2222	1.483 0.2234	1.564 0.2222	1.554 0.2126
Angrist–Pischke F test for first-stage regressions			12.76 0.0000	12.76 0.0000	12.77 0.0000	12.77 0.0000

FEM = fixed effects model, GMM = generalized method of moments, IV = instrumental variable, LIML = limited information maximum likelihood, Obs. = observations.

Notes: 1. Robust standard errors are in parentheses, with P-value below.
  2. *, **, and *** stand for significant at 10%, 5%, and 1%.

Source: Authors.

Table 11.6 summarizes the results when Δp_{irn} is the dependent variable. The Hausman test is in favor of the fixed effects model (FEM); therefore, we first apply the FEM to estimate the regression Eq. (2). As shown in column 1 of Table 11.6, the estimated coefficient of local policy $plan_{irn}$ is positive (0.333) and significant, which means that local industrial policy does promote the growth of the preferential industry's share in local industrial structure. If we further control time-fixed effect, the results remain (column 2 in Table 11.6). Columns 3 to 6 in Table 11.6 report two-step GMM estimator or LIML estimation when using $cplan_n$ and $rplan_n$ as the instrumental variables for local policy $plan_{im}$. In the first stage regression, the Angrist–Pischke F-statistic is at 12.8, which exceeds the threshold (F=10) suggested by Stock, Wright, and Yogo (2002). Thus, it is believed that there is no severe weak instrument bias. Still, columns 4 and 6 use LIML estimation since it is much less sensitive to weak instrumental variables. The coefficients of LIML estimators are quite close to those of GMM estimators. Judged from the results of columns 3 to 6, the coefficients of control variables are quite stable. Since local policy $plan_{im}$ has a significant and positive effect on the growth of industrial share out of local gross output, it can be concluded that local governments' industrial policies in 5-year plans do significantly influence local industrial structure and specialization.

Table 11.7 summarizes the results when Δs_{im} is the dependent variable. A provincial dummy variable is added to the pooled OLS regression (column 1 in Table 11.7). As indicated by the results, the estimated coefficient $plan_{im}$ is 0.447, which means that local industrial policy promotes provincial output share growth where this industry is listed as policy-oriented. Columns 2 to 5 in Table 11.7 apply a fixed effects model to address the time-invariant heterogeneity of unobservable or omitted variables. According to the results in Table 11.7, the estimated coefficient of $plan_{im}$ by fixed effects model and pooled regression model are relatively close. However, the F test of joint significance of the fixed effects model refuses the null hypothesis (p=0.00). Thus the fixed effects model is more appropriate. The estimated coefficient of $plan_{im}$ is positive and significant, indicating that, compared with those provinces that do not list some industry as policy-oriented, local industrial policies do grow its share of nationwide output in the province where this industry is offered with preferential policies. In addition, the estimated coefficient of variable $lntrs_{m}$, which measures the improvement of local transportation infrastructures, is positive. And again it proves the beneficial effect of decreasing transportation costs on geographic concentration.

The coefficients of the lagged dependent variable Δs_{iml} and the lagged development speed ar_{mL} are both positive and significant, showing that historical factors have continuous influence on economic geography.

Table 11.7: **Impacts of Preferential Industry Policy on Geographic Concentration** (Δs_{im} as dependent variable)

Variable	(1) Pooled OLS	(2) FEM	(3) FEM	(4) FEM	(5) FEM
$plan_{im}$	0.447*** (0.071)	0.460*** (0.073)	0.454*** (0.068)	0.438*** (0.078)	0.421*** (0.073)
s_{irL}	-0.112*** (0.022)	-1.044*** (0.057)	-1.080*** (0.056)	-1.047*** (0.056)	-1.083*** (0.056)
ar_{imL}	0.021 (0.021)	0.149** (0.053)		0.152*** (0.055)	
Δs_{imL}			0.502*** (0.118)		0.510*** (0.118)
$Intrs_m$				0.017 (0.014)	0.026** (0.013)
Province Dummy	Yes	None	None	None	None
_cons	-0.176*** (0.040)	3.325*** (0.196)	3.293*** (0.186)	3.324*** (0.216)	3.179*** (0.204)
Obs.	2,211	2,211	2,294	2,211	2,294
F-Statistic	8.89	135.25	152.26	109.91	125.70
R^2	0.1506	0.6273	0.6515	0.6277	0.6525

FEM = fixed effects model, Obs. = observations, OLS = ordinary least squares.

Notes: 1. Robust standard errors are in parentheses, with P-value below.

2. *, **, and *** stand for significant at 10%, 5%, and 1%.

Source: Prepared by the authors.

11.6 | Conclusions

New Economic Geography predicted that market integration would increase industrial specialization and reduce geographic concentration, which has been confirmed in developed countries. However, the evolution of economic geography in the PRC from 1999 to 2010 follows a different path: specialization and concentration started to decrease simultaneously after 2005 and the similarity of industrial structure among provinces began to increase. Though geographic concentration is doomed to change from increase to decrease along with the progress of domestic market integration, it turns around to decrease at a relatively low level of concentration verified by the previous literatures. Meanwhile, the situation of industrial and interprovincial specialization is also deteriorating with decreasing geographic concentration. As shown by the stylized facts, the evolution of economic geography in the PRC is "disturbed" by unique non-market factors other than economic and geographic determinants.

We found that local governments' policy intervention plays an important role in the evolution of the PRC's economic geography. Through industrial policy, local governments could directly interfere with development. As shown by the empirical results, the interference is so effective that it profoundly changes the industrial structures inside a province and regional specialization among industries, and, as a result, influences the domestic economic landscape. The effectiveness of the instrumental variables used here further proves the guiding role of the central government on provincial industrial policy. The central government's preference usually reflects more about industrial structures in developed regions, which is itself a function of its long-term goal of pursuing economic efficiency. Since local governments thus have incentives to follow the central government's lead when drawing up their own policies, this would lead to deviations from comparative advantage and misallocation of production, especially for less-developed provinces. Overall, there are pros and cons about the behavior pattern of "local governments following central government." It is helpful in achieving the central government's goal of industrial structure adjustment and transformation throughout the country.

However, its negative effect is that some provinces sacrifice too much to cater for the central government's support. Furthermore, the negative effect is much more obvious in underdeveloped provinces, which is also supported by empirical results. Since the early stage of economic reform in the PRC, provinces in the coast region have been striving for the central government's support, resulting in severe similarity of industrial structures across regions; nowadays, similar trends among underdeveloped provinces in the hinterland are observed. Learning from the experience of the developed regions is to some extent helpful in realizing the potential of underdeveloped provinces, but low concentration and insufficient specialization will definitely bring efficiency loss to such a large economy as the PRC.

References

Aiginger, K., and S. W. Davies. 2004. Industrial Specialisation and Geographic Concentration: Two Sides of the Same Coin? Not for the European Union. *Journal of Applied Economics* 7(2): 231–248.

Aiginger, K., and E. Rossi-Hansberg. 2006. Specialization and Concentration: A Note on Theory and Evidence. *Empirica* 33(4): 255–266.

Amiti, M. 1999. Specialization Patterns in Europe. Weltwirtschaftliches Archiv 135(4): 573–593.

Bai, C.-E., Y. Du, Z. Tao, and S. Y. Tong. 2004. Local Protectionism and Regional Specialization: Evidence from China's Industries. *Journal of International Economics* 63(2): 397–417.

Brülhart, M. 1998. Economic Geography, Industry Location and Trade: The Evidence. *World Economy* 21(6): 775–801.

Brülhart, M., and R. Traeger. 2005. An Account of Geographic Concentration Patterns in Europe. *Regional Science and Urban Economics* 35(6): 597–624.

Cowell, E. A. 1995. *Measuring Inequality.* London: Prentice Hall.

Ellison, G., and E. Glaeser. 1997. Geographic Concentration in U.S. Manufacturing Industries: A Dartboard Approach. *Journal of Political Economy* 105(5): 889–927.

Fujita, M., P. Krugman, and A. Venables. 1999. *The Spatial Economy.* Cambridge, MA: MIT Press.

Glaeser, E., and J. Kohlhase. 2004. Cities, Regions and the Decline of Transport Costs. *Papers in Regional Science* 83(1): 197–228.

Henley, A. 1994. Industrial Development in U.K. Manufacturing since 1980. *The Manchester School* 62(1): 40–59.

Hoover, E. 1936. The Measurement of Industrial Location. *Review of Economics and Statistics* 18(2): 162–171.

Kim, S. 1995. Expansion of Markets and the Geographic Distribution of Economic Activities: The Trends in U. S. Regional Manufacturing Structure, 1860–1987. *Quarterly Journal of Economics* 110(4): 881–908.

Krugman, P. 1991a. *Geography and Trade.* Cambridge, MA: MIT Press.

———. 1991b. Increasing Returns and Economic Geography. *Journal of Political Economics* 99(3): 483–499.

Krugman, P., and A. Venables. 1995. Globalization and the Inequality of Nations. *Quarterly Journal of Economics* 110(4): 857–880.

Lu, J., and Z. Tao. 2009. Trends and Determinants of China's Industrial Agglomeration. *Journal of Urban Economics* 65(2): 167–180.

Midelfart-Knarvik, K., H. Overman, P. Lane, and J.-M. Viaene. 2002. Delocation and European Integration: Is Structural Spending Justified? *Economic Policy* 17(35): 321–359.

Midelfart-Knarvik, K., H. Overman, S. Redding, and A. Venables. 2000. The Location of European Industry. European Commission European Economy—Economic Papers, No. 142.

Palan, N. 2010. Measurement of Specialization—The Choice of Indices. FIW Working Paper series. Vienna: Austrian Institute of Economic Research.

Rosenthal, S., and W. Strange. 2010. Small Establishments/Big Effects: Agglomeration, Industrial Organization and Entrepreneurship. In *Agglomeration Economics*, edited by E. Glaeser. Chicago, IL: University of Chicago Press.

Rossi-Hansberg, E. 2005. A Spatial Theory of Trade. *American Economic Review* 95(5): 1464–1491.

Stock, J. H., J. H. Wright, and M. Yogo. 2002. A Survey of Weak Instruments and Weak Identification in Generalized Method of Moments. *Journal of Business and Economic Statistics* 20(4): 518–529.

Venables, A. 1996. Equilibrium Locations of Vertically Linked Industries. *International Economic Review* 37(2): 341–359.

Wooldridge, J. M. 2004. *Introductory Econometrics: A Modern Approach* (International Edition). Beijing: Tsinghua University Press.

Young, A. 2000. The Razor's Edge: Distortions and Incremental Reform in the People's Republic of China. *Quarterly Journal of Economics* 115(4): 1091–1135.

Literature in Chinese

Fan, J. 2004. Market Integration, Regional Specialization and Tendency of Industrial Agglomeration: An Implication for Regional Disparity. *Social Science in China* 6: 39–51.

———. 2008. Unbalanced Industrial Structure, Spatial Agglomeration and Change of Regional Disparity. *Shanghai Economic Research* 2: 3–13.

Fan, J., and F. Li. 2011. Effect of Spatial Concentration of Manufacturing in China: A Review. *South China Journal of Economics* 6: 53–66.

Huang, J., and K. Li. 2006. Foreign Trade, Local Protectionism and Industrial Location in China. *China Economic Quarterly* 5(3): 733–760.

Industry Statistics Department of the National Bureau of Statistics of China. 2001 (since 2001 to 2011). China Industry Economy Statistical Yearbook-2001 (since 2001 to 2011). Beijing: China Statistics Press.

Jin, Y., Z. Chen, and M. Lu. 2006. Industry Agglomeration in China: Economic Geography, New Economic Geography and Policy. *Economic Research* 4: 79–89.

Lin, J. Y. 2012. *New Structural Economics: A Framework for Rethinking Development and Policy*. Beijing: Beijing University Press.

Lu, J., and Z. Tao. 2006. Industrial Agglomeration and Co-agglomeration in China's Manufacturing Industries: with International Comparison. *Economic Research* 3: 103–114.

———. 2007. Determinants of Industrial Agglomeration in China: Evidence from Panel Data. *China Economic Quarterly* 6(3): 801–816.

Luo, Y., and L. Cao. 2005. A Positive Research on Fluctuation Trend of China's Manufacturing Industrial Agglomeration Degree. *Economic Research* 8: 106–115.

Ma, J. 1989. *The Skewed Pyramid: Unbalancing Industrial Structure in China.* Beijing: Academy Press.

National Bureau of Statistics of China. 2000 (since 2000 to 2011). *China Statistical Yearbook–2000 (since 2000 to 2011).* Beijing: China Statistics Press.

———. 2006. *China Economic Census Yearbook–2004.* Beijing: China Statistics Press.

———. 2010. *China Economic Census Yearbook–2008.* Beijing: China Statistics Press.

Nie, H., T. Jiang, and D. Yang. 2012. A Review and Reflection on the Use and Abuse of Chinese Industrial Enterprises Database. *World Economy* 5: 142–158.

Song, L., and X. Wang. 2013. Industry Policy, Resource Allocation and Productivity. *Management World* 12: 63–77.

Urban Social and Economic Investigation Department of the National Bureau of Statistics of China. 2011. *China Urban Life and Price Yearbook–2011.* Beijing: China Statistics Press.

Wang, Y., and H. Wei. 2007. Characteristics of Industries, Competition for Space and the Geographic Concentration in Manufacture. *Management World* 4: 68–77.

Wang, F., Y. Wang, Y. Tang, and J. Fang. 2010. Whether the Time has Come for Manufacturing Dispersion. *Zhejiang Social Sciences* 9: 2–10.

Wen, M. 2004. Relocation and Agglomeration of Chinese Industry. *Journal of Development Economics* 73(1): 329–347.

Xu, X., X. Wang, and Y. Shu. 2007. Local Officials and Economic Growth. *Economic Research* 9: 18–31.

Zhou, L. 2004. The Incentive and Cooperation of Government Officials in the Political Tournaments: An Interpretation of the Prolonged Local Protectionism and Duplicative Investments in China. *Economic Research* 7: 36–50.

———. 2007. Governing China's Local Officials: An Analysis of Promotion Tournament Model. *Economic Research* 7: 36–50.

APPENDIX 1

1. Data Source and Collection

Data used in the paper are collected from the *China Industry Economy Statistical Yearbook,* the first and the second *China Economic Census Yearbook,* the *China Statistical Yearbook,* the *Almanac of China's Economy,* and provincial statistical yearbooks. First, we used the first and the second *China Economic Census Yearbook* and *China Industry Economy Statistical Yearbook* from 2001 to 2011 to collect the gross product of industrial enterprises above designated size of 37 two-digit industries in the PRC's 31 provinces as follows: 25 industries from 1999 to 2010 (See note 1), 10 industries in 2004 and 2008 (see note 2) and nonmetal mining and clothing industries from 2004 to 2010. Second, we collected the gross product of nonmetal mining and clothing industries in 2003 and 10 other industries in the remaining years from the provincial statistics yearbooks. Last, due to the inconsistency in some provinces, some data were recalculated or adjusted. The adjustments are as follows:

(1)   The yearbooks of Henan and Liaoning provinces do not provide the gross product of these 10 industries from 2005 to 2010. Thus, we calculated the gross product of these 10 industries from 2005 to 2007 through the added value and the ratio of added value in *Liaoning Statistical Yearbook.* Because of the lack of a ratio of added value in 2009 and 2010, we calculated the gross product by main operating income and the average ratio between main operating income and gross product in previous years. The missing data in *Henan Statistical Yearbook* was also calculated by the above approach.

(2)   Since the statistical data reported in 2000 *Shanghai Statistical Yearbook* is at village and above level, the data of plastic product industries in Shanghai in 1999 were adjusted by the ratio between industrial enterprises above designated size and enterprises in villages and above.

(3) Zhejiang and other six provinces miss some data or have changed statistical criteria. The missing data of Zhejiang province (from 1999 to 2003) were collected from *60 Years' Collections of Statistics of Zhejiang Province (Zhejiang 60 Nian Tongji Ziliao Huibian)*. The missing data of Guangxi province (2003, from 2005 to 2007) were collected from the relevant years' *Almanac of China's Yearbook*. The missing data of Inner Mongolia (from 2000 to 2001), Qinghai (2002), and Gansu (from 2000 to 2002) provinces were calculated by the average rate of growth of adjacent years. The missing data of Chongqing (from 1999 to 2002) were calculated by the average rate of growth from 2004 to 2010.

2. Data Cleaning

Since the panel data of the 37 industries used in this paper come from different yearbooks, some of which are even by calculation, it is necessary to check for consistency and accuracy. The verification is conducted at two levels.

First, we adjust the unit of gross product into 100 million with two digits. The 10,354 data from the *China Industry Economy Statistical Yearbook,* the first and the second *China Economic Census Yearbook* are denoted as x_{irt}^{china}, and the corresponding data from provincial yearbooks are marked as x_{irt}^{local}. The difference between the above data sets is defined by $\mu_{irt} \equiv \left| x_{irt}^{china} - x_{irt}^{local} \right| / x_{irt}^{china}$. As shown in Table A11.1 below, 98.33% of the data are consistent and 99.42% are less than 1% difference. Therefore, we believed the industrial data calculated by the National Bureau of Statistics and local bureaus of statistics are highly consistent. As for the different data, we found that most were caused by the discrepancy between classification of some industries, and some were caused by the lagged effect of criteria adjustment in local statistics. When difference occurred, we took the data compiled by the NBS.

Table A11.1: The Comparison of National and Provincial Statistics from 1999 to 2010 (%)

Δ	Δ=0	0<Δ≤0.5%	0.5%<Δ≤1%	1%<Δ≤5%	5%<Δ≤10%	10%<Δ	Total
%	98.33	0.79	0.29	0.26	0.11	0.20	100

Second, we have checked the consistency of data from *China Statistical Yearbook* and data used in this paper from the perspective of sum value. First of all, we add up the output of the 37 industries and from the 31 provinces, respectively. The difference between the added-up value by industry $\left(x_{it}^{\sigma}\right)$ or by province $\left(x_{rt}^{\sigma}\right)$ and corresponding data from *China Statistical Yearbook* (x_{it}^{c} and x_{rt}^{c} respectively) is defined as $\mu_{it} \equiv \left|x_{it}^{c} - x_{it}^{\sigma}\right|/x_{it}^{c}$ and $\mu_{rt} \equiv \left|x_{rt}^{c} - x_{rt}^{\sigma}\right|/x_{rt}^{c}$, respectively. Due to the data limitation and a major change in the criteria of industry classification in 2003, we select 37 industries (GB/T4754-2002) as the object. Thus, the comparison above should pay attention to the influence of the added-up value from the following industries: (1) from 1999 to 2002, wood and bamboo processing, other minerals processing and weapons and ammunition manufacturing; (2) after 2003, other minerals processing and wasted resources and materials recovery and processing. As shown by the results, the differences of the 372 values by province are all below 0.5%. As for the values by industry, the 434 differences out of 436 are below 0.5%, except for furniture manufacturing (0.846%, 1999) and stationery and sports products manufacturing (0.501%, 2000) (since *China Statistical Yearbook* lacks relevant data, the added-up of crafts and others manufacturing from 1999 to 2002 were not verified, leaving 436 pairs of data).

By verification at the above two levels, the statistical data this research relies on are highly consistent. In a word, the construction of the provincial and industrial database by the statistics from *China Industry Economy Statistical Yearbook*, the census data, and provincial statistical yearbooks is feasible and reliable.

Note 1: These 25 two-digit industries refer to Mining and Washing of Coal, Extraction of Petroleum and Natural Gas, Mining and Processing of Ferrous Metal Ores, Mining and Processing of Non-Ferrous Metal Ores, Processing of Food from Agricultural Products, Processing of Foodstuff, Manufacture of Beverages, Manufacture of Tobacco, Manufacture of Textile, Printing Reproduction of Recording Media, Processing of Petroleum, Coking, Processing of Nuclear Fuel, Manufacture of Raw Chemical Materials and Chemical Products, Manufacture of Medicines, Manufacture of Chemical Fibers, Manufacture of Non-metallic Mineral Products, Smelting and Pressing of Ferrous Metals, Smelting and Pressing of Non-ferrous Metals, Manufacture of Metal Products, Manufacture of General Purpose Machinery, Manufacture of Special Purpose Machinery, Manufacture of Transport Equipment, Manufacture of Electrical Machinery and Equipment, Manufacture of Communication Equipment, Computers and other Electronic Equipment, Manufacture of Measuring Instruments and Machinery for Cultural Activity and Office Work, and Producing and Supply of Electric Power and Heat Power.

Note 2: These 10 two-digit industries refer to Manufacture of Leather, Fur, Feather, and Related Products; Processing of Timber; Manufacture of Wood, Bamboo Rattan, Palm and Straw Products; Manufacture of Furniture; Manufacture of Paper and Paper Products; Manufacture of Articles for Culture, Education and Sport Activities; Manufacture of Rubber; Manufacture of Plastics; Manufacture of Artwork and Other Manufacturing; Producing and Supply of Gas; and Producing and Supply of Water.

Table A11.2: Time Series for Geographic Concentration ($CONC_i$) and the Relative Rate of Change

Industry Code	1999	2000	2001	2002	2003	2004	2005
06	2.705	2.735	2.690	2.647	2.599	2.576	2.574
07	2.328	2.289	2.326	2.372	2.418	2.417	2.427
08	2.537	2.521	2.503	2.521	2.479	2.673	2.678
09	2.644	2.630	2.666	2.644	2.544	2.593	2.626
10	2.896	2.896	2.902	2.883	2.842	2.809	2.764
13	2.917	2.861	2.828	2.799	2.801	2.777	2.750
14	2.914	2.919	2.912	2.940	2.931	2.947	2.901
15	3.012	3.008	3.002	3.003	2.997	3.027	2.999
16	2.744	2.744	2.782	2.816	2.838	2.846	2.862
17	2.508	2.511	2.450	2.395	2.374	2.286	2.280
18	2.250	2.246	2.235	2.220	2.194	2.208	2.220
19	2.306	2.294	2.286	2.205	2.207	2.246	2.262
20	2.735	2.736	2.734	2.741	2.771	2.732	2.718
21	2.667	2.671	2.578	2.541	2.438	2.384	2.393
22	2.781	2.729	2.713	2.663	2.605	2.561	2.577
23	2.867	2.838	2.819	2.798	2.690	2.665	2.666
24	1.961	1.935	1.956	1.980	1.960	1.930	1.956
25	2.872	2.850	2.855	2.870	2.884	2.901	2.920
26	2.957	2.940	2.898	2.873	2.857	2.840	2.804
27	3.101	3.095	3.086	3.086	3.074	3.061	3.041
28	2.464	2.417	2.374	2.320	2.113	2.035	1.968
29	2.729	2.712	2.631	2.538	2.504	2.497	2.475
30	2.462	2.462	2.489	2.456	2.423	2.435	2.444
31	2.937	2.939	2.929	2.929	2.902	2.871	2.834
32	2.976	2.966	2.972	2.967	2.936	2.914	2.894
33	3.133	3.135	3.129	3.133	3.106	3.064	3.033
34	2.552	2.536	2.528	2.493	2.436	2.446	2.464
35	2.652	2.632	2.618	2.604	2.560	2.580	2.587
36	2.716	2.697	2.698	2.708	2.810	2.786	2.794
37	2.879	2.886	2.889	2.883	2.881	2.910	2.923

continued next page

Table A11.2: *Continued*

Industry Code	1999	2000	2001	2002	2003	2004	2005
39	2.513	2.489	2.462	2.438	2.404	2.389	2.392
40	2.293	2.289	2.227	2.179	2.077	2.024	2.013
41	2.312	2.251	2.296	2.309	2.224	2.230	2.241
42	2.469	2.466	2.448	2.425	2.294	2.371	2.315
44	3.099	3.086	3.098	3.101	3.114	3.089	3.085
45	2.894	2.821	2.875	2.820	2.856	2.820	2.776
46	2.839	2.968	2.977	3.000	2.975	2.949	2.944
TYPCONC	2.724	2.709	2.694	2.672	2.638	2.627	2.612
Hoover1	0.364	0.366	0.369	0.371	0.379	0.376	0.381
Hoover2	0.350	0.351	0.353	0.356	0.361	0.353	0.356

Industry Code	2006	2007	2008	2009	2010	99–05	05–10
06	2.559	2.587	2.658	2.688	2.707	−0.131	0.133
07	2.453	2.474	2.492	2.575	2.542	0.098	0.115
08	2.623	2.658	2.603	2.547	2.611	0.141	−0.067
09	2.738	2.681	2.670	2.619	2.636	−0.018	0.009
10	2.804	2.799	2.847	2.858	2.892	−0.132	0.128
13	2.755	2.769	2.812	2.827	2.875	−0.167	0.124
14	2.897	2.892	2.918	2.919	2.971	−0.012	0.069
15	3.020	3.034	3.048	3.035	3.029	−0.013	0.030
16	2.872	2.876	2.899	2.915	2.910	0.118	0.048
17	2.267	2.277	2.280	2.313	2.354	−0.227	0.074
18	2.223	2.253	2.301	2.353	2.406	−0.030	0.187
19	2.272	2.306	2.322	2.335	2.345	−0.044	0.083
20	2.704	2.699	2.718	2.724	2.761	−0.017	0.043
21	2.427	2.419	2.431	2.486	2.545	−0.274	0.152
22	2.571	2.571	2.600	2.648	2.695	−0.204	0.118
23	2.701	2.720	2.735	2.742	2.761	−0.201	0.095
24	1.962	1.973	1.999	2.019	2.071	−0.006	0.115
25	2.930	2.958	2.971	2.987	3.006	0.048	0.087
26	2.783	2.792	2.800	2.764	2.805	−0.153	0.001
27	3.040	3.029	3.016	3.011	3.014	−0.061	−0.027
28	1.868	1.911	1.853	1.837	1.809	−0.496	−0.159

continued next page

Table A11.2: Continued

Industry Code	2006	2007	2008	2009	2010	99–05	05–10
29	2.489	2.485	2.474	2.453	2.496	−0.254	0.022
30	2.455	2.454	2.524	2.566	2.601	−0.018	0.157
31	2.826	2.826	2.849	2.886	2.930	−0.103	0.096
32	2.891	2.904	2.900	2.888	2.911	−0.082	0.017
33	3.015	3.001	2.971	2.950	2.975	−0.099	−0.058
34	2.458	2.472	2.543	2.591	2.618	−0.088	0.154
35	2.577	2.597	2.620	2.628	2.661	−0.064	0.074
36	2.802	2.814	2.832	2.836	2.831	0.078	0.037
37	2.913	2.905	2.895	2.897	2.902	0.044	−0.021
39	2.406	2.437	2.483	2.535	2.552	−0.122	0.161
40	2.037	2.055	2.038	2.047	2.072	−0.280	0.059
41	2.277	2.290	2.351	2.393	2.387	−0.071	0.146
42	2.312	2.320	2.366	2.425	2.457	−0.154	0.142
44	3.085	3.090	3.121	3.133	3.142	−0.015	0.057
45	2.791	2.791	2.811	2.850	2.887	−0.118	0.111
46	2.844	2.838	2.868	2.905	2.944	0.105	0.000
TYPCONC	2.612	2.625	2.641	2.664	2.687	−0.112	0.074
Hoover1	0.383	0.384	0.380	0.378	0.376	0.017	−0.005
Hoover2	0.356	0.353	0.345	0.342	0.337	0.006	−0.019

Notes: Hoover1 and Hoover2 are simple average and weighted average, respectively. Two-digit industry code in the table are explained as follows: Mining and Washing of Coal (06); Extraction of Petroleum and Natural Gas (07); Mining and Processing of Ferrous Metal Ores (08); Mining and Processing of Non-Ferrous Metal Ores (09); Mining and Processing of Nonmetal Ores (10); Processing of Food from Agricultural Products (13); Processing of Foodstuff (14); Manufacture of Beverages (15); Manufacture of Tobacco (16); Manufacture of Textile (17); Manufacture of Textile Wearing Apparel, Footwear, and Caps (18); Manufacture of Leather, Fur, Feather, and Related Products (19); Processing of Timber, Manufacture of Wood ,Bamboo Rattan, Palm and Straw Products (20); Manufacture of Furniture (21); Manufacture of Paper and Paper Products (22); Printing Reproduction of Recording Media (23); Manufacture of Articles for Culture, Education and Sport Activities (24); Processing of Petroleum, Coking, Processing of Nuclear Fuel (25); Manufacture of Raw Chemical Materials and Chemical Products (26); Manufacture of Medicines (27); Manufacture of Chemical Fibers (28); Manufacture of Rubber (29); Manufacture of Plastics (30); Manufacture of Non-metallic Mineral Products (31); Smelting and Pressing of Ferrous Metals (32); Smelting and Pressing of Non-ferrous Metals (33); Manufacture of Metal Products (34); Manufacture of General Purpose Machinery (35); Manufacture of Special Purpose Machinery (36); Manufacture of Transport Equipment (38); Manufacture of Electrical Machinery and Equipment (39); Manufacture of Communication Equipment, Computers and other Electronic Equipment (40); Manufacture of Measuring Instruments and Machinery for Cultural Activity and Office Work (41); Manufacture of Artwork and Other Manufacturing (42); Producing and Supply of Electric Power and Heat Power (44); Producing and Supply of Gas (45); Producing and Supply of Water (46).

Table A11.3: Time Series for Industrial Specialization ($SPEC_R$) and the Relative Rate of Change

Province Name	1999	2000	2001	2002	2003	2004	2005
Beijing	2.877	2.736	2.732	2.788	2.775	2.772	2.649
Tianjin	3.056	3.001	2.967	2.934	2.909	2.801	2.728
Hebei	3.122	3.117	3.104	3.073	2.961	2.858	2.830
Shanxi	2.538	2.570	2.530	2.523	2.437	2.379	2.374
Inner Mongolia	2.743	2.742	2.761	2.772	2.800	2.801	2.805
Liaoning	2.974	2.961	2.962	2.955	2.953	2.933	2.987
Jilin	2.633	2.586	2.498	2.344	2.193	2.321	2.399
Heilongjiang	2.229	2.342	2.429	2.507	2.578	2.670	2.679
Shanghai	3.110	3.095	3.038	3.014	2.895	2.889	2.821
Jiangsu	3.138	3.130	3.126	3.106	3.043	2.960	2.942
Zhejiang	3.175	3.186	3.172	3.154	3.165	3.142	3.143
Anhui	3.186	3.198	3.173	3.178	3.149	3.113	3.113
Fujian	3.201	3.211	3.207	3.146	3.126	3.089	3.103
Jiangxi	3.092	3.103	3.093	3.047	3.046	3.069	3.103
Shandong	3.253	3.238	3.244	3.237	3.233	3.237	3.222
Henan	3.208	3.215	3.213	3.198	3.183	3.175	3.178
Hubei	3.138	3.135	3.115	3.053	3.051	2.851	2.947
Hunan	3.122	3.141	3.157	3.176	3.162	3.137	3.175
Guangdong	3.189	3.142	3.068	2.989	2.889	2.830	2.784
Guangxi	3.032	3.023	3.005	2.930	2.869	2.804	2.835
Hainan	2.973	3.033	2.979	2.905	2.780	2.733	2.797
Chongqing	2.825	2.665	2.611	2.581	2.492	2.543	2.575
Sichuan	3.076	3.069	3.061	3.077	3.101	3.118	3.107
Guizhou	2.762	2.802	2.789	2.808	2.837	2.718	2.684
Yunnan	2.485	2.473	2.445	2.447	2.460	2.543	2.563
Tibet Autonomous Region	2.470	2.507	2.435	2.407	2.191	2.087	2.132
Shaanxi	3.009	3.019	2.986	2.990	2.980	3.007	2.996
Gansu	2.794	2.856	2.786	2.834	2.796	2.612	2.577
Qinghai	2.256	2.182	2.294	2.325	2.364	2.277	2.358
Ningxia	2.735	2.759	2.742	2.782	2.762	2.703	2.712
Xinjiang	2.107	2.222	2.313	2.367	2.399	2.392	2.351
TYPSPEC	3.053	3.045	3.030	3.011	2.972	2.940	2.931
Hoover3	0.454	0.458	0.463	0.470	0.475	0.472	0.478
Hoover4	0.360	0.359	0.363	0.371	0.370	0.365	0.368

continued next page

Table A11.3: *Continued*

Province Name	2006	2007	2008	2009	2010	99–05	05–10
Beijing	2.569	2.544	2.625	2.656	2.641	−0.228	−0.008
Tianjin	2.635	2.656	2.773	2.781	2.843	−0.328	0.116
Hebei	2.826	2.833	2.819	2.829	2.871	−0.292	0.041
Shanxi	2.375	2.350	2.352	2.378	2.430	−0.164	0.056
Inner Mongolia	2.820	2.871	2.884	2.935	2.966	0.063	0.160
Liaoning	3.019	3.053	3.076	3.073	3.054	0.013	0.067
Jilin	2.415	2.431	2.592	2.547	2.495	−0.234	0.096
Heilongjiang	2.735	2.777	2.842	2.862	2.925	0.449	0.246
Shanghai	2.782	2.716	2.721	2.700	2.649	−0.289	−0.171
Jiangsu	2.936	2.914	2.905	2.903	2.884	−0.196	−0.058
Zhejiang	3.140	3.132	3.127	3.123	3.122	−0.032	−0.021
Anhui	3.114	3.112	3.103	3.083	3.096	−0.074	−0.017
Fujian	3.114	3.139	3.155	3.178	3.167	−0.098	0.064
Jiangxi	3.106	3.114	3.105	3.112	3.106	0.011	0.003
Shandong	3.212	3.210	3.203	3.181	3.171	−0.032	−0.051
Henan	3.200	3.160	3.206	3.209	3.215	−0.030	0.036
Hubei	2.950	2.960	2.913	2.959	2.925	−0.191	−0.022
Hunan	3.181	3.185	3.211	3.203	3.198	0.053	0.023
Guangdong	2.769	2.801	2.794	2.802	2.783	−0.405	−0.002
Guangxi	2.843	2.878	2.899	2.876	2.924	−0.197	0.088
Hainan	2.807	2.591	2.671	2.654	2.668	−0.177	−0.128
Chongqing	2.515	2.477	2.588	2.577	2.619	−0.250	0.044
Sichuan	3.129	3.150	3.208	3.200	3.184	0.031	0.077
Guizhou	2.678	2.683	2.718	2.716	2.735	−0.078	0.051
Yunnan	2.591	2.608	2.660	2.700	2.700	0.078	0.136
Tibet Autonomous Region	2.157	2.215	2.263	2.217	2.209	−0.338	0.077
Shaanxi	2.986	2.969	2.988	3.000	2.995	−0.013	−0.001
Gansu	2.593	2.597	2.674	2.725	2.753	−0.217	0.177
Qinghai	2.399	2.446	2.496	2.546	2.519	0.102	0.161
Ningxia	2.689	2.696	2.704	2.767	2.757	−0.023	0.045
Xinjiang	2.430	2.542	2.594	2.651	2.710	0.244	0.359
TYPSPEC	2.928	2.931	2.948	2.954	2.947	−0.122	0.015
Hoover3	0.479	0.476	0.467	0.459	0.452	0.024	−0.026
Hoover4	0.366	0.362	0.355	0.351	0.346	0.009	−0.022

Note: Hoover3 and Hoover4 are simple average and weighted average, respectively.

Table A11.4: Definitions and Summary Statistics of Key Variables

Name	Definition	N	Mean	SD	Min	Max
Δp_{ir}	$\Delta p_{ir}=(x_{ir2010}/x_{r2010}-x_{ir2005}/x_{r2005})\cdot 100\%$, change of industry i's output in province r out of the gross output of province r from 2005 to 2010.	1,147	0.000	1.691	−15.579	21.752
Δs_{ir}	$\Delta s_{ir}=(x_{ir2010}/x_{i2010}-x_{ir2005}/x_{i2005})\cdot 100\%$, change of industry i's output in province r out of the gross output of industry i from 2005 to 2010.	1,147	0.000	1.494	−12.384	10.454
$plan_{ir}$	Dummy variable, $plan_{ir}=1$ for industry chosen as priority one in province r's 11th 5-year plan, otherwise $plan_{ir}=0$.	1,147	0.462	0.499	0	1
Δp_{irL}	$\Delta p_{irL}=(x_{ir2004}/x_{r2004}-x_{ir1999}/x_{r1999})\cdot 100\%$, change of industry i's output in province r out of the gross output of province r from 1999 to 2004.	1,147	0.000	2.068	−21.597	14.319
Δs_{irL}	$\Delta s_{irL}=(x_{ir2005}/x_{i2005}-x_{ir2004}/x_{i2004})\cdot 100\%$, change of industry i's output in province r out of the gross output of industry i from 2004 to 2005.	1,147	0.000	0.605	−5.764	4.607
$ar_{ir\text{-}L3}$	$ar_{ir\text{-}L3}=[(x_{ir2005}/x_{ir2002})^{1/3}-1]\cdot 100\%$, growth rate of industry i's output in province r from 2002 to 2005.	1,110	1.960	13.008	−1	425.5
$ar_{ir\text{-}L6}$	$ar_{ir\text{-}L6}=[(x_{ir2004}/x_{ir1999})^{1/5}-1]\cdot 100\%$, growth rate of industry i's output in province r from 1999 to 2004.	1,110	0.227	0.351	−1	3.659
Rplan	Dummy variable, $rplan=1$ for provinces listed in regional development plan during the 11th 5-year plan, otherwise $rplan=0$.	1,147	0.677	0.468	0	1
Cplan	Dummy variable, $cplan=1$ for industry chosen as priority one in the central government's 11th 5-year plan, otherwise $cplan=0$.	1,147	0.459	0.499	0	1
p_{ir03}	$p_{ir03}=x_{ir2003}/x_{r2003}\cdot 100\%$, share of industry i's output in province r out of the gross output of province r in 2003.	1,147	2.703	4.384	0	48.005

continued next page

Table A11.4: *Continued*

Name	Definition	N	Mean	SD	Min	Max
s_{ir03}	$s_{ir03} = x_{ir2003}/x_{i2003} \cdot 100\%$, share of industry i's output in province r out of the gross output of industry i in 2003.	1,147	3.226	5.077	0	37.778
scl_{ir04}	$scl_{ir04} = (x_{ir2004Small}/x_{ir2004}) \cdot 100\%$, share of output of industry i's small enterprise in province r out of the gross output of industry i in 2004.	924	0.473	0.396	-7.64	1
$firm_{ir}$	Number of province r's firms in industry i in 2000. (100 firms)	1,144	1.371	2.333	0	20.56
sfm_{ir}	quadratic term of $firm_{ir}$.	1,144	7.319	30.304	0	422.714
$isfm_i$	Number of firms in industry i in 2000. (10,000 firms)	1,147	0.293	0.418	0	1.894
$lngdp_r$	Logarithm of gross regional product of province r in 2003.	1,147	8.939	1.081	6.027	10.737
$lnpop_r$	Logarithm of population of province r in 2004.	1,147	8.036	0.886	5.598	9.176
$trans_r$	$trans_r = \Sigma b_k \cdot \Delta tr_{rk}/area_r$, Δtr_{rk} stands for change of province r's length of type k (road, rail, river) transportation infrastructure during the implementation period of the 11th 5-year plan, b_k stands for the share of cargo turnover of type k (road, rail, river) transportation infrastructure, $area_r$ stands for area of province r (10,000 km²).	1,147	1.129	1.039	0.003	4.336
$ntrans_r$	$ntrans_r = \Sigma_j a_{rj} \cdot \Sigma_k b_k \cdot \Delta tr_{rk}/\Sigma_j a_{rj} \cdot area_r$, Δtr_{rk}, b_k and $area_r$ as above, $a_{rr}=1$, if province r is adjacent to province j, then $a_{rj}=1$, otherwise $a_{rj}=0$	1,147	0.111	0.072	0.000	0.259
$plan_{irn}$	Dummy variable, $plan_{irn}=1$ for industry chosen as priority one in province r's nth 5-year plan, otherwise $plan_{irn}=0$.	2,294	0.417	0.493	0	1
Δp_{irn}	$\Delta p_{irn} = (x_{irt}/x_{rt}-x_{ir\,t-5}/x_{r,t-5}) \cdot 100\%$, change of industry i's output in province r out of the gross output of province r from year t-5 to t, year t is the last implementation year of the nth five year plan.	2,294	0.000	1.780	-15.677	21.751

continued next page

Table A11.4: *Continued*

Name	Definition	N	Mean	SD	Min	Max
Δs_{irn}	$\Delta s_{irn} = (x_{irt}/x_{it} - x_{ir,t-5}/x_{i,t-5}) \cdot 100\%$, change of industry i's output in province r out of the gross output of industry i from year t-5 to t, with t as above.	2,294	0.000	1.663	-16.992	23.260
fm_{irnL}	number of province r's firms in industry i in year t-7, t as above. (100 firms)	2,254	1.899	4.116	0	66.47
x_{irnL}	output of industry i in province r in year t-5, t as above (billion yuan)	2,294	1.369	3.89	0	108.477
x_{irnL2}	output of industry i in province r in year t-6, t as above (billion yuan)	2,294	1.154	3.154	0	85.172
ar_{irnL}	$ar_{irnL} = (x_{ir,t-5}/x_{ir,t-6}) - 1$, t as above.	2,211	0.192	0.574	-1	12.5
s_{irnL}	share of industry i's output in province r out of the gross output of industry i in year t-6, t as above.	2,294	3.226	4.937	0	37.431
$lntrs_{rn}$	$lntrs_{rn} = \ln(\Sigma b_{kn} \cdot \Delta tr_{rkn}/area_r)$, Δtr_{rkn} stands for change of province r's length of type k (road, rail, river) transportation infrastructure during the implementation period of the nth 5-year plan, b_{kn} stands for the share of cargo turnover of type k (road, rail, river) transportation infrastructure $area_r$ stands for area of province r (10,000 km²).	2,294	5.357	1.758	0	8.375

Does Fiscal Decentralization Help Indonesia Avoid the Middle-Income Trap?

Darius Tirtosuharto

12.1 | Introduction

The implementation of decentralization has elevated the pivotal role of local governments in managing economic development. Supporting economic growth and development at the regional level relies on various policies and strategies by local governments, particularly in providing public services along with incentive structures for private sector advancement. A sufficient public services delivery itself is key to supporting private sector development and stimulating economic activities in the regions. But the effectiveness of local government policies and programs to ensure optimal public services delivery is still questionable, considering the extent of fiscal inefficiency within the local government institutions. This becomes a major issue in many developing countries since good public services are considered to be a critical enabler to accelerate economic growth and sustain the development process to avoid the middle-income trap.

A paper by the World Bank to mark the 10 years since the term "middle-income trap" was first introduced in 2006, highlights the importance of the institutional aspect of governments. Gill and Kharas (2015) argued that one of the main challenges faced by many middle-income countries now is how to manage the distribution of growth benefits at all levels. This is considered to be of key importance for escaping the middle-income trap, primarily through better and more efficient public service delivery (health, education, low-cost housing) as enablers of economic development particularly in the manufacturing sector. Following the Solow growth model that emphasizes physical and human capital accumulation, improving the skills of a pool of cheap labor in most middle-income countries would trigger the higher growth necessary to move up the ladder to become a high-income country.

Among the roles of local governments in a decentralized system is the responsibility for and capability to manage fiscal resources. Fiscal decentralization transfers the fiscal responsibility to subnational governments based on the premise that local governments are more efficient in allocating fiscal resources than the central government. The main reason for that premise is the fact that local governments have closer interactions with their constituents (Bird and Wallich 1993; Oates 1993). However, due to differences in the political and socioeconomic landscapes between regions, the net fiscal benefits from the implementation of fiscal decentralization differ from one region to another. Consequently, the impact of fiscal decentralization on regional growth also varies. It is crucial, therefore, to identify determining factors that affect fiscal efficiency at the local government level as it becomes one of the factors for economic development and transition to a high-income country.

In reviewing the concept of fiscal efficiency as an indication of the effectiveness and responsiveness of local government institutions, the major issue is how to measure and identify its factor determinants.[1] Lack of reliable data and methodology, and the fact that many policies and strategies of development are inconsistent, have made it difficult to measure fiscal efficiency. Assessing the performance of state governments using comparative data is not a simple task, therefore.

---

[1]   In the literature, the efficiency of government institutions has generally been assessed through the size of government and public services delivery. It is commonly assumed that bigger governments are bad since they are less efficient. Efficiency of governments is also measured through the cost structure associated with public services delivery. Following Tiebout's hypothesis, people are concerned about the net fiscal benefits, as they compare the quality of public services and taxes that are levied to provide those services.

DOES FISCAL DECENTRALIZATION HELP INDONESIA
AVOID THE MIDDLE-INCOME TRAP?

385

One approach to evaluate fiscal efficiency is by analyzing part of the fiscal expenditure side. Allocation of fiscal expenditure has an embedded assumption of utility maximization. This is based on the assumption that local governments face budget constraints in allocating their spending. Thus, under rational expectations theory, local governments are to maximize the utilization of their fiscal resources to reap the greatest benefits for public welfare in their respective regions. In this regard, allocation of fiscal expenditure becomes a proxy for the institutional quality of local governments.

Other factors that determine the efficiency of state governments in allocating their fiscal expenditure is the degree of fiscal decentralization, following the argument that decentralization will improve efficiency levels of local governments due to their ability to identify the priorities and needs of their respective regions (Bardhan 2002). If it is confirmed that a higher degree of fiscal decentralization will lead to higher fiscal efficiency, then decentralized middle-income countries are likely to become high-income countries more quickly.

With the growing concern over implementation and policies of decentralization in developing countries, this study contributes to the policy discourse on whether decentralization supports the goal of transitioning to a high-income country. With limited sources of public financing, it becomes more vital for local governments to avert further waste in fiscal resources. More importantly, the finding of this study also supports further enhancement of policies related to decentralization that can prevent Indonesia from falling into the middle-income trap due to inefficiency in the allocation of fiscal resources.

This empirical study attempts to measure local government fiscal efficiency in Indonesia and establish its determining factors. The empirical analysis consists of a two-stage analysis: a non-parametric data envelopment analysis (DEA) to calculate fiscal efficiency scores of state (provincial) governments in Indonesia, and a Tobit panel data model to analyze the determining factors of state fiscal efficiency. This study uses regional fiscal data in Indonesia from 1996 to 2005, which includes approximately 5 years of data before and after the implementation of decentralization in 2001.

12.2 | Institutional Setting and Development in Asia

Only a few Asian economies have managed to escape the middle-income trap since the 1960s and of those economies, three (Japan; the Republic of Korea; and Taipei,China) were initially set up as a centralized government system before they made the transition to a decentralized government system.[2] Following a global wave of liberalization in the 1990s, those three economies, as well as other countries in Asia and the Pacific, began to decentralize their system of government. Decentralization was seen as a means to liberalize the political and economic aspects of the governance system. Hence, there has been lack of evidence on whether the institutional setting of decentralization plays a major role in the transition to becoming a high-income country.

In general, there are three phenomena that can describe the process of decentralization worldwide (Huang 2009): (1) comprehensive big-bang political-economic devolution (Indonesia, South Africa); (2) comprehensive political devolution and uneven or partial economic devolution (Brazil, India); and (3) limited political devolution with more significant administrative and economic devolution (People's Republic of China). These differences in the institutional setting of decentralization may affect the outcomes both in political and economic aspects. To a certain degree, the outcomes of decentralized systems of government will also affect the stages of economic development. Japan's transition to a decentralized system of government was not followed by a shift in political ideology and therefore provided relatively stable governments. On the other hand, decentralization was part of a democratic transition in Indonesia; the Republic of Korea; and Taipei,China.

Countries also experience different stages of systemic change in decentralization, which is in line with the challenges faced in improving the institutional quality of local governments. There are primarily four stages of

---

[2]   The others are island economies (Singapore and Hong Kong, China) that adopt a centralized government system.

DOES FISCAL DECENTRALIZATION HELP INDONESIA
AVOID THE MIDDLE-INCOME TRAP?

387

decentralization as measured by the degree of systemic change (Fritzen and Lim 2006): The first stage is bureaucracy reform, which is considered the hardest as it changes not only the system, but also the people within the system. The second stage is fiscal efficiency, which is considered the riskiest since it will affect the effectiveness of policy or program implementation. The third stage is democratization, which is critical for a country due to the potential conflicts associated with political friction at the regional level and between central and local governments. The fourth stage is market-preserving decentralization, which is considered to be the optimal condition as the decentralized system of government manages to support a sustainable market mechanism.

Early on, the characteristics of a centralized system of government could still be seen in the local government system in Japan. To supervise local governments, two systems of government operations were formed. Under the Agency Delegated Function System, the authority of local government was limited (Ikawa 2008). A central government minister or prefectural governor had the authority to supervise local governments under their jurisdiction. Beginning in the 1980s, there were several studies that promoted the revision of decentralization law by offering to reform the authority of local governments. The Omnibus Decentralization Law was finally enacted in 1999, and under this law the intervention (control) by central government was curtailed and local governments were given more authority over local revenue sources.

Among other considerations in reforming the relationship between central and local governments in Japan, the following points were considered important (Ikawa 2008): (1) a centralized system of government that prioritizes uniformity and efficiency in governing is effective when a country is in the catch-up stages of development; and (2) it is necessary to promote decentralization to be competitive in a dynamic global society.

The Republic of Korea experienced a similar transition from a centralized to a decentralized system of government. But despite the strong control by the central government, residents and civic organizations at the local level pushed for decentralization reform particularly from a political aspect.

One of the reasons for a strong state-led system of government was to ensure the direction of industrialization in the Republic of Korea from the 1960s to the 1980s (Park 2013). Under this strong state-led system of government, the authoritarian regime abolished the law that mandated a certain degree of decentralization and implemented a "command and control" system of intergovernmental relations. The democratization reform after 1987 brought a sociopolitical movement by local civil societies, which mainly focused on the practice of democracy at the local level. This became the embryo for decentralization reform later in the 1990s.

Despite a push for the implementation of local democracy, decentralization reform was delayed until the financial crisis hit in 1998. Under the agreement with the International Monetary Fund (IMF), the Government of the Republic of Korea agreed to implement public sector reform, which it directed toward more market economy. This reform was also aimed at strengthening the role of local governance as a means of gaining competitiveness and a speedy recovery of the economy. The shift to a democratic system in the Republic of Korea has proven to be relatively successful. After the implementation of post-crisis decentralization, most local governments focused on economic development and innovation. This was the reason for the continued economic progress that eventually lifted the Republic of Korea out of the middle-income trap after the 1998 crisis.[3]

For almost 50 years, Taipei,China followed a central state system of government due to the unique setting of its political institutions. Not until the enactment of the Law on Local Governments System in 1999 had decentralization finally been implemented to improve the local public service provisions. Similar to the case of the Republic of Korea, local governments played a significant role in improving public services after acquiring greater authority in managing local revenue sources. Health and education are two key sectors of public services that local governments have mainly prioritized.

---

[3]   Despite an increase in fiscal decentralization, central government transfers are still dominant in the Republic of Korea. The fiscal autonomy of local governments was even reduced from 1991 to 2005.

DOES FISCAL DECENTRALIZATION HELP INDONESIA
AVOID THE MIDDLE-INCOME TRAP?

389

Due to differences in the characteristics and complexity of each Asian
economy, the impact of decentralization can vary. The experiences of the
three Asian economies that managed to become high-income countries show
that the key is to achieve a market condition that preserves decentralization
through administrative (bureaucratic) and fiscal reform. Japan; the Republic
of Korea; and Taipei,China have been quite successful in implementing
bureaucratic and fiscal reform along with democratization. The systemic
change in these economies was implemented sequentially and also through
better planning and preparation. Even in the case of the Republic of Korea,
local democracy flourished before the 1988 financial crisis hit, which became
a trigger for further democratic reform. In the case of Indonesia, bureaucratic
and fiscal reform along with democratization took place in the same period
following the 1998 crisis, which resulted in a lack of preparation for improving
the capacity and capability of local institutions.

12.3 | Fiscal Decentralization and the Middle-Income Trap

The theoretical arguments for decentralization are primarily based on
allocative efficiency, which suggests that local governments should have
better knowledge of the needs in their respective regions. Local governments
also have an advantage in terms of planning and executing policies with
broader citizen participation (Maddick 1963). Rationally, local governments
are more capable and have greater credibility to deliver public goods in a
more efficient and innovative way compared with the central government,
which does not have a presence at the local level (Jin et al. 2001; Azis 2003).[4]
Thus, decentralization has the potential to improve efficiency due to the
ability of local governments to strategically mobilize and allocate resources.

---

[4]   Another way decentralization promotes democracy is through transparency and accountability,
in which citizens have a role in preserving good governance. In a democratic system, local district
elections provide a means for citizens to give their opinion.

It has also been argued that decentralization increases competitiveness among local governments and could potentially limit the size of the public sector, which leads to increased productivity (Gil et al. 2002).

Fiscal decentralization is defined as the mechanism of expenditure and revenue allocation within the intergovernmental finance system to ensure efficient delivery of public services (Rao 2003). The degree of fiscal decentralization, which is commonly used to measure the extent of decentralization, is defined as the share of subnational spending/revenue over total government spending/revenue (Oates 1993; Davoodi and Zou 1998; Woller and Phillips 1998; Ebel and Yilmaz 2003).

Based on the premise of allocative efficiency, fiscal decentralization can make the local economy more efficient and also promotes intergovernmental competition (Bardhan 2002). This implies that local governments should optimize the utilization of limited fiscal resources to increase public welfare. Excessive spending or a mismatch of expenditure assignments may hurt economic growth and regional development (Davoodi and Zou 1998; Devarajan 1998). Misallocation of fiscal resources is also influenced by the extent of rent seeking and corruption activities (Prud'homme 1995).

Theoretically, efficiency focuses on the relationship between inputs and outputs, which is also applied to measure the efficiency of fiscal allocation.[5] Hence, the term efficiency is quite different from effectiveness. Efficiency refers to the utilization of minimum resources to produce optimum outputs, whereas effectiveness refers to the extent allocated resources can produce positive results or meet targets. Given limited fiscal resources, both the efficiency and effectiveness of fiscal allocation is of crucial importance for local governments.

---

[5]   Neoclassical theory argues that organizations are not always efficient, consistent with the theory of X-inefficiency (Liebenstein 1996) that argues organizations do not necessarily operate at the optimum level.

DOES FISCAL DECENTRALIZATION HELP INDONESIA
AVOID THE MIDDLE-INCOME TRAP?

391

Figure 12.1: Efficiency and Effectiveness Matrix

High Effectiveness

	Effective, but excessively costly	Best, all-around performers	
Low Efficiency			High Efficiency
	Problematic and also underperforming	Efficiently managed, but insignificant results	

Low Effectiveness

Source: Adapted from the Standard Performance Management Best Practice.

High efficiency and high effectiveness is the ideal combination for the performance matrix depicted in Figure 12.1. The second-best situation is the case in which the allocation of resources produces a highly effective outcome but is very costly. The third-best scenario is the situation in which the allocation of resources is efficient, but the types of resources that are being allocated are not productive or effective. Finally, the worst circumstances are when allocation of resources is neither efficient nor produces a positive outcome. In the context of fiscal decentralization, the choices made by local governments about the four possible combinations of resource allocation and the decision to limit nonproductive allocation will ultimately affect development and economic growth.

The expected result of fiscal decentralization is higher efficiency levels of state governments in line with the basic premise of decentralization. In a democratic system, the incentive for state governments to allocate resources efficiently to support development in their respective region is also that people vote in local elections. This is tantamount to a referendum on the success and failure of state governments. Hence, the problem that persists in many developing countries is a lack of transparency and accountability.

There have so far been only a few studies on the relationship between fiscal decentralization and the middle-income trap, particularly when it comes to identifying the role of state governments. Gill and Kharas (2015) specifically stated that policy options to escape the middle-income trap are better formulated through democratic and decentralized government. Effectiveness and responsiveness of the local governments is a concern due to the speed of implementing policies and putting them into action, which will also affect the speed of moving up the ladder of development. Thus, it is critical to be able to measure the level of efficiency and effectiveness of state governments as part of an effort to promote good governance.

Another paper by the Brookings Institute (Woo 2009) and one by the Asia Foundation (Burke et al. 2014) stressed the need for having the right institutional setup to avoid the middle-income trap. Burke et al. (2014) argued that decentralized economic policy making will promote investment initiatives and induce growth competition among local governments. Specifically related to fiscal decentralization, an independent fiscal base (revenues) will allow local governments to respond promptly to infrastructure bottlenecks—a crucial issue in most middle-income countries. Woo (2009) also supported reforms and policy action that further decentralization and could offer more effective incentives, higher accountability, and transparency in the delivery of public services.

12.4 | Measuring Fiscal Efficiency

To measure the fiscal efficiency of local governments, we employ a two-stage method to calculate the fiscal efficiency scores and a Tobit panel data model to analyze the determinants of state fiscal efficiency. In the first stage, we use data envelopment analysis (DEA) to construct a measure of technical efficiency of local governments. In the second stage of the analysis, we use Tobit panel data regression to reveal the factors that determine fiscal efficiency.

DOES FISCAL DECENTRALIZATION HELP INDONESIA
AVOID THE MIDDLE-INCOME TRAP?

393

Two analytical methods are commonly used to measure comparative performance in terms of technical efficiency. The first is the parametric technique that utilizes statistical regression analysis with single input–multiple outputs or single output–multiple inputs. Simple ordinary least square (OLS) regression can be used to estimate performance levels in the parametric models. Hence, the major limitation of the parametric model is the risk of dealing with inaccurate specifications since it is necessary to have several assumptions or hypotheses to be able to run an OLS regression.

To overcome the limitation of the standard parametric model with OLS regression in measuring technical efficiency, the second option is to utilize the Stochastic Frontier (SF) or DEA model. This study uses the non-parametric technique of DEA that constructs an efficient production frontier from a number of observed inputs and outputs. In constructing the efficient production frontier, it is assumed that all observed inputs and outputs operate under the same production function. The efficient production frontier represents the optimum efficiency under the model. All units on the frontier curve, also known as "envelope," are assumed to be fully efficient and given the highest efficiency score of 1.

Performance is comparatively measured in terms of efficiency with references to a set of units that are compared with each other. In this study, the analytical framework of the DEA model aims to measure the relative performance of state (provincial) governments as the decision-making units (DMUs). Below is the analogy diagram representing the function of state governments as the DMU within the decentralization framework:

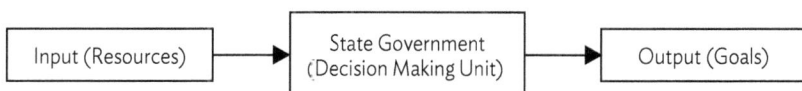

Each unit of assessment or DMU has control over the decision to transform inputs into outputs to achieve technical efficiency. The DEA model in this study is based on an input-oriented model in which inputs are controlled as they reflect the capability of state governments to maximize fiscal resources. As in many other countries, state governments in Indonesia face a budget constraint and they should therefore optimize the limited amount of public spending at their disposal as input to produce public goods that will impact economic growth.

Following Farrell (1957), technical efficiency is defined as a condition under which, for a set of inputs, an optimum quantity of outputs is produced or when, given a set of outputs, an optimum quantity of inputs is needed. The technical efficiency of a DMU is calculated as the ratio of output produced to input consumed.

Technical Efficiency = Σ weighted outputs / Σ weighted inputs

The traditional DEA model developed by Charnes, Cooper, and Rhodes (CCR) was constructed under the assumption of constant return to scale (CRS), where an increase in inputs consumed would lead to a proportional increase in outputs produced. Hence, not all DMUs in this study operate optimally as assumed in the CRS, and therefore the variable return to scale (VRS) assumption ought to be used.

The linear programming of the DEA model with the CRS assumption is as follows:

(1) $\underset{\mu,v}{Max}^{\theta_0} = \sum_r \mu_{r0} y_{r0} / \sum_i v_{i0} x_{i0}$

Subject to:

(2) $\sum_r \mu_{rk} y_{rk} / \sum_i v_{ik} x_{ik} \leq 1$ for all k-1,2,...j

(3) $\mu_{r0} \geq 0$

(4) $v_{i0} \geq 0$

DOES FISCAL DECENTRALIZATION HELP INDONESIA
AVOID THE MIDDLE-INCOME TRAP?

395

The description of each parameter is as follows:

θ_0	efficiency score of DMU_0;
i	number of DMUs;
r	number of outputs used by the DMUs;
i	number of inputs generated by the DMUs;
Y_k	vector of outputs r used by DMU_k;
X_k	vector of inputs i used by DMU_k;
μ and v	vector on multipliers respectively set on Y_k and X_k where
μ_r, v_i	the respective weights for output r and for input i.

The model determines that for each DMU_0 the optimal set of input weights $\{v_{i0}\}_{i-1}$ and output weights $\{\mu_{rc}\}_{r-1}$ that maximize its efficiency score is θ_0.

Considering the time dependent setting of panel data that will be used, the DEA model in this analysis is structured as a dynamic operation rather than a static condition. For that purpose, window analysis technique is used to validate the consistency of the efficiency scores over time. Window analysis in this study includes 26 DMUs (n), 10 observed years (k), and a 3-year window length (p), which produces an eight-window analysis (w) with associated DMUs under observation (see Appendix for an example of the window analysis application).

The first input variable is state capital expenditure, which is considered to be productive spending to finance public capital investment projects such as roads, ports, and utilities.[6] The model uses a 1-year lag for capital expenditure since public capital investment projects typically do not have an immediate impact on the economy. The second input variable is current expenditure, which is mainly state spending on operating costs including rent, wages, and other expenses to cover government operations.[7]

---

[6]   This spending excludes the mandated special allocation funds from the central government.
[7]   Due to the population imbalances between regions, normalization of state spending using per capita numbers does not depict the true fiscal capacity of a region. Hence, all the numbers used in the DEA model are adjusted for inflation as a means of normalizing both input and output variables.

Following the DEA model for regional analysis developed by Stimson, Stough, and Roberts (2002), the outcome of state expenditure is gross regional domestic product (GRDP) as the total output of all economic activities that are influenced by state spending and state own-source revenues.[8] Despite the fact that state expenditure is generally a small fraction of GRDP, the impact of state spending on GRDP varies depending on the structure and size of a region's economy. It also depends on the extent of the trickle-down effect from government spending on the region. State own-source revenue is the second output that comprises local taxes, fees, and charges. It also includes profits generated by state-owned enterprises (SOE) such as banks and public utility companies owned by state governments.

Table 12.1: Descriptive Analysis of Input–Output Variables

Variable	Pre-Decentralization (1996–2000), n = 130			
	Mean	St. D.	Min	Max
Capital Expenditure	149,159	192,605	36,907	1,229,105
Current Expenditure	301,708	540,725	27,850	3,826,516
Revenue	175,441	386,940	9,841	2,668,535
GRDP	31,920,834	40,832,564	2,101,872	189,075,401
Variable	Post-Decentralization (2001–2005), n = 130			
	Mean	St. D.	Min	Max
Capital Expenditure	504,412	1,470,387	14,432	15,800,000
Current Expenditure	971,035	1,462,443	61,741	9,041,520
Revenue	678,847	1,210,385	15,667	7,597,868
GRDP	68,283,175	70,797,332	2,954,380	436,251,000

GRDP = gross regional domestic product, Max = maximum, Min = minimum, St. D. = standard deviation.
Note: In million rupiah (*Indonesian currency*).
Source: Ministry of Finance, Bureau of Central Statistics.

---

[8]　In determining the input and output variables to be used in the DEA model, a Granger causality test is utilized to identify causal relationship between the input and output variables.

DOES FISCAL DECENTRALIZATION HELP INDONESIA
AVOID THE MIDDLE-INCOME TRAP?

397

Table 12.2 shows the average fiscal efficiency scores of the 26 state governments for three periods during the time of observation.[9] State fiscal efficiency scores declined most noticeably following the financial crisis in 1997. However, aggregate fiscal efficiency scores were at the lowest level after the implementation of decentralization in 2001. This indicates that state governments in Indonesia were not well prepared to manage a rapid increase in fiscal resources at the early stage of decentralization.

At the disaggregated regional level, fiscal efficiency scores vary between stable and conflict regions. Conflict states such as Aceh, Papua, and Maluku recorded a significant decline in the levels of fiscal efficiency due to a disruption in the functioning of government. With the exception of Maluku, conflict arose in those states was due to, among others, the unequal revenue-sharing schemes from the exploitation of natural resources.

Despite a windfall from the sharing of profits from the exploitation of natural resources, the levels of fiscal efficiency in rich resources regions such as Riau and East Kalimantan are at the lower end of the scale. A rapid expansion of fiscal resources without sound management may actually lead to higher levels of fiscal inefficiency due to increased unproductive spending.

The majority of states in the Java region, but not West Java and East Java, experienced a modest decline in their levels of fiscal efficiency after the 1998 crisis. Compared with most eastern regions, the levels of state fiscal efficiency in the western regions have been higher, which could be driven by better capacity and capability of their institutions, the quality of their leaders, and better supporting infrastructure. Various programs have been provided by international donors to assist with the implementation of fiscal decentralization in Indonesia, particularly in the eastern region. Besides the technical assistance with fiscal management, the assistance programs have also focused on improving good governance through greater transparency and accountability.

---

[9] A complete result of fiscal efficiency scores for the 10-year period of observation is provided in the Appendix.

Table 12.2: **Relative Fiscal Efficiency Scores**

DMUs (States/Provinces)	Pre-Crisis 1996	Crisis 1997–1998	Decentralization 2001–2005
Nanggroe Aceh	0.7873	0.7439	0.5937
North Sumatra	0.7956	0.7257	0.8436
West Sumatra	1.0000	0.8681	0.8270
Riau	0.9511	0.9165	0.7107
Jambi	1.0000	0.9655	0.8288
South Sumatra	0.8947	0.8119	0.7646
Bengkulu	1.0000	0.9507	0.9230
Lampung	0.9042	0.8568	0.8177
DKI Jakarta	1.0000	1.0000	0.9715
West Java	0.8641	0.9153	0.9555
Central Java	1.0000	0.7665	0.9396
Di Yogyakarta	1.0000	0.9813	0.8837
East Java	0.8238	0.8001	0.9928
Bali	1.0000	0.8467	0.8226
West Nusa Tenggara	0.9581	0.6939	0.6918
East Nusa Tenggara	0.8915	0.8453	0.8046
West Kalimantan	0.9474	0.7422	0.6524
Central Kalimantan	0.7103	0.9361	0.8975
South Kalimantan	0.8547	0.7618	0.8748
East Kalimantan	0.7911	0.8596	0.8172
North Sulawesi	0.8824	0.9505	0.8698
Central Sulawesi	0.7767	0.9653	0.9145
South Sulawesi	0.9382	0.9847	0.8808
Southeast Sulawesi	1.0000	0.8763	0.8309
Maluku	0.8725	0.8610	0.7513
Papua	0.7505	0.6705	0.5757
	0.8998	**0.8575**	**0.8245**

Western Region spans Nanggroe Aceh through Bali; *Eastern Region* spans West Nusa Tenggara through Papua.

DMUs = decision-making units.

Source: Author estimates using DEA application.

DOES FISCAL DECENTRALIZATION HELP INDONESIA
AVOID THE MIDDLE-INCOME TRAP?

399

Among the problems with the implementation of decentralization in Indonesia, lack of institutional ntegrity is the major one. Decentralization has established new powerful leaders in the regions ("local kings"), which has led to widespread rent seeking and corruption practices due to lack of integrity and oversight particularly at the start of the decentralization era. Accordingly, limited fiscal resources may be justifiable when sound institutional arrangements such as the rule of law and oversight mechanisms are not well established.

A greater constraint on regions' fiscal resources during the 1997 economic crisis could be lower own-source revenues and transfers from the central government.[10] This eventually will force state governments to manage the allocation of fiscal resources more responsibly, particularly since state governments are also required by law to balance their budget. However, it also means that state governments will limit their spending during a crisis period, which would not help to speec up the recovery process.

12.5 | Determinants of State Fiscal Efficiency Using the Tobit Model

The second stage of the empirical analysis is to examine fiscal indicators that determine fiscal efficiency levels of state governments in Indonesia. With a skewed distribution of the fiscal efficiency scores from the DEA analysis, a Tobit panel data regression is used in this study to identify the determinant factors of fiscal efficiency. The Tobit model is a maximum-likelihood random effect model that operates under a non-negative dependent variable. This model enables fiscal efficiency scores to be constrained within the range cf 0 to 1.

---

[10]   Most states still depend on transfers from the central government to close their budget gap and fund the mandated spending since they are not permitted to issue debt through bond issuance.

The Tobit model is expressed as the level of y_{it} (efficiency scores) in terms of an underlying latent (unobservable) variable y_{it}^* as the dependent variable:

$$y_{it}^* = \beta_0 + \beta_1 x_{it} + \varepsilon_{it} \tag{7}$$
$$y_{it} = \beta_0 + \beta_1 x_{it} + \varepsilon_{it} \quad \text{if } y_{it}^* > 0, \text{ and} \tag{8}$$
$$y_{it} = 0 \qquad\qquad\qquad \text{if } y_{it}^* \le 1$$

The error term (ε_{it}) in the efficiency distribution of the Tobit model is assumed to be independent and normally distributed with a function of $N(0, \sigma^2)$, where σ^2 is the variance. While ε_{it}, x_{it} and β are unknown parameters of the explanatory variables. The maximum likelihood estimation (MLE) is used to estimate β and σ.

The standard estimation for the likelihood function (L) for the censored normal distribution is as follows:

$$\log L = \sum_{y_{it}>0} -\tfrac{1}{2}\left[\log(2\pi) + \log \sigma^2 \frac{\left(y_{it} - [y_{it} - \beta x_{it}]\right)^2}{\sigma^2} \right] + \sum_{y_{it}=0}\left[1 - F\left(\frac{\beta x_{it}}{\sigma}\right) \right] \tag{9}$$

The estimated coefficients in the Tobit model represent the marginal effect of x_{it} on y_{it}^*. To determine the expected marginal effect of x_{it} on y_{it}, the following equation is calculated in the Tobit model:

$$E\left[y_{it} \mid y_{it} > 0\right] = \beta_0 + \beta_1 x_{it} + \sigma\left[\frac{\phi(\beta_0 + \beta_1 x_{it})/\sigma}{\Phi(\beta_0 + \beta_1 x_{it})/\sigma} \right] \tag{10}$$

In this study, there are four key variables that are likely to influence the fiscal efficiency scores of state governments:

- Degree of fiscal decentralization is defined as the share of state expenditures over total government spending. A higher share of state expenditures represents a higher degree of fiscal decentralization.
- Ratio of capital expenditure is defined as the share of state capital expenditure in total state spending. Capital expenditures are both capital improvements and new capital investment projects.

DOES FISCAL DECENTRALIZATION HELP INDONESIA
AVOID THE MIDDLE-INCOME TRAP?

401

- Ratio of operating costs is defined as the share of state operating costs in total state spending. They are direct and indirect spending associated with operating costs. Spending on goods and services is direct spending, whereas wages are considered to be indirect spending.
- Ratio of revenue independence is defined as the share of taxes, charges, and fees independently collected by state governments. A higher ratio of revenue independence implies either a higher portion of state own-source revenues or a decrease in central government transfers.

The result of the Tobit panel data regression for the period of analysis from 1996 to 2005 is shown in Table 12.3. In the Tobit model, the magnitude of likelihood for each determinant factor is measured by the marginal effect of each factor. If the marginal effect has a negative sign this indicates that the factor variable is inversely related to a higher fiscal efficiency level. The odds ratio's confidence level in the model is determined by the z-ratio.

Table 12.3: Determinants of State Fiscal Efficiency in Indonesia, 1996–2005

Dependent Var.	Fiscal Efficiency	n = 260 Obs (26 States)	
Independent Var.	Coefficients	z-ratio	Marginal
Fiscal Decentralization	0.79	2.94*	0.72
Ratio of Capital Expenditure	−0.07	−2.64*	−0.06
Ratio of Operating Costs	−0.09	−2.82*	−0.08
Ratio of Revenue Independence	0.04	2.96*	0.04
Lagging States Dummy	0.01	1.00	0.01
Per capita Spending	−0.20	−2.77*	−0.19
Constant	0.86	36.39*	
Log-Likelihood	139.78		
R-squared	0.21		
Wald chi2	74.20		

Note: * The point estimate is significant at the 1% level.
Source: Author's regression result.

Fiscal decentralization is identified as the factor with the highest marginal effect in terms of influencing the levels of fiscal efficiency compared with other factors. As the sign of the marginal effect is positive, the argument that fiscal decentralization is likely to provide incentives to allocate fiscal resources more efficiently can be supported. This finding supports the reasoning behind further enhancing fiscal decentralization in Indonesia, which had initially been motivated by trying to maintain national unity and prevent states from failing, rather than by trying to improve the quality of local government institutions.

On the other hand, the finding from the Tobit panel model indicates that a higher ratio of capital expenditure is likely to lower fiscal efficiency. A higher ratio of operating costs and per capita spending are also associated with lower levels of fiscal efficiency. This finding is in line with the phenomenon of rising corruption and rent-seeking activities at the regional level after the implementation of fiscal decentralization. An increase in state governments' spending tends to escalate waste spending and therefore constrains the potential regional outputs as the level of development is far from optimal.

Inefficiencies of current expenditures to cover operating costs are proven to be higher than capital spending, which implies there has been more waste spending and mark-up from the acquisition of goods and services, whereas capital spending inefficiency is more likely related to rent-seeking activities in land acquisition, permits, and construction. One way for state governments to achieve fiscal efficiency is by pursuing cost reduction programs without sacrificing basic public services. Hence, these efficiencies are more likely to occur under budget constraint conditions, such as in periods of crisis.

The finding suggests that fiscal efficiency associated with a higher degree of fiscal decentralization is driven from the revenue side. As evidenced by the model, states that can generate their own revenue independent of central government transfers are likely to have a significantly higher level of fiscal efficiency. Higher revenue independence implies that state governments are more capable of fulfilling their responsibility and allocate fiscal resources in a productive and efficient manner. Hence, there is also a risk that when states

DOES FISCAL DECENTRALIZATION HELP INDONESIA
AVOID THE MIDDLE-INCOME TRAP?

403

rely too much on additional taxes, charges, or fees to generate their own revenue this has a negative impact on trade and investment.

The lagging state dummy variable appears to be of no significance in the regression, which indicates that fiscal efficiency levels are not necessarily affected by the level of economic (scale) and resource capacity (structure), as initially predicted. It means that a number of lagging regions actually have a sound institutional quality that enables them to manage fiscal resources properly. Another factor is the quality of leaders in the leading and lagging regions that are not significantly different.

To test if the determining factors of state fiscal efficiency changed after the implementation of fiscal decentralization in 2001, separate panel data are constructed for the periods from 1996–2000 and 2001–2005. The results are shown in Tables 12.4 and 12.5. Greater fiscal decentralization is significantly more likely to have an effect on the level of fiscal efficiency. This finding defends the claim that allowing a larger degree of fiscal decentralization will improve the institutional quality of state governments, which potentially supports the transition to a high-income country. Thus, to some extent, the decision to implement the new decentralization law in 2001 is well justified. For other developing countries, the key reform should also focus on improving the quality of institutions, considering the extent of global competition in pursuing high growth and competitiveness through institutional reform.

In the post-decentralization panel, the sign of the capital expenditure ratio turns negative, which indicates that a higher ratio of capital expenditure is more likely to lower fiscal efficiency. This finding confirms the presumption that decentralization in Indonesia has increased corruption and rent-seeking activities associated with capital spending. Capital spending is more prone to corruption and rent-seeking practices due to local governments' discretion in awarding contracts. In addition, there is a lack of oversight and transparency in local governments' projects due to limited resources and capacity. In the old regime, which was more centralized, most decision-making about capital project developments was in the hands of central government.

Table 12.4: Determinants of State Fiscal Efficiency in Indonesia, 1996–2000

Dependent Var:	Fiscal Efficiency	n = 130 Obs (26 States)	
Independent Var.	Coefficients	z-ratio	Marginal
Fiscal Decentralization	0.35	2.09**	0.22
Ratio of Capital Expenditure	0.34	3.96*	0.31
Ratio of Operating Cost	−0.09	−0.89	−0.08
Ratio of Revenue Independence	0.06	2.75*	0.05
Lagging states Dummy	−0.03	−1.37	−0.03
Per capita Spending	0.06	0.20	0.05
Constant	0.71	13.01*	
Log-Likelihood	77.19		
R-squared	0.21		
Wald chi2	37.79		

Notes: * The point estimate is significant at the 1% level; ** the point estimate is significant at the 5% level.
Source: Author.

Table 12.5: Determinants of State Fiscal Efficiency in Indonesia, 2001–2005

Dependent Var:	Fiscal Efficiency	n = 130 Obs (26 States)	
Independent Var.	Coefficients	z-ratio	Marginal
Fiscal Decentralization	0.86	2.87*	0.82
Ratio of Capital Expenditure	−0.10	−3.96*	−0.09
Ratio of Operating Cost	−0.06	−1.83***	−0.05
Ratio of Revenue Independence	0.14	1.95**	0.03
Lagging states Dummy	0.02	0.86	0.02
Per capita Spending	−0.25	−3.24*	−0.24
Constant	0.74	21.28*	
Log-Likelihood	88.26		
R-squared	0.46		
Wald chi2	99.93		

Note: * The point estimate is significant at the 1% level; ** the point estimate is significant at the 5% level; *** the point estimate is significant at the 10% level.
Source: Author.

DOES FISCAL DECENTRALIZATION HELP INDONESIA
AVOID THE MIDDLE-INCOME TRAP?

405

Looking at the coefficient of variable operating cost ratio and per capita spending that is only significant post decentralization, it can be concluded that inefficiency in state governments' spending associated with a higher ratio of operating costs and per capita spending is more likely to occur after the expansion of fiscal decentralization.

The variable revenue independence ratio is significant in both panel regressions. Hence, the likelihood of a larger revenue independence positively affecting the fiscal efficiency level is more than doubled in post decentralization as state governments were able to raise their own source of financing through the taxation mechanism. One factor to consider is that the new decentralization law controls the type of taxes that state and local governments can impose. The law also limits the maximum rate for specific taxes to prevent excessive taxation.

The results of the empirical analysis confirm the potential benefits and risks of fiscal decentralization. They should be taken into consideration when determining challenges of migrating to a high-income country. So far, the risks have been identified on the expenditure side, hence clarity and consistency in implementing the rule of law is crucial to prevent misallocation of spending. Further enhancement of policies related to fiscal decentralization is necessary, but it should be accompanied by a commitment to eradicate any corruption and rent-seeking activities.

The findings of this chapter also imply that centralized control over capital projects in the short term might actually reduce inefficiency in the decentralized system of government. However, it would be a challenge to revert back to the centralized system as it may face resistance from local governments and the public.

12.6 | Conclusion

The degree of fiscal decentralization is the dominant factor determining state fiscal efficiency. This finding indicates that giving greater responsibility to state governments to manage their fiscal resources, despite the considerable political and economic risks, is well justified. More importantly, it also serves the purpose of more efficient public service delivery that will boost development in the Indonesian regions. Related to that, the effectiveness and responsiveness of state government institutions is also considered to be the key factor that will determine the speed of reform and Indonesia's migration to a high-income country.

Despite the positive impact from fiscal decentralization in Indonesia, the expansion of the fiscal spending of states has also caused inefficiencies due to growing waste spending, corruption, and rent seeking. This could jeopardize the economic development of the Indonesian regions. On the other hand, by being granted greater revenue independence, state governments are more compelled to improve their capacity and capabilities to boast revenue collection. This means streamlining the process of tax collection to increase efficiency and use favorable tax rates to achieve revenue targets. With regard to high inefficiency in the current expenditures, which are associated with the costs of government operations, it is necessary to provide clear guidelines on spending allocation and also efforts to strengthen the rule of law associated with misallocation of government spending.

In sum, while enhancing fiscal decentralization by giving local governments a greater role in managing their own finances is key, it is even more important to commit to the eradication of corruption and rent-seeking activities. As lessons learned from Indonesia's experience with decentralization, the following policies should be considered as guidance for minimizing the risks of taking a slower path to becoming a high-income country while expanding the degree of fiscal decentralization.

- Increase the capacity of local bureaucrats to draw up government budgets that prioritize the most needed and productive public services to support

DOES FISCAL DECENTRALIZATION HELP INDONESIA
AVOID THE MIDDLE-INCOME TRAP?

407

economic development and accelerate Indonesia's migration to a
high-income country.

- Support a good governance policy that ensures oversight, transparency,
  and accountability. This also means enforcing corruption law and
  committing to upholding the rule of law consistently without political
  intervention.
- Optimize technology to strengthen fiscal monitoring and contract
  procurement. It is also necessary to create a benchmark (standard)
  for each item of government spending with some variations in the
  logistics cost.

References

Azis, I. J. 2003. Concepts and Practice of Decentralization: Some Notes
    on the Case of Indonesia. Paper presented at the Policy Dialogue on
    "Empowering Women in Autonomy and Decentralization Processes."
    United Nations, New York.

Bardhan, P. 2002. Decentralization of Governance and Development.
    Journal of Economic Perspectives 16(4): 185–205.

Bird, R., and C. Wallich. 1993. Fiscal Decentralization and Intergovernmental
    Relations in Transition Economics: Toward a Systematic Framework
    of Analysis. World Bank Policy Research Working Paper 1122.
    Washington, DC: The World Bank.

Davoodi, H., and H. F. Zou. 1998. Fiscal Decentralization and Economic
    Growth: A Cross-Country Study. *Journal of Urban Economics* 43(2):
    244–257.

Ebel, R., and S. Yilmaz 2003. Fiscal Decentralization in Developing Countries:
    Is It Happening? How Do We Know?. World Bank Policy Research
    Working Paper 2809. Washington, DC: The World Bank.

Farrell, M. J. 1957. The Measurement of Productive Efficiency. *Journal of the
    Royal Statistical Society* 120(3): 253–290.

Fritzen, P., and P. W. Lim. 2006. *Problems and Prospects of Decentralization
    in Developing Countries*. Singapore: LKY School of Public Policy,
    National University of Singapore.

Gil, C., R. Ezcurra, P. Padro, and M. Rapun. 2002. Decentralization and Regional Economic Disparities. Newcastle, United Kingdom: Center for Urban & Regional Development Studies.

Gill, I. S., and H. Kharas. 2015. The Middle-Income Trap Turns Ten. World Bank Policy Research Working Paper 7403. Washington, DC: The World Bank.

Huang, X. M. 2009. *Politics in Pacific Asia*. New York, NY: Palgrave Macmillan.

Ikawa, H. 2008. *15 Years of Decentralization Reform in Japan*. Up-to-date Documents on Local Autonomy in Japan No. 4. Tokyo: CLAIR and COSLOG.

Jin, H. et al. 2001. Regional Decentralization and Fiscal Incentives: Federalism, Chinese Style. Stanford, CA: The Center for Research on Economic Development and Policy Reform.

Leibenstein, H. 1996. Fiscal Allocative Efficiency vs. X-Efficiency. *American Economic Review* 56(3): 392–415.

Maddick, H. 1963. *Democracy, Decentralization and Development*. London: Asia Publishing House.

Oates, W. E. 1993. Fiscal Decentralization and Economic Development. *National Tax Journal* 46(2): 237–243.

Park, S. C. 2013. *Decentralization Reform under the Economic Crisis in Korea*. Siheung, Republic of Korea: Korea Polytechnic University.

Prud'homme, R. 1995. The Dangers of Decentralizations. *World Bank Research Observer* 10 (2): 201–220.

Ramanathan, R. 2003. *An Introduction to Data Envelopment Analysis: A Tool for Performance Measurement*. Beverly Hills, CA: Sage Publications.

Rao, P. K. 2003. *Development Finance*. Berlin: Springer.

Stimson, R. J., R. R. Stough, and B. H. Roberts 2002. *Regional Economic Development*. Berlin: Springer.

Woller, G. M., and K. Phillips. 1998. Fiscal Decentralization and LDC Growth: An Empirical Investigation. *Journal of Development Studies* 34: 138–148.

Table A12.1
Sample of Window Analysis for Aceh

States	1996	1997	1998	1999	2000	2001	2002	2003	2004	2005
Nanggroe Aceh	78.73%	73.91%	72.36%							
		75.52%	74.06%	70.16%						
			75.80%	71.82%	74.14%					
				73.62%	77.46%	63.13%				
					78.03%	63.22%	58.17%			
						68.65%	65.18%	56.54%		
							52.63%	56.99%	57.99%	
								56.99%	57.99%	58.34%
Mean	0.7873	0.7472	0.7407	0.7187	0.7654	0.6500	0.5866	0.5684	0.5799	0.5834

Note: Refer to Ramanathan (2003) for more details on DEA and window analysis theories and applications.
Source: Author's estimates.

Table A12.2: Fiscal Efficiency Scores of 26 States in Indonesia between 1996 and 2005

INPUT Indicators: (1) Capital Expenditure, (2) Current Expenditure										
OUTPUT Indicators: (1) State Government Revenue (2) Private Investments										
DMUs (States/Provinces)	1996	1997	1998	1999	2000	2001	2002	2003	2004	2005
DI Aceh	0.787	0.747	0.740	0.718	0.765	0.650	0.586	0.568	0.579	0.583
North Sumatra	0.795	0.749	0.702	0.736	0.837	0.838	0.910	0.991	0.894	0.702
West Sumatra	1	0.879	0.857	0.819	0.870	0.794	0.839	0.836	0.834	0.830
Riau	0.951	1	0.832	0.782	1	0.719	0.725	0.756	0.687	0.664
Jambi	1	1	0.930	0.928	0.909	0.971	0.818	0.805	0.769	0.779
South Sumatra	0.894	0.819	0.803	0.741	0.807	0.733	0.774	0.840	0.724	0.749

continued next page

Table A12.2: *Continued*

DMUs (States/Provinces)	1996	1997	1998	1999	2000	2001	2002	2003	2004	2005
Bengkulu	1	0.958	0.943	0.903	0.988	1	0.978	0.745	0.898	0.992
Lampung	0.904	0.851	0.861	0.795	0.813	0.833	0.798	0.797	0.827	0.831
DKI Jakarta	1	1	1	1	0.995	1	1	0.888	0.969	1
West Java	0.864	1	0.830	1	0.877	0.960	0.969	0.868	0.978	1
Central Java	1	0.764	0.768	0.751	0.734	0.975	0.899	0.862	0.960	1
DI Yogyakarta	1	0.980	0.981	1	0.907	0.956	0.955	0.849	0.827	0.829
East Java	0.823	0.814	0.785	0.968	0.943	1	0.996	1	0.967	1
Bali	1	0.858	0.835	0.774	0.810	0.798	0.788	0.905	0.777	0.843
West Nusa Tenggara	0.958	0.692	0.695	0.718	0.812	0.716	0.751	0.685	0.622	0.683
East Nusa Tenggara	0.891	0.834	0.856	0.725	0.776	0.769	0.789	0.805	0.822	0.836
West Kalimantan	0.947	0.754	0.729	0.635	0.660	0.598	0.682	0.658	0.628	0.693
Central Kalimantan	0.710	0.872	1	0.824	0.868	1	0.745	0.790	1	0.951
South Kalimantan	0.854	0.779	0.744	0.826	0.864	0.912	0.923	0.853	0.852	0.831
East Kalimantan	0.791	0.899	0.819	0.751	0.698	0.797	0.846	0.844	0.830	0.767
North Sulawesi	0.882	0.963	0.937	0.849	0.877	0.989	0.805	0.735	1	0.818
Central Sulawesi	0.776	1	0.930	1	1	0.738	0.918	0.915	1	1
South Sulawesi	0.938	0.969	1	0.857	1	0.955	0.758	1	0.885	0.805
Southeast Sulawesi	1	0.884	0.868	0.794	0.852	0.912	0.773	0.780	0.868	0.819
Maluku	0.872	0.877	0.844	0.837	0.824	0.794	0.788	0.661	0.792	0.720
Papua	0.750	0.661	0.679	0.654	0.627	0.684	0.542	0.537	0.551	0.562

Note: Efficiency scores are within the range of 0 to 1 with 1 being the most efficient.

Source: Author's estimates using DEA application.

CHAPTER 13

Credit Market Development and Firm Innovation: Evidence from the People's Republic of China

Hua Shang, Quanyun Song, and Yu Wu

13.1 | Introduction

Innovation, as the engine of a firm's development, has been considered a major driving force of economic growth (Solow 1957). However, what drives innovation is still worth investigating. There is a growing literature exploring the factors affecting innovation from various perspectives. In this chapter, we contribute to this literature by analyzing how the development of the credit market affects firms' product innovation through improved credit resource allocation.

As Levine (2005: 6) argued, "if finance is to explain economic growth, we need theories that describe how financial development influences resource allocation decisions in ways that foster productivity growth." If the financial intermediaries are active in researching firms, monitoring firms, and pooling risks, they are likely to allocate more credit to firms and projects that increase productivity growth. Knowing that financial intermediaries are allocating credit more effectively and efficiently, firms might be more willing to engage in projects that are risky but foster productivity growth. Therefore, credit market development, through improved credit allocation, is expected to enhance firms' product innovation incentives and outcomes.

Compared with financial depth, credit allocation might play a more important role in fostering firms' product innovation in the People's Republic of China (PRC). Financial depth can only represent the increase of the total credit to gross domestic product (GDP). However, it cannot reveal how the credit is allocated in a financial system. As argued by King and Levine (1993), a well-developed financial system should be able to allocate more credits to firms or projects that promote economic growth. A financial system that passively allocates credits only to non-state-owned enterprises (non-SOEs) is quite different from that allocating to private firms. The PRC financial system used to be inefficient and ineffective. The financial intermediaries lent most of their credit to state-owned enterprises (SOEs), which are known to be less efficient and less profitable (Guariglia and Poncet 2008). On the other hand, the non-SOEs, especially privately-owned firms,[1] were discriminated by financial intermediaries due to their short credit history and low status in the socialist economy (Guariglia and Poncet 2008; Brandt and Li 2003). Even though the non-SOEs, on average, are much more efficient and profitable than SOEs, most of them are in shortage of credit for further development. If the credit allocation of the PRC financial intermediaries become more efficient and effective, it can reduce non-SOEs' cost of external fund on average and enable savers to invest in more risky but productive firms and projects (Rajan and Zingales 1998). Therefore, non-SOEs with better performances and/or more promising are expected to obtain more credit. It is likely to induce these firms, especially those with large credit constraints, to be concerned about their long-term growth and engage in innovative projects. On the other hand, the SOEs could also be forced to care about their performances in case they are not able to get enough credit.

We examine how credit market development, through improvement of credit allocation, affects firms' product innovation incentives and outcomes. Our data are obtained from the National Bureau of Statistics of China (NBS of China) from 2000 to 2007, based on annual surveys of industrial firms,

---

[1]   Privately owned firms are part of non-SOEs.

including SOEs and non-SOEs, with sales of more than CNY5 million in each province. One advantage of the data set is that it allows us to analyze the product innovation behavior of the non-listed firms, which make up more than 99% of the firms in this data set. Since the non-listed firms account for a much larger part of the PRC economy, it is important to explore the factors affecting non-listed firms' product innovation incentives and outcomes. Further, unlike the listed firms, non-listed firms do not have access to capital market. Therefore, we do not need to include the local capital market development, which is difficult to measure correctly (Rajan and Zingales 1998). Another advantage of this data set is that banks make commercial lending judgments, to a larger degree, for the manufacturing industry, as argued by Firth et al. (2009) using 2002 data.

One of the important problems in the financial market development–innovation literature is the endogeneity problem caused by omitted variables and the reverse causality of finance and innovation. The traditional way to investigate how financial market development affects innovation is to rely on cross-country-level or state-level (province) financial market development and innovation data. Therefore, the control variables can only include cross-country-level or state- evel (province) variables. Following the most recent researches (i.e., Ayyagari, Demirguc–Kunt, and Maksimovic 2011; Amore, Schneider, and Zaldokas 2013; etc.), we minimize the omitted variable problem by using firm-level innovation data. Firm-level analysis allows us to control for many unobserved variables such as firm-, industry-, and province-level variables that might affect both credit market development and firm innovation. We then lag the credit market development for one period to minimize the reverse causality problem. In addition, we apply the instrumental variable method to solve the endogeneity problem.

Our results indicate that credit market development enhances firms' product innovation incentives and outcomes through improved credit allocation, which is consistent with the theories established by King and Levine (1993) and Morales (2003). We further demonstrate that there are two possible channels for this: first, relaxing firms' credit constraints is marginally more beneficial for credit-restrained firms than for other firms. Credit market development has more of an effect on the product innovation incentives and outcomes of credit-restrained firms, such as privately owned firms and small and medium-sized enterprises (SMEs), as opposed to other types of firms. Second, financial institutions are more willing to lend to firms with better performances in better developed credit markets. Therefore, credit market development affects the product innovation incentives and outcomes of firms with better performances more than those of firms with worse performances. In addition, we demonstrate that our results are driven by improvement of credit allocation rather than by an increase in the quantity of total credit or an increase in the number of non-SOEs in a province. Our results are also robust for different estimation methods, different samples, and alternative measures for credit market development.

Our chapter is closely related to the literature on whether and how credit market development affects innovation. One part of the literature argues that credit market development mobilizes and provides appropriate financing to firms and projects, which promotes economic growth; and in a well-developed credit market, research, evaluation, and monitoring services are more effective and less expensive. Financial intermediaries may promote innovation by identifying those entrepreneurs with the best chances of successfully initiating new goods and production processes, and monitoring them to generate more innovation outputs (King and Levine 1993, Morales 2003, Levine 2005). The other part of the literature argues that credit market development discourages innovation. First, banks are conservative and dislike risky innovative projects (Weinstein and Yafeh 1998, Morck and Nakamura 1999). Second, banks prefer to use physical assets to secure loans, favoring firms that have large investments in plants and equipment, rather than those that have substantial research and development investments to generate intangible assets.

The most recent cross-country and within-country empirical analyses[2] also reach contradictory conclusions. For example, Ayyagari, Demirguc-Kunt, and Maksimovic (2011) found that bank financing enhances the innovation of SMEs in developing countries. Xiao and Zhao (2012) argued that credit market development enhances innovation in countries with lower government ownership of banks. Hsu, Tian, and Xu (2014) found that credit market development discourages innovation for more high-tech-intensive industries and industries that are more dependent on external finance. Benfratello, Schiantarelli, and Sembenelli (2008) argued that for firms in Italy, banking development accelerates the probability of process innovation, but this is less true for product innovation. Amore, Schneider, and Zaldokas (2013) found that for United States-listed firms from 1976 to 1995, credit market development enhanced the quantity and quality of innovation activities.

The contributions of this chapter are the following: first, we provide within-country analysis to investigate how credit market development affects firms' product innovation incentives and outcomes. Compared with cross-country analysis, within-country analysis can avoid the problems caused by the incomparability of variables between countries. Second, our analysis can be distinguished from many within-country studies because we focus on the perspective of credit allocation. We show that firms' product innovation incentives and outcomes are promoted by credit allocation rather than the quantity of credit (financial depth) in the PRC. Third, compared with country-level and industry-level analyses, we provide a firm-level analysis, which allows us to control for many unobserved firm-, industry-, and province-level variables that might affect both firms' product innovation and credit market development. Firm-level analysis also helps us to minimize the endogeneity problem caused by omitted variables and make the results more trustworthy.

---

[2]   In the financial development and firm innovation literature, it is common to analyze how macro-level financial development affects micro-level firm innovation. For example, Ayyagari, Demirguc-Kunt, and Maksimovic (2011); Xiao and Zhao (2012); and Hsu, Tian, and Xu (2014) analyzed how country-level financial development affects industry-level and firm-level innovation. Benfratello, Schiantarelli, and Sembenelli (2008) and Amore, Schneider, and Zaldokas (2013) analyzed how state-level financial development affects firm innovation.

Fourth, the non-listed firms make up more than 99% of our sample, which means that our research is much less affected by the development of the capital market. Our further analysis shows that even after we exclude all the listed firms, our results still hold. Fifth, as far as we know, this is the first study investigating whether credit market development, through improvement of credit allocation, enhances PRC firms' product innovation incentives and outcomes. The PRC financial system is evolving toward a more well-developed system. It is important to understand whether the development improves PRC firms' innovative capacities.

The rest of the chapter is organized as follows: in Section 13.2, we provide institutional background; Section 13.3 describes the data and provides summary statistics; Section 13.4 presents the results; Section 13.5 provides a robustness check; and Section 13.6 concludes.

13.2 | Institutional Background

After several years of development, the PRC financial system is gradually becoming a more well-developed system wherein credit allocation is also becoming more efficient and effective.

The PRC financial system originates from a monobank system, with the credit allocating to SOEs only. Since 1986, with the development of various types of financial institutions, the credit has been extended to more diversified customers. A bit more credit has been allocated to non-SOEs since 1997 (Lin 2011). It was when the PRC government pointed out that non-SOEs were important components of socialist market economy. However, the four state-owned banks with the largest market shares continue to lend to SOEs only (Guariglia and Poncet 2008) because the central and local governments issued lending quotas to firms which submitted investment plans. The non-SOEs are excluded from submitting investment plans. The banks discriminate against the non-SOEs due to their short credit history and low chances of being bailed out by the government (Guariglia and Poncet 2008; Brandt and Li 2003).

In 1998, the central bank, People's Bank of China, reformed the commercial banks' lending behavior, abolishing the loan-size restrictions on the four state-owned commercial banks. The management style of the People's Bank of China also changed from mandatory plans to guiding plans, and all commercial banks were required to rank their loans into five categories according to loan risk from 1998 to 2000. After the PRC's entry to the World Trade Organization in 2001, the PRC banks further went through several reforms, including attracting foreign strategic investors, going public, and reconstructing themselves. The financial institutions thus became more efficient and the credit allocation started to become more commercialized (Lin 2011). Using World Bank survey data from 2002, Firth et al. (2009) also argued that the state-owned banks allocating credits to non-state-owned sectors tend to use commercial judgments. Even though the proportion of lending to non-SOEs has been increased gradually, the non-SOEs are still financially constrained as argued by Poncet, Steingress, and Vandenbussche (2010) using data from 1998 to 2005.

13.3 | Data and Summary Statistics

13.3.1 Sample

The sample is taken from annual surveys on industrial firms, including SOEs and non-SOEs with sales above CNY5 million, conducted by NBS of China from 2000 to 2007. The industrial firms include manufacturing firms, mining firms, and public utilities. The database includes firm characteristics, financial information, and production information. We employ the method in Brandt, Biesebroeck, and Zhang (2012) to construct the panel. The firms in the sample are those adopting the enterprise accounting standard. Firms whose fixed assets are higher than total assets and whose new product production is higher than total production have been excluded from the analysis. To further remove the outliers, firms in the 1st and 99th percentiles of each variable have been excluded. Firms changing industries have also been excluded because the characteristics of the firms may differ if they switch from one industry to another (Ouyang, Zhang, and Dong 2015).

13.3.2 Innovation Measure

Following Zhang (2015), we measure the product innovation incentive and outcomes by using two measures constructed from the value of new products.[3] According to NBS of China, new products "refer to brand new products produced with new technology and new design, or products that represent noticeable improvement in terms of structure, material, or production process for improving significantly the character or function of the older versions. They include new products certified by relevant government agencies within the period of certification, as well as new products designed and produced by enterprises within a year without certification by government agencies. This indicator reflects the direct contribution of science and technology output to economic growth."[4]

One measure is the firms' product innovation incentives, NP, a dummy variable.

$$\text{NP}_{i,t} = \begin{cases} 1 \ \textit{if firm i produce new product in year t} \\ 0 \ \textit{if firm i doesn't produce new product in year t} \end{cases}, \textit{for } i = 1, ...N; \ t = 2000, ... 2007$$

However, this can only measure whether a firm would like to engage in innovative activities and cannot distinguish firms with more innovative activities from those with less innovative activities. Therefore, the second measure we construct is called product innovation outcome, NPr, which is measured as the ratio of the new product production of a firm in 1 year to its total production in that year. The higher the NPr, the more innovative the firm is in a particular year. Panel A of Table 13.1 provides the summary statistics for NP and NPr in the full sample and for innovative companies only.

---

[3]   According to Griliches (1990); Ayyagari, Demirguc-Kunt, and Maksimovic (2011); and the definition of innovation by the Organisation for Economic Co-operation and Development, product innovation is far beyond research and development and patent, especially for emerging economies.

[4]   See Explanatory Notes on Main Statistical Indicators in Section 20, Education, Science, and Technology available at http://www.stats.gov.cn/tjsj/ndsj/2008/indexeh.htm (accessed 30 December 2016).

Table 13.1: Summary Statistics

	Panel A							
	Full Sample				Innovative Companies			
Var	N	Mean	Std	Median	N	Mean	Std	Median
NP	891,462	0.067	0.250	0	127,959	0.400	0.490	1
NPr	891,462	0.030	0.139	0	127,959	0.190	0.303	0.021
	Panel B							
Year	1999	2000	2001	2002	2003	2004	2005	2006
CMD_mean	3.27	4.03	4.38	5.27	6.63	7.52	8.32	8.73
CMD_median	2.76	3.38	4.40	5.20	6.58	7.52	8.41	9.03
CMD_std	3.03	3.07	2.47	2.43	2.24	2.09	2.21	2.07

Panel C					
Variable	N	Mean	p50	Min	Max
size	891,462	9.750	9.583	6.717	13.985
lnage	891,462	2.068	1.946	0.693	4.094
lnage2	891,462	4.975	3.787	0.480	16.764
Leverage	891,462	0.567	0.590	0.011	1
Investment intensity	891,462	0.370	0.347	0.007	0.909
Export	891,462	0.153	0	0	1
HHI	891,462	0.008	0.005	0.001	1
ROA	891,462	0.067	0.030	−0.200	0.787
subsidy	891,462	0.002	0	0	0.078
SOE	891,462	0.124	0	0	1
COE	891,462	0.136	0	0	1
private	891,462	0.460	0	0	1
HMT	891,462	0.106	0	0	1
foreign	891,462	0.096	0	0	1
secondary industry	891,462	0.485	0.492	0.197	0.574
third industry	891,462	0.400	0.395	0.300	0.719
lngdppc	891,462	9.630	9.640	7.842	10.913
FD	891,462	0.985	0.920	0.562	2.139
nonSOE_ratio	891,462	0.827	0.884	0.128	0.983

Note: The definitions of variables are in Table 13.2.

Source: Authors.

The sample size for the full sample is 891,462 and that for the innovation companies is 127,959. For NP, the mean is 0.067 and the standard deviation is 0.250. For NPr, the mean is 0.03 and the standard deviation is 0.139. The medians for both NP and NPr are zero, indicating that there are many zeros in the data. For the sample including innovative companies only, the mean is 0.4 and the standard deviation is 0.490. For NPr, the mean is 0.19 and the standard deviation is 0.303. The median is 0.021.

13.3.3 Credit Market Development Measure

Following King and Levine (1993),[5] we measure the credit market development from the perspective of credit allocation by using an index constructed from a ratio of the amount of credit allocated to non-SOEs to the total credit amount for 31 provinces as the measure of credit market development. King and Levine (1993) argue that a financial system allocating more financial resources to private firms is more efficient and effective than that allocating financial resources to SOEs or publicly owned enterprises only. Because in such a financial system, the financial intermediaries are more active in researching, monitoring firms, and managing risks. As argued by Fan, Wang, and Zhu (2011), this index denotes the marketization of credit allocation of financial institutions in the PRC. A higher value of this index indicates that the financial institutions are more active in researching firms rather than just allocating credit to SOEs.[6]

The credit market development index is a subindex of the National Economic Research Institute (NERI) index. The NERI index was constructed by Fan, Wang, and Zhu (2011) and sponsored by the NERI of the PRC and the China Reform Foundation.[7] The original data is from China Banking Yearbooks

---

[5]   King and Levine (1993) used the ratio of credit allocated to private firms (firms not owned by the state) to total credit, to proxy the credit allocation of the financial market development.

[6]   Some might argue that this measure might be affected by the relative number of non-SOEs and SOEs. In our robustness check, after controlling the proportion of the number of non-SOEs to total number of firms in each province, our results remain the same.

[7]   Please refer to www.cerdi.org/uploads/sfCmsContent/html/192/Fangang.pdf for a detailed description of the data.

compiled by the China Banking Association, statistical yearbooks of various provinces, related statistical data on banking and finance, and surveys on finance and banking for each province. This measure has been used in Qian and Yeung 2014.[8] The NERI index had been used in many papers (e.g., in Firth et al. 2009 and in Qian, Strahan, and Yang 2015).[9]

The measure we used in this study can reflect the credit allocation in the PRC well (Fan, Wang, and Zhu 2011). The PRC financial system used to be very inefficient and ineffective The financial intermediaries used to allocate credit to SOEs only even though the performances of the SOEs were less efficient than those of non-SOEs. The system has gradually evolved to become a more well-developed system after a series of reforms since 1978 until now.[10] The financial intermediaries have grown to more actively investigate and monitor firms due to improvement of the status of non-SOEs, the reform of the PRC financial system, the increasing competition among the financial institutions, etc. Since non-SOEs, in general, are having better performances and are more promising than SOEs, the proportion of credit allocated by the PRC financial institutions to non-SOEs to total credit has increased gradually.

Panel B of Table 13.1 presents the mean, median, and standard deviation of the credit market development index from 1999 to 2006. The mean of the credit market development index increases from 3.27 to 8.73. The median is close to the mean. These show that credit allocation of the PRC financial intermediaries has improved throughout these years. The standard deviation of the credit market development index in each year ranges from 2.07 to 3.07, indicating that credit allocation varies from one province to another.

---

[8]   Qian and Yeung (2014) used the same index as we used to proxy banking industry development (page 3).

[9]   Firth et al. (2009) used the NERI index as an indicator of market development conditions (page 1154). Qian, Strahan, and Yang (2014) used the NERI index as the coastal indicator (page 20). The credit market development index used in our chapter is one of the components of the NERI index.

[10] Please see Section 13.2 for a detailed overview of the PRC financial system.

13.3.4 Control Variables

Following the literature, we include firm, industry, and province control variables that might affect firms' product innovation. The firm control variables include firm size, firm age, age square, leverage, investment intensity, whether it is an export firm, return on asset (ROA), and ownership types. The industry control variable is industry concentration (measured by Herfindahl–Hirschman Index). Province control variables include the secondary-industry production ratio, third-industry production ratio, and provincial GDP per capita. In addition, we include the government subsidy variable since the PRC government subsidizes companies that engage in more innovative activities.

Table 13.2 provides the definitions for all of the variables, including the control variables, the credit market development (CMD) variable, NP, NPr, and the variables used in the following sections. Panel C of Table 13.1 presents the summary statistics for the sample mean, median, minimum value, and maximum value of the control variables.

Table 13.2: Definitions of Variables

Variable	Definition
NP	New product dummy, equals 1 if new product production is greater than zero and zero otherwise.
NPr	Ratio of new product production on total production.
CMD	Credit market development index from Fan, Wang, and Zhu (2011), constructed from the ratio of credits allocated to non-SOEs on total credits for each province.
size	Firm size, constructed as natural log of total asset of a firm at the end of a fiscal year.
lnage	Firm age, defined as natural log of current year minus firm establish year.
lnage2	Firm age square
leverage	Leverage, defined as total debt dividing total asset of a firm at the end of a year.
Investment intensity	Fixed asset, defined as fixed asset dividing total asset of a firm at the end of a year.

continued next page

Table 13.2: *Continued*

Variable	Definition
export	Export, defined as total export dividing total production of a firm at the end of a year.
HHI	Industry concentration, measured as the Herfindahl–Hirschman Index based on 3-digit industry code.
ROA	Firm return on asset, measured as profit dividing total asset of a firm at the end of a year.
subsidy	Government subsidy to a firm, defined as government subsidy dividing the asset of a firm at the end of a year.
SOE	State-owned enterprises, equals 1 if the firms are state-owned enterprises, and 0 otherwise. The state-owned enterprises are defined according to the ownership type provided by the National Bureau of Statistics of China (NBS of China). We also include firms whose share of the state capital exceeds 50%.
COE	Collectively owned enterprises, equals 1 if the firms are collectively owned, and 0 otherwise. It is defined by the NBS of China as assets owned collectively, including township–village enterprises.
private	Privately owned enterprises, equals 1 if the firms are privately owned, and 0 otherwise. It is defined by the NBS of China as assets owned by natural persons.
HMT	Companies owned by investors from Hong Kong, China; Macau, China; and Taipei,China, equals 1 if the firms are HMT, and 0 otherwise.
foreign	Companies owned by foreign investors
secondary industry	Ratio of gross domestic product (GDP) from industries including mining, manufacturing, electricity, gas and water producing and supplying, and construction, defined as GDP of secondary industry dividing total GDP of a province at the end of a year
third industry	Ratio of GDP from industries excluding agriculture and those in secondary industry, defined as GDP of third industry dividing total GDP of a province at the end of a year
lngdppc	Ln GDP per capita defined as logarithm of provincial GDP dividing provincial population at the end of a fiscal year
small	Small-sized firms, equals 1 if the size of the companies are small as defined by NBS of China, and 0 otherwise
mid	Middle-sized firms, equals 1 if the size of the firms are middle as defined by NBS of China, and 0 otherwise
fp50	Firm performance dummy, equals 1 if the return on asset of the firm is above the 50% of all firms in the same province, industry, and year. It equals zero otherwise.
nonSOE_ratio	The ratio of the number of non-SOEs on total number of firms in one province at the end of a year
FD	Financial depth, defined as the total credits of a province dividing the GDP of that province at the end of a year

Source: Authors.

13.4 | Results

13.4.1 Empirical Models

In this subsection, we describe the models used in our analysis. To test whether credit market development affects firms' product innovation incentives, we estimate two models. The first model is

$$\ln\left(\frac{p_{i,t}}{1-p_{i,t}}\right) = \beta_1 + \beta_2 \times CMD_{k,t-1} + \lambda' \times X_{i,j,k,t-1} + v_k + w_j + \alpha_t + \varepsilon_{i,j,k,t}$$

where $p_{i,t} = Prob(NP_{i,t} = 1)$, the possibility that firm i produces new products at time t; $CMD_{k,t-1}$ represents the credit market development for province k in year $t-1$; $X_{i,j,k,t-1}$ denotes the control variables for firm i, in industry j, province k, at time $t-1$; v_k, w_j and α_t represent province-level, industry-level, and year fixed effects, respectively; $\varepsilon_{i,j,k,t}$ is the error term; β_1 is the constant term; β_2 represents the effect of credit market development through improving credit allocation on firms' product innovation incentives; λ' are vectors of coefficients of the control variables.

In the second model, we use the conditional logit method. The second model is

$$\ln\left(\frac{p_i}{1-p_i}\right) = \beta_2 \times CMD_{k,t-1} + \lambda' \times X_{i,j,k,t-1} + u_i + v_k + w_j + \alpha_t + \varepsilon_{i,j,k,t}$$

where u_i represents firm-level fixed effect.

To test whether credit market development affects firms' product innovation outcomes, we estimate the third model using the fixed effect regression method and the fourth model using the tobit method. The third model is

$$NPr_{i,t} = \beta_1 + \beta_2 \times CMD_{k,t-1} + \lambda' \times X_{i,j,k,t-1} + u_i + v_k + w_j + \alpha_t + \varepsilon_{i,j,k,t}$$

where $NPr_{i,t}$ is the ratio of the new product production to total production for firm i at time t.

The fourth model is

$$NPr_{i,t}^* = \beta_1 + \beta_2 \times CMD_{k,t-1} + \lambda' \times X_{i,j,k,t-1} + v_k + w_j + \alpha_t + \varepsilon_{i,j,k,t}$$

$$\text{where } NPr_{i,t} = \begin{cases} NPr_{i,t}^*, & \text{if } NPr_{i,t}^* > 0 \\ 0, & \text{if } NPr_{i,t}^* \leq 0 \end{cases}.$$

13.4.2 Baseline Results

From two perspectives, we analyze how credit market development
affects product innovation by improving credit allocation. First, we explore
whether the improvement in allocation affects firms' incentives to produce
new products in general. Second, we investigate whether improved credit
allocation encourages firms to produce more products.

Table 13.3 provides the results for firms' product innovation incentives and
outcomes. For the product innovation incentives, we apply both pooled
logit and conditional logit estimation methods. The advantage of the pooled
logit is that it can utilize the information in all observations and provide
the average partial effect of a variable. In comparison with the pooled logit
method, the advantage of the conditional logit is that it allows us to control
for the unobserved firm fixed effect. In other words, the method allows us
to include many time-invariant firm characteristics that affect both credit
market development and firms' product innovation incentives. This reduces
the endogeneity problems caused by omitted variables. Nevertheless, the
conditional logit method only considers the within variation of the variables.
The firms which always or never produce new products are dropped during
the estimation, and this therefore results in a big loss of observations.
The standard errors are clustered by industry and province.

The results from the pooled logit method, which are shown in column (1)
of Table 13.3, demonstrate that credit market development, through
improvement of credit allocation, enhances the probability of firms producing
new products. This finding is statistically significant at the 1% level, holding

other factors constant. When credit market development increases by 1 point, around 471 (891,384/7 ×0.0037) firms will be induced to engage in producing new products in 1 year, on average. The magnitude is similar to that of Benfratello, Schiantarelli, and Sembenelli (2008) who have shown that credit market development induces 133 (6,025/9×0.2) firms in Italy to engage in product innovation. Column (2) provides the results of the conditional logit method: credit market development is also significantly positive at the 1% level. All of the results confirm the idea that credit market development, by improving credit allocation, does increase firms' product innovation incentives.

Table 13.3: Credit Market Development and Firm Innovation: Full Sample

	(1) NP_logit	(2) NP_xtlogit	(3) NPr_xtreg	(4) NPr_tobit
CMD	0.0593*** [0.0037] (0.0087)	0.0654*** (0.0053)	0.0005** (0.0002)	0.0216*** (0.0011)
size	0.5573*** (0.0144)	0.5728*** (0.0204)	0.0073*** (0.0009)	0.1888*** (0.0014)
lnage	-0.6672*** (0.0533)	-0.0904 (0.0730)	-0.0054** (0.0018)	-0.2210*** (0.0089)
lnage2	0.1853*** (0.0129)	0.0499** (0.0166)	0.0014*** (0.0004)	0.0587*** (0.0020)
leverage	-0.2213*** (0.0612)	-0.1082* (0.0585)	-0.0011 (0.0009)	-0.0968*** (0.0072)
Investment intensity	-0.5097*** (0.0986)	0.2107** (0.0719)	0.0025* (0.0013)	-0.1989*** (0.0085)
export	0.3468*** (0.0854)	0.1904*** (0.0518)	0.0027* (0.0015)	0.1290*** (0.0056)
HHI	2.8389*** (0.7528)	-2.3018** (1.0191)	-0.0473** (0.0225)	1.3456*** (0.1240)
ROA	0.7062*** (0.1454)	0.4606*** (0.1119)	0.0024 (0.0022)	0.2574*** (0.0155)

continued next page

Table 13.3: *Continued*

	(1) NP_logit	(2) NP_xtlogit	(3) NPr_xtreg	(4) NPr_tobit
subsidy	−0.1908 (1.1373)	1.8736 (1.2853)	0.0471* (0.0263)	0.0785 (0.1940)
SOE	−0.0582 (0.0381)	0.2985*** (0.0549)	0.0027* (0.0014)	−0.0343*** (0.0072)
COE	−0.5163*** (0.0454)	0.0442 (0.0490)	0.0018 (0.0011)	−0.1861*** (0.0072)
private	−0.2226*** (0.0305)	0.0005 (0.0375)	0.0010 (0.0009)	−0.0838*** (0.0056)
HMT	−0.6137*** (0.0584)	0.1308 (0.0806)	0.0015 (0.0022)	−0.2160*** (0.0072)
foreign	−0.5674*** (0.0488)	0.1943** (0.0815)	0.0031 (0.0021)	−0.1900*** (0.0070)
secondary industry	−3.9274** (1.4428)	−5.1391*** (1.1289)	−0.1345** (0.0430)	−1.9515*** (0.2062)
third industry	8.4675*** (1.7083)	15.5376*** (1.3172)	0.2124*** (0.0528)	2.6136*** (0.2450)
lngdppc	0.7966* (0.4348)	1.1845*** (0.2496)	0.0220** (0.0111)	0.3290*** (0.0464)
constant	−18.5556*** (3.9894)		−0.2642** (0.1096)	−6.5475*** (0.3781)
Prov FE	Y	Y	Y	Y
Year FE	Y	Y	Y	Y
Industry FE	Y	Y	Y	Y
Firm FE		Y	Y	
N	891,384	96,497	891,462	891,462

* significant at the 10% level, ** significant at the 5% level, *** significant at the 1% level.

Notes: The first two columns provide results for firms' innovation incentives. Coefficients are estimated by logit and conditional logit methods. The third and fourth columns provide results for firms' innovation outcomes. Coefficients are estimated by fixed effect regression and tobit methods. All independent variables are lagged by one period. The standard errors are clustered by province and industry. CMD is credit market development index. The definitions of all other control variables can be found in Table 13.2. Standard errors are in parentheses. Marginal effect for CMD is in square brackets.

Source: Authors.

The results also indicate that firm size, the ratio of firms' exports to production, firms' performances, GDP per capita in a province, and the proportion of third-industry production in GDP have statistically positive effects on firms' incentives in engaging in innovative activities. In contrast, firms' leverage and the proportion of secondary-industry production in GDP in a province have statistically negative effects on firms' product innovation incentives. In addition, as firms' age increases, their product innovation incentives first decrease and then increase.

For firms' product innovation outcomes, the estimation methods we use include the fixed effect regression method and the tobit method. The fixed effect regression method is commonly used, is very easy to apply, and can help reduce the endogeneity problem caused by omitted variables. However, this method cannot account for the fact that the data are censored. Since not all firms produce a new product each year, there are many zeros in the data, which might make the fixed effect regression less trustworthy. In comparison with the fixed effect regression method, the tobit method is more suitable for censored data. In addition, the standard errors are also clustered at the province and industry levels.

The results for firms' product innovation outcomes are presented in columns (3) and (4) in Table 13.3. In column (3), we provide the results estimated by the fixed effect regression method, which show that the coefficient of credit market development is positive and significant at the 5% level. When credit market development increases by 1 point, a firm will produce CNY33 (66,739.79×0.05%)[11] more in new products in 1 year on average. The magnitude of the coefficients is close to that of Ayyagari, Demirguc-Kunt, and Maksimovic (2011) who have shown that when bank financing increases by 1 point, the core innovation of firms increases by 0.2%. The results estimated by the tobit method are presented in column (4).

---

[11]   The average production in our sample is 66,739.79.

The coefficient of credit market development is positive and significant at the 1% level. After accounting for the fact that the data are censored, the coefficient of credit market development on firms' product innovation outcomes increases substantially. This illustrates that, when credit market development increases by 1 point, a firm is predicted to produce CNY1,441 (66,739.79 × 2.16%) more in new products in 1 year on average. All of the results in Table 13.3 reinforce the idea that credit market development, by improving credit allocation in the PRC, does promote industrial firms' product innovation incentives and outcomes.

13.4.3 Mechanisms

In this subsection, we investigate the mechanism through which credit market development affects firms' product innovation incentives and outcomes by improving credit allocation. Specifically, we examine the credit constraint channel. We hypothesize that, if financial intermediaries can effectively alleviate firms' credit constraints over time, more credit-constrained firms should be more affected by credit market development. This is because the marginal utility provided by credit market development is higher for more credit-constrained firms than for less constrained firms.

To examine whether the more credit-constrained firms are more affected by credit market development, we first test whether privately owned firms are more affected by credit market development than other types of firms. We then test whether SMEs are more affected by credit market development than large firms.

Firm size has been widely used as a measure of credit constraint (Guariglia 2008). In the PRC, firm ownership has also been used as a proxy for firm credit constraint (Poncet, Steingress, and Vandenbussche 2010). SMEs and privately-owned firms have been found to be more credit constrained than other firms First, the PRC financial system originated from a state-owned monobank system. The financial institutions tend to allocate credit following the directives of the central government or local governments

(Cull and Xu 2003). Second, due to non-listed privately-owned firms' and SMEs' short credit history and non-standardized financial reports, the financial institutions tend to discriminate against them (Brandt and Li 2003; Guariglia and Poncet 2008; Chong, Lu, and Ongena 2013). We construct a dummy variable, private, where private is equal to one if the firm is privately owned and zero otherwise. We then add the interaction of private and credit market development to the models in Section 13.4.1. The coefficient of the interaction term captures the effect of credit market development on privately owned firms' innovative capacities compared with those of SOEs. In Table 13.4, we provide the results for product innovation incentives and outcomes for both types of firms. Columns (1) and (2) show the results for firms' product innovation incentives using the logit and conditional logit methods. The coefficients of the interaction of the variables private and credit market development are positive and significant at the 5% level in both regressions. This means that credit market development has a greater effect on the product innovation incentives of privately owned firms compared with other types of firms. The effect of credit market development on privately owned firms' product innovation incentives is 0.12% higher than it is for other types of firms. Columns (3) and (4) present the results for firms' product innovation outcomes. The coefficients of the interaction of the variables private and credit market development are also positive and significant at the 5% level. Compared with other types of firms, the effect of credit market development on privately owned firms' product innovation outcomes is 0.09% higher using the fixed effect regression method and 0.59% higher for the tobit method.

We then test whether the SMEs are more affected than large firms by improved credit allocation as a result of credit market development. We construct two dummy variables: middle and small. Middle is equal to one if the size of the firm is middle and zero otherwise. Small is equal to one if the size of the firm is small and zero otherwise. The variables small dummy, middle dummy, interaction of small dummy and credit market development, and interaction of middle dummy and credit market development are added to the models in Section 13.4.1. The results are presented in Table 13.5.

Table 13.4: Credit Market Development and Firm Innovation:
Private versus Others

	(1) NP_logit	(2) NP_xtlogit	(3) NPr_xtreg	(4) NPr_tobit
CMD	0.0552*** [0.0034] (0.0093)	0.0559*** (0.0055)	0.0003 (0.0002)	0.0204*** (0.0033)
CMD*private	0.0198** [C.0012] (C.0078)	0.0427*** (0.0072)	0.0009*** (0.0002)	0.0059** (0.0028)
private	-0.3984*** [-0.0246] (C.0712)	-0.3678*** (0.0724)	-0.0066** (0.0022)	-0.1352*** (0.0262)
Constant	-17.6119*** (3.8884)		-0.2329** (0.1050)	-6.2811*** (1.3520)
Controls	Y	Y	Y	Y
Prov FE	Y	Y	Y	Y
Year FE	Y	Y	Y	Y
Industry FE	Y	Y	Y	Y
Firm FE		Y	Y	
N	891,384	96,497	891,462	891,462

* significant at the 10% level, ** significant at the 5% level, *** significant at the 1% level.

Notes: The first two columns provide results for firms' innovation incentives. Coefficients are estimated by logit and conditional logit methods. The third and fourth columns provide results for firms' innovation outcomes. Coefficients are estimated by fixed effect regression and tobit methods. All independent variables are lagged by one period. The standard errors are clustered by province and industry. CMD is credit market development index. Private is a dummy of private firms. CMD*private denotes the interaction of private and CMD. The other control variables are the same as those in Table 13.3. For simplicity, we do not report the estimation results for other control variables. Standard errors are in parentheses. Marginal effects are in square brackets.

Source: Authors.

All coefficients of the interaction terms in columns (1) and (2) are positive and significant at the 1% level. The results indicate that, compared with large firms, credit market development affects SMEs' product innovation incentives by 0.63% (0.4% + 0.23%) more. Both coefficients of the interaction terms are also positive and significant at the 5% level using the tobit method. This finding shows that compared with large firms, the effect of credit market development on SMEs is 3.14% higher.

Table 13.5: Credit Market Development and Firm Innovation: Small and Medium-Sized Enterprises versus Others

	(1) NP_logit	(2) NP_xtlogit	(3) NPr_xtreg	(4) NPr_tobit
CMD	0.0159 [0.0010] (0.0106)	0.0087 (0.0070)	0.0001 (0.0003)	0.0073* (0.0038)
CMD*small	0.0644*** [0.0040] (0.0090)	0.0727*** (0.0062)	0.0003 (0.0002)	0.0200*** (0.0032)
CMD*mid	0.0370*** [0.0023] (0.0081)	0.0783*** (0.0084)	0.0018*** (0.0005)	0.0114*** (0.0030)
small	−1.2171*** [−0.0748] (0.0764)	−0.6196*** (0.0681)	−0.0017 (0.0029)	−0.3874*** (0.0289)
mid	−0.5665*** [−0.0348] (0.0687)	−0.3498*** (0.0830)	−0.0070 (0.0045)	−0.1786*** (0.0243)
constant	−16.2577*** (4.1117)		−0.2646** (0.1110)	−5.9158*** (1.4206)
Controls	Y	Y	Y	Y
Prov FE	Y	Y	Y	Y
Year FE	Y	Y	Y	Y
Industry FE	Y	Y	Y	Y
Firm FE		Y	Y	
N	891,384	96,497	891,462	891,462

* significant at the 10% level, ** significant at the 5% level, *** significant at the 1% level.

Notes: The first two columns provide results for firms' innovation incentives. Coefficients are estimated by logit and conditional logit methods. The third and fourth columns provide results for firms' innovation outcomes. Coefficients are estimated by fixed effect regression and tobit methods. All independent variables are lagged by one period. The standard errors are clustered by province and industry. CMD is credit market development index. Small is a dummy of small-sized firms. Middle is a dummy of middle-sized firms. CMD*small denotes the interaction of small and CMD. CMD*mid denotes the interaction of mid and CMD. The other control variables are the same as those in Table 13.3. For simplicity, we do not report the estimation results for other control variables. Standard errors are in parentheses. Marginal effects are in square brackets.

Source: Authors.

All of the results in Tables 13.4 and 13.5 show the heterogeneous effects of
how credit market development promotes firms' product innovation incentives
and outcomes. Credit market development, through improved credit allocation,
encourages credit-constrained firms to innovate more than firms that are less
constrained.

Financial Performance of Firms

We then examine whether credit market development, by improving credit
allocation, has a different effect on product innovation incentives and outcomes
based on the firm's financial performance. We hypothesize that, as the financial
institutions become more active in investigating firms and projects instead
of just allocating credit to SOEs fo lowing government directives, they will be
more likely to lend to firms with better performances. First, firms with better
performances have the ability to repay loans on time. Second, firms with better
performances might also have superior operations, management, and strategy
than other firms, and they might care more about their long-term growth.
Third, firms with better performance might be better able and more willing to
engage in risky innovative projects. Therefore, banks might be more willing to
lend to the innovative projects of firms with better performances than those
which have underperformed.

We use ROA as a proxy for firm performance: the higher the ROA, the better
the firm performance. Table 13.3 shows that firms' ROA has a positive and
significant effect on firms' product innovation incentives and outcomes.
We generate a dummy variable, fp50, by first sorting the firms within the same
industry, province, and year based on their ROAs. The dummy variable fp50
is equal to one if the firms' performances are above the 50th percentile, and
zero otherwise. The variable fp50 and the interaction term of fp50 and credit
market development are added to all of the models in Section 4.1. A positive and
significant interaction term indicates that the firm performance is indeed a factor.

In Table 13.6, we present our results. Column (1) shows the results for firms'
product innovation incentives estimated by the logit method, and column (2)
shows those estimated by the conditional logit method. Column (3) shows

the results for firms' product innovation outcomes estimated by the fixed effect regression model, and column (4) shows those estimated by the tobit method. The coefficients associated with the interaction terms of credit market development and fp50 are all positive and significant at the 5% level, which indicates that, compared with low-performance firms, the effect of credit market development on high-performance firms' product innovation incentives and outcomes is 0.09% higher—0.04% higher using the fixed effect regression method, and 0.48% higher with the tobit model.

Table 13.6: **Credit Market Development and Firm Innovation: Better Performance versus Others**

	(1) NP_logit	(2) NP_xtlogit	(3) NPr_xtreg	(4) NPr_tobit
CMD	0.0540*** [0.0033] (0.0097)	0.0539*** (0.0060)	0.0003 (0.0002)	0.0197*** (0.0033)
CMD*fp50	0.0138** [0.0009] (0.0070)	0.0241*** (0.0055)	0.0004** (0.0001)	0.0048** (0.0024)
fp50	0.1026** [0.0063] (0.0523)	−0.0862* (0.0508)	−0.0012 (0.0009)	0.0388** (0.0185)
constant	−18.9447*** (3.9437)		−0.2664** (0.1092)	−6.6912*** (1.3675)
controls	Y	Y	Y	Y
Prov FE	Y	Y	Y	Y
Year FE	Y	Y	Y	Y
Industry FE	Y	Y	Y	Y
Firm FE		Y	Y	
N	891,384	96,497	891,462	891,462

* significant at the 10% level, ** significant at the 5% level, *** significant at the 1% level.

Notes: The first two columns provide results for firms' innovation incentives. Coefficients are estimated by logit and conditional logit methods. The third and fourth columns provide results for firms' innovation outcomes. Coefficients are estimated by fixed effect regression and tobit methods. All independent variables are lagged by one period. The standard errors are clustered by province and industry. CMD is credit market development index. The variable fp50 is a dummy of profitable firms in the first 50% percentile of all firms in the same province and industry. CMD*fp50 denotes the interaction of fp50 and CMD. The other control variables are the same as those in Table 13.3. For simplicity, we do not report the estimation results for other control variables. Standard errors are in parentheses. Marginal effects are in square brackets.

Source: Authors.

13.5 | Robustness Check

In this section, we check the robustness of our results. We first check the validity of our results using the instrumental variable method. We then examine whether our results are driven by an increase in the number of non-SOE firms or an increase in total credit rather than improvement of credit allocation. Afterwards, we evaluate our results using firms that produce new products only. Furthermore, we investigate our results by employing an alternative credit market development measure. In the end, we check our results by excluding listed firms in the sample.

13.5.1 Instrumental Variable Regression

In this subsection, we solve the endogeneity problem using the instrumental variable (IV) method. Similar to Chong, Lu, and Ongena (2013), we construct an IV as follows: we use the average of the credit market development in neighboring provinces as the IV. First, the innovative capacities of firms in one province might not affect credit market development in other provinces. Second, the credit market development of other provinces is not likely to affect the local firms' innovative capacities because the PRC credit market is region specific (Qian and Yeung 2014). Bank branches are discouraged from lending to firms in other regions to minimize the overlapping competition. Third, the first-stage F-test shows that our instrument is valid. Since the logit methods cannot accommodate the IV method, we use a linear probability model to estimate how credit market development affects firms' product innovation incentives.

Table 13.7 presents the results. Column (1) presents the results for firms' product innovation incentives using a linear probability model, and column (2) presents those using the fixed effect linear probability model. Column (3) provides the results using the fixed effect regression method, and column (4) provides those using the tobit model. The first-stage F-statistics shows that the IV variable is statistically significant at the 1% level. The coefficients obtained by these four methods are all statistically significant at the 1% level, further reinforcing the idea that credit market development, by improving credit allocation, promotes firms' product innovation.

Table 13.7: Credit Market Development and Firm Innovation: Instrumental Variable Method

	(1) NP	(2) NP	(3) NPr_reg	(4) NPr_tobit
CMD	0.0027*** (0.0007)	0.0064*** (0.0012)	0.0024*** (0.0004)	0.0338*** (0.0050)
size	0.0407*** (0.0019)	0.0407*** (0.0019)	0.0074*** (0.0009)	0.1889*** (0.0044)
Ln(age)	−0.0531*** (0.0048)	−0.0527*** (0.0048)	−0.0056** (0.0018)	−0.2194*** (0.0189)
Ln(age)^2	0.0150*** (0.0013)	0.0149*** (0.0013)	0.0014*** (0.0004)	0.0584*** (0.0046)
leverage	−0.0217*** (0.0034)	−0.0217*** (0.0034)	−0.0010 (0.0009)	−0.0967*** (0.0227)
Investment intensity	−0.0340*** (0.0053)	−0.0341*** (0.0053)	0.0025* (0.0013)	−0.1992*** (0.0359)
export	0.0249*** (0.0061)	0.0247*** (0.0061)	0.0026* (0.0015)	0.1282*** (0.0343)
HHI	0.2618*** (0.0757)	0.2609*** (0.0756)	−0.0468** (0.0230)	1.3411*** (0.3037)
ROA	0.0607*** (0.0085)	0.0599*** (0.0085)	0.0017 (0.0022)	0.2553*** (0.0480)
Subsidy_ratio	−0.0662 (0.0809)	−0.0691 (0.0808)	0.0458* (0.0264)	0.0638 (0.4103)
SOE	−0.0043 (0.0037)	−0.0039 (0.0038)	0.0027* (0.0014)	−0.0325** (0.0136)
Collectively-owned	−0.0395*** (0.0036)	−0.0394*** (0.0036)	0.0017 (0.0011)	−0.1853*** (0.0173)
private	−0.0246*** (0.0027)	−0.0244*** (0.0027)	0.0012 (0.0009)	−0.0830*** (0.0118)
HMT	−0.0566*** (0.0046)	−0.0563*** (0.0047)	0.0016 (0.0022)	−0.2149*** (0.0216)
foreign	−0.0502*** (0.0046)	−0.0498*** (0.0046)	0.0035* (0.0021)	−0.1889*** (0.0183)
secondary industry	−0.4119*** (0.1100)	−0.3670*** (0.1078)	−0.1126** (0.0411)	−1.7973*** (0.5238)
third industry	0.4956*** (0.1102)	0.5146*** (0.1150)	0.2020*** (0.0532)	2.6534*** (0.6277)
Ln(gdppc)	0.0643** (0.0264)	0.0699** (0.0262)	0.0225** (0.0107)	0.3419** (0.1498)

continued next page

Table 13.7: *Continued*

	(1) NP	(2) NP	(3) NPr_reg	(4) NPr_tobit
constant	-0.8719*** (0.2325)	-0.9589*** (0.2396)	-6.4420*** (1.3562)	-6.7775*** (1.4023)
Prov FE	Y	Y	Y	Y
Year FE	Y	Y	Y	Y
Industry FE	Y	Y	Y	Y
Firm FE		Y	Y	
N	891,462	891,462	798,324	891,462
F-statistics first stage		733.92		

* significant at the 10% level, ** significant at the 5% level, *** significant at the 1% level.

Notes: The first column presents estimated results under fixed effect regression method. The second column presents results for ur der tobit method. All independent variables are lagged by one period. The standard errors are clustered by province and industry. CMD is credit market development index. Standard errors are in parentheses.

Source: Authors.

13.5.2 Improvement of Credit Allocation or Not?

Since the credit market development variable is constructed as an index of credit extended to non-SOEs relative to total credit, a larger number of non-SOEs might lead to a higher value. This would indicate that the increase in credit market development might not be due to improved credit allocation, instead resulting from the increase in the number of non-SOEs. To check whether our results are due to improved credit allocation or a higher number of non-SOEs, we construct a variable nonSOE_ratio, as the ratio of the number of non-SOEs to the total number of firms. We then add the nonSOE_ratio into the equations in Section 4.1.

Our results show that the credit market development variable is still significant for all cases after controlling for the nonSOE_ratio (Table 13.8).

Table 13.8: **Credit Market Development and Firm Innovation: Control Number of Non-State-Owned Enterprises**

	(1) NP_logit	(2) NP_xtlogit	(3) NPr_xtreg	(4) NPr_tobit
CMD	0.0640*** [0.0040] (0.0090)	0.0822*** (0.0054)	0.0007*** (0.0002)	0.0231*** (0.0011)
nonSOE	-0.9595** (0.3497)	-3.5345*** (0.2020)	-0.0492*** (0.0129)	-0.3094*** (0.0373)
constant	-14.1391*** (3.8220)		-0.1124 (0.0913)	-5.2146*** (0.4109)
controls	Y	Y	Y	Y
Prov FE	Y	Y	Y	Y
Year FE	Y	Y	Y	Y
Industry FE	Y	Y	Y	Y
Firm FE		Y	Y	
N	891,384	96,497	891,462	891,462

* significant at the 10% level, ** significant at the 5% level, *** significant at the 1% level.

Notes: The first two columns provide results for firm innovation incentive. Coefficients are estimated by logit and conditional logit. The third and fourth columns provide results for firm innovation ability. Coefficients are estimated by fixed effect regression and tobit method. All independent variables are lagged by one period. The standard errors are clustered by province and industry. CMD is credit market development index. nonSOE denotes the ratio of the number of non-SOEs on total number of firms in a province. The definitions of all other control variables can be found in Table 13.2. Standard errors are in parentheses. Marginal effect for CMD is in square brackets.

Credit market development consists of various dimensions, including improvement of credit resource allocation and an increase in total credit (financial depth). To further investigate whether our results are driven by an increase in the quantity of credit or improvement in credit allocation, we add the financial depth variable to the equations in Section 13.4.1. Following the literature, financial depth is defined as total credit/GDP for each province in each year.

The results indicate that the increase in the industrial firms' product innovation incentives and outcomes are more likely to be driven by improved credit allocation rather than financial depth (Table 13.9).

Table 13.9: **Credit Market Development and Firm Innovation: Control Financial Depth**

	(1) NP_logit	(2) NP_xtlogit	(3) NPr_xtreg	(4) NPr_tobit
CMD	0.0606*** [0.0037] (0.0086)	0.0742*** (0.0053)	0.0006** (0.0002)	0.0218*** (0.0011)
FD	0.2114 (0.2147)	1.6633*** (0.0987)	0.0283*** (0.0074)	0.0184 (0.0191)
constant	−17.5551*** (3.7531)		−0.2490** (0.1064)	−6.4741*** (0.3857)
controls	Y	Y	Y	Y
Prov FE	Y	Y	Y	Y
Year FE	Y	Y	Y	Y
Industry FE	Y	Y	Y	Y
Firm FE		Y	Y	
N	891,384	96,497	891,462	891,462

* significant at the 10% level, ** significant at the 5% level, *** significant at the 1% level.

Notes: The first two columns provide results for firm innovation incentive. Coefficients are estimated by logit and conditional logit. The third and fourth columns provide results for firm innovation ability. Coefficients are estimated by fixed effect regression and tobit method. All independent variables are lagged by one period. The standard errors are clustered by province and industry. CMD is credit market development index. FD denotes the financial depth. The definitions of all other control variables can be found in Table 13.2. Standard errors are in parentheses. Marginal effect for CMD is in square brackets.

Source: Authors.

After controlling for financial depth, the credit market development variable is significant in all cases. However, the financial depth variable is only statistically significant using the conditional logit method and fixed effect regression method.

13.5.3 Firms with New Products Only

Our primary results apply to all firms regardless of whether they have new products or not. In this part, we restrict our sample to firms producing new products to further check our results. We select firms producing new products in at least 1 year of our sample period. The sample size is then reduced to 129,131.

We report all results using the fixed effect regression and tobit methods in Table 13.10. These results are consistent with our primary results. The credit market development term for the full sample is positive and statistically significant at the 1% level for both methods. The interactions of the private variable and the credit market development term, the small variable and the credit market development term, and the middle variable and the credit market development term are also positive and significant for both methods.

13.5.4 An Alternative Credit Market Development Measure

In this part, we employ an alternative measure to proxy the credit market development. The variable CMD only represents the credit side of the credit market development. Nevertheless, the deposit side also affects the availability of the credits to firms. Therefore, we use a composite index by combining both the credit side and the deposit side of the credit market development as a proxy for credit market development. The index is constructed as a combination of deposits to non-state-owned financial institutions on total deposits and credit allocated to non-SOEs on total credit. The higher this index, the more marketization the financial market is (Fan, Wang, and Zhu 2011). The results shown in Table 13.11 are consistent with our primary results.

13.5.5 Excluding Listed Firms

We check our results by excluding listed firms in the sample, matching the firms by name, and removing listed firms. Listed firms comprised only 0.5% of the sample. The results are also consistent with our primary results and are available upon request.

Table 13.10: Credit Market Development and Firm Innovation: Firms with New Products Only

	Full Sample		Private		Scale		Profit	
	(1) xtreg	(2) Tobit	(3) xtreg	(4) Tobit	(5) xtreg	(6) Tobit	(7) xtreg	(8) Tobit
CMD	0.0036*** (0.0009)	0.0141*** (0.0018)	0.0029** (0.0009)	0.0123*** (0.0019)	0.0012 (0.0010)	0.0064** (0.0022)	0.0029*** (0.0009)	0.0122*** (0.0018)
CMD*private			0.0032** (0.0010)	0.0082*** (0.0019)				
private			−0.0223** (0.0092)	−0.0873*** (0.0183)				
CMD*small					0.0031** (0.0011)	0.0122*** (0.0023)		
CMD*mid					0.0033** (0.0011)	0.0054** (0.0022)		
small					−0.0142 (0.0094)	−0.1528*** (0.0178)		
mid					−0.0085 (0.0102)	−0.0861*** (0.0166)		
CMD*fp50							0.0015** (0.0007)	0.0043*** (0.0014)
fp50							−0.0026 (0.0053)	0.0020 (0.0119)
constant	−1.1011** (0.4637)	−3.2691*** (0.9755)	−0.9443** (0.4533)	−2.8567** (0.9419)	−1.2094** (0.4852)	−3.1127** (1.0141)	−1.1249** (0.4606)	−3.3290*** (0.9646)
controls	Y	Y	Y	Y	Y	Y	Y	Y
Prov FE	Y	Y	Y	Y	Y	Y	Y	Y
Year FE	Y	Y	Y	Y	Y	Y	Y	Y
Industry FE	Y	Y	Y	Y	Y	Y	Y	Y
Firm FE	Y		Y		Y		Y	
N	127,959	127,959	127,959	127,959	127,959	127,959	127,959	127,959

* significant at the 10% level, ** significant at the 5% evel, *** significant at the 1% level.

Notes: The first two columns provide full sample results for firms' innovation outcomes. Columns (3) and (4) are comparisons of private and other types of firms. Columns (5) and (6) are comparisons of small and medium-sized enterprises, and large firms. Columns (7) and (8) are comparisons of profitable and other firms. Coefficients are estimated by fixed effect regression and tobit methods. All independent variables are lagged by one period. The standard errors are clustered by province and industry. CMD is credit market development index. The variable fp50 is a dummy of profitable firms in the first 50% percentile of all firms in the same province and industry. CMD*fp50 denotes the interaction of fp50 and CMD. Small is a dummy of small-sized firms. Middle is a dummy of middle-sized firms. CMD*small denotes the interaction of small and CMD. CMD*mid denotes the interaction of mid and CMD. Private is a dummy of private firms. CMD*private denotes the interaction of private and CMD. The other control variables are the same as those in Table 13.3. For simplicity, we do not report the estimation results for other control variables. Standard errors are in parentheses. Marginal effects are in square brackets.

Source: Authors.

Table 13.11: Credit Market Development and Firm Innovation: Alternative Measure of Credit Market Development

	Full Sample		Private		Scale		Profit	
	(1) xtreg	(2) Tobit	(3) xtreg	(4) Tobit	(5) xtreg	(6) Tobit	(7) xtreg	(8) Tobit
Fmkt	0.0015*** (0.0004)	0.0366*** (0.0024)	0.0010** (0.0004)	0.0345*** (0.0068)	0.0011*** (0.0003)	0.0245*** (0.0065)	0.0012*** (0.0004)	0.0352*** (0.0069)
Fmkt*private			0.0016*** (0.0003)	0.0060* (0.0033)				
Private			-0.0111*** (0.0027)	-0.1328*** (0.0271)				
Fmkt*small					0.0004 (0.0003)	0.0233*** (0.0040)		
Fmkt*mid					0.0033*** (0.0007)	0.0127** (0.0044)		
Small					-0.0022 (0.0032)	-0.3981*** (0.0325)		
Mid					-0.0167** (0.0059)	-0.1816*** (0.0289)		
Fmkt*fp50							0.0006** (0.0002)	0.0032 (0.0033)
Fp50							-0.0025** (0.0013)	0.0541** (0.0228)
controls	Y	Y	Y	Y	Y	Y	Y	Y
Prov FE	Y	Y	Y	Y	Y	Y	Y	Y
Year FE	Y	Y	Y	Y	Y	Y	Y	Y
Industry FE	Y	Y	Y	Y	Y	Y	Y	Y
Firm FE	Y		Y		Y		Y	
N	891,462	891,462	891,462	891,462	891,462	891,462	891,462	891,462

* significant at the 10% level, ** significant at the 5% level, *** significant at the 1% level.

Notes: The first two columns provide results for firms' innovation incentives. Coefficients are estimated by logit and conditional logit methods. The third and fourth columns provide results for firms' innovation outcomes. Coefficients are estimated by fixed effect regression and tobit methods. All independent variables are lagged by one period. The standard errors are clustered by province and industry. Fmkt is an alternative credit market development index constructed as a composite index of deposit for non-state-owned financial institutions divided by total deposits and CMD. The definitions of all other control variables can be found in Table 13.2. Standard errors are in parentheses. Marginal effect for Fmkt is in square brackets.

Source: Authors.

13.6 | Conclusions

In this chapter, we examine the effects of credit market development, and the resulting improvement in credit allocation, on firms' product innovation incentives and outcomes in the PRC. Using a large data set of industrial firms in 31 provinces in the PRC from 2000 to 2007, we find that provincial-level credit market development enhances firms' product innovation incentives and outcomes. We show that firms' credit constraints and performances are two channels through which credit market development affects firms' product innovation abilities. The product innovation incentives and outcomes of more credit-constrained firms and firms with better performances are more affected by credit market development than other types of firms. We also show that our results are not due to a higher number of non-SOEs, nor are the results driven by the increase in the quantity of total credit (financial depth) in each year.

Our results are also robust for different estimation methods, different samples, and alternative measures for credit market development. To solve the endogeneity problem caused by omitted variables, we control for many unobserved variables, including firm fixed effect, industry fixed effect, and province fixed effect. We also used the IV method to solve the reverse causality problem.

To our knowledge, this is the first study to investigate whether provincial credit market development enhances PRC firms' innovation abilities through improved credit allocation. Distinct from research that provides country-level and industry-level data, we provide firm-level evidence for the ongoing debate on whether and how credit market development affects innovation.

References

Amore, M. D., C. Schneider, and A. Žaldokas. 2013. Credit Supply and Corporate Innovation. *Journal of Financial Economics* 109: 835–855.

Ayyagari, M., A. Demirguc-Kunt, and V. Maksimovic. 2011. Firm Innovation in Emerging Markets: The Role of Finance, Governance, and Competition. *Journal of Financial and Quantitative Analysis* 46: 1545–1580.

Benfratello, L., F. Schiantarelli, and A. Sembenelli. 2008. Banks and Innovation: Microeconometric Evidence on Italian Firms. *Journal of Financial Economics* 90: 197–217.

Brandt, L., J. V. Biesebroeck, and Y. Zhang. 2012. Creative Accounting or Creative Destruction? Firm-level Productivity Growth in Chinese Manufacturing. *Journal of Development Economics* 97: 339–351.

Brandt, L., and H. B. Li. 2003. Bank Discrimination in Transition Economies: Ideology, Information, or Incentives? *Journal of Comparative Economics* 31: 387–413.

Chong, T. L., L. Lu, and S. Ongena. 2013. Does Banking Competition Alleviate or Worsen Credit Constraints Faced by Small and Medium-Sized Enterprises? Evidence from China. *Journal of Banking & Finance* 37: 3412–3424.

Cull, R., and L. C. Xu. 2003. Who Gets Credit? The Behavior of Bureaucrats and State Banks in Allocating Credit to Chinese State-Owned Enterprises. *Journal of Development Economics* 71: 533–559.

Fan, G., X. Wang, and H. P. Zhu. 2011. NERI Index of Marketization of China's Provinces. Economics Science Press, Beijing (in Chinese).

Firth, M., C. Lin, P. Liu, and M. L. Wong. 2009. Inside the Black Box: Bank Credit Allocation in China's Private Sector. *Journal of Banking & Finance* 33: 1144–1155.

Griliches, Z. 1990. Patent Statistics as Economic Indicator: A Survey. *Journal of Economic Literature* 28: 1661–1707.

Guariglia, A. 2008. Internal Financial Constraints, External Financial Constraints, and Investment Choice: Evidence from a Panel of UK Firms. *Journal of Banking & Finance* 32: 1795–1809.

Guariglia, A., and S. Poncet. 2008. Could Financial Distortions Be No Impediment to Economic Growth after All? Evidence from China. *Journal of Comparative Economics* 36: 633–657.

Hsu, P. H., X. Tian, and Y. Xu. 2014. Financial Development and Innovation: Cross-country Evidences. *Journal of Financial Economics* 112: 116–135.

King, R. G., and R. Levine. 1993. Finance, Entrepreneurship and Growth: Theory and Evidence. *Journal of Monetary Economics* 32: 513–542.

Levine, R. 2005. Finance and Growth: Theory and Evidence. In *Handbook of Economic Growth*, edited by P. Aghion and S. Durlauf. Amsterdam: Elsevier Science.

Lin, H. D. 2011. Foreign Bank Entry and Firms' Access to Bank Credit: Evidence from China. *Journal of Banking & Finance* 35: 1000–1010.

Morales, M. F. 2003. Financial Intermediation in a Model of Growth through Creative Destruction. *Macroeconomic Dynamics* 7: 363–393.

Morck, R., and M. Nakamura. 1999. Banks and Corporate Control in Japan. *The Journal of Finance* 54: 319–340.

Ouyang, P., T. Zhang, and Y. Dong. 2015. Market Potential, Firm Exports and Profit: Which Market Do the Chinese Firms Profit From? *China Economic Review* 34: 94–108.

Poncet, S., W. Steingress, and H. Vandenbussche. 2010. Financial Constraints in China: Firm-Level Evidence. *China Economic Review* 21: 411–422.

Qian, J., P. E. Strahan, and Z. Yang. 2015. The Impact of Incentives and Communication Costs on Information Production and Use: Evidence from Bank Lending. *Journal of Finance* 70: 1457–1493.

Qian, M., and B. Y. Yeung. 2014. Bank Financing and Corporate Governance. *Journal of Corporate Finance* 32: 258–270.

Rajan, R. G., and L. Zingales. 1998. Financial Dependence and Growth. *The American Economic Review* 88: 559–586.

Solow, R. M. 1957. Technical Change and the Aggregate Production Function. *The Review of Economics and Statistics* 39: 312–320.

Weinstein, D. E., and Y. Yafeh. 1998. On the Costs of a Bank-Centered Financial System: Evidence from the Changing Main Bank Relations in Japan. *The Journal of Finance* 53: 635–672.

Xiao, S., and S. Zhao. 2012. Financial Development, Government Ownership of Banks and Firm Innovation. *Journal of International Money and Finance* 31: 880–906.

Zhang, H. 2015. How Does Agglomeration Promote the Product Innovation of Chinese Firms? *China Economic Review* 35: 105–120.

CHAPTER 14

Foreign Direct Investment Spillovers and Pharmaceutical Innovation: The Role of Intellectual Property Rights

Chun-Yu Ho, Xin Li, and Weimin Zhou

14.1 | Introduction

Foreign direct investment (FDI) has been widely introduced into developing countries in the expectation that foreign-invested enterprises (FIEs) can facilitate knowledge spillover to the host countries, yet FIEs' impact on domestic innovation remains ambiguous. With a global trend of increasingly strengthening intellectual property rights (IPR), how knowledge spillover performs in this context becomes even more complex. Some scholars argue that a stronger IPR regime would encourage FIEs to conduct research and development, which is beneficial to developing countries (Diwan and Rodrik 1991). This is because those FIEs would enable domestic firms to build up their innovation capacity through the "market for technology" (Chen and Puttitanum 2005), training of local staff in subsidiaries and joint ventures, turnover of skilled labor from foreign to domestic firms (Fosfuri, Motta, and Rønde 2001; Gorg and Strobl 2005), and learning within the supply chain from FIEs (Rodriguez-Clare 1996; Javorcik 2004). Therefore, a stronger IPR would promote knowledge spillover of FDI.

Though there are many empirical works examining the impacts of IPR or FDI on innovation in developing countries, there are few studies investigating how IPR protection affects the knowledge spillover of FDI in developing countries.

This chapter examines how IPR protection affects the effect of FDI on domestic innovation based on a data set covering the pharmaceutical industries across 29 provinces in the People's Republic of China (PRC) over the period 1998–2007. One year before joining the World Trade Organization (WTO) in 2001, the PRC amended its IPR laws and regulations to comply with the WTO Agreement on Trade-Related Aspects of Intellectual Property Rights (TRIPS). The TRIPS agreement is particularly significant, as it specifies strong minimum standards for the protection and enforcement of various types of IPR, including copyrights, patents, and trade secrets. The resulting IPR regime in the PRC became stronger in order to be more aligned with the IPR regimes in other WTO member countries. We show that there was a negative horizontal spillover effect of FDI on domestic innovation when the IPR regime was weak before the PRC's accession to the WTO. This spillover effect became more positive when the IPR regime strengthened after the PRC's accession to the WTO. We also show that there is a positive upstream spillover effect of FDI on domestic suppliers of pharmaceutical intermediates. Taken together, our findings provide important policy implications on why developing countries should encourage FDI and strengthen the IPR regime together to enhance domestic innovation for promoting productivity and economic growth.

This chapter contributes to three strands of literature. First, it extends the literature on the role of the IPR regime in promoting innovation in developing countries. Qian (2007) examined 26 countries that established pharmaceutical patent laws during the period 1978–2002 and concluded that such laws only stimulate domestic pharmaceutical innovation for countries with higher levels of economic development, educational attainment, and economic freedom. Kyle and McGahan (2012) found that the introduction of patent protection due to the TRIPS agreement in developing countries has not been followed by greater research and development (R&D) investment by domestic firms. Our study extends the literature in showing that stronger IPR can promote domestic innovation by facilitating knowledge spillover from FIEs to domestic firms.

This chapter also adds to the growing literature on investigating the spillover effect of FDI along the supply chain. Javorcik (2004) and Liu, Wang, and Wei (2009) showed that FDI increases the productivity of domestic suppliers in the upstream industry for Lithuania and the PRC, respectively. Our work differs from the existing studies in two aspects. First, we focus on the spillover effect of FDI on innovation. Second, we examine both horizontal and vertical linkages within an industry instead of relying on aggregate input–output tables to examine those linkages across industries. Specifically, we show that pharmaceutical FDI fosters not only domestic pharmaceutical innovation, but also the innovation of domestic pharmaceutical upstream suppliers.

Finally, our chapter adds to the literature on the spillover effect of FDI on domestic patenting activities at provincial level in the PRC. Cheung and Lin (2004) and Yang and Lin (2012) reported that FDI promotes patent application across provinces in the PRC, but Fu (2008) and Yueh (2009) reported mixed results for patents granted. However, their data include the patent applications submitted by foreign applicants and are aggregated across industries in a province. An exception is Huang and Wu (2012), who used the patent data provided by the State Intellectual Property Office (SIPO) of the PRC, which distinguishes domestic applicants from foreign applicants, to explore the effect of FDI on domestic innovation in nanotechnology. They showed that there is a negative effect of horizontal FDI on nanotechnology patent applications across provinces in the PRC. However, they do not examine FDI spillover along the supply chain.

The rest of the chapter is organized as follows. Section 14.2 provides background on the pharmaceutical industry in the PRC. Section 14.3 presents the model and data. Section 14.4 reports the empirical results. The last section concludes and provides policy implications.

14.2 | Industry Background

Despite the recent global financial crisis, the PRC's economic growth is still surpassing expectations as the world's fastest-growing economy. As of 2014, the PRC is the second-largest economy (in purchasing power parity) in the world with a gross domestic product (GDP) of an estimated international $17.6 trillion, which is growing at a rate of 8.9% (IMF 2015). Driven by the strong economic growth, increasing urbanization, and the health demands of an aging population, the country's pharmaceutical industry has also experienced a surge over the last few decades.

Figure 14.1 illustrates the PRC's gross pharmaceutical industry output value and profit from 2001 to 2014. The PRC's pharmaceutical industry output value increased from CNY2,188 billion in 2001 to CNY25,798 billion in 2014, and its profit increased from CNY179 billion to CNY2,322 billion during the same period. In addition, the compound annual growth rates (CAGR) of the PRC's pharmaceutical sector output value and profit between 2008 and 2013 were 21.9% and 21.0%, respectively. The PRC pharmaceutical market is currently the second-largest pharmaceutical market globally, after the United States (US), and in 2014 was worth $105 billion. It is forecast to increase dramatically to $200 billion by 2020 and increase its dominance as a leading player in Asia.[1]

Despite the rapid development of the pharmaceutical sector, it has some unique characteristics that may hinder its sustainable development in the future. More specifically, PRC pharmaceutical firms remain extremely fragmented with low capacity utilization. The total number of pharmaceutical firms was more than 4,500 by 2009; most of them were small-scale, duplicative producers of generic drugs. The sales revenue of the top 10 pharmaceutical enterprises accounts for only 10% of total pharmaceutical sales and the top 100 firms account for only 33% of total sales, compared with the top 10 international pharmaceutical companies, which account for about 42% of global pharmaceutical sales revenue.

---

[1]   *Pharmaceutical Industry in China to 2020: An In Depth Analysis of Multinational and Chinese Biopharma Companies, Industry Trends, Environment, Regulation, Market Drivers, Restraints, Opportunities & Challenges*, Kelly Scientific Publications, 2015.

Figure 14.1: Output Value and Profit of the PRC's Pharmaceutical Industry, 2001–2014

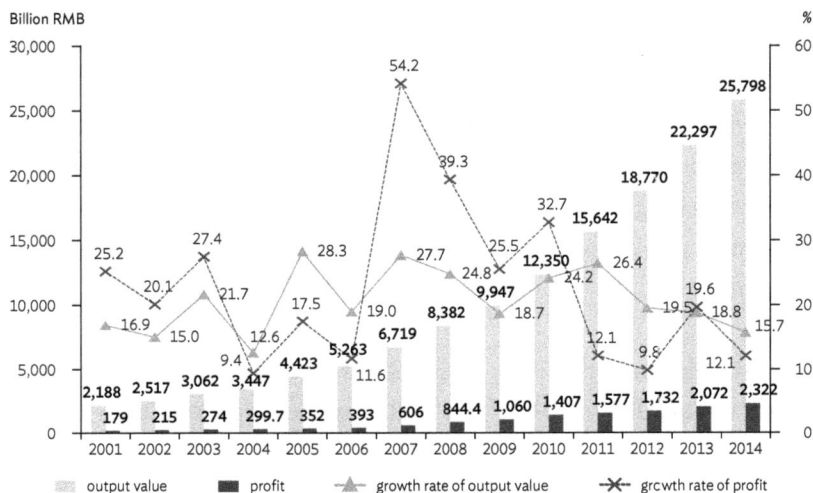

PRC = People's Republic of China.
Source: China Statistical Yearbook on Medicine.

Moreover, compared with international pharmaceutical giants, PRC pharmaceutical firms are not only small but also weak in terms of technology. On average, R&D spending accounts for only 2.7% of sales revenue (Kermani and Zhou 2007), which is far lower than the 17.4% of their US counterparts (phRMA 2009). From 2000 to 2008, PRC firms independently developed only 2 new chemical entities (NCEs), whereas the US had 193 NCEs during the same period (Liang, Ding, and Xue 2011). Having realized and tried to solve these problems, the PRC government has implemented a series of policies to encourage innovation in the pharmaceutical industry. Specifically, the National Development and Reform Commission (NDRC) specified that the focus of the Eleventh Five-Year Plan (2006–2010) is to improve the PRC's fundamental capacity for independent innovation. Companies are expected to invest at least 5% of their revenue in R&D and develop a total of 20 to 30 patented drugs and vaccines for diseases relevant to the PRC population. In addition, in December 2007, the State Council approved the

Key New Drug Creation and Development Program. Under this initiative, the government will invest CNY4 billion in the first 5 years and CNY10 billion in the following 10 years on pharmaceutical R&D, with a specific focus on selected major diseases. Overall, the PRC's domestic R&D activities are expected to gradually catch up with other countries.

14.2.1 The Relevance of Pharmaceutical Patent Data

This subsection discusses the features of pharmaceutical industries that fit our objective in using patent data to examine the impact of IPR protection on knowledge spillover. The pharmaceutical industry is one of the few industries where patents can capture, to a large extent, innovation capacity. On the one hand, the invention of pharmaceuticals is extremely time-consuming and costly: It takes on average 10 years and a substantial sunk cost to develop a new medicine successfully (Mansfield 1986; Levin et al. 1987). On the other hand, the cost of imitation is extremely low: For example, the critical part of a medicine—active ingredients defined by a molecular formula—is easy to identify by reverse engineering. As a result, pharmaceutical firms are forced to consistently resort to patent rights to protect their innovations. Therefore, patents can mostly represent the innovation capacity of the pharmaceutical industry.

In contrast, the inventions of other industries, such as machinery, are hard to imitate due to the complexity of the technology and the intricacy of the manufacturing process, so patent protection is not so critical for these industries. In addition, some industries may resort to other forms of protection, such as trade secrets, to attain more secure protection. Therefore, the patent data of these industries may reflect only a fraction of their innovation capacity and the size of the missing portion differs given firms' varied situations and purposes. For these industries, patents are less reliable as a measure of innovation capacity. Our argument on these unique features of the pharmaceutical industry is supported by a series of papers. For example, Mansfield (1986) and Levin et al. (1987) documented that the value of patent protection for pharmaceuticals is way above the average for all industries.

14.3 | Empirical Model and Data

14.3.1 Empirical Model

Our approach of examining pharmaceutical innovation in different provinces is based on the knowledge production function used in endogenous growth theory (Romer 1990; Grossman and Helpman 1991; Aghion and Howitt 1992). In alignment with the theory, we specify a knowledge production function as follows:

$$\Delta A_{it} = \delta(FDI_{it})A_{it}{}^{\varphi}H_{it}{}^{\sigma} \qquad (1)$$

The province and year are denoted by i and t, respectively. ΔA_{it} represents the flow of new innovations, A_{it} represents the stock of useful knowledge available to drive future knowledge production, and H_{it} represents the total resources devoted to knowledge production. The parameter φ characterizes the return-to-scale effect of the existing knowledge stock on producing new knowledge. The parameter σ is the duplication parameter and ranges from 0 if all innovations are duplicates to 1 if no innovation is duplicated. In addition, FDI_{it} refers to FDI in a province, and $\delta(FDI_{it})$ captures the FDI spillover effect on domestic innovation.

We specify the following empirical model to examine the horizontal spillover of FDI to domestic pharmaceutical innovation:

$$lnPG_{it} = \beta_1 FShare_{it} + \beta_2 FShare_{it} * WTO_t$$
$$+ \beta_3 lnPS_{it-1} + \beta_4 \left(\frac{RD}{FA}\right)_{it} + \beta_5 lnTA_{it} + \delta_i + \delta_t + u_{it}. \qquad (2)$$

The dependent variable is PG, the number of patents granted per 1,000 employees in pharmaceuticals, to measure domestic pharmaceutical innovation. Patents have been widely used, not without controversy, as measures of innovation output (Griliches 1990). Although not all inventions are patented, those that are must meet minimal standards of novelty, originality, and potential use. Therefore, patents are an appropriate proxy for economically significant innovation.

The main explanatory variable of interest is *FShare*, the ratio of foreign pharmaceutical firms to all pharmaceutical firms in a province, to measure FDI intensity. The coefficient β_1 captures the horizontal spillover of FDI in pharmaceutical industries on domestic pharmaceutical innovation. The variable *WTO* takes the value one in and after the year 2001, and zero otherwise. The choice of the year 2001 is based on the PRC's accession to the *WTO* in November 2001. We use the interaction term between *FShare* and *WTO* to capture how strengthening the IPR regime affects the horizontal spillover effect of FDI on domestic pharmaceutical innovation.

Moreover, we include a set of control variables in equation (2). To incorporate the effect of existing knowledge stock on new innovation, we include the variable *PS*, which is the number of patent stocks per 1,000 employees in pharmaceuticals. To incorporate the effect of the resources devoted to innovation, we include the ratio of *RD* to fixed assets (*RD/FA*) and total assets (*TA*) of the pharmaceutical industry.

Equation (2) also includes a full set of province dummies, δ_i, which capture any time-invariant provincial factors that affect the equilibrium levels of innovation. For example, these dummies eliminate the effect of constant, potentially institutional factors. Additionally, a full set of year dummies, δ_t, are included to capture common shocks to pharmaceutical innovation in all provinces. This includes the potential common effect of strengthening the IPR regime on domestic pharmaceutical innovation in all provinces. The error term uit captures all of the other omitted provincial factors, where E[uit] = 0 for all i and t.

To examine the FDI spillover effect on an upstream industry, i.e., pharmaceutical intermediates, we specify the following empirical model:

$$\ln PG - PI_{it} = \beta_1 FShare_{it} + \beta_2 FShare_{it} * WTO_t$$
$$+ \beta_3 \ln PS - PI_{it-1} + \beta_4 \left(\frac{RD}{FA}\right)_{it} + \beta_5 \ln TA - PI_{it} + \delta_i + \delta_t + u_{it} \qquad (3)$$

The dependent variable is *PG-PI*, which is the number of patents granted per 1,000 employees in pharmaceutical intermediates. Since pharmaceutical intermediates are input for drug manufacturing, the coefficient β_1 captures the upstream spillover of FDI in pharmaceutical industries on domestic innovation in pharmaceutical intermediates. The coefficient on *FShare*WTO* indicates how the strengthening of IPR protection affects that upstream spillover effect of FDI. The control variables include patent stock (*PS-PI*), ratio of RD to fixed assets (*RD/FA*), and total assets in pharmaceutical intermediates (*TA-PI*).

14.3.2 Data

We compile a novel panel data set at provincial level from various sources to conduct our empirical analysis. The sample period of the annual data is 1998–2007.[2] All variables have variations at province-year level. First, we collect the patent information from a unique database—the Chinese Pharmaceutical Patent (CPP) Database, developed by the SIPO of the PRC. Our analysis focuses on invention patents only because they represent higher quality and innovation capacity than other types of intellectual property.[3] To the best of our knowledge, there has not been any unified concordance approach that can be used to categorize patents into different industries. The challenge for defining such an approach lies in the complexity of the technology knowledge required (such as sections and search terms of patents) for the categorization. The CPP database provides a reliable source based on professional judgment to obtain pharmaceutical patents from among various overlapping International Patent Classification (IPC) classes.

The CPP database contains nearly 110,000 patent application entries for chemical medicine submitted by domestic and foreign applicants to the SIPO since 1985.[4] The information for each entry includes patent application and publication number, application and publication date, patent number,

---

[2] The sample period of our panel data is limited by the availability of firm-level data.
[3] There are three types of patents that can be granted, namely invention, utility model, and design. Invention patents must meet the requirements of "novelty, inventiveness, and practical applicability," which is more innovative than the requirements of the other two patent types.
[4] We exclude about 70,000 patent application entries for traditional Chinese medicine.

title, IPC code, abstract, claims, legal status, therapeutic effect, and so on. Furthermore, this database identifies whether patents applied for and granted belong to the category of drugs (including preparation methods) or pharmaceutical intermediates. Thus, we can aggregate patent applications and patent grants for drugs (*PA* and *PG*) and those for pharmaceutical intermediates (*PA-PI* and *PG-PI*) that have been submitted by domestic applicants at provincial level in each year.

Second, we use the firm-level data set from the Annual Surveys of Industrial Firms (ASIF) collected by the National Bureau of Statistics (NBS) of the PRC. We use the sample from Sector 272 (Chemical Medicine Preparation Pharmaceutical Industry) to compute the foreign firm penetration in pharmaceutical industries across PRC provinces. To identify foreign firms, we exploit the ownership information of our firm-level panel data set to define foreign firms with the following criteria. First, we define foreign firms as firms with at least 25% of shares owned by foreign investors. Based on this definition, we compute *FShare25*, the ratio of foreign firms to all firms in pharmaceutical industries at province-year level, to measure the foreign firm penetration. We also compute *FShare50* and *FShare100* in analogous ways as alternative measures for foreign firm penetration. Further, we compute the variables *TA* and *TA-PI* with the total assets across firms in Sector 272 and Sector 271 (Raw Chemical Medicine Pharmaceutical Industry) at provincial level in each year, respectively.

Third, we compute the ratio of R&D expenses to fixed assets to measure *RD/FA*. The provincial-level data on R&D expenses and fixed assets are collected from the Statistical Yearbook of High-Technology Industry published by the NBS of the PRC. We employ this data set because the ASIF does not provide information on R&D expenses over the sample period. The drawback of using this data set is that it reports data at a two-digit level for the pharmaceutical industry, which aggregates the information over Sectors 271–277. We use *RD/FA* as an imperfect proxy of R&D intensity for pharmaceutical and pharmaceutical intermediates in equations (2) and (3), respectively.

14.3.3 Descriptive Statistics

We report the variable definitions and summary statistics in Table 14.1.

Table 14.1: Variable Definitions and Summary Statistics

	Mean	SD	Min	P25	Median	P75	Max
Dependent variables							
PG	1.13	1.53	0	0.31	0.60	1.31	11.9
PG-PI	0.15	0.25	0	0	0.05	0.18	1.80
PA	3.12	5.52	0	0.77	1.48	3.33	67.1
PA-PI	0.28	0.49	0	0.02	0.09	0.33	3.98
Control variables							
PS	13.6	15.2	1.84	5.09	8.31	13.8	90.4
PS-PI	0.68	1.08	0	0.15	0.30	0.71	7.22
RD/FA	0.018	0.014	0	0.007	0.016	0.025	0.078
TA	3,752	3,912	38.1	1,146	2,397	4,874	22,279
TA-PI	3,952	5,646	6.28	632.2	1,892	4,455	30,051
FDI variables							
FShare25	0.085	0.086	0	0	0.069	0.122	0.458
FShare50	0.059	0.071	0	0	0.034	0.091	0.333
FShare100	0.026	0.037	0	0	0	0.044	0.167
MNC	0.979	2.314	0	0	0	1	14

PG = number of domestic patents of drugs granted per 1,000 employees; PG-PI = number of domestic patents of pharmaceutical intermediates granted per 1,000 employees; PA = number of domestic patent applications of drugs per 1,000 employees; PA-PI = number of domestic patent applications of pharmaceutical intermediates per 1,000 employees; PS = stock of domestic patents of drugs granted per 1,000 employees; PS-PI = stock of domestic patents of pharmaceutical intermediates granted per 1,000 employees; RD/FA = ratio of the expenses for research and development to fixed assets; TA and TA-PI = total assets (in RMB1,000,000) for drug and pharmaceutical intermediate industries, respectively; FShare25 = share of foreign firms in all firms, where we define foreign firms as firms with at least 25% of shares owned by foreign investors; FShare50 and FShare100 are defined in analogous ways; MNC = number of subsidiaries of MNCs.

Note: Number of observations = 290 (29 provinces for 10 years). Each observation represents a province in a year.

Data source for PG, PG-PI, PA, PA-PI, PS, PS-PI: State Intellectual Property Office (SIPO). Data source for FShare25, FShare05, FShare100, TA, and TA-PI: a firm-level data set on Sectors 271 (Raw Chemical Medicine Pharmaceutical Industry) and 272 (Chemical Medicine Preparation Pharmaceutical Industry) from the Annual Surveys of Industrial Firms (ASIF). Data source for MNC: 18 company websites for Fortune 500 pharmaceutical firms and various transnational corporation reports (2001–2012) in the PRC edited by Zhile Wang and published by China Economic Publishing House. Data source for RD and FA: China Statistics Yearbook on High-Technology Industry, published by the National Bureau of Statistics (NBS) of the PRC.

On average, there are 1.1 patents granted per 1,000 employees for drugs and 0.2 patents granted per 1,000 employees for pharmaceutical intermediates. The patent stock per 1,000 employees for drugs is 13.6 and that for pharmaceutical intermediates is 0.7. The average ratio of R&D expenses to fixed assets is about 0.02. On average, about 8.5% of total pharmaceutical firms enjoy no less than 25% foreign ownership; about 5.9%, no less than 50% foreign ownership; and about 2.6% with 100% foreign ownership.

Table 14.2 reports the correlation matrix of the key variables, which shows that patents granted in drugs positively correlate with patent stock, R&D intensity, total assets, and foreign firm penetration. Nonetheless, the correlations among most explanatory variables are statistically significant, thus we need to employ multivariate regression to establish the relationships between innovation and each explanatory variable.

Table 14.2: Correlation Matrix for Key Variables

	InPS	InPS-PI	RD/FA	InTA	InTA-PI	FShare25	FShare50	FShare100	MNC
InPG	0.459***	0.740***	0.336***	0.434***	-0.019	0.492***	0.486***	0.329***	0.565***
InPG-PI	0.326***	0.869***	0.430***	0.382***	0.147**	0.443***	0.480***	0.366***	0.631***
InPA	0.479***	0.804***	0.427***	0.466***	0.014	0.495***	0.504***	0.399***	0.593***
InPA-PI	0.359***	0.943***	0.486***	0.405***	0.158***	0.456***	0.496***	0.427***	0.645***
InPS	1.000	0.366***	-0.029	-0.288***	-0.492***	0.041	0.090	0.126**	0.172***
InPS-PI		1.000	0.481***	0.419***	0.129**	0.489***	0.507***	0.410***	0.645***
RD/FA			1.000	0.494***	0.374***	0.416***	0.447***	0.417***	0.402***
InTA				1.000	0.492***	0.570***	0.549***	0.457***	0.356***
InTA-PI					1.000	0.238***	0.232***	0.113***	0.458***
FShare25						1.000	0.926***	0.635***	0.171***
FShare50							1.000	0.707***	0.496***
FShare100								1.000	0.543***
MNC									1.000

Note: Number of observations = 290. Each observation represents a province in a year. *** $p < 0.01$, ** $p < 0.05$, * $p < 0.1$.

Source: Authors' estimation.

14.4 | Empirical Results

In this section, we first discuss the empirical results of equations (2) and (3) that are obtained from the fixed-effect model.[5] Then, we discuss two robustness checks.

14.4.1 Horizontal Spillover

Table 14.3 reports the results for equation (2). The variables of interest in column 1 are *FShare25* and *FShare25*WTO*. The coefficient of *FShare25* is negative and significant at the 1% level, and the coefficient of *FShare25*WTO* is positive and significant at the 1% level. Facing competition from foreign firms, domestic pharmaceutical firms reduce their innovation when the IPR regime is weak, but they increase their innovation when the IPR regime becomes stronger. These results suggest that domestic pharmaceutical firms increase their innovation to compete with foreign firms when the domestic firms have a stronger IPR protection. These results are in contrast to the study of Branstetter, Fisman, and Foley (2006) in which they find that a stronger IPR increases the knowledge transfer from US-based parent companies to their affiliates in patent-reforming countries, yet they fail to find any impact on domestic innovation in terms of local resident patent filings with the stronger IPR.

Column 1 of Table 14.3 also shows that the coefficients of ln*PS* and ln*TA* are positive and significant at the 1% and 5% level, respectively. However, the coefficient of *RD/FA* is positive but statistically insignificant. Provinces have a higher number of patents granted for drugs in the current year when they

---

[5]   We reject the unit root null hypothesis for all variables used in equations (2) and (3) with the panel unit test proposed by Levin, Lin, and Chu (2002), and conclude that all variables are stationary. We employ the Hausman specification test to compare the estimates from the fixed-effect models with those from the random effect models (Hausman 1978), and we reject the null hypothesis that the provincial effects are uncorrelated with the other regressors in the empirical model. We conclude that the random effect model produces biased estimators, and therefore the fixed-effect model is preferred.

have a larger knowledge stock in innovating drugs and have a larger scale of operation. Our results suggest that there is a decreasing return to scale for knowledge production and not all new knowledge duplicates existing knowledge. Further, the results reported in column 1 of Table 14.3 are confirmed by the results reported in columns 2 and 3, in which we define foreign firms as firms with at least 50% and 100% of shares owned by foreign investors, respectively.

Although the results from columns 1–3 in Table 14.3 show that all three types of foreign firms (FShare25, FShare50, and FShare100) affect domestic pharmaceutical innovation, this specification does not allow us to examine which particular type of foreign firm penetration has the strongest impact on domestic pharmaceutical innovation. In order to achieve this goal, we investigate this issue by defining three types of foreign firms, namely firms with 25%–49 % of shares owned by foreign investors, firms with 50%–99% of shares owned by foreign investors, and firms with 100% of shares owned by foreign investors, with the following specification:

$$
\begin{aligned}
lnPG_{it} &= \beta_1 FShare100_{it} + \beta_2 FShare100_{it} * Policy_t + \beta_1 FShare5099_{it} \\
&+ \beta_2 FShare5099_{it} * Policy_t + \beta_1 FShare2549_{it} + \beta_2 FShare2549_{it} * Policy_t \\
&+ \beta_3 lnPS_{it-1} + \beta_4 \left(\frac{RD}{FA}\right)_{it} + \beta_5 lnTA_{it} + \delta_i + \delta_t + u_{it}.
\end{aligned} \tag{4}
$$

Column 4 in Table 14.3 reports the results. The coefficient on FShare5099*WTO is positive and significant at the 5% level and that on FShare100*WTO is positive and significant at about the 13% level. Our results suggest that horizontal spillover of FDI on domestic innovation is stronger for joint ventures with majority foreign ownership than that for wholly foreign-owned enterprises. However, joint ventures with minority foreign ownership have no spillover effect no matter whether the IPR regime is strengthened or not.

Table 14.3: **Horizontal Spillover**

Variables	(1) lnPG	(2) lnPG	(3) lnPG	(4) lnPG	(5) lnPG
FShare25	−1.260*** [0.469]				
FShare25*WTO	1.433*** [0.389]				
FShare50		−1.912*** [0.596]			
FShare50*WTO		1.746*** [0.484]			
FShare100			−3.243** [1.301]	−2.631* [1.351]	
FShare100*WTO			2.837** [1.240]	2.040 [1.291]	
FShare5099				−1.441** [0.686]	
FShare5099*WTO				1.650*** [0.599]	
FShare2549				−0.240 [0.870]	
FShare2549*WTO				1.032 [0.904]	
MNC					−0.168*** [0.0398]
MNC*WTO					0.0499*** [0.0155]
lnPS(t-1)	0.125** [0.0593]	0.123** [0.0595]	0.204*** [0.0574]	0.133** [0.0614]	0.186*** [0.0633]
RD/CAP	0.650 [1.424]	0.513 [1.428]	0.572 [1.455]	0.325 [1.437]	1.323 [1.415]
lnTA	0.0910*** [0.0339]	0.0991*** [0.0335]	0.0977*** [0.0342]	0.0935*** [0.0343]	0.0935*** [0.0330]
Province FE	Yes	Yes	Yes	Yes	Yes
Year FE	Yes	Yes	Yes	Yes	Yes
Observations	260	260	260	260	260
R-squared	0.598	0.598	0.584	0.605	0.606
No. of provinces	29	29	29	29	29

continued on next page

Table 14.3: *Continued*

Variables	(6) nPA	(7) lnPA	(8) lnPA	(9) lnPA	(10) lnPA
FShare25	-2.032*** [0.683]				
FShare25*WTO	1.942*** [0.566]				
FShare50		-2.749*** [0.869]			
FShare50*WTO		2.249*** [0.706]			
FShare100			-6.620*** [1.857]	-6.264*** [1.953]	
FShare100*WTO			6.612*** [1.770]	6.034*** [1.866]	
FShare5099				-1.691* [0.992]	
FShare5099*WTO				0.924 [0.866]	
FShare2549				-0.725 [1.258]	
FShare2549*WTO				1.664 [1.307]	
MNC					-0.104* [0.0586]
MNC*WTO					-0.0325 [0.0228]
lnPS(t-1)	0.190** [0.0864]	0.194** [0.0868]	0.285*** [0.0819]	0.221** [0.0887]	0.444*** [0.0931]
RD/CAP	2.150 [2.075]	1.968 [2.083]	1.784 [2.078]	1.657 [2.077]	3.478* [2.080]
lnTA	0.0794 [0.0493]	0.0873* [0.0489]	0.0752 [0.0488]	0.0688 [0.0496]	0.0680 [0.0485]
Province FE	Yes	Yes	Yes	Yes	Yes
Year FE	Yes	Yes	Yes	Yes	Yes
Observations	260	260	260	260	260
R-squared	0.628	0.626	0.631	0.640	0.628
No. of provinces	29	29	29	29	29

Note: *** $p<0.01$, ** $p<0.05$, * $p<0.1$. Dependent variable: patents granted per 1,000 employees for drugs for columns 1–5 and patent applications per 1,000 employees for drugs for columns 6–10.

Source: Authors' estimation

14.4.2 Upstream Spillover

Table 14.4 reports the results for equation (3). The coefficients on *FShare25*, *FShare50*, and *FShare100* in columns 1–3 are negative but insignificant. The coefficients on *FShare25*WTO* and *FShare50*WTO* in columns 1–2 are positive and significant at the 1% level. Our results indicate that domestic innovation in pharmaceutical intermediates increases for provinces with a higher foreign firm penetration in pharmaceutical industries after strengthening the IPR regime. Column 4 reports that the coefficient of *FShare5099*WTO* is positive and significant at the 1% level. This indicates that a higher penetration of firms with majority foreign ownership in pharmaceutical industries is key to inducing domestic innovation of pharmaceutical intermediates after strengthening the IPR regime.

There are two potential reasons for these results to occur. First, foreign firms do not outsource their input to domestic suppliers when the IPR regime is weak. After strengthening the IPR regime, foreign firms outsource to domestic suppliers, which raises the innovation capacity of domestic suppliers. Second, after strengthening the IPR regime, domestic firms compete with foreign firms by producing higher-quality drugs. Consequently, domestic firms demand high-quality inputs from local suppliers.

Furthermore, our findings suggest that there is an upstream spillover effect of FDI on boosting domestic innovation. Liu, Wang, and Wei (2009) showed that FDI increases the productivity of domestic suppliers in upstream industry for the PRC. Our results show that FDI raises not only the productivity of domestic firms in upstream industry but also the innovation of domestic firms in upstream industry. Finally, columns 1–4 in Table 14.4 report that domestic innovation in pharmaceutical intermediates depends positively on patent stocks.

Table 14.4: Upstream Spillover

Variables	(1) lnPG-PI	(2) lnPG-PI	(3) lnPG-PI	(4) lnPG-PI	(5) lnPG-PI
FShare25	-0.187 [0.227]				
FShare25*WTO	0.538*** [0.187]				
FShare50		-0.295 [0.289]			
FShare50*WTO		0.707*** [0.234]			
FShare100			-0.254 [0.639]	0.0679 [0.661]	
FShare100*WTO			0.645 [0.610]	0.273 [0.632]	
FShare5099				-0.338 [0.333]	
FShare5099*WTO				0.824*** [0.292]	
FShare2549				-0.000499 [0.426]	
FShare2549*WTO				0.115 [0.443]	
MNC					-0.0211 [0.0195]
MNC*WTO					0.0358*** [0.00727]
lnPS-PI(t-1)	0.218*** [0.0441]	0.206*** [0.0447]	0.236*** [0.0439]	0.205*** [0.0458]	0.121** [0.0510]
RD/FA	0.480 [0.783]	0.545 [0.781]	0.628 [0.801]	0.546 [0.793]	0.644 [0.753]
lnTA-PI	0.00343 [0.0116]	0.00338 [0.0115]	0.00277 [0.0118]	0.00317 [0.0117]	0.00850 [0.0113]
Province FE	Yes	Yes	Yes	Yes	Yes
Year FE	Yes	Yes	Yes	Yes	Yes
Observations	247	247	247	247	248
R-squared	0.522	0.525	0.502	0.527	0.555
No. of provinces	28	28	28	28	28

continued on next page

Table 14.4: *Continued*

Variables	(6) lnPA-PI	(7) lnPA-PI	(8) lnPA-PI	(9) lnPA-PI	(10) lnPA-PI
FShare25	−0.132 [0.249]				
FShare25*WTO	0.626*** [0.205]				
FShare50		−0.130 [0.318]			
FShare50*WTO		0.721*** [0.258]			
FShare100			−0.217 [0.700]	0.207 [0.727]	
FShare100*WTO			0.920 [0.668]	0.485 [0.695]	
FShare5099				−0.152 [0.366]	
FShare5099*WTO				0.671** [0.321]	
FShare2549				−0.256 [0.469]	
FShare2549*WTO				0.508 [0.486]	
MNC					0.0489** [0.0207]
MNC*WTO					0.0327*** [0.00773]
lnPS-PI(t-1)	0.574*** [0.0483]	0.566*** [0.0493]	0.589*** [0.0481]	0.567*** [0.0503]	0.386*** [0.0542]
RD/FA	0.730 [0.859]	0.848 [0.860]	0.926 [0.877]	0.827 [0.871]	0.954 [0.800]
lnTA-PI	−0.0175 [0.0127]	−0.0178 [0.0127]	−0.0176 [0.0130]	−0.0172 [0.0128]	−0.00739 [0.0120]
Province FE	Yes	Yes	Yes	Yes	Yes
Year FE	Yes	Yes	Yes	Yes	Yes
Observations	247	247	247	247	248
R-squared	0.768	0.767	0.759	0.769	0.797
No. of provinces	28	28	28	28	28

Note: *** $p < 0.01$, ** $p < 0.05$, * $p < 0.1$. Dependent variable: patents granted per 1,000 employees for pharmaceutical intermediates for columns 1–5 and patent applications per 1,000 employees for pharmaceutical intermediates for columns 6–10.

14.4.3 Robustness Checks

In this subsection, we discuss two robustness checks. First, we employ an alternative measure of foreign firm penetration as an explanatory variable. We look into the Fortune 500 pharmaceutical corporations over the period 2001–2010. We collect the information on the location of their subsidiaries and starting operation year in the PRC from their company websites. We cross-check the location information with various transnational corporation reports in the PRC, which report information about local subsidiaries (including starting operation year, location, and ownership) for Fortune 500 corporations.

We compute a variable *MNC*, the number of subsidiaries of Fortune 500 pharmaceutical corporations in each province, to measure foreign firm penetration. We reestimate equations (2) and (3) by replacing the variable *FShare* with *MNC*, and report the results in column 5 of Tables 14.3 and 14.4, respectively. The results of column 5 in Table 14.3 are consistent with those of columns 1–3 in Table 14.3, in which the coefficient on *MNC* is negative and significant at the 1% level and the coefficient on *MNC*WTO* is positive and significant at the 1% level. Furthermore, the results of column 5 in Table 14.4 are consistent with those of columns 1–3 in Table 14.4, in which the coefficient on *MNC* is negative and insignificant and the coefficient on *MNC*WTO* is positive and significant at the 1% level.

The second robustness check employs patent applications as our measure of innovation. Compared with patent grants, patent applications have the advantage of timeliness: It usually takes 2–3 years for a patent application to be granted if successful. Thus, the measure of patent applications is better at reflecting the current innovation capacity. However, it also has a disadvantage—lack of quality control. Not all patents applied are qualified for granting, so a higher number of patent application rate does not necessarily mean higher innovative capacity.

Table 14.1 reports that, on average, there are 3.1 patent applications per 1,000 employees for pharmaceuticals and 0.3 patent applications per 1,000 employees for pharmaceutical intermediates. Table 14.2 reports the correlation matrix of the key variables, which shows that patent applications in drugs and pharmaceutical intermediates positively correlate with patent stock, R&D intensity, total assets, and foreign firm penetration. Moreover, columns 6–10 in Tables 14.3 and 14.4 report the results of equations (2) and (3) with patent application in drug and pharmaceutical intermediates as the dependent variable, respectively. The results are consistent with those reported in columns 1–5 of Tables 14.3 and 14.4.

14.5 | Conclusions

This chapter employs provincial panel data on the pharmaceutical industry to examine the impact of FDI spillover on domestic innovation. Using a fixed-effect panel data model, we show that FDI promotes domestic innovation only after strengthening the IPR regime. Under a stronger IPR regime, FDI in pharmaceutical industries not only induces more innovation from domestic pharmaceutical firms, which compete with foreign firms in the same market, but also induces more innovation from domestic suppliers in upstream industry, i.e., pharmaceutical intermediates. These relationships are robust to the use of alternative measures for foreign firm penetration and innovation, and the inclusion of knowledge stock, R&D expenses, total assets, provincial fixed effects, and year fixed effects as control variables. In line with the literature, we show that innovation depends on the existing knowledge stock and the resources devoted to knowledge production.

Our empirical findings shed light on the policy debate regarding IPR protection in the pharmaceutical sector in developing countries. Our results suggest that developing countries can learn pharmaceutical innovation from FIEs more effectively under a stronger IPR protection. Although there is a potential cost in that developing countries are adversely affected by high-price patented medicines, our results suggest that developing countries may trade off these benefits and costs to design their IPR protection in pharmaceuticals.

Finally, our empirical findings provide implications for innovation policy
in general, which should be of interest to policy makers aiming to sustain
economic growth. Policy makers need to take the strength of the IPR regime
into consideration when they try to attract FDI, as FDI is more efficient
in boosting domestic innovation under a stronger IPR regime. Besides a
strengthened IPR regime, policy makers also need to take the composition
of FDI into account: FDI in the form of joint ventures with foreign majority
shareholding seems more effective in improving domestic innovation. Also,
when policy makers assess the benefits of FDI for domestic innovation, they
need to examine its effect throughout the supply chain.

References

Aghion, P., and P. Howitt. 1992. A Model of Growth through Creative
Destruction. *Econometrica* 60: 323–351.

Branstetter, L., R. Fisman, and C. F. Foley. 2006. Do Stronger Intellectual
Property Rights Increase International Technology Transfer? Empirical
Evidence from US Firm-level Data. *Quarterly Journal of Economics* 121:
321–349.

Chen, Y., and T. Puttitanum. 2005. Intellectual Property Rights and Innovation
in Developing Countries. *Journal of Development Economics* 78(2):
474–493.

Cheung K. Y., and P. Lin. 2004. Spillover Effects of FDI on Innovation in
China: Evidence from the Provincial Data. *China Economic Review* 15(1):
25–44.

Diwan, I., and P. Rodrik. 1991. Patents, Appropriate Technology, and
North–South Trade. *Journal of International Economics* 30(1–2): 27–47.

Fosfuri, A., M. Motta, and T. Rønde. 2001. Foreign Direct Investment and
Spillovers through Workers' Mobility. *Journal of International Economics*
53: 205–222.

Fu, X. 2008. Foreign Direct Investment, Absorptive Capacity and Regional
Innovation Capabilities: Evidence from China. *Oxford Development
Studies* 36(1): 89–110.

Gorg, H., and E. Strobl. 2005. Spillovers from Foreign Firms through Worker Mobility: An Empirical Investigation. *Scandinavian Journal of Economics* 107(4): 693–709.

Griliches, Z. 1990. Patent Statistics as Economic Indicators: A Survey. *Journal of Economic Literature* 28(4): 1661–1707.

Grossman, G. M., and E. Helpman. 1991. *Innovation and Growth in the Global Economy*. Cambridge, MA: MIT Press.

Hausman, J. A. 1978. Specification Tests in Econometrics. *Econometrica* 46: 1251–1271.

Huang, C., and Y. Wu. 2012. State-led Technological Development: A Case of China's Nanotechnology Development. *World Development* 40(5): 970–982.

International Monetary Fund (IMF). 2015. *World Economic Outlook: Adjusting to Lower Commodity Prices*. Washington, DC: IMF.

Javorcik, B. S. 2004. Does Foreign Direct Investment Increase the Productivity of Domestic Firms? In Search of Spillovers through Backward Linkages. *American Economic Review* 94: 605–627.

Kermani, F., and Y. Zhou. 2007. China Commits Itself to Biotech in Healthcare. *Drug Discovery Today* 12: 501–503.

Kyle, M., and M. McGahan. 2012. Investments in Pharmaceuticals Before and After TRIPS. *Review of Economics and Statistics* 94(4): 1157–1172.

Liang, H., J. Ding, and Y. Xue. 2011. China's Drug Innovation and Policy Environment. *Drug Discovery Today* 16: 1–3.

Liu, X., C. Wang, and Y. Wei. 2009. Do Local Manufacturing Firms Benefit from Transactional Linkages with Multinational Enterprises in China? *Journal of International Business Studies* 40: 1113–1130.

Levin, A., C. F. Lin, and C. S. J. Chu. 2002. Unit Root Tests in Panel Data: Asymptotic and Finite-sample Properties. *Journal of Econometrics* 108(1): 1–24.

Levin, R. C., A. K. Klevorick, R. R. Nelson, and S. G. Winter. 1987. Appropriating the Returns from Industrial R&D. *Brookings Papers on Economic Activity* 18(3): 783–820.

Mansfield, E. 1986. Patents and Innovation: An Empirical Study. *Management Science* 32: 173–181.

phRMA. 2009. *Pharmaceutical Industry Profile 2009.* Washington, DC:
    Pharmaceutical Research and Manufacturers of America.

Qian, Y. 2007. Do National Patent Laws Stimulate Domestic Innovation
    in a Global Patenting Environment? A Cross-country Analysis of
    Pharmaceutical Patent Protection, 1978–2002. *Review of Economics
    and Statistics* 89(3): 436–453.

Rodriguez-Clare, A. 1996. Multinationals, Linkages, and Economic
    Development. *American Economic Review* 86(4): 852–873.

Romer, P. M. 1990. Endogenous Technological Change. *Journal of Political
    Economy* 98(5): S71–S102.

Yang, C.-H., and H.-L. Lin. 2012. Openness, Absorptive Capacity, and
    Regional Innovation in China. *Environment and Planning A* 44: 333–355.

Yueh, L. 2009. Patent Laws and Innovation in China. *International Review of
    Law and Economics* 29(4): 304–313.

CHAPTER 15

Innovation and Firm Performance in the People's Republic of China: A Structural Approach with Spillovers

Anthony Howell

15.1 | Introduction

Innovation is noted as being at the heart of economic growth and is essential for firms to maintain a competitive advantage in the market and to achieve long-term success (Porter 1990; Berthon, Hulbert, and Pitt 1999; Noble, Sinha, and Kumar 2002). In the literature, three dominant strands of research have emerged focusing on some aspect of the innovation process: (i) the innovation–performance relationship, (ii) the knowledge production function, and (iii) the structural framework that links knowledge production to firm performance.

The first strand has led to a general consensus that the role of innovation enhances firm productivity (Griliches 1958; Wakelin 2001; Wang and Tsai 2003; Griffith, Redding, and van Reenen 2004). The second strand has developed largely out of the seminal paper written by Pakes and Griliches (1980). The authors ascribe the positive association between innovative inputs (research and development [R&D] activities) and innovative output (patent activities) as the "knowledge production function." A slew of subsequent works has emerged linking innovative inputs to innovative outputs (Zahra and George 2002; Roper, Du, and Love 2008; Love and Roper 2009).

In the third strand, Crépon, Duguet, and Mairesse (1998) extended the knowledge production framework developed in Pakes and Griliches (1980), embedding it into a recursive system of equations that links the knowledge production function to firm performance (referred to as CDM framework). The structural model has become a popular approach to examine the linkages between innovation and firm performance.[1] The main advantages of the CDM framework over previous approaches is that it corrects for the undesirable effects produced by selectivity and simultaneity bias (Lööf and Heshmati 2006); moreover, it is parsimonious and empirically tractable (Griffith et al. 2006).

Building upon the structural approach, the current chapter estimates an "augmented" version of the CDM model to examine the process of the People's Republic of China's (PRC) "indigenous" innovation and estimate its impact on firm performance. Informing our analysis is an unusually rich source of panel data comprising almost 70,000 private firms operating in the PRC's manufacturing sector from 2004 to 2007. Our data is unique not only because of its representativeness of PRC firms during the time period, but it also provides the necessary detailed firm-level information—location, 4-digit industry, innovative sales, R&D expenditures, value added, gross output, and so forth—to carry out our analysis. Using panel data methods, we employ 3SLS with fixed effects to estimate the structural model, controlling for unobserved firm specific effects, simultaneity, and endogeneity.

This chapter makes contributions to the general innovation literature in the following ways. First, our study is set apart from previous structural approaches by its theorization and subsequent empirical analysis of a complex set of direct and indirect effects that attempt to disentangle the sources of technological learning. Technological learning is defined as the process of

---

[1]   See Jefferson et al. (2002); Kemp et al. (2003); Lööf and Heshmati (2006); Griffith et al. (2006); Arvanitis (2006); Benavente (2006); Johansson and Lööf (2009); Hashi and Stojcic (2010); Antonietti and Cainell (2011); and Howell (2017).

building and accumulating technological capability: the ability to effectively use technological knowledge in production, engineering, and innovation to become competitive in the marketplace (Kim 2001).

To disentangle the various sources of technological learning, we identify multiple learning interaction effects that take place: (1) within the firm (learning by doing); (2) between the firm and the environment (learning by exporting; and a firm's absorptive capacity to acquire intra- and inter-industry learning spillovers); and (3) external to the firm (intra- and inter-industrial learning spillovers mediated by institutions). These direct and mediating effects of learning are found to be important determinants of the innovation process and firm performance, albeit their respective impacts vary depending on both the different types of interactions, as well as the stage of innovation under examination.

Making a second contribution to the literature, we apply the CDM framework to a transitioning and dirigiste economy, thereby extending the CDM model to a non-Western context. Johansson and Lööf (2009) argued that applying a "general structural model" for multiple (European) countries is problematic and infeasible for advanced econometric models that attempt to examine the particularities of the knowledge production function as part of the CDM model. It is even more important to examine the unique aspects of the innovative process in transitioning countries like the PRC, where substantial changes in political, economic, and legal institutions present new opportunities and challenges to innovative activities for enterprises (Child and Tse 2001).

On a related point, a growing number of firm-level studies in the PRC have emerged in the innovation literature (Tan 2001; Sun 2002; Naidoo 2010; Guan et al. 2009; Zhou 2006; Wang and Lin 2013). These studies largely confirm the positive role of innovation and significance of location and policy instruments, in enhancing firm performance; however, the brunt of these empirical works fall into either the first or second strand of the innovation literature, thereby restricting the investigation to studying separately the knowledge production function from its impact on firm performance (with the exception of Jefferson et al. 2002). The structural framework adopted in this paper—capable of studying the entire process of PRC innovation and its impact on firm performance—improves the current literature on innovation in the PRC.

The outline of the chapter is as follows. The next section discusses the relevant literature on the PRC's innovation strategy and its particularities. Section 15.3 develops the theoretical framework. Section 15.4 introduces the structural framework, modeling strategy, and variable development. Section 15.5 provides information on the summary statistics. Section 15.6 reveals the research findings from the structural model, and Section 15.7 provides an overview of the main findings and concludes with some final remarks.

15.2 | Background: The PRC's Indigenous Innovation

Since economic reforms were implemented in 1978, and subsequent large-scale dismantling of inefficient state-owned enterprises during the 1990s, the PRC has experienced tremendous economic growth and emerged as a key actor in the global economy. In 2000, the PRC's share of global manufacturing output was approximately one-quarter that of the United States (US) output, representing only 5.7%. By 2011, the PRC surpassed the US to become the top global manufacturing producer, increasing its share to 19.8% of global output.

What accounts for the PRC's prenomenal growth in manufacturing in such a short time period? The conventional view is that the PRC capitalizes on several advantages, such as cheap, abundant labor supply, state subsidies, and a growing local demand for consumer items. While this perspective may explain, in part, the PRC's manufacturing success, it does not account for why other countries with low factor prices, state incentives and even a large domestic market have not achieved the same level of success as the PRC.

Offering new insight, Nahm and Steinfeld (2012) argue that "innovative manufacturing" is a critical part of, and the missing explanatory factor that accounts for the PRC's economic growth story. This perspective is in stark contrast to the conventional view that the manufacturing—physical assembling—process takes place in strict isolation from the innovation process (Steinfeld 2004a). Moreover, recognizing the important role of innovation in the PRC's manufacturing challenges the stereotypical perceptions of the PRC as being merely "the world's factory," rather PRC innovation, or "innovation with Chinese characteristics" explores the unique learning strategies adopted by PRC firms.

According to the "innovative manufacturing" perspective, the accumulation of diverse, firm-specific know-how is a central component to the PRC's competitive specialization in manufacturing. This firm-specific knowledge, combined with the ability to access foreign technology and, subsequently employ backward design strategies, enables PRC firms to recreate "imitated" products at a cheaper cost, crowding out foreign suppliers (Howell 2016). Although products can be made cheaper in other developing countries, multinational firms choose the PRC for more than just its cheap labor costs and emerging consumer market, but also because of its engineering capabilities and quick tempo to reorient a product for large-scale production with the lowest cost possible.

The 2011 US–PRC Economic and Security Review Commission Report confirms that PRC innovation has made substantial in-roads in a relatively short period of time, expanding into everything from design, to genuine innovation, development, and commercialization of new products and processes. Based on this report, Nahm and Steinfeld (2012) argued that the PRC's place *within* global manufacturing is enabling it to develop the propriety know-how *beyond* manufacturing. In effect, PRC firms are doing things differently than pioneer firms from developed countries, which leads to different learning outcomes, and as pointed out in Hall (1995), this type of imitator strategy leads the imitator firms to become, in essence, innovators in their own way.

The innovative manufacturing perspective also complements arguments made by some PRC scholars who claim that the PRC's learning process model of development is unique, deviating from that of other transitioning countries (Qian and Xu 1993; Chen and Qu 2003). For example, Chen and Qu (2003) argued that PRC firms integrate operational, tactical, and strategic learning, amalgamating to produce a specific form of technological learning that differs from other newly industrializing economies (NIEs). As opposed to fitting the PRC experience into that of other NIEs, the PRC-centric approach that accounts for how PRC firms incorporate technological learning into the innovation process, provides the necessary contextualized knowledge regarding the PRC's spatial, institutional, and organizational features to account for its phenomenal growth.

15.2.1 The PRC Industrial Policy

The process of internationalization has exposed domestic firms in the PRC to large amounts of foreign capital, reorienting them toward an export-based development strategy. Coinciding with the PRC's opening up strategy, firms in the PRC also face new, intense competition from foreign competitors. The increasing competition, in turn, has urged the PRC authorities to focus on promoting indigenous innovation through strong state interventionist policies to protect local profits and preserve state revenues (Peng and Heath 1996; Jefferson and Rawski 1994).

For example, then Premier Wen Jiabao delivered a speech in 2006 emphasizing the two main drivers for the PRC's continued progress and development include the persistence to promote opening and reform, and to "rely on the progress of science and technology and the strengths of innovation." In the same year, the promotion of innovation received center stage in the PRC's National Medium- and Long-Term Plan for the Development of Science and Technology (2006–2020) (Howell 2015; Liu et al. 2011). The plan unveiled the "blueprint" for innovation that will bring about the "great renaissance of the Chinese nation," with stated goals to transform the PRC into a technology powerhouse by 2020 and a global leader by 2050.

The relative ease of PRC firms to access foreign technology is buttressed by the industrial policy of the state, which has relied on a "market-access-for-technology" strategy since the early 1990s. In 2011, the National Development and Reform Commission and the Ministry of Commerce issued a revised version (originally released in 1995) of the Catalogue of Industries for Guiding Foreign Investment. In that document, the government identifies three categories where foreign investment is "Encouraged," "Restricted," or "Prohibited."

Over 450 industries are identified in the catalogue, nearly 100 of which are subject to ownership restrictions that require foreign companies, for example, to form joint ventures—equity, cooperative, or contractual—with partners in the PRC. To form a joint venture, foreign companies are often obligated to transfer technology once the joint venture is established as a precondition for its establishment (Shea 2012).

Scholars note several problems with the PRC's industrial policy that gives market access to foreign companies in exchange for tech transfer (Young and Lan 1997; Cheung and Lin 2004). According to Huang (2003b), the return benefits to the PRC have been incommensurate to the deep discounts by which foreigners are able to purchase industrial assets and gain a foothold in the PRC's market. There is also growing recognition that PRC firms may be over reliant on the transferring of the physical assets, overlooking the importance of training and experience needed to absorb those technologies.

For instance, Hu, Jefferson, and Qian (2005) suggested that the actual effect of foreign direct investment (FDI) on improving innovation capabilities of the PRC's domestic firms is close to nonexistent. From a different view, Young and Lan (1997) found that the potential for utilizing FDI as an instrument of technological development is greater than theory suggests. Going one step further, Liu and Buck (2007) found that the absorptive capacity of the firm positively mediates its utilization of the foreign knowledge inputs leading to higher levels of innovation performance.

15.2.2 Institutional Barriers to Innovation

The legal and institutional environment is important because investing in innovation is inherently risky and, in theory, can enhance firm performance or lead to financial distress and failure (Buddelmeyer, Jensen, and Webster 2010). The risk of engaging in innovative activities is comparatively high in the PRC, compared with advanced market economies, due to widespread intellectual property theft, unlawful abrogation of legal contracts and unfair competitive practices, the shortage of venture capital, poor institutional protection, and insufficient market demand (Guo 1997; Sun 2002; Wang and Lin 2008; Zhou 2008). These barriers not only increase the risk of innovation, but also diminish incentives for PRC firms to pursue indigenous innovation activities engendered from purely domestic inputs.

Building stable institutions can mitigate certain risks associated with pursuing innovation, whereas low state-capacity leads to unclear rules, distrust, and rent-seeking activities, all of which impinge upon the capacity and inclination of the firm to innovate (Steinfield 2004b). Promoting the rule of law is an essential component to institution building, incubating indigenous innovation, and promoting sustained growth. Taking into account the direct and mediating impact of institutions is an important issue for examining the innovation–performance linkages (Li and Atuahene-Gime 2001; Rodriguez-Pose and Crescenzi 2008a) and helps to conceptualize the dynamic interplay between actors and structures (Geels 2004).

At present, as a result of poor institutional and legal frameworks in the PRC, innovative firms must depend heavily on state intervention and protectionism to survive (Li and Atuahene-Gime 2001). On the one hand, a strong state-presence may increase the risk of innovation by undermining the benefits normally accrued from innovation in a competitive environment (Carlin, Schaffer, and Seabright 2004). Conversely, policy instruments may create demand for technological learning and increase the supply of technological capability (Lall 1992), especially in certain key industries.

For instance, He and Qing (2011) found that policy mechanisms directly impact the performance of industrial catch-up for private firms in the PRC's telecommunication and automobile industries.

15.3 | Theoretical Framework: Disentangling the Sources of Learning

Along with the institutional environment, the learning ability—absorptive capacity—of the firm becomes especially critical in the ability of the firm to capture and incorporate external knowledge inputs into its production function (Zahra and George 2002). According to Cohen and Levinthal (1990), the idea behind absorptive capacity is that firms need a preexisting set of related capabilities and knowledge to acquire and assimilate new knowledge. Geroski, Machin, and van Reenen (1993) highlighted the importance of not only innovation in itself, but also the learning process that takes place as a firm engages in innovative activities.

Several potential sources have been identified in the literature that can facilitate a firm's learning process, which in turn can influence the process of innovation and firm performance. Pertinent to the scope of this chapter, we identify the following sources of learning grouped into three categories: learning internal to the firm (learning by doing), firm-environment learning interaction (export by doing and absorptive capacity of the firm mediated by learning spillovers), and learning external to the firm (learning spillovers mediated by institutions).

15.3.1 Learning I: Internal to the Firm

Learning by doing (LBD) is the process by where the accumulation of production experience leads to increased performance and growth. The literature distinguishes between passive and active learning, with the former suggesting that LBD is an incidental and costless by-product of the firm's production activities, and the latter occurring as the result of intentional activities of the firm to increase organizational know-how, such as R&D investments (Thompson 2009). Early studies by Rapping (1965) and Sheshinski (1967) found evidence for significant learning effects as firms accumulate experience. Similarly, research confirms the positive and significant role of active learning, based on R&D investments, on firm performance (Jovanic 1982; Pakes and Ericson 1988; Liu and Buck 2007).

15.3.2 Learning II: Firm-Environment Learning

In addition to LBD, the geographic environment is a potentially important source of supplemental knowledge generated external to the firm (Lööf and Nabavi 2013). Two main sources of firm- environment learning interactions are learning by exporting (LBE) and absorptive capability of the firm to capture learning spillovers.

Learning by Exporting

LBE occurs as exporting firms benefit from their foreign buyers' technical and managerial expertise or the expertise from other foreign contacts, such as competitors, suppliers, or scientific agents (Rhee, Ross-Larsen, and Pursell 1984; Clerides, Lach, and Tybout 1998; Silva, Afonso, and Africano 2012). In addition, foreign buyers apply pressure for exporters to produce cheaper, yet higher quality products, which generates incentives for the exporting firm to become more efficient (Evenson and Westphal 1995). The accumulation of external knowledge inputs by exporting firms is not available to firms confined to the domestic market. This difference in access to external knowledge is thought to be a key factor that explains why exporting firms tend to be more productive than non-exporters, although the direction of causality between exports and productivity is debatable (Balasubramanayam, Salisu, and Sapsford 1996). Despite the existence of anecdotal evidence purporting the significance of LBE, the econometric evidence so far provides little support (Salomon and Shaver 2005).

Geography of Learning Spillovers

The spatial concentration of economic activity is believed to be an essential aspect of the learning process and generation of learning spillovers, which in turn fosters growth, innovation and productivity (Fujita and Thisse 2003; Henderson 2003, 2005; Acs, Armington, and Zhang 2007; Rodriguez-Pose and Crezcenzi 2008b: Baldwin et al. 2008; Kesidou and Romijn 2008; He 2009). According to Keller (2010), the benefits derived from learning spillovers in urban regions can be as large as the return from firms' own investments.

Learning spillovers occur when the firm is able to incorporate these external knowledge inputs into its knowledge production function. Research based on the initial works of Cohen and Levinthal (1989, 1990) agreed that the production of innovation and new technological knowledge increasingly depends on the firm's ability to search the external environment to access complementary knowledge inputs.

The literature discerns between two types of externalities. Within-industry knowledge spillovers result from the spatial concentration of firms in the same industry, leading to localization economies, while the increased diversity of economic activity within a region leads to urbanization economies. Although a large literature examining the impact of spatial externalities on firm productivity exists, their relationship remains undetermined (Antonietti and Cianelli 2011).

On the one hand, learning spillovers are advantageous because they enable the firm to overcome the financial and technological limitations of attempting to produce new knowledge solely based on in-house innovation (Antonellia, Patruccoa, and Quatraro 2001). At the same time, learning spillovers may cannibalize some of the benefits normally generated from the LBD process. As a greater stock of knowledge generated external to the firm becomes freely available, the firm may avoid investing in learning opportunities, such as in-house R&D, as a cost-saving strategy (Ghemawat and Spence 1985; Barrios and Strobl 2004).

Several studies from developed countries found that learning spillovers result in positive firm performance (Thornton and Thompson 2001; Gruber 1998). In a study on Spain, Barrios and Strobl (2004) found that both firm-level LBD and learning spillovers positively influenced firm performance. It is perhaps even more important to disentangle the sources of learning internal to the firm and between the firm and environment in developing countries, since these firms are much more likely to rely solely on learning spillovers in lieu of carrying out in-house R&D.

15.3.3 Learning III: External to the Firm

As developed in section 15.2.2 above, the legal and institutional environment is also likely to directly impact both the innovation process, as well as firm performance. Moreover, the mediating impact of institutions on learning spillovers is expected to facilitate the ease at which tacit knowledge can be transmitted at the organizational or industrial level. These expectations of institutions are in line with previous research that contends that the effects of innovation on firm performance and economic growth cannot be fully understood without considering the social and institutional conditions in an economy (Rodriguez-Pose and Crescenzi 2008b).

15.4 | The Structural Framework of Indigenous Innovation

In the previous two sections, we identified several sources of learning— LBD, LBE, and learning spillovers—emphasizing the importance of firm experience and its absorptive capacity to utilize foreign knowledge inputs, as well as acknowledge the PRC's state as a key player in the innovation and performance outcomes of the firm. Building on this theoretical groundwork, the current section introduces the structural model framework with learning, learning spillovers, and institutional effects.

15.4.1 Modeling Strategy

Following in the spirit of Crépon, Duguet, and Mairesse (1998), we model the process of innovation using four main equations. Equation (i) is the firm's decision to engage in innovation determined by a positive value for R&D expenditure. Equation (ii) is the intensity of the firm's R&D effort and equation (iii) is the knowledge production function based on the intensity of new product or process sales. Equation (iv) is the performance equation, where knowledge is an input for a firm's total factor productivity (TFP).

The model combines aspects of the original CDM model, along with the adapted CDM model developed by Antonietti and Cainelli (2011), which controls for spatial externalities. Developing our own structural model of innovation, we estimate firm characteristics, environmental conditions, and learning interactions at each stage of the model (Figure 15.1).

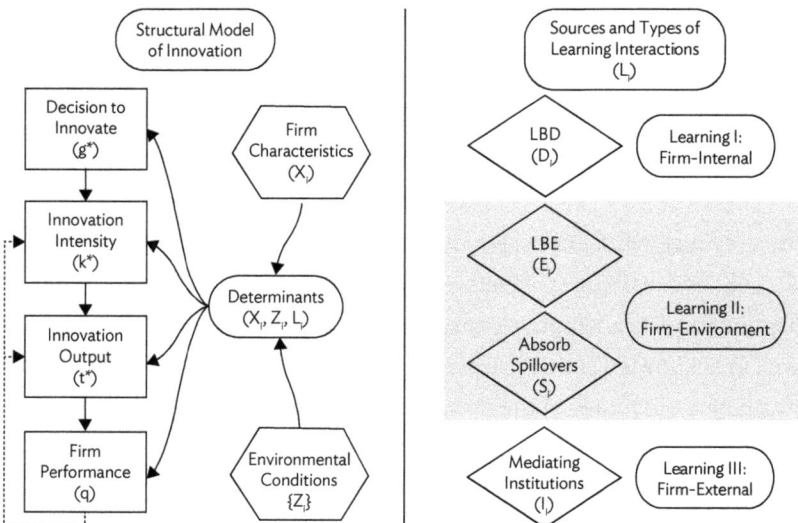

Figure 15.1: Augmented Structural Model of Innovation with Learning Interactions

Source: Author.

Three sets of learning interactions take place that account for learning by doing (D_i), learning by exporting (E_i), and absorptive capacity to utilize foreign knowledge inputs (S_i), and the effect of mediating institutions (I_i). Both S_i and I_i include two learning spillover terms, one for intra-industry spillovers and another for inter-industry spillovers. In total, our model takes into account six learning interaction effects.

To estimate the model, we employ panel 3SLS with fixed effects to control for unobserved firm specific effects, simultaneity, and endogeneity. This is a modest improvement over the original CDM model (and many of the related empirical works thereafter), which relies on cross-section data, and is thus incapable of accounting for specific effects across firms. Similar to the CDM model, we assume innovation to be endogenous in the performance equation (iv), and R&D intensity to be endogenous in the innovation equation (iii). We develop proper instruments to further control for this endogeneity—firm's market share, distance to port, industry and year dummies. The remaining explanatory variables are assumed to be exogenous, which is a difficult assumption to make. Therefore, when possible, the assumed exogenous variables are lagged by 1 year.

In line with Griffith et al. (2006), we estimate the CDM model for all firms, not just those with positive innovation sales. That is, we estimate the R&D equations and use the predicted values for all firms as the proxy for the innovation effort in equation (iii). This approach departs from the majority of other studies and is based on the idea that all firms exert (imitative) innovative effort to some extent, but not all firms report their efforts (Griffith et al. 2006).

15.4.2 The Structural Equations

The set of four structural equations will first be introduced, along with the dependent variables and latent independent variables. Following the explanation of the models, the set of independent variables $\{X_i, Z_i, L_i\}$ will be explained and discussed. Lowercase denotes logged values.

To obtain the innovation effort of the firm, we employ the estimation method developed by Wooldridge (1995) based on the Heckman two-step procedure (Heckman 1976). In the first step, maximum likelihood is used to estimate the panel probit model with fixed effects—a firm's decision to invest in R&D (1 = yes, 0 = no). In the second step, pooled ordinary least squares (OLS) is used to estimate the linear regression model for firms with a positive value of R&D with the dependent variable being the ratio of expenditures on R&D to the number of employees.

The first equation relates to the decision to pursue innovation and the second equation relates to the intensity of resources—R&D expenditures divided by total sales—utilized in the innovation process. We assume g_i^* is the unobserved dependent variable for whether a firm invests in innovation and k_i^* is the latent or true intensity of a firm's investment in innovation, with g_i and k_i being their observed counterparts. The first equation is defined as follows:

$$g_i^* = x_{i0}b_0 + z_{i0}\gamma_0 + l_{i0}\eta_0 + u_{i0} \tag{1}$$

and

$$k_i^* = x_{i1}b_1 + z_{i1}\gamma_1 + l_{i1}\eta_1 + u_{i1} \tag{2}$$

where x_{i0} and x_{i1} are vectors of firm characteristics, and b_0 and b_1 are their corresponding coefficient vectors. z_{i0} and z_{i1} represent the environmental conditions of the firm, with γ_0 and γ_1 as the associated vector coefficients. l_{i0} and l_{i1} are the learning interaction terms, and η_0 and η_1 are the associated vector coefficients. We assume marginal normality for u_0 and a linear conditional mean assumption for u_1.

In the innovation equation, we assume t_i^* is the latent dependent variable for innovation output based on the new product and process sales divided by the number of employees. k_i^* is the predicted values for R&D obtained from equation 2. The equation can be expressed as follows:

$$t_i^* = \alpha_k k_i^* + x_{i2}b_2 + z_{i2}\gamma_2 + l_{i2}\eta_2 + u_{i2} \tag{3}$$

Total factor productivity (TFP) is used to measure firm performance, which assumes the contribution from technological progress or institutional change, and is the difference between output growth and the weighted average of the growth rate of input factors. To construct the TFP variable we follow the semi-parametric approach of Olley and Pakes (1996), grouping firms into the same 2-digit industry to control for technological differences, and estimate TFP for each enterprise. t_i^* is the predicted value of innovation sales generated from equation 3 above.

The performance equation is: $\quad tfp_i = \alpha_i t_i^* + x_{i3} b_3 + z_{i3} \gamma_3 + l_{i0} \eta_3 u_{i3}$ $\qquad$ (4)

where *tfp* are estimates of the firm's TFP, derived from the Olley and Pakes (1996) method. The other coefficients have the same interpretation as before.

15.4.3 Variable Development

The set of firm characteristics (x_i's) include market share, distance to port, age, *age squared*, R&D intensity, export intensity, direct subsidy intensity, and leverage of the firm (assets-to-debt). All firm-level variables are reported in 1-year lags. Market share is excluded from the second R&D equation as an exclusion restriction. It is assured and supported in the literature that market share—an indicator of firm size—is related to the decision to engage in R&D, but not R&D intensity (Griffith et al. 2006). Market share and distance to port are identified as instrument variables for equations 3 and 4, respectively, along with industry and year dummies. Therefore, except for the exclusion of market share and distance to port, $x_{i0} = x_{i1} = x_{i2} = x_{i3}$.

The set of environmental conditions (z_i) consist of proxies for state industrial protection, local regional protection, quality of institutions, and learning spillovers. The same set of environmental conditions are used at all phases of the model. That is $z_{i0} = z_{i1} = z_{i2} = z_{i3}$. To control for potential endogeneity, we report learning by exporting and spatial externalities in 1-year lags; institutional development is reported in 4-year time lags times a constant value in 2004.

The set of learning interactions (z_i's) are equivalent for all four models and include the following six terms: learning by doing (LBD), learning by exporting (LBE), absorptive capacity of a firm to capture intra- and inter-industry spillovers, and mediating effects of institutional quality on intra- and inter-industry spillovers. Learning by doing is obtained by taking multiplying firm experience (age) by the firm's labor productivity in the previous year. Learning by exporting is obtained by interacting firm experience with the firm's export intensity in the prior year.

To proxy for the spatial concentration of economic activity, we construct the Ellison and Glaeser (EG) index developed by Ellison and Glaeser (1997) to capture the localization economies generated from the Marshall–Arrow–Romer (MAR) externalities.

Our second agglomeration proxy—labor density—is calculated as the size of the working population in each city divided by the area of the city (km^2). This proxy captures the urbanization economies generated by knowledge spillovers that result from the diversity of local industries. Moreover, labor density also is related to the size of the agglomeration, the significance of collective resources and information, and the size of the local labor market (Antonietti and Cianelli 2011).

We develop a simple proxy for institutional quality based on average spending on labor insurance (2001–2003) multiplied by a constant of the proportion of union workers in the labor force in 2004 for each city. No proxy for institutional quality is perfect. The main drawback of our proxy is that neither higher labor insurance expenditures, nor higher proportions of union workers in the labor force necessarily equates to stronger structural support for innovation, such as the protection of intellectual property laws or infrastructure that facilitate technology transfers. Despite its drawbacks, our institutional proxy does capture the aspects of institutional building that improves employment and social protections, which will likely be attractive to high-skilled workers engaged in innovative activities.

Moreover, our proxy takes into account the lagged time effects that usually occur with institutional change. Our choice of 4-year time lags seems reasonable and is partially driven by data availability.

Besides issues with proxy variables, a primary concern is that the addition of interaction terms leads to inefficient coefficients due to the presence of high collinearity. To alleviate concerns, we exclude all interaction terms in a baseline model that does not suffer from collinearity problems. In general, the subsequent inclusion of interaction terms does not lead to serious disturbances within the mode although we interpret some coefficients with caution in some cases.

15.5 | Data and Summary Statistics

This study utilizes the Annual Report of Industrial Enterprise Statistics (ASIF) compiled by the State Statistical Bureau of the PRC for the years 2004–2007. The data comprises all firms w th an annual turnover of approximately CNY5 million (approximately $600,000), which accounts for 95% of industrial output in the PRC (Lu and Tao 2009; Brandt, van Viesebroeck, and Schott 2012). An unusually rich set of variables is observed in the data, including information on R&D investments, total sales, gross output, employment, geographic location, industry affiliation, new product or process sales, and sources of finance.

The scope of our study is the process of PRC "indigenous" innovation and its impact on firm performance, therefore, our sample is restricted to domestic firms in the PRC where the majority of the firm's capital is privately owned. A balanced panel is constructed resulting in approximately 70,000 domestic PRC firms born in 1990 or after. Firms with missing information or illogical negative values (i.e., for R&D, new product sales, etc.) are excluded from the sample (Please see Table A15 in the Appendix for summary statistics and correlations of the main variables).

Table 15.1: Summary Information for Dependent Variables

	2004	2005	2006	2007	AvgChge(%)
TFP	2.59	2.62	2.65	2.68	6.91
Innov	...	9.20	12.30	14.64	91.31
RDint	...	0.29	0.37	0.52	115.14
RDchoice	...	0.09	0.10	0.11	39.22

TFP = total factor productivity.
Source: ASIF.

Table 15.1 presents the annual size-weighted means for the four dependent variables used in the structural model. The average percentage change in TFP from 2004 to 2007 is reported at just under 7%. R&D witnessed the highest average percentage change, increasing by 115% over the 2005–2007 period. This large percentage change in R&D intensity is facilitated, in part, by the 40% increase in the number of firms that chose to invest in R&D, as well as by firms investing a larger percentage of sales toward R&D activities.

Table 15.2: Firm Innovation Persistence

Innovation Effort	N	Percent	Innovation Output	N	Percent
RD-3Yrs	2,999	4.38	Innov-3Yrs	2,569	3.76
RD-2Yrs	3,033	4.43	Innov-2Yrs	3,945	5.77
RD-1Yr	5,785	8.46	Innov-1Yr	4,660	6.81
RD-None	56,594	82.73	Innov-None	57,237	83.67
Total	68,411	100	Total	68,411	100

Source: ASIF.

Table 15.2 reports a summary of firm persistence in R&D and innovation intensity over the 2005–2007 period. Less than 18% of firms report positive R&D sales and less than 17% report positive innovation sales. Of the firms engaged in innovative-related activities, 8.46% of firms engage in R&D

activities and 6.81% report positive innovation sales for at least one of the observed periods. Slightly less than half of those respective firms report positive R&D expenditures and innovation sales for all three reporting periods.

Table 15.3 reports the market share and size-weighted averages for TFP and innovation effort by industry. Textiles (12.5%) is the largest industry represented in the sample, followed by general equipment manufacturing (10.1%). Electrical machinery and equipment manufacturing observed the highest average TFP (3.9), as well as experienced the highest average percentage change (9.7%). Pharmaceutical manufacturing reported the highest average innovation sales (35.5), followed by instruments, meters, and office machinery (33.7) and communications, computers and electronics (31.5). The fastest movers in innovation output are in the resource-intensive industries, nonferrous metal smelting and processing (158%), and wood processing (149%). Interestingly, all industries reported positive changes in innovation output, indicating a growing reliance on developing new products or processes.

15.6 | Results

In the baseline model we are most interested in the role of LBD (proxied by age), absorptive capacity of the firm (AbsCap), export intensity (Exp), learning spillovers (EG3 and Labor density), and institutional effects at each stage of the innovation. To take into account learning interaction effects, additional models are subsequently estimated.

The Learning I model offers an improved proxy for LBD by interacting firm experience in years with its previous year's labor productivity (learning interaction internal to the firm). The Learning II model further examines the potential for learning spillovers conditioned on the firm's absorptive capacity (firm–environment learning interaction). The Learning III model adds an additional interaction term for learning spillovers mediated by institutions (learning interaction external to the firm). Each of the four model specifications are briefly discussed for each stage of the innovation process.

Table 15.3: Firm Innovation and Productivity by Industry

SIC	Industry	Firms	TFP	$\% \Delta TFP_{04-07}$	Innov	$\% \Delta Innov_{05-07}$
13	Agro-food processing	2.1	2.4	2.4	4.1	34.8
14	Food manufacturing	1.8	1.1	−6.8	11.9	35.9
15	Beverage manufacturing	1.1	1.2	−2.4	10.7	116.8
17	Textiles	12.5	2.8	0.2	8.9	104.9
18	Textiles, garments, shoes, hat manufacturing	3.8	3.1	4.5	5.3	17.1
19	Leather, fur, feather products	2.0	2.5	2.2	7.8	120.9
20	Wood processing/wood, bamboo, rattan, brown, grass products	2.8	1.8	11.0	7.3	149.8
21	Furnish making	1.3	2.5	1.6	8.7	88.4
22	Paper/Paper products	3.7	2.1	1.1	4.8	40.1
23	Printing/record medium reproduction	2.0	1.2	−10.3	9.5	17.9
24	Educational/sports goods	1.1	3.5	4.8	9.3	34.6
26	Chemical materials/chemical products	7.2	2.4	1.0	14.7	30.6
27	Pharmaceutical manufacturing	1.8	1.5	0.7	35.5	51.0
28	Chemical fiber	0.5	2.9	−3.5	6.6	48.6
29	Rubber products	1.4	2.3	4.3	7.6	58.8
30	Plastic products	5.4	2.8	1.3	9.9	66.5
31	Nonmetallic mineral products	8.8	2.5	4.2	7.8	42.7
32	Ferrous metal smelting/rolling processing	2.1	1.9	8.7	5.9	70.3
33	Nonferrous metal smelting/rolling processing	0.3	2.8	−9.9	9.4	158.2
34	Metallic mineral products	6.6	2.8	2.6	9.0	50.5
35	General equipment manufacturing	10.1	3.0	4.8	12.2	72.1
36	Special equipment manufacturing	4.5	3.1	5.0	21.9	82.5
37	Transportation equipment	4.9	2.1	2.7	17.5	64.8
39	Electrical machinery/equipment manufacturing	6.9	3.9	9.7	21.5	73.2
40	Communications equipment, computers/other electronic equipment	2.4	2.2	6.0	31.5	55.1
41	Instruments, meters, cultural/office machinery	1.3	2.8	1.7	33.7	68.0
42	Artwork/other manufacturing	1.7	3.5	2.8	7.8	124.4

Source: ASIF.

15.6.1 Innovation Effort Equations

The R&D equations relate to the firm's innovation effort (Table 15.4).
We find that firms with larger market shares are more likely to choose to
innovate. Distance from the port (access to foreign knowledge proxy) does
not affect the decision to innovate, but the larger distance tends to reduce
R&D intensity.

Older firms are more likely to choose to innovate, but younger firms pursue
a more intensive innovative strategy. Allowing for nonlinear effects of
experience, we find the opposite relationship. The most experienced firms
are less likely to choose to innovate, but pursue more intensive innovation
strategies. This result is confirmed in three of the four models, and provides
mixed results with regard to LBD expectations. While age is expected to
enhance through learning effects a firm's R&D capabilities, it also may impair
R&D strategy as a result of organizational sclerosis.

Absorptive capacity plays a positive role in the firm's decision to both
choose to innovate and in intensity of R&D activities. The higher the export
intensity the more likely to choose to innovate, but are less R&D intensive.
Direct subsidies both increase the likelihood of choosing to innovate and
increases the R&D intensity. Higher debt-to-equity (leverage) increases
likelihood a firm will choose to innovate, but reduces R&D intensity.

Interestingly, industrial specialization does not impact the choice to innovate
or affect the R&D intensity, whereas labor density increases the likelihood
a firm will choose to innovate, but leads to lower levels of R&D intensity.
State industrial subsidies increase both the probability that a firm will choose
to innovate, as well as increase the R&D intensity. On the other hand, regional
protectionism does not impact the choice to innovate, and is found to
negatively impact R&D intensity. The quality of institutions increases both the
decision to innovate, as well as the R&D intensity.

Table 15.4: Research and Development Equations

	Baseline		Learning I		Learning II		Learning III	
	Probit	Tobit	Probit	Tobit	Probit	Tobit	Probit	Tobit
(Intercept)	-1.687***	0.271***	-1.460***	0.119***	-1.457***	0.112***	-1.437***	0.113***
	(0.139)	(0.018)	(0.139)	(0.018)	(0.139)	(0.018)	(0.139)	(0.018)
mrktshr	0.221***	...	0.268***	...	0.267***	...	0.267***	...
	(0.004)	...	(0.005)	...	(0.005)	...	(0.005)	...
DistPrt	0.005	-0.002***	0.000	-0.001***	0.000	-0.001**	-0.002	-0.001**
	(0.003)	(0.000)	(0.003)	(0.000)	(0.003)	(0.000)	(0.003)	(0.000)
age	0.139*	-0.007	0.482***	-0.049***	0.481***	-0.049***	0.482***	-0.049***
	(0.059)	(0.007)	(0.062)	(0.007)	(0.062)	(0.007)	(0.062)	(0.007)
age2	0.005	0.001	-0.035*	0.006***	-0.037*	0.007***	-0.036*	0.007***
	(0.015)	(0.002)	(0.015)	(0.002)	(0.015)	(0.002)	(0.015)	(0.002)
AbsCap	1.393***	0.353***	1.464***	0.392***	1.581***	0.458***	1.547***	0.458***
	(0.042)	(0.007)	(0.042)	(0.007)	(0.076)	(0.012)	(0.076)	(0.012)
Exp	0.422***	-0.022***	0.344***	0.008*	-0.031	0.105***	-0.046	0.105***
	(0.028)	(0.004)	(0.029)	(0.004)	(0.200)	(0.028)	(0.200)	(0.028)
Subs	2.785***	0.288***	2.734***	0.411***	2.738***	0.413***	2.719***	0.411***
	(0.143)	(0.022)	(0.143)	(0.022)	(0.143)	(0.022)	(0.143)	(0.022)
Levg	0.293***	-0.023***	0.236***	-0.001	0.236***	-0.001	0.239***	-0.001
	(0.048)	(0.006)	(0.049)	(0.006)	(0.049)	(0.006)	(0.049)	(0.006)
EG3	0.286	-0.046	0.089	-0.014	0.219	-0.021	0.167	-0.019
	(0.242)	(0.031)	(0.243)	(0.031)	(0.245)	(0.032)	(0.245)	(0.032)
Den	0.052***	-0.012***	0.051***	-0.009***	0.052***	-0.008***	0.065***	-0.008***
	(0.011)	(0.001)	(0.011)	(0.001)	(0.011)	(0.001)	(0.011)	(0.001)
IndProt	0.041***	0.005***	0.055***	0.005***	0.055***	0.005***	0.056***	0.005***
	(0.009)	(0.001)	(0.009)	(0.001)	(0.009)	(0.001)	(0.009)	(0.001)
RegProt	0.008	-0.009***	0.018	-0.010***	0.018	-0.010***	0.020	-0.010***
	(0.012)	(0.001)	(0.012)	(0.002)	(0.012)	(0.002)	(0.012)	(0.002)
InstQ	0.022***	0.002**	0.023***	0.002***	0.023***	0.002***	0.077***	0.000
	(0.004)	(0.001)	(0.004)	(0.001)	(0.004)	(0.001)	(0.008)	(0.001)
LrnDo	...	...	-0.105***	0.015***	-0.105***	0.015***	-0.106***	0.015***
	...	...	(0.005)	(0.001)	(0.005)	(0.001)	(0.005)	(0.001)
LrnExp	...	...	...	...	0.338	-0.069**	0.358*	-0.069**
	...	...	...	...	(0.179)	(0.021)	(0.179)	(0.021)
AbsCap*EG3	...	...	...	...	-6.127***	0.204	-5.979**	0.183
	...	...	...	...	(1.990)	(0.283)	(1.991)	(0.283)
AbsCap*Den	...	...	...	...	0.018	-0.184***	0.073	-0.185***
	...	...	...	...	(0.133)	(0.020)	(0.133)	(0.020)
EG3*InstQ	...	...	...	...	...	...	-0.219	0.087***
	...	...	...	...	...	...	(0.198)	(0.026)
Den*InstQ	...	...	...	...	...	...	-0.099***	0.001
	...	...	...	...	...	...	(0.011)	(0.001)
IMR	-0.102***	...	-0.154***	...	-0.102***	...	-0.101***	...
	(0.003)	...	(0.003)	...	(0.003)	...	(0.003)	...
Adj. R²	...	0.122	...	0.119	...	0.119	...	0.119
Num. obs.	205,233	205,233	205,233	205,233	205,233	205,233	205,233	205,233
Num. Firms	68,411	68,411	68,411	68,411	68,411	68,411	68,411	68,411
LL	...	-60,777.6	...	-60,593.3	...	-60,583.8	...	-60,546.6

*** $p < 0.001$, ** $p < 0.01$, * $p < 0.05$.

Source: ASIF.

In the subsequent models—Learning I, II, and III—we add the learning interaction terms. Learning by doing diminishes the need for firms to invest in innovative activities, yet firms able to benefit from learning by doing will dedicate a larger amount of resources toward R&D intensity. Conversely, learning by exporting is found to not affect the choice to innovate, and reduces R&D intensity.

The higher the firm's ability to absorb knowledge from spatial externalities reduces its likelihood of choosing to carry out internal R&D in the case of knowledge generated from industrial specialization, and will reduce the R&D intensity in the case of knowledge generated from labor density. Building high-quality institutions, such as protecting intellectual property rights, plays an important role in providing confidence to firms to combine knowledge absorbed from spatial externalities with internal R&D expenditures. In other words, when firms are specialized and located in a region with higher-quality institutions, this leads to higher R&D intensity.

15.6.2 Innovation Output Equation

As shown in Table 15.5, in all four models, R&D intensity increases innovative output. With regard to firm experience, we find older firms are less likely to innovate, yet firms with the most experience are associated with higher levels of innovation. The absorptive capacity of the firm is found to statistically increase innovation output in all four models. Export intensity is also found to be positively associated with innovation output for all three models. The financial structure of the firm plays an important role in innovation. Both direct subsidies and access to loans lead to positive effects on innovation. Both industrial specialization and labor density are found to lead to increased innovation output, although industrial specialization plays a much stronger role in facilitating knowledge spillovers. Interestingly, industrial protectionism does not persist through the innovation effort stage, having no effect on innovation output. Regional protectionism on the other hand remains significant, increasing innovative output.

Table 15.5: Innovation Equations

	Baseline	Learning I	Learning II	Learning III
(Intercept)	1.106***	1.098***	1.109***	1.105***
	(0.086)	(0.086)	(0.086)	(0.086)
RDint	1.404***	1.370***	1.368***	1.368***
	(0.012)	(0.012)	(0.012)	(0.012)
age	−0.112**	−0.270***	−0.270***	−0.270***
	(0.037)	(0.038)	(0.038)	(0.038)
age2	0.047***	0.067***	0.066***	0.066***
	(0.010)	(0.010)	(0.010)	(0.010)
AbsCap	0.286***	0.267***	0.809***	0.815***
	(0.035)	(0.035)	(0.062)	(0.062)
Exp	0.677***	0.699***	0.631***	0.629***
	(0.020)	(0.020)	(0.154)	(0.154)
Subs	1.017***	1.062***	1.055***	1.054***
	(0.114)	(0.114)	(0.114)	(0.114)
Levg	0.144***	0.156***	0.158***	0.157***
	(0.033)	(0.033)	(0.033)	(0.033)
EG3	1.354***	1.430***	1.345***	1.370***
	(0.171)	(0.171)	(0.172)	(0.172)
Den	0.087***	0.087***	0.102***	0.101***
	(0.007)	(0.007)	(0.007)	(0.007)
IndProt	0.002	−0.001	−0.001	0.000
	(0.006)	(0.006)	(0.006)	(0.006)
RegProt	0.106***	0.106***	0.108***	0.108***
	(0.008)	(0.008)	(0.008)	(0.008)
InstQ	0.000	0.000	0.000	−0.017**
	(0.003)	(0.003)	(0.003)	(0.005)
LrnDo	...	0.045***	0.045***	0.045***
	...	(0.003)	(0.003)	(0.003)
LrnExp	...	...	0.186	0.188
	...	...	(0.116)	(0.116)
AbsCap*EG3	...	...	6.451***	6.263***
	...	...	(1.545)	(1.545)
AbsCap*Den	...	...	−1.704***	−1.709***
	...	...	(0.108)	(0.108)
EG3*Inst	...	...	...	0.656***
	...	...	...	(0.142)
Den*Inst	...	...	...	0.011
	...	...	...	(0.008)
Adj. R²	0.089	0.090	0.092	0.092
Num. obs.	205,233	205,233	205,233	205,233
Num. Firms	68,411	68,411	68,411	68,411

*** $p < 0.001$, ** $p < 0.01$, * $p < 0.05$.

Source: ASIF.

Institutional quality does not impact innovation output, except in the last model. One way to understand this finding is that in order for policy and infrastructure to have a positive effect on innovation, the enterprises within a particular region must have the appropriate absorptive capabilities and resources (Guan et al. 2009). The statistically negative coefficient in the last model should be interpreted with caution, considering it only becomes significant when the interaction term with institutions is entered in the model.

The models Learning I, II, and III add the learning interaction effects. We find that learning by doing leads to higher innovation output in all three models. Learning by export remains insignificant. The role of spatial externalities is further mediated by institutional quality. Firms located in specialized industries and supported by strong local institutions will generate higher levels of innovative output.

Firms with higher absorptive capacity are positively mediated by industrial specialization. Surprisingly, labor density is found to have negative mediating effects on a firm's absorptive capabilities. One explanation for this unlikely finding lays in the construction of the absorptive capacity variable, which itself is interacted by the proportion of professional staff in 2004 by the annual amount of spending on professional training from 2005 to 2007. A possible interpretation of the coefficient is that urbanization economies lead to higher levels of innovation for low-skilled, labor-intensive firms. This finding is consistent with the innovative manufacturing perspective that even in remedial tasks, such as assembly, PRC firms create new processes or products to reduce costs.

15.6.3 Firm Performance Equation

As shown in Table 15.6, innovation intensity is statistically significant and leads to higher TFP performance in all four models. Similar to the innovation equation, we find the same relationship between firm experience and TFP. Older firms tend to be less productive, but the most experienced firms are the most productive. The absorptive capacity of the firm is statistically significant and positive in the Baseline and Learning I models, but becomes insignificant once the learning interaction terms are included in Learning II and III models.

The role of exports on firm performance remains a puzzle. In the baseline model, export intensity decreases TFP output, but is found to increase TFP when the learning-by-doing interaction term is included in the model, and then becomes insignificant once the other learning and institutional interaction terms are included. One interpretation of this finding suggests that exporting firms that exhibit learning by doing are able to become more productive than exporting firms that fail to learn from their experiences.

Unlike in the innovation effort stage, subsidized and indebted firms experience lower levels of TFP. Similarly, industrial specialization is found to diminish TFP in the baseline model, but becomes insignificant in the subsequent models. The statistically significant negative coefficient in the baseline model likely reflects the "competition effect" generated by industrial specialization, which leads to greater entry rates and lower productivity output. Labor density is found to increase TFP output in all model estimations. State industrial protection is found to reduce TFP and is significant in three of the four models. Likewise, regional protectionism also harms TFP output, but is significant in only the baseline model. Quality institutions positively impact TFP performance and is significant in all four models.

Including the learning interaction terms, we find that learning by doing leads to higher levels of TFP, whereas there is no evidence to suggest that learning by exporting leads to increased TFP. Although industrial specialization (above) resulted in lower TFP output, we find that firms with a high-skilled labor force will absorb intra-industry knowledge spillovers, which in turn increases TFP performance. There is no evidence to suggest that labor density interacted with the absorptive capacity of the firm impacts TFP. In the Learning III model, we find that institutional quality positively mediates both industrial specialization and labor density, leading to higher levels of TFP.

Table 15.6: Total Factor Productivity Equations

	Baseline	Learning I	Learning II	Learning III
(Intercept)	0.694***	0.730***	0.603***	0.611***
	(0.029)	(0.025)	(0.035)	(0.035)
Innov	0.115***	0.031***	0.088***	0.085***
	(0.005)	(0.005)	(0.014)	(0.014)
age	-0.011	-0.779***	-0.781***	-0.781***
	(0.012)	(0.011)	(0.011)	(0.011)
age2	0.013***	0.109***	0.110***	0.110***
	(0.003)	(0.003)	(0.003)	(0.003)
AbsCap	0.171***	0.030**	-0.008	-0.001
	(0.011)	(0.010)	(0.019)	(0.019)
Exp	-0.114***	0.015*	-0.004	-0.002
	(0.007)	(0.006)	(0.045)	(0.045)
Subs	-0.654***	-0.464***	-0.459***	-0.453***
	(0.038)	(0.034)	(0.034)	(0.034)
Levg	-0.176***	-0.110***	-0.109***	-0.109***
	(0.011)	(0.010)	(0.010)	(0.010)
EG3	-0.275***	0.082	0.076	0.087
	(0.056)	(0.050)	(0.050)	(0.050)
Den	0.049***	0.054***	0.054***	0.052***
	(0.002)	(0.002)	(0.002)	(0.002)
IndProt	-0.003	-0.018***	-0.018***	-0.018***
	(0.002)	(0.002)	(0.002)	(0.002)
RegProt	-0.009***	0.000	0.000	0.001
	(0.003)	(0.002)	(0.002)	(0.002)
InstQ	0.030***	0.031***	0.031***	0.021***
	(0.001)	(0.001)	(0.001)	(0.002)
LrnDo	...	0.215***	0.215***	0.215***
	...	(0.001)	(0.001)	(0.001)
LrnExp	...	...	0.020	0.018
	...	...	(0.034)	(0.034)
AbsCap*EG3	...	...	1.038*	0.995*
	...	...	(0.451)	(0.451)
AbsCap*Den	...	...	0.048	0.039
	...	...	(0.032)	(0.032)
EG3*Inst	...	...	...	0.093*
	...	...	...	(0.042)
Den*Inst	...	...	...	0.019***
	...	...	...	(0.002)
Adj. R²	0.327	0.468	0.468	0.468
Num. obs.	205,233	205,233	205,233	205,233
Num. Firms.	68,411	68,411	68,411	68,411

*** $p < 0.001$, ** $p < 0.01$, * $p < 0.05$.

Source: ASIF.

15.7 | Summary of Results and Concluding Remarks

The structural innovation framework introduced in this chapter helps reveal the mediating effects of learning spillovers on the PRC's innovation and firm performance. Consistent with the existing literature, firms that engage in indigenous research and development increase their innovative throughput, which in turn, is found to increase firm performance. Moreover, a firm's learning by doing helps spur each stage of innovation, while learning by exporting is found to not have any effect. The lack of learning by exporting supports previous studies that bring into question the effectiveness of the PRC's market-access-for-foreign-capital strategy (Young and Lan 1997; Cheung and Lin 2004), as domestic firms in the PRC do not appear to benefit from their interactions with foreign buyers' technical and managerial expertise.

In the early stages of innovation, there is no evidence to suggest that PRC firms are capturing spillovers and incorporating them into their innovation effort, even when the firm's absorptive capacity is taken into account. Conversely, in the later stages of innovation, learning spillovers are found to positively increase the firm's innovation output, as well as its performance, especially for firms with high absorptive capacity. This result confirms previous work that suggest the effects of learning spillovers on innovation vary according to the stage of innovation (Ghemawat and Spence 1985; Barrios and Strobl 2004): the presence of learning spillovers reduces the firm's incentives to invest in innovation—in-house R&D, yet leads to higher levels of innovation output—imitation, and enhances firm productivity.

In view of the firm's inability to integrate learning spillovers with pursuing indigenous innovation strategies, the role of the state becomes particularly important. The state plays a key role in encouraging firms to pursue innovation through various policy tools, including subsidies for firms that open R&D labs, tax breaks, and unfettered access to loans, especially for firms in strategic industries. From this perspective, industrial policy and local protectionism may help to minimize the high risks associated with pursuing innovation, as well as mitigate the negative effects of potential market failures that disrupt the transfer of tacit knowledge from the environment to the firm.

To become a global "innovative powerhouse," the results presented in this chapter highlight the importance of institution building, along with contemporaneous efforts to reduce the role of state and local governments in the market. Building a solid institutional environment reduces the high risks associated with pursuing innovation and will help facilitate the transferring of tacit knowledge leading to both intra- and inter-industrial spillovers, thereby reducing firm dependency on state protectionism, and spurring firm competitiveness. Combined with the limited, strategic policy instruments and further accumulation of learning by doing, PRC firms will better absorb learning spillovers and integrate them with in-house R&D activities. In time, it is likely that the PRC will continue to contribute widely to the global stock of knowledge and increase its value added at all points of the global production chain.

References

Acs, Z. J., C. Armington, and T. Zhang. 2007. The Determinants of New-firm Survival Across Regional Economies: The Role of Human Capital Stock and Knowledge Spillover. *Papers in Regional Science* 86(3): 367–391.

Antonellia, C., P. P. Patruccoa, and F. Quatraro. 2011. Productivity Growth and Pecuniary Knowledge Externalities: An Empirical Analysis of Agglomeration Economies in European Regions. *Economic Geography* 87: 23–50.

Antonietti, R., and G. Cainelli. 2011. The Role of Spatial Agglomeration in a Structural Model of Innovation, Productivity and Export: A Firm-level Analysis. *The Annals of Regional Science* 46(3): 577–600.

Arvanitis, S. 2006. Innovation and Labour Productivity in the Swiss Manufacturing Sector: An Analysis Based on Firm Panel Data. KOF Working Paper 149. Zurich, Switzerland: KOF Swiss Economic Institute.

Balasubramanayam, V. N., M. Salisu, and D. Sapsford. 1996. Foreign Direct Investment and Economic Growth in EP and IS Countries. *Economic Journal* 106: 92–105.

Baldwin, J. R., D. Beckstead, W. M. Brown, and D. L. Rigby. 2008. Agglomeration and the Geography of Localization Economies in Canada. *Regional Studies* 42(1): 117–132.

Barrios, S., and E. Strobl. 2004. Learning by Doing and Spillovers: Evidence from Firm-Level Panel Data. *Review of Industrial Organization* 25(2): 175–203.

Benavente, J. M. 2006. The Role of Research and Innovation in Promoting Productivity in Chile. *Economics of Innovation and New Technology* 15(4–5): 301–315.

Berthon, P., J. Hulbert, and L. Pitt. 1999. To Serve or Create? Strategic Orientations towards Customers and Innovation. *California Management Review* 42(1): 37–58.

Brandt, L., J. van Viesebroeck, and P. Schott. 2012. Creative Accounting or Creative Destruction? Firm-Level Productivity Growth in Chinese Manufacturing. *Journal of Development Economics* 2: 339–351.

Buddelmeyer, H., P. H. Jensen, and E. Webster. 2010. Innovation and the Determinants of Company Survival. *Oxford Economic Papers* 62(2): 261–285.

Carlin, W., M. Schaffer, and P. Seabright. 2004. A Minimum of Rivalry: Evidence from Transition Economies on the Importance of Competition for Innovation and Growth. *Contributions to Economic Analysis & Policy* 3(1): 1284–1327.

Chen, J., and W. Qu. 2003. A New Technological Learning in the PRC. *Technovation* 23(11): 861–867.

Cheung, K.-Y. and P. Lin. 2004. Spillover Effects of FDI on Innovation in the PRC: Evidence from the Provincial Data. *China Economic Review* 15(1): 25–44.

Child, J., and D. Tse. 2001. China's Transition and its Impact on International Business. *Journal of International Business Studies* 32(1): 8–21.

Clerides, S., S. Lach, and J. Tybout. 1998. Is Learning by Exporting Important? Micro-dynamic Evidence from Colombia, Morocco and Mexico. *Quarterly Journal of Economics* 113(3): 903–948.

Cohen, W., and D. Levinthal. 1989. Innovation and Learning: The Two Faces of R&D. *Economic Journal* 99: 569–596.

Cohen, W., and D. Levinthal. 1990. Absorptive Capacity: A New Perspective on Learning and Innovation. *Administrative Science Quarterly* 25: 128–152.

Crépon, B., E. Duguet, and J. Mairesse. 1998. Research and Development, Innovation and Productivity: An Econometric Analysis at the Firm Level. *Economics of Innovation and New Technology* 7(2): 115–185.

Evenson, R., and L. Westphal. 1995. Technological Change and Technology Strategy. In *Handbook of Development Economics* (3rd edition), edited by T. Srinivasan and J. Behrman. Amsterdam: North-Holland.

Ellison, G., and E. Glaeser. 1997. Geographic Concentration in U.S. Manufacturing Industries: A Dartboard Approach. *Journal of Political Economy* 105(5): 889–927.

Fujita, B. M., and J.-F. Thisse. 2003. Does Geographical Agglomeration Foster Economic Growth? And Who Gains and Loses from It? *The Japanese Economic Review* 54(2): 121–145.

Geels, F. 2004. From Sectoral Systems of Innovation to Socio-technical Systems: Insights about Dynamics and Change from Sociology and Institutional Theory. *Research Policy* 33(6–7): 897–920.

Geroski, P., S. J. Machin, and J. van Reenen. 1993. The Profitability of Innovating Firms. *RAND Journal of Economics* 24(2): 198–211.

Ghemawat, P., and A. M. Spence. 1985. Learning Curve Spillovers and Market Performance. *Quarterly Journal of Economics* 100: 839–852.

Griffith, R., E. Huergo, J. Mairesse, and B. Peters. 2006. Innovation and Productivity Across Four European Countries. *Oxford Review of Economic Policy* 22(4): 483–498.

Griffith, R., S. Redding, and J. van Reenen. 2004. Mapping the Two Faces of R&D: Productivity Growth in a Panel of OECD Industries. *Review of Economics and Statistics* 86(4): 883–895.

Griliches, Z. 1958. Research Cost and Social Return: Hybrid Corn and Related Innovations. *Journal of Political Economy* 66(5): 419–431.

Gruber, H. 1998. Learning by Doing and Spillovers, Further Evidence from the Semi-conductor. *Industry Review of Industrial Organization* 13: 697–711.

Guan, C. J., R. C. Yam, E. P. Tang, and A. K. Lau. 2009. Innovation Strategy and Performance during Economic Transition: Evidences in Beijing, China. *Research Policy* 38: 802–812.

Guo, K. 1997. The Transformation of China's Economic Growth Pattern—Conditions and Methods. *Social Sciences in China* 18(3): 12–20.

Hall, P. 1995. *Innovation, Economics and Evolution, Theoretical Perspectives on Changing Technology in Economic Systems*. New York, NY: Harvester Wheatsheaf.

Hashi, I., and N. Stojcic. 2010. The Impact of Innovation Activities on Firm Performance using a Multi-Stage Model: Evidence from the Community Innovation Survey 4. CASE Network Studies and Analyses Working Paper 410. Warsaw: Center for Social and Economic Research.

He, C. 2009. Industrial Agglomeration and Economic Performance in Transitional China. In *Reshaping Economic Geography in East Asia*, edited by Y. Huang and A. M. Bocchi. Washington, DC: The World Bank.

He, X. and M. Qing. 2011. How Chinese Firms Learn Technology from Transnational Corporations: A Comparison of the Telecommunication and Automobile Industries. *Journal of Asian Economics* 23(3): 270–287.

Heckman, J. 1976. The Common Structure of Statistical Models of Truncation, Sample Selection and Limited Dependent Variables and a Simple Estimator for such Models. *Annals of Economic and Social Measurement* 5: 475–492.

Henderson, V. 2003. Marshall's Scale Economies. *Journal of Urban Economics* 53(1): 1–28.

Henderson, V. 2005. Urbanization and Growth. In *Handbook of Economic Growth*, edited by S. Aghion and N. Durlauf: Amsterdam: Elsevier, North-Holland.

Howell, A. 2015. "Indigenous" Innovation with Heterogeneous Risk and New Firm Survival in a Transitioning Chinese Economy. *Research Policy* 44(10): 1866–1876.

Howell, A. 2016. Firm R&D, Innovation and Easing Financial Constraints in China: Does Corporate Tax Reform Matter? *Research Policy* 45(10): 1996–2007.

Howell, A. 2017. Picking "Winners" in China: Do Subsidies Matter for Indigenous Innovation and Firm Productivity? *China Economic Review* 44: 154–165.

Hu, A., G. Jefferson, and J. Qian. 2005. R&D and Technology Transfer: Firm-Level Evidence from Chinese Industry. *The Review of Economics and Statistics* 87(4): 780–786.

Huang, Y. 2003. Selling China: Foreign Direct Investment during the Reform Era. New York: Cambridge University Press.

Jefferson, G. H., B. Huamao, G. Xiaojing, and Y. Xioyun. 2002. R&D Performance in Chinese Industry. *Economics of Innovation and New Technology* 15(4/5) 345–366.

Jefferson, G. H., and T. G. Rawski. 1994. *How Industrial Reform Worked in China: The Role of Innovation, Competition and Property Rights*. Washington, DC: The World Bank.

Johansson, B., and H. Lööf. 2009. Innovation, R&D and Productivity: Assessing Alternative Specifications of CDM-Models. CESIS Working Paper Series 159. Stockholm. Centre of Excellence for Science and Innovation Studies.

Jovanovic, B. 1982. Selection and the Evolution of Industry. *Econometrica* 50(3): 649–670.

Keller, W. 2010. International Trade, Foreign Direct Investment, and Technology Spillover. In *The Economics of Innovation*, edited by B. Hall and N. Rosenberg. Amsterdam: Elsevier, North-Holland.

Kemp, R., M. Folkeringa, J. de Jong, and E. Wubben. 2003. Innovation and Firm Performance. Scientific Analysis of Entrepreneurship and SMEs. Report H200207.

Kesidou, E., and H. Romijn. 2008. Do Local Knowledge Spillovers Matter for Development? An Empirical Study of Uruguay's Software Cluster. *World Development* 36(10): 2004–2028.

Kim, L. 2001. The Dynamics of Technological Learning in Industrialisation. *International Social Science Journal* 53(168): 297–308.

Lall, S. 1992. Technological Capabilities and Industrialization. *World Development* 20: 155–186.

Li, H., and K. Atuahene-Gime. 2001. Product Innovation Strategy and the Performance of New Technology Ventures in China. *Academy of Management Journal* 44(6): 1123–1134.

Liu, F.-C., D. F. Simon, Y.-T. Sun, and C. Cao. 2011. China Innovation Policies: Evolution, Institutional Structure, and Trajectory. *Research Policy* 40(7): 917–931.

Liu, X., and T. Buck. 2007. Innovation Performance and Channels for International Technology Spillovers: Evidence from Chinese High-tech Industries. *Research Policy* 36(3): 355–366.

Lööf, H., and A. Heshmati. 2006. On the Relationship between Innovation and Performance: A Sensitivity Analysis. *Economics of Innovation and New Technology* 15(4/5): 317–344.

Lööf, H., and P. Nabavi. 2013. Learning and Productivity of Swedish Exporting Firms: The Importance of Innovation Efforts and the Geography of Innovation. Working Paper Series at Centre of Excellence for Science and Innovation Studies. Stockholm.

Love, J. H., and S. Roper. 2009. Organizing the Innovation Process: Complementarities in Innovation Networking. *Industry and Innovation* 16: 273–290.

Lu, J., and Z. Tao. 2009. Trends and Determinants of China's Industrial Agglomeration. *Journal of Urban Economics* 65(2): 167–180.

Nahm, J., and E. S. Steinfeld. 2012. Reinventing Mass Production: China's Specialization in Innovative Manufacturing. SSRN Working Paper 2012-25. The Social Science Research Network.

Naidoo, V. 2010. Firm Survival through a Crisis: The Influence of Market Orientation, Marketing Innovation and Business Strategy. *Industrial Marketing Management* 39: 1311–1320.

Noble, C., R. Sinha, and A. Kumar. 2002. Market Orientation and Alternative Strategic Orientations: A Longitudinal Assessment of Performance Implications. *Journal of Marketing* 66(3): 25–39.

Olley, G. S., and A. Pakes. 1996. The Dynamics of Productivity in the Telecommunication Equipment Industry. *Econometrica* 64(6): 1263–1297.

Pakes, A., and R. Ericson. 1998. Empirical Implications of Alternative Models of Firm Dynamics. *Journal of Economic Theory* 79(1): 1–45.

Pakes, A., and Z. Griliches. 1980. Patents and R and D at the Firm Level: A First Look. NBER Working Paper 0561. Cambridge, MA: National Bureau of Economic Research.

Peng, M., and P. Heath. 1996. The Growth of the Firm in Planned Economies in Transition: Institutions, Organizations, and Strategic Choice. *Academy of Management Review* 21(2): 492–528.

Porter, M. 1990. *The Competitive Advantage of Nations*. New York, NY: Free Press.

Qian, Y. and C. Xu. 1993. Why China's Economic Reforms Differ: The M-Form Hierarchy and Entry/Expansion of the Nonstate Sector. *The Economics of Transition* 1(2): 135–170.

Rapping, L. 1965. Learning and World War II Production Functions. *Review of Economics and Statistics* 47(1): 81–86.

Rhee, Y., B. Ross-Larsen, and G. Pursell. 1984. *Korea's Competitive Edge: Managing the Entry into World Markets.* Baltimore, MD: The Johns Hopkins University Press.

Rodriguez-Pose, A., and R. Crescenzi. 2008a. Research and Development, Spillovers, Innovation Systems, and the Genesis of Regional Growth in Europe. *Regional Studies* 42(1): 51–67.

Rodriguez-Pose, A., and R. Crescenzi. 2008b. Research and Development, Spillovers, Innovation Systems, and the Genesis of Regional Growth in Europe. *Regional Studies* 42(1): 51–67.

Roper, S., J. Du, and J. Love. 2008. Modelling the Innovation Value Chain. *Research Policy* 37: 961–977.

Salomon, R., and J. Shaver. 2005. Learning by Exporting: New Insights from Examining Firm Innovation. *Journal of Economics and Management Strategy* 14(2): 431–460.

Shea, D. 2012. The Impact of International Technology Transfer on American Research and Development. In *Committee on Science, Space, and Technology Subcommittee on Investigations and Oversight United States House of Representatives*

Sheshinski, E. 1967. Tests of the "Learning by Doing" Hypothesis. *Review of Economics and Statistics* 49(4): 568–578.

Silva, A., O. Afonso, and A. P. Africano. 2012. Learning-by-Exporting: What We Know and What We Would Like to Know. *The International Trade Journal* 3(1): 255–288.

Steinfeld, E. S. 2004a. China's Shallow Integration: Networked Production and the New Challenges for Late Industrialization. *World Development* 32(11): 1971–1987.

Steinfeld, E. S. 2004b. Chinese Enterprise Development and the Challenge to Global Integration. In *Global Production Networking and Technological Change in East Asia,* edited by S. Yusuf, M. Altaf, and K. Nabeshima. Washington, DC and New York, NY: The World Bank and Oxford University Press.

Sun, Y. 2002. Sources of Innovation in China's Manufacturing Sector: Imported or Developed In-house? *Environment and Planning A* 34(6): 1059–1072.

Tan, J. 2001. Innovation and Risk-taking in a Transitional Economy: A Comparative Study of Chinese Managers and Entrepreneurs. *Journal of Business Venturing* 16(4): 359–376.

Thompson, P. 2009. Learning by Doing. In *Handbook of Economics of Technical Change.* Amsterdam: Elsevier, North-Holland.

Thornton, R. A., and P. Thompson. 2001. Learning from Experience and Learning from Others: An Exploration of Learning and Spillovers in Wartime Shipbuilding. *American Economic Review* 91: 1350–1368.

Wakelin, K. 2001. Productivity Growth and R&D Expenditure in UK Manufacturing Firms. *Research Policy* 30: 1079–1090.

Wang, C., and C. Lin. 2008. The Growth and Spatial Distribution of China's ICT Industry: New Geography of Clustering and Innovation. *Issues & Studies* 44(2): 145– 192.

Wang, C. C., and G. C. Lin. 2013. Emerging Geography of Technological Innovation in China's ICT Industry: Region, Inter-firm Linkages and Innovative Performance in a Transitional Economy. *Asia Pacific Viewpoint* 54(1): 33–48.

Wang, J., and K. Tsai. 2003. NBER Working Paper 9724. Cambridge, MA: National Bureau of Economic Research.

Wooldridge, J. M. 1995. Selection Corrections for Panel Data Models under Conditional Mean Independence Assumptions. *Journal of Econometrics* 68: 115–132.

Young, S., and P. Lan. 1997. Technology Transfer to China through Foreign Direct Investment. *Regional Studies* 31(7): 669–679.

Zahra, S. A., and G. George. 2002. Absorptive Capacity: A Review, Re-conceptualization, and Extension. *Academy of Management Review* 27: 195–203.

Zhou, K. Z. 2006. Innovation, Imitation, and New Product Performance: The Case of China. *Industrial Marketing Management* 35(2006): 394–402.

Zhou, Y. 2008. *The Inside Story of China's High-tech Industry: Making Silicon Valley in Beijing*. Lanham, MD: Rowman & Littlefield.

Table A15: Summary Statistics and Pearson's Correlation Coefficients

Panel A: Summary Statistics				
Variable	Mean	St. Dev.	Min	Max
TFP	2.685	0.978	0.0002	12.610
Innov	12.566	77.933	0.000	3,701.362
RDint	0.489	3.613	0.000	214.857
RDch	0.102	0.302	0	1
mktshr	0.280	0.365	0.001	4.672
DistP	347.587	308.231	0.000	2,732.400
age	6.716	3.511	1	17
Exp	0.094	0.244	0.000	1.000
Subs	0.005	0.026	0.000	0.355
Levg	0.035	0.096	0.000	0.763
HCap	0.012	0.078	0.000	3.242
EG3	0.016	0.017	−0.014	0.151
Den	0.754	1.093	0.002	11.196
Glob	0.162	0.194	0.000	18.755
IndPr	175.633	127.422	2.939	1,850.756
RegPr	0.000	1.000	−1.956	22.122
InstQ	0.000	1.000	−0.961	10.130
LrnDo	10.571	3.070	1.118	23.658

Panel B: Correlations

	TFP	Innov	RDint	RDch	mktshr	DistP	age	Exp	Subs	Levg	AbsCap	EG3	Den	IndPr	RegPr
TFP															
Innov	0.07*														
RDint	0.05*	0.28*													
RDch	0.03*	0.18*	0.40*												
mktshr	0.22*	0.05*	0.01*	0.10*											
DistP	-0.06*	0.01	-0.02*	0.02*	0.00										
age	0.06*	0.02*	0.03*	0.07*	0.10*	-0.02*									
Exp	0.03*	0.03*	-0.01*	0.03*	0.09*	-0.11*	0.06*								
Subs	-0.04*	0.03*	0.05*	0.05*	0.00	0.03*	0.03*	-0.01*							
Levg	-0.05*	0.00	-0.01	0.01*	0.03*	0.08*	0.01*	-0.04*	0.01*						
AbsCap	0.05*	0.08*	0.17*	0.14*	0.02*	0.02*	0.02*	-0.03*	0.02*	0.00					
EG3	-0.01*	0.02*	0.01*	0.03*	0.01*	0.02*	0.03*	0.07*	0.00	-0.01*	0.00				
Den	0.04*	-0.02*	-0.02*	-0.01*	0.03*	0.09*	0.00	-0.03*	-0.03*	0.02*	-0.02*	-0.03*			
IndPr	-0.11*	0.03*	0.05*	0.06*	-0.06*	0.11*	-0.01*	-0.14*	0.11*	0.07*	0.05*	0.06*	0.00		
RegPr	-0.03*	-0.01	-0.05*	-0.02*	-0.03*	0.05*	-0.07*	0.05*	0.00	0.02*	-0.08*	0.01	0.18*	0.02*	
InstQ	-0.04*	0.01	0.01*	0.02*	-0.03*	0.45*	-0.10*	-0.13*	0.03*	0.07*	0.02*	-0.03*	0.06*	0.14*	0.04*

Notes:

1. Correlations are Pearson.

2. $*\,p < 0.001$.

Source: ASIF.

Index

Figures, notes, and tables are indicated by "f," "n," and "t" following page numbers.

G

H

Lightning Source UK Ltd.
Milton Keynes UK
UKHW011146221218
334434UK00004B/62/P

9 784899 740797